Queerly
Canadian

Queerly Canadian

An Introductory Reader in Sexuality Studies

Edited by Maureen FitzGerald and Scott Rayter

Canadian Scholars' Press Inc.

Toronto

Queerly Canadian: An Introductory Reader in Sexuality Studies
edited by Maureen FitzGerald and Scott Rayter

First published in 2012 by
Canadian Scholars' Press Inc. / Women's Press
180 Bloor Street West, Suite 801
Toronto, Ontario
M5S 2V6

www.cspi.org / www.womenspress.ca

Canadian Scholars' Press Inc. gratefully acknowledges financial support for our publishing activities from the Government of Canada through the Canada Book Fund (CBF)

Library and Archives Canada Cataloguing in Publication

Queerly Canadian : an introductory reader in sexuality studies /
edited by Maureen FitzGerald and Scott Rayter.

Includes bibliographical references.
Issued also in electronic formats.
ISBN 978-1-55130-400-7

    1. Gays--Canada--Social conditions. 2. Homosexuality--
Canada. 3. Gay rights--Canada. I. FitzGerald, Maureen, 1942-
II. Rayter, Scott, 1970-

HQ76.3.C3Q44 2012   323.3'2640971   C2012-904663-9

Text and cover design by Aldo Fierro
Cover image © Kent Monkman, *Charged Particles in Motion* (2007)

Printed and bound in Canada by Marquis

Canadä

MIX
Paper from
responsible sources
FSC® C004071

TABLE OF CONTENTS

Alternative Table of Contents • ix

Acknowledgements • xiii

Introduction • xv

PART ONE: THINKING QUEERLY ABOUT IDENTITY, COMMUNITY, AND NATION • xxvii
1 On the Myth of Sexual Orientation: Field Notes from the Personal, Pedagogical, and Historical Discourses of Identity, *Margot Francis* • 1
2 Outside in Black Studies: Reading from a Queer Place in the Diaspora, *Rinaldo Walcott* • 23
3 Our Bodies Are Not Ourselves: Tranny Guys and the Racialized Class Politics of Incoherence, *Jean Bobby Noble* • 35

PART TWO: THE STATE, THE LAW, AND THE CRIMINAL JUSTICE SYSTEM • 49
4 The Regulation of First Nations Sexuality, *Martin Cannon* • 51
5 The Canadian Cold War on Queers: Sexual Regulation and Resistance, *Gary Kinsman* • 65
6 Unknowable Bodies, Unthinkable Sexualities: Lesbian and Transgender Legal Invisibility in the Toronto Women's Bathhouse Raid, *Sarah Lamble* • 81
7 Faith, Politics, and the Transformation of Canada, *Tom Warner* • 99

PART THREE: ORGANIZING AND RESISTANCE • 119
8 Identity and Opportunity: The Lesbian and Gay Rights Movement, *Miriam Smith* • 121
9 Like Apples and Oranges: Lesbian Feminist Responses to the Politics of *The Body Politic*, *Becki Ross* • 139

Part Four: Health, Medicine, and the Experts • 151

10 On the Case of the Case: The Emergence of the Homosexual as a Case History in Early Twentieth-Century Ontario, *Steven Maynard* • 153

11 The Criminal Sexual Psychopath in Canada: Sex, Psychiatry, and the Law at Mid-Century, *Elise Chenier* • 171

12 Continental Drift: The Imaging of AIDS, *Richard Fung* and *Tim McCaskell* • 191

13 Emergence of a Poz Sexual Culture: Accounting for "Barebacking" among Gay Men, *Barry D. Adam* • 197

Part Five: Work • 211

14 From Modern Babylon to a City upon a Hill: The Toronto Social Survey Commission of 1915 and the Search for Sexual Order in the City, *Carolyn Strange* • 213

15 We Are Family: Labour Responses to Gay, Lesbian, Bisexual, and Transgender Workers, *Gerald Hunt* and *Jonathan Eaton* • 229

16 Reframing Prostitution as Work, *Deborah Brock* • 243

17 Working the Club, *Chris Bruckert* • 255

Part Six: Education • 275

18 Gay and Out in Secondary School: One Youth's Story, *John Guiney Yallop* • 277

19 Canadian School Lethargy, *David Rayside* • 293

20 Sexing the Teacher: Voyeuristic Pleasure in the Amy Gehring Sex Panic, *Sheila L. Cavanagh* • 311

Part Seven: Marriage, Parenting, and the Family • 329

21 'That Repulsive Abnormal Creature I Heard of in That Book': Lesbians and Families in Ontario, 1920–1965, *Karen Duder* • 331

22 Heterosexuality Goes Public: The Postwar Honeymoon, *Karen Dubinsky* • 349

23 A New Entity in the History of Sexuality: The Respectable Same-Sex Couple, *Mariana Valverde* • 361

24 Queer Parenting in Canada: Looking Backward, Looking Forward, *Rachel Epstein* • 367

Part Eight: Sport • 387

25 Sex and Sport, *Brian Pronger* • 389

26 Transsexual Bodies at the Olympics: The International Olympic Committee's Policy on Transsexual Athletes at the 2004 Athens Summer Games, *Sheila L. Cavanagh* and *Heather Sykes* • 409

27 Consuming Compassion: AIDS, Figure Skating, and Canadian Identity, *Samantha King* • 427

PART NINE: MEDIA, POPULAR CULTURE, AND YOUTH CULTURE • 449

28 The "Blood Libel" and the Spectator's Eye in Norwich and Toronto, *David Townsend* • 451

29 Queering "Pervert City": A Queer Reading of the Swift Current Hockey Scandal, *Debra Shogan* • 467

30 Beyond Image Content: Examining Transsexuals' Access to the Media, *Viviane Namaste* • 477

31 Queer as Citizens, *Brenda Cossman* • 487

32 FOBs, Banana Boy, and the Gay Pretenders: Queer Youth Navigate Sex, "Race," and Nation in Toronto, Canada, *Andil Gosine* • 507

PART TEN: VISUAL CULTURES • 521

33 The "Hottentot Venus" in Canada: Modernism, Censorship, and the Racial Limits of Female Sexuality, *Charmaine A. Nelson* • 523

34 Porn Wars and Other Hysteries, *Kiss & Tell* • 539

35 Forbidden Love, or Queering the National Film Board of Canada, *Thomas Waugh* • 551

36 The Noble Savage was a Drag Queen: Hybridity and Transformation in Kent Monkman's Performance and Visual Art Interventions, *Kerry Swanson* • 565

About the Authors • 577

Copyright Acknowledgements • 583

ALTERNATIVE TABLE OF CONTENTS

In organizing the material for this book in the way we have, we are aware that categorization raises its own particular issues and narratives. We therefore propose an alternative Table of Contents that reflects the different ways these articles could be grouped, read, and taught. In this way, we believe we do justice to the full range and diversity of topics these chapters cover.

PART ONE: THINKING QUEERLY ABOUT IDENTITY, COMMUNITY, AND NATION

The Regulation of First Nations Sexuality, *Martin Cannon*

The Noble Savage was a Drag Queen: Hybridity and Transformation in Kent Monkman's Performance and Visual Art Interventions, *Kerry Swanson*

On the Myth of Sexual Orientation: Field Notes from the Personal, Pedagogical, and Historical Discourses of Identity, *Margot Francis*

The Canadian Cold War on Queers: Sexual Regulation and Resistance, *Gary Kinsman*

Forbidden Love, or Queering the National Film Board of Canada, *Thomas Waugh*

Consuming Compassion: AIDS, Figure Skating, and Canadian Identity, *Samantha King*

Outside in Black Studies: Reading from a Queer Place in the Diaspora, *Rinaldo Walcott*

Our Bodies Are Not Ourselves: Tranny Guys and the Racialized Class Politics of Incoherence, *Jean Bobby Noble*

FOBs, Banana Boy, and the Gay Pretenders: Queer Youth Navigate Sex, "Race," and Nation in Toronto, Canada, *Andil Gosine*

PART TWO: THE STATE, THE LAW, AND THE CRIMINAL JUSTICE SYSTEM

The Regulation of First Nations Sexuality, *Martin Cannon*

From Modern Babylon to a City upon a Hill: The Toronto Social Survey Commission of 1915 and the Search for Sexual Order in the City, *Carolyn Strange*

On the Case of the Case: The Emergence of the Homosexual as a Case History in Early Twentieth-Century Ontario, *Steven Maynard*

The Criminal Sexual Psychopath in Canada: Sex, Psychiatry, and the Law at Mid-Century, *Elise Chenier*

The Noble Savage was a Drag Queen: Hybridity and Transformation in Kent Monkman's
  Performance and Visual Art Interventions, *Kerry Swanson*
The "Blood Libel" and the Spectator's Eye in Norwich and Toronto, *David Townsend*
Identity and Opportunity: The Lesbian and Gay Rights Movement, *Miriam Smith*
Porn Wars and Other Hysteries, *Kiss & Tell*
Like Apples and Oranges: Lesbian Feminist Responses to the Politics of *The Body Politic*,
  Becki Ross
Unknowable Bodies, Unthinkable Sexualities: Lesbian and Transgender Legal Invisibility in
  the Toronto Women's Bathhouse Raid, *Sarah Lamble*
Faith, Politics, and the Transformation of Canada, *Tom Warner*
A New Entity in the History of Sexuality: The Respectable Same-Sex Couple, *Mariana
  Valverde*
Sexing the Teacher: Voyeuristic Pleasure in the Amy Gehring Sex Panic, *Sheila L. Cavanagh*
Queer Parenting in Canada: Looking Backward, Looking Forward, *Rachel Epstein*

PART THREE: ORGANIZING AND RESISTANCE

Identity and Opportunity: The Lesbian and Gay Rights Movement, *Miriam Smith*
The Canadian Cold War on Queers: Sexual Regulation and Resistance, *Gary Kinsman*
Like Apples and Oranges: Lesbian Feminist Responses to the Politics of *The Body Politic*,
  Becki Ross
We Are Family: Labour Responses to Gay, Lesbian, Bisexual, and Transgender Workers,
  Gerald Hunt and *Jonathan Eaton*
Canadian School Lethargy, *David Rayside*
Faith, Politics, and the Transformation of Canada, *Tom Warner*
Continental Drift: The Imaging of AIDS, *Richard Fung* and *Tim McCaskell*
Reframing Prostitution as Work, *Deborah Brock*
Unknowable Bodies, Unthinkable Sexualities: Lesbian and Transgender Legal Invisibility in
  the Toronto Women's Bathhouse Raid, *Sarah Lamble*
Beyond Image Content: Examining Transsexuals' Access to the Media, *Viviane Namaste*
The Noble Savage was a Drag Queen: Hybridity and Transformation in Kent Monkman's
  Performance and Visual Art Interventions, *Kerry Swanson*
Queer Parenting in Canada: Looking Backward, Looking Forward, *Rachel Epstein*

PART FOUR: HEALTH, MEDICINE, AND THE EXPERTS

On the Case of the Case: The Emergence of the Homosexual as a Case History in Early
  Twentieth-Century Ontario, *Steven Maynard*
On the Myth of Sexual Orientation: Field Notes from the Personal, Pedagogical, and
  Historical Discourses of Identity, *Margot Francis*
The Criminal Sexual Psychopath in Canada: Sex, Psychiatry, and the Law at Mid-Century,
  Elise Chenier
'That Repulsive Abnormal Creature I Heard of in That Book': Lesbians and Families in
  Ontario, 1920–1965, *Karen Duder*

Heterosexuality Goes Public: The Postwar Honeymoon, *Karen Dubinsky*

Continental Drift: The Imaging of AIDS, *Richard Fung* and *Tim McCaskell*

Emergence of a Poz Sexual Culture: Accounting for "Barebacking" among Gay Men, *Barry D. Adam*

Our Bodies Are Not Ourselves: Tranny Guys and the Racialized Class Politics of Incoherence, *Jean Bobby Noble*

Transsexual Bodies at the Olympics: The International Olympic Committee's Policy on Transsexual Athletes at the 2004 Athens Summer Games, *Sheila L. Cavanagh* and *Heather Sykes*

Queer Parenting in Canada: Looking Backward, Looking Forward, *Rachel Epstein*

Part Five: Work

From Modern Babylon to a City upon a Hill: The Toronto Social Survey Commission of 1915 and the Search for Sexual Order in the City, *Carolyn Strange*

We Are Family: Labour Responses to Gay, Lesbian, Bisexual, and Transgender Workers, *Gerald Hunt* and *Jonathan Eaton*

Reframing Prostitution as Work, *Deborah Brock*

Working the Club, *Chris Bruckert*

Our Bodies Are Not Ourselves: Tranny Guys and the Racialized Class Politics of Incoherence, *Jean Bobby Noble*

Part Six: Education

Gay and Out in Secondary School: One Youth's Story, *John Guiney Yallop*

Canadian School Lethargy, *David Rayside*

Sexing the Teacher: Voyeuristic Pleasure in the Amy Gehring Sex Panic, *Sheila L. Cavanagh*

Outside in Black Studies: Reading from a Queer Place in the Diaspora, *Rinaldo Walcott*

The "Hottentot Venus" in Canada: Modernism, Censorship, and the Racial Limits of Female Sexuality, *Charmaine A. Nelson*

Our Bodies Are Not Ourselves: Tranny Guys and the Racialized Class Politics of Incoherence, *Jean Bobby Noble*

Part Seven: Marriage, Parenting, and the Family

"That Repulsive Abnormal Creature I Heard of in That Book": Lesbians and Families in Ontario, 1920–1965, *Karen Duder*

Heterosexuality Goes Public: The Postwar Honeymoon, *Karen Dubinsky*

Queering "Pervert City": A Queer Reading of the Swift Current Hockey Scandal, *Debra Shogan*

Queer as Citizens, *Brenda Cossman*

A New Entity in the History of Sexuality: The Respectable Same-Sex Couple, *Mariana Valverde*

Queer Parenting in Canada: Looking Backward, Looking Forward, *Rachel Epstein*

PART EIGHT: SPORT

Sex and Sport, *Brian Pronger*

Transsexual Bodies at the Olympics: The International Olympic Committee's Policy on Transsexual Athletes at the 2004 Athens Summer Games, *Sheila L. Cavanagh* and *Heather Sykes*

Consuming Compassion: AIDS, Figure Skating, and Canadian Identity, *Samantha King*

Our Bodies Are Not Ourselves: Tranny Guys and the Racialized Class Politics of Incoherence, *Jean Bobby Noble*

Queering "Pervert City": A Queer Reading of the Swift Current Hockey Scandal, *Debra Shogan*

PART NINE: MEDIA, POPULAR CULTURE, AND YOUTH CULTURE

The "Blood Libel" and the Spectator's Eye in Norwich and Toronto, *David Townsend*

Heterosexuality Goes Public: The Postwar Honeymoon, *Karen Dubinsky*

Consuming Compassion: AIDS, Figure Skating, and Canadian Identity, *Samantha King*

Continental Drift: The Imaging of AIDS, *Richard Fung* and *Tim McCaskell*

Queering "Pervert City": A Queer Reading of the Swift Current Hockey Scandal, *Debra Shogan*

Beyond Image Content: Examining Transsexuals' Access to the Media, *Viviane Namaste*

A New Entity in the History of Sexuality: The Respectable Same-Sex Couple, *Mariana Valverde*

Queer as Citizens, *Brenda Cossman*

Sexing the Teacher: Voyeuristic Pleasure in the Amy Gehring Sex Panic, *Sheila L. Cavanagh*

FOBs, Banana Boy, and the Gay Pretenders: Queer Youth Navigate Sex, "Race," and Nation in Toronto, Canada, *Andil Gosine*

Outside in Black Studies: Reading from a Queer Place in the Diaspora, *Rinaldo Walcott*

PART TEN: VISUAL CULTURES

The "Hottentot Venus" in Canada: Modernism, Censorship, and the Racial Limits of Female Sexuality, *Charmaine A. Nelson*

Heterosexuality Goes Public: The Postwar Honeymoon, *Karen Dubinsky*

Porn Wars and Other Hysteries, *Kiss & Tell*

Sex and Sport, *Brian Pronger*

Continental Drift: The Imaging of AIDS, *Richard Fung* and *Tim McCaskell*

Forbidden Love, or Queering the National Film Board of Canada, *Thomas Waugh*

The Noble Savage was a Drag Queen: Hybridity and Transformation in Kent Monkman's Performance and Visual Art Interventions, *Kerry Swanson*

ACKNOWLEDGEMENTS

We would like to thank the people at Canadian Scholars' Press who first approached and really pushed us to create a reader in sexuality studies for the Canadian classroom. They were so supportive of the project and, without that, the book simply would not have happened. Jack Wayne, Susan Silva-Wayne, and Sarah Wayne worked with us early on, and most recently, Daniella Balabuk has worked tirelessly and skillfully to pull the entire project together and get it to press. This is a big book (36 pieces) and had the added cost of permissions, because all of the essays (with the exception of Epstein) had been previously published in some form. Despite those costs, and the real challenges in (academic) publishing today, CSP shared our vision, and it is tremendously gratifying to work with people so committed to publishing queer scholarship. And thanks to all the other people at CSP who had a hand (or two) in putting this all together and making it such a stunning visual object.

And a very grateful acknowledgement to all those contributors to the book whose dedication to queer and sexuality studies scholarship was the very impetus for creating this reader in the first place. We read a great deal of material for this book and many other works by these contributors in making our choices, and we hope the excellence of that work is as obvious to everyone who reads this book as it is to us.

INTRODUCTION
Thinking Queerly about Canada

Scott Rayter

At the tenth annual comedy night Accent on Toronto, held in October 2011 by CBC Radio One, queer Nicaraguan-Canadian comedian Martha Chaves remarked, "I love this country. When Jack Layton died, the funeral for the leader of Her Majesty's Loyal Opposition was presided over by a gay minister married to a man. And the right-wing prime minister had to pay for it!"

Chaves, of course, would not be the first to point out what many in a long line of cultural critics, historians, and, yes, comedians have noted: there appears to be something contradictory or paradoxical about this country, a quality often remarked upon whenever someone attempts to define Canadian identity. And yet, as others have suggested, we seem to take great pleasure in pointing this out, just as Chaves does above. Linda Hutcheon, in a chapter entitled "As Canadian as … Possible … Under the Circumstances," argues that "[o]bsessed, still, with articulating its identity, Canada often speaks with a doubled voice, with the forked tongue of irony."[1] She does not want "to suggest that irony is any kind of master narrative, any total explanatory system that will reveal the key to all Canadian mythologies,"[2] but rather, that irony is a strategy we often see deployed (most notably in the postmodern Canadian art and literature she examines) to confront the binary oppositions with which we endlessly seem to struggle: "native/colonial, federal/provincial, not to mention English/French."[3]

No doubt there is irony to be found in Chaves's study in contrasts. While Canadians in our most recent federal election (May 2011) sent the largest-ever NDP cohort of politicians to the House of Commons in Ottawa (more than double that of any previous election, making this left-of-centre party the Official Opposition for the first time), we also handed Stephen Harper's Conservative Party its first majority government (after two previous minorities), which has become what many describe as the most socially conservative government Canada has seen in recent memory. The August 2011 funeral for NDP leader Jack Layton—whose unexpected death from cancer created a rather singular moment of national outpouring—was presided over by Reverend Brent Hawkes, a gay rights activist who, in January 2001, performed a same-sex marriage ceremony at the Metropolitan Community Church in Toronto, a key moment in the history of the fight for same-sex marriage in Canada, which was ultimately legalized by Parliament in July 2005. Is it a sign of contradiction or deep division to elect the most gay-positive party leader this country has ever seen alongside a prime minister and political party who used their opposition to same-sex marriage as a rallying cry to unify disparate conservative and religious factions in the country and eventually take government? Indeed, Warner, in his essay here, looks at how a number of issues concerning sexuality and sexual minorities have played out under Harper's government.[4]

If the same-sex marriage debate appears as an obvious example of how matters of sexuality and sexual politics are not private concerns, but rather issues of national attention, this collection of essays brings to the fore the way in which sexuality has played a fundamental role not only in the building of our nation, but in the creation of national narratives, myths, and indeed anxieties about Canadian identity. To wit, when in 2009 the Conservative government introduced its new citizenship guide, *Discover Canada: The Rights and Responsibilities of Citizenship*, many were quick to point out the Conservative ideology at work in the way the new treatise seemed to place greater emphasis on responsibilities than on rights.[5] Compared to the previous 1995 Liberal government guide, there is no mention of important achievements in social policy, such as universal health care (and the man who helped make it a reality—Tommy Douglas), in favour of a much lengthier description of Canada's military history. When it was learned—through an access to information request—that the reference to same-sex marriage had been dropped from the final version (along with the mention of the decriminalization of homosexuality in 1969), mounting criticism, including from the national LGBT human rights organization Egale Canada, and a motion tabled in the House of Commons by NDP immigration critic Olivia Chow prompted Minister of Immigration Jason Kenney to have the marriage reference reinstated for the second edition, released in 2011.[6]

In a section titled "Diversity in Canada," which addresses immigration, language, and religion, the conclusion now reads:

> Canada's diversity includes gay and lesbian Canadians, who enjoy the full protection of and equal treatment under the law, including access to civil marriage. [...] Together, these diverse groups, sharing a common Canadian identity, make up today's multicultural society.[7]

It may seem petty to quibble with the substance of the text, particularly if we contrast the Canadian government's stance with that of most other countries, where LGBT people lack basic freedoms, rights, and protections. Still, a number of questions persist: Where are bisexual, transgender, or two-spirited people? And, in this great story in which diversity and multiculturalism are celebrated, what precisely is the "common identity" we all share? More to the point, how did we get there?

While it is perhaps not surprising that any government document on Canadian identity is bound to be met with criticism and debate, the initial exclusion—the *deletion* to be precise—

of LGBT people and history in Canada is a reminder to some of how precarious "citizenship" can actually be. If the inclusion of sexual diversity in our official citizenship guide is meant to signal to the world that Canada is a tolerant, inclusive, and accommodating nation (and that homophobia is an external problem), certainly both past and current practices tell a different story: one that is told here in this collection of essays. That said, no matter how skeptical some LGBT people might be about the actual experience of tolerance and inclusion, most queer people would likely agree that adding a reference to sexual diversity is an important message to the rest of the world. Indeed, many Canadians take pride in this image of ourselves and would see the addition as a commitment to and representation of our core values and freedoms.

If, in 2012, we appear to be a country that celebrates and welcomes diversity, such inclusion did not come easily, and many would point out that the difference between policy and practice is still great. In her critique of Canada's national mythology, including its policy of multicultural-ism, Eva Mackey, for example, looks at how when it comes to the First Nations, "this notion of Canada's tolerance coexisted with brutal policies of extermination and cultural genocide."[8] In a similar vein, we only need to look at practices such as the Chinese Head Tax, the internment of Japanese-Canadians during the Second World War, the "none is too many" stance of the Depart-ment of Immigration (then a division of the Department of Mines and Resources) towards Jews during the 1930s and 1940s, or the FLQ crisis of 1970. If such critiques are becoming more familiar in demonstrating the ways in which the nation and the national imaginary have been built upon racial and ethnic exclusions—including specific policies about who belongs and who does not—less familiar is the role of sexual minorities in this narrative, and the way in which the relationship between governmentality and sexuality has been, and continues to be, a key part of that nation-building project. The story of same-sex marriage in Canada (and for equal rights and protections for LGBT people more generally) is composed of many court battles over the years because of the government's steadfast opposition—at all levels—to recognize sexual minorities as full citizens. Today we are still witnessing ongoing struggles to address school and health-care policy around sexual and gender diversity, disputes over the criminalization of HIV, and, most recently, court challenges to the country's prostitution laws.

Debates about sexuality—and our country's attitudes towards it—are front and centre. On a daily basis, we hear about sexual abuse (in Residential Schools, the Catholic Church, Scouts Can-ada, and in organized sports such as hockey), polygamy (the legal proceedings in Bountiful, British Columbia, for example), the inclusion of sex education and sexual diversity in school curricula and policy, bullying and queer teen suicide, "sex addiction" (Tiger Woods et al.), and even "gay" penguins.[9] And indeed government and politicians' stances on such matters are now standard topics of debate and media coverage, particularly during elections. It may be easy to say that "sex is everywhere" or that "sex sells," but to attribute the prevalence of sex to the media or to corporate interests does not take into account the fundamental role that sexuality plays in our everyday lives and in our understandings of ourselves, our communities, and our nation; nor does it explain the fundamental historical role that sexuality has played in shaping our country or the state's interest in—and its policies dealing with—matters sexual. In response, those of us who teach sexuality studies and those who have contributed to this book argue that "sex matters."

Sexuality studies (including LGBT/queer studies) programs and courses today are a feature of most major universities in the country and, in many instances, they barely meet the student demand for them at both the undergraduate and graduate level. Scholars from a variety of disciplines, employing a range of methodologies and frameworks, and asking questions about sexuality here and elsewhere, past and present, have come together to offer interdisciplinary courses to show students *how* and *why* sexuality matters. And students choosing careers in law, health and medicine, education, public and social policy, journalism, government, research, the arts, and business are looking for a grounding in the field of sexuality studies as a way to reimagine and restructure what those jobs might look like, how those workplaces might function, and what their roles as global citizens might be.

Queerly Canadian: An Introductory Reader in Sexuality Studies brings together some of the best work in the field of sexuality studies by some of its most important contributors. We believe the collection can be used in a variety of courses depending on instructors' needs and particular course designs. Having taught many such courses—and surveyed many more while researching this book—we also wanted to offer a remedy to what we and others have often seen as an obstacle: most edited collections on sexuality for use in the classroom have little Canadian content. If educators and historians in this country consistently bemoan the fact that students today don't know Canadian history, this is even more true of *queer* Canadian history. And while not all of these pieces are historical or even focussed on Canada, many of them do address some key moments in LGBT oppression, resistance, and activism in this country. In addition, many of the authors look to wider issues of sexuality, such as those in relation to the First Nations, race, gender, sexual representation, the media, art, film, politics, labour, health and medicine, law, education, religion, marriage, family, sport, sex work, and HIV/AIDS, which have played out in ways that are necessary for understanding the important differences from (and at times similarities to) other countries, particularly the United States. All too often there is a sense of universalism when it comes to American texts and examples, so it is crucial that we—as teachers and students—probe some of the assumptions that go along with that way of thinking. In one of the opening essays here, for instance, Rinaldo Walcott asks us to think about the way a queer diasporic interrogation of the Black studies project can interrupt national, imperialist, and heteronormative discourses and allow for "transnational identification." For many who teach sexuality studies in Canadian universities (be they from Canada, the U.S., or elsewhere), it is all too easy to (unconsciously) perpetuate this universalism because they are unaware of particular local and national histories, or even the breadth of scholarship in Canada. We hope that this collection will not only offer a worthy alternative, but will stand in its own right as a testament to how a focus on Canadian subjects and scholarship can indeed push the field of sexuality studies further and thereby prompt our students to think more critically about their own national and cultural narratives and the role they themselves play in shaping, (re)producing, challenging, and (re)writing them.

To begin to question what nation means, and therefore what national belonging means when it comes to sexuality and sexual identity, we need to ask critical—and queer—questions about identity itself. As Maynard writes in his essay here, "[i]t was Foucault who famously remarked that sometime beginning in the nineteenth century the homosexual became, among other things, a 'case history.' ... Of course what Foucault meant was not so much that the homosexual became a case history, but that the case history helped to bring the homosexual into existence." And if, as he urges, we need to look at medical discourses as "concrete practices generating relations of power and knowledge in local settings," what agency, he asks, did individual men exert under such circumstances, or, as he puts it, what are the "relative roles played by discourse and the material in shaping identities and experience"? Looking at sexual psychopath laws that were passed in the 1940s and 1950s in Canada, Chenier explores how the "sexual deviant" came to be a new object of psychiatric study and how the term's popularization provided the public with a new understanding of "the homosexual"; in addition, "women whose sexual activities violated social and moral standards were also likely to be labelled psychopathic." Duder warns us of seeing the new discourse on sexuality as "monolithic": "emerging ideas about lesbianism [...] had both positive and negative effects. [...] [S]ome were able to frame their feelings within the new discourse without internalizing its more negative aspects." Still further, Francis reminds us that "straightforward notions of identity fail in the extraordinarily complex tasks of intimacy and desire. How then to construct a language which 'names the self' in less unitary and restrictive ways?"

If the scholarship in queer studies, following Foucault in particular, has made it clear that identity categories are a recent phenomenon, these scholars remind us that the coming together of medical and juridical discourses to create a new object of study—of discipline and surveillance—needs to be properly historicized when we are looking at sexuality. Other contributors to *Queerly Canadian* look at the historical legacy of those identity categories and the role of representation in helping to naturalize and (re)produce them. For example, in her examination of Modernist art practices of representing white and black female bodies, Nelson argues that "censorship was used in an effort to monitor and carefully delimit the boundaries of female sexuality. However, this practice was not arbitrary but directed specifically at representations of the white female body in an effort to protect the idealization of white womanhood." Such policing had the effect of figuring blackness as "primitive" and whiteness "as 'civilized,' beautiful, rational, and intelligent." Martin Cannon interrogates the social construction of the "Indian" in government policy such as the *Indian Act*, and the way the term *berdache* served to conflate homosexuality with more complex gender, sexual, and spiritual practices. More recently, Kiss & Tell, in their contemporary artwork exploring lesbian sexuality, look at the role that feminism and gay rights have had in shaping lesbian understandings of the self and what it means to "transgress" and even "betray" those identities in relation to sadomasochistic and "pornographic" representations. Namaste asks questions about who is in control of identity in current media representations of trans people and what effects—that is, what knowledges and power relations—are (re)produced through those images. Cavanagh and Sykes, building on the work of Pronger and others, look to the world of organized sports for the way in which binary concepts of gender are reinforced and policed and how the strict regulations around competition indeed manifest anxieties about border-crossings and "non-normative" bodies.

Still other authors examine both personal and institutional confrontations with putative and abject identities. Townsend describes the shock of identity when moving to Canada in the months following the murder of the Portuguese shoeshine boy Emanuel Jaques and Anita Bryant's "Save the Children" campaign visit to Toronto, and the effect that these two 1977 events had in dramatically conflating homosexuality with pedophilia. Shogan looks at the homophobia at work that prevented NHL hockey player Sheldon Kennedy from speaking out about his abuser Graham James for fear of being identified as gay. Kinsman interrogates what it meant, during the wake of anti-communist witch hunts, to be identified as a "pinko commie fag." In relation to sex work and the way in which workers are governed and policed, Brock asks how they have "been prevented from entering into discourses which determine their work and construct their identities." In strip clubs, Bruckert looks at the way a female worker is "required to assume a role that is neither her own nor of her making." If "she is always performing" a role, "to what extent can she transcend her-self through the body and reproduce sexuality without internalizing an alienating and oppressive regime of physical representation?"

Further distinguishing between acts and identities, Yallop looks at queer youth and how sexual identity develops, and the struggles youth face in adopting those identities. How do "gay" and "straight" fail to "capture the complexities of sexuality"? He reminds us that "awareness of same-sex attraction is not the same as adopting a gay identity" and that "the belief that one has to be sexually active in order to credibly self-identify as gay is a double standard. This same measure is not used for heterosexuals because heterosexuality is assumed." Indeed for many male youth, their "first sexual experience is not as significant as falling in love with another male." Gosine looks at the way "[q]ueer, immigrant youth ... are perpetually cast outside the nations they cross: bad ethnic citizens who betray the reproductive prerogatives of the 'home,' and racialized bodies read as abnormal, incompetent, and/or inferior in the 'host,' including in its principal gay and lesbian venues." Fung and McCaskell remind us how, if the AIDS epidemic initially turned people into "pariahs," a "new 'poz' identity—a brotherhood (and soon sister-hood) of infection located within, but also outside, the gay communities ... claimed to reach beyond the divisions of race, gender, and class. At times it almost did. Impending common death tended to intensify the need for solidarity." Adam examines barebacking culture, which raises still new questions about the relationship between acts and identities. In confronting the AIDS epidemic, "by the 1990s gay men [had] responded with a massive reorientation of their sexual practices." And now, for a number of reasons which he examines, "a converging set of social, psychological, and physiological factors [... have] created the conditions for the begin-nings of a bareback microculture and identity"—one that "remains ... emergent, inchoate, and contested." In yet another more recent challenge to queer identity, Epstein asks us to think about new and emerging categories in (and outside) law such as "parent," "family," "queer spawn"/"kids of queers," or "pregnant man."

Such interrogations of identity lead to larger questions about community and activism. Smith, for instance, looks at "the ways in which collective identity is constructed through social and political processes. While same-sex behaviour has existed in many societies, it is only in the Western world since the 1960s that the identities of 'gay' and 'lesbian' have been formulated as identity options that are currently available." More to the point, she examines how the "gay liberation movement early on encountered a tension between the idea that categories of gender and sexuality should be erased and the need to construct lesbian and gay identities as a necessary prerequisite to the building of the movement." Ross looks at how debates about gay liberation created schisms within and between the lesbian and gay communities over issues such as public and bathhouse sex, pornography, and intergenerational sex, particularly following the Toronto and Ontario Provincial Police raid on the *Body Politic* offices in 1977 over Gerald Hannon's article, "Men Loving Boys Loving Men." According to Ross, this was a particular "moment in the consolidation of a white, middle class Lesbian Nationalist identity and community [… and] the subsequent fracturing of hegemonic lesbian feminism in the 1980s and the emergent possibility for new queer alliances in the 1990s."

For a number of contributors here, such questions about alliances, belonging, and communal identity have taken on new dimensions. Noble asks about the relationship between trans men and the lesbian feminist communities that were central to his politics and activism, once he was no longer "seen" to be a member of the latter group. Namaste challenges the presumption that trans people are even a part of the gay and lesbian/queer community, especially for those who have no history or ties there. And of course sex work, as Brock examines, continues to both unite and divide queer and feminist communities. For Cossman, these questions of identification and community are better framed in terms of citizenship, particularly in the wake of gay marriage. "Gay and lesbian subjects are in the process of becoming citizens. This process may be incomplete and uneven. But, it is a process that is underway." "How," she then asks, are "gay and lesbian subjects" transformed when they "cross the border into legitimate citizenship," and how are they also destabilizing "the borders between gay and straight"? As such identities are transformed, Valverde asks us to think critically about "the vanishing homosexual" and the way the "gay community is [instead] constructed as a quasi-ethnic group" in recent legal rulings. If sexuality itself is no longer seen to be central to that identity, by extension, the "community's future [is not] embodied" in the media as "a young queer person or a transsexual activist, but, predictably, in images of a respectable same-sex couple." Examining the Toronto Police raid on the Pussy Palace (and the resulting court case, *R. v. Hornick* [2002]), Lamble notes the way the terms "lesbian" or "transgender" do not appear in the legal ruling. But, "[r]esisting the temptation to see legal invisibility as simply the consequence of state indifference or repression, [she] suggest[s] legal discourses and organizational rationalities constitute queer bodies and sexualities as unthinkable and unknowable." Ultimately, "[a]n event originally designed to promote a public, transgressive, queer sexuality was tamed and desexualized by legal discourse in order to produce victims worthy of state protection."

These questions about the status of queerness and about what gay identity might mean or look like today in turn have new and profound ramifications for our understanding of ourselves and our relationship to communal and national histories and narratives. What effect do nationalism and national identity have on gay identity or attempts to que(e)ry identity? King, in her examination of the "problem" of Canadian identity, argues that

> [b]oth Canada's size … and its racial, ethnic, linguistic, and sexual diversity ensure that this question is not easily resolved.… For similar reasons, attempts to define Canadianness in the past three decades have rarely begun with the notion of a unitary, distinct identity (as is the case in many modern Western nation states) but instead with a state-sanctioned recognition of difference, contradiction, and tension—most obviously illustrated in its policies of official bilingualism and multiculturalism, and fondly known as the Canadian

"mosaic." … The problem with the mosaic, particularly for aboriginal peoples, Quebec sovereigntists, recent non-Anglo immigrants, and gays, is that this recognition of difference frequently fails to translate into economic, political, or cultural autonomy, and indeed often translates into state-sanctioned oppression and violence. Thus, for marginalized populations in Canada, the struggle for Canadian national identity is not the most pressing issue on the political agenda (as saturation-point media coverage of this question suggests) and, indeed, the national preoccupation with the search for the meaning of Canada often works as a tool to make invisible the relations of power and privilege that work to constitute such populations as marginal.

How then, we might ask, can an interrogation of the politics of sexuality expose these relations of power and lead us to an understanding of how the nation works at the expense of sexual diversity? Or, perhaps more accurately, how have narratives of sexuality and sexual minorities been necessary to create the very idea of Canadian national identity? Dubinsky looks at the construction of the honeymoon, and Niagara Falls, as integral to the national imaginary: "The honeymoon was not just popular, it was *important*.… [P]ostwar sex experts imagined a direct line that began at the honeymoon and extended to the health and well-being of the marriage and, hence, society itself." There was a wealth of "expert" advice and popular discourse about the honeymoon; the health of the nation was at stake. But such a narrative relied heavily on the "conformity to gender roles." All we have to do is look at the experience of police harassment of gay people in places such as Niagara Falls to realize that the very experience of the "nation" was different for gay and straight people. In Kinsman's analysis of the role of sexuality in Cold War politics, he argues that we need to contest "[t]he hegemonic view of the Cold War [as] a conflict between the American and Soviet empires" and expand "the analysis … to include relations of ethnicity, immigration, race, gender, and sexuality." By constructing queer people as a national security threat, the RCMP was able to exercise power and surveillance in extreme ways in Canada.

A number of contributors here look at various moral panics and how they have played out in relation to, for example, the "Sex Wars" around sexual representation and Canada's obscenity laws (Kiss & Tell), prostitution and its regulation in this country (Brock), the Emanuel Jaques murder and the "cleanup" of Yonge Street in Toronto in the late 1970s (Townsend), the AIDS epidemic and the Canadian response (King, Fung, and McCaskell), and the sex-abuse scandal in hockey and how it played out in the Canadian media and in Swift Current where Sheldon Kennedy was coached by Graham James (Shogan). Moral panics are typically manifestations of other local and national anxieties (about gender, race, and class, for example), and in turn they demonstrate how the discourse surrounding sexuality allows for both overt and insidious operations of power. For Chenier, "[c]riminal sexual psychopath legislation in Canada was the product of a moral panic that took shape during a particular historical period, but it also must be seen as but one point along a century-old trajectory of psycho-medical thinking about criminality, sexuality, and the law." Strange looks at how the social and moral reform movements at the beginning of the twentieth century "traced some of the greatest sources of immorality to … working women and their changing leisure patterns." The "working girl" was not seen as a worker, but as an "index of urban immorality; her leisure received more attention than her work because [… it was] believed that it was in leisure pursuits that moral choices were made." In a more recent example of a moral panic, Cavanagh analyzes the "sensationalist media coverage surrounding the twenty-six-year-old former teacher Amy Gehring and the allegations that she indecently assaulted two former [male] students in the British school to which she was recruited in 2000 from her native Canada." In light of Gehring's acquittal, Cavanagh argues we must view this case as scandalous

> because it taps into a fear of who the feminine subject can be in sexualized power dynamics. […] Female teachers like Gehring seem to violate Western conventions of gender associated with the prototype of the younger, presumably passive female subject and the older, allegedly more aggressive male counterpart of the heterosexual encounter; intergenerational prohibitions on sex (with its associated refusal of ascetic motherly love imbued in the construction of the feminine teacher role); and the mythology of the "good girl" attributed to the sexual subjectivity of girls and young men in the school.

And it is because schools play such a fundamental role in shaping young people's understandings and experiences of gender and sexuality that they are such contested spaces when it comes to raising issues of sexual diversity. Looking at the coming out experience, Yallop directs us to survey results indicating that gay youth hardly ever first discuss their sexual orientation with a teacher or school counsellor—a telling reminder of how hostile an environment schools can be for queer youth. Rayside examines in detail the history and policy of addressing sexual and gender diversity in schools and the debates surrounding them throughout the country. From bullying and suicide to "safe schools" policies, from book-banning and heterosexism in the curriculum to same-sex couples being allowed to attend high-school proms, from religious and right-wing opposition over the issue of inclusion to queer student and teacher activism, he documents the overwhelming complacency when it comes to policy and implementation on the part of many teachers, school boards, and provincial ministries of education. "Most Canadians believe that the acceptance of same-sex relationships, up to and including marriage, speaks to overall policy inclusiveness, and they probably believe that schools have moved further than they have." In the workplace, Hunt and Eaton look at the labour movement's changing policy regarding discrimination against LGBT workers and where that policy still falls short. Not surprisingly, trans rights and protections have been the most difficult to achieve, particularly putting in place specific language addressing discrimination based on gender, rather than sex or disability. "Few unions have yet achieved this goal."

The gap between policy and practice can be great in Canadian schools, workplaces, and in our cultural institutions, such as the National Film Board of Canada. As Waugh explains, "GLBTQ Canadians have a rollercoaster love-hate relationship with John Grierson's studio, founded in 1939 to construct our national imaginary," because of both the long silence and the homophobia when it came to giving voice to sexual minorities. Such representations are not only important for artists and individual Canadians who are members of these groups, but NFB films and videos make the domestic rounds of the proverbial church basements, school AV centres, and community library loan shelves, flow out through cassette and DVD merchandising online and over the counter, occasionally make it onto cablecast, and even stream down from increasingly common cyber servers. This everyday product is unrecognized by cultural arbiters but reaches huge numbers of people efficiently and quietly, providing invaluable resources for isolated individuals and grass roots groups.

But the battles over censorship and representation are also part of a larger story told in this book about queer resistance to state control and discrimination and to our national narratives of tolerance, inclusion, and diversity. Taking us back to where we began this introduction, and the place of irony as a Canadian and queer strategy for resistance, let us conclude by looking at the cover art for this book: *Charged Particles in Motion* (2007, acrylic on canvas, 121.9 x 182.9 cm), by queer Canadian Cree artist Kent Monkman. Although Swanson's essay about Monkman in this collection does not discuss this particular image, the painting is nonetheless an extraordinary illustration of her argument of how his work interrogates canonical colonial images of Aboriginal peoples by a number of important nineteenth-century painters such as Paul Kane, Albert Bierstadt, and the Hudson School of painters who "mythologized the 'dying' race of Red Men while propagating their own personas as heroic adventurers in a wild, undiscovered land." Taking up Kane's *Scene in the Northwest: Portrait of John Henry Lefroy* (c. 1845), also known as *The Surveyor*,[10] Monkman literally enters the frame by way of his alter ego, Miss Chief Share Eagle Testickle, to throw into turmoil a number of binaries we would normally rely upon to interpret the Kane work: artist and model, colonial explorer and colonized subject, gazer and gazed upon, male and female, straight and queer, past and present, real and imaginary. In the Kane painting, the British Lefroy, who set out in 1843 to map the magnetic North Pole, poses confidently for the artist, clothed in *coureur de bois* attire and snowshoes next to his bobsled and dog-pack. Having achieved his goal (part of the larger Enlightenment project), Lefroy stands fully assured of his place in history and as a national icon. And time has proven him correct, particularly when we consider the fact that Kane's piece sold in 2002 at Sotheby's in Toronto to Canadian media baron Ken Thomson for $5 million— double the price of any previous sale of a Canadian painting.[11] Later donated by Thomson to the Art Gallery of Ontario, the painting is one of many such works that foreground European explorers in a Canadian landscape "authenticated" through the use of Aboriginal characters to fill out the background, in this case a woman standing next to a teepee.

In the Monkman work, however, the tranquility and stasis of the scene is interrupted as Miss Chief, white leather whip in hand, charges across the foreground from right to left in her bobsled driven by a pack of six white huskies, none of which appears to touch the ground (as though she were Santa Claus flying a reindeer-driven sled). Against the more muted shades used in the rest of the painting, we see the striking contrast with the bright colours used to depict Miss Chief and her dogs, where the bright pink satin, feathered, and beaded harness coverings on the dogs' white fur backs are echoed in Miss Chief's pink gloves, pink-feathered white fur pillbox hat, and full-length white fur coat blowing open to reveal the matching satin material of her coat lining and her pink stiletto leather boots—and a very muscular male body. Always fashion conscious—and anachronistic, as if she just flew in from our own era—Miss Chief's bobsled is imprinted with the Louis Vuitton logo and design pattern. If Lefroy is the central focus of the Kane painting, clearly Miss Chief takes centre stage here, literally bowling him over as he lies prone on the ground in a state of confusion, bobsled overturned, his own dogs fallen or jumping anxiously, one a very coiffed black poodle that reminds us of the iconic queer poodle image used so famously (and as an alter ego) by gay Canadian art trio General Idea, and which does not appear in Kane's painting.

The work operates on many levels, not least of which is the other painting that Monkman "highjacks" here: Albert Bierstadt's *Yosemite Winter Scene* (1872).[12] Indeed the entire landscape is not that of Kane; rather, detail by detail, brushstroke by brushstroke, Monkman's landscape is an exact match for the earlier work. Bierstadt's painting, void of people, and paradigmatic of the explorer fantasy of discovering virgin territory, is a classic romantic landscape painting, and with the leafless trees catching the light coming from behind the clouds, it could be a Caspar David Friedrich graveyard scene. Reclaiming, reinvigorating, and reimagining this solemn, sublime, and perhaps spiritual (if overdone in the attempt to be an "awe-inspiring"[13]) landscape in Bierstadt's work, and upsetting the colonial authority and "knowledge" of the Kane work, Monkman intervenes in the historical record and the national mythology to counter ideas of the "noble savage" and the "'dying' race of Red Men." Miss Chief is very much alive—and kicking—and functions as a trickster figure who blurs gender binaries, comically wreaking havoc with order and reason, as a way of insisting on Aboriginal subjectivity, agency, and survival. If Miss Chief looks like a drag queen we may encounter in any gay bar performance, Monkman fuses this contemporary queer and camp icon with earlier Aboriginal notions of both the gender-bending, shape-shifting trickster and the two-spirited individuals who held elevated status in many indigenous cultures because they were seen to contain both genders. Nearly wiped out by Christian colonization through violence and shame, this character is reappropriated by Monkman to challenge monolithic notions of authenticity and purity, and signify and embody queer and Aboriginal power.

Resistance, adaptation, and hybridity all feature strongly in Monkman's work and serve as a queer thematic for the tensions, contradictions, and multiplicity of identity we have been discussing here in this introduction and which many of the contributors try to work through in their essays. *Charged Particles in Motion* is not just a reference to the mapping of the magnetic North Pole, but an indication of the dynamic, transformative, erotically charged, and radicalizing force of queer interrogation and affirmation that is also documented and manifested in the essays and scholarship in this book. And to do it with the aplomb, flamboyance, and style of Miss Chief is something to which we all can aspire.

I want to acknowledge here how incredibly fortunate I am to be a part of the Mark S. Bonham Centre for Sexual Diversity Studies. To teach the courses on sexuality that I do, to have the full support to carry out the research I care about, and to be in an environment where others are also committed to doing that work has consistently challenged me to do better. Colleagues including Brenda Cossman, Maureen FitzGerald, David Rayside, David Townsend, and Mariana Valverde are not just extraordinary role models to have but colleagues who make the job so rewarding. I wish that other academics who work in sexuality studies (and in other areas) all had this kind of collegiality and institutional support. Don Ainslie, Emily Gilbert, Linda Hutcheon, Don McLeod, and Vikki Visvis at University College and at University of Toronto, and Elise Chenier at SFU, along with the Steering Committee, Advisory Board, and Fellows of the Centre, and our program assistant Wendy Koslow, have all directly and indirectly supported my work and this project. And of course the students in our program, at both the undergraduate and graduate level, offer great insight and opportunity for my own critical thinking in this field. Andrew Lesk helped out early on in the project and has continued to offer his expert advice. Lee Frew, my research assistant, has also proven himself to be a remarkable asset and colleague.

NOTES

1 Linda Hutcheon, *Splitting Images: Contemporary Canadian Ironies* (Toronto: Oxford UP, 1991), 1.

2 Hutcheon, 2–3.

3 Hutcheon, 15.

4 Also see, Marci McDonald, *The Armageddon Factor: The Rise of Christian Nationalism in Canada* (Toronto: Random House, 2010).

5 Harris MacLeod, "Feds' new citizenship guide reflects Canada's becoming more conservative," *Hill Times* 23 Nov. 2009. http://www.hilltimes.com/news/2009/11/23/feds-new-citizenship-guide-reflects-canadas-becoming-more-conservative/22812. Accessed 30 Dec. 2011.

6 Dale Smith, "Revamped citizenship guide still light on gay content," *Xtra!* 15 Mar. 2011. http://www.xtra.ca/public/National/Revamped_citizenship_guide_still_light_on_gay_content-9873.aspx. Accessed 30 Dec. 2011.

7 Citizenship and Immigration Canada, "Who We Are," *Study Guide—Discover Canada: The Rights and Responsibilities of Citizenship,* 2011. http://www.cic.gc.ca/english/resources/publications/discover/section-05.asp. Accessed 30 Dec. 2011.

8 Eva Mackey, *The House of Difference: Cultural Politics and National Identity in Canada* (Toronto: University of Toronto Press, 2002), 14.

9 Oliver Moore, "Toronto Zoo decision to separate 'gay' penguins sparks international outcry," *Globe and Mail* 10 Nov. 2011. http://www.theglobeandmail.com/news/national/toronto/toronto-zoo-decision-to-separate-gay-penguins-sparks-international-outcry/article2231781/. Accessed 2 Jan. 2012.

10 "Kent Monkman, *Charged Particles in Motion.*" Heffel.com. http://www.heffel.com/auction/Details_F.aspx?ID=36477. Accessed 15 Jan. 2012.

11 Adams, James, "Canadian painting sells for record $5-million," *Globe and Mail*, 26 Feb. 2002: A1.

12 I would like to thank my research assistant, Lee Frew, for pointing this out to me and whose doctoral dissertation, "A Kinship with Otherness: Settler Subjectivity and the Image of the Wild Animal in Canadian Fiction in English," York University, 2011, helped me in my own thinking here, particularly for the way, as he argues, traditionally "[b]oth the image of the indigene and the image of the wild animal are … symbolically managed within a discourse of landscape in order to foreclose any claim either might have *to* the land" (12–13).

13 "Albert Bierstadt Oil Paintings." FineArt-China.com. www.fineart-china.com/htmlimg/image-02509.html. Accessed 15 Jan. 2012.

PART ONE
Thinking Queerly About Identity, Community, and Nation

CHAPTER 1

On the Myth of Sexual Orientation: Field Notes from the Personal, Pedagogical, and Historical Discourses of Identity

Margot Francis

In *The History of Sexuality*, volume I, Michel Foucault argues that the notion of 'sexual identities' as constitutive of the 'truth' of our being is one influential means by which modern subjectivities are managed. However, he also suggests that this same notion has made possible a 'reverse discourse,' through which homosexual subjects have spoken back against the terms of a medico-scientific project which has relied on our existence to establish its own legitimacy.[1] While the development of this reverse discourse has been of critical importance in the lobby for lesbian and gay civil rights and the right to an everyday not organized by violence and erasure, it has *not* typically called into question the grounds of the very heterosexual/homosexual binary itself. In fact, the pedagogy of much liberal antihomophobia discourse has reinforced static notions of sexuality as identity.[2] In addition, this discourse has often failed to address sexuality as a socially and historically constituted set of relations, which may not be as settled as is generally presumed. It is precisely the possibilities inherent in this unsettling of sexual binaries that provides the axis around which this project will turn.

This chapter attempts to ground an argument regarding the instability of sexual categories in an investigation of the shifting borders of sexuality as this is mapped in three different sites: the personal, the pedagogical, and the historical. The argument will proceed in several stages.

In the first I use field notes from the personal and pedagogical as a method of reflecting on my three years of work as an antiheterosexism educator in secondary schools and in community settings. Here I investigate the construction of sexuality *not* as a discovery regarding the 'truth of one's being,' but as that which requires explanation and about which knowledge might be produced. This methodology is rooted in historian Joan Scott's analysis that 'it is not individuals who have experience, but subjects who are constituted through experience.'[3] Thus I use field notes as a self-reflexive method of drawing attention to the contradictory ways in which individual subjects and educational practices are formed, in, and through, resistance to heteronomative ideals.

The second stage uses the theoretical frameworks suggested by Jennifer Terry and Gayatri Spivak to explore one avenue through which historical research can be used to shift the grounds for political activism. I will argue that the first large-scale, empirical study of women's sexuality in America, titled *Factors in the Sex Life of Twenty-Two Hundred Women* (Davis [1929]),[4] suggests that textual representations of women's sexual *practice* were remarkably dissimilar from the *discourses* about white, middle-class women's sexuality which were emerging during this same period. Thus while empirical research indicated a remarkable complexity and fluidity in women's sexual choices, the discourses *about* women posited same-sex attractions as the result of congenital, biologically based, and binary sexual identities.[5] To explain this disjuncture I will argue that the practice of labelling sexuality as identity served a range of strategic and contradictory purposes for *both* the emerging medico-scientific *and* homosexual communities.

In the postscript to this chapter I suggest that a deconstructive approach such as the one suggested here can contribute to the project of developing a pedagogy which recognizes that the homo/hetero binary is far from pure; and can, in addition, challenge the limitations inherent in an identity-based politic. However, as my field notes from the personal and pedagogical will suggest, and as Janet E. Halley notes in her essay 'The Construction of Heterosexuality,' deconstruction itself cannot accomplish the work of politics. As she observes, 'An analysis of the definitional knots (exposed by the deconstruction of the binarism hetero/homosexuality), however necessary, is not at all sufficient to disable them. Quite the opposite: I would suggest that an understanding of their irresolvable instability has been continually available, and has continually lent discursive authority, to antigay as well as to gay cultural forces of this century.'[6]

Indeed, from the use of electric shock therapy to reprogram gay patients, to the mobilization of groups to 'cure' gay students, the knowledge of the 'irresolvable instability' of the hetero/homo binary continues to be used against queer communities. But then the protection of essentialism is no protection either, as knowledge about the supposed 'gay' gene is as likely to be used to allow parents to select *not* to have gay children as it is to further the project of establishing that homosexuality is inborn, and thus not deserving of moral condemnation. But perhaps deconstruction can take yet another turn. Perhaps the instability of the term *queer* can pose the production of *normalization* as the problem. In this context the interrogation of binaries themselves—normal/deviant, biological/social, straight/gay—can open up quite a different approach. As Deborah Britzman suggests, 'in its positivity, Queer Theory offers methods of imagining difference on its own terms: as eros, as desire, and as the grounds of politicality. It is a particular articulation that returns us to practices of bodies and bodies of practices.'[7]

This project then, examines how practices of deconstruction might be used more effectively to further the project of thinking ethically about discourses of difference and visibility in our bodies, in history, and in pedagogy—and in the risking of the self that is the grounds of all political action.

FIELD NOTES FROM THE 'PERSONAL'

> Work which 'rashly jettisons' essentialism takes away an interventionary strategy of
> the oppressed who can use it in an Irigarayian move 'to undo by overdoing,' a 'displace-
> ment and redeployment of essentialism' which thinks through the body.[8]

Thinking through the body is no simple project. For twelve years of my life I was primarily attracted to men, and for eleven years after, my sustained attractions and relationships have been with women. While this shift was neither sudden nor complete, desire, as I have experienced it, has been far from coherent. 'Go the way your blood beats,' writes James Baldwin.[9] And I do. Yet a discourse which locates desire, agency, and personal truth solely within the body or the blood, fails the task.

The story of my coming out was at first a coming into my 'No.' This involved a body know-ledge that I *could not* continue in heterosexual relationships, not for lack of sexual pleasure but because I could not (again) involve myself in a partnership where I was not *seen*. This is not a coming out story I will tell in a classroom, because the popular culture's discourse of sexuality as the essential ground of one's being has been too widely dispersed for this story not to reinforce stereotypes about lesbians as 'women who are bitter about men, and therefore turn to other women and deny the "true" nature of their desire.'

But what about my 'Yes?' This story is about intense intimacy and lust, and for better or worse it is about the most profoundly affecting relationships of my life. It is also about connec-tions which have been lived in a context of growing possibilities for autonomy and fierce desires for equity. While my attraction to masculinity has been consistent I now prefer my boys to be girls.[10] Throughout, my curiosity, hunger, and courage have been stoked by queer intellectual and cultural communities, and by the unapologetic material on sexuality produced by queer and straight cultural workers. However, this also is not a story easily told within the constraints of a secondary school classroom.

Thus both the terms *lesbian* and *bisexual* are an incomplete description of the desire in my blood. They are a historical construction of identity I have both claimed and resisted; and in the end they comprise provisional strategies embraced for the possibilities they have created in resistance to heteronormative and misogynist norms. Clearly, straightforward notions of identity fail in the extraordinarily complex tasks of intimacy and desire. How then to construct a language which 'names the self' in less unitary and restrictive ways? How did the concept develop that anyone is really anything? Does the fact that the question can be asked at all attest to the instability of this category we call essential: the scent of desire?

FIELD NOTES FROM AN ANTIHETEROSEXISM EDUCATOR

> What sort of difference would it make for everyone in a classroom if gay and lesbian
> writing were set loose from confirmations of homophobia, the afterthoughts of inclu-
> sion, or the special event?[11]

In a classroom I survey the sea of faces in front of me and struggle with the binary which constructs this pedagogical moment—even before I step into it. We are the queers, here to educate about heterosexism and challenge the 'othering' which always and already confounds this encounter. I often wonder at the shoals that frame anti-oppression work for all of us who do antisexism, antiracism and antihomophobia education. How is it that the structure of the questions may undermine the very project we engage in? As James Baldwin suggests, when talking about racism, 'as long as I protest my case on evidence or assumptions held by others, I'm simply reinforcing those assumptions. As long as I complain about being oppressed, the oppressor is in consolation of knowing that I know my place, so to speak.'[12]

How then to proceed? In the context of the heteronormative assumptions of the classroom, where we are the *queers* come to educate the *straights,* constructing a pedagogy which disrupts and challenges these objectifying paradigms is a troubling and difficult task.

Between 1993 and 1996 I served as the coordinator for a diverse team of youth called TEACH—Teens Educating and Confronting Homophobia.[13] Over the years youth involved with TEACH have identified in a range of ways, including queer, gay, lesbian, bisexual, undecided, and heterosexual; also lesbians who are occasionally attracted to men and those who refuse identification. In our work, tactics of critical analysis, storytelling, and subversion all had their use. The pedagogies we employed explored the effects of heterosexism on gay youth, and examined how the stigma of the epithets *faggot* and *dyke* are used to police all our performance of gender—masculinity and femininity—in addition to policing desire.

Most antiheterosexism educational work in North America, including my own, has relied to some degree on the narrative of the coming out story.[14] The invisibility imposed by a heteronormative culture ensures that storytelling can often disrupt and problematize the objectifying label 'gay.' In addition, the youth with whom I have worked have *performed* antiheterosexism educational work as an act of resistance, generosity, anger, and pride. However, a host of significant problems remains. Even where the 'traditional' coming out story is unsettled by descriptions of a range of sexualities, the assumption of sexuality itself as an essential and individualizable truth of one's being is nevertheless reinforced. Thus I ask: Does this work participate in re/forming subjectivities through the very labeling process which makes stories of *identity* possible? How then do human beings become simultaneously turned as they turn themselves into subjects? And how might this process of naming end up re/producing the very essentialist categories I want clearly to avoid?

In their article 'Queer Pedagogy: Praxis Makes Im/Perfect,' Mary Bryson and Suzanne de Castell engage a similar issue in their analysis of a lesbian studies course they co-taught in 1991:

> We attempted to reflect on what it might mean ... (to) re-think, or *queer*(y) normatively sanctioned pedagogies—to insist on the 'right to speak as one,' to make pedagogical spaces where the hitherto unsayable could be uttered ... within the oppressive confines of the always-already heterosexualized classroom. How to accomplish some of this while, concurrently, resisting the incredible pressures to instantiate and reify essentialized representations of queer sexuality ...[15]

These are questions I have felt in my body; they have also engaged my curiosity as an educator and a scholar. However, after three years of working with youth to facilitate workshops I found myself falling silent. My body refused the lack of complexity as I asked, like Denise Riley, 'Am I That Name?'[16]

These are the problems with identity, yet how might one engage in a political practice without it? The very act of pedagogy has kept me cognizant of just how important visibility is, as it has brought us face to face with the heterosexist erasure that is always and everywhere present. While individual student responses to TEACH were overwhelmingly positive, myriad restrictions confounded the possibility of real change. As Deborah Britzman suggests, so long as consideration of sexualities is confined to the 'afterthoughts of inclusion, or the special event,' only the most superficial changes are possible, leaving the structure of curriculum and everyday heteronormative practices unchallenged. TEACH workshops were considered disruptive, or marginal, or both, and often ended up sandwiched into the least amount of time possible. In addition, the pervasive subtext of threat rooted in cultural taboos about sex, as well as homo-sex, continues to keep the vast majority of queer students and teachers silent about the complex realities of their lives.

And then there was the hate. Or was it desire?

At a workshop in Toronto in 1995 several young men engaged in escalating heckling and harassment of the team of presenters, and one announced that 'if he ever had a gay son, he would kill him.' Our team refused to come back to the class unless the young men were asked to leave. Their parents, fundamentalist Christians, forbade them to come back in any case.

The follow-up workshop was conducted without similar disruption and with significantly more space for other students to speak. However, as this second workshop ended, the young men who had attended the first appeared at the classroom door, anxious to speak with us. Fascinated and repelled in the same moment, they could not leave us, or the issue, alone.

On reading through the evaluation forms, which include the request that students list 'some things they learned about themselves,' five of the twenty forms contained the following comments: 'Nothing, I'm not a fag'; 'I'm not gay'; 'I don't like you, and I glad I'm strait' [sic]; 'Im not gay' [sic]; 'I'm a heterosexual and I will respect others, to an extent.' In response to the question 'What were the most helpful aspects of the workshop?' one student responded, 'When you left the building.' Heterosexual panic—and obsession—indeed.

Judith Butler suggests that sexuality and gender are embodied, but not essentialist, social practices. Encounters like the one detailed above, and the palpable discomfort evidenced by some young men when we challenged heteronormative *gender* as well as *sexual* roles, illustrates the panic felt when this embodied 'self' is unsettled. Butler continues: 'that heterosexuality is always in the act of elaborating itself is evidence that it is perpetually at risk, that is, that it "knows" its own possibility of becoming undone …'[17] Thus while there is no underestimating the importance of being 'out,' the terms of the discourse may nevertheless reinforce notions of sexuality that undermine the very space one seeks to create. How to unsettle this pedagogical, and crucially political, dilemma?

For the task of pushing the boundaries of what is thinkable in resistance to hegemonic norms I can find no better tool than history. I turn, then, to research from turn-of-the-century

America to examine possibilities for looking at the connections between gender, sex, and hegemonic notions of identity in more complex and thoughtful ways.

SOURCES AND THE HISTORY OF THE SUBALTERN

As Joan Scott has suggested, the proliferation of historical narratives occasioned by feminist, antiracist, and queer scholarship has generated a crisis for orthodox history and pushed debates about 'objectivity' to a new and critical juncture. The new histories generated in this context have multiplied not only stories, but also subjects, and insisted that histories are written from fundamentally different and sometimes irreconcilable standpoints, none of which may be completely true.[18] Current historiographic research has increasingly turned to considering how multiple social positionings—shaped by race, gender, class, and sexuality, among other things—form the diverse fields of power regulating agency and resistance in local sites.

For historians of sexuality one of the central dilemmas is the problem of sources. Most of the documents which provide information about same-gender relationships have been destroyed through heterosexist vandalism, effacement, and suppression. The remaining historical materials are most often made up of elite accounts which focus on the sin, criminality, or pathology inherent in a deviant sexuality.

In her article 'Theorizing Deviant Historiography' Jennifer Terry suggests that historians face the task of searching for a subaltern presence and consciousness, and yet must 'rely on the dominant account, not only for source material but also for tracing how these sources constructed the very conditions of subalternity.'[19] Terry emphasizes the necessity for historians to read against the grain of these largely hostile accounts. Using the deconstructive work of Gayatri Spivak, she suggests that 'instead of looking for another *identity* (the subaltern) the reader should watch for *difference* within textual operations of elite accounts.'[20]

Spivak's suggestions are particularly useful in deconstructing the development of the notion of identities, as these were applied to the homosexual or the 'sex pervert' by the medico-scientific discourse at the turn of the century. As Terry elaborates:

> For Spivak, the notion of a coherent and autonomous subaltern subject whose history can be disentangled from colonial accounts is preposterous; similarly, a lesbian and gay history which hopes to find homosexuals totally free of the influences of pathologizing discourses would be an historiographic optical illusion. At best, we can map the techniques by which homosexuality has been marked as different and pathological, and then locate subjective resistances to this homophobia.[21]

Thus, the next part of this chapter is an attempt to provide a set of historiographic field notes that chart the cartography of regulation, agency, resistance, and desire evident in textual accounts of women's sexuality in turn-of-the-century America.

SEX LIVES AND ARCHIVES

In 1918 Katherine Bement Davis embarked on the first major survey of women's sexual behaviour to be undertaken in America. Sponsored by the John D. Rockefeller Jr. Bureau of Social Hygiene, the research was first published in 1929 under the title *Factors in the Sex Life of Twenty-Two Hundred Women*, and represents women's sexuality *across* the homosexual-heterosexual divide. The only other empirically based accounts of women's sexual behaviour during this period can be found in two smaller surveys representing case studies of fewer than fifty women.[22]

Davis solicited information from women who were graduates of women's colleges and coeducational universities and members of women's clubs, to ensure that her study would be perceived as legitimate. These groups, which were likely to be almost exclusively white and middle or upper class, were considered to be a 'respectable class of women.' Thus Davis's research methods both reflected and reproduced racialized and classed assumptions about Black, Chicana, Asian, Native American, and working-class white women who were, in different ways, always/already sexualized and seen as deviant and marginal from the norms of respectability.

Two other historians, Rosalind Rosenberg (1982) and Lillian Faderman (1981, 1991), have examined this study and both have provided only a cursory analysis of the data relating to same-sex relationships between women. As Rosenberg notes, the social discourses which legitimated the Rockefeller investigation can be found in the relatively conservative operations of maternal feminism and moral reform, while the specific impetus for this research came from the foundation's commitment to the abolition of prostitution and the eradication of venereal disease. Ironically, the actual results of the study cast doubt on white middle-class women's ability to fit within the norms of respectability—a consequence which was precisely the reverse of what the sponsors of the study had intended.[23]

The final sample for the Davis survey was composed of the first 1,000 married and 1,200 unmarried women who replied to the 20,000 surveys distributed to women's club members and alumnae from colleges and universities across the country. The majority of respondents were born about 1880 and had completed their degree at the turn of the century; the average age was thirty-seven years. College women made up almost 70 per cent of the married group, and 100 per cent of the unmarried group.

WOMEN RESISTING SEXUAL NORMALCY

The results of Davis's study challenged several then-common notions about women's sexuality. While many middle-class commentators and medico-scientific experts at the beginning of the twentieth century considered white, bourgeois women to be passionless, the Davis study demonstrated that they were far more sexual than most people believed. Of particular interest for our purposes are the results relating to same-sex relationships. As Davis reports, 'Slightly over 50% of a group of [single] women … state that they have experienced intense emotional relations with other women, and that in slightly more than half these cases, or 26% of the entire group, the experience has been accompanied by overt physical practices' [identified in the questionnaire as 'mutual masturbation, contact of the genital organs, or other physical expressions generally recognized as sexual in character'].[24] In the group of 1,000 married women, 30 per cent had had intense emotional relations with other women, and in half of this group, that is 15 per cent of the total, these relations were accompanied by 'physical practices' (298).

Davis had to contend with extensive criticisms for these findings, but chose to stand by the veracity of her figures. Commenting on the controversy in her introduction she notes that 'others have felt that college women are being slandered and that those who replied are not representative of college women as a whole, but are, to an extent at least, those whose experiences are abnormal ... Our own judgment would be that the figures given ... may be taken as a minimum for the group studied ...' (xiv).

As the reaction to these figures suggests, they alone are significant enough to disrupt binary assumptions about the exclusive and contradictory nature of hetero- and homosexualities among this group, at least in turn-of-the-century America. Given this, it is troubling that earlier historians of women's sexuality devoted little attention to the Davis survey. For example, in *Surpassing the Love of Men: Romantic Friendships and Love between Women from the Renaissance to the Present*, Lillian Faderman accords just one page to Davis's findings, despite the fact that the report is the *sole* empirical study of romantic friendships in existence. While the study provides a remarkable store of data indicating that women's romantic friendships *were* often sexual, Faderman leaves this material unexamined.

Faderman has explained what some have seen as her desexualization of women's relationships by arguing that her central purpose was to establish that women who had romantic friendships in this earlier period could be claimed as foremothers to the more recent lesbian feminist movement. For this connection to work it was neither possible or necessary to prove that women's relations were explicitly sexual. Other critics have argued that the definition of nonsexual relationships between women as lesbian may also have suited the larger goal of promoting solidarity between feminists and lesbians—during a period when feminist organizing was often split along these lines.

While there are indeed significant connections between turn-of-the-century romantic friendships and current lesbian practices, there are also significant differences, as the wealth of newer local and historical studies attest.[25] However, of more interest for our purposes here is the observation that not only did Faderman suggest that early romantic friendships need not have been sexual, her analysis downplayed textual evidence that indeed *many were*. These elisions reflect a continuing fault line within lesbian and gay historical research,[26] and a debate to which I hope the present study will contribute. For, as Eve Sedgwick argues, sexuality does transform other languages and relations through which we know. Thus I would argue that the project of mapping the conditions that made these explicitly sexual relationships possible is an important one.

CONSTRUCTING A STUDY, CONSTRUCTING IDENTITY

Despite the fact that same-sex desires cut a broad swath across all the participants in the Davis study, the report nevertheless seems to reflect the researchers' interests in reproducing and stabilizing heteronormative categories. Thus the fundamental axis around which the participants' responses were organized was women's status as married or unmarried.

Introducing the chapter 'Homosexuality: The Unmarried College Woman,' Davis classifies her responses into two categories. Out of a sample of 1,200 unmarried women, 605 of whom had had relationships with women, Davis categorizes the 293 who had 'intense emotional relationships with women' into Group H1 and the 312 women who had intense emotional relationships which were accompanied by sexual expression into Group H2.[27]

The Davis researchers were relentless in their inquiries about the 'single' women's 'failure to marry.' Similarly, the unmarried group are asked about homosexual experiences and nervous breakdowns while at no point are the married women asked to speculate about whether their heterosexuality or their married life have provoked a 'breakdown.'

In the unmarried category Davis's selection of case studies highlights those whom she characterizes as 'naturally' homosexual, which meant they rarely experienced attractions to men. Consequently the relatively uncomplicated narratives provided in the case studies fail to reflect the complexity suggested in her actual figures. However, the two case studies Davis presents of single women who had relationships with both women and men provide an ironic and amusing commentary. One reads, 'I have met so few eligible men that I could count them. Homosexualism has interfered. So have my brains' (291). The second case study presents a woman who has had three sexual relationships with women and more than one encounter with men. As Davis comments, 'She does not regret not having married, as she says that since leaving college "my emotional life has been fed on the sex side … I do not need the financial help of a husband. The many husbands I observe possessed by other women do not seem to me to have developed much of a genius for companionship with their wives"' (293).

In eight out of the nine 'naturally homosexual' case studies Davis conducted the women characterize their experiences in remarkably positive terms. For example, in case number four, a thirty-six-year-old music teacher asserts that she has been aware of strong attractions towards girls and women since she was a child. Claiming the right to judge her own choices and engage in sensual pleasure, she writes, 'It has arisen as an expression of love, which is the only way I have experienced it, and I am qualified to judge. It has proved helpful and has made my life inexpressibly richer and deeper. I would not have been without the experience for worlds' (283).

However, the possibility of finding subaltern subjects 'totally free of the influences of pathologizing discourses would be a historiographic optical illusion.'[28] This woman did not come to her sense of the legitimacy of her relationship alone, but in relation not only to the discourses of pathology but also to those in resistance. Earlier in Davis's case history she tells us: 'I realized that my emotional experiences were more or less out of the ordinary. For a while this worried me frightfully. After six months or more of great mental anxiety in this regard I finally went to a woman physician and made a clean breast of everything. She was most wonderfully wise with me, explained that this was quite natural with some people, and gave me further help and information that has stood by me ever since.'[29] Clearly not all of those who participated in the medical hierarchy accepted the pathologizing discourse of the sexologists.

In case number one a nurse who had received honours for distinguished service suggests that she has 'never met a man [she has] had the slightest desire to marry.' She continues:

> I have come to think that certain women, many, in fact, possibly most of those who are unmarried, are more attracted to women than to men, through no fault of their own, but inherent in their nature; and I am somewhat inclined to think that to mate with one woman is as natural and as healthful and helpful for them as are marital relations between husband and wife. In my own case it has had a decidedly softening and sweetening effect on my temper and general attitude. (280)

However, for each of these subjects pathologizing discourses are never far from view. But where the Davis study tries to obscure this with individualizing questions about 'present sex problems,' this participant replies by contextualizing the 'problem' in relation to these larger discursive practices. In response to the question about 'present sex problems' she replies that the conflict between the moral code of the church and her choice of a sexual relationship with another woman disturb her. However, she continues, 'I cannot believe that large numbers of women must forgo full development because they are attracted to a woman rather than to a man … It seems very prevalent among humans and I feel cannot be wholly bad' (280).

Thus, despite powerful discourses mobilized to deter women's same-sex intimacy, over one-quarter of the single women in this study had sexual relationships with other women, and resisting the condemnation meted out to them, put pen to paper to document the power of connections they 'would not have been without for the world.'

In her section 'Homosexuality: The Married Woman' Davis suggests that the questionnaires for this (assumed heterosexual) group made less detailed enquiries about same-sex experiences, no doubt because they did not expect to find many. However, the problems with notions of sexual identity based on an exclusive heterosexual/homosexual binary are even more evident in Davis's research on married women's same-sex relationships. Out of a total of 1,000 women, 306 (30 per cent) said they had had 'intense emotional relations with other women,' and 157 (15 per cent) had engaged in physical practices (298).

Countering the now popular assumption that sexuality can be described as an individualizable 'orientation,' this section suggests that external factors may have had a significant effect on women's opportunity to have a choice of relationships. In this study married women who had also had same-sex relationships tended to have more education and were more often employed than their counterparts (308).

Of the 157 married women who had same-sex relationships, Davis presents the reader with eight case studies. Here she tells us her selection was based on her desire to 'illustrate several different points of homosexual experiences or raise important questions' (313). Thus some case studies characterize same-sex experiences as 'helpful' and 'a very perfect form of love,' and others are saturated in moral admonitions about the 'menace' of a 'particular kind of girl.' However, these women certainly did *not* see their same-sex relationships as any less compelling or passionate than their heterosexual relationships. Indeed, those who condemned same-sex relationships seemed particularly aware that the 'danger' related precisely to their extraordinary intensity and thus to the intense pain of ending them or to the possibility of betrayal. For example, as case number five explains:

> [T]his girl was my grand passion. She was a boyish girl [and] we had the most radiant and spotless of comradeships. I have never before nor since, felt for any man the rapture and ecstasy and self-immolating devotion that I felt towards that girl. When, after a long time it began to dawn on me that she was not on the square with me; that there were half a dozen girls who felt toward her as I did; and that she liked to receive what we gave and to give nothing of value to any of us in return I quit. The process of disillusionment was long and painful. It left a scar on me that none of my relations with men have ever left. (321)

Case number six provides another example of this theme: 'In college several older women approached me with what, owing to an affair at the time I knew to be perverted sex appeal. It repelled me unspeakably. About six years later I experienced the strongest love of my life for a much older woman who had had at least three such passions before. My whole life was deranged …' (323).

None of these case studies describes a relationship that was entered into lightly. On the contrary, each narrates a passionately felt emotional and sexual connection, all of which existed either prior to or alongside these women's relationships with men.

It is precisely *this* terrain of passion and contradiction—evident in both the single and married women's accounts—that historians have often glossed over or failed to explore. A variety of historians are culpable, both those who assume an always/already straight universe, and sometimes also those investigating lesbian and gay history. Thus, in so far as the either/or of identity politics shapes our investigation, we fail to allow history's real challenge: to go beyond categories into the messy contradictions which have made up women's daily lives.

There are no large-scale empirical studies to provide a textual indication of whether or not large numbers of working-class white, Black, Asian, Latina, or Native American women also engaged in same-sex relationships. Indeed, the rationale for seeking out predominately white, middle-class participants for the Davis study was that this group could be considered a 'respectable class of women.' Ironically, the notion that 'respectable' women were passionless, and the belief that 'real' sex was procreative, may have provided the protective cover which allowed this group to engage in same-sex relationships with relative impunity. While working-class women, especially those of colour, were always/already sexualized, white middle-class women, precisely because they were assumed *not* to be sexual, may have had sufficient discursive protection *to be sexual.*

MEN, GENDER, AND SEX

Interestingly, new research on male same-sex relationships during the same period indicates a similar complexity. However, for men it was more often working-class surroundings which provided the setting for the 'bachelor subcultures' which nourished these connections. In *Gay New York* George Chauncey argues that between 1850 and 1940 an all-male culture played a significant role in the lives of urban Italian, Irish, African-American, and Anglo-American men. Although many would go on to marry, about 40 per cent of men over fifteen years of age were unmarried at any given time.[30]

Marshalling a wide range of discursive and material indicators, Chauncey argues that 'in important respects the hetero-homosexual binarism, the sexual regime now hegemonic in American culture, is a stunningly recent creation' (13). At the turn of the century differing conceptions of gender played a pivotal role in the sexual activities considered permissible for 'normal' men. Particularly in working-class cultures, he asserts, normal men could and did engage in sexual activity with other men without regarding themselves, or being regarded by others, as gay, so long as they did not take the 'feminine' position in the sex act. Chauncey describes the working man's culture as one in which men could both confirm their gendered status as men, and demonstrate their sexual virility, by playing the 'man's part' in sexual encounters. Thus 'in a world in which "every woman is just another place to enter," as one Italian teenager described the attitude of men at his neighbourhood pool hall in 1930, the body to enter did not necessarily have to be a woman's (84).

In middle-class male culture, however, the hetero- homo-sexual binary became hegemonic somewhat earlier, as the late nineteenth century saw bourgeois men utilizing sexual self-control as one crucial element in the attempt to distinguish themselves from the working classes. However, only a few decades earlier, in the first two-thirds of the nineteenth century, romantic friendships between men had been both common and accepted. Anthony Rotundo, who has studied the diaries of dozens of nineteenth-century men, argues that young men frequently slept together and felt free to express passionate love for each other. Drawing on Rotundo, Chauncey writes:

> [T]hese ardent relationships were 'common' and 'socially acceptable.' Devoted male friends opened letters to each other with greetings like 'Lovely Boy' and 'Dearly Beloved'; they kissed and caressed one another; and, as in the case of Joshua Stead and the bachelor lawyer Abraham Lincoln, they sometimes shared the same bed for years. Some men explicitly commented that they felt the same sort of love for both men and women. 'All l know,' wrote one man quoted by Rotundo, 'is that there are three persons in this world whom I have loved, and those are, Julia, John, and Anthony. Dear beloved trio.' It was only in the late nineteenth century that such love for other men became suspect, as men began to worry that it contained an unwholesome, distinctly homosexual element. (120)

While Rotundo argues, correctly, that these men cannot be classified as 'homosexual,' as no such concept existed in their culture, he nevertheless persists in calling them 'heterosexual.' However, one side of this binary relies on the other. As Jonathan Katz has argued in *The Invention of Heterosexuality*, *normal* men and women only began to become *heterosexual* in the late nineteenth and early twentieth century, when they started to make their normalcy contingent on renouncing such intimacies. This process proceeded at a different pace in different contexts and was dependent, as we have seen, on gender, class, and race, among other things.

While it is impossible to determine just how widespread the sexual practices documented in Davis's and Chauncey's research actually were, Alfred Kinsey's studies, published in 1948 but compiled in the 1930s and 1940s, do provide a fuller picture. Kinsey himself intended his work to be used to demonstrate the extent of various kinds of sexual behaviour, rather than the incidence of particular kinds of 'identity.' In his research, fully one-quarter of his male respondents acknowledged having had 'more than incidental homosexual experience or reactions' for at least three years between the ages of sixteen and fifty-five.[31]

In addition, Kinsey's own remarks 'indicate that many of the men he interviewed believed their sexual activity with other men did not mean they were homosexual so long as they restricted that behaviour to the "masculine role."'[32] In women Kinsey found that 19 per cent of the women he interviewed had had 'overt lesbian relationships.'[33]

What are we to make of the instability evident in these accounts? I would argue that twentieth-century notions of sexuality as identity provide little of the nuance and complexity necessary for understanding the notions of sexuality, gender, power, experimentation, friendship, and intimacy evident here. Both the Davis study and the research by Chauncey and Rotundo suggest a rich mine of historical investigation, indicating both the range of women's and men's sexual practices and the process by which identities were inscribed, embraced, and resisted. However, the larger question of this research consists in investigating the rationale for the binary notion of identities in the first place. It is to this issue that we must next turn.

UNSTABLE RELATIONS

In 'Imitation and Gender Insubordination,' Judith Butler argues that both sexuality and gender are sites of 'necessary trouble,' where the dominant patterns of relationships are reinscribed through a compulsive repetition, designed to produce the effect of naturalness, originality, and authenticity. She asserts:

> [I]f the category were to offer no trouble, it would cease to be interesting to me: it is precisely the *pleasure* produced by the instability of those categories which sustains the various erotic practices that make me a candidate for the category to begin with. To install myself within the terms of an identity category would be to turn against the sexuality that the category purports to describe; and this might be true for any identity category which seeks to control the very eroticism that it claims to describe and author-ize, much less 'liberate.'[34]

Building on Butler's argument I would argue that rigid and binary notions of identity have served both to *acknowledge* sexual differences, and, paradoxically, have operated to *contain, regulate, and polarize* this instability.

How then do we understand the implications of this notion for the construction of sexual categories in history? Postmodern theorists have characterized modernist discourse as a grand narrative consisting in a steady movement towards increased freedom and tolerance. Foucault, however, suggests that we must develop a strategic awareness of the possibilities existing in par-ticular historical moments and discourses, and argues that '"effective history" exposes not the events and actors elided by traditional history, but instead lays bare the *processes* and *operations* by which these elisions occurred.'[35] Through what operations, then, did the idea of binary sexual identities come to take prominence over eighteenth-century notions of a procreative sexuality or a sensuality legitimized by 'true love'?

As noted above, a complex range of material and economic factors, all of which threatened the traditional family unit, affected this shift. Key elements included changes in the wage labour system, which allowed a larger number of men and some women to live independent of the family;[36] increasing rates of urbanization; challenges to gender relations through women's involvement in the paid work force; the influence of first wave feminism; and an increased flex-ibility in sexual relationships occasioned by the dancehalls and speakeasies that developed in urban areas, particularly during Prohibition.

However, among the most contradictory and influential of the forces shaping the new idea of sexual identity was the emerging medico-scientific discipline of sexology. Michel Foucault has argued that this discourse constituted a new technology of power used by the bourgeoisie to extend their influence through ever more elaborate definitions of *normalcy* and *perversion*.[37] However, as Jeffery Weeks has countered, the language of sexuality is often a metaphor for larger and more intractable battles. With rapidly changing social and economic conditions, and major shifts in gendered relations, sexuality became a symbolic battleground. Carroll Smith-Rosenberg agrees:

> Social, not sexual, disorder lies at the heart of this discourse. The control of literal sexual behaviour at all times constitutes a secondary goal. Male sexologists were obsessed not with sex but with imposing order through the elaboration of categories of the normal and the perverted. Perverted behaviour did not have to cease. Quite the contrary. A proxy, it existed to be railed against and thus to give the sexologists a sense of power over chaos and reaffirm their faith in their ability to restore order.[39]

In this drive for control sexology moved with, not against, the grain of other nineteenth-century 'reform' movements such as social purity and eugenics.[40]

However, sexology itself was not a monolithic or unified movement. Some, like Edward Carpenter and Havelock Ellis, took strong stands in support of the decriminalization of male homosexual relationships in Britain. However, many sexologists also spoke out against the emerging influence of the New Woman. For Ellis, like Freud, the instability of sexual identities was explicitly acknowledged. However, this perspective served not as the basis for affirming a plurality of sexual choices; instead, it occasioned his lobby for the reverse. Ellis believed, above all, in the complementarity of the genders, and in the supremacy of men. The social changes occasioning women's independence profoundly threatened these values. The sexological discourse on women's same-sex relationships was profoundly different from that developing about male homosexuals, and was used largely to discredit the influence of the New Woman. Thus Smith-Rosenberg concludes:

> And so Havelock Ellis transformed the New Woman into a sexual anomaly and a political pariah. Citing Ellis as an unimpeachable scientific expert, American physicians and educators launched a political campaign against the New Woman, the institutions that nurtured her, and her feminist and reform programs. 'Female boarding schools and colleges are the great breeding grounds of artificial (acquired) homosexuality,' R.N.Shufeldt wrote in the Pacific Medical Journal in 1902.[41]

However, the history is yet more complex, as homosexual activists themselves also took a role in this debate. While some spoke under the protective cover of professional identities as sexologists (Edward Carpenter, Karl Heinrich Ulrichs), others, like Radclyffe Hall, entered the public discourse in a more direct manner. With the publication of her widely read *The Well of Loneliness*, Hall initiated a literary 'reverse discourse' of homosexual women speaking for themselves. For Hall, as for some sexologists, a binary and biologically determined sexual identity allowed her to argue that homosexuality was inborn, and thus should not be subject to moral condemnation.[42]

Thus the discourse of sexuality as identity, and of a binary juxtaposition of homo- and heterosexualities served a range of strategic purposes, for *both* the emerging sexological and homosexual communities. When the instability of sexual categories *was* acknowledged, this perspective served primarily to fuel the antifeminist campaigns then taking shape in response to women's increased social and political power.

POSTCRIPT

This chapter has attempted to ground an argument regarding the instability of sexual categories in a personal, pedagogical, and historical study that explores the shifting and porous borders between homosexual and heterosexual definitions and desires within the past century. In addition I have highlighted the conflicted uses to which the notion of sexuality *as constitutive* of identity has been put, both by the medico-scientific establishment and by homosexual communities themselves. The thrust of this text is towards challenging biological determinists—straight and gay, establishment and activist—who have attempted to convince us that sexual and relational feelings must be physiologically located and fixed in order to be considered natural and normal. This argument is in substantial agreement with the poststructuralist turn to questioning the possibility of a unified or homogenizing 'self.' However, the implications of this analysis for pedagogy and activism remain unclear. As Steven Seidman suggests, poststructuralist approaches, as they have been articulated to date, have serious limitations:

> As disciplining forces, identities are not only self limiting and productive of hierarchies but are enabling or productive of social collectivities, moral bonds, and political agency. Although the post-structural problematization of identity is a welcome critique of the essentialist celebration of a unitary subject and tribal politic, post-structuralism's own troubled relation to identity edges toward an empty politics of gesture or disruptive performance that forfeits an integrative, transgressive politic ... Whereas identity politics offers a strong politics on a weak, exclusionary basis, post-structuralism offers a thin politics as it problematizes the very notion of a collective in whose name a movement acts.[43]

Thus we end where we began. Deconstruction cannot do the work of politics, yet how can we do the work of politics within oppressively naturalized notions of identity?

Despite the intractability of this dilemma I would argue that deconstruction *does* provide a starting place for a different kind of discussion. The possibilities inherent in an activist historiography proceed not from the abandonment of notions of a collectivity, but from a commitment to illuminating the possibilities *and* contradictions inherent in notions of identity *within our pedagogy.* To this end, the research by Davis and Chauncey might be mobilized to serve as an example, not of coming out as *something/someone*, but as puzzles and unsettlings for the ways we can think about and represent sexuality, gender, and the self.[44] Can we then use this analysis to illustrate how particular historical moments, including our own, may make certain forms of desire, friendship, exploration, and intimacy possible, *at the same time* as they preclude others?

Social construction theory argues that the 'fact' that a certain percentage of the population engages in same-sex practices in the 1990s does not mean that the same percentage did so fifty years ago when Kinsey conducted his research, or seventy years ago when the Davis survey was completed, or one hundred and seventy years ago when Abraham Lincoln and Joshua Stead shared their bed. One of the considerable ironies implied in this research is that the post-gay liberation, identity-based culture of the 1980s and 1990s may well constitute a context in which it is *more* difficult for some individuals to explore same-sex desires than in the turn-of-the-century period documented by Davis and Chauncey. As Davis implies and Chauncey concludes, if sexuality is culturally organized and subject to change, then the prewar sexual culture may have made it easier for some women and men to engage in casual same-sex relationships when these did not ineluctably mark them as a homosexual.[45]

Thus the historical tension evident in this data is indicative of that hesitant and scary movement from *sexual practice* to *deviant sexual identity.*[46] Does the current historical moment suggest a reverse discursive strategy might be in order, in which we begin to shift the emphasis from identities to practices? As Cindy Patton argues, one indication of the utility of such an approach can be found in the cultural politics surrounding HIV and AIDS. In this context the discourse of 'risk groups' instead of 'risk behaviours' has already had life and death implications. While most heterosexuals continue not to employ safer sex practices with their partners, the definition of the category heterosexual remains problematic. As data collected in a 1990 study of HIV-positive male blood donors suggests, of the 129 men who reported having sex with both men and women since 1978, 30 per cent self-identified as homosexual, 34 per cent as bisexual, and 36 per cent as heterosexual. Further, behaviourally bisexual white men were more likely to identify as homosexual, whereas Black and Latino men were more likely to identify as bisexual and heterosexual, respectively.[47] Once again, we see the problems with identity. While in most parts of Canada and the United States young adults demonstrate sufficient knowledge about HIV and AIDS, few actually practise safer sex.[48] It is 'other people' who develop AIDS, and those others are associated not with the performance of specific acts, but with specific identities or subcultures.

However, the utility of a pedagogy which deconstructs notions of identity can be seen not just in relationship to AIDS, but must also be recognized in the broader discourse about sex. I would argue that a shift in emphasis from identities to practices may open up options for desire, intimacy, friendship, and exploration beyond those which are possible within a unitary conception of the self. In addition, this starting point is better suited to acknowledging that sexuality is constructed in profoundly different ways in different cultural and geographic sites. Two stories from more recent pedagogical experiences will help to illustrate this point.

From 1994 until 1997 I was employed as a teaching assistant for the Introduction to Women's Studies course at the University of Toronto. During the fall of 1996, in the week when we were to talk about lesbianism and bisexuality, I told my students a story from Dutch sociologist Ingrid Foeken in order to illustrate how very different meanings can be attached to similar acts:

> Benin, West Africa. The year is 1976. Two women get to chatting on a bus. One is a local woman, the other a European. Towards the end of their journey the African invites the other to stay with her large family. That night they sleep together in one bed.
>
> They talk for a while, then, responding to each other's gestures, they make love. The next morning the European woman asks her new friend whether she often has such experiences with other women, and how she feels about being a lesbian.
>
> Astonished, the African woman answers that it is quite usual for her to let a friend comfort her in this way.[49]

In the discussion that followed a student who had recently immigrated to Canada from Nigeria commented that indeed women and men in Nigeria do comfort each other this way, but few would identify these activities with the terms lesbian or gay.

Also in the fall of 1996, Lynne Fernie, the director of the National Film Board's recent coproduction about lesbian and gay youth, *School's Out,* previewed the video with a Toronto secondary school audience. In the discussion following the screening a student who was originally from India and had come to Canada after several years' stay in the Middle East, suggested that films such as *School's Out* should also talk about non-Western notions of sexuality. The student suggested that in some areas of the Middle East the bride price made it difficult for men who were poor to get married.[50] In his view this situation resulted in some men choosing to have relationships with each other. However, the lens through which these same-sex relationships were understood was fundamentally different from Western notions of identity implied in the terms lesbian or gay.[51]

In the multiracial context of most large North American cities these stories are far from uncommon. Yet the pedagogical strategies used by anti-heterosexism educators usually seem to assume a mythical and homogeneously Western context, untouched by colonial and imperial legacies. As Didi Khayatt has argued, our failure to theorize these contradictions can lead to the erasure of new (to some) epistemological frameworks for thinking about sexuality, gender, and the self:

> The West's global intellectual hegemony leads us to suppose that everyone everywhere understands exactly what we mean by the sexual categories that identify homoerotic behaviour, as evidenced by the number of books and articles which attempt to discuss 'homosexuality' on an international level, and in doing so, subsume all homoerotic activities under one rubric. This tendency renders different notions of same-sex activities invisible. However, it is important to recognize that it is not merely a difference in words that we are discussing, nor is it just particular meanings of corresponding terms. It is a distinctive conceptualization, different in theory as well as in substance, and thus could be said to refer to a different reality ... Not only do such sexual categories exclude the experiences of men and women of the 'Third World,' but the terms seem to be insufficient to capture the myriad differences in sexual expression.[52]

Thus I would argue that while educational strategies may include the language of identity they must, at the same time, extend an invitation to examine the problematics inherent in this process. For it is only through making the messy contradictions of 'our' various histories and movements visible that we will have constructed a pedagogy that does justice to any of our sexualities. I am suggesting here that the task of understanding the discursive processes by which identities are ascribed, resisted, or embraced is fraught with contradictions. Nevertheless I would assert that 'queerying' these usually unremarked operations which 'indeed achieve their effect because they aren't noticed'[53] can be a critical function of an activist pedagogy and historiography.

If sexual categories are both inevitable and inevitably troubling, I would argue that we must *wear* these notions of identity lightly, so they do not contain us, or contain the work of understanding desire. To do this we must not erase the profound differences and contradictions found in historical texts or in community and classroom settings, but instead mine them. For it is only in so doing that our pedagogy can reconstruct the passions which have made up both our movements and our lives.

NOTES

1 Foucault, *History of Sexuality*, 101.

2 See, for example, the pedagogy workshop section of Blumenfeld, *Homophobia*.

3 Scott, 'Experience,' 26.

4 Two other, smaller studies of women's sexuality pre-date the Davis report. The first, titled *The Single Woman* by Robert Latou Dickinson and Laura Beam (Baltimore, 1934), was reviewed by Rosalind Rosenberg in *Beyond Separate Spheres* (New Haven: Yale University Press, 1982). Dickinson's report is based on forty-six case studies of the sexual life of working women in the 1890s. In Rosenberg's brief review of this study she suggests that Dickinson found that 'among his single patients, homosexuality, which he at first failed to notice, even among patients who were living together, represented, he gradually realized, a widespread practice' (202).

  The second study, titled 'Statistical Study of the Marriage of Forty-seven Women,' by Celia Duel Mosher is contained in volume 10 of her unpublished work, 'Hygiene and Physiology of Women,' compiled from 1892 to 1920. It has been examined by Carl Degler in 'What Ought to Be and What Was: Women's Sexuality in the Nineteenth Century' and by Rosalind Rosenberg (as above); however, there is no indication that Mosher inquired about same-sex experiences in her survey.

5 There was, of course, considerable diversity and conflict within the medico-scientific literature of the period regarding the etiology of same-sex relations. The binarist model of sexuality, however, was supported by two of sexology's most influential voices. Richard von Krafft-Ebing described same-sex relations as a biologically-based disease in *Psychopathia Sexualis* (New York: Stein and Day, 1978), and Havelock Ellis characterized them as a congenital condition in 'Sexual Inversion with an Analysis of Thirty-three New Cases,' in *Medico-Legal Journal* 13 (1895–1896). The major opposing view was championed by Sigmund Freud, who characterized same-sex attraction as originating in an arrested form of childhood sexual development. For a summary of Freud's position see C. Standford, M.D., 'Homosexuality' in *Journal of Mental Science*, vol. 67 (London, 1921). Havelock Ellis and others did acknowledge some instability in women's same-sex desire—however, as I will argue later, he deployed this perspective in specific, and for women, damaging ways.

6 Halley, 'The Construction of Heterosexuality,' 98.

7 Britzman, 'Is there a Queer Pedagogy'? 152–53.

8 Lather, *Getting Smart*, 30–31, referring to a point made by Diana Fuss.

9 Quoted in Goldstein, 'Go the Way,' 173.

10 For a discussion of one stream of thought about the pleasures and contradictions of en-gendered desire, see Pratt, *S/HE*; also Feinberg, *Stone Butch Blues*.

11 Britzman, 'Queer Pedagogy?' 11.

12 Goldstein, 'Go the Way,' 184.

13 TEACH was sponsored by the East End Community Health Centre and the Department of Public Health in Toronto. For a visual representation of the work of TEACH see the video *School's Out* (1996),

a Great Jane Production distributed by the National Film Board and directed by Lynne Fernie (of *Forbidden Love* fame).

14 Information is from 'Taking Risks: Anti-Homophobia education in America,' an unpublished paper completed for Dr Didi Khayatt in 1994, in which I surveyed numerous organizations doing anti-homophobic work in the United States and Canada.

15 Bryson and de Castell, 'Queer Pedagogy,' 296.

16 Riley, *Am I That Name?*

17 Butler, 'Imitation and Gender Insubordination,' 23.

18 Scott, 'Experience,' 24.

19 Terry, 'Theorizing Deviant Historiography,' 58.

20 Ibid.

21 Ibid.

22 See note 4 above.

23 Rosenberg, *Beyond Separate Spheres*, 200.

24 Davis, *Factors in the Sex Life of Twenty-Two Hundred Women*, 27.

25 For just two examples of published work in this steadily growing field see Kennedy and Davis, *Boots of Leather*; and Becki Ross, *The House That Jill Built*.

26 See for example Jeffreys, 'Does It Matter If They Did It?'

27 Davis, *Factors in Sex Life*, 247.

28 Terry, 'Theorizing Deviant Historiography,' 58, referring to a point made by Spivak.

29 Davis, *Factors in Sex Life*, 283.

30 Chauncey, *Gay New York*, 76.

31 Ibid., 70.

32 Ibid., 71.

33 Irvine, *Disorders of Desire*, 54.

34 Butler, 'Imitation and Gender Insubordination,' 14.

35 Quoted in Terry, 'Theorizing Deviant Historiography,' 56.

36 Although low wages made marriage a financial necessity for most women, for a small group in the upper and middle classes, their newly won right to education brought options for professionalized employment and for shaping an independent life. These 'New Women,' as they were called, represented over one-third of the students of higher education in America. (See Faderman, *Odd Girls and Twilight Lovers*, 14.) During this period the actual numbers of women receiving advanced degrees and entering the professions reached a peak not to be equalled again until the late 1970s (Smith-Rosenberg, *Disorderly Conduct*, 43). In addition, up until 1910 the majority of the graduates of women's colleges remained unmarried, and by 1920, 75 per cent of female professionals were single (Rapp, Rayna, and Ellen Ross, 'The Twenties Backlash,' 94).

37 Smith-Rosenberg, *Disorderly Conduct*, 268.

38 Weeks, *Sexuality and Its Discontents*, 74.

39 Smith-Rosenberg, *Disorderly Conduct*, 268.

40 Weeks, *Sexuality and Its Discontents*, 76.

41 Smith-Rosenberg, *Disorderly Conduct*, 280.

42 Newton, 'The Mythic Mannish Lesbian,' 281–93.

43 Seidman, 'Identity and Politics,' 134–35.

44 I want to acknowledge Barbara Williams, who suggested this way of thinking about using the historical material (OISE, 1995).

45 Chauncey, *Gay New York*, 71.

46 I am indebted to Kathleen Rockhill for suggesting this insight (OISE, 1995).

47 Tielman, Carballo, and Hendriks, eds., *Bisexuality and HIV/AIDS*, 28.

48 For Canadian figures see Michael Ornstein, *AIDS in Canada*, 50. For information on the United States see Cindy Patton, *Inventing AIDS*, 109.

49 This story was told by Dutch sociologist Ingrid Foeken at the 'Which Homosexuality?' International Conference on Lesbian and Gay Studies in Amsterdam, Holland, in 1987. It is documented by Vanessa Baird in her article 'Pride and Prejudice' in *The New Internationalist*, no. 201 (November 1989), 4.

50 Unfortunately I have not been able to speak to the student personally, and do not have the information that would specify which country in the Middle East he is referring to. I realize this phrasing may reproduce stereotypes about the Middle East as one homogeneous region, and that it fails to specify the extraordinary historical, ethnic, and cultural differences that exist in different regions.

51 Personal communication from Lynne Fernie to the author.

52 Khayatt, 'The Place of Desire: The Exclusion of Women in the Third World in Theorizing Sexual Orientation' (May 1993), 10–11. Work in progress, quoted with permission of the author.

53 Scott, 'Experience,' 33.

REFERENCES

Blumenfeld, Warren, J. *Homophobia: How We All Pay the Price*. Boston: Beacon Press, 1992.

Britzman, Deborah. 'Beyond Rolling Models: Gender and Multicultural Education.' In *Gender and Education*, ed. Sari Knopp Biklen and Diane Pollard. Chicago: University of Chicago Press, 1993.

Britzman, Deborah. 'Is There a Queer Pedagogy? Or, Stop Reading Straight.' *Educational Theory* 45, no. 2 (Spring 1995): 151–65.

Britzman, Deborah, and Alice Pitt. 'Pedagogy and Transference: Casting the Past of Learning into the Presence of Teaching.' *Theory into Practice* 35, no. 2 (1996): 117–23.

Britzman, Deborah, Kelvin Santiago-Valles, Gladys Jimenez-Munoz, and Laura Lamash. 'Slips That Show and Tell: Fashioning Multiculture as a Problem of Representation.' In *Race, Identity, and Representation in Education*, ed. Cameron McCarthy and Warren Crichlow. New York: Routledge, 1993.

Bryson, Mary, and Suzanne de Castell. 'Queer Pedagogy: Praxis Makes Im/Perfect.' *Canadian Journal of Education* 18, no. 3 (Summer 1993): 285–305.

Butler, Judith. 'Imitation and Gender Insubordination.' In *Inside/Out: Lesbian Theories, Gay Theories*, ed. Diana Fuss, 13–31. New York: Routledge, 1991.

Chauncey, George. *Gay New York: Gender, Urban Culture and the Making of the Gay Male World*, 1890–1940. New York: Basic Books, 1994.

Davis, Katherine Bement. *Factors in the Sex Life of Twenty-Two Hundred Women*. [1929]. New York: Arno Press, 1972.

Degler, Carl. 'What Ought to Be and What Was: Women's Sexuality in the Nineteenth Century.' *American History Review* 79 (December 1974).

Faderman, Lillian. *Surpassing the Love of Men: Romantic Friendship and Love between Women from the*

Renaissance to the Present. New York: Quill William Morrow, 1981.

Faderman, Lillian. *Odd Girls and Twilight Lovers: A History of Lesbian Life in Twentieth-Century America.* New York: Penguin, 1991.

Feinberg, Leslie. *Stone Butch Blues: A Novel.* Ithaca, NY: Firebrand Books, 1993.

Fernie, Lynne. *School's Out.* 25 min. Coproduced by Great Jane Productions and the National Film Board of Canada, 1996. Videocassette.

Foucault, Michel. *Histoire de la sexualite,* vol. I. *La volonte de savoir.* Paris: Gallimard, 1976.

Freud, Sigmund. 'Negation.' In *The Complete Psychological Works of Sigmund Freud.* Vol. 19 (1923–1925), 235–9. Trans. James Strachey. London: Hogarth Press, 1925.

Freud, Sigmund. 'Thoughts for the Times on War and Death' (1915). In The Complete Psychological Works of Sigmund Freud. Vol. 14, 275–302. Trans. James Strachey. London: Hogarth Press, 1957.

Freud, Sigmund. *Civilization and Its Discontents.* Trans. Joan Riviere. London: Hogarth Press, 1975.

Freud, Sigmund. 'Mourning and Melancholia.' (1915/1917). In *On Metapsychology: The Theory of Psychoanalysis,* 251–67. Trans. James Strachey. New York: Penguin, 1984.

Goldstein, Richard. 'Go the Way Your Blood Beats: An Interview with James Baldwin.' In *James Baldwin: The Legacy,* ed. Quincy Troupe, 173–85. New York: A Touchstone Book, 1989.

Halley, Janet E. 'The Construction of Heterosexuality.' In *Fear of a Queer Planet: Queer Politics and Social Theory,* ed. M. Warner, 82–102. Minneapolis: University of Minnesota Press, 1993.

Irvine, Janice. *Disorders of Desire: Sex and Gender in Modern American Sexology.* Philadelphia: Temple University Press, 1990.

Jeffreys, Sheila. 'Does It Matter If They Did It?' In *Not a Passing Phase: Reclaiming Lesbians in History, 1840–1985.* ed. Lesbian History Group, 158–187. London: The Women's Press, 1989.

Katz, Jonathan Ned. *The Invention of Heterosexuality.* New York: Penguin, 1995.

Kennedy, Elizabeth Lapovsky, and Madeline Davis. *Boots of Leather, Slippers of Gold: The History of a Lesbian Community.* New York: Penguin Books, 1994.

Khayatt, Didi. 'Legalized Invisibility: The Effects of Bill 7 on Lesbian Teachers.' *Women's Studies International Forum* 13, no.3 (1990): 185–93.

Khayatt, Didi. *Lesbian Teachers: An Invisible Presence.* Albany: State University of New York Press, 1992.

Khayatt, Didi. 'In and Out: Experiences in the Academy.' In *Resist! Essays against a Homophobic Culture,* ed. Mona Oikawa, Dionne Falconer, and Ann Decter, 210–17. Toronto: Women's Press, 1994.

Lather, Patti. *Getting Smart: Feminist Research and Pedagogy With/In the Postmodern.* New York: Routledge, 1991.

Newton, Ester. 'The Mythic Mannish Lesbian: Radclyffe Hall and The New Woman. In *Hidden from History: Reclaiming the Gay and Lesbian Past,* ed. Martin Duberman, Martha Vicinus, and George Chauncey, 281–93. New York: Basic Books, 1990.

Ornstein, Michael. *AIDS in Canada: Knowledge, Behaviour and Attitudes of Adults.* Toronto: University of Toronto Press, 1989.

Patton, Cindy. *Inventing AIDS.* New York: Routledge, 1990.

Pratt, Minnie Bruce. *S/He.* Ithaca: Firebrand Books, 1995.

Rapp, Rayna, and Ellen Ross. 'The Twenties Backlash: Compulsory Heterosexuality, the Consumer Family, and the Waning of Feminism.' In *Class, Race, and Sex: The Dynamics of Control,* ed. Amy Swerdlow and Hanna Lessinger. Boston: G.K. Hall Publishers, 1983.

Riley, Denise. *Am I That Name? Feminism and the Category of Women in History*. Minneapolis: University Of Minnesota Press, 1988.

Rosenberg, Rosalind. *Beyond Separate Spheres: Intellectual Roots of Modern Feminism*. New Haven: Yale University Press, 1982.

Ross, Becki. *The House That Jill Built: A Lesbian Nation in Formation*. Toronto: University of Toronto Press, 1996.

Scott, Joan. 'Experience.' In *Feminists Theorize the Political*, ed. Judith Butler and Joan Scott, 22–40. London: Routledge, 1992.

Sedgwick, Eve Kosofsky. *Between Men: English Literature and Male Homosocial Desire*. New York: Columbia University Press, 1985.

Seidman, Steven. 'Identity and Politics in a "Postmodern" Gay Culture: Some Historical and Conceptual Notes.' In *Fear of a Queer Planet: Queer Politics and Social Theory*, ed. Michael Warner, 105–42. Minneapolis: University of Minnesota Press, 1993.

Smith-Rosenberg, Carroll. *Disorderly Conduct: Visions of Gender in Victorian America*. New York: Oxford University Press, 1985.

Spivak, Gayatri Chakravorty. *The Post-Colonial Critic: Interviews, Strategies, Dialogues*, ed. Sara Harasym. New York: Routledge, 1990.

Spivak, Gayatri Chakravorty. 'Acting Bits/Identity Talk.' *Critical Inquiry* 18, no. 4 (1992): 770–803.

Spivak, Gayatri Chakravorty. *Outside in the Teaching Machine*. New York: Routledge, 1993.

Terry, Jennifer. 'Theorizing Deviant Historiography.' *Differences* 3, no. 2 (Summer 1991): 55–74.

Tielman, Rob, Manuel Carballo, and Art Hendriks, eds. *Bisexuality and HIV/AIDS: A Global Perspective*. Buffalo: Prometheus Books, 1991.

Weeks, Jeffrey. *Sexuality and Its Discontents: Meanings, Myths and Modern Sexualities*. London: Routledge, 1985.

CHAPTER 2

Outside in Black Studies:
Reading from a Queer Place in the Diaspora

Rinaldo Walcott

Kissing my ass could bring you closer to god.

—Dusty Dixon, in *Welcome to Africville*

Toward the end of the last millennium and the beginning of the new one, reassessments have been taking place of the black studies project and its emergent twin, black diaspora studies. Manning Marable's edited collection *Dispatches from the Ebony Tower;* Carole Boyce Davies's *Decolonizing the Academy: Diaspora Theory and African New-World Studies;* and several issues of the *Black Scholar* (vol. 30, no. 3-4; vol. 31, no. 1) are exemplary texts in these reassessments. A bevy of conferences have also taken place, for example, Black Queer Studies in the Millennium (University of North Carolina, Chapel Hill, April 2000); African, Afro-American and African Diaspora Studies in the Twenty-First Century (University of Pennsylvania, Philadelphia, April 2000); as well as the conference that led to the edited collection by Davies. These reassessments of the black studies project place on the table, at least for me, what might be at stake in our readings of what constitute the terms, codes, and conditions of the project. And, to this end, much of these conversations concerning the black studies project return us to its very recent past and clearly to memories of trauma, pain, injury, and what is recognized as a precarious triumph in its institutionalization. In this chapter I investigate what might be at stake when the black studies project, diaspora studies, and queer studies collide in our reading practices. I argue for what I call a diaspora reading practice, which can disrupt the centrality of nationalist discourses within the black studies project and thereby also allow for an elaboration of a black queer diaspora project.[1]

I initially wanted to title this chapter "Why Black Studies Won't Go Down, But I Keep Blowing Wid It," but I did not want to give the impression that I am only interested in oral or verbal forms of communicating. However, when Dusty Dixon tells us in Dana C. Inkster's film *Welcome to Africville* (1999) that kissing her ass could bring you closer to god, she places a premium on the relationship between the practice of the erotic and the erotics of pedagogy. It is the erotics of pedagogy or the lack thereof that I want to hint at (among other things) in relation to the black studies project. I want to comment on what I see as the potential of black queer diaspora studies to rejuvenate the liberatory moments of the black studies project. Let me state here that I think the possibilities of black queer studies within the black studies project can only act to elaborate the terms of a potential liberation, because queer studies interrupts the black studies project as it stands by putting on the agenda new and different positions and conditions for thinking. Let me be clear, I am not constituting black queer studies as the vanguard of a liberatory project but rather as the unthought of what might be thinkable within the confines of the black studies project proper and what might be the constitutive knowledge of a renewed black studies project proper. Is black queer studies the improper subject of the black studies project? Or can black queer studies even reside within the confines of the black studies project proper? These are important questions and are not meant to be immediately resolved but rather continually evoked as the basis for an ethicality to the black studies project. Further, I want to evoke a more troubling side of the black studies project—its inability to continue to render complex and shifting notions of community and, for my purpose, diaspora.[2] And yet community as a discourse and a practice remains the fetish of the black studies project. Why is this? My intervention is concerned with the thought of thinking and with the thought and practice of thinking queerly. I am primarily interested in issues of conceptualization as opposed to the empirical foundationality of the black studies project per se. In this regard I will conclude my comments by returning to and discussing the film *Welcome to Africville* as an example of what the exploration of a queer unthought can bring to questions of community, nation, diaspora, and therefore the black studies project.

The black studies project tends to produce community in two overlapping registers: first, community as homogenous, despite much noises to the contrary; and, second, black community as largely based in the United States and therefore relegated to the "national thing."[3] There are variations on these themes but they tend to largely remain steady. The 1980s witnessed the crashing of the community as one in the black studies project by the black British cultural studies invasion. In many senses this was a celebratory return of the repressed and therefore the diaspora to the black studies project. The various continual returns to the continental space of Africa complicates my reduction. However, these interventions into the black studies project tend to turn on how U.S. blackness is implicated and positioned and often the debate or the limit of analysis tends to get stuck there, even when the diaspora is at issue.[4] The Caribbean, Latin America, and Canada (the latter being the most queer of diaspora places) are hardly taken up within the black studies project.[5] Again, there are always some exceptions; but why is it that the black studies project has hung its hat so lovingly on U.S. blackness and therefore a "neat" national project? And how does a renewed interest in questions of the diaspora seem to only be able to tolerate U.S. blackness and British blackness? Finally, how does imperialism figure in national subaltern studies? Let me say that this is not an argument for inclusion—such arguments do not take seriously diaspora circuits and the identifications, disidentifications, and cultural sharing and borrowing that occur in that symbolic and political space. The brief point that I want to make here is that black diaspora queers have actually pushed the boundaries of transnational identification much further than we sometimes recognize.[6] Black diaspora queers live in a borderless, large world of shared identifications and imagined historical relations produced through a range of fluid cultural artifacts like film, music, clothing, gesture, and signs or symbols, not to mention sex and its dangerously pleasurable fluids. In fact, black diaspora queers have been interrupting and arresting the black studies project to produce a bevy of identifications, which confound and complicate local, national, and transnational desires, hopes, and disappointments of the post–Civil Rights and post–Black Power era.

I want to bring to bear the sensibilities of the diaspora to read the black studies project, but I also want to signal some difficult moments concerning conceptions of community and diaspora in the black studies project when queers cruise in that zone. In particular, I want to exorcise the repressed relationship between the black studies project as a national issue and therefore its limit—a limit that places it in disjunct time with diaspora desires and identifications. To exorcise this repression I need briefly to outline what I think is at stake in calling out the nation-centred heteronormativity of the black studies project. It is only too obvious to say that by and large the black studies project has in its thought produced black community as assumed and essentially heterosexual. Despite the evidence of difference, and even sometimes its celebration, the black studies project has not adequately incorporated nor engaged the thought of thinking blackness differently, especially when it encounters black queers. I think this lack has much to do with the pedagogical nature of the black studies project—its careful desire for "epistemological respectability"[7] and its continued ambiguous and ambivalent institutionalization. The historical precariousness of the black studies project in the U.S. academy means that its pedagogical impulse has been fashioned by an attempt to correct current and historical wrongs and to produce a relation to knowledge production that is irreducible to the so-called lived experiences of a homogenized blackness or black community. In this sense the black studies project is too narrowly fashioned as a corrective for wounds and/or injuries, and in a larger sense for African American dislocations from a Euro-normative nation-making project.[8] In short, the black studies project in its institutionalization has come to stand in for one kind of black respectable community through which its relation to its imagined community is a one-on-one match. Black queers mess with that desired respectability by bringing their shameful and funky sexual practices to it.[9] As we all know, it is exactly this attempt to have a one-on-one match that constitutes the major crises of the black studies project and projects for the making of community everywhere—even in queer studies proper. What is demanded is a rethinking of community that might allow for different ways of cohering into some form of recognizable political entity. Put another way, we must confront singularities without the willed effort to make them cohere into a oneness; we must struggle to make a community of singularities of which the unworking of the present ruling regime, a regime that trades on the myths of homogeneity, must be central. In short, a different sociality is required—a sociality of mutual recognitions.[10]

It is the wounds and injuries of African American positionality, and black peoples more generally, that have conditioned the monolingual voice of the black studies project. The wound of always seeming to be on the outside has worked to produce the black studies project as a constant corrective to the elisions of normative national narratives. Nonetheless, I want to augment and amend a question that William Haver asked of queer studies and research: What if black studies [queer studies] were to refuse epistemological respectability, to refuse to constitute that wounded identity as an epistemological object such as would define, institute, and thus institutionalize a disciplinary field?[11] Haver is insistent that subaltern studies and research might refuse, in his words, the "intellectual hegemony, to provide a better explanation of the world"[12] in favour of articulating a world in which we act politically. That is, a political theory of acts that concerns itself with "an active intervention, a provocation: an interruption rather than a reproduction.[13] What would such a practice of black studies do to our relation to knowledge? Would this queer black studies produce a kind of knowledge that would allow "for something queer to happen" to all of us in the black studies project, as Deborah Britzman has asked of the discipline of education? Can the black studies project "stop being straight"?[14] I would like to suggest that it could.

Haver further argues that research is an "unworking without destination, thinking as departure, 'research' is essentially nomadic, something that happens."[15] Haver calls for a queer research that does more than reproduce recognizable social and cultural wounds of queer identity. He is neither dismissing nor undermining the evidence of the punishing nature within which proclaiming such identities occurs, but rather he would have us think the thought of thinking identity when those thoughts result in something queer happening to all of us in the contexts of the institutional sites of "research," pedagogy, and importantly disciplinarity. But his comments are important to me for other reasons as well, in particular his suggestion that "research" as a departure accords with conceptualizations of the diaspora, which has as one of its tenets the problematics of departure. In fact, I am suggesting that the interruption of the black studies project by black diaspora queers is in part a departure from the project only to return to it in ways that elaborate it by extending its discourse and potential as a liberatory project reaching beyond the institutional site and location.

I want to ask what queer positions might mean for the remaking of the black studies project as a multidisciplinary and cross-disciplinary configuration. I want to ask why the "difficult knowledge" of the black queer diaspora remains on the edges. In particular I want to use Deborah Britzman's notion of "difficult knowledge"[16] to ask what is difficult about black queer positions in the black studies project and what might be at stake when black queer positions continue to occupy the edges of the black studies project. To draw on Marlon Riggs, I want to ask some questions along with him that speak to the problematic utterances of community within current black diaspora discourses. As Riggs suggests concerning community: "All terms denoting an ideological frame of reference that enforces a rigorous exclusion of certain kinds of difference, that erects stifling enclosures around a whole range of necessary debates, or, alternately, confines them within an easily recognisable—and controllable—psychosocial arena should be suspect and questioned."[17] On the agenda here is to think simultaneously a number of overlapping concerns—community, black queer positions, and what I call the "whatever" of black studies. In terms of the "whatever" of black studies, I draw on and develop Giorgio Agamben's formulation of the "whatever" to suggest one way in which the uncertainties and commonalities of blacknesses might be formulated in the face of some room for surprise, disappointment, and pleasure without recourse to disciplinary and punishing measures.[18] This is a whatever that can tolerate the whatever of blackness without knowing meaning—black meaning, that is—in advance of its various utterances.

By making use of the whatever in conjunction with (black) queer theory and the recognition of the difficult knowledge it brings to bear on the black studies project I mean to ask tough questions concerning the nature of black diasporic communities and the disciplinary weakness of the black studies project as a community building and making exercise. In this sense I am attempting to grapple with the thorny question of the making of black community via the routes of academic disciplinarity and what might be at stake in the making of this community. I am particularly driven to these questions by the challenge, and may I say limit, of Charles H. Rowell's afterword to *Shade: An Anthology of Fiction by Black Gay Men of African Descent.* In "Signing Yourself: An Afterword" Rowell argues against both racism and heteronormativity by both white and black Americans, gay and straight alike. I am exercised by Rowell's claims in his afterword for a number of reasons, and I share both a solidarity and an antagonism with his argument. He is particularly interested in charting one specific aspect of the black diaspora—its queer twists and turns. I stand in solidarity with that aspect of the project, but in concentrating on this one element Rowell takes a rather punishing twist when he calls the "Third World" into question for prohibiting gay men from "signing themselves gay."[19] It is not the evidence of this inability that I take issue with concerning Rowell's indictment of some parts of the black diaspora and Africa, but rather what I read as the "ideological frame" from which he utters his critique. His inability to account for the contradictions within his argument is surprising. For as he calls the Third World into question he must simultaneously also call the First World into question. And yet he leaves us with the bitter taste that somehow the possibility for queer life in the Great Free North is so much better than it is in the so-called Third World. What I find troubling about his speech acts in his afterword is that they take quite an imperialist U.S. stance, particularly reading from my queer place in the diaspora (Canada). This imperialist stance is of the kind that does not adequately (or does only in nuanced ways) account for the disjunctures of desire, political utterances, and disappointment in various spaces and places, even nations. In some respects Rowell fails to see when the sexual is not intellectual, to paraphrase one of my favourite songs from the queer party circuit. Instead, his argument suggests that even if things are bad in the United States then elsewhere the situation is dire, and that folks elsewhere have a long developmental path to take, almost along the lines of UNESCO. Such utterances are rampant in the "new" sexiness of diaspora discourse in the contemporary black studies project. It is Rowell's attempt to make African American and therefore U.S. exceptionality singular that I contest. But what Rowell does not consider are all the ways in which men in the Third World might sign themselves queer in ways that might not constitute an intelligible speech act for him. I am exercised by Rowell because he is both pushing and elaborating the limits of the black studies project at the same time that his push contracts for what it cannot adequately account for elsewhere. His diaspora desire is ultimately, despite its claim otherwise, a national thing.

I contest Rowell's assertions because I think that politically the invocation of the diaspora requires us to think in ways that simultaneously recognize the national spaces from which we speak and gesture to more than those spaces. In fact, sometimes it might require a subversion or at the least an undermining of the national space. In the contemporary black studies project the sexy trendiness of the diaspora is continuously being appropriated to speak to a singular context of African American concerns. On the one hand, it seems impossible for Rowell to really traverse the space of the black diaspora and in particular of crossing the forty-ninth parallel and heading north to another moment of blackness, much less than heading to the Third World to liberate it; yet, on the other hand, black Canadian Courtnay McFarlane makes the journey south in his poem "Gill's Paradise."

> Crown Heights
> Paradise found/Brooklyn black/crumbles
> Through gypsy cab/Classon and Pacific streets
> a hell/to eyes not seein' home/
> On this neglect paved/urban artery
> apathy's pothole/open hydrant/piss stained wall
> street corners/"the Dream"
> Burned-out shell/stands/three-stories
> three sets of eyes/concrete sealed
> willful/blind/remembers better days
> Next door Gill's Paradise/is overpainted 'ho
> gaudy yellow façade/single palm/Rastaman
> and lion of Judah/testify to longings/distant/unfilled
> romance defiant/in decay
> Gill's beckons

Or, in McFarlane's "Craig":

> was jumping/in Tracks/
> capital T/D/C/Washington
> carryin' on/makin' noise/being loud
> in black and white/polka dotted pantihose
> tight white tank top/matching canvas Keds/the slip on kind
> dancin'/and cruising/in disco drag[20]

What is at stake here are the ways in which some black diaspora queers find African American queers, yet the reverse always seems impossible. This sexual/textual economy of unequal exchange is important in how we conceptualize the limits of contemporary discourses of the diaspora and questions of community within the black studies project. The inability within some versions of the black studies project to think of the nation alongside the outernational is in some senses also a queer diaspora position, at least in its inconsistency. But as we know, the diaspora by its very nature, its circumstances, is queer. What do I mean by this? I mean that the territories and perambulations of diaspora circuits, identifications, and desires are queer in their making and their expressions. Reginald Shepherd's *Some Are Drowning,* a collection of poetry, charts the sexual desiring racialized territories of the New World by highlighting the (homo)erotics of the conquest of the Americas and transatlantic slavery.[21] In a different way, which is even more troubling and disturbing, Gary Fisher takes us deeper into uncharted, at least textually, territories of racialized sex acts, fantasies, and desires.[22] These black queer territorial claims rewrite blackness in ways that require us to examine blackness beyond the singularity of victim or resistor so that a more nuanced rendering is at least approached. Drawing on Arjun Appadurai's notion of "scapes" of various sorts, we might understand Fisher's, Shepherd's, and McFarlane's poetics as those of sexscapes.[23] These sexscapes chart the difficult territories of "streets and residences" and "peaks of nipples" as Shepherd puts it in one of his poems. Even more concretely, however, these sexscapes chart the politics of the black queer diaspora in both its ephemera and its varying political acts. What is at stake here is an understanding of a black queer diaspora across and within, in which artifact, desire, pleasure, and disappointment can sometimes be the basis of the struggle over and the making of imaginary community. Isaac Julien's film art, Joseph Beam's anthology *In the Life,* Pat Parker's poetry, Audre Lorde's oeuvre, and Samuel Delany's memoir are just examples of artifacts used in the making of this black queer diaspora.[24] The more difficult and intangible moments of interiority, sensibility, and political utterance play out in localized and transnational political alliances, desires, pleasures, and disappointments.

My investment in questioning the boundaries of a heteronormative black studies project, in particular its diaspora perambulations, have much to do with my own investment in the black studies project as a liberatory project. But I want to qualify this project by suggesting that some of the questions that made the black studies project the site of radicality at one particular historical moment might now require that we seek new questions.[25] I am grandly suggesting, then, that black queer studies is both the edge and the cutting edge of a reinvigorated black studies project. In this aspect, a black queer studies might go a long way in producing formulations of community and the rethinking of community conceptually that might be more useful for our postmodern, outernational times. This, in essence, is why I find Charles Rowell's afterword troubling and limiting in its conception of the black queer diaspora. His inability to really go down—that is, to really go south—is ultimately a queer political disappointment. His argument, despite the material object of the anthology, still fits the frame of a black studies project discourse that Kobena Mercer identifies as disappointment. Mercer argues, and I agree, "that questions of sexuality have come to mark the interior limits of decolonisation, where the utopian project of liberation has come to grief."[26]

I want to make clear that I still understand the black studies project as marginal within the contemporary North American academy. But the marginality of the black studies project and its resistance through the reproduction of a minoritarian discourse of assertiveness is particularly important historically and politically for black queer studies. A black queer studies partakes of this assertive tradition and extends it into new and politically troubling territories. In this sense, black queer studies is attempting to reclaim the ground that Mercer marks as disappointment in the black studies project. Mercer attends to this by charting territories for thinking about blackness that are reflective of national political positions and events but also, importantly, far exceed the demands of the national. This is the demand of a "postconceptual" black studies project that can do more than tolerate sexual difference and that can take the diaspora seriously enough to seek outside national concerns and narratives.

The tensions and relations between the black studies project and diaspora sensibilities sorely require revisiting in this era of renewed interests in invoking the term diaspora. Such a study could begin with the debates between DuBois and Garvey and DuBois and McKay. The debate between Gilroy and Chandler, Gilroy and Dyson, and a plethora of nation/diaspora skirmishes would then be important to flesh out the significance of the tensions of diasporic discourses within the black studies project. In addition, the ways in which different intellectuals and scholars within the black studies project are positioned in terms of both their political utterances and the nuances of their politics is crucial: for example, the political difference between Harold Cruse and Larry Neal; or, in more general terms, the difference between nation-centred approaches as opposed to more diasporic orientations—that is, pan-African or outernational. What is important here is to signal the distinction between different inflections of the black studies project. One component of the distinction is how different individual intellectuals and scholars see themselves in relation to the desires of national narrations and narratives. The black studies project has never been a singular project, despite contemporary attempts to rewrite its history into a singular, nation-centred one. So while an argument can be made for the continuing marginalization of the black studies project in the North American academy, it is also important to point out that within the black studies project its own self-generating discourses have produced what can be described as "official positions." These positions provide particular confines and directives of what might and might not count as a part of the black studies project. One of the first incursions into "official black studies" was that of feminism. Others, like queer theory, have since arrived. Therefore, by the "official black studies" moniker I mean to signal the terms on which the originary project conceptualized a singular blackness, thereby foreclosing other moments that could only then return as the unruly, or the whatever, of a fabricated homogeneity and offer a different perspective and reading. William Haver, in "Of Mad Men Who Practice Invention to the Brink of Intelligibility," an essay on Samuel Delany's *Mad Men*, argues that "queer theory is queer only to the extent that it sustains an erotic relation/nonrelation to the extremity that interrupts it: queer theory is queer precisely in its incompleteness."[27] Haver's insistence on the possibilities of queer theory lying in its incompleteness is also where I see the possibilities of the unfinished project of black studies in its encounters with black queer theory and/or queer positions. The pedagogy of the black studies project in its suggestion of possible liberation and its insistence on narratives of liberation bares a historiography that requires a continual reassessment of the politics of dispossession among its imagined community. The thing that must be thought as the content and politics of the black studies project is definitely a queer thing—community. I am suggesting here that it is because queer communities reside at various assorted edges that the queering of the black studies project in a sustained way holds the potential for the continual attempt to think about the difficult politics of liberation at its limits.

For example, Houston Baker's now-notorious claim at the Black Popular Culture conference in 1992 that he is not gay is a case in point. Such an utterance (and I am referring only to what is printed in the book *Black Popular Culture* that resulted from the conference) is the expressed place where some versions of the black studies project encounter the difficult terrain of community or, put another way, the tensions and antagonisms of family, which underwrite the black studies project, come to the fore. Baker's claim is a moment, which I think is pedagogical in many ways for the black studies project. Particularly crucial is the edge that black queer bodies occupy in our concerns within the field as histories of the field are being written. Here I think of Baynard Rustin and Lorraine Hansberry, both of whom are cutting edge and also currently occupying the edge of the black studies project.

But let me express a provocation not of my making but rather in the words of another black gay guy. In "Making Ourselves from Scratch" Joseph Beam writes: "As African-Americans, we do not bequeath financial portfolios. We pass from generation to generation our tenacity. So I ask you: What is it that we are passing along to our cousin from North Carolina, the boy down the block, our nephew who is a year old, or our sons who may follow us in the life? What is it that we leave them beyond this shadow play: the search for a candlelit romance in a poorly lit bar, the rhythm and the beat, the furtive sex in the back street? What is it that we pass along to them or do they, too, need to start from scratch?"[28] In response, Dana Inkster's film *Welcome to Africville* takes up the challenge made by Beam. With this in mind I turn to a reading of Inkster's film as an example of a diaspora reading practice to demonstrate what might be at stake when we risk reading for and creating works that think the unthought of blackness.

Welcome to Africville is a fifteen-minute film that recalls the thirtieth anniversary (in 1999) of the destruction of one of black Canada's oldest communities, which was founded in the 1800s by ex-African Americans. The narrative of the destruction, or rather the interruption in the narrative of the destruction and dispersal, is told through three generations of women from the Dixon family, and also through a bartender. These actors do not tell the why of the destruction—they refuse to do so—but rather they tell the why of their sexual practices, desires, disappointments, pleasures, and adventures as well as their loss. The grandmother (Anna Dixon) tells of a strong desire to have what she calls a "numb love," being too old for anything else. Her daughter (Mary Dixon) tells of her sexual adventures in the big city and her fantasies. And the granddaughter (Mary Dixon) tells of the possibility of finding love. The bartender (Julius Johnson) details the possibility of finding love, with a commentary on masculinity. Some of the images in the film, such as the archival footage of the demolition of the community, tell the story of the Canadian state's racist action. The actors' stories arrive through an off-screen interviewer's attempt to gather responses to the impending demolition. The film opens with these lines: "Yes they making us move ... but I don't want to talk about that ... history will tell the story." Instead, these characters tell the story of a black history of erotics often demolished in heterosexist acts parallel to those of racist acts. These characters tell of love, loss, and desire defying what kind of history and what history can tell as a necessary part of black community and queer community.

What makes this film useful for my purpose here is not only its complex layering of writing history but also the way in which Inkster queers the history of Africville by making something queer happen to viewers. She tells the story of Africville through the voices of at least two generations of black women who love other women. Anna Dixon (played by Kathy Imre of *Shaft's Big Score)* is the grandmother. Me'shell Ndegeocello composed and performed the original blusey, soulful score. The film brings together a cast of diasporic players to tell a national story of pain and loss, which not only gestures to the historical dispersal across U.S. borders—before and after Africville—but has echoes across the black diaspora. The film participates in a rather large project—a project of diaspora desires and connections—yet it is still able to productively engage its local context. It is a product that through fiction is able to complicate the historical record of blackness. By telling the now-sacred story of Africville through the eyes of black lesbians, Inkster creates the opportunity for reflecting differently on historical context and memory and not only what is remembered but who is allowed to remember and how. Inkster tells the sex of memory; hers is a queer memory with much significance for interrupting disciplinarity.

Welcome to Africville takes its immediate influences from Isaac Julien's and Marlon Riggs's meditations on history and black queerness. Inkster is, however, closer to Julien than to Riggs in the subtlety of her cinematic styling—her shots are posed like photographs. But, importantly, she is among a group of black lesbian filmmakers returning to the archives and opening them up in challenging ways; the black queer living-dead is placed to rest with cinematic love and care. These queer cinematic returns and departures force new kinds of questions concerning what the black studies project has often only whispered about and might not be publicly ready for yet. At the same time, these returns make something queer happen to all of us in the black studies project. In many ways, then, *Welcome to Africville* is in conversation with Cheryl Dunye's *Watermelon Woman* (1997) and Julie Dash's *Daughters of the Dust* (1991). At the same time, it engages the many documentaries chronicling Africville's demolition[29] and also moves away from them to bring a different or a queer look to black Canadian historiography. In addition, Inkster's film fixes a black lesbian feminist gaze on critical cinematic diasporic representations, in particular the chronicling of black queer histories that have been overwhelmingly male in cinematic presentation.

It was reported that when Inkster's film was screened in Halifax, Nova Scotia (Africville was located just outside Halifax's city's limits), it came as a shock to the local black audience. Apparently the audience was aghast that the sacred story of Africville might be fictionalized and told through the eyes of at least two lesbians. This response is similar, I think, to the institutional positioning of the black studies project. Because Inkster refuses epistemological respectability by refusing to represent the wound as only the loss of property—a representation that potentially might elicit the collective respect of black folks by white folks and therefore serve as evidence of black victimization—her film was a shock to some. Instead, Inkster's erotics of loss can provoke a different possibility of encountering the demolition of Africville. The site thus becomes symbolic of all that is loss/lost when history forecloses certain kinds of knowledge, especially queer queries and feminist queries concerning the past and what David Scott calls the "changing present."[30] These queries do not only return, recover, and correct but they tell a cautionary tale opening up new "problem-spaces"[31] that can act to effectively allow for a more politically inflected changing present that is in accord with the continued ambivalent and ambiguous nature of the institutionalization of the black studies project. But what queer black studies requires the black studies project to risk is its wounded "specialism," so that a queer pedagogy of erotics might allow something queer to happen to all who enter the disciplinary zone of the black studies project. But if only the black studies project could do more than think the unthought of queer conditionality and encounter the sensuality of—to paraphrase Dusty Dixon—kissing some queer ass, the possibility of the continuation of this audacious project for liberation might proceed unabated until liberation is a condition of our being.

NOTES

1 An elaboration of diaspora reading practice can be found in my essay "Beyond the 'Nation Thing': Black Studies, Cultural Studies, and Diaspora Discourse (or the Post-Black Studies Moment)," in *Decolonizing the Academy: African Diaspora Studies,* ed. Carole Boyce Davies et al. (New York: African World Press, 2003).

2 For exemplary critiques of family as community and the inherent conceptual problem in that kind of theorizing, see Hazel Carby, *Race Men* (Boston: Harvard University Press, 1998); Paul Gilroy, *There Ain't No Black in the Union Jack: The Cultural Politics of Race and Nation* (London: Hutchinson, 1987); Stuart Hall, "Cultural Identity and Diaspora" in *Identity: Community, Culture, Difference,* ed. Jonathan Rutherford (London: Lawrence and Wishart, 1990), 222–37.

3 Slavoj Žižek, *Looking Awry: An Introduction to Jacques Lacan through Popular Culture* (Cambridge, Mass.: MIT Press, 1991).

4 See Paul Gilroy, *The Black Atlantic: Modernity and Double Consciousness* (Cambridge, Mass.: Harvard University Press, 1993) and Michael Hanchard, *Orpheus and Power: The Movimento Negro of Rio de Janeiro* (Princeton, N.J.: Princeton University Press, 1994).

5 See Jane Rhodes on Mary Ann Shadd and her attempt to make her United States black again in *Mary Ann Shadd Cary: The Black Press and Protest in the Nineteenth Century* (Bloomington: Indiana University Press, 1998). See also my reply to Rhodes's book: "'Who Is She and What Is She to You?': Mary Ann Shadd Cary and the (Im)possibility of Black Canadian Studies," in *Rude: Contemporary Black Canadian Cultural Criticism,* ed. Rinaldo Walcott (Toronto: Insomniac Press, 2000), 27–48.

6 An example of this is the popularity of Isaac Julien and Marlon Riggs, which extends across the black diaspora. Other examples include the invitation of Pomo Afro Homos to Toronto or the popularity of Bill T. Jones among black gay men who are otherwise not interested in dance.

7 William Haver, "Queer Research; or, How to Practice Invention to the Brink of Intelligibility," in *The Eight Technologies of Otherness,* ed. Sue Golding (London: Routledge, 1997), 280.

8 For a discussion of the injury and rights discourse that informs my argument in this essay, see Wendy Brown's *States of Injury* (Princeton: Princeton University Press, 1995).

9 See Cornel West, *Race Matters* (Boston: Beacon Press, 1993).

10 See Jean-Luc Nancy, *The Inoperative Community* (Minneapolis: University of Minnesota Press, 1991); Giorgio Agamben, *The Coming Community* (Minneapolis: University of Minnesota Press, 1993); William Haver, *The Body of This Death: Historicity and Sociality in the Time of AIDS* (Stanford: Stanford University Press, 1996); Sylvia Wynter, "On Disenchanting Discourse: 'Minority' Literary Criticism and Beyond," in *The Nature and Context of Minority Discourse,* ed. Abdul Janmohamed and David Lloyd (New York: Oxford University Press, 1990): and Sylvia Wynter, "1492: A New World View," in *Race, Discourse, and the Origin of the Americas: A New World View,* ed. Vera Hyatt and Rex Nettleford (Washington, D.C.: Smithsonian Institution Press, 1995).

11 Haver, "Queer Research," 280.

12 Ibid., 282.

13 Ibid., 283.

14 Deborah Britzman, "Is There a Queer Pedagogy? or, Stop Being Straight," *Educational Theory* 45 (spring 1995): 151–66.

15 Haver, "Queer Research," 283.

16 Deborah Britzman, *Lost Subjects, Contested Objects* (Albany: State University of New York Press, 1998).

17 Marlon Riggs, "Unleash the Queen," in *Black Popular Culture*, ed. Gina Dent (Seattle: Bay Press, 1992), 101.

18 Agamben, *The Coming Community*.

19 Charles Rowell, "Signing Yourself: An Afterword," in *Shade: An Anthology of Fiction by Black Gay Men of African Descent* (New York: Avon, 1996).

20 Lynn Crosbie and Michael Holmes, eds., *Plush: Selected Poems of Sky Gilbert, Courtnay McFarlane, Jeffery Conway, R. M. Vaughan, and David Trinidad* (Toronto: Coach House Press, 1995), 46–49.

21 Reginald Shepherd, *Some Are Drowning* (Pittsburgh: University of Pittsburgh Press, 1994).

22 Gary Fisher, *Gary in Your Pocket: Stories and Notebooks of Gary Fisher*, ed. Eve Sedgwick (Durham: Duke University Press, 1996); for a reading of Fisher, see Robert Reid-Pharr, "The Shock of Gary Fisher," in *Dangerous Liaisons: Blacks, Gays, and the Struggle for Equality*, ed. Eric Brandt (New York: New Press, 1996), 243–56.

23 Arjun Appadurai, "Disjuncture and Difference in the Global Cultural Economy," in *Colonial Discourse and Postcolonial Theory: A Reader*, ed. Patrick Williams and Laura Chrisman (New York: Columbia University Press, 1994), 324–39.

24 For a sample of some of these artifacts, see Joseph Beam, ed., *In The Life: A Black Gay Anthology* (Boston: Alyson, 1996); Audre Lorde, *Sister Outsider* (Freedom, Calif.: The Crossing Press, 1984) and *Zami: A New Spelling of My Name*, (Freedom, Calif.: Crossing Press, 1982); Samuel Delany, *The Motion of Light in Water: Sex and Science Fiction Writing in the East Village, 1957-1965* (New York: Plume, 1988); Essex Hemphill, ed., *Brother to Brother: New Writings by Black Gay Men* (Boston: Alyson, 1991); and Essex Hemphill, *Ceremonies* (New York: Plume, 1992). Also see the films of Isaac Julien, Marlon Riggs, and the oeuvre of James Baldwin, as well as house music and disco.

25 See David Scott, *Refashioning Futures: Criticism after Postcoloniality* (Princeton: Princeton University Press, 1999).

26 Kobena Mercer, "Decolonization and Disappointment: Reading Fanon's Sexual Politics," in *The Fact of Blackness: Frantz Fanon and Visual Representation*, ed. Alan Reed (Seattle: Bay Press, 1999), 116.

27 William Haver, "Of Madmen Who Practice Invention to the Brink of Intelligibility," in *Queer Theory in Education*, ed. William Pinar (Mahwah, N.J.: Lawrence Erlbaum Associates, 1998), 290.

28 Joseph Beam, "Making Ourselves from Scratch," in *Brother to Brother: New Writings by Black Gay Men*, ed. Essex Hemphill (Boston: Alyson, 1991), 262.

29 For example, see *Remember Africville*, 1992, dir. Shelagh Mackenzie, National Film Board of Canada.

30 Scott, *Refashioning Futures*, 110.

31 Ibid.

CHAPTER 3

Our Bodies Are Not Ourselves: Tranny Guys and the Racialized Class Politics of Incoherence

Jean Bobby Noble

That was when I realized a shocking thing. I couldn't become a man without becoming The Man. Even if I didn't want to.

—Jeffrey Eugenides (2002: 518)

I n my first department meeting as a professor at York University, one held during the CUPE strike on our campus in 2000, the department was attempting to address the gender imbalance among its rank of full professors. Given that many of the full professors are male, the department was taking the very important step of finding a remedy to this situation. One senior professor (but not full professor), a woman who teaches, among other things, feminist literature, made the very curious claim that given how easy it is these days to change one's gender—and this even after the Ontario government de-listed sex-reassignment surgeries—that she would volunteer to do so if it would allow her to access the pay increase that accompanied a full professorship. A round of laughter ensued in which all seemingly agreed that this was indeed an easy process and the meeting continued. I sat a little dumbfounded that—in the midst of the CUPE 3903 union labour action on the campus, a local that has been remarkably progressive in its inclusion of trans issues in its mandate, and in the face of the aggressive de-listing of sex-reassignment procedures *and* the sad reality that male full professors still outranked the females—any of these matters would be so easily the source of laughter among faculty. This work is addressed to, in part, not only the female professor in question but to those folks inside of feminism who might claim that trans is not a feminist issue.

[I]ssues around the prefix *trans-* present not only theoretical but lived opportunities to refine our intersectional reading practices. The perspective I want to explore here is one that will allow us to see trans issues as not only those of gender but also those of race and class as well. The titles of two significant feminist books on class—Dorothy Allison's *Skin* and bell hooks's *Where We Stand*—signal the precise articulation I want to explore here: that between (trans-)[1] embodiment, class, and labour. Each text argues, among other things, that materializing class within feminist theoretical paradigms is often accomplished through corporeal metaphors. Moreover, each also suggests to us that class, the one term within our intersectional frameworks that is often neglected, is itself perceived to be about a kind of hyper-embodiment and hyper-visibility, especially for those of us who are working class and racialized White. If the anti-racist field of whiteness studies is correct, as I will argue later it is, then being classed as White is whiteness racialized as visible, especially since whiteness operates through ironic codes of invisibility and, hence, epistemological and discursive power. That is, whiteness comes into visibility as whiteness when it is articulated through class. If that is true, then under what conditions can transed bodies, bodies that similarly matter when invisible and/or fetishized, emerge within the feminist analytical intersections of capitalism, class, and race? I want to play in those fields by offering my own trans body—which is White but formerly off-White,[2] formerly lesbian but now female-to-male trans-sexual—as a case study in resistance. A practice of strategically unmaking the self—that is, working the labour of self-making against the categorical imperative—is a class, trans, anti-racist, and union politic I want to cultivate in this era where "self" is the hottest and most insidious capitalist commodity.[3]

The union motto that I want to borrow—an injury to one is an injury to all—has been in my life since I was very young.[4] My maternal grandmother was a member of CUPE for her entire working life; she was a hospital worker when services, like laundry and food, were still provided in-house. She worked in a hospital laundry for almost 40 years. I spent one summer as a young teenager working in that same laundry with her and just barely lasted the first month. Conditions were horrific. Unpacking the laundry from the hospital hampers was one of the nastiest jobs I have ever witnessed. Thankfully, I suppose, the staff wouldn't let me near the job of separating soiled sheets, bloodied towels from the operating rooms, and so on. Temperatures were extremely high and dangerous. Between massive pressing machines that ironed linens and sheets, the huge dryers, and washers that laundered sheets at very high temperatures, workers were dehydrated on a regular basis. After working for 40 years in daily conditions like these, my grandmother was given a CUPE ring that I still have and wear on a chain around my neck. I remember visiting her on her lunch break when I was much younger; I would wait for her in the hospital cafeteria and when the laundry women came into the room, they certainly were quite a sight. Into that otherwise unremarkably populated cafeteria walked a group of White, working-class, big, tough-looking, often hard-drinking women dressed in white dress-uniforms that looked out of place on them. They lumbered into the cafeteria, lit cigarettes, opened their homemade lunches, and stared down all who dared to look. Those women, a formidable bunch of working-class women who were literally at the bottom of the health-services industry but upon whom it depended, made a mark on me. Much later when I walked the CUPE 3903 picket line at York University with my teaching assistants as a new faculty member, something of those early workers infused my determination to see that strike through to its conclusion. I doubt that much of CUPE 3903's current work on trans-sexual issues would have made much sense to those women with whom my grandmother worked, although I suspect a couple of them might have understood the stakes. Because of the political commitment to social justice issues, CUPE 3903 has passed a number of resolutions that include the struggles of trans-sexual peoples into their primary mandate. They also support their trans-sexual members with funding; when I had surgery, CUPE 3903's Ways and Means fund helped me pay for a procedure that has been de-listed in the Conservatives' butchery of Ontario health care.[5]

The men in my family were less union-affiliated but just as affected by the class-based issues of labour activism. My grandfather was one of the "Little Immigrants," groups of White, working-class, orphaned British children shipped to Canada from the homes of Thomas John Barnardo, a philanthropist in 19th-century London, England. Thomas Barnardo, along with others, established a series of reformatory and industrial schools known as "ragged schools" (because of the ragged clothing of the attendees) for homeless and abandoned children. In the 19th century, they struck a deal with the Canadian government whereby they would export large numbers of these children to Canada to work as "farm" help and "mother's helpers" in Canadian homes and farms (Bagnall 1980: 91). At its peak, this emigration was responsible for shipping between 80,000 and 100,000 (orphaned or abandoned) children to Canada, a ready-made, exploitable "servant" class (Bagnell 1980: 9). Most of these children, now known as the Barnardo kids, would end up working as indentured domestic servants. My grandfather was one of those who came to Canada via Montreal in 1916 as a young boy to be adopted into a farm family, or so he thought. Instead, he lived in the barn, was ill fed, beaten, and overworked until he was old enough to run away. He did, and set up a life for himself in Canada as a labourer, eventually marrying my grandmother in Northern Ontario. As one of the students of a ragged school, my grandfather was still unable to read and write when he died in 1992.

About one thing I felt certain: these were the primary influences on my gender. My grandfather had an entirely ambivalent relationship with England: I suspect he had always felt abandoned and banished from it, although as a young boy from a very poor family, he had already lived the life of an exile on the streets of London. He remained vehemently class-identified and anti-British for his entire life, continuously evoking cultural traces of England and, unknowingly, its particular form of class whiteness while constantly disparaging both at the same time. I find traces of both grandparents in the words I use to describe myself ("a guy who is half lesbian") and, in finding these traces, have built a sense of self quite different from their own. The rough and yet somehow vulnerable masculinity of the butches and FtMs brings my grandmother back to me, while, in some kind of temporal and geographical displacement, I find traces of my grandfather's off-whiteness in the class-based traces of manhood I now wear as corporeal signifiers.

To be sure, my family and I are all White. When I say "off-White," I do not mean to suggest at all that somehow being poor and/or working class means that one is no longer White. What I mean is that whiteness, like gender and class, has a history of invention, construction, and utility. Embedded in those histories are the processes that manufacture whiteness in the service of modern nation building. [...]

If racialized bodies are the product of both our own labour and the work of a racial social manufacturing machine, then developing not just a tolerance, but an acquired taste, for destabilizing paradoxes within our feminist vocabularies might be one way to trouble that machinery. Female-to-male trans-sexuals embody but are also articulated by paradox: Loren Cameron's (1996) photographs in *Body Alchemy* visually represent this paradox. The guys whom Cameron photographs, especially those without clothes, really are half guy, half something else. My own body does this too: from the waist up, with or without clothes, I display a White male chest. Naked, from the waist down, my body reads closest conventionally female body even though that is not how it reads to me. Clothed, from the waist down, my body is overdetermined by signifiers of whiteness and masculinity and I am just a guy. Given that the surgical production of a penis leaves much to be desired—and the penis they can build costs so much that it is out of reach for most guys—trans men cannot leave the "trans" behind and be "men." Self-naming and, by implication, self-definition, then, these crucial axioms that feminist movements fought long and hard for become tricky: I find myself at an even greater loss when it comes to finding a language to describe myself. Just recently, I have settled upon the following paradox: "I am a guy who is half lesbian." I have a long lesbian history, which I do not deny despite tremendous pressure, but have just recently come out as a straight (albeit trans-sexual) man or "I am a lesbian man": Identifying myself through paradox as a "guy who is half lesbian" really comes closest to bringing a number of historical moments together to form *something like an identity*.

Refracting identity through simile ("something like" or "closest to") is crucial to my sense of self. While I am suggesting *something like*—that is, something comparable or similar to—I am also suggesting but *something that fails to*—that is, something that fails to cohere as a thing unto itself, hence the need for the comparison to begin with. In the case of my own sense of self, for instance, the tension between "guy" and "lesbian" does the work of articulating in language what my body is currently doing through gender signifiers. The result, of course, is that many FtMs cannot always be read as "men" (without the quotation marks) in every circumstance, presuming, of course, that any man can. Take gym locker rooms as an example. These are sites of poignant contradiction within our current capitalist discourses about bodies. Gyms and health clubs are strange sites of Marxist alienation and disembodiment even in the face of an apparent hyper-embodiedness. Fragmenting bodies into "legs," "abs," "chest," "shoulders," and "arms" (and then systems like "cardio"), the class culture of working out before or after work (not employment/work as physically demanding) requires one to become, quite literally, subject to or to step into a machine that has been designed to isolate a muscle or set of muscles and work them with the goal of having them look like they do more than get worked on at the gym. The gym body is developed not necessarily from use but from an extreme form of docility, repetition, and discipline. Capitalism requires each of these when manufacturing labouring bodies. Don't get me wrong: working out is not necessarily a terrible thing to do. After years of disembodiment, I decided to take the plunge and sign up with a fitness program. Like most gyms, it relies heavily on a gendered division of space determined by conventional understandings of the supposed self-evidence of the body. Given that I read completely as male, showering in public would compromise that reading. Being undressed in a locker room—and given the degree to which straight men furtively but quite decidedly look at each other—would, quite literally, be my undoing.

Then again, signifying as a guy, which I do more consistently now that I no longer have breasts, I do so with a success that makes me politically suspect to some lesbians while at other times interesting to gay men. Toronto's Pride 2003 was an interesting experience; two things happened that marked a shift in my identity from very masculine lesbian to guy. First, I seemed to be much more interesting to gay men as an object of desire. This is evident by the way in which I am now just more noticeable; gay men flirt with me now in a way they've not done so before. At dinner, in a queer-esque restaurant, a number of men stopped by our table to say hello, pass on a pride greeting or, in one case, to invite me upstairs to an event that was happening later that night. But let me describe myself to you: in my life as a "woman," I failed miserably. I signified as extremely butch, stone butch, macho even. I am heavy-set, continue to wear a kind of crew cut, dress in black pants and crisp shirts, and do not communicate signals that could be easily construed as gay (read: gay man) in any way at all. And yet precisely because of my gender performance (if categories are necessary, I could be considered a smallish bear), I am cruised on a regular basis by gay men.

But masculinity is not the only subject of unmaking found in No Man's Land. The other thing I felt quite compelled to do during the weekend's activities was to insist that my very out lesbian-femme girlfriend of African descent hold my hand as much as possible.[6] This irony resonates even more strongly for several reasons. In a historical moment where femmes are accused of not being lesbian enough, or where queer femininity is cast in a suspicious light, it was a bit of an oddity to realize that I passed as *less than bio-guy* when outed as *something else* through my lesbian partner. Queer femininity or, as Anna Camilleri calls it, femininity gone wrong, is equally bound by contradiction, paradox, and, in the best sense of the term, perversion. The curious difference, though, where trans-folks often need to be recognized for their gender resignifications, queer femmes often rearticulate sexual scripts and do not receive enough credit for that very political work. That is, to be very specific, as a trans guy it is extremely important to me to be seen as male whereas for my femme partner, it's far more important for her to be seen as lesbian. My partner is a woman of African descent, which means that, because of our impoverished and anti-intersectional economies, a battle of dualities plays out on her body to claim her—through identification or disidentification—either as "Black" or "queer" (but rarely both) in No Man's Land. This is not her battle but a battle over how her body is being read. The signifiers most easily read as femme and/or lesbian in our culture are those of White femininity. Lesbians of colour, including many femmes and butches, have written extensively about the whiteness of gay, lesbian, bisexual, and trans language, signifiers, histories, and so on. The semiotic deficiencies of subjectivity within White supremacy disallow signifying as Black and femme simultaneously. For my partner, visibility is frequently conditional: either she is read as her sexuality or she is read as her race. Being a racialized, gendered, and sexualized subject all at the same time is seen as unthinkable within our current paradigms of identity, which privilege—indeed, demand—singularity of identification. Models of intersectionality, which allow me, for instance, to read myself as raced (White, British), gendered (masculine), and sexualized (hetero-gendered and queerly straight) all at the same time are still sadly missing in our political lexicons. If FtMs wear masculinity as what Jay Prosser calls a second skin in order to feel visible and, strangely, invisible at the same time, femmes, on the other hand, wear a queer gendered-ness as a second skin that renders them invisible as lesbians. Femmes of colour, to risk an awkward phrase, are hailed as racialized subjects, which can render them invisible as queers *inside* queer communities. Each of these are accomplished through a triangulation, each through the other, and tell us that despite the work we have done, we have still so much more to do.

One of the most significant things I have done to unmake this supposedly femininely signified body is to have top surgery to remove my breasts. On June 9, 2003, I underwent top surgery, a euphemism for a surgical procedure properly known as bilateral mastectomy with male chest reconstruction. As I sat at my desk several days after the procedure, I wore a wide binder around my now scrawny-looking white chest. Underneath that binder, strangely similar to one I had worn when I wanted to bind my breasts, are two lateral scars where those breasts used to sit. Just above those scars are my nipples, grafted onto my newly configured chest but still healing under dressings to ensure that the grafts take. To be clear, in this procedure, the graft (the nipples) are removed completely from the skin. Once the breast tissue is removed, the nipples are then reattached as grafts. After about two weeks, the "new" nipples have attached again to the skin, only this time in a new position on the newly configured chest. But the *metaphor* of grafting is an interesting one and all too relevant to what I have just come through in this "transition."

I prefer the trope of "grafting" to "transition" because it allows me to reconfigure what I mean by trans-gender or trans-sexual. All too often, the relation between the "trans" and either "gender" or "sexual" is misread to mean that one transcends the other or that trans people, in essence, are surgically and hormonally given "new" bodies. That is, the terms "trans-gender" or "trans-sexual" are often misread to suggest a radical departure from birth bodies into squeaky clean new ones. But the terms are often misread as transcending the gender of those birth bodies into an entirely new gender. I counter that belief in my earlier book *Masculinities without Men?* but also now on and through my body; indeed, even more so now since my nipples were literally grafted back onto my chest: neither of these misreadings is as helpful as they could be.[7] My *gender* now looks different from the one I grew up with but my body is, paradoxically, almost still the same. I have the same scars, the same stretch marks, the same bumps, bruises, and birthmarks that I have always had, only it is all different now. Grafting allows me to think that relation. Not only does this trope allow me to look at the way my "new" body is grafted out of, onto, through my "old," but it is also a way of rethinking trans-gendered (read: differently gendered) bodies as effects of the sex/gender system in crisis and transition. It means my newish-looking gender is the effect of a productive failure of that manufacturing system, not its success. In those failings, trans men can become "men" in some contexts; some, but not all. But neither do trans-sexual and trans-gender folks transcend the sex/gender system; instead, trans-folks are an important site where its inabilities, as Judith Butler argues, to live up to its own imperatives (that gender be the artifact of sex) are rendered obvious.

The process of grafting, as self-remaking and queer reproduction outside of a heteronormative model, spawns (certainly for FtMs) something else outside of our sexual vocabularies and grammars. But this is not androgyny, a mix, or blending of both (read: natural) genders. As Doan (1994: 153) puts it, "the notion of hybridity resonates with doing violence to nature, which results […] in the scientific equivalent of freaks, mongrels, half-breeds and crossbreeds." This is a strategy of naturally denaturalizing biological essentialisms with a "sexual politics of heterogeneity and a vision of hybridized gender constructions outside an either/or proposition" in order to naturalize "cultural oddities, monstrosities, abnormalities, and [what appear to be] conformities" (Doan 1994: 154). The trope of grafting thus allows me to articulate the paradox signalled by "I am a lesbian man" or "I am a guy who is half lesbian." This picture of transed bodies as grafted, where one materialization is haunted by the other, as opposed to crossing or exiting, also allows me to articulate the radical dependencies that these identities (lesbian and trans guy or, to update the lexicon, female masculinity and trans-sexual masculinity) have for me but also with each other historically (the invert + the lesbian + the trans-sexual). To say "I am a lesbian man" or "I am a guy who is half lesbian" both materializes or externalizes a body that is not always immediately visible yet is still absolutely necessary for the performative paradox to work. It means to answer "yes" to "Am I that name?"[8] and to amend the question so that it reads multiply instead of singularly: "Am I this and that at the same time?" Thus, intelligibility for the female-to-male trans-sexual man means contesting the alignment of bodies, genders, and sexualities to force a crisis by grafting articulations onto each other in the same way that my nipple grafts work. I remember the day I heard a trans man say about his former breasts: "It's such a paradox to have to cut some part of myself off in order to feel whole." Those words are inscribed painfully across my chest today more than ever, but make no mistake: this is the body not as foundation but as archive; this is the same chest, the same body, the same flesh I have always known, only now its text is totally different.[9]

For all my bravado around top surgery, one of the things I have learned through the process is that these are costly choices. Certainly they are costly financially and now that many provincial governments have de-listed these services, trans-folks are left to their own devices to pay for vital procedures. In addition, there's something about going to my extremely trans-friendly doctor that I find profoundly disturbing. My anxiety traces a particular distress around the medically overdetermined conditions of embodiment. This is still the medicalization of bodies, genders, and lives, and as much as the diagnosis "gender identity disorder" is a formal alibi, it still reflects the reality that trans-folks are forced to make the best choices for ourselves in a field of over-determined possibilities. Even though Toronto's Clarke Institute is no longer the sole gatekeeper of sex-reassignment procedures, the job of dispensing hormone therapies and giving referrals to surgeons, etc., still rests with usually non-transed physicians. And the means of rendering oneself intelligible, which is especially true for FtMs who do not achieve full embodiment of their chosen gender, is still the clinical alibi of "gender identity disorder."

That said, politically, the pressure to complete paperwork to change my former F to an M is tremendous. While I signify a version of White masculinity, I have chosen to keep the F. The existence of that F, though, has led me to draw some rather interesting conclusions about its limits. When I have handed that document over to various individuals, most people seem to pay little attention, if any, to the F. I am often, because of my gender presentation, disidentified with that F. Similarly, my image of myself as masculine is becoming reoriented in the process as well. Such incommensurability between self and body is the No Man's Land in which transed lives are lived. While medicalized interventions render this gap less dangerous, they do not, at least for FtMs, render the gap non-existent. Since my surgery, I am aware that I signify quite differently and that I need to transform my own consciousness to keep up. I now find myself asking what kind of *guy* am I presenting because masculinity on the perception of a male body is quite different than masculinity on the perception of a female body. But I am still a guy with an

F designation. This discursive contradiction, paradox even, allows me, as Duggan and McHugh suggest (1996: 110) in the "Fem(me)inist Manifesto," to "inhabit normal abnormally." It means, as the best feminist interventions have always told us, that I need to be painfully aware of how I signify, of what kinds of power accrue to my whiteness and masculinity, and then work against both of those to challenge those power grids. It means, as a White man, outing myself whenever and wherever possible as a race traitor, not because I am partnered with a woman of colour but because of my commitment to an antiracist critical practice that includes doing the pedagogical work of challenging racism among other straight White men. Who better to occupy the space of *guy* but former lesbians who have walked the streets as women, loved as fierce and sometimes stone butches, and who have come of political age in the context of lesbian-feminism? For me, that's a proud history that does not get left behind in the operating room.

But it is precisely *because* of that same gender performance that some lesbians, on the other hand, have expressed frustration when I, a straight White man, appear in lesbian (although not lesbian/woman only) spaces. The most pernicious of these chills occurred at United Kingdom 2: International Drag King Show, a trans-friendly and literate event produced in Toronto that showcases drag king performances from across North America and, this year, Amsterdam. The irony resonates strongly: at an event that offers female and trans masculinity for consumption, I passed so well as a non-transed person—indeed, as just a straight White guy—that my presence was troubling to one young woman in particular who felt little discomfort about communicating her disapproval. That chill was repeated a number of other times during Toronto's Dyke March day (I did not go on the dyke march) so that I quite aggressively hunted down a t-shirt that would, at the very least, dis-identify my seemingly heterosexual masculinity with heteronormativity.

That said, then, if it is possible to render my masculinity anti-heteronormative, then might it also be possible to remake whiteness, not necessarily just self-conscious but similarly incoherent? That is, if I've been suggesting that trans men risk incoherence, can White masculinity also risk incoherence as a political strategy, one that refuses the hegemonic bargains offered to White trans manhood? White masculinity is, of course, an intersection of parts where a fantasy of singularity is privileged instead. [For] James Baldwin, whiteness is secured by its violent imperative of universal, categorical singularity (that is, non-intersectionality). Trans manhood has the ability to exist on a similar frequency as biological masculinity without the coherence or clarity of meaning. Trans White masculinity is key for its failure to cohere [...] into hegemonic or visible *matter*. (Again, simile is key here.) Dionne Brand presents a similar argument about this in her work, *A Map to the Door of No Return*, when she writes of bodies as matter being socially constructed with extremely potent stakes:

> There are ways of constructing the world—that is, of putting it together each morning, what it should look like piece by piece—and I don't feel that I share that with the people of this small town. Each morning I think we wake up and open our eyes and set the particles of forms together—we make solidity with our eyes and with the matter in our brains. [...] We collect each molecule, summing them up into "flesh" or "leaf" or "water" or "air." Before that everything is liquid, ubiquitous and mute. We accumulate information over our lives which brings various things into solidity, into view. What

I am afraid of is that waking up in another room, minutes away by car, the mechanic wakes up and takes my face for a target [...] He cannot see me when I come into the gas station; he sees something else [...] as if I do not exist [...] or as if something he cannot understand has arrived—as if something he despises has arrived. A thing he does not recognize. Some days when I go to the gas station [...] I drive through the possibility of losing solidity at any moment. (Brand 2002: 141–42)

Brand argues for race what Fausto-Sterling and Butler argue about sex and gender and what I want to advocate as a trans practice of masculinity:

To be material is to speak about the process of materialization. And if viewpoints about [identity] are already embedded in our philosophical concepts of how matter forms into bodies, the matter of bodies cannot form a neutral, pre-existing ground from which to understand the origin of [...] different. Since matter already contains notions of [identity], it cannot be a neutral recourse on which to build "scientific" or "objective" theories of [the trans subject] ... the idea of the material comes to us already tainted, containing within it pre-existing ideas about [identity] ... the body as a system [...] simultaneously produces and is produced by social meanings. (Fausto-Sterling 2000: 22–23)

Entrance into these fictionalities of matter, of coherent White skin, is purchased through an ideological belief in a naturalized whiteness and naturalized masculinity. The reading of a body as gendered male and racialized White involves presenting signifiers within an economy where the signifiers accumulate toward the appearance of a coherently gendered and racialized body.

Baldwin's work on the price of the White ticket is crucial here. "White people are not white," writes James Baldwin (1985: xiv), "part of the price of the white ticket is to delude themselves into believing that they are." [...] Entrance into the fictionality of whiteness is purchased through an ideological class belief in naturalized whiteness. What White is, then, is a class-based race: the higher up you go, the whiter you get. One is not born White, one buys his or her way into whiteness and *becomes* White. That price, Baldwin writes, includes, necessitates even, believing in the fiction of whiteness as signifier of the universal subject, the just plain, simple, and singular Man and Woman. But the price is afforded by what later theorists of whiteness will call its psychological and social wages: skin colour and class (upward) mobility. This is what the men and women of my ancestry purchased for me off the labour of their class-based whiteness (what I previously called off-White, White, but not middle-class White): entrance, as an educated adult, into a whitened middle class. While I grew up on welfare, we became *whiter* through the generations.

While I am no longer working class (the transition into that whitened middle class was a far harder transition for me than "changing" genders), I continue to be very aware of a rising discourse of whiteness, which, as some writers detail, is racializing class-based whiteness in what seem to me to be all the wrong ways. Five years ago I would have argued that self-consciousness for White people could be anything but wrong. But as many race theorists have taught us, White supremacy, like other colonial systems, is historical and amenable to new circumstances and critique. In the last few decades, there has been a huge proliferation of thinking and writing about whiteness. [...]

The first cultural theorist whose work is seminal to whiteness scholarship is film critic Richard Dyer. In 1988, he published an extremely important essay simply called "White." In that early essay (subsequently published later as part of a full-length book of the same name), Dyer enacts a theoretical shift that enables us to ask the questions about whiteness that we are asking today. This shift shares much in common with the contradictions about sexuality detailed by Eve Sedgwick in *Epistemology of the Closet* (1990). Questions about race and sexuality have been bound by a set of epistemological contradictions: on the one hand, some questions of identity race theory have been conservatively constructed as what Sedgwick calls a *minoritizing* discourse (seeing that identity as an issue of active importance only for a small, distinct, relatively fixed group, like Caribbean-Canadians or First Nations peoples, for instance). On the other hand, what we need to do instead is to retheorize race and sexuality as what Sedgwick dubs a "universalizing discourse," an issue or discourse of active importance in the lives of subjects across the spectrum of identity categories. This particular shift in thinking allows us, like Dyer and Sedgwick in their work, to ask particular kinds of questions about whiteness and heterosexuality, questions that shift the critical gaze from the so-called racialized object (Black people, etc.) to the so-called racial subject (White folks doing the looking). In other words, instead of allowing the White critical gaze to look and taxonomize colours or cultures, a universalizing discourse allows us to turn the gaze back onto whiteness. And shifting that gaze is exactly what Dyer's essay accomplishes. Where race theory interrogates the production of racialized identities, critical whiteness studies examines the ways that whiteness *qua* whiteness has somehow been left out of those terms.

[...] One of the consequences of allowing whiteness to remain unmarked as a race, as Dyer suggests, is that whiteness becomes the norm. Whiteness, in other words, constructs itself as coterminous with the endless plenitude of human diversity, with the non-particularizable general. [...] What this means is that whiteness remains so entirely hyper-visible as everything that it also becomes, paradoxically, invisible as nothing, the norm, as an invisible backdrop against which all other races are produced. It also means that whiteness was not a found category but one that was historically invented and/or constructed.

*****

What's at stake in a particular set of arguments [made by Frankenberg] is a denaturalization of whiteness. That is, denaturalizing whiteness means to universalize whiteness, not as the norm but as just another race among a spectrum of racial identities that could do the work of articulating both whiteness and antiracism work differently, albeit another race with systemic power. As I began to research, [...] I realized that whiteness, like many of the things I have been exploring in this work, has a history and representational currency. Thinking through representations of whiteness in popular culture and fiction allows me to argue not just the persistence of racism around us but also the ways in which identities can either challenge or be complicit with that persistence. [...]

Whiteness will always force its subjects to privilege their own unmarked invisibilities over any other marker of "difference" among its subjects (class, gender, and sexuality). But the price of becoming White is quite different than the price and, or, more accurately, the cost of knowing one is White. These two things are not exactly the same thing at all; *becoming* White means that one is no longer aware of oneself as a race and believes that one simply melts into the amorphous mass of the norm; *knowing* one is White means understanding oneself as a product of White supremacy or systemic racism that is larger than one individual and that also precedes our entry into the public domain. How can whiteness be used to dismantle that larger system? [...]

*****

[Annalee] Newitz argues that there are some forms of whiteness that have had a particular kind of visibility. In her thesis, she argues further that one way we might understand White racial identity at the close of the 20th century is as a social construction characterized most forcefully by a growing awareness of its own internal contradictions and a growing deployment of class divisions within whiteness. These are manifested in White-on-White class conflicts that produce a White racial self-consciousness based on various forms of divisiveness and self-loathing. White consciousness, she argues, emerges as a distinct and visible racial identity when it can be identified as class or as primitive, inhuman, and, ironically, hyper-visible: poor White trash. She continues to suggest that lower-class whiteness functions as a racially marked identity (Newitz 1997: 138). Whites who are not "trash" seem innocent of racially marked whiteness. Poor Whites are, in other words, less White and guilty of a "savagery" that upper-class Whites have transcended.

At the same time this particular deflection and deferral can be converted into what Newitz calls a confession of whiteness or a racialized look or positioning of redemption, a gesture of concern that will give us the appearance of innocence or redemption as White but which takes the place of real action to eliminate social injustice (Newitz 1997: 139). It becomes, in other words, a form of self-punishment that gets played out within and among White groups, producing a White nihilism. Nihilism was a doctrine that denied purpose, hope, a larger order, and that translated quickly into the self-destructive behaviours we've seen before. In a racial context, it is the actualization of what she argues is at the core of White supremacy to begin with: fear, inferiority, and failure. "When whites," she argues, "are put in touch with that fear, a kind of self-destructive nihilism results" (Newitz 1997: 139). This then converts into a pre-emptive self-hatred. Whites, in her estimation, imagine themselves as people of colour might and then name themselves preemptively to circumvent the power of being named by others. "One might understand these narratives," she argues, "as fantasies about whites resolving their racial problems without ever having to deal with people of colour" (Newitz 1997: 139). This is, in other words, a form of psychological defence, one that is racist and "a politically reactionary form of ideological defense" (Newitz 1997: 144). No one, after all, can insult you if you insult yourself first.

*****

[...] I have been suggesting all along that the labour of making oneself—indeed, of becoming a man—is fraught with responsibilities that go with the territory whether we know it or not. This labour is not unlike the labour of capitalized waged work, especially when, as the whiteness theorists have told us, whiteness accrues with it an additional social and psychological wage. The question then is less how much of ourselves do we sell with intention and more how much we are willing to articulate our bodies against the hegemonic bargain offered to us. For me, that is the measure of the privilege of masculinity without also being The Man.

I like to think that my grandmother and her co-workers understood something of these stakes as working-class and union women. If class and race are the subject of invention and ideological production, then theorizing trans-sexual issues as *labour* also does not seem that strange to me. In many ways, that's precisely the argument of this book. Gender identities—that is, gendered selves—are the product of, but also condition, particular kinds of labour. If the sex/gender system works, like any other ideological system, through misrecognition where we misperceive ourselves as natural human beings rather than as ideologically produced subjects, then it requires, as many theorists have pointed out, our complicit co-operation in order to accomplish that misrecognition. One of the rewards of that activity is the belief in a natural gender that is not man-made. Feminism has been arguing now for over a century that active insubordination with the imperatives of that system is one of the ways to make change happen and to refuse to allow that system to accomplish itself. A new century demands that feminism also begin to acknowledge its own complicity with the biological essentialisms at the core of the sex/gender systems. If it is true that gender identities are acts of coproduction, then the process of becoming a self, of making a self, which is so much a part of what trans-identities tell us, is also labour that can be used against the sex/gender system. A North Carolina drag king named Pat Triarch calls gender queers and trans-folks "deconstruction workers," who, by quite literally putting misfitting bodies on the (dis-assembly) line, begin to resist and rebuild the *man-made* gender imperatives that pass as those of nature. These bodies are not bodies as foundation but trans-bodies as archive, witness, risking political incoherence.

NOTES

1 The pedantic distinction between "trans-gender" and "trans-sexual" cannot hold, especially for female-to-male trans-sexual men for whom surgeries are always incomplete. To avoid being repetitive here, I used the prefix *trans-* to signify subjectivities where bodies are at odds with gender presentation, regardless of whether that misalignment is self-evident in conventional ways or not. The entire question of what's visible, when, how, and by whom is precisely what is at stake in this chapter, so policing or prescribing or hierarchizing kinds of political embodiment is a topical identity politic and moral panic that I eschew.

2 I am not claiming to be outside of White supremacy, nor am I claiming that somehow working-class whiteness is not White. What I am trying to explore here is the possibility within intersectionality of different kinds of whiteness, positioned at different angles to power in White supremacy, where the type of power is mitigated by overlapping and intersecting vectors of power by class, able-bodied-ness, sexuality, gender, and so forth. But the relation to racialized power is constant and I am not at all suggesting otherwise.

3 There is a curious and undertheorized history of what has come to be known as the "self-help discourse"; there was a time in early second wave feminism, due to the work of rape crisis and battered women's/shelter activists/workers, when recovering from the trauma and violence of the sex/gender system was an inherently political act of resistance. Hegemonic appropriations of these ideas rearticulated this notion of a reconfigured self in extremely conservative ways: self is what cosmetic procedures provide ("The Swan"); it's the product of an upper-class leisure-time activity (in most recent years, "Oprah"); self is what's taken up by the beauty myths and also what's used as an advertising strategy (see Subway's new campaign for lighter food consumption, which shows several people stating why they prefer Subway's new light menu, including a young, blonde, White woman from the anorexia demographic saying "I choose to actually eat"); a newly configured self is what Dr. Phil's diet campaign berates and shames folks into becoming. One of the few feminist texts to begin examining this history is Ann Cvetkovich's (2003) *An Archive of Feelings: Trauma, Sexuality and Lesbian Public Cultures.*

4 This is, of course, the primary trope and political rallying cry of Leslie Feinberg's (1991) novel, *Stone Butch Blues*, one of the most important working-class and trans narratives to call for a practice of strategic unmaking.

5 The CUPE 3903 Women's Caucus has not only counted trans-sexual women amongst its members, but in a truly unprecedented intervention in this border war, recently changed its name (it is now the "Trans Identified and   Identified" Caucus) to create space for trans-sexual men as well. It is clear that this local i   old the concerns of its trans-sexual and trans-gendered members into its mandate as issues of labour, not "lifestyle" as the Ontario Conservative government has so deemed.

6 The work of this section owes a debt to OmiSoore H. Dryden, my partner, with whom I have spent many pleasurable hours in delightful conversation.

7 *Masculinities without Men?* (2004).

8 This is an allusion to Denise Riley's (1988) extremely important work, *"Am I That Name?": Feminism and the Category of "Women" in History.*

9 See Ann Cvetkovich, *An Archive of Feelings.* On the relation between trauma and counter-cultural resistance movements as an archive or record of trauma but also of resistance, Cvetkovich (2003: 20) writes: "I am interested [...] in the way trauma digs itself in at the level of the everyday, and in the incommensurability of large-scale events and the ongoing material details of experience ... I hope to seize authority over trauma discourses from medical and scientific discourse in order to place it back in the hands of those who make culture, as well as to forge new models for how affective life can serve as the foundation for public but counter-cultural archive as well."

REFERENCES

Allison, Dorothy. 1994. *Skin: Talking about Sex, Class and Literature.* Ithaca: Firebrand Books.

Bagnell, Kenneth. 1980. *The Little Immigrant: The Orphans Who Came to Canada.* Toronto: Macmillan of Canada.

Baldwin, James. 1985. *The Price of the Ticket: Collected Nonfiction, 1948–1985.* New York: St. Martin's Press.

Brand, Dionne. 2002. *A Map to the Door of No Return.* Toronto: Coach House.

Butler, Judith. 1990. *Gender Trouble: Feminism and the Subversion of Identity.* New York and London: Routledge, Chapman & Hall, Inc.

Cameron, Loren. 1996. *Body Alchemy: Transsexual Portraits*. Pittsburgh: Cleis Press.

Camilleri, Anna. 2004. *I Am a Red Dress: Incantations on a Grandmother, a Mother, and a Daughter*. Vancouver: Arsenal Pulp Press.

Cvetkovich, Ann. 2003. *An Archive of Feelings: Trauma, Sexuality and Lesbian Public Cultures*. Durham: Duke University Press.

Doan, Laura. 1994. "Jeanette Winterson's Sexing the Postmodern." In *The Lesbian Postmodern*, edited by Laura Doan, 137–55. New York: Columbia University Press.

Duggan, Lisa, and Kathleen McHugh. 1996. "A Fem(me)inist Manifesto." *Women & Performance: A Journal of Feminist Theory* 8, no. 2: 107–10.

Dyer, Richard. 1988. "White" *Screen* 29, no. 4: 44–64.

Eugenides, Jeffrey. 2002. *Middlesex*. Toronto: Random House.

Fausto-Sterling, Anne. 2000. *Sexing the Body: Gender Politics and the Construction of Sexuality*. New York: Basic Books.

Feinberg, Leslie. 1991. *Stone Butch Blues*. Ithaca, NY: Firebrand.

Frankenberg, Ruth. 1993. White Women, Race Matters: The Social Construction of Whiteness. Minneapolis: University of Minnesota Press.

hooks, bell. 2000. *Where We Stand: Class Matters*. New York and London: Routledge.

Newitz, Annalee. 1997. "White Savagery and Humiliation, or a New Racial Consciousness in the Media." In *White Trash: Race and Class in America*, edited by Matt Wray and Annalee Newitz, 131–54. New York: Routledge.

Noble, Jean Bobby. 2004. *Masculinities without Men?* Vancouver: University of British Columbia Press.

Prosser, Jay. 1998. *Second Skins: The Body Narratives of Transsexuality*. New York: Columbia University Press.

Riley, Denise. 1988. *"Am I That Name?": Feminism and the Category of "Women" in History*. Houndmills: Macmillan Press.

Sedgwick, Eve Kosofsky. 1985. *Between Men: English Literature and Male Homosocial Desire*. New York: Columbia University Press.

Sedgwick, Eve Kosofsky. 1990. *Epistemology of the Closet*. Berkeley and Los Angeles: University of California Press.

PART TWO
The State, the Law, and the
Criminal Justice System

CHAPTER 4
The Regulation of First Nations Sexuality

Martin Cannon

INTRODUCTION

Several aspects of Canadian political reality have led historical sociologists to maintain that race, gender and sexuality are not separate categories of experience and analysis but dynamic sets of social constructions which, as they interconnect, impact upon individuals and their (re)productive activities in distinctive, historically specific ways (Ng, 1993: 50; Parr, 1995: 356–360; McClintock, 1995). Informed by this understanding, any comprehensive analysis of Canada's *Indian Act* and early Indian policy should examine how configurations of racist, sexist and heterosexist knowledges were manifested in the process(es) of colonization. Such an analysis would seek to document the endeavours toward making (European) heterosexuality compulsory within status Indian communities (Rich, 1993). Such an analysis, in its most ambitious sense, would illuminate the convergent discrimination(s) directed toward those preferring same-sex intimacies, and make a contribution toward an integrated theory of race, gender and sexuality. Such an endeavour, though far from exhaustive, is the primary focus of this chapter.

The first part of the chapter will provide a critical review of the literature which suggests that a broad range of gender and erotic relationships existed among Aboriginal populations at early contact. Part of this exercise will be to specify homosexuality as an analytic category describing in turn the difficulty with using terms such as "gay" and "lesbian" to describe historic First Nations sexual categories (Sun, 1988: 35; Whitehead, 1993). The second part of the chapter will then document how racist sexism and heterosexism worked together to legislate and define First Nations political reality. Upon illustrating the interactive relationship among these systems of domination, I will conclude that none of the development of class relations, the regulation of sexuality, racism or patriarchy can be explained as mutually exclusive.

SEXUALITY AND GENDER IN NATIVE NORTH AMERICA

Even prior to Confederation and the emergence of the first statute entitled the *Indian Act* in 1876, the colonial enterprise in Canada had virtually enforced a system of Eurocentric policies, beliefs and value systems upon First Nations. The earliest missionaries, for example, were determined to "civilize" the Indian populations by attempting to indoctrinate a Christian ethos and patriarchal familial structure (Brodribb, 1984). It was within the context of such a conversion mission that same-sex erotic and sexual diversity was negatively evaluated and often condemned (Kinsman, 1987: 71; Katz, 1983: 28). This mission was a project fueled by heterosexism.[1]

One of the often quoted passages related to the views of the early missionaries is that of the Jesuit, Joseph Francois Lafitau. Speaking of the erotic and gender relations which he observed among Native North Americans from 1711–1717, he noted:

> If there were women with manly courage who prided themselves upon the profession of warrior, which seems to become men alone, there were also men cowardly enough to live as women ... they believe they are honoured by debasing themselves to all of women's occupations; they never marry... (Joseph Francois Lafitau, quoted in Katz, 1976: 288).

The later diaries of the Jesuit, Pedro Font, resonated with the observations made by Lafitau. Only Pedro Font also identified an impending need to eradicate all such erotic or sexual relations and in their place establish a system of Christian morality. Making an assessment based on his observations taken from the expedition of Juan Bautista de Anza from 1775–1776, he noted:

> Among the women I saw men dressed like women, with whom they go about regularly, never joining the men... From this I inferred they must be hermaphrodites, but from what I learned later I understood that they were sodomites, dedicated to nefarious practices. From all the foregoing I conclude that in this matter of incontinence there will be much to do when the Holy Faith and the Christian religion are established among them (Pedro Font, quoted in Katz, 1976: 291).

Missionary accounts of sodomy were not always so subtly expressed. Jean Bernard Bossu, whose translated journals from the interior of North America between 1751 and 1762 spoke of "perverse" addictions among the Aboriginal nations he observed, expressed it thusly:

> The people of this nation are generally of a brutal and coarse nature. You can talk to them as much as you want about the mysteries of our religion; they always reply that it is beyond their comprehension. They are morally quite perverted, and most of them are addicted to sodomy. These corrupt men, who have long hair and wear short skirts like women, are held in great contempt (Jean Bernard Bossu, quoted in Katz, 1976: 291).

The spectrum of erotic and gender diversity recorded in times of early contact suggests that same-sex relations were considered to be of some moral and political consequence.[2] Labelled as "nefarious," the relations that did exist were seen as illegitimate. Clearly, there is no superior foundation for such "common sense" forms of paternalistic judgement, but we can explain the claims to Euro-Christian preeminence as grounded in the ethos of the historical period.[3] Informed by notions of supremacy, ideologies of racial inferiority and of "civilized" (hetero) sexual behaviour, the early Europeans saw First Nations (indeed all non-Europeans) as subordinate and underdeveloped entities (Miles, 1989; Said, 1978).[4] Of pertinent interest in the aforementioned passages is also the way they reveal the interrelated nature of all systems of oppression.

Configurations of racist, patriarchal and heterosexist knowledges worked together to influence the views of the missionaries. Being a "nefarious sodomite," for example, not only meant "debasing" oneself by "cowardly" appropriating the gender and assumed sexual roles of a devalued (in this case) female class, it was an "unproductive" realm that, as I will describe in further detail, required complete refashioning. Salvation (sexual and otherwise) was to rest under the auspices of a religiously superior race of Europeans: a motive that was clearly racist. Salvation was something that required the regulation of a "savage" sexuality thought antithetical to Christian decorum, gendered domestic relations, and moral rationality. There may be reason to suggest, however, that the view toward individuals referred to as "nefarious" by the missionaries was an unshared sentiment among some of the original inhabitants of North America. It has been suggested that the *berdache* enjoyed an esteemed role within certain communities prior to contact.[5]

Among the Bella Coola Nation located in what is now called British Columbia, Franz Boas noted the special status accorded to the *berdache,* a status that was central to an origin myth on food (Boas, reprinted in Roscoe, 1988: 81–84). Toleration of the *berdache* and even "institutionalized homosexuality" is suggested in more contemporary anthropological literature and Native testimonials (Benedict, quoted in Roscoe, 1988: 16–17; Mead, quoted in Roscoe, 1988: 19; Owlfeather, 1988: 100; Kenny, 1988: 153). Sharing a similar perspective, Kenny (1988: 26) has noted that

> [s]ome tribes, such as the Minois, actually trained young men to become homosexuals and concubines of men. The Cheyenne and Sioux of the plains may not have purposely trained young men to become berdaches but certainly accepted homosexuals more readily than perhaps other tribes.

In short, some have been inclined toward emphasizing the *berdache* as a recognized and legitimate social institution. Nonetheless, is it necessary to look upon this claim with some scepticism.

First, there is some difficulty in making cross-cultural comparisons like the one made by Kenny (1988) in the above noted excerpt. In his postulation, the tradition of *berdache* gets conflated with "homosexual" leaving little or no recognition of Native sex/gender systems. Such an interpretation is limited, for as Harriet Whitehead has argued, "sexual practices and beliefs must be understood within the context of the specific gender-meaning system of the culture in question" (Whitehead, 1993: 523; Rubin, 1975: 159). If we take a brief look at Native North American cultures, we grow increasingly familiar with the weaknesses of "homosexual" as an analytic category (Sun, 1988: 35).

The evidence to substantiate the claim that the Native North American *berdache* was an equivalent to the modern "homosexual" is limited. As Harriet Whitehead explains, such cross-cultural investigations tend to posit a *shared sexual identity* between the gender-crossing *berdache* and modern "homosexual": the very place where contradictions start to emerge (1993: 498). Alluding to the importance of sex/gender systems, Whitehead explains:

> Western society foregrounds erotic orientation as the basis for dividing people into socially significant categories, but for Native North Americans, occupational pursuits and dress/demeanour were the important determinants of an individual's social classification, and sexual object choice was its trailing rather than leading edge (1993: 498).

Whitehead does not suggest that the role of the *berdache* excluded same-sex sexual behaviour (1993: 514). She illuminates instead a sex/gender system that renders one's chosen occupational behaviour of much greater importance than sexual object choice when it comes to social (re) classification (Whitehead, 1993: 511, 513). The role of the *berdache*, according to Whitehead, was more about gender-crossing than it was about sexual relations. In making this point, she alerts anthropologist and social historian alike to the weaknesses of "homosexual" as an analytic category. In an historic or cross-cultural interpretation, modern-day Western categories may be unknown to the culture or past under study. The categories' applicability is subsequently limited. This is a position that is broadened by constructionist theorists who are interested in the history of sexuality. Foucault is exemplary.

For Foucault, sexuality is not a natural given, but the name that is granted to a historical construct (1990: 105, 127). Sexuality, in other words, is never more than a set of ever-varying developments tied to the mode of production and prevailing social/political realities (Foucault, 1990: 5–6; Padgug, 1989: 58). In short, sexuality and subsequently related behavior is socially constructed. Failing to recognize this category as such presents the social historian with conceptual and interpretive difficulties. Kenny's postulation in the above noted excerpt on Native "homosexuals" is again problematic.

The inclination to extract some *modern-day notion* of "homosexual," "gay" or even "lesbian" Native identity from the missionary statements on "sodomy" cannot be clearly substantiated. Nor can references to Indigenous sexualities be referred to as "homosexual" as this is known in the historical present. There are at least two reasons for this. First and foremost, the history of sexuality does not permit a conclusion such as the second. Foucault, for example, reminded us that the concept of "homosexuality" did not even emerge in Western discourse until the 19th century (1990: 43). To be sure, and this is my second point, the missionaries were speaking of "sodomy" and "nefarious practices" as a set of sex-related acts. The missionary statements, though they may speak of "morally perverse" behaviour and the outwardly physical attributes of the *berdache,* make no explicit mention of a specific personality type, sexual sensibility or sexual identity. It is not possible to make such an inference on that basis.

It is necessary to distinguish between behaviour and identity when we apply an analytic category such as "homosexual" to the historic past. We cannot take the sexual acts reported to have been witnessed by the missionaries and convert them to a history of personality or contemporary "gay" identity. For on this question of identity, Robert Padgug insists:

> These identities are not inherent in the individual. In order to be gay … more than individual inclinations (however we might conceive of those) or homosexual activity is required; entire ranges of social attitudes and the construction of particular cultures, subcultures, and social relations are first necessary (1989: 60).

In sum, while it may be true that *homosexual behaviour* existed in history, we cannot call those whose behaviour was so inclined either "gay," "lesbian" or homosexual as these are known in the historic present.[6]

The third problem with postulating on and about "Native homosexuality" is in alluding to its prevalence as "institutionalized." This suggestion, as noted by Kenny and others, tends to overshadow any critical understanding of the practice from a culturally-informed point of view. This characterization of homosexuality threatens to foreground the homosexual sex act over and above gender-crossing, occupational choice and the distribution of (cross-gendered) tasks. The effect of this characterization is to suggest that sexual object choice was more important than gender-crossed behaviour in Native social classification systems. A mistaken consequence is thereby afforded to the homosexual or even heterosexual sex act since some *berdaches* "lapsed into anatomic heterosexuality and on occasion even marriage without any loss of their cross-sex status" (Whitehead, 1993: 512; also see Schnarch, 1992: 115). In sum, it is important to recognize when we speak of "institutionalized homosexuality" that

> [h]omosexual acts were not in any way immediately suggestive of an enduring disposition such as that which characterized the gender-crosser (or the "homosexual" in our culture), and such acts were not confused with gender-crossing in the Native mind (Whitehead, 1993: 511).

This brief investigation on sexuality and cross-gendered behaviour in Native North America provides some insight into the diversity of erotic and gender relations that existed among a selection of Aboriginal populations at early contact. Through the use of secondary documents provided by Katz (1976), this investigation also illustrates the missionary response to such interactions. By no means exhaustive, what I have sought to illuminate is merely the care required when using "homosexuality" to describe or interpret the historic past. To that extent, the preceding discussion permits at least three conclusions.

First, missionary statements confirm the existence of "sodomy" following (and likely even prior to) contact and nothing more. While it may be tempting to transform the Jesuit accounts to reveal a history of homosexual identity, we can deduce only that homosexual *behaviour* existed in a selection of Native communities. Neither homosexual or heterosexual behaviour was definitive to the (re)classification of social identity under Native sex/gender systems (Whitehead, 1993). On that account, the history of First Nations sexuality may be better thought a history of cross-gender behaviour.

A second conclusion is that heterosexual behaviour could not have been as "mandatory" for Native North Americans as it was for the Euro-Jesuit newcomers since sexual behaviour did not set into motion an entire process of gender reclassification (see Schnarch, 1992: 111). Contrary to a European sex/gender system that characterized or equated the homosexual sex act with some enduring (cross)gendered disposition, the Native North American could engage in same-sex sexual contact without necessarily acquiring the recognized status of (gender-crossing) *berdache*. Later colonial policy would work to alter this system through institutionalizing a structure of power and kinship relations that were both patriarchal and heterosexist. In the next section of this chapter, this proposition will be further elaborated.

A third and more central conclusion based on the preceding analysis and evidence is the way that racism, patriarchy and heterosexism are witnessed to have developed in relation to one another. In the selected descriptions, the sexuality of Native North Americans was quite simply racialized and engendered. "Sodomy," for example, was viewed as a practice engaged in by a "morally perverted" and "coarse natured" *race* of people. By extension, the cross-gendered effeminacy and homosexual behaviour of the male *berdache* was socially constructed as "cowardly" or effeminate. In short, the dynamic interplay between "racial," sexual and gendered types of knowledge both produced and organized missionary recordings. A similar set of ethnocentric understandings would later translate into a set of policy objectives. These colonial knowledges would influence the contemporary circumstances of Native "gays" and "lesbians," some of whom continue to identify as "two-spirited" people. In the following section I explore the interactive relationship between racism, patriarchy and heterosexism in early "Indian" policy and the *Indian Act*.

RACISM, PATRIARCHY AND HETEROSEXISM IN THE *INDIAN ACT*

In this section I will highlight the way in which the *Indian Act,* in the assumptions that it made about the kinship and social organization of First Nations, assumed homosexual behaviour out of existence. Further research is needed to illustrate more precisely the actual impact, or causal effect, that government initiatives and legislation had on the suppression of homosexual behaviour and same-sex intimacies. For an initial analysis of how the *berdache* tradition is no longer as recognized an institution as it once was in Native communities, see Williams (1986: 183–192), Roscoe (1988, Part II), and Brown (1997).

For well over 100 years, the *Indian Act* has been the central legislation governing the affairs of First Nations in Canada. Since its inception in 1876, the *Act* consolidated earlier policy and appointed the Federal Government in control of all aspects of "Indian" life including education, social services, health care and lands administration. For the purposes of this chapter I will concentrate largely upon those sections of the *Indian Act* that deal with "Indian" status and citizenship. These were the sections that fundamentally reorganized kinship relations and delineated who was, and who was not, eligible to be registered as an "Indian" under the jurisdiction of the *Indian Act*.[7] While the historical development of these sections are most blatantly patriarchal, I will also illustrate how they combine to reveal an interactive relationship between racism, patriarchy and heterosexism. It is necessary, in other words, to understand patriarchal discrimination *in relation to* racism and heterosexism. Moreover, these systems of domination cannot be understood outside of the formation of capitalist relations.

The implementation of the Reserve system in 1830s Upper Canada was among the earliest of statutory policies to affect First Nations prior to Confederation. This was a policy intended to resocialize First Nations into recognized "British-agricultural-Christian patterns of behaviour" (Frideres, 1983: 22). To that extent, the agricultural policy of the Reserve system revealed underlying ideologies of racism and ethnocentrism. The Reserve system was intended to "civilize" the "Indian" who, in the eyes of the European, would be otherwise susceptible to nomadism and societal decline.

The agricultural component of the Reserve system was also among the earliest of policies to commence with the social construction of gendered tasks. Commenting on the sexual division of labour associated with this policy, Ng has observed that "men were taught farming skills such as how to clear land and hold a plow, [and] women, under the tutelage of the missionaries' wives and daughters were taught "'civilized' domestic skills" (1993: 54). The Reserve system policy thus represented a further endeavour toward the re-construction of gender relations among Aboriginal populations. These "common-sense" assumptions about the gendered division of tasks likely impacted upon First Nations women. At the same time, these assumptions likely influenced the position of the *berdache* discussed earlier in the chapter. Had systems that recognized and affirmed an engagement in cross-gendered occupations existed prior to European contact, they would not have been possible during the 1830s.

A continued emphasis toward gender hierarchicalization continued well into the late 1800s. Most notably, it emerged in the status and citizenship sections of "Indian" policy. These were the sections that defined who was, and who was not, entitled to "Indian" status. In the tradition of earlier statutes, these initiatives made invidious distinctions between male and female "Indians."

The status and citizenship sections of the *Indian Act* have historically excluded Aboriginal women from recognition as status "Indians." As early as 1869, for example, Native women marrying non-Native men lost status, along with their children, as defined under section 6 of *An Act for the Gradual Enfranchisement of Indians* ([S.C. 1869, c. 6 (32-33 Vict.)], reprinted in Venne, 1981: 11–15).[8] This same loss of status did not apply to Native men or their children. In law, Native men retained their entitlement to status along with an ability to bestow it regardless of whom they married.

The exact motive for making invidious distinctions between Native men and women is not immediately discernable, but as one author has put it: "[T]he 1869 legislation ... was intended to reduce the number of Indians and 'half-breeds' living on reserves" (Jamieson, 1986: 113). The surface motivation behind the 1869 *Act*, then, was doubtlessly assimilationist. It may also have been about protecting "Indians" from White male encroachment onto Reserve lands (Sanders, 1972: 98). To be sure, the mandate of the 1869 *Act* was to institutionalize a system of patrilineal descent and heterosexual marriage.

The status and citizenship sections of the 1869 policy carried connotations that were simultaneously racist, patriarchal and heterosexist. As Jamieson (1986: 118) has asserted, "the statute of 1869, especially section 6 ... embodied the principle that, like other women, Indian women should be subject to their husbands." At the level of "common sense," in other words, it went unstated that all Native women (and children) take on the "racial" status of their husbands at marriage. It also went unstated that Native women and men ought to be inclined toward the

Euro-Christian institution of heterosexual marriage. Had there ever been a time where hetero-sexual behaviour was not judged "mandatory" in First Nations communities, it was unlikely to have been during the mid to late nineteenth century. By making marriage the only possible avenue through which to convey "Indian" status and rights, the 1869 *Act* simply legislated European forms of heterosexuality compulsory in First Nations communities.[9] Later legislation would only perpetuate such institutionalized domination.

In 1876, for example, the Federal Government passed the first legislation entitled the *Indian Act*. Like preceding legislation, this *Act* imposed patriarchal definitions of "Indian" by again emphasizing patrilineal descent. Section 6 of the 1869 statute became section 3(c) of the *Indian Act,* only later to become section 12(1)(b) in the revised 1951 *Indian Act.*[10]

Similar to previous legislation, the 1876 legislation did not require a loss of status for Native men. Native men retained their legal "Indian" status and, under section 3, were able to bestow it onto the non-Native women they married. Section 3 of the *Indian Act* would later become section 11(1)(f) in the revised 1951 *Act.*[11] Historically, these legislated changes institutionalized descent through the male line and simply "naturalized" the heterosexual nuclear family within First Nations communities.

Major changes to the *Indian Act* were common following 1876 and several systems of domination were upheld. In 1956, for example, an amendment to section 12(2) of the 1952 *Act* strengthened patriarchal definitions of "Indian" by enabling individual band members to contest the status and band membership of Native children thought to be "illegitimate." If an individual band member could prove that the father of a child was not an "Indian," then the child would not be entitled to statutory registration or band membership.[12] "Indian" women's status, henceforth from 1956, ceased to be of any official legal significance in and of itself since only men could bestow legitimacy (Department of Indian and Northern Affairs, 1991: 14). It was by entrenching this system of relations that a discourse of patrilineage was offered to First Nations. At the same time, notions of "illegitimacy" in the 1952 *Act* privileged heterosexual unions by emphasizing the importance of paternity to the exclusion of non-male partners. In this way, the existence—even possibility—of same-sex relationships in First Nations communities went unacknowledged.

This chronological selection of legislation provides some insight into the early provisions of the *Indian Act*. What I have sought to illustrate are the colonial assumptions made with respect to gender and sexuality. But in many ways, this brief explication requires further engagement. At least two considerations might guide this analysis. First, how can the *Indian Act* be considered a tool through which "Indians" were being "re-socialized" to become "productive" members of an emerging Nation? Second, why did racism and (hetero)sexism interrelate as they did within "common-sense" attitudes about kinship organization? To what larger project, or sets of know-ledges, was the interrelationship between these systems of domination tied? In short, what is so unique about the regulation of First Nations sexuality?

The historical development of the *Indian Act* and other "Indian" policy was a process coinci-dent with the building of Canada as a Nation. Between 1830 and 1950, for example, most of the *Act*'s central prescriptions were being created. These were the years when Canada was moving toward an urbanized industrial economy. On that account, it is reasonable to speculate that the

Indian Act and other "Indian" policies were informed by ideologies congruent with the impend-ing processes of social and economic change. The *Indian Act* may be (re)interpreted as a mech-anism fashioning the human infrastructure necessary for the growth of capitalism. Informed by that understanding, the Reserve system of the 1830s may be revisited.

The agricultural policy of the 1830s not only placed emphasis on the state's motivation toward socializing "Indians" into economically viable entities, it also made some fundamental distinc-tions between the male and female genders. Policy makers of this new legislation, as mentioned, simply presupposed that "Indian" men would learn agricultural skills; and women, domestic chores. In this way, policy makers made "common-sense" assumptions about the gendered distribution of tasks. These assumptions were informed by ideologies of the sexual division of labour and the private and public spheres. It was within the broader context of these knowledges that the State mandated the regulation of gendered behaviour among First Nations. The impera-tive to divide tasks on the basis of gender must certainly have impacted upon women and also those inclined toward cross-gendered activity.

For women, capitalist and patriarchal knowledges combined to require that their labour be restricted to the private sphere. The implication of capitalist and patriarchal knowledges was to relegate women to the lower strata of the institutionalized gender hierarchy.[13] For those inclined to cross-gendered behaviour, capitalist and patriarchal knowledges relating to the sexual div-ision of labour combined to mandate, even if unintentionally, the loss of gender flexibility. The effect of these knowledges was likely to have intensified gender classification systems making cross-gendered behaviour of considerable consequence. Seen in the 1880s as an *implicit* threat to the very project of Nation building and economic prosperity, the cross-gendered individual was seemingly confronting legislative regulation if not vigilant policing. A similar concern over discordant individuals inhered within the "Indian" status sections of 1869 and 1876.

The status and citizenship sections of the *Indian Act* were as much about extending a project of invidious gender distinctions into First Nations communities as they were about the regula-tion of sexuality. The formulation of these sections were shaped through an historical context that ideologically prescribed the types of sexual behaviour thought most compatible with the mode of production. Capitalist and patriarchal knowledge relating to the (re)productive modes of sexuality combined in the 1800s to require the disavowal of same-sex relationships. Since only heterosexual marriage ensured a form of reproductive sexuality, these would become the only recognized unions through which to convey status in the *Indian Act*. Later *Indian Act* prescrip-tions on "illegitimacy" would reveal a similar influence from the historical period.

The "legitimacy" sections of the *Indian Act* were just as much inspired by the patriarchal emphasis on paternity as they were by the emerging productive relations of the late 19th century. The imperative of "legitimacy," for example, was tied intimately to capitalist notions of private property. Those status provisions that upheld notions of "illegitimacy" simply reflected a legal and social system which tried to ensure that only men could bequeath wealth onto their own children (Engels, 1942: 76; O'Brien, 1981: 54). The way that wealth was bequeathed was to declare that wives were the sole and exclusive property of their husbands and that subsequently, a man's children were those that his wife bore. It was in the broader context of wealth and the transfer-ence of property that the state endeavoured toward the regulation of women's sexuality. The imperative of paternity was largely to bring all First Nations into further congruence with a patriarchal system of private property.

To sum up, the historical development of the *Indian Act* was a process that coincided with the building of Canada as a Nation. With that in mind, it is not possible to consider the *Indian Act*'s development outside of the pervasive ideologies of that period. Engrained within the *Act* itself are "common-sense" assumptions about the gendered distribution of tasks, the forms of reproductive sexuality and capitalist notions of private property. All of these knowledges were contained within early "Indian" policy.

CONCLUSION

A central conclusion of this chapter is that the regulation of First Nations sexuality cannot be explained apart from, or without reference to, racist and patriarchal configurations as those emerged in the Euro-Christian and subsequent colonial contexts.

For the early missionaries, descriptions of sexuality were informed by both "racial" and "gendered" knowledges. "Sodomy," for example, was a practice engaged in by a "coarse natured" "race" of people. The cross-gendered behaviour of the *berdache* was further constructed as effeminate. Informed by knowledges that linked sexuality with "racial" difference, along with ideas that linked gender with masculinity and femininity, the Euro-Christian missions made the first attempt toward a "civilizing" agenda. In any attempt to reconsider that agenda, the dynamic interrelationship among all systems of domination needs to be recounted.

Racist and patriarchal configurations also influenced the later agenda of Nation building. Capitalist and patriarchal knowledges relating to the (re)productive modes of sexuality, for example, combined to require the disavowal of same-sex relationships in the status and citizenship sections of the *Indian Act*. By extension, the sexual division of labour intensified gender classification systems in turn requiring the regulation of cross-gendered behaviour. All of these systems combined to deeply affect First Nations.

In short, the dynamic interplay between racist, patriarchal and capitalist knowledges all influenced the regulation of First Nations sexuality. Any account of the history of this regulation, or theory of state formation, needs to illuminate that interrelationship.

NOTES

1 By the term "heterosexism," I mean the system of knowledges or "political institution" through which heterosexuality is either implicitly or explicitly assumed to be the only acceptable or viable life option and/or sexual aim (Rich, 1993: 232; Blumenfeld and Raymond, 1988: 244–5).

2 The actual depth of missionary observation, comment and sentiment about "sodomic practices" cannot be thoroughly discussed in a chapter of this size. Testimonies can be analyzed more closely, however, in Katz (1983) and Williams (1986). Goldberg (1992) provides further analysis of the evidence in both Katz and Williams, along with an overview of the sexual practices of Indians from the vantage point of Spanish explorers.

3 I borrow the term "common sense" from Himani Bannerji (1987) who draws attention to the way that systems of discrimination "disappear from the social surface" and become ordinary ways of doing things of which we rarely have consciousness.

4 For a scholarly analysis of the genealogies of imperialist knowledge, see Anne McClintock (1995: 21–74).

5 As Burns has noted (1988: 1), *berdache* is the word used by early French explorers to describe male Indians who "specialized in the work of women and formed emotional and sexual relationships with other men" (also see Kinsman, 1987: 71).

6 It is worth noting—without delving too far into an analysis of "essentialist" versus "constructionist" theories of sexuality—that the (in)stability of analytic categories such as "gay," "lesbian" or "homosexual" are of some political urgency for communities interested in recounting "minority history" and validating an immemorial existence (Boswell, 1989: 20; also see Sharpe, 1992: 31, 38). This may represent one explanation as to why modern-day notions of "homosexuality" are sometimes conflated with the role of the *berdache*.

7 The very first attempt to define the term "Indian" and thereby racialize a heterogeneous and diverse group of people was made in 1850 under legislation entitled *An Act for the protection of the Indians in Upper Canada from imposition, and the property occupied or enjoyed by them from trespass and injury* (Indian and Northern Affairs Canada, 1991: 7).

8 As section 6 reads: "Provided always that any Indian woman marrying any other than an Indian, shall cease to be an Indian within the meaning of this *Act*, nor shall the children issue of such marriage be considered as Indians within the meaning of this *Act*…" (*An Act for the Gradual Enfranchisement of Indians…* [S. C. 1869, c. 6. (32-33 Vict.)] reprinted in Venne, 1981: 11).

9 Resistance to heterosexist status sections may have been possible by securing some alternate arrangement whereby the children of "two-spirited" people could obtain Indian status. However, this did not alter the fundamental effect of the legislation which was to privilege heterosexual over same-sex relationships. Had same-sex relationships ever been recognized and affirmed in First Nations communities—and it seems more than reasonable to suggest they were—the *Indian Act* would work toward ensuring that the legal and structural means with which to regain such systems were lost.

10 As section 3(c) of the 1876 *Act* reads: "Provided that any Indian woman marrying any other than an Indian or a non-treaty Indian shall cease to be an Indian in any respect within the meaning of this *Act*…"(*IndianAct* [S. C. 1876, c. 18], reprinted in Venne, 1981: 25).1n 1951, this section was amended to read: "The following persons are not entitled to be registered, namely… (b) a woman who is married to a person who is not an Indian" (*Indian Act* [S. C. 1951, c. 29], reprinted in Venne, 1981: 319).

11 As section 3 of the 1876 *Act* reads: "The term "Indian" means, First. Any male person of Indian blood reputed to belong to a particular band; Secondly. Any child of such person; Thirdly. Any woman who is or was lawfully married to such person" (*Indian Act* [S. C. 1876, c. 18), reprinted in Venne, 1981: 24). In 1951, this section was amended to read: "Subject to section twelve, a person is entitled to be registered if that person … (f) is the wife or widow of a person who is entitled to be registered by virtue of paragraph (a), (b), (c), (d) or (e)" (*Indian Act* [S. C. 1951, c. 29], reprinted in Venne, 1981: 318–319).

12 As section 12(2) of the 1952 *Act* reads: "The addition to a Band List of the name of an illegitimate child described in paragraph (e) of section 11 may be protested at any time within twelve months after the addition, and if upon the protest it is decided that the father of the child was not an Indian, the child is not entitled to be registered under paragraph (e) of section 11" (*Indian Act* [R.S.C. 1952, c. 149], reprinted in Venne, 1981: 360).

13 For many settlements, this meant a fundamental reconstruction of gender relations as some communities are said to have been egalitarian and matriarchal prior to contact. For a discussion of the matriarchal

kinship organization and egalitarian relations among the Iroquoian Nations see Druke (1986: esp. 305). Also see Native Women's Association of Canada (1992) and Kirkness (1987/88: 410–413).

REFERENCES

Bannerji, Himani. "Introducing Racism: Notes Toward an Anti-Racist Feminism." *Resources for Feminist Research* 16(1): 10–12, 1987.

Blumenfeld, Warren J. and Diane Raymond. *Looking at Gay and Lesbian Life*. Boston: Beacon Press, 1988.

Boswell, John. "Revolutions, Universals, and Sexual Categories," pp. 17–36 in Martin Duberman, Martha Vicinus and George Chauncey Jr. (Editors): *Hidden from History: Reclaiming the Gay and Lesbian Past*. New York: Meridian, 1989.

Brodribb, Somer. "The Traditional Roles of Native Women in Canada and the Impact of Colonization." *The Canadian Journal of Native Studies* 4(1): 85–103, 1984.

Brown, L. B. (Editor). *Two Spirit People: American Indian Lesbian Women and Gay Men*. New York: Haworth Press, 1977.

Burns, Randy. "Preface," pp. 1–5 in Will Roscoe (Editor): *Living the Spirit: A Gay American Indian Anthology*. New York: St. Martin's Press, 1988.

Department of Indian and Northern Affairs. 1991. (Note: the title of the document was not provided in the original version of this chapter.)

Druke, Mary. "Iroquois and Iroquoian in Canada," pp. 303–324 in R. Bruce Morrison and C. Roderick Wilson (Editors): *Native Peoples: The Canadian Experience*. Toronto: McClelland & Stewart, 1986.

Engels, Frederic. *The Origin of the Family, Private Property and the State*. New York: International Publishers, 1942.

Foucault, Michel. *The History of Sexuality. Volume One: An Introduction*. New York: Vintage Books, 1990.

Frideres, James S. *Indian and Northern Affairs Canada: The Indian Act Past and Present: A Manual on Registration and Entitlement Legislation*. Ottawa: Indian Registration and Band Lists Directorate, 1991.

Frideres, James S. *Native People in Canada: Contemporary Conflicts*. Scarborough: Prentice-Hall, 1983.

Goldberg, Jonathan. *Sodometries: Renaissance Texts/Modern Sexualities*. Stanford: Stanford University Press, 1992.

Jamieson, Kathleen. "Sex Discrimination and the *Indian Act*," pp. 112–136 in J. Rick Ponting (Editor): *Arduous Journey: Canadian Indians and Decolonization*. Toronto: McClelland & Stewart, 1986.

Katz, Jonathan. *Gay/Lesbian Almanac*. New York: Harper and Row, 1983.

Katz, Jonathan. *Gay American History*. New York: Thomas Y. Crowall, 1976.

Kenny, Maurice. "Tinselled Bucks: A Historical Study in Indian Homosexuality," pp. 15–31 in Will Roscoe (Editor): *Living the Spirit: A Gay American Indian Anthology*. New York: St. Martin's Press, 1988.

Kinsman, Gary. "Sexual Colonization of the Native Peoples," pp. 71–74 in Gary Kinsman (Editor): *The Regulation of Desire: Sexuality in Canada*. Montreal: Black Rose Books, 1987.

Kirkness, Verna. Emerging Native Women. *Canadian Journal of Women and the Law* 2: 408–415, 1987/88.

McClintock, Anne. *Imperial Leather: Race, Gender and Sexuality in the Colonial Contest*. New York: Routledge, 1995.

Miles, Robert. *Racism.* London: Routledge, 1989.

Native Women's Association of Canada. *Matriarchy and the Canadian Charter: A Discussion Paper.* Native Women's Association of Canada, 1992.

Ng, Roxana. "Racism, Sexism, and Nation Building in Canada," pp. 50–59 in Cameron McCarthy and Warren Crichlow (Editors): *Race, Identity and Representation in Education.* New York: Routledge, 1993.

O'Brien, Mary. *The Politics of Reproduction.* London: Routledge, 1981.

Owlfeather, M. "Children of Grandmother Moon," pp. 97–105 in Will Roscoe (Editor): *Living the Spirit: A Gay American Indian Anthology.* New York: St. Martin's Press, 1988.

Padgug, Robert. "Sexual Matters: Rethinking Sexuality in History," pp. 54–64 in Martin Duberman, Martha Vicinus and George Chauncey Jr. (Editors): *Hidden From History: Reclaiming the Gay and Lesbian Past.* New York: Meridian, 1989.

Parr, Joy. Gender, History and Historical Practice. *Canadian Historical Review* 76(3): 354–376, 1955.

Rich, Adrienne. "Compulsory Heterosexuality and Lesbian Existence," in Henry Abelove, Michele Aina Barale and David Halperin (Editors): *The Lesbian and Gay Studies Reader.* New York: Routledge, 1993.

Roscoe, Will. *Living the Spirit: A Gay American Indian Anthology.* New York: St. Martin's Press, 1988.

Rubin, Gayle. "The Traffic in Women: Notes on the Political Economy of Sex," pp. 157–210 in Reyna R. Reiter (Editor): *Toward an Anthropology of Women.* New York: Monthly Review, 1975.

Said, Edward. *Orientalism.* New York: Vintage Books, 1978.

Sanders, Douglas. "The Bill of Rights and Indian Status." *University of British Columbia Law Review* 7(1): 81–105, 1972.

Schnarch, Brian. "Neither Man nor Woman: Berdache—A Case for Non-Dichotomous Gender Construction." *Anthropologica* 34(1): 105–121, 1992.

Sharpe, Jim. "History from Below," pp. 24–41 in Peter Burke (Editor): *New Perspectives on Historical Writing.* Pennsylvania State University Press, 1992.

Sun, Midnight. "Sex/Gender Systems in Native North America," pp. 32–47 in Will Roscoe (Editor): *Living the Spirit: A Gay American Indian Anthology.* New York: St. Martin's Press, 1988.

Venne, Sharon Helen. *Indian Acts and Amendments 1868–1975: An Indexed Collection.* Saskatoon: University of Saskatchewan Native Law Centre, 1981.

Whitehead, Harriet. "The Bow and the Burden Strap: A New Look at Institutionalized Homosexuality in Native North America," pp. 498–527 in Henry Abelove, Michele Aina Barale and David Halperin (Editors): *The Lesbian and Gay Studies Reader.* New York: Routledge, 1993.

Williams, Walter. *The Spirit and the Flesh: Sexual Diversity in American Indian Culture.* Boston: Beacon Press, 1986.

CHAPTER 5

The Canadian Cold War on Queers: Sexual Regulation and Resistance

Gary Kinsman

We even knew occasionally that there was somebody in some police force or some investigator who would be sitting in a bar ... And you would see someone with a ... newspaper held right up and if you ... looked real closely you could find him holding behind the newspaper a camera and these people were photographing everyone in the bar. (12 May 1994)[1]

David is speaking in an interview about his experiences of police surveillance in the basement tavern at the Lord Elgin Hotel around 1964, which was by then one of the major gathering places for gay men in Ottawa. This surveillance was one way that the RCMP collected information on homosexuals during the Cold War against 'queers.' What is most remarkable, however, is how David described the response of the men in the bar to this surveillance:

We always knew that when you saw someone with a newspaper held up in front of their face ... that somebody would take out something like a wallet and do this sort of thing [like snapping a photo] and then of course everyone would then point over to the person you see and of course I'm sure that the person hiding behind the newspaper knew that he had been found out. But that was the thing. You would take out a wallet or a package of matches or something like that ... it was always sort of a joke. You would see somebody ... and you would catch everyone's eye and you would always go like this [snapping a photo]. And everyone knew watch out for this guy. (12 May 1994)

Rather than diving under the tables, these men acted to turn the tables on the undercover agents. David is among more than thirty-five gay men and lesbians whom Patrizia Gentile and I have interviewed about their experiences with the national security regime.[2] David's involvement in the security campaigns began when a friend gave the RCMP his name during a park sweep of one of the cruising (or meeting) areas for men interested in sex with men in Ottawa. The RCMP had jurisdiction over the parks in the capital, and these sweeps were fairly common. According to David, the RCMP was far more interested in getting the names of homosexuals than in arresting people for 'criminal' activities, and would threaten to lay 'criminal' charges against the men they rounded up unless they gave the names of other homosexuals. (At this time all homosexual acts were criminalized in Canada; a partial decriminalization took place only in 1969.) David was interrogated and followed by the RCMP and his home was searched, but he refused to cooperate. He was one of the more than 9,000 'suspected,' 'alleged,' and 'confirmed' homosexuals that the RCMP investigated in the 1960s.[3]

David's account indicates the extent of national security surveillance in the 1960s, as well as the awareness concerning this security campaign in the gay networks in which he participated. The resistance of gay men to this police surveillance has been confirmed in a number of our other research interviews, as well as in RCMP documents themselves.[4] [...] These men were thus not simply victims of the national security war against queers; they also tried to identify and isolate the spies. They exerted their own agency[5] and resistance in a creative fashion within major social constraints. The social and historical conditions that made such resistance possible emerge from David's story, which provides us with a sense of the social standpoints taken up by gay men and lesbians who were directly affected by the security campaigns. A major advantage of this standpoint is that it allows us to pursue Cold War issues from a position outside the confines of national security discourse and ideology. This standpoint is crucial to our investigation because 'national security' is an ideological practice or code that occludes the social practices that actually bring it into being.[6] This stance allows us to disrupt and decentre the master-narrative of heterosexual Cold War Canadian history by placing the social experiences and resistances of 'queers' at the centre of our analysis.[7] I use 'queer'[8] to reclaim a term of abuse and stigmatization in order to turn it back against our oppressors. I also use it as a term that is broader than 'lesbian and gay' in that it can include experiences of non-normalized consensual sexual and gendered practices that would not usually be included under 'lesbian and gay.' Finally, the term 'queer' helps to construct a place from which to challenge heterosexual hegemony and the dichotomous notion of gender that is hegemonic in society.[9]

QUEER HISTORY: SOCIOLOGY FROM BELOW

There are three main theories/methods that inspire this investigation.[10] The first is a history/ sociology from below that derives from the work of E.P. Thompson,[11] an approach that rewrites history from the standpoints of the exploited and oppressed, releasing the knowledges based on their lived experiences which are suppressed within ruling histories. I combine this approach with the work of Marxist-feminist Dorothy Smith, who has developed sociologies for women and the oppressed which attempt to produce social knowledge for the benefit of the oppressed rather than to govern and rule them,[12] an approach that has been productively extended into sociologies for gay men and lesbians.[13] In particular I draw upon Smith's notion of institutional ethnography[14] which I apply in a historical context.[15] The focus is on *how* cultures work, on *how* social organization operates, and on developing rich descriptions of cultural and social organization.[16] Such institutional ethnographies critique ruling relations in our society by critically interrogating the social organization of institutional relations.

[Here] I critically interrogate the social organization of the national security regime and the Cold War against queers by starting from the standpoint of the oppressed, in this case those directly affected by the national security campaigns. It is vital to this approach that one hold to this standpoint when interrogating security texts and operatives, since the goal of institutional ethnography is to analyse 'national security' itself as an ideological code. [...]

*****

Finally, I draw on dialectical theories of mediation that allow for the combination in social analysis of the mutually constructed character of social relations while also preserving the moments of autonomy of each specific form of social oppression and exclusion.[17] [...]

TOWARDS THE GENEALOGY OF 'COMMIE PINKO FAG'

'Commie pinko fag' used to be scrawled on my locker and used as a greeting in the halls when I was a student at Victoria Park Secondary School in Don Mills in the early 1970s. I was a member of the Young Socialists and later of the Revolutionary Marxist Group so the 'commie' part made some sense to me. I never understood where 'pinko' came from. The sole basis for the 'fag' part seemed to be my refusal to laugh at the anti-gay jokes that were all pervasive at my school. A 'cutting out' operation,[18] much as George Smith describes,[19] was mobilized against me, as I was socially cut out of 'normal' heterosexual interaction. During these years I was beginning to explore my sexuality and starting to come out to myself and to others as gay, and eventually I did become an anti-Stalinist 'commie fag.' My interest in the national security campaigns against queers flows from this association between commies and fags that has been integral to my experience. This association was forged in major part during the years of the national security campaigns against gay men and lesbians and also through the alliances between some queer activists and sections of the left.[20]

[...] I want to *remember* the deep roots of heterosexism in Canadian state and social formation and to interrogate the anti-queer history which continues to shape our present. As David McNally points out, drawing on cultural critic and theorist Walter Benjamin's Marxist and Freudian work, 'Rather than something laid down once and for all the past is a site of struggle in the present.'[21] Capitalism and oppression rule through what I call the social organization of forgetting, which seeks to annihilate our social and historical memories. This is also how strategies of 'respectability' and 'responsibility' gain hegemony in queer communities. We have been forced to forget where we have come from; our histories have never been recorded and passed down; and we are denied the social and historical literacies that allow us to remember and relive our pasts and therefore grasp our present. Thus, telling stories of the sort with which I began is an act of rebellion.

[...] The national security texts were an active part of constructing queers as a national security threat. Using institutional ethnography I read these texts for the social organization they reveal but I start outside this official discourse in the first-hand accounts of queers.[22]

QUEERING THE COLD WAR

The hegemonic view of the Cold War that I am contesting here is that it represented a conflict between the American and Soviet empires.[23] The present [work] thus follows from *Whose National Security?*, which argues a rethinking of the bases for the national security program and for expanding the analysis of the Cold War to include relations of ethnicity, immigration, race, gender, and sexuality.[24] The Cold War was not only about defending Western capitalism and the expanding U.S. empire against the bureaucratic class societies that emerged in the USSR and elsewhere.[25] It was also very much a neo-colonialist war against Third World liberation movements. It was thus not only a Cold War but also sometimes a very hot war. This imperialist war had a clear racial character which contributed to the construction of the hegemony of a white,[26] middle-class way of life. It was also a war against transformative working-class movements and movements of the oppressed, including anti-Stalinist working-class political movements. Similarly, it was very much a Cold War to reassert gender and sexual 'normality' after the social disruptions of the Second World War mobilizations.[27] The focus on queers was thus not simply about homophobia,[28] the anti-queer aspect of the Cold War was central to its deeply rooted social character.[29] Indeed, by the late 1960s and 1970s these anti-queer mobilizations were attempting to contain the broader political sphere of gender and sexual struggles.

A key objective of these Cold War mobilizations has been the making of the 'normal,' as Mary Louise Adams[30] has argued. Moral regulation[31] was always a key feature of these mobilizations. This 'making normal' was always constructed against 'others,' 'dangers,' and 'risks' outside the fabric of 'the nation.' But this is a relational social process. The other side of these mobilizations is that the Cold War fought for heterosexual hegemony, producing heterosexuality in the national interest as 'loyal' and 'safe,' such that heterosexuality becomes the 'national' sexuality.

The Cold War in its various phases was mobilized against forms of political, social, sexual, and cultural 'subversion.' [...] Subversion that is given the form of a 'national security risk' is an administrative collecting category[32] into which various social and political practices and movements can be placed so that they can be read as lying outside the 'normal' and 'national' social fabric. These conceptualizations can be expanded or contracted depending on the social and political context. Some groups get excluded from their rights and become targets of surveillance in a 'cutting-out operation'[33] of the sort I described above that separates them from 'the nation.' Once successfully claimed as a 'subversive' or a 'national security risk' these groups can then be denied their human and citizenship rights. At various points in Canadian history, communists, socialists, peace activists, trade unionists, Red power and Black power activists, Quebec sovereignists, immigrants, high school students, and queers have been designated as 'subversive.'[34]

We need constantly to ask which nation and whose security is being defended through these national security practices. It is important not to take constructions of the nation and national security for granted. The image of Canada as unitary is based on the suppression of all the national, linguistic, class, sexual, cultural, and other social differences that constitute the Canadian social formation. At the same time, some of these social differences get 'othered' as 'different' and as 'deviant.' National security rests on the interests of 'the nation,' defined in the Canadian context by capitalist, racist, heterosexist, and patriarchal relations. But notions of the nation and national security can easily draw people in by appearing to be consensual. These constructs can thus be very useful for the making of ruling-class hegemonies, obscuring who is being actively excluded through these 'cutting-out' mobilizations and also who is being actively placed at the centre of the social fabric through these mobilizations.[35] As Harold (one of the gay men purged from the Canadian Navy whom I spoke to in 1994) wrote in the early 1960s, 'security is a sacred cow of a word in the name of which highly dictatorial and sweeping actions are possible for which no explanation can be forced.'[36] Initially, queers were seen as 'fellow travellers' of communists because of our violation of political, class, social, and sexual boundaries. R.C. Waldeck, in 'The International Homosexual Conspiracy,' published in *Human Events* in 1960, gives us a taste of this right-wing discourse:

> Homosexual officials are a peril for us in the present struggle between West and East: members of one conspiracy are prone to join another … [M]any homosexuals from being enemies of society in general become enemies of capitalism in particular. Without being necessarily Marxist they serve the ends of the Communist International in the name of their rebellion against the prejudices, standards, ideals of the "bourgeois" world. Another reason for the homosexual-Communist alliance is the instability and passion for intrigue for intrigue's sake, which is inherent in the homosexual personality. A third reason is the social promiscuity within the homosexual minority and the fusion of its effects between upperclass and proletarian corruption.

There are some interesting dialogical connections[37] between this right-wing discourse and the discourse of the Canadian Security Panel, the interdepartmental committee set up to coordinate the national security campaigns within the Canadian state. In a 1959 memorandum they wrote:

> [...] The case of the homosexual is particularly difficult for a number of reasons. From the small amount of information we have been able to obtain about homosexual behaviour generally, certain characteristics appear to stand out—instability, willing self-deceit, defiance toward society, a tendency to surround oneself with persons of similar propensities, regardless of other considerations—none of which inspire [sic] the confidence one would hope to have in persons required to fill positions of trust and responsibility.[38]

While this discourse has shifted from its more overtly right-wing form, it still carries with it the notion that homosexuals are deviant towards 'society.'

GENDER AND HETEROSEXUALITY

The campaigns against queers were also integrally tied up with practices of gender regulation and the redrawing of the boundaries of heterosexual 'normality' following the Second World War. For example, gender regulations were imposed on women as they entered into the public service and the military. These included dress codes and beauty contests, in the attempt to secure the performance of heterosexual femininity in the civil service.[39] Sue tells us about these practices and also about resistance to them in the militia and at military camp in the late 1950s:

We would be out with sergeants, staff sergeants, corporals, privates, lieutenants ... no rank was untouched ... So we would be running all over camp. And the deal was you weren't allowed to leave the premises, so of course, we wanted wine, women, and song. So in order to get wine, women and song you had to leave the base. So you had to go out. But you weren't allowed to wear butchy clothing. You had to wear a *dress* [her emphasis]. So what we used to do was pull our pant legs up and hide them with our skirt. And you'd go out and through the gates in your skirt right, lookin' all femmy and lovely. Well this one night we came home and we got a little too drunk. Well trust me that the pants were down. And we, we were up on charges the next day for being in some place we weren't supposed to be, improper attire, all kinds of things. So we learned that we shouldn't drink too much. (23 February 1996)

There was also a redrawing of the boundaries around heterosexual and queer sex during these years. While in previous periods, emerging heterosexual identifications could have included some same-gender erotic sexual play or experimentation, this now became suspect. There was an uneven shift away from gender inversion as the queer problem—the effeminate man or butch woman—towards same-gender eroticism in general. In the military this meant that not only were the effeminate fairy[40] or the butch woman seen as a problem, but so too was the 'normal' masculine man who might engage in same-gender sex occasionally, or the 'feminine' normal woman who might occasionally engage in same-gender eroticism. Now all these individuals were supposedly vulnerable to blackmail and compromise by 'evil' Soviet agents.[41] There were important connections between this shift and the reconceptualization of homosexuality as a 'sexual orientation' based on sexual-object choice.[42]

MORAL FAILINGS AND BLACKMAIL FEARS

The major focus of the national security campaigns was thus on those individuals having a moral or 'character' weakness, rather than on 'ideological' or political subversives. These 'weak-nesses' were defined as an inability to perform oneself as 'normal.' Because queers were defined as being outside 'normality,' they were seen as having something to hide and therefore as subject to blackmail. The security regime's texts display an interesting grasp of the relations of living in the closet or living a double life,[43] but they nowhere note their own active participation in the construction of these relations.

The 'invisibility' of homosexuals during the Cold War was not a 'natural' aspect of their sexu-ality but instead was deeply rooted in the social relations produced by heterosexual hegemony. The national security campaigns of the postwar period played a central role in organizing the social relations of the closet; there is considerable evidence that there was far more openness to queer erotic and gender practices earlier in the twentieth century. This conclusion is arrived at by moving beyond the mainstream—and often gay—social mythology of monolithic oppression. In our research, for example, we have found that there was more openness to queer practices in Victoria, B.C., prior to the military and RCMP investigations of the murder by Leo Mantha of his estranged boyfriend, and also in Ottawa before the major campaigns against homosexuals began in the late 1950s.[44] It was in this context that fears over blackmail were constructed and mobilized. While the RCMP defined gay men and lesbians as the blackmail threat, from the point of view of those gays and lesbians who were interrogated it was the RCMP who were the blackmailers. In interview after interview we have heard that the RCMP asked for the names or identities of other homosexuals, trying to pressure homosexuals to inform on other homosexuals.[45] For instance, Hank stated that he was 'only ever blackmailed by the RCMP' (20 February 1995), and Harold wrote about the RCMP 'applying a form of blackmail very difficult to resist.'[46] The RCMP also counterposed people's loyalty to their gay/lesbian friends with their loyalty to the state. For instance, during one interrogation, Harold was asked 'Which is the greater treason, treason to your country or treason to your friends?'[47]

The anti-queer campaigns affected thousands of people from the 1950s to the 1990s. A 1960 RCMP document reveals that the security investigations intruded into many departments and especially into External Affairs and the Navy. The RCMP report discovered 76 'suspected' and 123 'confirmed' homosexuals in the Navy, and it appears (in a document with numerous deletions) that they found 17 'alleged,' 33 'suspected,' and 9 'confirmed' homosexuals in External Affairs in the same period, with totals of 139 'suspected,' 168 'alleged,' and 156 'confirmed' overall in the report.[48] The RCMP interrogations attempted to move those investigated from the 'suspected' or 'alleged' categories into the 'confirmed' category so that action could be taken against the individual;[49] to do so they relied on other homosexuals to confirm that these individuals were indeed gay. Fred, who worked in the character weakness subdivision of the Directorate of Security and Intelligence (Ottawa) of the RCMP in 1967–1969 described his work as hanging around with gay men, trying to make friends with them, and converting them into informants. He would ask the gay men he knew about any gay parties they had been at and whether there had been any public servants present at these events. If a public servant had been present, Fred would then try to have this person photographed in order to see if the gay informant could identify this person as homosexual so that they could be moved into the 'confirmed' category. Fred reported (21 October 1994) no similar dealings with lesbians, who tended to be more apprehensive; the RCMP only had male officers at this point. Once an individual was placed in the 'confirmed' category they could be purged from their position in the public service or the military, or demoted and transferred to lower-level positions where they would have no access to security information. This process of identification and confirmation was dependent on there being 'cooperative' and 'reliable' homosexual informants; ironically, reliance on gay informants became the weak link in the process.

THE FRUIT MACHINE

In response to costly RCMP field investigations of public servants, and perhaps in response to the non-cooperation of previously 'cooperative' homosexual informants, there was an attempt to develop an 'objective' scientific means of determining sexual orientation based on the research of 'experts' in the psychological and psychiatric disciplines. This program [dubbed "The Fruit Machine"] was part of the expanding social and state administration of the 1950s and 1960s;[50] the Security Panel, the RCMP, the military, and National Health and Welfare were engaged in this research for more than four years.[51] Professor Wake of Carleton University's Psychology Department was actively involved in the development of this detection technology, illustrating the linkage between the academy and Cold War research. At the centre of his research was the pupillary response test, which showed images of naked men and women to research subjects and photographed the level of dilation of their pupils to determine their 'involuntary' response. The research also drew on masculinity/femininity scales as a general marker of homosexuality, although Wake did not subscribe to theories of homosexuality as gender inversion. It also combined use of a word association test with the Palmer sweat test to examine anxious responses to 'homosexual' words such as 'queen,' 'circus,' 'gay,' 'bell,' 'whole,' 'blind,' 'camp,' 'coo,' 'cruise' 'drag,' 'dike' (i.e., 'dyke'), 'fish,' 'flute,' 'fruit,' 'mother,' 'punk,' 'queer,' 'rim,' 'sex,' 'swing,' 'trade,' 'velvet,' 'wolf,' 'blackmail,' 'prowl,' 'bar,' 'house,' 'club,' 'restaurant,' 'tea room,' and 'top men.'[52] There was resistance to this project from members of the RCMP who feared that even though they were supposed to be the 'normal' control group for the study, they might be exposed as 'fruits.'[53] The research was eventually abandoned, its technology deemed a failure.[54]

QUEER RESISTANCE

As David's story has already demonstrated, there were possibilities for non-cooperation and resistance to the Cold War against queers. [...] In 1962–1963 the RCMP reported that their security campaign 'was hindered by the lack of cooperation on the part of homosexuals approached as sources. Persons of this type, who had hitherto been [their] most consistent and productive informers, [had] exhibited an increasing reluctance to identify their homosexual friends and associates.'[55] This report is corroborated by Michael, who was employed as a civilian employee of the armed forces. Interrogated by the RCMP in the 1960s, he stated that the advice in the gay networks he was familiar with was to say nothing to the RCMP about people's names or identities and 'if anybody did give anything they were ostracized.' Michael also reported a conversation in the interrogation room with an RCMP officer:

> 'Is it true that you are a homosexual?' [the official asked]. And I said 'yes!' And he looked at me and I said, 'Is it true that you ride side-saddle?' and he laughed and that almost ended the interview. I mean, my intent was there, don't bother me any more, because I began to get the impression that it was a witch-hunt. It was a real witch-hunt. (15 July 1994)

This response and the response in the bar reported by David suggest that these men were using humour and camp[56] as a survival strategy. As David expressed it, 'I think that the way people coped with the whole situation of surveillance and harassment and so on was basically to make the best of it. And turn it as much as possible into a humorous situation' (12 May 1994).

These narratives of resistance begin to flesh out the social organization of the 'non-cooperation' the RCMP reports mention. Gays and lesbians had a sense of themselves and the networks they participated in that allowed them to engage in these collective and individual acts of defiance. Participants in these networks had an awareness of what the RCMP was up to but also had an awareness of a collective community response. The social basis for these forms of non-cooperation and resistance was in the development of gay networks and social space formed on the basis of eroticism, friendship, and love, and the concomitant development of queer solidarity and 'talk.'[57] The national security campaigns of the late 1950s and 1960s are thus not only about oppression and exclusion but are also about resistance and non-cooperation in difficult circumstances.

SPYING ON QUEER ORGANIZATIONS

The Cold War against queers did not end, as some have imagined, in the late 1960s or early 1970s,[58] but continued into the 1970s and 1980s through a policy of spying on the new gay liberation and lesbian feminist organizations as they emerged. These organizations challenged the national security policies of the Canadian state and thus came under RCMP surveillance. These groups were seen as subversive in their challenge to state policies, including those on national security questions, but they were also seen to be subversive because of the involvement of many of these early groups with Trotskyist organizations, the League for Socialist Action, and the Young Socialists. In this national security discourse, 'Trotskyist' was mobilized in the same way that 'communist' had been in other contexts. The RCMP also developed new classifications for 'gay political activist' and 'radical lesbian' as part of their attempt to survey, analyse, and thus contain these activists.[59]

When gay and lesbian activists gathered for the first time in a protest rally on Parliament Hill in August 1971, the RCMP were there conducting surveillance, as they were at the 1975 founding conference of the National Gay Rights Coalition conference in Ottawa. In their analysis of the activities of the Gay Alliance Towards Equality (GATE) in Vancouver in 1973 they even expressed the fear that 'unless another stronger group takes the initiative—a liberal grouping—leadership and direction of what could be a real force in the gay community and in the community as a whole could fall into the hands of GATE.'[60] RCMP surveillance of the feminist movement likewise led them to discover 'radical lesbians,' such as the lesbian group 'Wages Due,' who were part of the Toronto 'Wages for Housework' campaign. The RCMP report points out that the 'T.W.H.C.'s membership has been described by [blanked out] as being 'Born Losers' who in appearance and attitude are both lower working class and welfare cases and involved in living alternative life-styles [blanked out].' The next comment emphasizes the physical appearance of these women: 'This is especially true of the radical lesbians in W.D., who take a perverse pride in de-feminizing themselves by cultivating the dirty and unkempt appearance.'[61] Here the anti-working class and anti-poor perspective is combined with a particular gender standpoint defending hegemonic discourses of femininity.[62] The lesbians in 'Wages Due' are defined as taking a perverse pride in 'de-feminizing' themselves because they construct and perform their femininity differently and engage in specifically lesbian cultural practices of gender performance.[63]

The RCMP had great difficulty handling the new gay and lesbian feminist activists in the 1970s. These activists were no longer hiding their sexualities nor were they trapped within the relations of the closet or living a double life. Instead, by being out and building political movements they began to undermine the social relations of the closet and to undermine the notion of 'character weakness' based on the need to maintain the secrecy and invisibility of queers. These new movements and the emergence of broader gay and lesbian communities gradually undermined the main features of the Cold War against queers.

THE CONTINUING COLD WARS

The Cold War against queers continued at a high level of intensity within the military and the RCMP itself until at least the late 1980s and early 1990s, when official policies excluding gay men and lesbians were changed owing to lesbian and gay activism and legal challenges.[64] The Canadian Security and Intelligence Service (CSIS), which took over national security work from the RCMP following the revelations of RCMP 'dirty tricks' against the sovereignty and left movements in Quebec, can still to this day deny security clearances to gay men and lesbians who are not 'out' on the grounds that, since they have 'something to hide,' they could be 'blackmail-able.'[65] [...]

New targets for national security campaigns since the 1990s include Arab and Muslim Canadians during and since the Gulf War,[66] and again with the current 'war on terrorism' and the global justice movement against capitalist globalization.[67] Defending the new international trade and investment alliances the Canadian state is entering into has now become part of defending national security. [...] What this suggests is that a political Cold War in a broad sense continues against threats to capitalist social relations even though the USSR no longer exists.

A major and central part of the Canadian Cold War was the campaign against queers. Heterosexual hegemony has been key to the making of the Canadian state and its social formations, and sexual, gender, and moral regulation was at the heart of the social organization of the Cold War. The Cold War against queers had a detrimental impact on the lives of thousands of people and played a crucial part in constructing the 'normality' of heterosexuality that we continue to confront today. But there is also a history of resistance to this Cold War which provides an important resource for our continuing struggles.

NOTES

1 The dates when interviews took place are indicated in parentheses at the end of the interview extracts. To protect confidentiality, all names given for people I have interviewed are pseudonyms.

2 I thank Patrizia Gentile for her part in the research that this chapter is based on. See Gary Kinsman and Patrizia Gentile, with Heidi McDonell and Mary Mahood-Greer, '"In the Interests of the State": The Anti-Gay, Anti-Lesbian National Security Campaigns in Canada,' research report, Laurentian University, 1998; and Kinsman and Gentile, *The Canadian War on 'Queers': National Security as Sexual Regulation* (Vancouver: U British Columbia P: 2010).

3 RCMP, *Directorate of Security and Intelligence: Annual Report* 1967–1968.

4 For more on this see Kinsman and Gentile, *The Canadian War on 'Queers'.*

5 On the importance of an active sense of agency in developing liberationist social theory, see the work of Himani Bannerji, especially 'But Who Speaks for Us?' in *Thinking Through: Essays on Feminism, Marxism and Anti-Racism* (Toronto: Women's Press, 1995).

6 'Ideology refers to all forms of knowledge that are divorced from their conditions of production (their grounds),' writes Roslyn Wallach Bologh in *Dialectical Phenomenology: Marx's Method* (Boston: Northeastern UP, 1979), 19. On ideology see also the work of Dorothy Smith, including *The Everyday World as Problematic: A Feminist Sociology* (Toronto: U of Toronto P, 1987); *The Conceptual Practices of Power: A Feminist Sociology of Knowledge* (Toronto: U of Toronto P, 1990); and *Texts, Facts and Femininity: Exploring the Relations of Ruling* (London: Routledge, 1990); and the work of Himani

Bannerji, including *Thinking Through* (1995), and her articles on the ideological construction of India: 'Beyond the Ruling Category to What Actually Happens: Notes on James Mill's Historiography in *The History of British India*,' in Marie Campbell and Ann Manicom, eds., *Knowledge, Experience,and Ruling Relations: Studies in the Social Organization of Knowledge* (Toronto: U of Toronto P, 1995), 49–64; and 'Writing "India," Doing Ideology,' *Left History* 2.2 (1994): 5–17. On ideological codes see Dorothy Smith, 'The Standard North American Family: SNAP as an Ideological Code,' and '"Politically Correct": An Organizer of Public Discourse,' in Dorothy Smith, *Writing the Social: Critique, Theory and Investigations* (Toronto: U of Toronto P, 1999), 157–94. I find the notion (developed in this last text) of an ideological code which 'coordinates multiple sites within the intersecting relations of public text-mediated discourses' useful in the analysis of national security issues. At the same time, I have difficulty with Smith's suggestion that ideological codes are analogous to 'genetic codes' (159) since this suggests that these are automatic and cannot be disrupted or subverted. I want to hold on to the possibilities for disruption and subversion and to avoid the reification of human, social practices.

7   Kinsman and Gentile (1998) have been criticized for producing 'revisionist' history. While I reject this way of framing struggles over history, I do intend this to be a work of transformative historical sociology—a work that transforms and redefines what Canadian history and sociology is all about. This is not simply about adding the campaign against 'queers' to the established history of Cold War Canada but about 'queering' and transforming our overall analysis of the Cold War in the Canadian context.

8   On the use of 'queer' in this context see Annamarie Jagose, *Queer Theory: An Introduction* (New York: New York UP, 1996), 72–126.

9   On heterosexual hegemony see Gary Kinsman, *The Regulation of Desire: Homo and Hetero Sexualities* (Montreal: Black Rose, 1996). On the dichotomous notion of gender see Suzanne Kessler and Wendy McKenna, *Gender: An Ethnomethodological Approach* (Chicago: U of Chicago P, 1978) and Kessler's *Lessons from the Intersexed* (New Brunswick, NJ: Rutgers UP, 1998). For the concept of hegemony see Antonio Gramsci, *Selections from the Prison Notebooks* (New York: International Publishers, 1971).

10 I am blurring the distinction here between theories and methods to foreground the interrelationships of these terms as part of my practice of adopting theories and methods that are epistemelogically and ontologically committed to active agency and anti-reification.

11 While E.P. Thompson's *The Making of the English Working Class* (New York: Vintage, 1966) did not adequately take up relations of gender, race, or sexuality, or their mediated construction in and through class relations, Thompson's approach has been extended by others into these areas.

12 Campbell and Manicom, eds., *Knowledge, Experience, and Ruling Relations*.

13 See George Smith, 'Policing the Gay Community: An Inquiry into Textually-Mediated Social Relations,' *International Journal of the Sociology of Law* 16 (1988): 163–83, and 'Political Activist as Ethnographer,' *Social Problems* 37 (1990): 401–21; Madiha Didi Khayatt, *Lesbian Teachers, An Invisible Presence* (Albany, NY: State University of New York P, 1992), and 'Compulsory Heterosexuality: Schools and Lesbian Students,' in Campbell and Manicom, eds., *Knowledge, Experience, and Ruling Relations*, 149–63; and Gary Kinsman, 'The Textual Practices of Sexual Rule: Sexual Policing and Gay Men,' in Campbell and Manicom, eds., *Knowledge, Experience, and Ruling Relations*, 80–95.

14 Dorothy Smith, *The Everyday World as Problematic*, 147–207; Marjorie L. Devault, 'Institutional Ethnography: A Strategy for Feminist Inquiry,' in *Liberating Method: Feminism and Social Research*

(Philadelphia: Temple UP, 1999), 46–54.

15 Gary Kinsman, 'The Textual Practices of Sexual Rule,' in Campbell and Manicom, eds., *Knowledge, Experience, and Ruling Relations,* 80–95.

16 Dorothy Smith, 'On Sociological Description,' *Texts, Facts and Femininity,* 86–119.

17 Bannerji, *Thinking Through.*

18 Dorothy Smith, *Texts, Facts and Femininity,* 30–43.

19 George Smith, 'The Ideology of "Fag": The School Experience of Gay Students,' *Sociological Quarterly* 39.2 (1998): 309–35.

20 In the United States, leftist and ex-Communist Party members were centrally involved in the early 1950s in the formation of the Mattachine Society, the first attempt at a homophile organization. See John D'Emilio, *Sexual Politics, Sexual Communities* (Chicago: U of Chicago P, 1983) 57–74. At the height of the Cold War frenzy against communists and ex-communists, leaders were turfed out of such groups by their more conservative members (75–91). Left-wing activists were also centrally involved in the formation of gay liberation fronts after the Stonewall riots in New York City in 1969.

21 David McNally, *Bodies of Meaning: Studies on Language, Labor, and Liberation* (Albany, NY: State University of New York, 2001), 191.

22 On the postmodernist bias against 'experience' as 'contaminated' by discourse see Campbell and Manicom, eds., *Knowledge, Experience, and Ruling Relations,* 7–10; Rosemary Hennessy, *Profit and Pleasure: Sexual Identities in Late Capitalism* (New York: Routledge, 2000), 17–22; and Ellen Meiksins Wood, *Democracy against Capitalism* (Cambridge: Cambridge UP, 1995), 96–7. However, while accounts of social experience are not an absolute truth and are always shaped by forms of social discourse, they can exist in rupture with official accounts and discourse, as in David's story.

23 This is the underlying assumption in Reg Whitaker and Gary Marcuse, *Cold War Canada: The Making of a National Insecurity State* (Toronto: U of Toronto P, 1993).

24 Gary Kinsman, Dieter K. Buse, and Mercedes Steedman, eds., *Whose National Security? Canadian State Surveillance and the Creation of Enemies* (Toronto: Between the Lines, 2000) 2–5, 278–85.

25 Numerous theories of the social formation of the USSR have been put forward. The view I find most persuasive argues that after the initial revolutionary period, the new bureaucratic ruling class mobilized Marxism-Leninism as an ideology to obscure the oppression and the exploitation of the workers and peasants. On this and other approaches see Moshe Machover and John Fantham, *The Century of the Unexpected: A New Analysis of Soviet Type Societies* (London: Big Flame, 1979).

26 See Ruth Frankenburg, *White Women, Race Matters: The Social Construction of Whiteness* (Minneapolis: U of Minnesota P, 1993); David Roediger, *The Wages of Whiteness: Race and the Making of the American Working Class* (London: Verso, 1993).

27 Allan Berube, *Coming Out under Fire: The History of Gay Men and Women in World War Two* (New York: Free Press, 1990); Kinsman, *The Regulation of Desire,* 148–57.

28 On the limitations of conceptualizing homophobia as a strictly individual phenomenon, and of analysing heterosexist practices solely in terms of psychological phobia, thus obscuring how homophobia is shaped through broader social relations, see Kinsman, *The Regulation of Desire,* 33.

29 David Kimmel and Daniel J. Robinson, 'The Queer Career of Homosexual Security Vetting in Cold War Canada,' *Canadian Historical Review* 73.3 (1994): 319–45 neglects this aspect of the national security texts.

30 Mary Louise Adams, *The Trouble with Normal: Postwar Youth and the Making of Heterosexuality* (Toronto: U of Toronto P, 1997).

31 See Philip Corrigan, 'On Moral Regulation,' *Sociological Review* 29 (1981): 313–16, and Gary Kinsman, 'National Security as Moral Regulation: Making the Normal and the Deviant in the Security Campaigns against Gay Men and Lesbians,' in Deborah Brock, ed., *Making Normal: Social Regulation in Canada* (Toronto: Thomson/Nelson, 2003), 121–45.

32 Corrigan, *On Moral Regulation.*

33 Dorothy Smith, *Texts, Facts and Femininity,* 30–43.

34 See Kinsman et al., eds., *Whose National Security?*

35 Kinsman et al., eds., *Whose National Security?,* 2–5, 278–85. These Cold War mobilizations against queers also had major and lasting impacts on the left which affected not only those who identified with the USSR who already had overt positions against queers but also those who had broken with Stalinism. See Laura Engelstein, 'Soviet Policy toward Male Homosexuality: Its Origin and Historical Roots,' in Gert Hekma, Harry Oosterhuis, and James Steakley, eds., *Gay Men and the Sexual History of the Political Left* (New York: Harrington Park/Haworth, 1995), 155–78. In the United States, during the Cold War, the Trotskyist Socialist Workers Party came to view lesbian and gay members of the organization as 'security risks' to the party and prohibited lesbians and gays from membership in the SWP. See Gary Kinsman, 'From Anti-queer to Queers as "Peripheral": The Socialist Workers' Party, Gay Liberation and North American Trotskyism, 1960–1980' (unpublished manuscript, 2000); David Thorstad, ed., *Gay Liberation and Socialism: Documents from the Discussions on Gay Liberation inside the Socialist Workers Party (1970–1973),* Part 1 (New York: Thorstad, 1976); and Steve Forgione and Kurt T. Hill, eds., *No Apologies: The Unauthorized Publication of Internal Discussion Documents of the Socialist Workers Party (SWP) Concerning Lesbian/Gay Male Liberation* (New York: Lesbian/Gay Rights Monitoring Group, 1980). The Cold War mobilizations against queers helped to produce the heterosexism on the left that the gay and lesbian liberation movements confronted in the late 1960s and 1970s.

36 Harold, 'A Case Study with Observations' (unpublished manuscript, 1960–1), 17.

37 Dialogism and its variants are central terms used by Russian literary theorist M.M. Bakhtin to get at how '[e]verything means, is understood, as part of a greater whole—there is constant interaction between meanings, all of which have the potential of conditioning others.' See M.M. Bakhtin, *The Dialogic Imagination: Four Essays* (Austin: U of Texas P, 1981) 426–7. In this case we can see how the earlier, more explicitly right-wing, discourse came to condition and live on within national security discourse.

38 D.F. Wall, 'Security Cases Involving Character Weaknesses, with Special Reference to the Problem of Homosexuality,' Memorandum to the Security Panel, 12 May 1959, 12–13.

39 See Patrizia Gentile, 'Searching for "Miss Civil Service" and "Mr. Civil Service": Gender Anxiety, Beauty Contests and Fruit Machines in the Canadian Civil Service, 1950–1973,' MA thesis, Carleton University, Ottawa, 1996, and '"Government Girls" and "Ottawa Men": Cold War Management of Gender Relations in the Civil Service,' in Kinsman et al., eds., *Whose National Security?,* 131–41.

40 George Chauncey, 'Christian Brotherhood or Sexual Perversion? Homosexual Identities and the Construction of Sexual Boundaries in the World War One Era,' in M. Duberman, K. Vicinus, and George Chauncey, eds., *Hidden from History: Reclaiming the Gay and Lesbian Past* (New York: Meridian, 1989), 294–317; and George Chauncey, *Gay New York* (New York: Basic Books, 1994), 47–63.

41 Kinsman and Gentile, "In the Interests of the State," 469.

42 Kinsman, *The Regulation of Desire*, 200.

43 On the limited but significant distinction between the closet and living a double life see Chauncey, *Gay New York*, 375, n.9.

44 Kinsman, *The Regulation of Desire*, 173; Kinsman and Gentile, "In the Interests of the State," 38–49; Kinsman and Gentile, *The Canadian War on 'Queers.'*

45 Kinsman and Gentile, "In the Interests of the State," 98–106.

46 Harold, 'A Case Study with Observations' (1960–1).

47 Ibid.

48 J.M. Bella, 'Appendix "A": Homosexuality within the Federal Government Service—Statistics,' in Director of Security and Intelligence, *Homosexuality within the Federal Government Service*, 29 April 1960.

49 Kinsman, 'Constructing Gay Men and Lesbians as National Security Risks, 1950–1970,' in Kinsman et al., eds., *Whose National Security?*, 145–7.

50 Ellen Herman, 'The Career of Cold War Psychology,' *Radical History Review* (Special issue: 'The Cold War and Expert Knowledge') (1995): 52–85; Nikolas Rose, *The Psychological Complex: Psychology, Politics and Society in England, 1869–1939* (London: Routledge and Kegan Paul, 1985).

51 Kinsman and Gentile, "In the Interests of the State," 106–16.

52 Ibid.

53 John Sawatsky, *Men in the Shadows: The RCMP Security Service* (Toronto: Totem Books, 1983), 133.

54 Kinsman and Gentile, "In the Interests of the State," 106–16.

55 RCMP, *Directorate of Security and Intelligence: Annual Report 1962–1963*, 19.

56 Camp sensibility and humour is a cultural form produced by gay men to manage and negotiate the contradictions between our particular experiences of the world as gays and the institutionalized heterosexuality that hegemonizes social relations. A crucial part of this cultural formation is to denaturalize normality and heterosexuality by making fun of it. On this see Kinsman, *The Regulation of Desire*, 226–7.

57 Kinsman and Gentile, "In the Interests of the State," 118–29; Kinsman, 'Constructing Gay Men and Lesbians as National Security Risks, 1950–1970,' in Kinsman et al., eds., *Whose National Security?*, 149–51.

58 Kimmel and Robinson, 'The Queer Career.'

59 Kinsman and Gentile, *The Canadian War on 'Queers.'*

60 RCMP, 'Assessment of the Gay Alliance towards Equality' (Vancouver 1973); released under the Access to Information Act.

61 RCMP, 'Report on the Toronto Wages for Housework Committee (TWHC) and Unaligned Marxist and Pressure Groups' (Toronto 1976); released under the Access to Information Act.

62 Dorothy Smith, 'Femininity as Discourse,' in *Texts, Facts and Femininity*, 159–208.

63 On performances of lesbianism in relation to gender see Becki Ross, *The House That Jill Built: A Lesbian Nation in Formation* (Toronto: U of Toronto P, 1995), and her 'Destaining the Delinquent Body: Moral Regulatory Practices at Street Haven, 1965–1969,' *Journal of the History of Sexuality* 7.4 (1997): 561–95; Joan Nestle, 'Butch-Femme Relationships: Sexual Courage in the 1950s,' in Nestle, *A Restricted Country* (Ithaca: Firebrand, 1987), 100–9; Elizabeth Lapovsky Kennedy and Madeline D.

Davis, *Boots of Leather, Slippers of Gold: The Making of a Lesbian Community* (New York: Routledge, 1993); and *Forbidden Love,* Aerlyn Weissman and Lynne Fernie, directors, National Film Board of Canada, 1993.

64 Kinsman, *The Regulation of Desire,* 359–60.

65 Brian K. Smith, CBC Radio News, 14 April 1998; Jeff Sallot, 'The spy masters' talent hunt goes public,' *Globe and Mail,* 22 June 1999, A1, A14.

66 Zuhair Kashmeri, *The Gulf Within: Canadian Arabs, Racism and the Gulf War* (Toronto: James Lorimer, 1991).

67 Naomi Klein, *No Logo: Taking Aim at the Brand Name Bullies* (Toronto: Knopf, 2000); David McNally, *Another World Is Possible: Globalization and Anti-capitalism* (Winnipeg, Arbieter Ring Publishing, 2002).

CHAPTER 6

Unknowable Bodies, Unthinkable Sexualities: Lesbian and Transgender Legal Invisibility in the Toronto Women's Bathhouse Raid

Sarah Lamble

INTRODUCTION

Despite the recent proliferation of high-profile cases involving sexual orientation and gender identity discrimination claims, lesbian and transgender bodies and sexualities remain largely invisible in Anglo-American courts (Boyd and Young, 2003; Lloyd, 2005; Smith, 1997; Whittle, 2002). Even in Canada, where significant sexual orientation rights have been won, lesbians appear as disembodied, desexualized legal subjects (Valverde, 2006). Likewise, although transgender people are gaining increased legal protection from discrimination, their corporeal experiences and sexual identities remain largely unintelligible. For transgender persons, such invisibility results from federal and provincial legal frameworks that do not formally recognize gender identity as a distinct discrimination ground, and from social norms that marginalize gender-variant people (Durnford, 2005; Namaste, 2000; Ontario Human Rights Commission, 1999). For lesbians, legal invisibility is often attributed to similar social exclusion and to policing practices which historically criminalized lesbian sexuality less vigorously than gay men (Mason, 1995: 70–2; Robson, 1992; Valverde, 2007: 248). Indeed, lesbian sexuality is often assumed to fall below the radar of state surveillance. Yet the capacity to 'not see' or 'not know' queer bodies and sexualities is not simply a matter of inadvertent omission, but involves wilful acts of ignorance. Particular facts must remain unspoken, details unquestioned, lines of thinking unpursued—especially in the legal domain where selection of evidence is crucial to case outcomes. As such, I argue that discourses of limited knowledge and rationalities of ignorance play an active part in the legal disappearance of lesbian and transgender bodies and sexualities.

Examining *R. v Hornick* (2002), a Canadian case involving the police raid of a women's bathhouse, this chapter explores how lesbian, queer and transgender bodies and sexualities are actively rendered invisible via legal knowledge practices, norms and rationalities. Resisting the temptation to see legal invisibility as simply the consequence of state indifference or repression, I suggest legal discourses and organizational rationalities constitute queer bodies and sexualities as unthinkable and unknowable. *R. v Hornick* provides an important case study because lesbian and transgender bodies and sexualities were initially quite visible within the courtroom, but then dramatically disappeared in the final ruling. As such, lesbian and transgender bodies did not simply fall below the state's radar, but were actively reconfigured as non-queer disembodied subjects. Drawing from governmentality literatures which examine ways of knowing as techniques of regulation, I suggest legal forms of *limited knowledge* and *limited thinking* regulate borders of (in)visibility, and play an active part in shaping identities, governing conduct and producing subjectivity.

THE 'PUSSY PALACE' CASE

On 15 September 2000, five male officers from Toronto Police Services entered a women's sexual bathhouse at Club Toronto and proceeded to investigate for liquor licence violations and criminal sex acts. The sold-out event, known as the 'Pussy Palace'[1] was the fourth of its kind in Toronto and attracted several hundred patrons, the majority of whom were scantily clad when the police arrived. The police spent more than an hour on the premises, searching private rooms and questioning half-naked women, actions that were widely denounced by local press (Addis, 2000; Gallant, 2000; Giese, 2000; Gilbert, 2000). Two members of the Toronto Women's Bathhouse Committee were subsequently charged with several violations of Ontario's Liquor Licence Act, including disorderly conduct and serving liquor outside prescribed areas and hours. When brought to court, however, Judge Peter Hryn dismissed the charges, ruling that police had violated the women's security, privacy and equality rights under the Canadian Charter of Rights and Freedoms. Hryn deemed the police conduct analogous to a male-on-female strip search, which, in the absence of exigent circumstances, could not be justified. The police evidence was declared inadmissible and the charges withdrawn.

Though hailed as a victory by the Bathhouse Committee, the ruling itself, as Bain and Nash (2007) argue, did not mark an entirely progressive decision for queer women's sexuality. For both judge and defence, the key concern was neither the state's efforts to monitor queer sexuality, nor the police abuse of liquor laws to do so, but simply that a search of semi-naked females was conducted by males. Why the women were naked, or what they were doing while naked was largely irrelevant to the court, as were their sexualities. In fact, nowhere in the final judgment do the words 'lesbian', 'queer' or even 'homosexual' appear (Bain and Nash, 2007: 27). Likewise, despite considerable discussion during the court proceedings about the presence of transgender persons at the event (inclusive of male-to-female transwomen and female-to-male transmen), the words 'transgender' or 'transsexual' were also non-existent in the ruling. The absence of these terms is not trivial; such omission not only marks a gap in the legal representation of queer identities, but affects how the case is classified and read in future. If a law student conducts a Westlaw search using the term "lesbian" or "transgender", for example, the case will not appear.

The legal erasure of such identities is particularly striking in a context where promoting visibility of queer women's sexuality was a clear objective of the organizers (Gallant and Gillis, 2001: 153). An event originally designed to promote a public, transgressive, queer sexuality was tamed and desexualized by legal discourse in order to produce victims worthy of state protection. 'In the end', argue Bain and Nash, 'the classic argument of the danger of the heterosexual male gaze on the defenceless and naked female body was successfully used by the state to contain the transgressive potential of queer spaces and queer identities' (2007: 31).

It is tempting to see this case as an example of deliberate state repression of queer desire. Yet such a reading is too simplistic, for it assumes the case outcome was the direct result of state intentions, and fails to interrogate the conditions that made such power effects possible. Further examination suggests the police actions were a culmination of social, institutional and political forces, rather than a singular ideological mission by a monolithic state (Lamble, 2006). Moreover, the key legal arguments that effectively contained transgressive bathhouse sexuality were not initiated by the state, but were brought forth by the lawyer representing the Bathhouse Committee, thereby raising questions about the conditions in which subjects participate (albeit strategically) in their own regulation. Such regulation arguably arose in part from appealing to a human rights framework, which, despite its benefits, relies on universal humanity claims that often erase lesbian and transgender specificities. Invisibility also emerged from right to privacy arguments, which required that queer women's bodies and sexualities find their 'proper' place in a private rather than public realm (Bain and Nash, 2007: 24–6). Given the legacy of failed privacy claims for queers (e.g., *Bowers* v *Hardwick,* and *R.* v *Brown),* the successful deployment of privacy rights in the Bathhouse case is laudable, but nevertheless reinforced conservative gender norms. The court's capacity to employ liberal rhetoric while simultaneously confining queer bodies and sexualities is therefore best understood through a governmentality lens which recognizes how regulation operates through individual freedoms (Rose, 1999/2004).

LESBIAN AND TRANSGENDER LEGAL INVISIBILITY

Despite the long-standing legal invisibility of lesbian bodies and sexualities, explanations for such absences are surprisingly under-explored. Conventional wisdom suggests that lesbian sexuality poses less threat to heterosexual norms than gay male sexuality, such that lesbians fall below the radar of state policing. Indeed, while gay male sexuality has been historically criminalized by anti-sodomy laws, same-sex acts among women have generated less state interest.[2] In England and Wales, for example, lesbians could not be prosecuted under buggery laws that criminalized gay men.[3] This legacy extends to Canada (and the US), where anti-sodomy laws technically applied to women, but were rarely enforced (Valverde, 2007: 233, 248). Noting the relatively few cases of criminalized lesbianism is not to suggest that female-female eroticism has been unregulated by the state; such legal silences may constitute a deliberate attempt to regulate lesbian sexuality through denial of its existence (Mason, 1995: 71; Robson, 1992). Family law rulings, welfare provision, civil service and military employment mark other areas where lesbians have been highly regulated by the state (Arnup, 1989; Kinsman, 1996; Millbank, 1997). However, since state efforts to regulate lesbian sexuality have been largely manifest within non-criminal and non-legal domains, lesbians have made few public appearances in Canadian legal history.

Even since the enactment of the Canadian Charter of Rights and Freedoms, which ushered in a new era of gay rights litigation, lesbians are surprisingly absent. Of the 16 Supreme Court decisions to date that reference the word 'lesbian', only one significant case (*M. v H.*, 1999) directly involved lesbians.[4] The remaining cases fall into one of three groupings: (1) cases that address or reference published representations of gays and lesbians rather than embodied persons (e.g., *Little Sister's*, 2007; *Little Sister's*, 2000; *Chamberlain v Surrey School District*, 2002; *R. v Tremblay*, 1993; *Towne Cinema Theatres v The Queen*, 1985; *WIC Radio Ltd v Simpson*, 2008); (2) cases that make passing reference to the sexual orientation of suspects or witnesses in criminal proceedings (e.g., *R. v Davis*, 1999; *R. v O.N.E.*, 2001); or (3) cases that simply reference lesbians within a generic, abstract homosexuality that is indistinguishable from gay men (e.g., *Granovsky*, 2000; *Hodge*, 2004; *Trinity Western*, 2001). The key Charter cases that address sexual orientation claims involve gay men, with rulings that impact lesbians, but do not directly represent them (e.g., *Egan*, 1995; *Canada (Attorney General) v Mossop*, 1993; *Vriend*, 1998). Even the 2004 Supreme Court reference on same-sex marriage did not involve actual same-sex couples and the words 'lesbian', 'gay', or 'sexuality' were absent from the decision (*Reference re Same-Sex Marriage*, 2004).

Where lesbians do appear before Canadian courts, they are constituted as disembodied, desexualized legal subjects (Valverde, 2006). The most prominent Supreme Court case involving a lesbian couple, *M. v H.* (1999), made virtually no reference to the sexual aspect of the litigants' relationship. Although the key question was whether or not the same-sex couple's legal status was equivalent to a heterosexual common-law relationship, the case was framed as a property dispute. The sexual nature of their relationship was not discussed (Valverde, 2006: 162). Not only was their sexuality missing; their bodies were absent too. Although customary to use initials to protect litigants' anonymity, the initials M. and H. did not even refer to the litigants' own names, but to their respective lawyers (M. for Martha McCarthy and H. for Julia Holland).[5] In their extended anonymity, M. and H. mark another example of disembodied, desexualized lesbians.

The absence of lesbian bodies and sexualities in law is partly an effect of legal strategy and partly a consequence of the legal conceptualization of 'sexual orientation'. Gay and lesbian litigants are unlikely to reveal intimate sexual details, lest such information jeopardize their legitimacy in court. Same-sex couples are desexualized or treated as heterosexual-like; any references to sexual relations are framed as evidence of long-term, stable, loving, spousal relationships (see e.g., *K. (Re)*, 1995). De-sexing and disembodiment function as both a condition of receiving equal treatment and a prerequisite for intelligibility (Cooper, 2006). Sexual orientation itself tends to be desexualized in Canadian law, treated more like a socio-cultural group than a sexual identity (Boyd and Young, 2003; Valverde, 2006: 106).

Transgender bodies and sexualities have also remained largely invisible in Canadian law. While courts have historically scrutinized transgender bodies with respect to marriage cases (where the capacity for penile-vaginal penetration, whether functional or aesthetic, provided a key threshold for legal recognition of gender identity), such cases generally treat transgender persons as biological, medical and psychological 'specimens', rather than fully-embodied legal subjects (Sharpe, 2007; Whittle, 2002). Although legalization of same-sex marriage has rendered moot the Canadian applicability of some of this older case law, it has not resolved issues of invisibility, since legal recognition of transgender relationships can conflict with couple's self-defined identities. For example, a transgender (male-to-female) woman is now eligible to marry a non-transgender man, but the state will likely recognize the relationship as same-sex, even if the couple identifies as heterosexual (Cowan, 2005: 81). Similarly, although the 2004 UK Gender Recognition Act enables transgender persons to obtain legal status in their self-identified gender, recognition is conditional on dissolution of any previous marriage (Sharpe, 2007: 70). While these frameworks mark an improvement over other jurisdictions—such as Germany, Denmark, Sweden, the Netherlands and some US states—where sterilization is a precondition for identity recognition, UK and Canadian law nonetheless obscures transgender sexualities and relationships (Whittle, 2002: 162).

Most Canadian provinces also require evidence of sex-reassignment surgery for a legal change of sex, thereby excluding individuals who do not choose, or are unable to access, medical interventions. Further, because both federal and provincial human rights legislation in Canada (with the exception of the Northwest Territories) does not formally recognize gender identity as a specific category of discrimination, transgender persons must graft their claims to other grounds (such as sex, sexual orientation or disability), which fail to address the specificity of transgender issues (Durnford, 2005). To date, no case specifically involving transgender issues has reached the Supreme Court of Canada, despite vital appeals by transgender persons to have their cases heard (e.g., *Nixon v Vancouver Rape Relief*, 2007).

Visibility is particularly fraught for transgender persons, adding further complexity to questions of legal erasure. For many transgender people, visibility is not in fact desirable, as it often signals a failure to 'pass' in one's self-defined gender. Particularly if one has undergone the state's arduous legal and medical requirements of transitioning, successful passing can be liberating. Passing is also a safety issue, since transpeople are at high risk of harassment and violence. Yet passing carries the burden of secrecy and fear of discovery.

Visibility thus poses a dilemma for many transgender persons, as tensions arise between wanting to pass and wanting to be acknowledged (Green, 1999). These tensions become more acute as transgender issues come to court, because transpeople simultaneously experience hypervisibility, and stark invisibility, since legal narratives and media spectacle often prevent transpeople from fully representing themselves and their experiences (Whittle, 1999). For example, while transgender persons are disproportionately criminalized and imprisoned, the concerns and experiences of transgender prisoners have received scant public attention (Findlay, 1999; Mann, 2006). When transgender identities *are* acknowledged, it is usually without recognizing the material, embodied experiences of transgender lives (Namaste, 2000).

R. v Hornick marks both a departure from, and an adherence to, the standard legal treatment of lesbian and transgender bodies and sexualities. Generating mainstream news coverage and attracting sold-out crowds, women's bathhouse events were by no means below the police radar (Gallant and Gillis, 2001: 153–4). When police entered the premises, physical bodies were the primary target of surveillance, with officers counting each of the 330 semi-nude bodies in attendance. Likewise, lesbian and transgender bodies were initially visible in the courtroom. Defence lawyer Frank Addario asked each bathhouse witness detailed questions about her body: how exactly she was clothed ('how were you dressed that evening?'); the degree of bodily exposure ('nude or partially nude?'), the visibility of particular areas of the body; ('was your chest area covered?'); what type of material was worn ('by sheer, do you mean see through?'); and the exact position of women's towels on their bodies ('you wrapped it around below your armpit?''It came just to the top of your thighs?') (R. v Hornick Proceedings, 22 Oct. 2001: 22, 28, 65, 66). Police described explicit sex acts among women at the bathhouse, including 'genital rubbing' and 'penetration' (R. v Hornick Proceedings, 23 Oct. 2001: 31, 33). The physical bodies of transgender persons also garnered significant attention, with a police witness even describing in detail the genital area of one patron, referring to a 'slight bulge in the underwear' as evidence of biological maleness (R. v Hornick Proceedings, 23 Oct. 2001: 34, 54, 57). While the officer did not consider [that] the 'bulge' in question could have been a strap-on dildo (common attire at women's bathhouses), such attention to queer corporeality nonetheless evoked a striking image in court. Although bathhouse bodies and sexualities eventually transformed into disembodied, desexualized legal subjects, they were initially visible in very explicit and corporeal ways.

Making queer women's sexuality visible was, in fact, a clear goal of the Pussy Palace (Gallant and Gillis, 2001: 153). Promoting such visibility not only required physical space, but also conceptual space. As two organizers describe, the bathhouse

> created new possibilities for how women could think about, organize, and enact their sexual desires. Whether or not women attended the Pussy Palace, it existed as an option, as a possibility, as a problem for how women think of themselves as sexual beings. (Gallant and Gillis, 2001: 153)

Yet the court's capacity to think, know and see queer bodies and sexualities on such terms proved difficult. As the courtroom drama unfolded, bathhouse patrons were transformed from public, active, queer subjects to private, passive, heterosexual victims. The construction of such bodies was not simply a consequence of the judge's decision, but also the product of entrenched legal rationalities that rendered queer bodies and sexualities unthinkable and unknowable.

GOVERNING THROUGH KNOWING/UNKNOWING

Governmentality, simply stated, concerns the conduct of conduct (Dean, 1999/2006: 10; Foucault, 1991; Gordon, 1991: 2; Rose, 1999/2004: 3). As Nikolas Rose describes, governmentality includes 'all endeavours to shape, guide, direct the conduct of others' (Rose, 1999/2004: 3). Governing in this sense does not function through repressive force, but 'seeks to shape our conduct by working through our desires, aspirations, interests and beliefs' (Dean, 1999/2006: 11). Hence, governmental power works through individual freedom (Rose, 1999/2004). This capacity to shape conduct is contingent on particular knowledge practices, since working through individual desires requires knowledge of the subject to be guided and the conditions that foster intended conduct. Mitchell Dean describes four dimensions of governing, each linked to ways of knowing: (1) forms of visibility, which emerge from particular ways of seeing and perceiving; (2) modes of thinking and questioning, which rely on specific vocabularies and rationalities for producing truth; (3) techniques of acting, intervening and directing, which are comprised of practical rationalities, expertise and 'know how'; and (4) modes of forming subjects, which elicit, foster and attribute various capacities, statuses and orientations to particular agents (Dean, 1999/2006: 23, 30–2). Collectively, these modes of knowledge shape the capacity to conduct ourselves and others (Dean, 1999/2006). In short, governing operates through knowing.

But what if *unknowing* or *limited knowing* also function as regulatory techniques? How might discourses of ignorance work to produce certain kinds of subjects, orders and power relations (Cooper, 2006)? No doubt, *unknowing* is inextricably bound with *knowing* as there are few clear boundaries for determining where knowing begins and ends. But what if a focus on unknowing reveals something different than what attention to knowing can yield?

Eve Kosofsky Sedgwick raises such questions in claiming that 'ignorance is as potent and as multiple a thing there as is knowledge' (Sedgwick, 1990: 4). Quoting Foucault, she notes:

> [T]here is no binary division to be made between what one says and what one does not say; we must try to determine the different ways of not saying such things. There is not one but many silences, and they are an integral part of the strategies that underlie and permeate discourse. (Sedgwick, 1990: 3)

In other words, ignorances 'are produced by and correspond to particular knowledges and circulate as part of particular regimes of truth' (Sedgwick, 1990: 8). Drawing from Sedgwick and Foucault, but broadening the category of ignorance to incorporate other forms of limited thought, I explore how limited knowing/thinking play a significant role in the governmentality of lesbian and transgender legal subjects. By limited knowing/thinking I refer to stoppages, gaps, limits and refusals upon thinking and knowing that occur within a particular logic or rationality, including: explicit references to what one doesn't know; deliberate and less intentional refusals to know or think; logics and norms which render some facts as relevant and others as easily cast aside.

Limited thinking is not simply the opposite of knowing, nor a partial fragment of a more pure logic or authentic mode of thought. As Donna Haraway reminds us, all knowledges are situated and partial, meaning they are bound by the time, place and particular location of the subject making knowledge claims (Haraway, 1991). Nor is limited thinking synonymous with irrationality. If rationality, in a governmentality sense, refers to deployments of knowledge that enable an activity to become thinkable and practicable (whether a theoretical framework, political paradigm, or pragmatic method), then limited thinking—which achieves similar results by rendering particular activities unthinkable and impractical—can be understood as a kind of inverse or hyper-rationality (Dean, 1999/2006: 211; Foucault, 1991: 96; Rose, 1999/2004: 24–8). Such limited thinking reflects what Linsey McGoey, drawing from Nietzsche, describes as the 'will to ignorance' within bureaucracies—a tendency to deploy ignorance strategically for highly functional outcomes (McGoey, 2007: 213, 228). Investigating the utility of limited thinking as a conceptual tool, I hope to make visible knowledge-power relations that might otherwise be taken for granted. This task should not be confused with a polemic against judicial ignorance, whereby lesbian and transgender people are positioned to enlighten judges (although I am not ruling out such a strategy either); rather, it is an attempt to interrogate the conditions which make certain kinds of ignorance possible and with what effect.

I locate limited thinking within the realm of social practice, rather than individual psyches. Limited thinking of individual agents (e.g., police, lawyers, judges) is not simply the product of an autonomous rationality, but is sculpted and invoked by specific governing regimes (e.g., administrative rules, bureaucratic culture, duties and obligations) that compel agents to self-identify in particular ways, to ask some questions and not others, and to use particular forms of knowledge that foreclose upon others. Such techniques structure a field of vision that illuminates certain objects, while shadowing and obscuring others (Dean, 1999/2006: 32).

Multiple forms of limited thinking/knowing were deployed throughout the bathhouse case: lack of thought; refusal to know and think; self-proclaimed ignorance; limited reasoning. These manifestations of limited thinking were not uniform, but served different purposes and created varied effects, whether providing a means to avoid self-reflexivity, evade responsibility, claim innocence, provide distance from dangerous knowledge, maintain norms, or perpetuate hierarchies. Limited knowing was not a sporadic imperfection in logic, but played a vital role in the police capacity to carry out the raid, the lawyer's capacity to defend, and the judge's capacity to rule. Below, I examine three examples: first, *careless thinking* on the part of the police officers carrying out the raid; second, *limited thinking* of both judge and defence lawyer in upholding the ban on cross-gender strip searches; and third, the judge's *refusal to know* when determining matters of relevance.

QUEERLY UNTHINKING COPS: THE PRIVILEGE OF UNKNOWING

Discourses of limited thinking played a key role in the police justification for using male officers to search a women's bathhouse. As lead detective Dave Wilson testified in court, *it did not occur to him* that using male officers might be upsetting for bathhouse patrons; he simply assumed entitlement to gaze upon semi-naked bodies *(R. v Hornick Proceedings,* 23 Oct. 2001: 82, 90, 118). Here, lack of thought denotes carelessness. Wilson's actions reflect lack of attentiveness, failure to deliberate, negligence and obliviousness. Whether Wilson actually failed to consider the feelings of bathhouse patrons or simply dismissed them, he used discourses of careless thought as an alibi (i.e., 'I didn't know I was causing harm'). These claims of ignorance, which Sedgwick calls 'the privilege of unknowing', are not simply a lack of knowledge, but an epistemological position which enables otherwise unacceptable practices to occur (Howe, 2000; Sedgwick, 1990: 5).

Wilson's ignorance also blurred into wilful unknowing. When asked why he did not seek additional female officers to conduct the raid, Wilson again claimed limited knowledge:

> *Addario [Lawyer]:* Would you agree with me that the investigation conducted by the men on your crew could have been conducted equally well by qualified female members of the Toronto Police Service?
>
> *Wilson:* I don't think so.
>
> *Addario:* Why not?
>
> *Wilson:* I knew the capabilities of these officers that were with me at the time. I couldn't certainly speak to the officers that you're speaking of, somebody's who's qualified, that doesn't necessarily mean they've got the same professionalism, integrity that my officers did ...

Addario: Are you telling us that there were no female members of the force who would qualify to conduct the type of investigation that was done that evening?

Wilson: Qualified, no, I wouldn't know. There may have been.

Addario: You don't know because you didn't call around to see who was available.

Wilson: Correct …

Addario: —what I'm asking you about is whether or not you're suggesting that there aren't women on the Toronto Police Service who are capable of behaving professionally and with integrity on an investigation?

Wilson: Perhaps.

Addario: You just don't know?

Wilson: That's right.

(*R. v Hornick Proceedings,* 23 Oct. 2001: 90–1, 95)

Wilson's limited knowledge serves multiple functions in this exchange. Wilson relies on his own ignorance (not knowing if there were qualified females) to justify using male rather than female officers. His logic is also contingent upon an association between uncertainty and risk; Wilson claims that choosing male officers he 'knows' is a better guarantor of professionalism than seeking female officers whom he 'doesn't know'. Uncertainty serves another function in this passage: evasiveness. Claiming to be unaware if there were qualified female officers, Wilson attempts to side-step Addario's accusations of sexism.

Wilson's reliance on tensions between knowing and unknowing proved crucial to the rationale that officially governed his actions. When further questioned on his decision to conduct the raid with male officers, Wilson testified that his officers had a 'special knowledge' of the Church and Wellesley community, an area in downtown Toronto known as the 'gay village' (*R. v Hornick Proceedings,* 23 Oct. 2001: 91).[6] Wilson noted his officers had several years experience in the community, having undertaken previous investigations at local establishments, namely the Bijou Club and the Barn (men's sex bars). Wilson claimed this experience gave his officers special 'expertise', 'where other qualified … officers, scholastically might be prepared to do a liquor inspection, [but] practically speaking they wouldn't do as good a job' (*R. v Hornick Proceedings,* 23 Oct. 2001: 90, 93). Yet Wilson's logic was spectacularly circular, revealing a striking combination of naïve ignorance and unguarded arrogance. According to Wilson, if women went to a bathhouse where there is sex but no men, they must be lesbians; if they were lesbians, they must be from the Church and Wellesley community; if from Church and Wellesley, then expertise about gay male residents in the area applies (*R. v Hornick Proceedings,* 23 Oct. 2001: 90–3). It did not occur to Wilson that non-lesbian-identified women might have sex with other women, that lesbians (or other bathhouse patrons) reside outside the Church and Wellesley area, or that lesbians might require different policing responses than gay men. For Wilson, the ability to conduct a proper investigation came not simply from knowing the law, but from knowing his target subjects, even if that knowledge was blatantly spurious.

So well did Wilson 'know' the bodies of the bathhouse patrons, he claimed not to be looking at them at all. Indeed, Wilson and his officers did not consider the investigation to be equivalent to a strip search; officers claimed to be searching a space rather than bodies (*R. v Hornick,* 2002:

para. 61). Wilson described himself as undertaking a 'verbal liquor inspection' as though he questioned women without looking at their bodies (*R. v Hornick Proceedings*, 23 Oct. 2001: 71). Evident here are key tensions between knowing and not knowing: Wilson emphasized his 'expertise' regarding the Church and Wellesley community to justify the inspection, but simultaneously claimed not to know what would occur at the bathhouse to counter the argument that he should have known to send female officers. Both his expertise and his ignorance served as the 'rational' foundation to justify his actions.

LIMITED THINKING IN THE COURTROOM: UPHOLDING THE CROSS-GENDER SEARCH BAN

The crux of the final ruling in *R. v Hornick* lies in a simple legal ban on cross-gender searches, whereby men cannot strip search women and vice versa. Yet the capacity to apply this principle in the bathhouse case required wilful ignorance of the rationale behind such a ban, as well as deliberate bracketing of sexual and gender identities. Judge Hryn never elaborated on the reasons for the ban; he simply proclaimed 'policy and law clearly sets out that a male on female strip search is wrong'(*R. v Hornick*, 2002: para. 83). The policy and law referenced by Hryn offer little elucidation; neither the acts, the case law nor academic articles provide any explanation for the ban on cross-gender searches (Newman, 1999; *R. v Flintoff*, 1998; *R. v Mattis*, 1998). Even the Arbour Inquiry, which dealt specifically with male-on-female searches, provides no clear rationale, other than a vague reference to societal intolerance for the presence of 'non-intimate members of the opposite sex during the performance of private functions'(*Arbour Inquiry*, 1996: section 2.4).[7]

Only one case sheds light on the reasons for the prohibition, but it is noted within a Toronto Police Services report, and not directly cited by Hryn (Lyons, 1999: 4–5). In *Conway v Attorney General of Canada* (also cited as *Weatherall*), the Supreme Court recognized differential power relations among men and women as well as the 'historical trend' of male violence against women as a justification for prohibiting men from searching women in prison, but not vice versa (*Weatherall*, 1993). However, *Weatherall* is not considered authoritative on searches, as it concerned 'pat-down' searches (rather than strip searches, which were the issue in *Hornick*) and it involved prisoners who are subject to reduced privacy rights. Moreover, the strip-search policies applicable in *Hornick* were implemented subsequent to the *Weatherall* decision and prohibit *all* cross-gender strip searches, not just searches of women by men.

On the surface, then, 'gender' functions as the official regulatory boundary for the strip-search policy. Yet, as Judge Hryn's comments made clear, 'sexuality' is also at stake. Hryn not only ruled that the bathhouse raid constituted the 'functional equivalent of a strip search' but likened male officers' conduct to 'visual rape'(*R. v Hornick*, 2002: para. 45, 80). Hryn did not denote a particular way of looking as the source of the rights breach (e.g., police ogled patrons); rather, the violation arose simply because male officers had seen semi-nude women without consent. Implicit in the rape analogy is a presumed heterosexuality; the male gaze upon the female body is deemed dangerous because it is sexualized. Hence, it is not simply gender that governs the ban on cross-gender searches, but also sexuality.

Yet this sexuality-based rationale is limited in so far as it cannot reconcile non-heterosexualities.

If, for example, the male officers were gay and sexually uninterested in the women, would the gaze be considered benign and the search considered lawful? Conversely, would the gaze of a lesbian police officer upon a lesbian body constitute a similar form of 'visual rape'? One of the undercover officers who investigated the bathhouse prior to the arrival of the male officers did in fact identify as lesbian, thus disrupting the ban's heteronormative logic (Millar, 2002). Here a paradox emerges, for the court draws upon sexuality to justify the ban on cross-gender searches, but cannot consider sexuality outside of heteronormativity, lest its logic unravel. Applying the ban thus requires that non-heterosexuality become invisible and unintelligible.

The application of the cross-gender ban is further challenged by the presence of transgender men at the bathhouse. If the ban is taken seriously, then male officers could not conduct the search as it would violate the rights of female patrons, and female officers could not conduct the search as it would violate the rights of male-identified transgender patrons. Since both male-to-female transwomen and female-to-male transmen were present at the bathhouse, the search paradox arises regardless of how one legally recognizes transgender identity. Hence, even if sexuality is set aside, a purely gender-based prohibition is troubled by the presence of transgender persons.[8] Accordingly, the court could not formally recognize the presence of transgender men at the bathhouse; transmen had to be absorbed into the female social body.[9]

Unpacking the ban on cross-gender searches reveals what feminists, transgender and queer theorists have long argued: namely that sex, gender and sexuality are not discrete categories, but are inextricably bound up with one another, each concept relying on the others for its logic. The rationale of the ban thereby functions only when given coherence through a male/female binary governed by a presumed heterosexuality. Queer and transgender identities exceed the ban's logic, thereby becoming legally unintelligible.

MATTERS OF LEGAL 'RELEVANCE': REFUSING TO KNOW, UNWILLING TO THINK

> *Don't ask; You shouldn't know.* It didn't happen; it doesn't make any difference; it didn't mean anything; it doesn't have interpretive consequences. Stop asking just here; stop asking just now ... it makes no difference; it doesn't mean. (Sedgwick, 1990: 53)

While Detective Wilson relied on discourses of 'ignorance' to justify his actions, the judge could not make similar claims. Since the presence of transgender persons and the sexuality of bathhouse patrons were explicitly discussed during the witness proceedings, the court was well informed of these facts. To exclude these matters, however, the court need not render them unintelligible; the judge could simply dismiss such details as irrelevant. To render sexuality as inconsequential rather than inappropriate side-steps controversies over imposed morality and reinstalls claims of judicial objectivity. Perhaps seeking to avoid potential accusations of homophobia (under the assumption that if one does not acknowledge identity-based differences, one cannot be accused of discriminating against them), the judge did not want to utter the word 'lesbian' in court (Valverde, 2003: 71, 82, 97). Indeed, Hryn expressed discomfort stating aloud the words 'Pussy Palace', perhaps symptomatic of another kind of unknowing—a deliberate distancing from knowledge that 'one doesn't know because one shouldn't know' (Cooper, 2006: 934).

Such epistemological distancing also characterizes the rationale of 'relevance' albeit in less moralistic terms. Deciding something is irrelevant marks an intentional setting aside of knowledge, a deliberate refusal to know or consider. Irrelevant details are purposefully cast aside lest they confuse, complicate or contaminate more significant facts. Accordingly, the curious absence of references in the final ruling to transgender, lesbian and queer sexuality would seem perfectly reasonable to the court: such details were simply inconsequential.

Indeed, one might argue that the presence of trans people at the bathhouse was legally irrelevant because the individuals charged were not (according to the court) trans-identified. The crown made a similar claim, arguing the defendants were never seen by male officers in a state of undress and therefore could not seek remedy under the Charter. However, Judge Hryn rejected this argument, stating that the expectation of privacy was not limited to the organizer's personal state of dress, but extended to the event as a whole.

According to Hryn, the event 'by definition would have nude or partially nude women present exploring their sexuality with the expectation that men were excluded'(R. v Hornick, 2002: para. 54). Hyrn's language choice is significant; he carefully extends privacy rights to other patrons, while sidestepping any reference to transgender persons. Whether Hryn deliberately excluded transgender people here, or simply failed to consider their presence, the effect is the same; transgender bodies were located outside the realm of thinkability, and thereby rendered invisible.

No doubt the judge would deny he had engaged in any form of censorship. In one sense this is correct, for the judgment does not constitute conventional repression of queer gender and sexuality. Ultimately, the ruling chastised police rather than bathhouse patrons. However, the court's refusal to speak about queer bodies and sexualities reflects a more subtle kind of prohibition, one perhaps more insidious. Limited thought did not take the form of 'irrational' homophobia or explicitly transphobic logic, but arose within carefully argued legal rationalities. The very act of sorting through evidence, a crucial component of any judgment, marked a form of limited thinking that is deeply imbedded within legal processes. Such modes of thinking foreclose particular questions before they are even asked. The danger of such epistemological prohibition lies in its apparent reasonableness.

CONCLUSION

R. v Hornick provides an important case study for examining the legal regulation of bodies and sexualities through modes of invisibility and unthinkability, particularly because Canada is frequently revered for its embrace of lesbian, gay and (to a lesser extent) transgender rights. However, these regulatory trends arguably persist elsewhere. The West Australian Gender Reassignment Act 2000, for example, offers legal protection to post-operative transgender persons, but excludes those who are pre- and non-operative, thus rendering them legally invisible (Sharpe, 2002: 189). The UK's Gender Recognition Act 2004 does not necessarily demand surgery, but requires 'permanent crossing' from one gender to another, thereby denying recognition to transgender persons who shift between or contest the male/female binary (Sandland, 2005: 48-50; Sharpe, 2007: 71). In the US, current federal prison policy refuses to recognize any gender change (such that transgender men are placed in women's prisons and transgender women are placed in men's prisons at huge risk to their safety), signalling a particularly violent form of denial (Spade, 2008). The numerous jurisdictions that have annulled marriages involving transgender persons provide further examples of wilful ignorance. Unlike divorce, which declares the end of a marital relationship, annulment denies one ever existed (Flynn, 2006: 39). The UK Civil Partnership Act 2004 extends a marriage model to same-sex couples, but does so on the condition of sexual erasure; the act removes the consummation requirement and excludes adultery as grounds for divorce. The government noted that consummation and adultery each have 'a specific meaning within the context of heterosexual relationships and it *would not be possible* nor desirable to read this across to same-sex civil partnerships' (quoted in Stychin, 2006: 907, my emphasis). Although the absence of sex in the Act may be politically desirable for other reasons (see Barker, 2006), the legal 'impossibility' of same-sex consummation and adultery arguably marks a refusal to think of sex beyond heterosexual penetration (Stychin, 2006: 907). These examples suggest that despite winning important legal gains, lesbian and transgender bodies and sexualities often remain unthinkable in law.

Although I have mapped the ways in which limited thinking and knowing produce invisibility as both effect and mode of regulation, I do not wish to suggest that promoting visibility is a necessary or desirable antidote. Indeed, queer visibility in the legal domain has often led to criminalization and social stigma. The infamous *R. v Brown* (1993), which involved private consensual acts of sadomasochism among gay men, provides a UK case in point, where the hypervisibility of gay male sexuality not only invoked a pathologized queer body, but resulted in job loss, social hardship and imprisonment (Moran, 1995: 225; Stychin, 1995: Chap. 7). Even when legal visibility does not invoke punishment, recognition-based politics can facilitate other undesirable consequences, such as assimilation of transgressive practices or entrenchment of new normative hierarchies. In this sense, '[v]isibility is a trap; it summons surveillance and the law; it provokes voyeurism, fetishism, the colonialist/imperial appetite for possession' (Phelan, 1998: 6). More importantly, as Evelynn Hammonds argues, 'visibility in and of itself does not erase a history of silence nor does it challenge the structure of power and domination, symbolic and material, that determines what can and cannot be seen' (Hammonds, 1994: 141). Accordingly, a bathhouse judgment that recognized the embodied, sexual identities of lesbian and transgender patrons may not have been more politically advantageous than the judgment that was delivered.

Moreover, the boundaries between visibility and invisibility, and between thinkability and unthinkability are highly fraught, with unpredictable and often conflicting effects. The bathhouse raid generated public attention, which furthered the organizers' goal of making queer sexuality more visible, even though the terms of that visibility were considerably 'flattened' by both court and media (Bain and Nash, 2007: 27–30). Similarly, the ruling will likely deter future raids, even though it ultimately affirmed the state's right to intrude upon queer sexual spaces. Just as increased visibility of queer identities can usher in new forms of political freedom *and* enable more intensive regulation, discourses of 'limited thinking' have contradictory and unpredictable effects.

The remedy for 'limited thinking' is not 'better thinking,' but rather a critical interrogation of the conditions that make such rationalities possible. The task is not only to expose the process by which discourses of ignorance are mobilized as techniques of governance, but to provide a basis upon which to challenge the socio-political consequences and 'truth effects' of such modes of thought (Valverde, 2003: 7). If, as Michael Taussig argues, 'knowing what not to know' is one of the most powerful forms of social knowledge, then paying attention to discourses of unknowing is crucial for contesting normative power relations (Taussig, 1999: 2). The challenge, then, is to seek new ways of disrupting the conditions of knowing and unknowing, to continuously unsettle the terms by which law claims both knowledge and ignorance.

NOTES

1 The Toronto Women's Bathhouse Committee was founded in 1998 by a group of queer activists who wanted to create spaces for women to have 'casual, kinky and public sex' with other women. The Committee has since hosted several events each year, renting gay male bathhouses (which have existed for decades in Toronto) for use by women and transgender persons. Similar women's bathhouses have been hosted in other Canadian cities, including Hamilton and Halifax. See Gallant and Gillis (2001).

2 This is not to diminish the significance of cases where same-sex acts among women were punished by criminal law in Europe and North America (see Crompton, 1981/2; Robson, 1990; Sorainen, 2006).

3 The legal history of sodomy in Britain is itself characterized by wilful ignorance. Not only was sodomy described as 'a crime not fit to be named' but the decision to exclude women from the statute arose from a fear that verbalization of such acts would make otherwise ignorant women aware of, and thereby more prone to engage in, such behaviour. See Valverde (2007) and Arnup (1989).

4 Although the recent decision in *Alliance for Marriage and Family* v *A.A.* (2007) technically involved two lesbian litigants, I have excluded it here because the case reached the Supreme Court solely over a procedural matter of whether an intervener group (Alliance for Marriage and Family) had standing to appeal a lower court decision (which held that two lesbian partners could both be considered as mothers of a child born to one of them, in addition to the parental status of the biological father). The case was dismissed because none of the original parties wished to continue litigation. Even if considered significant, the case nonetheless supports my broader argument about disembodied, desexualized lesbian legal subjects.

5 Thanks to Mariana Valverde for bringing this point to my attention.

6 The Toronto neighbourhood at the intersection of Church and Wellesley Streets is home to many gay-owned businesses, residences and community organizations, as well as the city's annual Gay Pride Parade. While associated with the broader lesbian, gay, bisexual and transgender community, the area is primarily populated by gay men, particularly those who can afford its increasingly high rents.

7 The report notes concerns about sexual harassment and assault by male guards against female prisoners, but nowhere is a direct reason given for the cross-gender ban.

8 Police searches of transgender persons have been subsequently addressed in Ontario law; transgender persons can now choose between male or female officers for search purposes; see Chung (2006).

9 Curiously enough, the term 'trans' appears once in the ruling, perhaps another case of careless thinking, for it suggests the judge did not fully appreciate the implication of recognizing transgender identities. Significantly, it is 'trans' and not 'transgender' or 'transsexual', as these terms would challenge more directly the search policy logic. 'Trans' arguably functions as an empty signifier: a placeholder which denotes formal inclusion, but lacks substantive meaning.

CASES CITED

Alliance for Marriage and Family v *A.A.*, [2007] 3 S.C.R. 124, 2007 SCC 40.

Arbour, Louise. *Commission of Inquiry into Certain Events at the Prison for Women in Kingston. Public Works and Government Services Canada*, 1996.

Bowers v *Hardwick*, 478 U.S. 186 (1986).

Canada (Attorney General) v *Mossop*, [1993] S.C.J. No. 20.

Chamberlain v *Surrey School District No. 36*, [2002] S.C.J. No. 87.

Egan v *Canada*, [1995] S.C.J. No. 43.

Granovsky v *Canada (Minister of Employment and Immigration)*, [2000] S.C.J. No. 29.

Hodge v *Canada (Minister of Human Resources Development)*, [2004] S.C.J. No. 60.

K (Re) 23 O.R. (3d) 679 [1995] O.J. No. 1425.

Little Sister's Book and Art Emporium v *Canada (Minister of Justice)*, [2000] S.C.J. No. 66.

Little Sister's Book and Art Emporium v *Canada (Commissioner of Customs and Revenue)*, [2007] 1 S.C.R. 38, 2007 SCC 2.

M. v *H.*, [1999] S.C.J. No. 23.

Nixon v *Vancouver Rape Relief Society* [2007] 147 C.R.R. (2d) 376 (note), 364 N.R. 394 (note).

R. v *Brown*, [1993] 2 All ER 75.

R. v *Davis*, [1999] S.C.J. No. 67.

R. v *Flintoff* (1998), 126 C.C.C. (3d) 321 (Ont. C.A.).

R. v *Hornick*—Proceedings at Court Before the Honourable Mr Justice P. Hryn (2001) Ontario Court of Justice, Toronto, 22 & 23 October.

R. v *Hornick*, [2002] O.J. No. 1170.

R. v *Mattis* (1998), 20 C.R. (5th) 93 (Ont. Court of Justice).

R. v *O.N.E.*, [2001] S.C.J. No. 74.

R. v *Tremblay*, [1993] 2 S.C.R. 932.

Reference re Same-Sex Marriage, [2004] S.C.J. No. 75.

Towne Cinema Theatres Ltd. v *The Queen*, [1985] 1 S.C.R. 494.

Trinity Western University v *British Columbia College of Teachers*, [2001] S.C.J. No. 32.

Vriend v *Alberta*, [1998] S.C.J. No. 29.

Weatherall v *Canada (Attorney General)*, [1993] 2 S.C.R. 872 [sub nom Conway v Canada].

WIC Radio Ltd. v *Simpson*, 2008 SCC 40.

REFERENCES

Addis, Richard (2000) 'Barging In', *Globe and Mail* 25 September: A12.

Arnup, Katherine (1989) '"Mothers Just Like Others": Lesbians, Divorce, and Child Custody in Canada', *Canadian Journal of Women and the Law* 3: 18–32.

Bain, Alison and Catherine Nash (2007) 'The Toronto Women's Bathhouse Raid: Querying Queer Identities in the Courtroom', *Antipode* 39(1): 17–34.

Barker, Nicola (2006) 'Sex and the Civil Partnership Act: The Future of (Non)Conjugality?', *Feminist Legal Studies* 14(2): 241–59.

Boyd, Susan B. and Claire F.L. Young (2003) '"From Same-Sex to No Sex"? Trends Towards Recognition of (Same-Sex) Relationships in Canada', *Law and Sexuality* 1(3): 757–93.

Chung, Matthew (2006) 'Ontario Upholds Transsexual Rights', *Globe and Mail* 25 May: A2.

Cooper, Davina (2006) 'Active Citizenship and the Governmentality of Local Lesbian and Gay Politics', *Political Geography* 25(8): 921–43.

Cowan, Sharon (2005) '"Gender Is No Substitute for Sex": A Comparative Human Rights Analysis of the Legal Regulation of Sexual Identity', *Feminist Legal Studies* 13(1): 67–96.

Crompton, Louis (1981/2) 'The Myth of Lesbian Impunity: Capital Laws from 1270 to 1791', *Journal of Homosexuality* 6(1/2): 11–25.

Dean, Mitchell (1999/2006) *Governmentality: Power and Rule in Modern Society.* London: Sage.

Durnford, Frank (2005) 'The Mirror Has Many Faces: Recognizing Gender Identity in Canadian Anti-Discrimination Law', *Dalhousie Journal of Legal Studies* 14: 200–20.

findlay, barbara (1999) 'Transsexuals in Canadian Prisons: An Equality Analysis', URL (consulted 18 July 2007): www.barbarafindlay.com/articles/45.pdf

Flynn, Taylor (2006) 'The Ties That (Don't) Bind: Transgender Family Law and the Unmaking of Families', pp. 32–50 in P. Currah, R. M. Juang and S. P. Minter (eds) *Transgender Rights.* Minneapolis: University of Minnesota Press.

Foucault, Michel (1991) 'Governmentality', pp. 87–104 in G. Burchell, C. Gordon and P. Miller (eds) *The Foucault Effect: Studies in Governmentality.* Chicago: University of Chicago Press.

Gallant, Chanelle and Loralee Gillis (2001) 'Pussies Bite Back: The Story of the Women's Bathhouse Raid', *Torquere: Journal of the Lesbian and Gay Studies Association* 3: 152–67.

Gallant, Paul (2000) 'Our Wanking Boys in Blue', *Xtra!* 21 September.

Giese, Rachel (2000) 'Police "Panty Raid" Was All about Sex, Not Crime', *Toronto Star* 12 October: A31.

Gilbert, Sky (2000) 'Bathhouse Raid a Sexist Outrage', *Eye Weekly* 21 September.

Gordon, Colin (1991) 'Governmental Rationality: An Introduction', pp. 1–51 in G. Burchell, C. Gordon and P. Miller (eds) *The Foucault Effect: Studies in Governmentality.* Chicago: University of Chicago Press.

Green, Jamison (1999) 'Look! No, Don't! The Visibility Dilemma for Transsexual Men', pp. 117–31 in K. More and S. Whittle (eds) *Reclaiming Genders: Transsexual Grammars at the Fin de Siecle.* London: Cassell.

Hammonds, Evelynn (1994) 'Black (W)holes and the Geometry of Black Female Sexuality', *Differences: A Journal of Feminist Cultural Studies* 6(2/3): 126–45.

Haraway, Donna (1991) *Simians, Cyborgs, and Women: The Reinvention of Nature.* London: Free Association Books.

Howe, Adrian (2000) 'Homosexual Advances in Law: Murderous Excuse, Pluralized Ignorance and the Privilege of Unknowing', pp. 84–99 in C. Stychin and D. Herman (eds) *Sexuality in the Legal Arena.* London: Athlone Press.

Kinsman, Gary (1996) *The Regulation of Desire: Homo and Hetero Sexualities.* Montreal: Black Rose Books.

Lamble, Sarah (2006) 'The Politics of Policing the Lesbian Body: Contesting Moral and Corporeal Order in the "Pussy Palace" Bathhouse Raid', unpublished Masters research paper, Toronto, Criminology Centre, University of Toronto.

Lloyd, Abigail W. (2005) 'Defining the Human: Are Transgender People Strangers to the Law?', *Berkeley Journal of Gender, Law & Justice* 20: 150–95.

Lyons, Jeffrey S. (1999) 'The Search of Persons—A Position Paper', *Toronto Police Services Board Review—Search of Persons Policy.*

Mann, Rebecca (2006) 'The Treatment of Transgender Prisoners, Not Just an American Problem—A Comparative Analysis of American, Australian, and Canadian Prison Policies Concerning the Treatment of Transgender Prisoners and a "Universal" Recommendation to Improve Treatment', *Law & Sexuality* 15: 91–133.

Mason, Gail (1995) '(Out)Laws: Acts of Proscription in the Sexual Order', pp. 66–88 in M. Thornton (ed.) *Public and Private: Feminist Legal Debates*. Oxford: Oxford University Press.

McGoey, Linsey (2007) 'On the Will to Ignorance in Bureaucracy', *Economy and Society* 36(2): 212–35.

Millar, Cal (2002) 'Lesbian Officer Seen as Traitor after Club Raid', *Toronto Star* 5 June: B7.

Millbank, Jenni (1997) 'Lesbians, Child Custody, and the Long Lingering Gaze of the Law', pp. 280–303 in S. B. Boyd (ed.) *Challenging the Public/Private Divide: Feminism, Law, and Public Policy*. Toronto: University of Toronto Press.

Moran, Leslie J. (1995) 'Violence and the Law: The Case of Sado-Masochism', *Social & Legal Studies* 4(2): 225–51.

Namaste, Viviane (2000) *Invisible Lives: The Erasure of Transsexual and Transgender People*. Chicago: University of Chicago Press.

Newman, Dwight (1999) 'Stripping Matters to their Core: Intrusive Searches of the Person in Canadian Law', *Canadian Criminal Law Review* 4: 85–118.

Ontario Human Rights Commission (1999) 'Towards a Commission Policy on Gender Identity—Discussion Paper', Government of Ontario, Policy and Education Branch.

Phelan, Peggy (1998) *Unmarked: The Politics of Performance*. London: Routledge.

Robson, Ruthann (1990) 'Lesbianism in Anglo-European Legal History', *Wisconsin Women's Law Journal* 5: 1–42.

Robson, Ruthann (1992) *Lesbian (Out)Law: Survival Under the Rule of Law*. Ithaca, NY: Firebrand Books.

Rose, Nikolas (1999/2004) *Powers of Freedom*. Cambridge: Cambridge University Press.

Sandland, Ralph (2005) 'Feminism and the Gender Recognition Act 2004', *Feminist Legal Studies* 13(1): 43–66.

Sedgwick, Eve Kosofsky (1990) *Epistemology of the Closet*. Berkeley: University of California Press.

Sharpe, Andrew (2002) *Transgender Jurisprudence: Dysphoric Bodies of Law*. London: Cavendish.

Sharpe, Andrew (2007) 'Endless Sex: The Gender Recognition Act 2004 and the Persistence of a Legal Category', *Feminist Legal Studies* 15(1): 57–84.

Smith, Anna Marie (1997) 'The Regulation of Lesbian Sexuality through Erasure: The Case of Jennifer Saunders', pp. 181–97 in J. Dean (ed.) *Feminism and the New Democracy: Resiting the Political*. London: Sage.

Sorainen, Antu (2006) 'Productive Trials: English and Finnish Legislation and Conceptualisations of Same-Sex Sexualities in Course of Trials of Oscar Wilde, Maud Allan, Radclyffe Hall and Herb Grove, from 1885 to 1957', *SQS—Journal for Queer Studies in Finland* 1(1): 17–38.

Spade, Dean (2008) 'Documenting Gender', *Hastings Law Journal* 59(4): 731–822.

Stychin, Carl (1995) *Law's Desire: Sexuality and the Limits of Justice*. London: Routledge.

Stychin, Carl (2006) '"Las Vegas is Not Where We Are": Queer Readings of the Civil Partnership Act', *Political Geography* 25: 899–920.

Taussig, Michael (1999) *Defacement: Public Secrecy and the Labor of the Negative*. Stanford: Stanford University Press.

Valverde, Mariana (2003) *Law's Dream of a Common Knowledge*. Princeton: Princeton University Press.

Valverde, Mariana (2006) 'A New Entity in the History of Sexuality: The Respectable Same-Sex Couple', *Feminist Studies* 32(1): 155–62.

Valverde, Mariana (2007) 'Bodies, Words, Identities: The Moving Targets of the Criminal Law', pp. 224–51 in M. Dubber and L. Farmer (eds) *Modern Histories of Crime and Punishment*. Stanford, CA: Stanford University Press.

Whittle, Stephen (1999) 'Introduction', pp. 6–11 in K. More and S. Whittle (eds) *Reclaiming Genders: Transsexual Grammars at the Fin de Siècle*. London: Cassell.

Whittle, Stephen (2002) *Respect and Equality: Transsexual and Transgender Rights*. London: Cavendish.

CHAPTER 7
Faith, Politics, and the Transformation of Canada

Tom Warner

In recent years, some politicians and commentators have asserted that in order to maintain separation of church and state, legislators should not be influenced by religious belief ... The notion of separation refers to the state not interfering in religious practice and treating all faith communities impartially. It does not mean that faith has no place in public life or the public square.

—Stephen Harper, 2006

Afol fter four decades of concerted political and social action, the modern social conservative movement has experienced more defeats than victories. It has fought a losing battle to stem the tide of secularism, to halt the severing of the historic link between church and state. It has been resoundingly set back in its desperate efforts to reclaim Canada as a staunchly Christian democracy in which the laws, culture, and institutions preserve and promote Judeo-Christian values and identity. Social conservatism has failed in its substantial and persistent efforts to recriminalize abortion. It was defeated in its campaigns to prevent legislated human rights for gays and lesbians, the legal recognition of same-sex relationships, and the state's recognition of same-sex marriage. While the social conservative movement was a leading participant in the successful campaigns to achieve tough child pornography legislation, new criminal offences purportedly to address child sexual exploitation, and an increased age of consent, it was the new morality of rights and equality of treatment, especially as applied to women and children, that formed the basis of new laws to regulate sexual behaviour; it was not the old Christian religious morality. Nevertheless, by continuing to agitate, not just through those intensive campaigns focusing on key issues and through court challenges but also in the political arena proper, social conservatives remain hopeful that eventually the tide may be turned: that Canada will be taken back from the atheists and secularists and restored as a religiously moral state in which God and God's laws have supremacy.

As social conservatives sensed that they were losing control over the moral agenda of the country they sought to increase their influence on the political agenda. Happily for them, in electoral politics they have found no shortage of political support—primarily but not exclusively among the various conservative parties, from the old Progressive Conservative Party through the Reform Party and its successor, the Canadian Alliance, to the united-right Conservative Party of Canada. Indeed, social conservatives were the founders, leaders, and dominant forces within the Reform Party and Canadian Alliance and carried that involvement into the Conservative Party under Stephen Harper.

Just as importantly, social conservatives have constituted an indispensible electoral constituency that can be marshalled at election time to support their favoured candidates. While, as the various opinion polls show, social conservatives represent a minority of Canadians overall, their numbers, strategically dispersed across the country, remain significant. A survey carried out during the 2000 federal election by academics from three Canadian universities indicated that fully 27 per cent of voters identified as social conservative. According to a 2003 poll conducted for the Evangelical Fellowship of Canada, 19 per cent of Protestants and 7 per cent of Catholics identified themselves as "evangelical."[1] As the election of both the Mulroney and Harper governments attest, the path to power requires forming and sustaining a coalition of both social and economic conservatives. That goal in turn requires that close attention be paid to the moral issues that social conservatives view as primary.

In "Rediscovering the Right Agenda," Harper articulated the importance of social conservatives as an electoral constituency. [...] Uniting the right, he emphasized, required re-discovering the conservative agenda, which means that "we must give greater place to social values and social conservatism, broadly defined and properly understood."[2]

Harper's appeal to include social conservatives and their moral issues within a political coalition of the right was also a pragmatic recognition that, as an electoral constituency, social conservatives have been passionately motivated to use partisan politics and the political process to advance their agenda. In contrast, the majority of Canadians are not similarly motivated. A Carleton University study conducted in 2003 found that most Canadians do not feel a similar need to get involved in the political process and generally decline to become politically involved. Indeed, in the years leading up to 2003, the number of Canadians who had attended political rallies, signed petitions, or joined political parties had actually declined.[3] In contrast, members of the social conservative movement in Canada are active in all of these political pursuits, as well as in making financial donations to their political allies.

Social conservatives also have allies among legislators who accept the notion that religious faith should guide public policy decisions. A number of current members of Parliament have publicly expressed the importance of drawing upon their religious faith to influence their political decision-making. [...] The leaders of social conservatism have also encouraged Christians involved in the political process to bring their religious beliefs to that role. In a 2002 edict the Roman Catholic Church commanded Catholics involved in the political process not to espouse "ethical pluralism." It declared, "A well-formed Christian conscience does not permit one to vote for a political program or an individual law which contradicts the fundamental contents of faith and morals."[4] In a 2004 position paper, the Catholic Civil Rights League articulated the obligation of the faithful to follow the laws of God if those rules collide with the laws of the state. [...][5]

Evangelical Protestants have been equally insistent about the imperative of bringing religious faith to political involvement. [...] In a similar vein, the CFAC's [Canada Family Action Coalition] Brian Rushfeldt lambasted governments for promoting the "negative moral and financial consequences of social liberalism." He lamented, "The family—God's fundamental institution for society—is labeled destructive by feminists, discriminatory by homosexuals, outdated and unnecessary by liberals." To address this alarming situation, and to defend "the biblical view of humanity," Rushfeldt encouraged people of faith to become "an elected official or other public servant in your community and influence decision-making."[6]

TOWARDS AN ELECTORAL BREAKTHROUGH

To this end social conservatives have assiduously pursued their objective of regaining control of the moral agenda through activism within conservative political parties—an effort that has been going on since at least the Mulroney years, if not longer. But it was a basic dissatisfaction with the Mulroney government that, in 1987, led social conservatives, especially in Western Canada, to establish the Reform Party, which would more faithfully reflect their ideology, especially in regard to moral issues. Its first leader, Preston Manning, was a fervent evangelical Protestant who with his father Ernest, an evangelist and former Social Credit premier of Alberta, sought the privatization of most services provided by government, including health care, regional development, and education. Those beliefs formed the basis of the Reform Party platform. Reform called for strong opposition to abortion; support for traditional family values and measures to strengthen and support the family unit, which included strong opposition to legislating rights for gays and lesbians; opposition to affirmative action; the cessation of government support for women's and advocacy groups; tightening of immigration laws; opposition to state-funded day care; a reduction in taxes; and the slashing of social assistance programs.[7]

The Reform Party scored a stunning political success in the 1993 federal election campaign. The result was due in no small measure to the shattering of the coalition that had elected Mulroney a decade earlier. The Quebec nationalists had split from the Progressive Conservatives to form the Bloc Quebecois. Angry and disillusioned social conservatives embraced the new Reform Party. [...] Like their leader, Manning, the Reform MPs were, as Brooke Jeffrey noted, "quite unrepresentative of Canadian society as a whole." They were made up of "predominantly older, middle-class, white males." In addition, wrote Jeffrey, "Their religious commitments far exceeded those of legislators from other parties, with at least 40 per cent indicating they were connected with fundamentalist or evangelical religious groups and many of them claiming experience in formal or lay positions."[8] The Reform Party immediately became the preferred political entity of social conservative activists, gaining the support of REAL Women of Canada and other groups. Later, Manning's executive assistant, Darrel Reid, went on to become president of Focus on the Family (Canada).

Still, a couple of elections later the Reform Party had failed to make the electoral breakthrough it needed to become a truly national party. It was not able to attract in any significant numbers the support of economic conservatives in Eastern Canada, especially Ontario, and its support in Quebec was practically nonexistent. Political scientists and the news media held that a major cause for the failure was its social conservative agenda. The party had become identified in the public mind with bigotry and intolerance. Many political conservatives saw this image as an obstacle to the movement to unite the right. In response, Manning and others conceived of a new political party. The Canadian Reform Conservative Alliance, popularly known as the Canadian Alliance, was founded at a convention in March 2000.

The Canadian Alliance proved to be short-lived, lasting only three years and failing, like the Reform Party before it, to establish itself as a national party capable of forming a government. [...] After the calamity of the federal election of 2000, [Stockwell] Day was replaced as leader by fellow evangelical Protestant [Stephen] Harper. Both Day and Harper were massively supported by social conservative groups during their leadership campaigns. Equally important, the Canadian Alliance retained within its ranks a strong social conservative core of former Reform Party MPs.[9]

In late 2003 the Progressive Conservative Party and Canadian Alliance merged to form the Conservative Party of Canada. Social conservative groups organized aggressively to sign up members and to influence both the policies of the new party and the choice of its leader. The Canada Family Action Coalition mounted a campaign urging its members to join the new party to ensure that it opposed same-sex marriage and other "progressive" issues.[10] A few weeks later the Social Conservative Caucus for Members of the Conservative Party of Canada was formed. Its mission was to "bring together various groups such as pro-life and pro-family advocacy organizations." The group would "cross religious lines," including "Muslims, Christians, Jews and even non-religious social conservatives"—anyone who shared objectives on issues such as gay marriage, the defeat of legislation such as Bill C-250 [the amendment to the Criminal Code on hate crimes to include sexual orientation], euthanasia, and abortion. "United we can ensure that the values we all share are recognized and adequately represented." One of the organization's stated objectives was to recruit as many social conservatives as possible to become members of the Conservative Party during the leadership campaign and policy discussions.[11] These efforts were rewarded not just through the election of Harper to party leadership, but by the party's official policy statements. The party decided, among other concessions to social conservative sentiment, to make a commitment to give Parliament, not the courts, the final decision on issues such as marriage.

Conservative Party candidates in the 2004 election also reflected the strong social conservative bent of the new party. Ottawa-area candidate Cheryl Gallant stated that abortions were "absolutely no different" from a recent beheading of a hostage in Iraq by Islamic militants. [...] Other Conservative candidates [...] promised that bilingual services would be reduced by a Conservative government, and suggested that women considering abortions should first seek out independent counselling.[12] Although the election returned the Liberals to power with a fragile minority government, the new Conservative Party formed the official opposition and stood as the only other party in Parliament with a realistic chance of forming a government.

At the party's grassroots level, an intense battle erupted between social moderates and social conservatives over policy. The first policy conference, held in early 2005, featured organizing by social conservatives to secure the party's support for policies opposing abortion and for an opposite-sex definition of marriage. The Campaign Life Coalition and REAL Women, among other groups, urged their members to become involved in the party and to secure election as delegates to the policy conference. REAL Women exhorted its supporters to resist the efforts of the "Red Tories" to move the new party towards the centre of the political spectrum. That tendency must be stopped, the group said, by "ensuring that the Conservative National Convention in Montreal in March is filled with true conservatives who are prepared to stand up for genuine conservative values."[13] In the end the social conservatives lost on the abortion question. The party members pledged that a Conservative government would not introduce a new law to ban abortions. But the social conservative faction scored a victory on same-sex marriage. The party committed itself to holding a free vote in Parliament on the question of defining marriage in law as the union of one man and one woman.

The battle within the party continued at the local constituency level as prominent social conservatives were nominated to be Conservative Party candidates in the next election. In British Columbia, Darrel Reid and Cindy Silver, a former executive director of Christian Legal Fellowship, were elected as candidates. Rondo Thomas, an official with the Canadian Christian College, and David Sweet, former president of Promise Keepers, secured Conservative nominations in Ontario. So too did Harold Albrecht, a Kitchener, Ontario, evangelical pastor. In a letter sent to his local newspaper, Albrecht had charged that recognition of same-sex marriage would destroy society within a generation. In Nova Scotia the party nominated three candidates, including a church minister, who had received strong public support from Tristan Emmanuel, the head of a new social conservative group called Equipping Christians for the Public Square.[14]

During the 2006 federal election the Conservative Party made a number of commitments intended to retain the support of its social conservative constituency. It was on the very first day of the election campaign that Harper made his promise about the holding of a free vote on whether or not the same-sex marriage law adopted by the Liberals should be overturned and replaced with a law stating that marriage would be limited to opposite sex couples. He restated his intention that, upon receiving a positive outcome from such a vote, the government would establish a new category of civil union for same-sex couples.[15] The Conservatives also campaigned on other policies designed to appeal to social conservative electors: increasing the age of consent for sexual activity to sixteen years (from fourteen years) and to ending "all defence loopholes for child pornography." Focus on the Family, Canada Family Action Coalition, and Evangelical Fellowship of Canada had aggressively promoted both measures. Similarly, the Conservative child-care policy catered strongly to social conservatives. […][16]

Despite these manoeuvres, the Conservatives succeeded in presenting Harper as a moderate conservative, as someone who was not an extremist on social issues and looked "prime ministerial." The party strategists effectively muzzled the social conservative ideologues, and rumblings about activist judges, threats to recriminalize abortion, and even the policy to repeal the same-sex marriage law were noticeably absent in the rest of the campaign. The strategy succeeded: the Conservatives won enough votes to secure a minority government. […] Outright expressions of concern about what a Conservative government would do on social issues were replaced, for many Canadians, with a more benign suspicion that perhaps Harper and his crew of evangelical Christians had a hidden agenda that would be revealed only after they took command of government.

That suspicion remained a feature of public discourse following the election and was certainly not alleviated by the exultant nature of social conservative commentary on the outcome of the vote. For social conservatives, the arrival of the Harper government presented the prospect of securing victory over the secularists, social engineers, and activist judiciary who had brought the country so perilously close to ruin. Noting that about thirty Liberal MPs who had voted in favour of same-sex marriage had gone down to defeat in the 2006 election, [Charles] McVety declared the outcome a "tremendous victory for families nationwide … and a great victory for marriage." The Catholic Civil Rights League's [Philip] Horgan noted pointedly in a press release, "The League, our individual members, and our colleagues in inter-faith coalitions, devoted a great deal of time and effort to electing candidates who support the traditional definition of marriage, and whose views on moral issues are in line with those of the majority of Canadians." The EFC [Evangelical Fellowship of Canada] also expressed optimism about the new Conservative regime. "We now have a government that will be more sympathetic to a number of the issues of concern to evangelicals," [Bruce] Clemenger [President, EFC] stated. For [Brian] Rushfeldt [Executive Director, EFC] the election of the Conservative government opened up the prospect of reclaiming the moral agenda: "Let us build on the hope that Election 2006 gave us for change in the moral and spiritual levels of Canada."[17]

THE SOCIAL CONSERVATIVES IN POWER
After assuming office as prime minister, Harper kept his election promises. The motion on same-sex marriage was introduced in the House of Commons but defeated as a result of the combined opposition of the other parties. Harper's government also moved quickly to introduce legislation to increase the age of consent for sexual activity to sixteen years from fourteen years, a move that Janet Epp Buckingham of the EFC saluted: "We took it as a message that we were being heard."[18] [...]

*****

The Harper government also dismantled some of the federally funded, socially liberal, and secularist infrastructure that it and its social conservative constituents had long attacked. They ended the world-renowned Law Commission of Canada, which had over many years generated a significant volume of studies and reports calling for a modernization of Canada's laws, including those that criminalize various forms of consensual sex. In 2001 the Law Commission had produced a ground-breaking report, *Beyond Conjugality*, which recommended that the federal government review the laws dealing with recognizing and supporting close personal adult relationships to ensure that they reflected the diversity of conditions in modern-day Canada. Social conservatives had branded the Commission as "anti-family."

Also axed was the Court Challenges Program, which provided funding for legal challenges alleging that a law or government policy contravened the equality rights guaranteed in the

Charter. The program had invoked the wrath of social conservative groups because it had, in particular, provided funding to a number of successful Charter challenge cases launched by gays and lesbians to strike down discriminatory laws, including the laws that gave legal recognition only to opposite-sex spousal relationships. The decision to kill the program was clearly driven by the ideology of the Harper government and not by economics. The budget for the program was, in government terms, insignificant at $5.6 million annually, especially in a time when the government had a $13-billion budget surplus. Yet the impact of the program in helping to reshape modern Canada in the age of Charter rights had been profound.

*****

Ideology, whether of a social conservative bent or one that simply despised government funding for social service and equity programs—especially those focused on equality for women or that were directed towards queer communities—manifested itself in other Harper government decisions. The Canadian Rainbow Health Coalition (CRHC), established to advocate for better access to health care for gay, lesbian, bisexual, and transgendered (LGBT) communities, issued urgent fundraising appeals in 2007 as a result of being confronted with the removal of federal government funding. Under the previous Liberal government, CRHC had received funding for a multi-year project to conduct education into health issues for LGBT communities and to provide resource materials for health-care professionals and organizations. But CRHC was unable to obtain funding under the Harper government to continue the project. [...] "Homophobia is rife within the federal government and the federal bureaucracy," wrote Gens Hellquist, CRHC's executive director, in a November 2007 fundraising letter. "Those few programs that have benefited our communities in the past have been cut or will be cut in the next budget."[19]

Ideological considerations also appear to have led in 2007 to reduced funding for HIV/AIDS community education programs in Ontario. The Harper government defended its action as part of its overall objective to reduce spending by realigning federal government investments. The added factor cited by the government was its commitment to fund research into an AIDS vaccine by the Bill & Melinda Gates Foundation. However, the principles of the Foundation required that donations to it by governments not result in a reduction of existing funding for AIDS programs and the Harper government was breaking those principles. The cuts, amounting to 30 per cent of total federal government funding of HIV/AIDS programs in Ontario, would, according to AIDS organizations, have their most severe impact on the gay male population, which had become the focus of renewed education efforts aimed at reversing an increase in the rate of HIV/AIDS. Other changes to federal funding provisions introduced by the Harper government had resulted in the loss of funding for operating AIDS organizations, with the focus being placed instead on funding certain kinds of projects. Funding had been removed, for instance, from the Legal, Ethical and Human Rights Fund of the Canadian HIV/ AIDS Legal Network.[20]

For the Harper government it was neither necessary nor politically advisable to articulate in anything other than fiscal terms its funding policies in relation to women's organizations that had a feminist bent, to gay and lesbian organizations, or to HIV/AIDS organizations. There was no political advantage in admitting that it was targeting certain groups and communities because of a strong social conservative tendency or even as a way of placating its most fervent social conservative supporters. The members of that important constituency would know what was motivating the cuts to programs, and would applaud those measures; and there was little likelihood that any of the groups or communities hurt by the funding cuts would in any significant way be or become supporters or allies of the Harper Conservatives. Few votes would be lost through such actions. The cutting of government funding of programs and projects is simply one of the many ways in which an ideological agenda can be effectively advanced without the need to introduce legislation or seek the approval of the electorate. It can also be defended as fiscally prudent. Moreover, it is also an effective means of helping social conservatives in their constant struggle against secularism and immorality.

In December 2006 the Harper government once more placed the interests of social conservatives in the foreground when it appointed members of the board of assisted Human Reproduction Canada, a federal agency established to influence Parliament and medical practice on issues of fertility treatments and research on human embryonic stem cells. The appointments to Assisted Human Reproduction Canada were especially concerning given the strident advocacy of social conservative groups on the issues of reproductive technologies, or assisted human reproduction, and research into the use of embryonic stem cells. [...][21]

The EFC has actively lobbied for stringent laws dealing with reproductive technologies. In successive briefs and submissions to the federal government, the organization has argued that Parliament should protect the dignity of every human life, which "includes prohibiting research on human zygotes and embryos, in addition to adopting legislative terminology which reflects respect for human dignity." The group has also been adamant in opposing sperm donations: "One reproductive practice we find objectionable is that of sperm 'donation,' particularly anonymous sperm donation, which breaks biological ties and denies children the answers to basic questions of identity." [...][22]

Similarly, Harper's government moved, in a small but symbolic way, to address the evil of judicial activism. In September 2006 Harper appointed a prominent social conservative lawyer, David Brown, as a judge on the Ontario Superior Court. Brown had represented social conservative groups in a number of anti-abortion and anti-gay rights interventions in significant court cases in recent years. Among those groups was the Association for Marriage and the Family in Ontario, which opposed a challenge by same-sex couples to the legal definition of marriage. [...]

*****

THE IMPORTANCE OF BEING INCREMENTAL

The various actions of the Harper government led to considerable speculation on what it all meant for the future of social conservatism. In that regard, some insight might be gleaned by looking once more at Harper's musings in "Rediscovering the Right Agenda."

"We must realize that real gains are inevitably incremental," Harper wrote. "This, in my experience, is harder for social conservatives than for economic conservatives. The explicitly moral orientation of social conservatives makes it difficult for many to accept the incremental approach. Yet, in democratic politics, any other approach will certainly fail.... Conservatives should be satisfied if the agenda is moving in the right direction, even if slowly."[23]

If incrementalism is indeed Harper's strategy, but the real agenda remains, as he stated, one of "social values," clearly there are grounds for concern among those who have a different vision for the future of the country.

Clearly, as well, the path taken by the movement must continue to appeal to a broad spectrum of conservatives, whose unity and support are essential to the long-term success of Harper's Conservative Party. [...] Proposing an agenda for Conservative electoral success in tellingly biblical terms—a "Ten Commandments of Conservative Campaigning"—Tom Flanagan, one of Harper's ideological mentors and his chief campaign organizer, observed: "Canada is not yet a conservative or Conservative country. We can't win if we veer too far to the right of the median voter." The task of conservatives and Conservatives over time, he contended, is to preserve the "traditional Conservative base of Anglophone Protestants" and draw in "Francophones, Roman Catholics (44 per cent in the 2001 Census of Canada), and other racial and religious groups." Echoing Harper's call for incrementalism, Flanagan declared, "We have to be willing to progress in small, practical steps." Noting approvingly that "incrementalism has marked Harper's leadership throughout," Flanagan lauded it as "intrinsically the right approach for a conservative party."[24]

[...] Harper and his cohort believe that through many small and possibly imperceptible steps—what Flanagan has termed "small conservative reforms [that] are less likely to scare voters than grand conservative schemes"—Canada can be transformed from a socially liberal into a socially conservative country.[25] That is the real objective—and in pursuit of that goal, issues such as same-sex marriage and abortion that may no longer have any immediate political traction will be replaced with a range of other issues or initiatives, presented as seemingly moderate and unthreatening.

Social conservatives have not universally embraced incrementalism. Some see it as simply a cynical and opportunistic political tactic to avoid taking stands on the issues that are most of concern to them. Despite the Harper government's various initiatives, these social conservatives have remained sceptical about the veracity of the administration's commitment to their values and issues. They have cited in particular the capitulation on the same-sex marriage legislation, the failure to take a strong stance in opposition to abortion, and a refusal to support pro-life legislation. That scepticism was expressed publicly in the months prior to the 2008 federal election. A March 2008 editorial in *Catholic Insight* contained a blunt warning for Harper. [...] In any upcoming election, the editorial declared, "These topics should be front and centre in the questioning of candidates. If answers are not forthcoming, moves should be made for replacement of Stephen Harper as party leader."[26]

A few weeks later Charles McVety pointed out that "the honeymoon" with Harper had "ended quite quickly" after the defeat of the same-sex marriage resolution and the prime minister's declaration that the issue was closed.[27] [...]

*****

Confronted with growing disenchantment within his social conservative constituency,

Harper persisted in promoting incrementalism as the way of achieving Canada's transformation into a conservative country. During the 2008 federal election campaign he told *Maclean's* magazine that the long-term objective was to hold his conservative coalition together and "to make Conservatives the natural governing party of the country." They needed, he said, "to pull conservatives, to pull the party, to the centre of the political spectrum. But what you also have to do, if you're really serious about making transformation, is you have to pull the centre of the political spectrum toward conservatism." [...] He declared, "We are also building the country towards a definition of itself that is more in line with conservatism."[28]

Most social conservatives apparently took solace from Harper's comments. The Prime Minister seemed to be speaking in code that they readily understood. He offered assurance that in the long term his government's objective of moving the political spectrum rightward included facilitation of an incremental shift in the national ethos to social conservatism, which would occur through the restoration of pride in the national institutions and the history of the old Christian Canada. In the end, enough social conservatives stuck with Harper and his Conservative Party to help ensure re-election, albeit without the majority that party members so desperately wanted.

The objective of casting Canadian values and identity in more traditional and conservative hues featured prominently in one of the government's more significant initiatives following re-election. Citizenship and Immigration Minister Jason Kenney put it forth that the government was reviewing the content of the civic literacy questions used on the test written by persons applying to become Canadian citizens—"with a mind to improving the test to ensure that it demonstrates a real knowledge of Canadian institutions, values, and symbols, and history."[29]

In fall 2009 Kenney introduced a new study guide for the citizenship test that placed a renewed emphasis on the importance of Christianity and religious faith in the development of "a common Canadian identity." *Discover Canada: The Rights and Responsibilities of Citizenship* noted that "the great majority of Canadians identify as Christians," while acknowledging in passing that members of other religions "as well as atheists" were increasing in numbers. Using language that undoubtedly appealed to ardent social conservatives, the guide emphasized, "In Canada the state has traditionally partnered with faith communities to promote social welfare, harmony and mutual respect; to provide schools and health care; to resettle refugees; and to uphold religious freedom and freedom of conscience." Similarly, the section describing the rights and responsibilities of citizenship presented the Canadian Charter of Rights and Freedoms in a manner that social conservatives would applaud. It noted that the Charter "begins with the words, 'Whereas Canada is founded upon principles that recognize the supremacy of God and the rule of law.' This phrase underlines the importance of religious traditions to Canadian society and the dignity and worth of the human person." In contrast, *Discover Canada* made no mention of the equality rights guaranteed by section 15. It tellingly omitted them from its short listing of the "most important" rights and freedoms set out in the Charter.[30]

The continuing presence of social conservative activists among Harper's circle of closest advisers also provided evidence that fostering social conservatism would remain an important element of the Conservative government's agenda. Early in 2009 Harper appointed Darrel Reid as his deputy chief of staff. Reid had previously served as director of policy, and replacing him in that position was Paul Wilson, a former executive director of Trinity Western University who had worked for Preston Manning and Stockwell Day. In fall 2009 Nigel Hannaford became a speech writer for Harper. As a former columnist with the *Calgary Herald,* Hannaford had championed social conservatism, disparaging equality rights for gays and lesbians and attacking human rights commissions.

These appointments caused alarm in gay and lesbian communities that were already apprehensive about the Harper government's agenda. Helen Kennedy, executive director of Egale Canada, cited the Reid and Wilson appointments as an acknowledgement of what "we've suspected for a long time—that Harper has deep roots with the religious right." She added, "We don't expect to see a lot of favourable recommendations coming out of the PM's office with respect to lesbian, gay, bisexual and trans human rights."[31] [...]

Lesbian and gay activist suspicions about social conservative influence on the Harper government were heightened in June 2009 following controversy generated over a $400,000 federal tourism stimulus grant awarded to help fund the annual pride celebrations in Toronto. The grant, approved and personally presented to Pride Toronto by Diane Ablonczy, the minister of State for Tourism, was condemned by outraged social conservatives. REAL Women urged its supporters to write to Harper and MPs in protest. The Institute for Canadian Values, a social conservative "think tank" launched in 2005 at the instigation of McVety, presented a petition to protest government funding for "sex parades" that added fuel to "a dangerous sex trade." "Unrepentant" conservative spokesperson Joseph Ben-Ami cited the grant as "the latest indication of how detached the Harper Conservatives have become from their key supporters and how incoherent their evolving electoral strategy is as a result." The Harper government, he lamented, "has ignored, obstructed or jettisoned virtually every prudent policy initiative that social conservatives have championed."According to Ben-Ami, the time had come "for rank and file members of the party to let their leaders and elected representatives know that they're mad as hell and they're not going to take it any more." The outcry led to a sharp rebuke of Ablonczy by the Harper government. Conservative MP Brad Trost stated on a pro-life website that the grant was not supported "by a large majority of the MPs," and that Ablonczy was being punished for awarding it. Responsibility for tourism stimulus grants was abruptly taken away from her and given to Industry Minister Tony Clement, who was swift in declaring that the funding program would be reviewed to ensure that "we have value for taxpayer money." Sure enough, shortly afterwards, the Harper government denied a tourism grant for Divers/Cité, Montreal's pride event.[32]

ORGANIZING TO RECLAIM THE MORAL AGENDA

Whatever the immediate strategic objectives of a Conservative government, social conservatives are hopeful that they are on the cusp of achieving a historic retransformation of Canada. For despite the many defeats and setbacks suffered over the last couple of decades, social conservatism in Canada is neither dying nor beaten. It has survived with astonishing resilience and tenacity. Indeed, it seems that the enactment of legislation recognizing same-sex marriage and the many perceived assaults on religious freedom by the courts and human rights commissions have galvanized social conservatives anew. They have spiked their determination to restore Judeo-Christian religious beliefs and moral values as the bedrock of Canada's laws and public policy.

In pursuit of that objective they have cast their eyes to their counterparts in the United States to find the means through which they can reclaim the moral agenda. They see the American social conservative movement as being fabulously successful in controlling the political and social agenda in that country. They hope that by adopting the strategies used south of the border they can enjoy the same degree of success here—although, like Harper, they also believe that the key to their success must also involve incrementalism. REAL Women, in its 2004 polemic "The Silencing of the Conservative Voice in Canada," acknowledged as much, stating: "It may take several generations to institutionalize a rightward trend in Canada. But we have to begin somewhere and it should begin now. Years ago, American conservatives began this journey: Do conservative Canadians have the will to do the same?"[33]

Social conservative and *National Post* scribe Adam Daifallah similarly wrote in a July 2004 opinion piece that what the country needs is "an overt campaign to shift the Canadian political goalposts to the right." The model for doing so, he suggested, could be found in the United States, where conservatives had built a powerful institutional structure. [...][34] The need to build a U.S.–style movement of social conservatism in Canada was also touted in a December 2005 essay published by Paul Tuns of the Christian think tank Work Research Foundation. Tuns suggested that politically viable social conservatism has been absent in Canada primarily because of three interrelated reasons: the lack of a conservative infrastructure such as foundations, think tanks, and publications; the failure to organize and become part of a larger conservative coalition; and Charter-era politics. [...][35]

Social conservative advocates remain optimistic that they will be able to succeed in the long run through continued agitation, public education, and involvement in the political process. Commenting in a December 2007 *Canadian Christianity* online article, Brian Stiller declared, "The pendulum of secularism has swung as far as it can, and now it's in retreat." Bruce Clemenger expressed a similar sentiment: "We are living in a post-Christian society which is secularized yet very religious and highly individualistic. ... In the aftermath of a period of rapid secularization, Canada is searching for a clearer sense of its identity amidst the diversity of culture, race, religion, lifestyle, social and political visions."[36]

Around the same time, Joseph Ben-Ami, then the executive director of the Institute of Canadian Values, proclaimed the determination of social conservatives to fight back against contemporary secularism, which he condemned as a "supremacist, fundamentalist religion." [...][37] Richard Bastien of the Catholic Civil Rights League [...] contended that "Canada, like most other Western countries, has been on the wrong road for quite some time and that our current social model is simply not viable in the long run." Taking a U-turn would be a progressive act resulting in a rediscovery of "the permanent human virtues" without which "no democracy can survive."[38]

Conservative mainstay Preston Manning [...] weighed in, expressing optimism that social conservatives had it within their power to gain control of the political agenda in the long run. They could do so by presenting a more moderate image and adopting more pragmatic tactics that would allow them to successfully navigate "the faith/political interface." The first step, according to Manning, must be "'legitimating the discussion' of faith-based convictions and issues in the Canadian political arena, including Parliament and the legislatures." [...][39]

*****

Canada is now indeed witnessing the persistent building of an organizational infrastructure that will support and sustain a social conservative resurgence. New political action groups and think tanks have formed. They join with and in some instances are spawned by the more established groups. Their mandates revolve around the challenge of restoring the union of church and state. One such group is the web-based Social Conservatives United. Founded in August 2006 by John Pacheco, a Catholic anti-gay marriage militant, it is dedicated to "faith family freedom." Its objective is to become a "network of social conservative groups to advance the principles of social conservatism in Canada through political and social activism." Another online venture, *C2C: Canada's Journal of Ideas,* launched in 2007, publishes quarterly issues containing analysis and opinion on both economic and social conservatism. Preponderantly made up of lawyers, academics, and journalists, *C2C's* editorial and advisory boards are a who's who of Canadian conservatism. They include Preston Manning, Tom Flanagan, Adam Daifallah, and David Frum (prominent North American social conservative and former speech writer for George W. Bush). Some have also served as policy advisers or political aides to conservative politicians.[40]

The more prominent Manning Centre for Building Democracy, founded in 2005 by Preston Manning, is another instance of the social conservative effort to promote both an active engagement in the political process and the construction of an infrastructure to enable movement members to do so. The Centre's mission is "the creation of a democratic society in Canada whose governments are guided by conservative ideas and principles—individual worth, free markets, freedom of choice, acceptance of responsibility, limited government, and respect for Canada's cultural, religious, and democratic values." Among the Manning Centre's projects is "[a] Faith and Politics program to assist faith-oriented Canadians to better understand, manage and involve themselves responsibly at the interface of faith and politics." The program claims to have partnerships with organizations and individuals within the various faith and cultural communities, faith-based volunteers, media and communication professionals, and others. Its seminars for Christian, Jewish, and Muslim communities have included, as speakers, social conservative politicians at both the federal and provincial levels. [...][41]

Meanwhile, too, the Roman Catholic Church remains adamantly committed to the "evangelization of culture," as dictated by Pope Benedict XVI, and to combating the "the split between the Gospel and culture, with the exclusion of God from the public sphere." In addresses made during a 2006 visit of Canada's Catholic bishops to the Vatican, the Pope lamented: "Certain values detached from their moral roots and full significance found in Christ have evolved in the most disturbing of ways. In the name of 'tolerance' your country has had to endure the folly of the redefinition of spouse, and in the name of 'freedom of choice' it is confronted with the daily destruction of unborn children." Benedict XVI warned about the "false dichotomies" that "are particularly damaging when Christian civic leaders sacrifice the unity of faith and sanction the disintegration of reason and the principles of natural ethics, by yielding to ephemeral social trends and the spurious demands of opinion polls."[42]

Apparently august think tanks and institutes play their part, making a concerted effort to present social conservative values and beliefs to the Canadian public with a patina of academic respectability. McVety's Institute for Canadian Values, for instance, is "dedicated to advancing knowledge of public policy issues from Judeo-Christian intellectual and moral perspectives, as well as promoting awareness of how such perspectives contribute to a modern, free and democratic society."[43]

In February 2006, amidst great fanfare, Focus on the Family also launched its own think tank, the Institute of Marriage and Family Canada, tasked with "presenting solid family-based policy research and ideas to Canada's decision makers."[44] [...] Yet another social conservative thinktank, the Institute for the Study of Marriage, Law and Culture, founded in 2003, includes contributions from high-profile academics who have crusaded against the legalization of same-sex marriage.[45]

*****

The alleged decline of marriage and family remains a critical issue. As Bastien declared, "In addition to being today's major cause of social instability, family breakdown compromises civic freedom." To reduce family breakdown, he stated, young couples needed to be made more aware of the dangers of common-law unions, which are "much less likely to survive the test of time." [...][46]

*****

For social conservatives, the strengthening of marriage and family also involves stronger laws against prostitution and one of its current manifestations, human trafficking. REAL Women, the EFC, and other groups campaigned intensively during 2009 for stronger Criminal Code provisions dealing with human trafficking, linking that issue to the need to retain or strengthen laws against prostitution. Decriminalizing prostitution, they maintained, would only create a social climate in which the trafficking of young girls and women would proliferate.[47]

The social conservative agenda also includes the abolition of the despised human rights commissions. In 2008 both REAL Women and the Canada Family Action Coalition ratcheted up their campaigns against the commissions. [...] CFAC has been even more extreme. In May 2008 it accused human rights activists and commissions of being influenced by "communist socialists" and having "immorality as an ethos." The human rights commissions, the group contended, have "a bias bordering on hatred of moral principles"—and especially if these morals emanate from a Christian organization. "We citizens who have rights, hold to religious beliefs and have a sense of morality must force governments to rescind the Human Rights Acts that interfere with normal functions of a civilized society and democracy."[48]

The war to recapture the public square for people of faith and to reclaim the moral agenda is not, then, a momentary or short-lived phenomenon. The social conservative leadership in Canada, whether prescient or simply deluded, has concluded that the changing consensus of Canadians about sexuality and moral issues, the pronouncements of the courts, and the actions of legislatures are merely transitory and changeable. They do not see the growing separation of church and state that has produced the incremental secularization of Canada's laws and public policy over the last several decades as being irreversible. They want more, not less, religious faith influence on the nation's public policy. They are determined to wage their war for the long term, convinced that they can still prevail over the forces of immorality, secularism, and "political correctness."

Social conservatism as a movement does face immense challenges. A crucial question is whether movement activists will attempt to position themselves more within the mainstream of a broad conservative renewal movement—and whether they will succeed if they do. Will they truly embrace the "moderation" and "incrementalism" championed by Harper and Flanagan in the interests of achieving significant and long-term progress? Can the coalition of political conservatives maintain a place for social conservatives? [...]

Indeed, the pluralistic, multicultural, multi-religious country of the twenty-first century is not the old Canada of predominantly European colonialists, firmly indoctrinated with Judeo-Christian beliefs and morality. Attempting to desecularize the state would be somewhat like trying to unscramble eggs. Myriad laws and public policies, as well as social and cultural institutions, would have to be repealed and replaced or at least substantially altered.

The biggest obstacle of all for the forces of social conservatism remains the Charter of Rights and Freedoms and the rights that it guarantees to every citizen, notwithstanding the fact that its preamble declares, "Canada is founded upon principles that recognize the supremacy of God." To achieve the total retransformation of Canada would require the amendment of the Charter, which, as part of the Constitution, would require that seven provinces having at least 50 per cent of the population of Canada must agree. That is a very high threshold. Alternatively, social conservatives could hope that, over a very long period of time, appointments to the judiciary by governments staunchly committed to reclaiming the religious moral agenda could rely upon the "supremacy of God" wording in the preamble to reinterpret the provisions of the Charter and undo the damage done by the hated secular judicial activists. But not even Harper has ventured down that highly contentious path.

Nonetheless, the stark reality is that social conservatism's call to take back Canada, to return it to the Christian democracy of the past, cannot be met with complacency. To simply label and ignore the social conservative constituency as a fringe element or to magnanimously dismiss the movement's leaders as extremists, as many suggest, *is* dangerously myopic. Contrary to what their own propagandists and many in the media contend, social conservatives continue to have great influence and vast resources to pursue their agenda. They have stamina, resources, and, increasingly, the infrastructure to wage their campaign over a long period of time—perhaps, as REAL Women notes, for several decades.

Most importantly, social conservatives have, at least for the time being, a fellow evangelical as prime minister and, in the Conservatives, a governing party in which evangelicals are disproportionately represented. The Harper government's election in 2006 and re-election in 2008 were undeniably historic—and reason enough for social conservatives to be optimistic about the future. Having secured the reigns of power and being determined to make the Conservatives the "natural governing party," Harper and his evangelical colleagues are well positioned to strive for the transformation of Canada that they and their crucial social conservative constituency so ardently desire. The Harper government is testament to how the holding of strong religious views is not an impediment to gaining political power. It is proof that the movement can effectively navigate Preston Manning's "faith/political interface."

Setting aside (at least for now) the issues of same-sex marriage and abortion, the legislative and policy agendas of the Harper government have confirmed the distinct possibility of using the many instruments and levers of political power to advance a radical agenda of lasting social conservatism. As Bastien stated in 2009, "One cannot ignore the fact that the Harper government has been in a minority position and, perhaps more importantly, confronted until recently with a very hostile media seeking every opportunity to make it appear extremist." Seen in that light, the "soft" response of the Harper government on some issues important to social conservatives "has been based more on tactical prudential judgment than on a lack of commitment." For Bastien and, it seems, a majority of other evangelicals, "The Conservatives remain the national party most capable of addressing the issues of particular concern to conservative-minded people." If for short-term pragmatic reasons they cannot achieve the transformation of Canada that they seek, they may very well do so once Harper and his Conservative Party achieve a majority government. Or it may fall to Harper's successor, or to that person's successor, to be the victor in social conservatism's righteous war. The prospect remains that transforming the nation is an attainable goal, perhaps even an imminent one.[49]

Resisting the many efforts by social conservatives to regain control of the moral agenda is not just an imperative for gays and lesbians, women, youth, those who are labelled as socialist, left-wing, or even for that matter liberal, or, most especially, all of those deemed to be moral transgressors. The challenge of doing so must necessarily be met by all Canadians who prefer the morality of rights and equality of treatment over the puritanical religious morality preached by evangelical Protestants and the Roman Catholic Church. This project requires confronting the social conservative groups and organizing uncompromising opposition to their disturbingly retrograde moral agenda. Because what the warriors of social conservatism really seek is not the right to practise their religion. Rather, it is entrenchment in the Constitution and the laws of the land of the presumption that religious and moral values should be imposed on everyone, and enforced by the instruments of the state.

The social conservatives may seemingly have lost control of the moral agenda, but we must all strive to make sure that they do not ever regain that control. Canadians who want to ensure the continued existence of a more secular state—to advance the continued expansion of the separation of church and state—must remain vigilant. When the need arises, they will need to respond swiftly and decisively to beat back the multitude of social conservative crusaders who are so fervently dedicated to bringing the nation back to God.

NOTES

1 Elisabeth Gidengil, André Blais, Richard Nadeau, and Neil Nevitte, "Making Sense of the Vote: The 2000 Canadian Election," a paper prepared for presentation at the Biennial Meeting of the Association for Canadian Studies in the United States (ACSUS), San Antonio, Texas, November 2001, 10; Aileen Van Ginkel, "Evangelical Beliefs and Practices: A Summary of the 2003 Ipsos-Reid Survey Results," Evangelical Fellowship of Canada, December 2003.

2 Stephen Harper, "Rediscovering the Right Agenda," *Citizens Centre Report*, June 2003, 72–77.

3 Brian Laghi, "Public Spurning Politics, Poll Finds," *Globe and Mail*, Feb. 10, 2003, A4.

4 Holy See, Congregation for the Doctrine of the Faith, "The Participation of Catholics in Political Life," Nov. 24, 2002, 2.

5 Catholic Civil Rights League, "The Laity and Political Affairs Position Paper No. 3," June 9, 2004, 2.

6 Bruce Clemenger, "Of Church, State and the Political Engagement of Evangelicals," June 2006 <http://www.christianity.ca>; Brian Rushfeldt, "How Individuals and Churches Can Make an Impact," Canada

Family Action Coalition.

7 Murray Dobbin, *Preston Manning and the Reform Party* (Halifax: Goodread Biographies, Formac Publishing Company, 1992), 144–145; Sydney Sharpe and Don Braid, *Storming Babylon* (Toronto: Key Porter Books, 1992), 310–311.

8 Brooke Jeffrey, *Hard Right Turn: The New Face of Neo-Conservatism in Canada* (Toronto: HarperCollins Publishers, 1999), 310–311.

9 Gordon Laird, "Inside the Little Town That Nurtured a Would-Be Prime Minister—and Some of the Most Notorious Hate-Mongers in Canada," *Now*, April 13–19, 2000, 18; William Walker, "Church Leaders Urged to Vote for Day," *Toronto Star*, June 6, 2000, A1; Paul Tuns, "Assessing the Pro-Life Credentials of Alliance Leadership Candidates," *The Interim*, May 2000 <http://www.theinterim.com>.

10 Brian Langhi, "Lobby Group Targets 'Progressive Policies' of Alliance-PC party," *Globe and Mail*, Nov. 6, 2003, A9.

11 Evangelical Missionary Church, Canada West Division, "Action Item—The New Social Conservative Caucus," Dec. 11, 2003 <http://www.emcwest.ca>.

12 CBC News, "Conservative MP Calls for Repeal of Hate Law," June 6, 2004 <http://www.cbc.ca>; Canoe cnews, "Conservative MP: Abortion Same as Terrorism," June 7, 2004 <http://cnews.canoe.ca>.

13 REAL Women of Canada, "Alert!!! Don't Let the Conservative Party Drift to the Left," Dec. 2, 2004 <http://www.realwomenca.com>; Gloria Galloway and Brian Laghi, "Harper Faces Split in Party," *Globe and Mail*, Feb. 4, 2005, A1.

14 Bill Curry, "Silence as a Strategy for Success, MP Says," *Globe and Mail*, Feb. 3, 2006, A5; Gloria Galloway, "Christian Activists Capturing Tory Races," *Globe and Mail*, May 27, 2005, A1; Jeffrey Simpson, "Why Stephen Harper Is Going to Lose More Sleep," *Globe and Mail*, May 27, 2005, A19.

15 Gloria Galloway and Brian Laghi, "Harper Reopens Same-Sex Debate," *Globe and Mail*, Nov. 30, 2005, A1; Brian Laghi and Daniel Leblanc, "Harper Won't Use Opt-Out Clause on Same-Sex," *Globe and Mail*, Dec. 16, 2005, A1; Bill Curry, "Silence as a Strategy for Success, MP Says," *Globe and Mail*, Feb. 3, 2006, A5.

16 Conservative Party of Canada, "Stand Up for Canada," Federal Election Platform 2006 <http://www.conservative.ca>.

17 Michael Valpy, Caroline Alphonso, and Rhéal Séguin, "Same-Sex Vote Likely to be Tight," *Globe and Mail*, Feb. 1, 2006, A1; Catholic Civil Rights League, "League Pledges to Work with New Government on Key Issues," press release, Jan. 24, 2006; EFC, "The Evangelical Fellowship of Canada Statement on Election 2006" <http://www.evangelicalfellowship.ca>; Michael Foust, "Canadian Christians Hopeful after Conservative Election Win," *Baptist Press*, Jan. 24, 2006 <http://www.bpnews.net>; Brian Rushfeldt, "The Enemy Is Not Done with Canada—But Neither is God!" *City Lights News*, March 2006 <http://familyaction.org>.

18 Marci McDonald, "Stephen Harper and the Theo-cons," The Walrus, Nov. 4, 2006, 8 <http://www.walrusmagazine.com>.

19 Gens Hellquist, fundraising letter, Canadian Rainbow Health Coalition, November 2007.

20 Gloria Galloway, "Ottawa Redirects AIDS Funds for Gates Initiative," *Globe and Mail*, Nov. 29, 2007, A1; Krishna Rau, "AIDS Funding under Attack," *Xtra!*, Dec. 6, 2007, 9.

21 Carolyn Abraham, "Critics Troubled by New Fertility Panel," *Globe and Mail*, Dec. 23, 2006, A1.

22 EFC, "Reponse to Bill C-47," Apr. 9, 1997, I, 2.

23 Harper, "Rediscovering the Right Agenda."

24 Tom Flanagan, *Harper's Team: Behind the Scenes in the Conservative Rise to Power* (Montreal & Kingston: McGill-Queen's University Press, 2007), 278, 279–30, 282.

25 Ibid., 282.

26 "When Lobbyists Speak in Tongues," *Ottawa Citizen*, Apr. 12, 2008.

27 *Catholic Insight*, "Easter, Reform and Prime Minister Stephen Harper," editorial, March 3, 2008 <http://www.catholicinsight.com>.

28 Paul Wells, "Harper's Canadian Revolution," *Maclean's*, Sept. 18, 2008 <http://www.macleans.ca>.

29 "Maclean's Interview: Jason Kenney," April 29, 2009, *Macleans.ca*<http://www2.macleans.ca>.

30 Dale Smith, "Evangelicals Get Top PMO Jobs after Shuffle," *Xtra!*, Feb. 19, 2009.

31 Citizenship and Immigration Canada, "Discover Canada: Rights and Responsibilities of Citizenship," 2009.

32 REAL Women of Canada, "President's Message," *REALity*, July/August 2009 <http://www.realwomenca.com>; Institute for Canadian Values, "Conservatives Announce New Program to Fund Sex Parades," <http://www.canadianvalues.ca>; Joseph Ben-Ami, "$400,000 to Toronto Gay ride Stimulant Too Far," June 24, 2009 <http://www.proudtobecanadian.ca>; Louise Elliott, "Ablonczy Punished for Giving Pride Parade Cash: Tory MP," CBC News, July 7, 2009 <http://www.cbc.ca>; Tonda MacCharles, "Ablonczy Finds Tory Support in Pride Controversy," thestar.com, July 10, 2009 <http://www.thestar.com>.

33 REAL Women of Canada, "The Silencing of the Conservative Voice in Canada," booklet, 2004.

34 Adam Daifallah, "Building a Conservative Canada—From the Ground Up," *National Post*, July 15, 2004, A18.

35 Paul Tuns, "Social Conservatism's Canadian Barriers," *Comment* magazine, December 2005, v.251.6 <http://www.wrf.ca>.

36 "The State of the Canadian Church—Part III: Are Christians in Danger of Becoming a Persecuted Minority?" *Canadianchristianity.com*, December 2007 <http://www.canadianchristianity.com>.

37 David Ben-Ami, "Endorsements," <http://christiangovernment.ca>.

38 Richard Bastien, "Social Conservatives and the Harper Government,"*C2C Canada's Journal of Ideas*, "Reclaiming Compassion," Volume 3, Issue 4, Nov. 26, 2009 <http://www.c2cjournal.ca>.

39 Preston Manning, "Navigating the Faith/Political Interface," *C2C Canada's Journal of Ideas*, June 19, 2009 <http://www.c2cjournal.ca>.

40 Social Conservatives United, "Welcome to Our Site" <http://www.socon.ca>; *C2C Canada's Journal of Ideas*, "About Us" <http://www.c2cjournal.com>.

41 Manning Centre for Building Democracy, "Our Vision," "Projects," and "Faith Political Interface" <http://www.manningcentre.ca>.

42 "Address of His Holiness Benedict XVI to the Bishops of the Episcopal Conference of Canada-Ontario on the 'Ad Limina' Visit," Sept. 8, 2006.

43 Institute for Canadian Values, "Welcome" <http://www.canadianvalues.ca>.

44 Institute of Marriage and Family Canada, "Welcome," brochure <http://imfcanada.org>.

45 Institute for the Study of Marriage, Law and Culture, "About the Institute" <http://www.marriage-institute.ca>.

46 Bastien, "Social Conservatives and the Harper Government;" *REALity*, March/April 2009.

47 Bastien, "Social Conservatives and the Harper Government"; EFC, "Human Trafficking: A Report on Modern Day Slavery in Canada," April 2009.

48 REAL Women of Canada, "Report by Professor Moon to Repeal S.13 of CHRA," media release, Nov. 26, 2008; Canada Family Action Coalition, "IMMORALITY an Ethos of Human Rights Activists," May 1, 2008 <http://www.familyaction.org/>.

49 Bastien, "Social Conservatives and the Harper Government."

PART THREE
Organizing and Resistance

CHAPTER 8

Identity and Opportunity: The Lesbian and Gay Rights Movement

Miriam Smith

Until the 1960s, lesbians and gay men led their personal lives in the shadows of Canadian society. Same-sex relationships were stigmatized and considered to be shameful and indicative of moral deviance or mental illness. The police routinely raided lesbian and gay gathering places such as bars, rounding up the clientele and sending them off to the police station to be charged with "gross indecency" or "buggery." The RCMP's "fruit machine" weeded out lesbians and gay men from government service, especially in the military and diplomatic services where their presence was thought to undermine moral and state security (Kinsman, Buse, and Steedman, 2000). Many lesbians and gay men socialized with each other in private networks, meeting only in each other's homes for fear of discovery; hiding their relationships and sexual lives from their families, co-workers, and communities; and living a veritable double life, in some cases, for all of their lives. Homosexuality was illegal, shameful, and hidden.

The status of lesbians and gay men in Canadian law, society, and politics has changed fundamentally since the 1960s. In 2002–2003, courts in Quebec, British Columbia, and Ontario ruled in favour of same-sex marriage, and, as these rulings were followed by courts in other provinces and territories, the Liberal government of Paul Martin legalized same-sex marriage in 2005. Anti-discrimination laws are on the books in all Canadian jurisdictions. Lively gay villages exist in Montreal, Toronto, and Vancouver. Huge Pride festivals in Canadian cities have brought lesbian and gay life out into the open. Courts no longer routinely bar lesbian mothers from custody of their children, and, in most Canadian jurisdictions, same-sex couples have gained the right to adopt (including the right of second-parent adoption) and to enjoy a range of partner benefits. In Quebec and British Columbia, lesbian partners enjoy full filiation rights, meaning that same-sex parents can be listed together on the birth certificate, obviating the need for second-parent adoption. Queer student organizations exist on most Canadian university campuses, and professional associations have recognized lesbian and gay networks in their midst, such as the Sexual Orientation and Gender Identity Conference of the Canadian Bar Association.

Like the women's movement, the environmental movement, and other new social movements of the 1960s and 1970s, the lesbian and gay movement challenges dominant social norms. As Alberto Melucci (1997) has pointed out, social movements do not always primarily dedicate themselves to changing public policies but also to changing the dominant "codes" of society. The lesbian and gay rights movement challenges heteronormative norms or social codes. Heteronormativity means that social organization is structured around the assumption that heterosexual sexual preference and heterosexual coupling is the dominant mode of sexual, intimate, and family organization and that homosexuality is deviant. Even when dominant norms are not openly homophobic or hostile towards homosexuality, lesbian and gay people are outside of the "norm." So, for example, people are usually assumed to be heterosexual unless they state or are shown to be otherwise, an assumption that is an example of "heteronormativity." Some lesbian and gay people label themselves "queer"—tradition-ally a hostile epithet aimed at them—in part to call attention to the power of "naming" as a means of enforcing social expectations and defining "normalcy." Heteronormativity is not confined to social attitudes, norms, and values but is also enshrined in public policies. Until very recently, same-sex couples were not entitled to benefits provided to heterosexual couples, such as pensions or medical benefits provided by private or public sector employers. Such policies are "heteronormative" because they assume that heterosexual couples are the only form of couple or the only form of couple that is worthy of the social and economic support they provide.

This chapter will present the contemporary history of the lesbian and gay rights movement in terms of its origins in the gay liberation and feminist movements and will survey the major issues that have been raised by lesbian and gay activists in light of various social movements. Theories that highlight the role of the political process in creating obstacles and opportunities for social movement action are particularly relevant to the Canadian lesbian and gay movement, which has successfully exploited the new political opportunities created by the empowerment of the judiciary under the *Charter of Rights and Freedoms*. While resource mobilization approaches stress the internal resources of the movement, the political process model stresses its external opportunities. The lesbian and gay movement has exploited external opportunities, despite the fact that it is not well resourced in terms of formal organizations or large-scale funding. At the same time, new social movement theories call attention to the role of identity in the mobilization of collective actors. While the lesbian and gay movement engages the dynamics of recognition by the state and other societal actors as well as that of redistribution (e.g., through the material stakes in relationship recognition; see Fraser, 1995), the movement calls our attention to the ways in which collective identity is constructed through social and political processes. While same-sex behaviour has existed in many societies, it is only in the Western world since the 1960s that the identities of "gay" and "lesbian" have been formulated as identity options that are cul-turally available. The lesbian and gay movement could not exist unless lesbians and gays were willing to "come out" and embrace their identity. This "coming out" process constituted a direct and open challenge to heteronormative social codes. Therefore, theories that pay attention to culture and identity as well as to the political process of movement mobilization are the most useful in understanding the dynamics of this movement.

THE 1960s: HOMOPHILE ORGANIZING AND THE 1969 REFORMS

A number of developments during the 1960s formed the essential backdrop for the emergence of the modern lesbian and gay rights movement as we know it in Canada today. In 1964, a homophile group called the Association for Social Knowledge (ASK) was founded in Vancouver to advocate for the legalization of homosexuality and for greater education and understanding of same-sex relationships. This group was similar to the homophile groups in the US such as the Mattachine Society and the Daughters of Bilitis, which had been founded over the postwar period. The 1960s were dangerous times for lesbians and gay men, making political organizing difficult. These dangers were called to public attention by the case of Everett George Klippert in the Northwest Territories, who was convicted of "gross indecency" after admitting that he had engaged in consensual sex with other men. Klippert was then labelled a dangerous sex offender, meaning that he could be imprisoned indefinitely, and his sex offender status was upheld on appeal to the Supreme Court of Canada in 1967. The Court's decision "raised the chilling prospect that any gay man could be imprisoned for life unless he could prove he was unlikely to recommit a same-sex act" (Warner, 2002: 46).

Partially in response to the public outcry over the Klippert case and to advocacy work by ASK and by the Canadian Bar Association, the federal government in 1967 followed the lead of Britain in tabling a bill to decriminalize homosexual acts between consenting adults 21 years of age or over. This bill, which was passed in 1969, meant that homosexual sex was "legal" in Canada, although the age of consent was higher for homosexual acts than for heterosexual acts. The 1969 reforms also provided for no-fault divorce and established a procedure by which women could obtain legal abortions. Therefore, the decriminalization of homosexuality was part of that package of legal reforms of the late 1960s that were epitomized by the famous quote from Pierre Trudeau: "[T]he state has no place in the bedrooms of the nation" (cited in English, 2006: 471). As for Klippert, he was released from prison in 1971, his only crime having been his relationships with other men.

Aside from the 1969 legal changes, the late 1960s and early 1970s also saw other developments that were important for the evolution of the lesbian and gay rights movement in Canada. The effervescent youth movement of this period and the rise of the women's movement were important precursors to the gay liberation movement. The women's movement politicized the questions of gender and sexuality as never before. It challenged traditional gender roles, the patriarchal nuclear family, and the regulation of women's bodies by men and by the state. Many lesbians were active in the women's movement, although the movement itself was not always friendly to lesbian politics. The youth movement of the late 1960s and the arrival of a large number of baby boomers in higher education helped fuel countercultural movements of the new left. Many of the early activists in the gay liberation movement were drawn from university campuses. They led the transition from the homophile organizing of the previous generation, which had focused on the guarded strategies of education, and transformed themselves into gay liberation groups in 1970–71. As we shall see, unlike the early homophile activists of the 1950s and 1960s, gay liberation and lesbian feminist activists directly challenged the idea that homosexuality and lesbianism should be stigmatized or that they were in any way inferior to heterosexuality.

THE 1970s: GAY LIBERATION AND LESBIAN FEMINISM

The 1969 Stonewall riots in New York City marked the beginning of a new phase of radical gay politics in the US that almost immediately had repercussions in Canada. The police raid on a New York bar was similar to many other police raids on such establishments in both the US and in Canadian cities such as Montreal and Toronto. The difference in 1969 was that a group of lesbians, transsexuals,[1] transvestites, and gay men at the Stonewall bar fought back against the police, defending their right to a public space—the bar—free from state repression (Duberman, 1993). By 1970 gay liberation groups, such as the Gay Liberation Front, had sprung up in New York.

An important aspect of the gay liberation movement was the way in which it was organized. While the homophile movement had been dominated by small groups of professionals who held educational evenings, the gay liberation movement held kiss-ins (or "zaps") and demonstrations. The more radical tactics were borrowed from strategies of the other countercultural movements of the 1960s. Further, the gay liberation movement was not centred in formal organizations but in a plethora of relatively small groups, which operated according to new left principles of democratic and participatory decision-making rather than by conventional majoritarian decision-making. Its resources were located much more in informal organizing networks rather than in large-scale social movement organizations.

With regard to its interpretation of homosexuality and its demands on society and the state, gay liberation went much further than the homophile movement. Early gay liberationists claimed that everyone was inherently bisexual and aimed to free everyone from the rigid categories of gender and sexual preference (Altman, 1993 [1971]). At the same time, however, the gay liberation movement early on encountered a tension between the idea that categories of gender and sexuality should be erased and the need to construct lesbian and gay identities as a necessary prerequisite to the building of the movement. If everyone was inherently bisexual and "polymorphously perverse" (in the Freudian term used by early gay liberationists), then what was the distinctive basis for a gay liberation movement? Like other social movements, the gay liberation movement eventually sought to build a collective identity. Boundaries were drawn around the idea of "gay" as innate sexual orientation. The claim that people were born lesbian or gay was used to advance the cause of human rights. After all, it would be unfair to discriminate against people based on an innate characteristic they could neither change nor control (Epstein, 1987: 13–20). Therefore, in terms of the networked methods of organization of the movement, the emphasis on the personal as political, and the importance of culture and identity in the process of political identity, the lesbian and gay movement conformed to the model of new social movements and, with respect to these characteristics, was similar to and inspired by the second-wave feminisms of the 1960s and 1970s.

The gay liberation movement took off in major Canadian cities over the course of the 1970s. Groups such as Toronto Gay Action, Gay Alliance Toward Equality in Toronto and Vancouver, the *Association des gai(e)s du Québec* in Montreal, the Coalition for Gay Rights in Ontario, and the Canadian Lesbian and Gay Rights Coalition worked on a common human rights agenda. Their demands were articulated in the document presented to Parliament by the protesters at the first gay liberation demonstration on Parliament Hill in August 1971. These included:

- removing "gross indecency" and "buggery" from the Criminal Code (and as a basis for declaration of dangerous offender status);
- equalizing penalties for sexual assault between heterosexual and homosexual acts;
- providing the same age of legal consent for heterosexual and homosexual sex;
- amending the *Immigration Act* to enable lesbians and gay men to immigrate to Canada;
- providing that lesbians and gay men may not be discriminated against in employment or promotion in public service;
- removing sodomy and homosexuality as grounds for divorce or for denial of child custody;
- permitting lesbians and gay men to serve in the Canadian Forces without discrimination;
- forcing the RCMP to publicly report on its witch hunt against lesbians and gay men in government service;
- providing equal status for homosexuals with respect to legal marriage, pensions, and income tax; and
- amending the *Canadian Human Rights Act* to include sexual orientation as a prohibited ground of discrimination. (Waite and DeNovo, 1971)

Gay liberation groups throughout the 1970s used different strategies in pursuing this agenda, including demonstrating, lobbying, and litigating. Except in Quebec, where sexual orientation was included in the province's human rights legislation in 1977, these efforts at public policy change were not successful (for examples, see Higgins, 2000; Korinek, 2003).

Like other social movements, gay liberation was deeply structured by gendered relations between women and men. Many women felt that the movement's emphasis on sexuality and discrimination was not as relevant for lesbians as it was for gay men. They argued that, as women, they occupied a different position in society than men. Discrimination based on sex was probably more important for many lesbians than discrimination based on sexual orientation, even assuming that these could be meaningfully separated. A plethora of women's issues—such as male violence, gender inequality in the labour market, and child care—were also important issues. Similarly, sexual freedom was not prioritized by many lesbians, who viewed gay male activities such as public sex, bathhouses, and bars as activities that were not particularly worthy of political energies (Ross, 1995).

While some women participated in the gay liberation movement, others participated in the women's movement or in the autonomous lesbian movement. The women's movement was not particularly friendly to lesbian issues during the 1970s and early 1980s; many lesbians worked mainly on "women's" rather than "lesbian" issues over this period. The autonomous lesbian movement focused on building social and political space to define the distinctive political interests of lesbians as separate from gay men or from straight women. Aside from the creation of social space and the building of collective identity, the autonomous lesbian movement spawned a range of groups such as the Lesbian Organization of Toronto and Lesbians Against the Right in Vancouver (Ross, 1995). One of the most important groups to emerge from lesbian politics of this decade in Canada were lesbian mothers' groups, which took up the important political and legal issue of securing child custody for lesbian parents (Stone, 1991).

Yet, over the course of the 1970s, the subcultures of lesbian and gay life grew substantially in Canada's major cities. Whether at Church/Wellesley in Toronto, the famous gay village of Montreal, or the West End of Vancouver, lesbian and gay male life was increasingly lived out in the open. The cultures of queer life spawned social institutions ranging from Pride Day to the women's chorus. Community institutions such as the 519 Community Centre in Toronto and queer media such as *RG, Fugues,* and (later) *Être* in Montreal or *The Body Politic* and, later, the *Xtra* chain in Ottawa, Toronto, and Vancouver, all permitted the construction of a collective culture and identity for Canadian gay men and, to a lesser extent, lesbians.

THE 1980s: AIDS AND THE CHARTER

The AIDS epidemic had important effects on the evolution of lesbian and gay politics in Canada as elsewhere. The epidemic resulted in the deaths of many of the pioneers of the gay communities of Canada's major cities, while, at the same time, it reinforced the rise of the new right by associating gay male sexuality with the spread of disease. The idea of open sexual expression became problematic as some argued that traditional gay spaces such as washrooms, parks, bars, and bathhouses should be regulated in the interests of public health. Others argued that what was needed was education about safe sex. Either way, the stigma of HIV/AIDS was very strong during the 1980s, and the liberatory potential of sex and sexual expression that had been so important in the gay liberation movement was undermined. The rise of the Moral Majority in the US, the election of the Progressive Conservative government of Brian Mulroney in 1984, and the establishment of the right-wing populist Reform Party in 1987, all indicated that the 1960s and 1970s had not been a one-way street to sexual openness and liberation but that traditional social conservative values, especially those associated with evangelical Protestantism, were still an important political force. The forces of moral regulation brought a new vulnerability to the lesbian and gay communities, which expressed itself in part in new forms of politics (Herman, 1994).

AIDS organizing shifted the balance in lesbian and gay organizing away from the human rights campaigns of the 1970s and toward political action centred on ending the epidemic. This does not mean that human rights issues went away. On the contrary, AIDS drew attention to the legal inequality of gay men, especially with regard to relationship recognition. When a gay man fell ill or died, his partner was often left with no legal rights and could be shut out by his partner's family of origin. A particularly important issue was that of medical decision-making. Same-sex partners were often prevented from participating in medical and health decisions.

The effects of AIDS were also felt in political organizing. The perceived lack of attention to HIV/AIDS in the medical community and the direction of resources for research and treatments sparked the revival of some of the earlier tactics of gay liberation as well as new forms of direct action. ACT UP (AIDS Coalition to Unleash Power), the radical American AIDS group, pioneered the use of direct action tactics to focus public action and attention on the AIDS crisis. With the slogan "Silence=Death," ACT UP used civil disobedience such as demonstrations and "die-ins" (a variation of a "sit-in") and directly targeted pharmaceutical corporations as well as the US Food and Drug Administration, which was responsible for certifying new drugs in the US (Sommella, 1997). In

Canada, groups such as AIDS Action Now! in Toronto played an important role in putting AIDS on the agenda of the federal government (Rayside and Lindquist, 1992: 37–70). Further, over the course of the late 1980s, a number of groups were established to deal with the specific needs of racialized people with HIV/AIDS. Toronto's Black Coalition for AIDS Prevention and Vancouver's Black AIDS Network were formed to provide services and education in black communities. Gay Asians Toronto established the Gay Asians AIDS project, and similar organizations were established in the early 1990s by other groups (Warner, 2002: 325–26).

The radicalization and decentring of social movement politics over this period can also be seen in the rise of groups such as Lesbian Avengers and Queer Nation. These focused on direct action tactics to counter bashing and homophobic attacks on lesbians and gays in urban areas, as well as other issues (Visser, 1990: 1). The ideology and tactics of Queer Nation formed a striking contrast to the mainstream political organizations. Instead of simply demanding that lesbians and gays be treated in the same way as straights through claims to equal rights, Queer Nation asserted a distinctive queer political identity while at the same time questioning the binary opposition of queer and straight. Instead of presenting briefs to government, Queer Nation engaged in direct action such as kiss-ins and street patrols. It represented a return to gay libera- tion ideology, especially in its assertion of a broader vision of social transformation. The tactic of kiss-in or "zap," for example, had been used in the early days of gay liberation in New York, Toronto, and elsewhere. While Queer Nation groups themselves were short-lived as political organizations in Canadian cities, they raised the flag on important issues that would animate lesbian and gay politics in the 1990s and after; in particular, groups such as Queer Nation and Lesbian Avengers called attention to the fact that lesbian and gay life constituted a distinctive culture or set of cultures of its own.

These forms of social movement politics highlighted the ways in which the movement over this period was not represented in a single movement or movement organization. Rather, lesbians and gay men organized in different locations, in AIDS organizing, in the women's movement, and in other locations. Often, as well, the targets of social movement activism were not only governments but also corporations, scientists, pharmaceutical companies, and the media. AIDS organizations such as ACT UP and urban groups such as Queer Nation and Lesbian Avengers often drew upon the radical template of the gay liberation and feminist movements, especially in their commitment to direct action (see Shepard and Hayduk, 2001). During this period, the resources of the movement were built up in AIDS organizations, yet much of the politics of the movement still occurred in decentred and decentralized social movement networks.

While the AIDS crisis and the radical politics of Queer Nation were emerging in the 1980s and early 1990s, another important development occurred that would shape lesbian and gay politics in Canada over the coming decades: the entrenchment of the *Charter of Rights and Freedoms* in the Canadian constitution. The Charter was proposed as part of Pierre Trudeau's "people's package" of constitutional reforms in 1980. It was intended to reinforce a sense of Canadian identity and to defuse regionalism and Quebec nationalism by reinforcing a sense of pan-Canadian political identity. The Charter became the object of a substantial political mobilization by First Nations, the disabled people's movement, the women's movement, and ethnocultural groups who were partially successful in shaping its equality rights guarantees in the debate over its enactment in 1980–81. [...] The lesbian and gay rights movement did not play a major role in these developments in part because it lacked a viable pan-Canadian organization at the moment of the Charter debates. In addition, the human rights agenda of the gay liberation groups of the 1970s had exhausted itself. As the pursuit of legislative and policy change had not been successful over the course of that decade, the fragmented gay rights groups were not very interested in the Charter, did not have the political and financial resources to mount a substantial mobilization, and were preoccupied with the first onset of the AIDS crisis. However, the issue was raised by MP Svend Robinson, who was unsuccessful in his efforts to have sexual orientation included in the proposed Charter. Despite this exclusion, it was understood that the open-ended wording of the equality rights section of the Charter (section 15) left the door open to the addition of sexual orientation in the future. The Liberal government was well aware that sexual orientation might be added to the Charter by the courts because of the wording of the clause (Smith, 1999).

Over the course of the mid-1980s and into the 1990s, political mobilizing in the lesbian and gay rights movement slowly began to focus on the political opening provided to the movement by the Charter. This realization was slow to take hold. In cities such as Toronto, Montreal, and Vancouver, this was the major period for AIDS activism. In Quebec, attention was not as focused on the Charter because of the impact of the Quebec nationalist movement, which perceived it as part of the politically illegitimate constitutional patriation of 1982. Lawyers were among the first to realize the potential impact of the Charter: lesbian and gay lawyers and law students began to organize both within law schools and bar associations, and lesbian and gay legal issues began to obtain coverage in law journals and legal scholarship (Duplé, 1984; Girard, 1986; Herman, 1989; Cossman, 1994). Moreover, lesbian and gay movement organizing at the pan-Canadian level was spurred in part by the political opportunity provided by the Charter. Therefore, rather than resources making the movement, as resource mobilization theory would contend, in this case it was the existence of political opportunities that galvanized resources and organization. The parliamentary sub-committee on section 15 equality rights, held in 1985, was a major fulcrum for legal and political debate. The equality rights hearings drew a large number of submissions from lesbian and gay groups and resulted in the creation in 1986 of Egale, a lesbian and gay rights group that would work on human rights issues at the federal level.

THE 1990s: THE CHARTER AND BEYOND

Over the course of the 1990s, lesbian and gay organizing occurred in many different institutions and organizations of Canadian society and across a broad range of issues ranging from the use of queer-positive reading materials in the education system to the issue of same-sex marriage. We will now explore these diverse forms of organizing in terms of the issues they raised, including discrimination in housing and employment, relationship recognition, sexual freedom, and policies and practices on lesbian and gay issues in the public education system. During this period, substantial social change took place in Canadian society, partly as a result of the movement's politicization of lesbian and gay identities. As we will see, the Charter provided an important opening for lesbian and gay litigation. In keeping with the political process model, the movement was able to take advantage of this opportunity and to secure public policy change through the courts in areas ranging from discrimination in employment to same-sex marriage. The movement was able to achieve this despite the fact that its main organization in federal politics—Egale—was poorly resourced.[2]

One of the major areas of public policy change has been that of freedom from discrimination based on sexual orientation in areas such as employment and housing. With regard to government policies, this was the main goal of gay liberation groups of the 1970s, although in most cases this type of discrimination is covered by provincial and federal human rights legislation. The Charter itself does not directly regulate relationships between private citizens (such as the relationship between landlord and tenant), although it indirectly shapes human rights legislation at both federal and provincial levels. Human rights campaigns in the provinces focused on amending provincial human rights legislation to include sexual orientation as a prohibited ground of discrimination, while at the federal level lobbying and litigation focused on the addition or "reading in" of section 15 to include sexual orientation and the amendment of the federal Human Rights Act along the same lines. Citizen-to-citizen discrimination is governed by a patchwork of provincial and federal human rights legislation, including the Charter itself, which governs state-to-citizen relationships. A major campaign to change the Ontario Human Rights Code in the 1970s failed, even in the wake of such high-profile employment discrimination cases as that of John Damien, a racing steward who was fired from his job with the Ontario Racing Commission for being gay (Warner, 2002: 145–52). In British Columbia, the Social Credit government gutted human rights protections in the province, and one case of discrimination—the *Vancouver Sun*'s refusal to publish an ad from a gay rights group—was defeated in the Supreme Court of Canada *(Gay Alliance Toward Equality v. Vancouver Sun;* see also Black, 1979). In other provinces, lesbian and gay communities of this period were too fragile to mount major campaigns for human rights changes.

In the 1980s, a sustained campaign in Ontario by groups such as the Coalition for Lesbian and Gay Rights in Ontario and by the Right to Privacy Committee finally led to the amendment of Ontario's Human Rights Code to include sexual orientation in 1986 (Rayside, 1988), while, at the federal level, a Charter challenge by litigants Haig and Birch resulted in the de facto addition of sexual orientation to the federal human rights code in 1992. However, even then, the Liberal government of Jean Chrétien prevaricated on the formal amendment of the federal *Human Rights Act* to include sexual orientation by 1996. The Alberta government only included sexual orientation in its human rights legislation when forced to do so by the Supreme Court decision in *Vriend* in 1998. Most provinces had amended their human rights legislation to include a formal ban on sexual orientation discrimination in provincial territorial jurisdiction by the early 1990s (Smith, 2005b).

The recognition of same-sex relationship and parenting rights is another important area of social movement mobilization. The question of recognizing same-sex relationships for the purpose of employment benefits became an issue almost as soon as the Charter came into effect. One of the first cases on relationship recognition was brought by Brian Mossop, a federal government employee and long-time gay liberation activist, in 1985; although Mossop did not directly invoke Charter rights in his claim for bereavement leave to attend the funeral of his partner's father, the final decision against Mossop in the Federal Court of Canada invited the recasting of the claim on Charter grounds. Meanwhile, the *Veysey* case had established the right of same-sex partners to spousal rights in prisons, a case in which the Federal Court of Canada recognized that sexual orientation was analogous to the other grounds of discrimination named in section 15. Finally, in the 1995 *Egan* case on same-sex spousal benefits under the Old Age Security program, the Supreme Court of Canada ruled that sexual orientation was included in section 15. However, the court ruled that the "reasonable limits" clause of the Charter provided grounds on which to deny benefits to same-sex couples. The Court's decision to subject the equality rights guarantees of section 15 to the general limitation clause in section 1 to deny government benefits to same-sex couples was taken as a threat to equality rights in general by other stakeholder groups, and, following the *Egan* ruling, a number of groups, including ethnocultural groups and women's groups, mobilized to work against this interpretation of section 15 across equality rights cases (Go and Fisher, 1998). In the late 1990s, two important cases were decided, one on the right of same-sex couples to access spousal benefits in employer pensions under federal tax rules (*Rosenberg*) and the other on the constitutionality of Ontario's *Family Law Act,* which denied spousal support to same-sex partners upon the break-up of their relationship (*M v. H*). In the latter case, the most important ruling on same-sex spousal rights to date, one of the former partners, "M," pursued "H" for support upon the break-up of their relationship, arguing that the family law of Ontario discriminated against same-sex couples in preventing former same-sex couples from making claims of spousal support. In ruling that Ontario's family law discrimin- ated against same-sex couples and violated their equality rights under the Charter, the Supreme Court of Canada moved away from the logic of the *Egan* case and indicated that it would not accept anything less than full equality under the law for same-sex couples and, in so doing, set the stage for the next step, which was the move to same-sex marriage.

Therefore, litigation and lobbying in response to litigation have constituted important polit- ical strategies for the movement. In this context, once again, we can see the impact of the struc- ture of political opportunity in social movement politics. The movement was not particularly well resourced during this period and did not have the means of bringing political pressure to bear on the Liberal government, except through the courts. It is highly unlikely that the Liberal government would have recognized lesbian and gay rights if it had not been for these court deci- sions. In the mid-1990s, Parliament voted on several occasions against spousal recognition for same-sex couples, and it was only in response to the Supreme Court decision in *M v. H* (which recognized the constitutional necessity of equality in spousal support laws) that the federal government passed the *Modernization of Benefits and Obligations Act* of 2000, which extended most benefits (except immigration rights) to same-sex couples in federal jurisdiction, short of marriage (Smith, 2005b). Similarly, the move from relationship recognition in common law (or *union de fait*) relationships to the recognition of same-sex marriage was also sparked by a series of court decisions in the early 2000s and not by the pressure brought to bear by the movement on the Liberal government.

Same-sex marriage litigation took place across Canada. In 1998, a Quebec gay couple brought a legal challenge to the heterosexual definition of marriage in Quebec's civil law. In 2000, the first of what would eventually be two sets of couples began their litigation on same-sex marriage in British Columbia. In 2001, four couples were married in Metropolitan Community Church in Toronto after the publication of banns, in a challenge to Ontario's laws governing marriage. Evangelical Christians and their supporters have been forceful opponents of such measures, arguing that recognizing same-sex benefits will undermine the traditional family or that such recognition will "condone" a "lifestyle" that leads to AIDS and other diseases (Canada, 2000). A wide range of religious organizations and lesbian and gay organizations spoke to the courts through the litigation in British Columbia, Quebec, Ontario, and other provinces which led to the key set of court decisions in 2002–2003. The first decision, in British Columbia, rejected the same-sex couples' claims for the right to access to legal marriage. The judge argued that marriage had always been heterosexual and that the Charter did not require marriage equality for same-sex couples. However, this decision was appealed to the provincial Court of Appeal, which ruled that barring same-sex couples from same-sex marriage was unconstitutional but that the legislature should have the right to devise a solution. At the same time, in Quebec, a long battle for parenting and partnership rights, led by a wide range of social movement organizations including the labour movement, resulted in the recognition of parenting rights and the creation of a new civil union regime in Quebec, one that included same-sex partners (Nicol, 2005). Nova Scotia passed domestic partnership legislation in 2001. For a time, therefore, it looked as though civil unions might emerge as the dominant policy in this area. However, this was brought to an end by the Court of Appeal decision in Ontario in 2003 in the case of *Halpern v. Canada*, in which the Ontario Court of Appeal not only agreed with the British Columbia court that same-sex marriage was constitutional but ruled that marriage licences had to be issued immediately. Quebec followed with a decision in favour of same-sex marriage in 2004. Rather than appealing these decisions, the Chrétien government developed legislation to legalize same-sex civil marriage and then referred the question of its constitutionality to the Supreme Court. The Court (*Reference* 2004) indicated that the government's same-sex marriage was constitutional and that it did not infringe on religious freedom. Under the Liberal government of Paul Martin, the same-sex marriage legislation became law in June 2005. Although the Conservative government elected in January 2006 opposes same-sex marriage, it did not roll back the measure, despite holding a vote on the possibility of doing so in December 2006.

A number of voices within the lesbian and gay communities questioned the extent to which same-sex marriage was a worthwhile expenditure of movement resources. Some opposed relationship recognition as a co-optation of the original goals of the gay liberation movement—sexual freedom—and as marking the conservatization of the movement (Hannon, 1999: 3), while others were critical of relationship recognition because they shared the feminist critique of family as a patriarchal institution. Others argued that relationship recognition might radicalize and transform the traditional family or mark the full recognition of lesbians and gay men as citizens (on this debate, see Herman, 1989; Cossman, 1994; Boyd and Young, 2003). Despite the debates that have occurred in lesbian and gay communities over same-sex marriage, in general lesbian and gay rights-seeking organizations are caught up in a political dynamic that demands the articulation of a clear-cut, almost "ethnic" identity in order to make their rights claims legible to the Canadian public, the media, the courts, the governing caucus, and policy-makers (Smith, 2005a, 2005b; see also Epstein, 1987). In this dynamic, it was very difficult for the movement(s)—especially as decentred networks of activism and community—to counter the dynamic generated by the course of litigation. In this sense, then, opportunities not only shaped the success of the movement but also its priorities, claims, and demands.

The settling of the debates over discrimination, relationship recognition, and parenting and same-sex marriage has had a profound effect on lesbian and gay organizing at the federal level. Many of the other policy issues for lesbian and gay communities are local, provincial, or urban, which creates challenges for the maintenance of stable pan-Canadian organizations (Grundy and Smith, 2005). Political mobilization to reduce homophobia in schools and to ensure that health research and health care delivery reflect the health needs of lesbian and gay citizens is another important area of political activism. A number of other political issues concern the regulation of sexual behaviour and pornography through the criminal law. In these areas, there are important differences in the lesbian and gay movement, especially between gay men and some lesbians over the ways in which the state should regulate sexual freedom and sexual expression. There is increasing recognition of the importance of transgender legal and political issues within lesbian and gay communities, especially with respect to the recognition of gender identity as a prohibited ground of discrimination and with respect to the availability of sexual reassignment surgery in the provinces (which are responsible for this policy as the administra- tors of the medicare system). For these reasons, lesbian and gay organizing faces challenges in maintaining the relatively high level of success that was achieved in the 1990s and early 2000s.

The lesbian and gay movement has been active in the area of sexual freedom, a central characteristic of the gay liberation movement. For some, sexual freedom is the main goal of the movement and a key dimension of lesbian and, especially, gay political identity (Cossman et al., 1997). Issues in this area include censorship of lesbian and gay bookstores, pornography, criminalization of anal sex, police attempts to regulate public sex, and age of consent laws. Sexual freedom is an issue that has the potential to openly challenge the line between "good sex" and "bad sex," and between sexual order and sexual chaos, in Gayle Rubin's terms (Rubin, 1984). While relationship recognition has the potential to (in part) fit lesbian and gay couples into an acceptable "family" model (precisely the point of the feminist and gay liberationist critiques of "family" in the lesbian and gay communities), the political issues surrounding sexuality and sexual expression such as pornography threaten this cozy picture of middle-class and monogamously coupled respectability by pushing at the line between "good" and "bad."

A series of legal cases on the issue of censorship and pornography results from the Little Sister's Book and Art Emporium in Vancouver. This lesbian and gay bookstore has been bat- tling Canada Customs since 1986 over the seizure and censorship of lesbian and gay materials shipped from the US. Lesbian and gay erotica is often deemed to be pornography by customs officials and is held up at the border. Even literary novels published in the US by well-known Canadian novelists, such as Jane Rule, have been stopped at the border (Fuller and Blackley, 1995). Little Sisters is not the only bookstore to have faced this kind of ongoing and systematic harassment by the state: Glad Day in Toronto, After Stonewall in Ottawa, and Androgyne in Montreal have all faced similar problems. State regulation of lesbian and gay sexual expression also continues to be at issue in police behaviour with regard to the lesbian and gay communities in Canada's major cities. In 2000, undercover police in Toronto raided the lesbian bathhouse, the Pussy Palace, and, reminiscent of the bath raids of the 1970s and 1980s, made a number of arrests in a seeming attempt to shut down the space (Gallant, 2001).

Another important arena of contestation by the lesbian and gay rights movement is the area of education and social policy. The legal advances of the movement at the level of public policy cannot obscure the fact that, at the local level, life is still very difficult for lesbian and gay people. There are still tremendous social sanctions and dangers in coming out, especially in Canada's smaller communities. Queer youth face bullying and harassment in school, and the stresses caused by facing such harassment are surely one of the factors behind the higher suicide rate for queer teens than for straight youth (Bagley and Tremblay, 1997). In some parts of Canada, notably Toronto, Vancouver, and the lower mainland of British Columbia, lesbian and gay activists have attempted to put the issue of heteronormativity on the educational agenda through the adoption of school board policies on homophobia and through the introduction of gay- and lesbian-positive reading materials in the schools. A sustained and concerted effort by activists in the Toronto boards of education (merged into the Toronto District School Board) over the course of the 1990s resulted in the adoption of equity policies on sexual orientation and gender identity, although there are still important problems with the implementation of these policies, especially because of budget cuts (Francis, 2000). In the lower mainland of British Columbia, the British Columbia Teachers' Federation has played a leading role in implementing anti-homophobia and anti-racism policies. Further, the province's lesbian and gay educators group, Gay and Lesbian Educators of British Columbia, has worked to create a social and support space for teachers and school administrators. From this effort came the campaign led by James Chamberlain and Murray Warren to introduce gay- and lesbian-positive reading materials into the elementary school grades in the Port Coquitlam and Surrey school districts. Chamberlain and Warren sought to use books that depicted families with same-sex parents for young children. This sparked a backlash from the evangelical movement, which had undertaken a concerted campaign to control school boards in the "bible belt" of the province. The Surrey School Board banned the gay- and lesbian-positive books from the elementary school classroom and was immediately challenged by parents, teachers (including Chamberlain and Warren), and others who undertook a successful Charter challenge to this censorship of reading materials.

The conflict between lesbian and gay equality rights and religious rights was also at issue in the case of Marc Hall, the gay Oshawa teen who claimed the right to take his boyfriend to the prom in a Catholic school (Kennedy, 2001). These challenges were not directed by social movement organizations such as Egale but were brought by individuals who decided to pursue a legal avenue in the face of what they believed to be discrimination or who were connected with lesbian and gay activism through their trade union (such as the British Columbia Teachers' Federation) or local lesbian and gay groups. The myriad networks of lesbian and gay activism span unions, the education system, and the workplace (Hunt, 1999). Strategically, litigation has been an effective political strategy for lesbian and gay activists in the late 1990s and beyond, and litigation, by its very nature, bubbles up when individuals choose to undertake a legal fight and cannot be directed by social movement organizations.

Finally, new forms of local and pan-Canadian organizing have arisen recently in the area of lesbian and gay health policy. The Canadian Rainbow Health Coalition, founded in Saskatoon, has been paralleled by local organizations across Canada, which centre on the health needs of lesbian and gay people with regard to issues including sexual health, breast cancer, domestic violence, mental health, sex reassignment surgery, and other health needs of trans people (Rainbow Health Coalition, 2006). In most major cities, queer youth projects have sprung up, in some cases funded by local government and public health agencies; these provide health and social services for queer youth, as well as facilitating organizing and community-building by them. To date, efforts to politicize social and economic policy to highlight the situation and needs of lesbian and gay youth communities have not succeeded. For example, they are at greater risk of homelessness than straight youth. Yet, social services for youth and the homeless do not clearly recognize how sexuality is intertwined with other bases of social and economic inequality (Grundy and Smith, 2005).

CONCLUSIONS: LESBIAN AND GAY POLITICS AND SOCIAL MOVEMENT THEORIES

Social movement theories from sociology and political science provide a useful perspective on some aspects of lesbian and gay social movement challenges in Canadian politics. Resource mobilization theory stresses the idea that movements arise when they are able to obtain economic and political resources, the political process model stresses that movements must have political opportunities in order to achieve success, and new social movement theory stresses the cultural dimension of movement challenges which lead to the formation of collective identity (Della Porta and Diani, 1999).

All three of these dimensions may be seen at work in the evolution of lesbian and gay organizing described here. Without a common sense of political identity and without a mass exit of lesbian and gay people from the closet, the modern lesbian and gay rights movement in Canada would not exist. The first step in the formation of the movement was the process of establishing a collective identity. In the early years of gay liberation, the very act of holding a gay dance posed a radical challenge to the dominance and raw economic, social, and political power of heteronormativity. By allowing lesbian and gay people to come together, if only for the purpose of recreation, such events helped to build and reinforce lesbian and gay cultures, which, in turn, formed the basis of social movement networks. Formal organizations such as Egale are the tip of the iceberg of these broader networks of organizing. New social movement theories highlight the creation of new social and political identities which underpin collective action. Similarly, they highlight post-materialism and historical specificity in the context of the politics of the 1960s and after, at least in the context of developed countries such as Canada. The women's movement, the gay liberation movement, and the lesbian feminist movements were the product of this period of youth revolt and, initially at least, drew on the template of 1960s organizing.

Resources have played less of a role in the politics of the lesbian and gay movement in Canada. The movement is not well resourced at the pan-Canadian level, and even at the height of the same-sex marriage debate in the early 2000s, the movement's organizational resources consisted of two small lobbying groups with meagre budgets. While the movement enjoys some material support from allies in the labour movement, lesbian and gay organizations in the US are much better resourced than organizations in Canada. Nonetheless, despite these far greater resources, the US is far behind Canada in its recognition of the legal equality of lesbian and gay citizens or the recognition of same-sex relationships and parenting rights (see Cahill, 2004). Therefore, the success of the gay and lesbian movement cannot be attributed to resources alone.

The political process model offers a more convincing account of the recent history of the lesbian and gay rights movement. In particular, the political and legal opportunities afforded by the Charter have provided an opening for lesbian and gay organizations and individual litigants to use the courts to force public policy changes on reluctant governments. These Charter challenges have also disrupted the normative status of straight life by calling media and public attention to issues ranging from censorship and discrimination to the right of one young man to take another young man to the prom. In the lesbian and gay rights case, the material consequences of changes to public policy such as the right of same-sex couples to pension, medical, and dental benefits are intertwined with the symbolic and cultural challenge to the traditional norms of Canadian (and other) societies. The Charter has proven to be a potent and effective weapon for lesbian and gay litigation and organizing and has forced governments to act where, otherwise, they were clearly unwilling to touch the "gay rights" hot button. The result has been a dramatic period of change in Canadian politics and one of the few successful stories of progressive social movements in the neoliberal era.

NOTES

1 This article does not treat the politics of transgender ("trans") and transsexual issues in any detail. Sexual orientation and gender identity are not the same thing. Many people who identify as "trans" do not identify as "lesbian" or "gay," and, indeed, transgender and transsexual people may be straight in their sexual orientation. The terms sexual orientation and gender identity are often used together to denote this distinction. For accounts of trans politics and law, see Namaste (2000) and findlay (2003).

2 Information on Egale's resources comes from a number of sources. For example, in several interviews with former executive director of Egale, John Fisher (in 1995 and 2001), he indicated to me that the Egale budget was very small—under $500,000. Egale's 2006 President Gemma Schlamp-Hickey estimated the budget at $350,000 in 2006, just before the Harper government held a free vote on rolling back same-sex marriage (see Barsotti, 2006).

CASES CITED

Egan & Nesbitt v. Canada (1995), 124 D.L.R. (4th) 609 SCC

Gay Alliance Toward Equality v. Vancouver Sun, [1979] 2 S.C.R. 435

Halpern v. Canada (2003) O.A.C. 405

Klippert v. the Queen, [1967] S.C.R. 822

M v. H, [1999] 2 S.C.R. 3

Canada (A. G.) v. Mossop, [1993] 1 S.C.R. 554

Reference re Same-Sex Marriage [2004] SCC 79

Rosenberg v. Canada (Attorney General) (1998), 38 O.R. (3d) 577 (C.A.)

Veysey v. Canada (Correctional Service) (1990), 109 N.R. 300

Vriend v. Alberta [1998] 1 S.C.R. 493

REFERENCES

Altman, Dennis. 1993 [1971]. *Homosexual Oppression and Liberation*. New York: New York University Press.

Bagley, C., and P. Tremblay. 1997. "Suicidal Behaviors in Homosexual and Bisexual Males." *Crisis, The International Journal of Suicide and Crisis Studies* 18(1): 24–34.

Barsotti, Natasha. 2006. "More Resignations Rock Egale." *Xtra West* [Vancouver], 6 December. <http://www.xtra.ca/public/Vancouver/More_resignations_rock_Egale-2416.aspx>.

Black, W.W. 1979. "Gay Alliance Toward Equality v. Vancouver Sun." *Osgoode Hall Law Journal* 17: 649–75.

Body Politic [Toronto]. 1976 (August) and various issues 1971–87.

Boyd, Susan B., and Claire F.L. Young. 2003. "From Same-sex to No Sex? Trends Towards Recognition of (Same-sex) Relationships in Canada." *Seattle Journal for Social Justice* 3: 757–93.

Cahill, Sean. 2004. *Same-Sex Marriage in the United States: A Focus on the Facts*. Lanham: Lexington Books.

Canada. 2000. *Minutes of Proceedings and Evidence*. Ottawa: House of Commons, Standing Committee on Justice and Human Rights (16 March): 1606.

Cossman, Brenda. 1994. "Family Inside/Out." *University of Toronto Law Journal* 44: 1–39.

Cossman, Brenda, Shannon Bell, Lise Gotell, and Becki Ross. 1997. *Bad Attitude/s on Trial: Pornography, Feminism, and the "Butler" Decision*. Toronto: University of Toronto Press.

Della Porta, Donatella, and Mario Diani. 1999. *Social Movements: An Introduction*. Oxford: Blackwell.

Duberman, Martin. 1993. *Stonewall*. New York: Dutton.

Duplé, Nicole. 1984. "Homosexualité et droits à l'égalité dans les Chartes canadienne et québécoise." *Les cahiers de droit* 25: 1–32.

English, John. 2006. *Citizen of the World: The Life of Pierre Elliott Trudeau, Vol. 1 1919–1969*. Toronto: Knopf.

Epstein, Steven. 1987. "Gay Politics, Ethnic Identity: The Limits of Social Constructionism." *Socialist Review* 17: 9–54.

findlay, barbara. 2003. "Real Women: *Kimberly Nixon v. Vancouver Rape Relief*." *University of British Columbia Law Review* 36: 58.

Francis, Margot. 2000. "Chalkboard Promises." *Xtra* (7 September): 19.

Fraser, Nancy. 1995. "From Redistribution to Recognition? Dilemmas of Justice in a 'Post-Socialist' Age." *New Left Review* 212: 68–93.

Fuller, Janine, and Stuart Blackley. 1995. *Restricted Entry: Censorship on Trial*. Vancouver: Press Gang.

Gallant, Paul. 2001. "Who Should Be Ashamed?" *Xtra* (1 November).

Girard, Philip. 1986. "Sexual Orientation as a Human Rights Issue in Canada, 1969–1985." *Dalhousie Law Journal* 10(2): 267–81.

Go, Avvy, and John Fisher. 1998. *Working Together Across our Differences: A Discussion Paper on Coalition-building, Participatory Litigation, and Strategic Litigation*. Ottawa: Court Challenges Program.

Grundy, John, and Miriam Smith. 2005. "The Politics of Multiscalar Citizenship: The Case of Lesbian and Gay Organizing in Canada." *Citizenship Studies* 9(4): 389–404.

Grundy, John, and Miriam Smith. 2007. "Activist Knowledges in Queer Politics." *Economy and Society* 36:2 (May): 295–318.

Hannon, Philip. 1999. "Sexual Outlaws or Respectable In-laws?" *Capital Xtra* (3 June).

Herman, Didi. 1989. "Are We Family? Lesbian Rights and Women's Liberation." *Osgoode Hall Law Journal* 28(4): 789–815.

Herman, Didi. 1994. *Rights of Passage: Struggles for Lesbian and Gay Legal Equality.* Toronto: University of Toronto Press.

Higgins, Ross. 2000. *De la clandestinité à l'affirmation.* Montreal: Comeau/Nadeau.

Hunt, Gerald. 1999. "No Longer Outsiders: Labor's Response to Sexual Diversity in Canada." In Gerald Hunt (ed.), *Laboring for Rights: Unions and Sexual Diversity Across Nations.* Philadelphia: Temple University Press.

Kennedy, Sarah. 2001. "Gay Teen Goes to the Prom." *Globe and Mail,* 10 May: A1.

Kinsman, Gary, Dieter K. Buse, and Mercedes Steedman (Eds.). 2000. *Whose National Security? Canadian State Surveillance and the Creation of Enemies.* Toronto: Between the Lines.

Korinek, Valerie J. 2003. "'The Most Openly Gay Person for at Least a Thousand Miles': Doug Wilson and the Politicization of a Province, 1975–1983." *Canadian Historical Review* 84(4): 517–50.

Melucci, Alberto. 1997. *Challenging Codes: Collective Action in the Information Age.* Cambridge: Cambridge University Press.

Namaste, Vivian K. 2000. *Invisible Lives: The Erasure of Transsexual and Transgendered People.* Chicago: University of Chicago Press.

Nicol, Nancy. 2005. *Politics of the Heart/La politique du coeur.* Film. Toronto.

Rainbow Health Coalition. 2006. *About Us.* <http://www.rainbowhealthnetwork.ca/about>.

Rayside, David. 1988. "Gay Rights and Family Values: The Passage of Bill 7 in Ontario." *Studies in Political Economy* 26: 109–47.

Rayside, David, and Evert Lindquist. 1992. "AIDS Activism and the State in Canada." *Studies in Political Economy* 39: 37–76.

Ross, Becki. 1995. *The House That Jill Built: A Lesbian Nation in Formation.* Toronto: University of Toronto Press.

Rubin, Gayle. 1984. "Thinking Sex: Notes for a Radical Theory of the Politics of Sexuality." In C.S. Vance (ed.), *Pleasure and Danger: Exploring Female Sexuality.* Boston: Routledge and Kegan Paul.

Shepard, Benjamin, and Ronald Hayduk (Eds.). 2001. *From ACT UP to the WTO: Urban Protest and Community Building in the Era of Globalization.* London: Verso.

Smith, Miriam. 1999. *Lesbian and Gay Rights in Canada: Social Movements and Equality-Seeking, 1971–1995.* Toronto: University of Toronto Press.

Smith, Miriam. 2005a. "Resisting and Reinforcing Neoliberalism: Lesbian and Gay Organizing at the Federal and Local Levels in Canada." *Policy & Politics* 33(1): 75–93.

Smith, Miriam. 2005b. "Social Movements and Judicial Empowerment: Courts, Public Policy, and Lesbian and Gay Organizing in Canada." *Politics & Society* 33(2): 327–53.

Sommella, Laraine. 1997. "This Is about People Dying: The Tactics of Early ACT UP and Lesbian Avengers in New York City." In G.B. Ingram, A.-M. Bouthillette, and Y. Retter (eds.), *Queers in Space: Communities, Public Places, Sites of Resistance.* Seattle: Bay Press.

Stone, Sharon Dale. 1991. "Lesbian Mothers Organize." In S.D. Stone (ed.), *Lesbians in Canada.* Toronto: Between the Lines.

Visser, Andy. 1990. "Queer Notions." *Xtra* (14 September): 1.

Waite, Brian, and Cheri DeNovo. 1971. *We Demand.* Toronto: August 28th Gay Day Committee.

Warner, Tom. 2002. *Never Going Back: A History of Queer Activism in Canada.* Toronto: University of Toronto Press.

CHAPTER 9

Like Apples and Oranges: Lesbian Feminist Responses to the Politics of *The Body Politic*

Becki Ross

INTRODUCTION

At the conclusion of my article for *FUSE Magazine* (1993), I speculate about future cultural and political "enactments of queerness" in myriad arenas of struggle. In the intervening two decades, queer debate, community building, and knowledge making have flourished across Canada. I am struck by the strength and verve of queer film festivals, the publishing house Arsenal Pulp Press, recent conferences (e.g., "Queerly Canadian," "We Demand: History/Sex/Activism," and "Queer U" in Vancouver), critical sexuality studies on college and university campuses, and the brilliant creative writing by Amber Dawn, Farzana Doctor, Drew Hayden Taylor, Ivan Coyote, and Anna Camilleri, among others. Young queer activists such as Aboriginal sex educator Jessica Yee, Egyptian-Canadian rap singer Jazz Kamal, and Singaporean-Canadian graphic novelist Elisha Lim are making their presence known, and their influence felt. The queerly multi-lingual and multi-ethnic poster campaign "Our City of Colours" was launched in 2011 by Chinese-Canadian Darren Ho. Trans folks are agitating for visibility and inclusion through support groups, art shows, research, films, and online forums.

While queer characters on mainstream TV and in Hollywood film remain stereotypically one-dimensional, the eclectic world of YouTube posts, Internet blogs, dating websites, porn sites, and Facebook pages offers sometimes brave, surprising meditations on queer love, family, kin, and belonging. Indeed, the Internet promises greater access to diverse, sexually explicit queer images, and yet high-quality lesbian porn remains elusive, and so much commercial gay porn is (still) stunted by racist tropes of white dominance and non-white submission. On the legal front, same-sex marriage was legalized in Canada in 2005; other policies concerning adoption, fostering, and immigration have been rendered more queer-friendly as a result of activists' political pressure. At the same time, an anti-queer backlash has manifested through an intensification of bullying, with a heartbreaking rash of suicides by queer and racialized youth over the past ten years. School boards across Canada are still cowed by the fear of "corrupting innocent youth" and have been slow to eradicate heterosexism, homophobia, and transphobia. Religious fundamentalists at home and abroad continue to hone and polish their sexist and anti-homosexual crusades.

Making manifest what I imagined as "future possibilities for conscious coalition," some queer activists today are joining others to oppose new forms of militarism, slut shaming, sexualized violence, racial profiling, and environmental degradation. However, as Jasbir Puar argues in *Terrorist Assemblages: Homonationalism in Queer Times*, white, middle-class queers in the global North seem preoccupied with citizenship privilege, capitalist consumption, and forms of homonational belonging. By contrast, the poor (queer and non-queer), sex workers, trannies, refugees, and queerly racialized populations worldwide experience exclusion, not solidarity or inclusion, much as they did decades ago. In 2012, there is an urgent need for new, queerly feminist, anti-racist assemblages that overturn complicities of privilege and, instead, install radical circuits of allegiance that know no bounds.

Becki Ross, 2012

A number of historians and theorists have recently remarked on the embattled relations that have persisted between post-Stonewall lesbian feminists and gay male activists.[1] This is a revisitation of one site of contestation: the 1977 police raid on *The Body Politic* (a now defunct radical gay liberation monthly with an international readership) by Project P—a joint Metropolitan Toronto/Ontario Provincial Police anti-pornography squad. This is a replaying of the debates that swirled around the article "Men Loving Boys Loving Men," focusing on the sharpening of lesbian feminist sexual discourse against and in contradistinction to gay men's sexual discourse. Indeed, the raid served as a lightning rod for the articulation of competing discourses on issues of sexual practice, representation and the role of the state in legislating matters of sex and morality. The focus on dominant lesbian feminist responses allows one to recapture one moment in the consolidation of a white, middle-class Lesbian Nationalist identity and community. It also allows a contextualization of the subsequent fracturing of hegemonic lesbian feminism in the 1980s and the emergent possibility for new queer alliances in the 1990s.

LESBIAN FEMINISTS ENTER THE MAELSTROM

On November 21, 1977, *The Body Politic* mailed out issue no. 39 to subscribers and bookstores. The issue contained "Men Loving Boys Loving Men" by Gerald Hannon—the third in a series of three articles on consent and youth sexuality.[2] Written from the standpoint of a boy-lover, the tone and content of the article suggested competing desires to confess, to educate and to provoke. And provoke it did. In five consecutive columns leading up to and following the publication of issue no. 39, Claire Hoy of *The Toronto Sun* vilified "radical homosexuals" and their "rag," *The Body Politic*."[3] Referring to homosexuals as "filthy garbage" and "child rapers," he called for immediate police action against the newspaper. The office of *The Body Politic* was raided on December 30, 1977, one month after issue no. 39 had appeared on newsstands,[4] and charged under Section 164 of the Criminal Code—use of the mail to distribute immoral, indecent and scurrilous materials.[5]

In early January 1978, a formal meeting of the Lesbian Organization of Toronto (LOOT—the city's largest constituency of lesbian feminists) was held to discuss the "Men Loving Boys Loving Men" crisis. Most LOOT members accused *The Body Politic* of bad timing in publishing the article. Lesbian, gay and feminist communities were still reeling from orange juice queen Anita Bryant's anti-homosexual "Save Our Children" crusade launched in July 1977, and the reported "homosexual orgy slaying" of twelve-year-old Emanuel Jaques in a Yonge Street establishment in August 1977.[6] The ensuing moral panic organized through the media not only focused hostility against the entire gay community, it provided rationale for an escalation of the "Clean Up Yonge Street" campaign (similar to the Times Square and Tenderloin clean-ups in New York and San Francisco) orchestrated by police, politicians and downtown real estate developers.[7]

By being published when it was, many lesbian feminists argued, "Men Loving Boys Loving Men" endangered the gay civil rights campaign which at that time seemed to be gaining momentum.[8] Bluntly told, void of nuance, the article worked to feed and reinforce the myth of the homosexual child molester, and thus some lesbian feminists claimed, provided right-wing organizers—Renaissance International, the Catholic Church, Positive Parents, the Western Front (later the League Against Homosexuals)—with fuel for their backlash and served to grease the wheels of Anita Bryant's powerful anti-gay, anti-feminist and "pro-family" machine.

More importantly, though, on a deep emotional level, the article evoked shock and disgust among most lesbian (and straight) feminists. At several public forums, lesbian feminist speakers denounced cross-generational sex as abusive and nonconsensual, and they condemned its exploitive portrayal in *The Body Politic*. Refusing the libertarian defense of the magazine by high-profile writers like Margaret Atwood and June Callwood, a number of lesbian feminists spoke out against the sexual, economic, physical and emotional inequalities between gay men and young boys. In interviews they remember being furious with the romanticization of adult/child love. Former psychiatric nurse and youth counsellor Pat Murphy was a vocal critic:

> [Gay men] didn't see the relationship between power and sexuality... they'd have sexual relationships with a young kid that they'd taken to McDonald's for a hamburger and they'd say he's all willing and likes it... It was all romantic sexuality that was to their own advantage. It's like paying five bucks at McDonald's for an all-day blow job.[9]

Disallowing the "Men Loving Boys" article as a "celebration of sex," members of LOOT railed against the lack of power and privilege of the young boys.[10] Not only, they argued, did Gerald Hannon's standpoint assure a foregrounding of adult male sexual desire, it secured the erasure of meaning/s that the boys themselves attached to cross-generational sexual encounters. In the aftermath of the raid, the statement formulated by a number of activist lesbians during anti-Bryant organizing—"pedophilia is neither a lesbian nor a feminist issue"—was recapitulated with a renewed, steely confidence. Feelings of rage cut across ideological differences that were beginning to fragment LOOT lesbians into socialist and radical feminist camps. A long-time member of the Revolutionary Marxist Group (later the Revolutionary Workers League), Amy Gottlieb recalls that:

> ...there was a general feeling that [the article] was awful and terrible and how could men do this to boys and there must be something wrong with these men and they're really beyond the pale, and no wonder we didn't want to have anything to do with them. I know for myself, I was pretty outraged at the time.[11]

Former collective member of *The Body Politic*, Ed Jackson remembers his shock and dismay at the intensely negative criticism of "Men Loving Boys" voiced by many lesbian feminists (and, not insignificantly, some gay men).[12] However, he is quick to note the absence of any gender-mixed infrastructure within lesbian and gay political organizing during this period which may have furnished a context for productive dialogue.

RE-ALIGNING MEMORY

Asked to recall their feelings about the "Men Loving Boys" debacle, a number of former LOOT members told of their girlhood experiences of unwanted, forced sexual pain and humiliation at the hands of straight adult men. In addition, a number of lesbian feminist leaders added the knowledge that they had gained from work with sexually abused women and children in hostels, rape crisis centres, counselling clinics, prisons and psychiatric hospitals. And it was, it seems, to a large degree these stories that influenced the reaction to the article (an example of the privileging of first-person narrative that was characteristic of dominant feminist ideology.)

Spokeswomen for the Lesbian Mothers Defense Fund (LMDF) were among the most vigorous and persuasive critics of cross-generational sex. Positioning themselves as moral guardians and recasting maternal feminist rhetoric of the nineteenth century, they argued for the "innocence" of children. Adult lesbian feminists, members of LOOT contended, were not child molesters, nor did they sexually desire children. As Amy Gottlieb recalls, "There was a need to say we were really different [from gay men] and by implication, we wouldn't do this with young girls."[13] In interviews for this piece only one narrator mentioned having had sex with an older woman, while two women mentioned the sex they had experienced with underage female partners. Perhaps a compulsion to disengage from the messiness of one's past in the service of a politically consistent present prevented others from disclosing similar acts.[14] Even the lesbian "crush" popularized by singer/songwriter Meg Christian's "Ode to a Gym Teacher" (Olive Records, 1974) was eulogized in language reminiscent of nineteenth-century ennobling of same-sex romantic friendships. Ultimately, notwithstanding Jane Rule's heretical wish "to make adults easier to seduce," breaking the cross-generational taboo was incongruent with 1970s right-on, reciprocal, relational love between adult, women-identified women.[15]

In light of their own personal and increasingly political awareness of male sexual violence, many lesbian and straight feminists were suspicious of claims to consensual sex, whether straight or gay.[16] As stated by Susan Cole, "Gay men were interested in eliminating age of consent laws so they could find many, many dozen more holes into which they could plug their penises."[17] Cole and others were not encouraged by the stories that some gay men, as teenagers, delighted in the sexual education they sought and received from older men, or that virtually all boys, as males, are taught to view themselves as sexual subjects. That intergenerational sex among males often entailed a positive and genuinely different experience from intergenerational heterosex was not something with which women, lesbian or straight, identified.[18]

However, while most activist lesbians were scornful of what they understood to be "anonymous," "penis-fixated," "recreational" and "public" gay sex-at-any-cost,[19] gay liberationists Chris Bearchell and Konnie Reich remember the envy they felt (and still feel) toward the richness of gay male sexual possibilities.[20] Comprising a tiny minority in the late 1970s, Bearchell, Reich and others were drawn to the complex dynamics of dominance and submission, lust and fantasy played out in some segments of the (white) gay male community, and made vivid in the sexually anarchic work of filmmaker Kenneth Anger, writers John Rechy and John Preston, and artist Tom of Finland.[21] The majority of LOOT members felt, though, that the worst forms of heterosexual power imbalance, objectification and insensitivity were intrinsic to gay male sexual activity. To LOOT members, the pursuit of young boys exemplified the vulgar opportunism already present in a gay male world that obsessively sought new, increasingly commercial outlets for sexual pleasure.[22] As Darlene Lawson quipped, "Would it really destroy the lesbian movement in this community or country if *The Body Politic* was not operating?"[23]

THE CONUNDRUM OF THE STATE

Against that hegemonic feminist current, a small collection of lesbian activists, many of whom had participated in the Stop Anita Bryant Coalition in the summer of 1977, argued that *The Body Politic* and the freedom to publish, more generally, must be defended. In particular, the five women who joined The Body Politic Free the Press Fund insisted that lesbian feminists needed to take a strong, principled stand against the danger of state control in the form of sexual censorship as well as bath and bar raids, police intimidation and entrapment. The lines, though, were not clearly drawn.

Lesbian feminists of all political stripes condemned the police seizure of twelve shipping cartons full of materials from *The Body Politic* office and the laying of charges against Pink Triangle Press. They were shaken by the blatant incursion—the depth and severity of which were then unknown to lesbian feminist institutions. And yet at the same time, in another context, many of these activists were exerting pressure on state agents to forbid the public screening and distribution of what they deemed "offensive" sexual materials. One month prior to *The Body Politic* raid, a band of radical feminists from LOOT and the newly formed "Snuff Out Snuff" (SOS) contingent descended upon mayor Crombie's office demanding the closure of the film "Snuff" at Cinema 2000. In a letter to *The Body Politic* in 1978, Pat Leslie cautioned against support for state censorship laws which "could conceivably be used against us."[24] And yet, at the same time, Eve Zaremba, Susan Cole and others began to argue for the necessary involvement of the state (via the Criminal Code, customs regulations and censor boards) to legislate against "pornographic material" that, according to Cole, not only "taught the hatred of women," but also "promoted child abuse."[25] In concert with feminist anti-porn organizations in the United States which also formed in late 1977, Zaremba, Cole and others began a call for state-administered penalties against the owners of the commercial pornography industry—"the purveyors of violence against women"—a call which foreshadowed the infamous Minneapolis Ordinance designed by anti-pornography crusaders Catharine MacKinnon and Andrea Dworkin in 1983.[26]

As Darlene Lawson avowed during the January 1978 debate on *The Body Politic* at the LOOT headquarters, enlisting the state to censor such "damaging" accounts as "Men Loving Boys Loving Men" was not only conceivable, it was a justified strategy.[27] Ironically, it was one that also appealed to right-wing lobbyists. Only weeks earlier, *Toronto Sun* columnist Claire Hoy demanded the repeal of two small Ontario Arts grants awarded to *The Body Politic* on the grounds that "our taxes are helping to promote the abuse of children" (a demand that anticipated Jesse Helms' homophobic assault on the NEA in 1989 and *Toronto Sun* columnist Christina Blizzard's attack on the "flagrant misuse of state funds" by the AIDS Committee of Toronto in 1992).[28]

In effect, then, lesbian and feminist criticism of all forms of male sexuality in the '70s led to both tacit and openly declared support (alongside moral conservatives) for state regulation of male homosexual pornography, and by extension, all gay male sexual expression. Having taken this stance, and without a pornographic tradition of their own, it is perhaps not surprising that lesbian activists did not mount a coordinated protest against the police seizure of *The Joy of Lesbian Sex* in the same raid on *The Body Politic* offices in late 1977.

GENDER LOYALTY

Reflecting upon the mid-to-late 1970s, the territories occupied jointly by lesbian feminists and activist gay men seem much more troubled than the mezzanine of the King Edward Hotel, Bowles Lunch, the Melody Room after-hours club or Hanlan's Point beach shared by semi-secret queer subcultures in the 1950s and '60s.[29] Requests to join gay men on the front lines stirred fears in post-Stonewall lesbian feminists of being railroaded into positions prematurely or of having their agenda co-opted by a slick, more experienced gay male leadership. Further, political lesbians in the '70s were not overly keen on joining forces with gay men given the spotty evidence of gay men's anti-sexism, measured in part by poor attendance at abortion rallies, anti-violence protests, International Women's Day events, strikes by women workers, and so on (though paradoxically it was not always clear that men, gay or straight, were welcome). Faced with scarce resources, the legacy of invisibility and the goals of coming out proud and united, white lesbian leaders were consumed by the desire to construct empowered, cultural identities and "gomer-free" wanderground: a forceful and utopian lesbian feminist mythos enacted to bind women together. They grappled with inventing language not only to describe and analyse sexism and heterosexism, but to give voice to the particularities of lesbian oppression and the need for women-only space.

Throughout the '70s, immersed in campaigns to end men's sexual violence, neither lesbian nor straight feminists battled to enshrine a politics of pleasure in arenas outside their own bedrooms.[30]

With so many lesbians just coming out, their often hurtful memories of heterosexual sex were deep, immediate reminders of their need to "do sex" differently. In this context, gay male sexuality (and gay male life which, to cite John D'Emilio, has often taken shape in pornographic zones) appeared threateningly "other" or "alien."[31] As such, feminist elevation of "the personal" to creed fed the disinclination, even resistance, of lesbian feminists to move beyond the limits of their own lived experience. Under siege and inventing things as they went along, they constituted a visible, proud presence against social forces that actively disavowed or condemned their existence. However, their emphases and practices also contained strands of a congealing, identity-based politics compelling (and exclusive) to insiders who feared dissolution, co-optation and assimilation.[32]

Indeed, gay men's sexual culture was not readily "personalized" by lesbians who themselves were vying to displace medical and popular images of The Lesbian as sexual deviate, pervert and predator. Most radical lesbians—who were largely white and middle-class—were embarrassed and repelled by talk and images of "dirty," "kinky" gay male "promiscuity."[33] Without supportive links to largely working-class sex workers, lesbian feminists unwittingly aligned themselves with the "Clean Up Yonge Street" campaign against prostitutes, dancers, porn models and masseuses who worked "the strip" and who became increasingly vulnerable to arrest and police harassment in the '70s. Thus the moral authority exercised by some white middle-class lesbian feminists vis-à-vis sex and sexual imagery in the mid-to-late '70s not only echoed the sexual conservatism of the Daughters of Bilitis in the 1950s; but it also reworked early twentieth-century temperance and social purity notions of essential, unchecked male lust from which women needed protection.[34]

Consonant with bourgeois norms of propriety, these lesbian radicals seemed partial to century-old notions of childhood as the age of vulnerability to be guarded at all costs from adult corruption. Championing the goodness of egalitarian, nurturant adult love, most middle-class lesbian activists seemed unaware of the state warehousing of minors—sexually active working-class girls—in detention centres on charges of sexual immorality. Regarding man/boy love, not only did lesbian feminists tend to re-invoke the potent spectre of pedophilia (against evidence that the overwhelming majority of child molesters are heterosexual men), they applied an analysis of unequal power in adult/child heterosexual relations to adult/youth homosexual relations without considering how same-gender sex might fundamentally alter the dynamic. Had girlhood memories of lust for older women been admissible, it is possible that recognition of the disjuncture between practice and ideology may have opened up space for dialogue and for the formulation of alternative strategies. Indeed, attention to the structuring of power within lesbian sexual exchanges was effectively stopped (or at least discredited) until volcanic debates about butch/femme and SM erupted in the early 1980s.

Significantly, by the end of the '70s, lesbian feminist attention to power and its abuses in sexual relations had raised vexing questions concerning the civil libertarian stance of *The Body Politic*. It also prefigured later criticisms of the race- and class-bound character of commercial porn, gay and straight.[35] However, the slide from criticism of sexual practice and representation to support for state sexual censorship was riddled with flaws, not least of all the deflection away from root causes of sexual and gender inequality in capitalist, racist and patriarchal culture.[36]

In the end, a preoccupation with mobilizing around female rage and pain, disconnection from pre-Stonewall queer experience of state sexual regulation, a separation from gay men and the yearning of many middle-class lesbian feminists for radical (yet respectable) power-free love, contributed to the dominant feminist interpretation of cross-generational sex, gay and straight, as indefensible. On the level of strategy in the mid-to-late 1970s, lesbian and straight feminists tended to support two courses of action: 1) the elimination of pornography by the state through obscenity legislation; 2) the rejection of demands made by gay and lesbian youth for modification, if not abolition, of "age of consent" laws. Importantly, the reluctance of the left to engage in the politics of sexuality, compounded by the long-standing anti-left hostility of radical (and liberal) feminists, accounted in part for feminist faith in the state's role as a facilitating force in social justice.[37] Over the past year, the short-sightedness of this approach has become crystal clear given the retooled obscenity legislation enshrined by the Supreme Court (i.e., the *Butler* decision) and recent interpretations of *Butler* that have criminalized sexually explicit matters, both lesbian/gay and straight.

THE 1990s: THE PROMISE OF QUEER

Between 1977 and when *The Body Politic* closed down in 1987, discussion of the content of the "Men Loving Boys" article was ostensibly squelched. Undoubtedly, the immeasurable amounts of community time, energy and money expended in defense of the paper chilled the collective's desire to encourage further debate on the subject. Today, as one consequence of this chill, nagging issues persist: If an imbalance of gender power relations is not relevant when we consider sex between men and boys (or women and girls), do unequal power relations based on age remain? In other words, what age limits (if any) are appropriate in determining when the impermissible becomes permissible? How do gay (and lesbian) youth who seek sex from adults make sense of this desire and the sexual activity that may ensue? And how can print and visual resources designed to foster sexual agency in young people (ideally produced by youth themselves) be made widely available?

To date, gay and lesbian movements have not mounted a successful defense of "man/boy love." Clearly, the stigmatization of gay men as lecherous child molesters is long-standing and resilient; however, the current lesbian/gay moratorium on cross-generational sex cedes authority to the already powerful emotional (and moral) force of a right-wing sexual agenda. Christina Blizzard of *The Toronto Sun*, the architects and supporters of Measure 9 in Oregon and Initiative 2 in Colorado during the 1992 United States' presidential campaign, have been successful in deploying the demonizing discourse of homosexual pedophilia in the service of a broad offensive against all lesbians and gay men.[38] In addition, the intense focus on the spectre of the perverts is being used to galvanize neo-conservative and fundamentalist activity on broader issues of welfare, unemployment, immigration, the family, people of colour and women.

In looking for allies to challenge the dominant ideology of young people's sexuality (and the control adults exert over children/youth), gay men will not readily discover friends among lesbian feminists. Still, factors that include the AIDS/HIV crisis, the efflorescence of queer discourses inspired in part by man/boy lovers, sex workers, bisexuals, SM dykes and lesbians and gay men of colour, as well as the state confiscation of lesbian-explicit materials (e.g., *Bad*

Attitude), have converged to herald new possibilities of conscious coalition, of political and social kinship.[39] Unlike (white, middle-class) lesbian feminist ideology of the 1970s, the distinction made between male and female sexualities no longer operates as the primary political cleavage. Moreover, there seems to be a growing awareness among feminists that radical issues are often transformed by the state into legal (as well as administrative and medical) categories which may bear little resemblance to original feminist (and anti-racist) demands or intents.[40] Whether queer-as-identity will operate as a set of rallying points, or yet another regulatory regime riven by inclusions and exclusions, will only become clear through the repetitive enactment of queerness in myriad private and public arenas of struggle.

NOTES

1 Analysis of relationships forged between activist lesbians and gay men in the post-Stonewall period remains underdeveloped. Brief references can be found in Margaret Cruikshank, *The Gay and Lesbian Liberation Movement* (New York and London: Routledge, 1992); Teresa de Lauretis, "Queer Theory: Lesbian and Gay Sexualities," *differences: A Journal of Feminist Cultural Studies*, vol. 3, no. 2 (1991), pp. iii-xviii; Jeffrey Escoffier, "Can Gay Men and Lesbians Work Together?" *Out/Look*, no. 6 (Fall, 1989), p. 1; Amy Gottlieb, "The Gay Movement," in Lesbians Against the Right (ed.) *Lesbians Are Everywhere, Fighting the Right* (Toronto: 1981), pp. 7–101; and, John D'Emilio, *Making Trouble: essays on gay history, politics and the university* (New York and London: Routledge, 1992).

2 Gerald Hannon, "Men Loving Boys Loving Men," *The Body Politic* (November, 1977), pp. 30–33. The standpoint of sexually active young gays and lesbians was explored in "Seven Years to Go: the plight of gay youth," *The Body Politic* (September, 1976), pp. 1, 14, 15.

3 Claire Hoy, "Stop the Bleeding Hearts," *The Toronto Sun* (October 30, 1977); 'The Limp Wrist Lobby," *The Toronto Sun* (November 2, 1977); "Gay Rights, Continuing Saga," *The Toronto Sun* (November 13, 1977); "Morality vs. Perversity," *The Toronto Sun* (December 21, 1977); "Our Taxes Help Homosexuals Promote Abuse of Children," *The Toronto Sun* (December 22, 1977); "Kids, Not Rights, Is Their Craving," *The Toronto Sun* (December 25, 1977).

4 Armed with a warrant, officers from the Metropolitan Toronto Police force and the Ontario Provincial Police carted away twelve shipping cartons filled with documents and records: subscription lists dating years into the past, distribution and advertising records, corporate and financial records (even the cheque book), classified ad records and addresses, manuscripts for publication and letters to the editors. Personal and business mail was opened and the Canadian Gay Archives was ransacked. Importantly, unlike gay men, there was not the same tension between the local character of the politics and everyday lives of LOOT members and the extra-local and textual organization of gay male life instructed by the Criminal Code. Lesbian oppression was, and is not, primarily organized through official categories of "indecency" and "obscenity."

5 *The Body Politic* editors were also charged under section 159 with "possession for the purpose of distribution, of obscene publications": the books *Loving Man* and *The Joy of Lesbian Sex*. On August 12, 1977, Norman Webster of *The Globe and Mail* reconsidered the value of sexual orientation legislation: "If that right is to include proselytizing or the teaching of homosexuality in the schools by homosexual instructors or swinging adult males having affairs with young boys—all things loudly demanded by militants in the movement, then forget it. It's just not on."

6 On the Jaques murder, see Yvonne Chi-Ying Ng, "Ideology, Media and Moral Panics: an analysis of the Jaques Murder" (Centre for Criminology, University of Toronto, M.A. thesis, 1981) and Gary Kinsman, "The Jaques Murder: an anatomy of a moral panic," in *The Regulation of Desire* (Montreal: Black Rose Books, 1986), pp. 204–205. This was not the first "homosexual" murder in Toronto. See Sidney Katz, "The Truth about Sex Criminals," which appeared in *Maclean's*, July 1, 1967, pp. 46–48. Here, Katz focuses on "homosexual" sex murders. The article also associates homosexuals with the molesting of children.

7 On the media, see Chris Bearchell, Rick Bébout, Alexander Wilson, "Another Look," *The Body Politic*, no. 51 (March/April 1979), where they state: "The 'molestation tactic' was tailor-made for the compressed and unsubtle world of the mass media. It was direct, unencumbered by sophisticated analysis and could make a dramatic impact in less than ten seconds" (p. 21).

8 A debate was scheduled in the Ontario Legislature in early February 1978 to consider the prohibition of discrimination on the basis of sexual orientation. Gay Alliance Towards Equality (GATE), the John Damian Defense Committee and the Coalition of Gay Rights in Ontario had made this a priority since the early 1970s.

9 Interview with Pat Murphy, 1986, conducted by myself and other members of the oral history collective, Lesbians Making History, Toronto.

10 "Editorial," *The Body Politic*, no. 39 (December/January, 1977) p. 1.

11 Interview with Amy Gottlieb, 1989.

12 Interview with Ed Jackson, 1992. As Education Coordinator of the AIDS Committee of Toronto, Jackson commented on how AIDS activism and service provision has facilitated some positive, respectful relations between lesbians and gay men, though these relations are far from conflict-free.

13 Interview with Amy Gottlieb, 1989.

14 In *The Safe Sea of Women: Lesbian Fiction, 1969–1989* (Boston: Beacon Press, 1990), critic Bonnie Zimmerman identifies the pressure lesbians face to "shape one's personal story in accordance with the communal tale, or myth" (p. 51).

15 Jane Rule's original article, "Teaching Sexuality" appeared in issue no. 53 (June, 1979) of *The Body Politic* and has been reprinted in her collection *Outlander: short stories and essays* (Tallahassee, Fla.: Naiad Press, 1982), pp. 157–162. Here, Rule adds: "[I would want] to make adults easier to seduce, less burdened with fear or guilt, less defended by hypocrisy. If we accepted sexual behaviour between children and adults, we would be far more able to protect our children from abuse and exploitation than we are now" (pp. 160–161).

16 It is hypothesized in the article "Incest and Other Sexual Taboos: A Dialogue between Men and Women," *Out/Look* (Fall, 1989) that "the feminist/lesbian movements may be anti-sexual because many of the women involved may have been sexually abused. Whether they remember it or not" (p. 53). I would submit that the connections between women's (lesbian, straight and bisexual) histories of sexual abuse, feminist politics and actual sexual practice require much more rigorous investigation.

17 Interview with Susan Cole, 1989.

18 This is not to argue that all cross-generational sexual experiences between gay youth and men are positive and pleasurable, as testimonies at the 1991 inquiry into widespread sexual abuse of young people at the Mount Cashel, Newfoundland, orphanage makes clear.

19 See Adrienne Rich, "The Meaning of Our Love For Women Is What We Have Constantly to Expand,"

in Adrienne Rich, *On Lies, Secrets and Silence: Selected Prose, 1966–1977* (New York: W.W. Norton and Co., 1980), p. 225. In this essay, as in her oft-quoted "Compulsory Heterosexuality and Lesbian Existence" (1980), she speaks to the tensions between activist lesbians and gay men. Specifically, she criticizes gay men's "gynephobia" and points to the difficulties of finding "real 'brotherly' solidarity in the gay movement." She also points to the "prevalence of anonymous sex and the justification of pederasty among male homosexuals, the pronounced ageism in male homosexual standards of sexual attractiveness, and so forth" (p. 193).

20 Interview with Chris Bearchell and Konnie Reich, 1990. In 1978, responding to the "Men Loving Boys" debacle, Gayle Rubin penned a letter to *The Body Politic* cautioning against the abandon of "already vulnerable and stigmatized groups such as boy-lovers, sadomasochists and transsexuals to further attack and isolation" (p. 90).

21 On gay male porn, see Nayland Blake, "Tom of Finland, an appreciation," *Out/Look* (Fall, 1988), pp. 36–45, and John Preston, "What Happened? An SM pioneer reflects on the leather world past and present,"*Out/Look* (Winter, 1992), pp. 8–15. For a post-Stonewall piece of gay male erotic writing, see John Rechy, *City of Night* (New York: Grove, 1977).

22 By the late '70s, especially in large urban centres like Toronto, many lesbian feminists extended their distaste for gay male political and sexual culture to what they viewed as signs of a rising gay capitalism. A burgeoning commercial and residential district complete with established cruising grounds, businesses, a publishing company, local bars, baths and clubs, and a pornography industry, signified the expansion of a gay male market.

23 Darlene Lawson, three-hour taped debate, "Men Loving Boys Loving Men" at LOOT, January, 1978, housed at the Canadian Women's Movement Archive (CWMA/acmf), Toronto, Ontario.

24 Pat Leslie, "Doing Our Own Work," *The Body Politic*, no. 46 (September, 1978), p. 2. For an early critique of the limitations of state sexual censorship legislation, see Mariana Valverde, "Freedom, Violence and Pornography," *The Body Politic*, no. 51 (March/April, 1979), p. 19.

25 See Eve Zaremba, "Porn Again," *The Body Politic*. no. 47 (October, 1978), p. 4.

26 Ibid.

27 Darlene Lawson, three-hour taped debate, "Men Loving Boys Loving Men" at LOOT, January, 1978, housed at the Canadian Women's Movement Archive (CWMA/acmf), Toronto, Ontario.

28 Claire Hoy, "The Limp Wrist Lobby," *The Toronto Sun* (November 2, 1977). And see Christina Blizzard, "Gay Pap Appalling Tax Waste," *The Toronto Sun* (January 25, 1992), p. 14; "Gay Flier Furor: Pamphlet Says Homosexuality 'Natural,'" *The Toronto Sun* (September 25, 1992), p. 4; "Gay Case for Fliers is Bizarre," *The Toronto Sun* (September 25, 1992), p. 14; "Personal Problem? Yes It Is," *The Toronto Sun* (October 15, 1992), p. 16.

29 I treat these themes in greater depth in my unpublished article, "Dance to 'Tie a Yellow Ribbon', Get 'Churched' and 'Buy the Little Lady a Drink,'" Toronto, 1993.

30 For a longer discussion of lesbian feminist sexual norms in the 1970s, see my article, "Sex, Lives and Archives: Pleasure/Danger Debates in 1970s Lesbian Feminism," Sandi Kirby, Michele Pujol, Kate McKenna, Michele Valiquette, Dayna Daniels (eds.) *Women Changing Academe* (Winnipeg: Sororal Publishing, 1991), pp. 74–91.

31 John D'Emilio, *Making Trouble: essays on gay history, politics and the university* (Routledge: New York and London, 1992), p. 202.

32 This is not to deny the multiple successes achieved by political lesbians in the 1970s which have seeded virtually all contemporary lesbian social, political and cultural initiatives. I roundly dispute trendy critiques that simplistically reduce this decade of lesbian nationalism to anti-male, anti-sex pessimism or naive, gender-separatist idealism. My point is one of self-criticism, i.e., by isolating and analysing pitfalls in past thought and practice, we become better able to effect change in our historical present.

33 Laura Kipnis, "(Male) Desire and (Female) Disgust: Reading Hustler," in Lawrence Grossberg, Cary Nelson and Paula Triechler (eds.) *Cultural Studies* (Routledge: New York and London, 1991), pp. 373–391.

34 On the history of the English Canadian social purity movement, see Mariana Valverde, *The Age of Light, Soap and Water: Moral Reform in English Canada, 1885–1925* (Toronto: McClelland and Stewart, 1991) and in Britain, Margaret Hunt, "The De-Eroticization of Women's Liberation: Social Purity Movements and the Revolutionary Feminism of Sheila Jeffreys," *Feminist Review*, no. 34 (Spring, 1990), pp. 23–45.

35 There is the beginning of a critical reconsideration of the genre largely led by working-class gay men and gay men of colour. See letters from Richard Fung, Pei Lim and Alan Li in *The Body Politic*, no. 113 (April, 1983), p. 30; Gary Kinsman, "The Porn Debate," *FUSE* (Summer, 1984), pp. 39–44, as well as Gary Kinsman, "Racism in Gay Male Porn: An interview with Pei Lim," *Rites* (February 1987), pp. 14–15; Richard Fung, "Looking for My Penis: The Eroticized Asian in Gay Video Porn," in Bad Object-Choices (eds.) *How Do I Look? Queer Film and Video* (Seattle: Bay Press, 1991), pp. 145–168. On reading the textual ambivalence in Robert Mapplethorpe's photographic representation of black male nudes, see Kobena Mercer, "Skin Head Sex Thing: Racial Difference and the Homoerotic Imaginary," in Bad Object-Choices (eds.) *How Do I Look? Queer Film and Video* (Seattle: Bay Press, 1991), pp. 169–222. And see Paul Leonard's review of The Bear Cult in *Rites* (January/February, 1992) where he argues: "Instead of the blond-surfers-with-massive-hairless-pecs-and-big-dicks, we are presented with older men—well, twenties to fifties, anyway—men who are bearded, hairy, tattooed, men whose body types range, for the most part, from 'husky' to very fat" (p. 19).

36 See Varda Burstyn's edited anthology, *Women Against Censorship* (Vancouver: Douglas and McIntyre, 1983).

37 See Varda Bursryn, "The Left and the Porn Wars," in Howard Buchbinder, Diana Forbes, Varda Burstyn and Mercedes Steedman (eds.) *Who's On Top: The Politics of Heterosexuality* (Toronto: Garamond Press, 1987), pp. 11–46.

38 On the chilling developments in Oregon and Colorado during the US federal election in 1992, see Sally Chew, "Ding, Dong, Mabon Calling," *Out* (March, 1993), pp. 41–47.

39 In April 1992, mostly young, in-your-face "queer girls" took to the streets to protest the police seizure of *Bad Attitude* from Glad Day bookshop (the content of which unapologetically adapted conventions of gay male porn). They were joined by others equally committed to the efflorescence of queer sexual discourses and the repudiation of newly entrenched obscenity legislation—i.e., the *Butler* decision, that heavily references anti-porn feminism. See Chris Bearchell, "Cut That Out," *This Magazine* (January/February, 1993), pp. 37–40; and Clare Barclay and Elaine Carol, "Obscenity Chill: Artists in a Post-Butler Era," *FUSE* (vol. 16, no. 2, Winter, 1992–93), pp. 18–28.

40 On the limitations of the categories "visible minority" and "multiculturalism," see Linda Carty and Dionne Brand, "'Visible Minority' Women—A Creation of the Canadian State," *Resources for Feminist Research* (September, 1988), pp. 39–42.

PART FOUR
Health, Medicine, and the Experts

CHAPTER 10

On the Case of the Case:
The Emergence of the Homosexual as a Case
History in Early-Twentieth-Century Ontario

Steven Maynard

In February 1911, Walter F., a butcher from Toronto's St. Lawrence Market, appeared in Police Court on several charges of gross indecency. The judge presiding over the preliminary hearing decided there was sufficient evidence to send the case on to a higher court. As Walter was remanded in jail, Magistrate Denison ordered: 'Let the doctors see that man before he goes up.' After several weeks awaiting trial in jail, Walter finally received a visit from the doctor. Beginning with Walter's name and age, the doctor proceeded to conduct a mental examination. Walter's answers to the doctor's many questions were recorded by the doctor in a case history: 'Walter F.—age 43—born 1869—July 15th—London, England—lived there the first twenty years of life—went to school until 16—afterwards went to learn the trade of butcher—been at it all my life—came to Canada four years ago—came to Toronto—went to Harris abattoirs—worked there three months—then went to St. Lawrence Market—married 21 years of age—5 living children—3 children dead—Father died age 46—alcoholic—Mother died age 25—childbirth—have always indulged freely in stimulants—20 drinks—has lead irregular life.' Aside perhaps from the taint of an alcoholic father and an intemperate, irregular life, the doctor was unable to find symptoms of mental disease and pronounced Walter fit to stand trial. Walter was found guilty. Although the doctor had discovered no evidence of mental illness in Walter's case, in passing sentence Judge Denton averred that Walter's behaviour was 'evidently due to some disease of the mind.'[1]

It was Foucault who famously remarked that sometime beginning in the nineteenth century the homosexual became, among other things, a 'case history.'[2] It was a mark of Foucault's brilliance that he was so often theoretically right when, as we historians are wont to remind everyone, he actually read very few case histories. But the psychiatric examinations performed by doctors on men like Walter—men charged with homosexual offences in early-twentieth-century Ontario courts—confirm Foucault's speculations on the way the law and medicine worked together to transform men and their homosexual activities into case histories.[3] Of course, what Foucault meant was not so much that the homosexual became a case history, but that the case history helped to bring the homosexual into existence. In this way, the case history was closely related to what Foucault identified as one of the linchpins of disciplinary power—the examination. The examination, surrounded by all its documentary techniques, makes each individual a "case": a case which at one and the same time constitutes an object for a branch of knowledge and a hold for a branch of power. In terms of the homosexual, Foucault singled out the 'psychiatrization of perverse pleasure,' or the mental examinations and case histories of homosexuals performed by psychiatrists and other medical professionals.[4]

Gay historians, especially those grounded in social history with its traditional emphases on human agency and the material, have been reluctant to wholly embrace Foucault's insistence on the discursive invention of the homosexual. George Chauncey, for one, has convincingly argued that 'medical discourse did not "invent" the homosexual … [Doctors] were investigating a subculture rather than creating one.' Against those who would privilege discourse in the formation of homosexual identities and subcultures, Chauncey has offered a powerful reconceptualization, one that stresses the role of homosexual men in the making of their own cultural worlds.[5]

The debates within gay history over the relative roles played by discourse and the material in shaping identities and experience have parallels in many other subfields of social history. They have in common a concern with the nature and status of historical evidence, a concern provoked by the poststructuralist critique of historical practice.[6] Case files have emerged as one particularly fractious site in the debates over evidence. Think back to the exchange between Joan Scott and Linda Gordon over the interpretation of the case files of social-welfare agencies. These debates also share a similar structure, one often marked by dichotomous, either/or positions. In the Scott-Gordon exchange, Scott argued that the historian should train his or her analytic gaze on the way the case files constructed the categories and subject positions of domestic abuse; Gordon maintained that the historian could use the case files to recover women's historical experience and resistance of abuse. Neither Scott nor Gordon really allowed any of the other's position. This unproductive stance, one that casts the relationship between the discursive and the material as mutually exclusive, has unfortunately characterized much of the discussion among historians.[7]

In what follows, I want to make a modest contribution to efforts currently under way to think through the material/discursive impasse in the writing of social history through a brief consideration of the psychiatric case histories from the legal case files of men charged with homosexual offences in early-twentieth-century Ontario.[8] If Chauncey is right, and I think he is, that doctors and medical discourse did not invent the homosexual, the question remains, What did they do? During mental examinations, doctors translated men's sexual experiences with other men into cases of 'insanity,' 'perversion,' and 'homosexuality.' Key to this process—and what I want to trace here—were the textual practices of the case history. I also want to look at the discursive linkages between case histories and the broader medical discourse. Worked up into articles in medical journals and texts, doctors' case histories became the basis for an emerging psychiatric discourse in Canada, one that linked homosexual behaviour with mental disease.

The Ontario case also allows us to explore what may be some interesting divergences between Canada and the United States vis-à-vis state formation and sexual regulation. Chauncey has suggested for the United States that medical professionals 'did not play a major role in the state regulation of homosexuality until World War II.'[9] That Ontario courts sent men charged with homosexual offenses for psychiatric examination beginning around 1910—the earliest examination I discovered dates from 1905—suggests that the Canadian state, at least at the local level, began to draw on the power of medical professionals and medical discourse sooner than in the United States. Chauncey further argues that until the mid-twentieth century, doctors and medical discourse had little impact on the lives and self-understandings of most homosexually active men. What influence doctors had specifically over men's sense of their sexual identities remains an elusive historical question, but it is clear that doctors *did* have an impact on the lives of homosexually active men, at least upon many of those hauled before the courts in Ontario. Thinking of Walter's case, doctors had the power to help determine whether a man stood trial or not. Doctors' expert testimony also had the power to influence the outcome of a man's trial and, if found guilty, whether he was sent to jail, committed to a hospital, or in some cases released on suspended sentence. Thinking of the judges involved in Walter's trials, it is clear that their understanding of sexual relations between men was shaped in part by the emerging medical/psychiatric conceptualization of homosexual behaviour as a 'disease of the mind.' Indeed, I would suggest that links established among criminality, insanity, and homosexuality in the early-twentieth-century Ontario court cases, doctors' case histories, and psychiatric discourse laid some of the groundwork for the intensification of medico-legal regulation during and after the Second World War, most notably in the creation of sexual psychopath laws and their particularly devastating effects on gay men.

Before attending to the discursive operations of the case history, I want to foreground what Judith Walkowitz has termed 'the material context of discursive struggle.'[10] I will do this by tracing the historical and material context of the emergence of the psychiatric case history.

THE HISTORY OF THE CASE HISTORY

Ironically, historians who often rely on case histories as primary sources have paid little attention to the historical emergence of the case history. But the case history does have a history. The medical case history, for instance, has a long genealogy, one stretching back to Hippocrates and the cases in his Epidemics. As Julia Epstein has noted, a renewed interest in Hippocratic medicine in the seventeenth century produced a flurry of treatises on case-taking. But, as Epstein demonstrates, 'not until the nineteenth century were these ... translated into particular techniques of notation and data organization in patient histories ... Case-taking did not become a formalized or systematic procedure until it became connected with clinical schools and institutions and their need to produce and codify a professional discourse.'[11] We need, then, to skip ahead to the nineteenth century, in which a changing material context established the preconditions for the emergence of the case history as we know it. Two processes were crucial here. First, rapid urbanization in the nineteenth century demanded the development of new devices, including statistics, social surveys, criminal identification methods, and, of course, case histories, in order to know and regulate increasingly large populations of urban dwellers. As Dorothy Smith explains: 'Case histories and case records evolved … when government welfare agencies or charitable organizations were confronted with the numbers and anonymities of the late-nineteenth-century city, when the particularized knowledge of people and their histories characterizing smaller communities no longer served.'[12] Second, the historical emergence of case histories was also intimately linked with the efforts of experts to professionalize their fields. In her work on the history of single mothers and social work, for instance, Regina Kunzel demonstrates how casework—'key to the professionalizing project of social workers'—'used a step-by-step procedure of collecting information about a person's experiences and background, followed by "diagnosis" and "treatment" of their problem.'[13]

Case histories, of course, also proved to be particularly integral to the nineteenth-century emergence of the professions of psychiatry and sexology. One of the pioneers of the sexological case history was Richard von Krafft-Ebing. His classic text *Psychopathia Sexualis,* published in 1886, was originally based on forty-five case histories. As Jeffrey Weeks has noted, Krafft-Ebing's 'case studies were a model of what was to follow, the analyses were a rehearsal for a century of theorizing.' From the beginning, the psychiatric case history was tied to the legal realm. Krafft-Ebing, who described *Psychopathia Sexualis* as a medico-forensic study, was a professor of psychiatry whose 'earliest concern was with finding proofs of morbidity for those sexual offenders dragged before the courts.'[14] Over the next several decades, the case history became central to the practice and professionalization of psychiatry. Elizabeth Lunbeck, for example, in her fine history of psychiatry based on the case records of the Boston Psychopathic Hospital (established in 1912), has drawn attention to the significance of 'the examination and the constitution of the case.'[15]

The reciprocal relationship between the law and medicine was forged in Ontario beginning in the late nineteenth century through the courts' referral of men charged with homosexual offences to doctors for examination. Medical examination took two different forms. Some men were sent to doctors for a regular physical exam to obtain medical evidence of sexual activity. Doctors probed what they preferred to call men's 'anal apertures' on the lookout for the tell-tale traces of penetration: semen, a 'dilated aperture,' and the like. But by the opening decade of the twentieth century, some men were sent by the courts specifically for mental examinations. The issue of an accused's mental condition was an extremely important matter in the courtroom. Lawyers defending men charged with a homosexual offence sometimes argued their clients were not guilty by reason of insanity. The prosecution might also claim an accused man was insane in order to secure a conviction, suggesting that an insane man posed a danger to himself and others. Either way it was necessary to have medical proof. The law required that at least two doctors concur that the accused was insane, and further stipulated that the doctors spell out their diagnoses in a 'Province of Ontario Physician's Certificate.' The physician's certificate was a rudimentary case history recording the doctor's examination of the accused along with a determination of whether the accused was sane or insane.[16] Certificates were entered as exhibits in the trial and sometimes accompanied by a doctor's testimony in court. The significance of the certificate and how to conduct a mental examination constituted a part of medical instruction in late-nineteenth-century Ontario. In his lectures to graduating medical students, published in

1895, Daniel Clark, the superintendent of the Toronto Insane Asylum, explained that the physician's certificate was 'a record of observed facts' and he stressed that the 'medical certificates are important documents, hence great care should be exercised in filling them up properly.'[17]

As one way to bolster the modern, scientific status of the emerging profession, psychiatrists devoted much energy to refining and making more complex the case history, both the mental examination and its corresponding documentary forms. In his annual report for 1906, S.A. Armstrong, the provincial inspector of prisons and public charities, announced that 'a new system of case book or clinical records, together with a filing system, has now been completed and will be installed in all the Asylums of the province at the beginning of the new year.' Armstrong noted that 'the system will be uniform throughout and will be in keeping with the most modern practice of recording the history and clinical records pertaining to a patient.' The following year, Armstrong was pleased to report that 'the new system of recording clinical notes of cases … has proved most satisfactory … In compiling the data necessary for completion of the history of a patient, greater attention will be paid to the case by the attending physician than has been possible heretofore.'[18] The introduction of the new case-history forms and procedures was greeted with enthusiasm by psychiatrists. In October 1907, the *Bulletin of the Ontario Hospitals for the Insane* noted with approval the introduction of the new 'history form.' Two years later, Dr Charles K. Clarke, one of the country's leading psychiatrists and the superintendent of the Toronto Hospital for the Insane after Daniel Clark's retirement in 1905, wrote in an article on 'The Relationship of Psychiatry to General Medicine' that 'in any study of mental disease you must scan closely: the family history, the whole life history of the patient, the history of the disease, and the present condition.' 'No wonder,' Clarke concluded, 'even a poor form of application is elaborate.' Clarke's was one of many similar articles pressing for the acceptance of psychiatry among general practitioners, and key to psychiatry's campaign for professional legitimacy was the case history.[19]

The case history assumed an increasingly central position in psychiatric practice in the opening decades of the twentieth century. This was evident at the Psychiatric Clinic of the Toronto General Hospital. Opened in 1909, the Psychiatric Out-Patient Clinic was the first of C.K. Clarke's efforts to establish a psychiatric practice separate from the asylum system. As Jennifer Stephen has demonstrated, central to the Clinic's work was 'a textual, clinical approach that was rooted in the identification of individual pathology: in other words, an emphasis on the psychiatric case study.' A good number of the Clinic's patients were those referred to it by the courts. As Stephen notes, Clarke became 'a significant contributor to the development of forensic psychiatry in Canada. His sphere of influence extended well beyond the Toronto Psychiatric Clinic into the criminal justice system; he was called upon frequently as an expert witness in notable trials during the period.'[20]

HOMOSEXUALITY AND ONTARIO DOCTORS

Before looking at a few examples of the case history, it will be helpful to situate them within the context of Ontario doctors' understandings of sexual relations between men in the late nineteenth and early twentieth centuries. For some Ontario doctors the ample evidence of sexual relations between men supplied by the courts was a sign of the degeneration of civilization in

Ontario. Degeneration theory held that sexual and other perversions were manifestations of a physical process of decline in which some people reverted to earlier moments in the evolution of the species. In 1898, Ezra Hurlburt Stafford, first assistant physician at the Toronto Asylum for the Insane, delivered an address on the subject of 'Perversion' before the Toronto Medical Society, subsequently published in the *Canadian Journal of Medicine and Surgery*. Drawing on Krafft-Ebing and Lombroso, Stafford was concerned mainly with prostitution and 'forms of perversion long familiar to readers of the later classical writers.' Stafford explained that these were 'indications of the insidious process of degeneration' and that 'many cases of sexual perversion may be set down as a reversion or a miscarriage in the chain of evolution.'[21]

Degeneration theory coexisted alongside other explanations for homosexual behaviour, theories that stressed homosexuality as a disease of the mind rather than as a reversion in the evolution of civilization. Even Stafford, who held firm to degeneration theory, allowed that some sexual perversion was 'not so often of the nature of a physical defect as of a mental aberration, and therefore a form of insanity.' Referring more specifically to sex between men, Stafford noted that 'in origin it is usually rather psychic than physical, and properly speaking comes under the study of the alienist rather than the surgeon or the physician.'[22] But there were different opinions among alienists as to the root of homosexuality. Under the influence of Freud, some believed that homosexuality, and mental illness more generally, resided in the subconscious. In Ontario, psychoanalytic theories were introduced by Ernest Jones, Freud's biographer and 'the man who almost singlehandedly forced a hearing for Freud's theories, first in North America, and later in England.' On the invitation of C.K. Clarke, Jones came to Toronto from London, England, in 1908 to be the first director of the Psychiatric Clinic. In addition, Jones worked as a pathologist at the Toronto asylum and as an associate professor of psychiatry at the University of Toronto.[23] He published numerous articles in Canadian medical journals, introducing physicians to the principles of psychoanalysis. In 'Psycho-Analysis in Psycho-Therapy,' published in 1909 in the *Bulletin of the Ontario Hospitals for the Insane,* Jones informed his readers that the psychoanalytic method had been used successfully in treating 'practically all forms of psycho-neuroses, the different types of hysteria, the phobias, obsessions, anxiety neuroses, and even certain kinds of sexual perversions.'[24]

But most Ontario doctors remained unpersuaded by psychoanalysis, in large part because it challenged the 'somatic interpretation of nervous and mental diseases that was established orthodoxy among Canadian neurologists and psychiatrists.' Somatic theories held that mental diseases had a physical basis, that they were manifestations of organic brain disease. While numerous factors were believed to give rise to insanity, most doctors agreed that heredity was the primary cause.[25] In arguing for the somatic, hereditary basis of mental disease, doctors went further, claiming that as outgrowths of insanity, immorality and criminality were also inherited. Not surprisingly, then, much of the medical commentary on insanity and perversion overlapped with the medical pathologization of the working class, especially working-class immigrants. Psychiatrists, many of whom were involved in the Canadian eugenics and mental-hygiene movements, never tired of providing statistics to demonstrate the disproportionate number of 'foreign born' among Ontario's insane and perverted. In his 1906 report, Inspector Armstrong claimed that, of fifty-four male patients admitted to the Toronto Asylum, thirty-seven were of foreign birth, one of whom was 'a sexual pervert of the worst possible type.' A 1907 article on 'The Importation of Defective Classes' noted that, of the thirty-four men admitted to the Toronto Insane Asylum between December 1906 and February 1907, two were 'sexual perverts.' Referring to the 'hordes of immigrants' entering the country, C.K. Clarke used his 1907 annual report on the Toronto Hospital for the Insane to propound, '[I]t is all very well to talk about pumping in the population, but surely the streams tapped should not be those reeking with degeneracy, crime and insanity.' 'One sexual pervert hailing from the London Slums,' Clarke warned, 'has induced others of his family to come here.' Finally, an article entitled 'The Defective and Insane Immigrant,' published in 1908, summed up the connections among immigrants, insanity, and perversion. The author began by noting 'how startling is the preponderance of the foreign born among the insane of the country' and claimed that an analysis of the characteristics of immigrants admitted to Canadian asylums was 'an interesting study in degeneracy of a type we rarely see among Canadians,' including 'sexual perverts of the most revolting kind.'[26] All of the different understandings of perversion can be found in doctors' case histories.

DOING A CASE HISTORY

Numerous articles in Canadian medical journals provided step-by-step instructions on how to perform a mental examination. As Dr H.C. Steeve wrote in a typical article that appeared in the *Canadian Journal of Medicine and Surgery* in 1922, 'the question of how to examine a patient for insanity is one which often arises.' Key to the answer was the case-history approach. Noting the 'overwhelming importance of the history,' Steeve explained that 'the keynote of all successful examinations … is thoroughness and system, bringing out each phase and feature of the case.' The bulk of Steeve's article was given over to the questions to be asked by the examiner. Once the examiner had 'brought out' the answers or the symptoms, they needed 'to be sorted out and classified' and Steeve provided the categories in which to classify and label the 'subjective and objective symptoms' of insanity. 'It is by such a process,' Steeve concluded, 'that the soundness or otherwise of the mind must be judged and I feel quite sure that any physician, whether experienced in psychiatry or not, who will follow out the examinations as suggested here will make very few errors.' The place to begin the psychiatric case history according to Steeve was with the patient's family history, reflecting the importance attached to heredity in the etiology of mental diseases. Beginning with family history 'not only supplies the examiner with information of inestimable value, but serves to gain the confidence of the patient, to put him at ease, and to make the intricate paths of his mind much more readily accessible to the examiner.' 'Begin with the father,' the article continued, 'learn whether he is alive or dead … If he is dead, at what age did he die, of what cause.' Crucial in this part of the investigation was the question of whether the father or other family members died at home. 'In answer to this question one will quite occasionally learn that the father or some other member of the family died in a mental hospital when the patient never had any intention of admitting that there ever was such a thing as insanity in the family.'[27] Dr Bruce Smith pursued this line of questioning during his mental examination of Carlo C., an Italian immigrant. Carlo's troubles began after Toronto police discovered his sexual involvement with several different young men over the summer of 1909. Smith learned that Carlo's 'father had died of apoplexy, his mother of epilepsy and a brother had died in the asylum.'

Carlo's was diagnosed as a case of 'chronic progressive paranoia, inciting to the most abominable practices.' Smith's diagnosis was corroborated in court by three other doctors, including C.K. Clarke.[28]

Another key element of the diagnostic procedure of the case history zeroed in on the patient's sexual past. As Steeve wrote, 'When the [case] history has brought the patient to the age of fourteen or fifteen the question of sexual development is inquired into with the idea of learning of unusual sexual irritations or excitements; of masturbation or other practices frequently developed at this period of life which may indicate a neurotic or nervous temperament which is so frequently the fertile soil for the later development of mental disease.' The doctor who examined Thomas M., a labourer from Sault Ste. Marie charged in 1926 with indecently assaulting a boy to whom he had offered a ride, noted that Thomas 'admits practising masturbation … Says he has wet dreams nearly every night.' Although Thomas told the doctor that he had not masturbated 'since he was circumcised about two years ago,' the doctor—likely convinced that Thomas's solitary vices were linked to his more public perversions—recorded in the case history that Thomas 'is a great liar. You cannot believe him at all.' This, along with other 'facts indicating insanity,' including a 'dull' appearance and the fact that Thomas 'will not stay at work,' were enough for the doctor to 'certify that the said Thomas M. is insane.'[29]

Other facts indicating insanity were numerous indeed. According to Steeve, insanity might be revealed by a patient's answers to questions as simple as 'Does he recognize the proper season of the year, day of the week, month, etc.?' One doctor had his own 'small test,' which he believed 'very often revealed serious mental weakness.' In 1905, Tennyson W., a married, thirty-six-year-old gardener, was caught having sex with three youths just off Toronto's Yonge Street. Tennyson's lawyer suggested he visit a doctor. As Dr James Richardson wrote in a letter to Tennyson's defence lawyer, 'Mrs W. called upon me last evening along with her husband and told me that you … wished me to examine him as to his mental condition. I had a long interview with him… I gave him to multiply four figures by four others … He soon put down the first, but pondered some time over every succeeding one.' The doctor included the math test along with the case history; Tennyson failed the test. The doctor admitted that 'this may be merely the result of want of education, but his writing … is not that of an ignorant man, and his figures were made correctly and clearly.' Therefore, the doctor concluded, 'I have no hesitation in giving the opinion that' Tennyson 'shows symptoms of incipient lunacy.' But perhaps more germane to the doctor's diagnosis of incipient lunacy was his belief, indicated in the concluding observations of his case history, that 'a married man, whose conduct had always been proper should have acted in the indecent, dirty, foul way he did on a public street in open day light would itself lead one to suspect that there was some mental defect.'[30]

In cases where doctors had a difficult time certifying a man as insane, there existed a whole range of other mental illnesses with which to explain men's homosexual behaviour. Based on intelligence tests that measured 'mental age' and were developed in the eugenics and mental-hygiene movements, the 'mentally defective' were divided into increasingly numerous and discrete categories of mental disorder, including 'idiots,' 'imbeciles,' and the 'feeble-minded.' In Toronto in 1920, Daniel L., a single, twenty-two-year-old tailor, was caught having sex with a labourer in a laneway off Ontario Street. Dr G. Boyer wrote to the court that Daniel had a mental development 'not more than that of a boy of eight or ten years of age' and concluded that 'he is mentally defective.' In another case, two exhibition-goers reported James C. and his friend Charles W. to the police after spying the two young men having sex at the 1913 Canadian National Exhibition. Awaiting trial in jail, James, a nineteen-year-old labourer, was examined by the assistant superintendent of the Ontario Hospital for the Insane. James had a 'mentality' of 'a child of four years of age.' 'In my opinion,' the doctor wrote, 'he is an idiot.' The assistant superintendent also noted about James that 'physically he is undeveloped; and shows many marks of degeneration such as asymmetry of the face, high palate, asymmetry of his legs and he is also unable to talk plainly.' The physical exam reflected the persistence of somatic theories in which the signs of perversity were read directly off the surface of the body.[31]

The doctors who examined David J., a seventy-one-year-old minister charged in 1925 with committing an act of gross indecency with a younger draughtsman, believed he was suffering from mental impairment and nervous exhaustion. Dr W.T. Parry, the surgeon at the Toronto jail, concluded that 'his mentality shows marked signs of deterioration and yet while he is not insane ... neither do I think that he is entirely responsible for his acts on account of his impaired mentality.' Another doctor, this one from the Ontario Hospital for the Insane at Mimico, noted that David, some thirty years prior to his offence, had suffered a spinal injury that for two years left him unable to work. 'At times during these two years he experienced discreditable impulses ... and sexual improprieties, but they were always of short duration.' At the time of his offence, David had travelled to Toronto and 'was greatly prostrated by the hot weather and the fatigue of the journey ... In his exhausted condition the old impulses re-appeared.' David's condition was also partly to be explained by historical circumstance, in particular, the great Methodist/Presbyterian church union crisis of 1925. David had come to Toronto to attend the General Assembly and was suffering 'disappointment and worry over the action of his congregation in church union and his own future status.' The third doctor, one less historically, more psychoanalytically, minded, believed that David's problem was not so much a spiritual crisis as it was a case of repressed sexual desire for men. 'In my opinion,' the third doctor stated, David was 'suffering from a Psycho-neurosis.' His examination of David revealed 'a short and unhappy married life' leaving him 'without anyone to confide in and rely on intimately and for many years there has been continual repression of emotions and impulses.' Perhaps the opportunity afforded by the psychoanalytic encounter to finally confide and be intimate was therapeutic for David, for as the doctor noted, David 'seemed perfectly frank with me and admitted having had to fight against sex impulses ... These impulses have been associated with men.' Even though one of the other doctors had discovered 'sexual improprieties' earlier in David's life, this doctor concluded that David's was 'probably not a long-standing or deeply rooted perversion.'[32]

THE HOMOSEXUAL TALKS BACK

In the cases of some men, doctors were unable to find any symptoms of insanity or other mental illness. Even Dr Bruce Smith, who endorsed 'asexualization' for 'perverts,' testified in court in 1909 that men who had sex with other men 'may appear perfectly normal in other respects and may display a fair amount of mental culture.'[33] Unable to find symptoms of mental pathology in their patients, some doctors (though certainly not Dr Bruce Smith) concluded that a man's sexual desire for another man was not a mental disease. This belief originated with the work of sexologists such as Havelock Ellis. Ellis first introduced his ideas in *Sexual Inversion,* a volume in his *Studies in the Psychology of Sex* published in 1897. Like Krafft-Ebing's *Psychopathia Sexualis,* Ellis's *Sexual Inversion* employed the case-history approach. Ellis wrote that 'when the sexual impulse is directed towards persons of the same sex we are in the presence of an aberration variously known as "sexual inversion" … or, more generally, "homosexuality."' Ellis argued that homosexuality or sexual inversion was a congenital or inborn characteristic, not an acquired vice nor the product of a diseased, degenerate mind. 'Congenital sexual inversion,' Ellis wrote, is 'akin to a biological variation … often having no traceable connection with any morbid condition.'[34] While still insisting on its biological basis, the move away from degeneration and disease toward the more neutral concept of 'variation' represented a major medical reconceptualization of homosexuality. While many Ontario doctors persisted in viewing sex between men as a vice or a disease of the mind, a letter written in 1907 suggests that at least one Ontario doctor was familiar with the emerging sexological concept of homosexuality. On 18 October 1907, Dr R.J. Dwyer wrote to His Honour Judge Winchester about the results of his examination of Thomas C., a manual warehouse labourer from Toronto. Beginning with the results of his physical examination of Thomas, Dr Dwyer noted that aside from 'marked atrophy of the sexual organs' and 'a diseased condition of one testicle … physically he is generally well developed.' Moving on to the results of the 'mental examination,' Dwyer explained to Judge Winchester that while Thomas's 'mental capacity' might be 'below the normal average,' 'he impresses one as being gentle and refined, even aesthetic, having no bad habits and quite far from coarseness or brutality.' Dwyer continued: 'He is evidently the victim of an unnatural and perverted sexual instinct—that form in which the natural attraction towards the opposite sex is replaced by an unnatural attraction for the same sex (Homosexuality).' 'It is further of importance to note,' Dwyer wrote, 'that this condition is one which has existed from birth and is not an acquired condition the result of vice and dissipation.' While Dwyer continued to use the language of the 'unnatural' and the 'perverted,' he used these terms in a very different way than many Ontario doctors. Rather than conclude that Thomas suffered from mental disease, Dwyer preferred to explain Thomas's behaviour as the product of an inborn 'sexual instinct,' his 'homosexuality.' Sexologists like Ellis believed their theories were politically progressive; insisting on the congenital basis of homosexuality rather than on homosexuals as wilful criminals or perverts with an acquired vice was one way to argue that homosexuals should be removed from the purview of the law. Indeed, Ellis and like-minded doctors supported the late-nineteenth- and early-twentieth-century reform movements to repeal anti-homosexual laws. Some doctors worked toward similar ends on a more case-by-case basis. Often the intent behind the insanity defence in homosexual trials was to save an accused from prison. As Dr Dwyer wrote to the judge, Thomas's homosexuality made him, if anything, 'mentally deficient … rather than criminal … I am of the opinion that to commit him to prison would be futile so far as curing him of his condition as he could not be kept there long enough to eradicate his perverted instinct, while on the other hand the factors upon which we depend most to suppress the manifestations of this instinct—his mental and moral faculties, would suffer disastrously by such an experience leaving him worse after than before. The ideal would be to have him placed in charge of some one or some institution which while he was kept actively employed, he could have medical treatment and at the same time have no opportunity or temptation to yield to his instinct. Moreover, it would be a matter of keeping such supervision over him for years as this is not an acquired habit but a congenital condition.'[35]

While claiming homosexuals were simply born that way or were insane did save some men from prison, it simultaneously delivered them into the hands of doctors. Those men sent by the courts to be examined before or during a trial and those later sentenced to be incarcerated in asylums and psychiatric wards of reformatories became case histories not only for the courts but also for psychiatrists. Psychiatrists used the case histories they conducted for the courts to write articles for medical journals and texts. This was another step in the professionalization of psychiatry, for 'as professions and professional discourses have been established, case histories and case records have become part of the knowledge basis of the professional discourse.' To give but one example, during the period January 1929 to September 1933, 150 people charged with sex offences were sent by the court to the Toronto Psychiatric Hospital for examination. Of the 150 case histories conducted at the hospital, 100 went on to form the basis of an article written by Dr A.J. Kilgour published in 1933 in the *Ontario Journal of Neuropsychiatry*, entitled 'Sex Delinquency—A Review of 100 Court Cases Referred to the Toronto Psychiatric Hospital.' Kilgour began his article by classifying the 'types of sex acts' committed by the sex offenders. Here, using the terms in a strictly descriptive manner, Kilgour classified the sex acts as 'homo-sexual' and 'heterosexual.' When he turned to a discussion of selected case histories, however, those involving homosexual acts were transformed into cases of what he called 'homosexuality,' while the discussion of the case histories involving heterosexual acts remained cases of 'sexual acts with female minors,' 'rape,' 'incest,' and so on, rather than cases of 'heterosexuality,' a term never used in the study.[36]

The introduction of the case-history approach aroused much debate among medical pro-fessionals. Doctors were suspicious of the case history because it challenged traditional med-ical techniques based on physical examination, but even more so because doctors believed it lacked scientific objectivity, relying as it did on the word of the patient. This very charac-teristic of the case history—the way it allowed the patient to speak—opened up possibilities for patients to resist doctors' efforts to pathologize them.[37] In her analysis of *Sex Variants: A Study of Homosexual Patterns,* a medico-scientific inquiry into homosexuality in New York City in the late 1930s, Jennifer Terry analyses the process 'by which a position or identity space is constructed discursively by sexology and medicine and strategically seized upon by its objects of study.' Terry traces how 'deviant subjects … have spoken back against the terms of a pathologizing discourse.' A similar process can be detected at work in the psychiatric case histories of Ontario men. In his study of sex delinquency, for example, Kilgour concluded about the homosexual cases that 'the sex life was unsatisfactory in all cases.' But the individual case histories told a different story. 'Case 1,' for example, a forty-year-old, single caretaker, told Kilgour that 'he enjoyed this form of sex act.' Similarly, about 'Case 2,' a thirty-six-year-old, single salesman, Kilgour recorded that 'he said he enjoyed this form of sex activity better than the normal heterosexual variety.' Kilgour was particularly surprised by 'Case 3.' The married labourer 'admitted the acts but did not feel that they were wrong and had no particular feeling of guilt or shame. He said "God said in the Bible if a man wants to be filthy, let him be filthy and He would judge him. The law that says it is wrong is only a man-made law, not God's law, and therefore it was all right for me to do as I did.'"[38]

CONCLUSION

I want to return to the issue of the status of the case histories as historical evidence. It is tempting to read in the psychiatric case histories the doctors' diagnoses of 'homosexuality' and 'sexual perversion' and on that basis argue that the case histories constitute the evidence of homosexual experience in the past. But it is unlikely that all or even many of the men sent for mental examinations thought of themselves as insane, as sexual perverts, or even as homosexuals. [...] [F]or some men in early-twentieth-century Ontario sexual relations with other men were an outgrowth of or gave rise to unconventional sexual/gender identities, while many other men who engaged in homosexual behaviour did not adopt such identities and remained within the bounds of what at the time was considered 'normal manhood.'[39] To read the case histories in a way that accepts the doctors' diagnoses at face value would be to assign to many men sexual identities they may never have embraced. It would also be to ignore the complicity of the case history in producing the categories and identities of insanity and homosexuality, and it is here that I find post-structuralist insights into the discursive operations of texts most helpful.

During their examinations, doctors did not objectively record symptoms of illness or simply note down a patient's own sense of identity; doctors actively constructed illnesses and identities for the men who appeared before them. The textual practices of the psychiatric case history—as set out, for example, in the article by Dr Steeve—organized doctors' examinations and diagnoses by providing them with 'standardized methods of observation and investigation, categories, interpretive schemata and practices.' As Jennifer Stephen has wryly observed about the case history in the work of the Psychiatric Clinic, '[T]he forms designed for use at the [Clinic] could hardly remain blank. The point was to locate and identify the abnormal.'[40] In identifying the abnormal, the textual practices of the case history abstracted men and their sexual experiences from their local, lived contexts. Men, some of whom were known in the street as 'pansies,' 'sissies,' and 'fairies,' were labelled by doctors during psychiatric examinations as 'insane,' 'perverts,' and 'homosexuals.' The resulting rupture or disjuncture between experience and text at the centre of the case history informs its status as historical evidence: rather than as the unmediated evidence of a pre-existing homosexual or homosexuality, the case histories and the broader psychiatric discourse of which they were a part are better viewed as constructed 'representations of the object of their knowledge.'[41]

That case histories were representations of men's sexual behaviours and identities, often distorted and inaccurate ones, does not mean they were without repercussions on men's lives. Chauncey has argued that early-twentieth-century medical professionals and discourse had only limited influence on homosexually active men, especially working-class men, because it is unlikely they read elite, obscure medical journals and texts.[42] While I concur with Chauncey that most men did not learn about their sexual identities by reading such literature, a broader range of doctors' impacts on men, especially on the predominantly working-class and immigrant men hauled before the courts, comes into view if we expand our notion of what constitutes 'medical discourse' beyond periodicals and textbooks. That the psychiatric examination/case history of an accused man took place in a jail cell, a doctor's office, a clinic, or even an accused's home, reminds us that medical discourse was a series of concrete practices generating relations of power and knowledge in local settings. In court, doctors and their case histories had the power to influence both judges' understandings of sexual relations between men and the outcome of a man's trial. Thinking of discourses as practices rather than solely as texts—or, to put it another way, thinking of discourses as texts that *work*—is one way to capture something of the materiality of discourse.[43]

As case histories were linked to broader psychiatric and legal discourses, the net of their power relations was cast further afield. To give just one example, in 1948 the Canadian Penal Association, in cooperation with the Canadian Bar Association, the Canadian Medical Association, the National Committee for Mental Hygiene, the Canadian Welfare Council and the federal Department of Justice, established a committee on the 'Problem of the Sex Offender.' Part of the movement that would culminate in the 1954 Royal Commission on the Criminal Law Relating to Criminal Sexual Psychopaths, the committee chose to open its preliminary report with a long, detailed 'case history' with commentary by a penitentiary psychiatrist. In relating the case of a twenty-year-old man, the psychiatrist noted there was no history of neuropathic traits, except that 'at the age of thirteen he developed a nervous state of mind ... responsible for queer behaviour such as chewing on handkerchiefs and shirt collars.' More significant was the fact that he 'was initiated, early in life, in sexual activities along homosexual lines. Persisted in that form of activity and has become a confirmed sexual invert ... He has been in trouble with the law since about the age of fourteen years over his abnormal sex life.' On the basis of this case history and others like it, the committee rested its conclusion that the problem of the sex offender was 'large in size' and required immediate changes in the law, increased resources for psychiatric treatment, and a public campaign of sex education.[44] The case history—first introduced into Ontario psychiatric/legal practice in the early twentieth century—was one of the principal forms of knowledge and power undergirding the intensified medico-legal regulation of homosexual relations in the post-war period.

While post-structuralism draws our attention to historical sources as active texts, there are also silences in much post-structuralist work. Post-structuralist critics urge historians to historicize all their foundational categories, such as experience and agency, but these same critics rarely bother to historicize discourse itself, often leaving it as a foundational category in their work.[45] Jennifer Terry, for example, makes no reference in her article to the historical or material context in which the *Sex Variants* study was produced. She does admit that 'the deviants' clash with medicine is not entirely dependent on the medical discourse for its enunciation. Much of this conflict comes from lesbian and gay subcultural practices which may overlap with the pathologizing discourse but whose origins, implications, and effects are locatable partially outside the hegemonic formations of science and medicine in a homosexual 'underworld.' In an article that aims to suggest new historiographic practices, this crucial point is relegated to a footnote.[46] But to step outside the text (or, more accurately, to read a text not in isolation but against other texts), whether to trace subcultural practices or to set out material contexts, is essential if only because it underlines the fundamental point that discursive forms are historically specific. Historicizing discourse helps us to explain how, why, and when the identities that discursive forms construct (as well as the identities they fail to register) emerge when they do. As I've tried to show briefly, the emergence of the homosexual as a case history was wrapped up in broader historical developments during the late nineteenth and early twentieth centuries, most notably the professionalization of psychiatry. Recognizing that discursive forms have a history, that is, analysing the material context of their emergence, is one interpretive move that makes the sharp differentiation between discourse and the material begin to fade from view. This, in turn, moves us beyond unhelpful, dichotomous positions, opening up a space in which to theorize the 'discursive construction of social experience' in a way that 'can enrich rather than erase our sense ... of material life.'[47]

NOTES

1 Archives of Ontario (AO), Crown Attorney Prosecution Case Files, York County, 1911, case 8. *Toronto Evening Telegram,* 20 February 1911, 7, and 22 May 1911, 6.

2 Michel Foucault, *The History of Sexuality: An Introduction,* trans. Robert Hurley (New York 1978), 43.

3 It is important to remember that the psychiatric case history was only one of many different types of documents that made up the homosexual's legal case file. Despite the array of textual material to be found in the legal case file, historians often treat it as a monolithic whole, pulling pieces of information willy-nilly from the different documents of the file as it suits the demands of their narrative. But many of the documents that make up the case file have their own distinct provenance and textual form, and there are important interpretive reasons for disaggregating the case file. At the very least, we need to distinguish between the *case file* and the *case history.* The legal case file is not itself a case history or, at least, it is unlike the many case histories it may contain, including those produced by medical, social-welfare, parole, and other agencies. Each of these case histories is rooted in the distinct history of its originating agency. If we are to attain a comprehensive theorization of the legal case file, each distinct textual element of the file will require its own discursive genealogy similar to the one I am attempting here for the psychiatric case history. As for the legal case file itself, part of what makes it unique is its discursive practice of centralizing a number of disparate case histories into one textual site, linking them all to the powerful truth effects of the law.

4 Michel Foucault, *Discipline and Punish: The Birth of the Prison,* trans. Alan Sheridan (New York 1979), 189–91; *History of Sexuality,* 105.

5 George Chauncey, 'From Sexual Inversion to Homosexuality: The Changing Medical Conceptualization of Female "Deviance,"' in Kathy Peiss and Christina Simmons, eds, *Passion and Power: Sexuality in History* (Philadelphia 1989), 109 and 106. See also Chauncey, *Gay New York: Gender, Urban Culture, and the Making of the Gay Male World, 1890–1940* (New York 1994), 125.

6 See James Chandler, Arnold I. Davidson, and Harry Harootunian, eds, *Questions of Evidence: Proof, Practice, and Persuasion across the Disciplines* (Chicago 1994) and the special issue of *PMLA* on 'The Status of Evidence,' *PMLA* 111 (January 1996).

7 For the Gordon-Scott exchange see *Signs* 15 (Summer 1990), 848–60.

8 My search through court records housed at the Archives of Ontario turned up 313 case files involving sexual offences between men for the period 1890–1935. The cases employed here come from Archives of Ontario, Criminal Court Records, RG 22, Crown Attorney Prosecution Case Files, various series (hereafter AO, Crown Attorney Prosecution Case Files, county/district name, year, case number). In

order to be granted research access to the crown attorney's files, I was required to enter into a research agreement with the Archives. In accordance with that agreement, all names have been anonymized and all case file numbers used here refer to my own numbering scheme and do not correspond to any numbers that may appear on the original case files.

9 Chauncey, *Gay New York,* 125. My thanks to George Chauncey for first drawing my attention to these national differences.

10 Judith Walkowitz, *City of Dreadful Delight: Narratives of Sexual Danger in Late-Victorian London* (Chicago 1992), 9. In addition to Walkowitz, I have found the following particularly helpful in thinking about the relationship between discourse and the material: Regina Kunzel, 'Pulp Fictions and Problem Girls: Reading and Rewriting Single Pregnancy in the Postwar United States,' *American Historical Review* 100 (December 1995), 1465–87; Kunzel, *Fallen Women, Problem Girls: Unmarried Mothers and the Professionalization of Social Work, 1890–1945* (New Haven 1993); Kathleen Canning, 'Feminist History after the Linguistic Turn: Historicizing Discourse and Experience,' *Signs* 19 (Winter 1994), 368–404; Lisa Duggan, 'The Trials of Alice Mitchell: Sensationalism, Sexology, and the Lesbian Subject in Turn-of-the-Century America,' *Signs* 18 (Summer 1993), 791–814; Mary Poovey, *Uneven Developments: The Ideological Work of Gender in Mid-Victorian England* (Chicago 1988), 17.

11 Julia Epstein, *Altered Conditions: Disease, Medicine, and Storytelling* (New York 1995), 36 and 38. See also 'The Art of the Case History,' a special issue *of Literature and Medicine* 11 (Spring 1992) and Harriet Nowell-Smith, 'Nineteenth-Century Narrative Case Histories: An Inquiry into Stylistics and History,' *Canadian Bulletin of Medical History* 12 (1995), 47–67.

12 Dorothy E. Smith, 'Cases and Case Histories,' in *The Conceptual Practices of Power: A Feminist Sociology of Knowledge* (Toronto 1990), 89.

13 Kunzel, 'Pulp Fictions and Problem Girls,' 1468, and *Fallen Women, Problem Girls,* esp. chapter 4.

14 Jeffrey Weeks, *Sexuality and Its Discontents: Meanings, Myths and Modern Sexualities* (London 1985), 67.

15 Elizabeth Lunbeck, *The Psychiatric Persuasion: Knowledge, Gender, and Power in Modern America* (Princeton, NJ 1994), 133.

16 On the medical certificate as case history and the process of committal to an insane asylum, see Wendy Mitchinson, 'Reasons for Committal to a Mid-Nineteenth Century Ontario Insane Asylum: The Case of Toronto,' in Wendy Mitchinson and Janice Dickin McGinnis, eds, *Essays in the History of Canadian Medicine* (Toronto 1988), 88–109, and S.E.D. Shortt, *Victorian Lunacy: Richard M. Bucke and the Practice of Late-Nineteenth-Century Psychiatry* (New York 1986), 50–1.

17 Daniel Clark, *Mental Diseases: A Synopsis of Twelve Lectures Delivered at the Hospital for the Insane, Toronto, to the Graduating Medical Classes* (Toronto 1895), 323–34.

18 'Thirty-ninth Annual Report of the Inspectors of Prisons and Public Charities upon the Lunatic and Idiot Asylums … of the Province of Ontario … 1906,' Ontario *Sessional Papers,* 1907, ix; 'Annual Report of the Inspectors of Prisons and Public Charities … 1907,' Ontario *Sessional Papers,* 1908, x.

19 *Bulletin of the Ontario Hospitals for the Insane* 1 (October 1907) and C.K. Clarke, 'The Relationship of Psychiatry to General Medicine,' *Bulletin of the Ontario Hospitals for the Insane* 2 (November 1909), 9–10.

20 Jennifer Stephen, 'The "Incorrigible," the "Bad," and the "Immoral": Toronto's "Factory Girls" and the Work of the Toronto Psychiatric Clinic,' in Louis A. Knafla and Susan W.S. Binnie, eds, *Law, Society,*

and the State: Essays in Modern Legal History (Toronto 1995), 406–7.

21 Ezra Hurlburt Stafford, 'Perversion,' *Canadian Journal of Medicine and Surgery* 3 (April 1898), 181–4. I first learned of Stafford's article reading Gary Kinsman, *The Regulation of Desire: Sexuality in Canada* (Montreal 1987), 91–2.

22 Stafford, 'Perversion,' 181–2, 183.

23 Thomas E. Brown, 'Dr Ernest Jones, Psychoanalysis, and the Canadian Medical Profession, 1908–1913,' in S.E.D. Shortt, ed., *Medicine in Canadian Society: Historical Perspectives* (Montreal 1981), 315.

24 Ernest Jones, 'Psycho-Analysis in Psycho-Therapy,' *Bulletin of the Ontario Hospitals for the Insane* 2 (November 1909), 32–43.

25 Brown, 'Dr Ernest Jones,' 339.

26 'Annual Report of the Inspectors of Prisons and Public Charities Upon the Lunatic and Idiot Asylums … 1906,' Ontario *Sessional Papers*, 1907, ix; 'The Importation of Defective Classes,' *Bulletin of the Ontario Hospitals for the Insane* 1 (1907), 3–6; Hospital for Insane, Toronto, 'Annual Report of the Medical Superintendent for the Year Ending December 31st, 1907,' Ontario *Sessional Papers*, 1908, 4; 'The Defective and Insane Immigrant,' *Bulletin of the Ontario Hospitals for the Insane* 2 (July 1908), 10, 8.

27 H.C. Steeve, 'The Physician's Responsibility in Connection with Insane and Their Committal to Hospital, Together with Suggestion for Examination of a Patient,' *Canadian Journal of Medicine and Surgery* 51 (May 1922), 199.

28 AO, Crown Attorney Prosecution Case Files, York County, 1909, case 93.

29 Ibid., Algoma District, 1926, case 203.

30 Ibid., York County, 1905, case 87.

31 On intelligence tests and the categories of mental illness see Stephen, 'The "Incorrigible," the "Bad," and the "Immoral,"' 421–2. AO, Crown Attorney Prosecution Case Files, York County, 1920, case 53; 1913, case 11.

32 AO, Crown Attorney Prosecution Case Files, York County, 1925, case 73.

33 *Toronto Evening Telegram*, 20 Sept. 1909, 6. For Smith's thoughts on the 'asexualization' of 'perverts' see Smith, 'Mental Sanitation,' *Canada Lancet* 40 (1906–7), 976, cited in McLaren, *Our Own Master Race: Eugenics in Canada, 1885–1945* (Toronto 1990), 42, 182.

34 Havelock Ellis, *Psychology of Sex: A Manual for Students* (New York, 1935), 218, 229. This is a condensed version of *Studies in the Psychology of Sex*.

35 AO, Crown Attorney Prosecution Case Files, York County, 1907, case 89.

36 Smith, 'Cases and Case Histories,' 89; A.J. Kilgour, 'Sex Delinquency—A Review of 100 Court Cases Referred to the Toronto Psychiatric Hospital,' *Ontario Journal of Neuropsychiatry* (September 1933), 34–50.

37 On the historical controversy surrounding the case history and the 'speaking pervert,' see Siobhan Somerville, 'Scientific Racism and the Emergence of the Homosexual Body,' *Journal of the History of Sexuality* 5 (October 1994), 263–4.

38 Jennifer Terry, 'Theorizing Deviant Historiography,' in the 'Queer Theory: Lesbian and Gay Sexualities' issue of *differences*, vol. 3 (Summer 1991), 59–60. Kilgour, 'Sex Delinquency,' 37–9.

39 Chauncey, *Gay New York*, esp. part I, 33–99.

40 Smith, 'Cases and Case Histories,' 90; Stephen, 'The "Incorrigible," the "Bad," and the "Immoral,"' 409.

41 Smith, 'Cases and Case Histories,' 89.

42 Chauncey, *Gay New York,* 125.

43 Mariana Valverde makes a similar point when she argues that discursive practices are 'much broader than relations among words. Insofar as material objects such as badges or clothes or church buildings function as signs, then the old dichotomy between idealism and materialism recedes from view.' See Valverde, *The Age of Light, Soap, and Water: Moral Reform in English Canada, 1885–1925* (Toronto 1991), 10. The idea that discourse is made up of textual and non-textual practices was Foucault's; he was particularly interested in architecture and space as discourse. It should be noted that there is some debate over whether Foucault meant there to be an analytical distinction between 'discourses' and 'practices.' Some argue that 'practices' represent a domain intimately connected to but distinct from 'discourse,' while others argue that Foucault intended no such analytical separation. With his repeated references to discourse versus 'concrete arrangements' and his insistence on the 'local centres' of power/knowledge, I believe Foucault did mean something unique by practices. The view that discourses are not free-floating but rooted and expressed in concrete practices is perhaps the view most amenable to social historians with a materialist bent. On these debates, see Jan Goldstein, ed., *Foucault and the Writing of History* (Oxford, UK, and Cambridge, Mass., 1994).

44 Canadian Penal Association, 'Interim Report: Committee on the Sex Offender,' June 1948. My thanks to Robert Champagne for passing on to me a copy of this report that he discovered in his research in the papers of the royal commission on the criminal sexual psychopath housed at the Public Archives of Canada. For historical background on the committee and the royal commission see Robert Champagne, 'Psychopaths and Perverts: The Canadian Royal Commission on the Criminal Law Relating to Criminal Sexual Psychopaths, 1954–58,' *Canadian Lesbian and Gay History Newsletter* 2 (September 1986), 7–9, and Kinsman, *The Regulation of Desire,* 125–9.

45 This point is made by Kathleen Canning in 'Feminist History after the Linguistic Turn.'

46 Terry, 'Theorizing Deviant Historiography,' 72.

47 Kunzel, 'Pulp Fictions and Problem Girls,' 1473.

CHAPTER 11

The Criminal Sexual Psychopath in Canada: Sex, Psychiatry, and the Law at Mid-Century

Elise Chenier

n the spring of 1947, Mrs. Geraldine M. had had enough. During a Saturday shopping excursion in downtown Toronto, a man had exposed himself just as she and her daughter boarded the bus home. Two days later, her daughter came home in "a hysterical condition. One of those indecently exposed pale creatures had approached her." Mrs. M. related these events in a letter to Ontario's Minister of Health, Russell Kelly. She wrote the Minister not only to express anger and fear but to share some very specific ideas about what the Ontario government should do with sex perverts. "We have raised our children with a chaste and modest upbringing in a Christian home," she argued, "and we feel that this class of men's childhood may have been sadly neglected, thus causing them to be what they are ... Any right thinking person is forced to believe there must be ... some brain disease to cause them to act in such a manner." For this reason, "such men needed treatment [because] jail meant nothing to this type."[1]

Mrs. M. was not alone in her thinking. As Canada set out to rebuild itself after the exhaustive effort to win World War II, sex crimes against children emerged as one of the most urgent social problems. Fuelled by sensational media coverage of sexual assaults and, in rare instances, the disappearance and murder of children, the sexual deviant, a pathological character popularized in the United States prior to WWII and revived almost as soon as the dust over Europe and Asia began to settle, emerged as the new sexual villain. In Toronto, thirteen-year-old and physically disabled Arlene Anderson was one of the earliest Canadian victims; in Winnipeg, the murder of two small boys inflamed local citizens; and in Vancouver, at least one child molestation made media headlines.[2] Perceiving a dangerous threat out of control, people across the country looked to the government for quick and meaningful responses.

While the call for action was predictable, what was unique to this era was the construction of the problem. Curiously, Mrs. M. did not address her letter to either the Minister of Justice or the Attorney-General. Instead, she directed her comments to the Minister of Health. That she did so places her at the forefront of an epistemological shift in the way Canadians thought about sexual danger, and human sexual behaviour in general. In the years following WWII, sex offenders were viewed as more mentally disturbed than criminally responsible, and sex crime was regarded as a major mental health problem waiting to be solved.

All across Canada, everyday citizens came to see criminal sexual psychopath laws as the solution. First introduced in the state of Michigan in 1937, such laws were premised on the notion that repeat sex offenders were neither deterred nor changed by incarceration because their actions were driven by an uncontrollable impulse to commit their horrible crimes. Those who came to accept this interpretation of sex crime, and sexually "deviant" behaviour in general, believed that the solution was to eliminate the impulse, or, in popular lay terms, cure the disease. To this end, sex psychopath laws married psychiatric expertise to political prerogative by allowing the state to incarcerate offenders until they were deemed "cured" by a psychiatrist. Adopted by only a handful of northeastern US states in the late 1930s, at the end of WWII public support for sexual psychopath laws resumed with fervour. In 1948 Parliament unanimously passed criminal sexual psychopath legislation into the *Criminal Code* of Canada, and by 1953 twenty-four American states had adopted some version of the law.[3]

Recently, historians have attributed the proliferation of sexual psychopath laws to pre- and post-WWII anxiety over the Great Depression and the Second World War's unhinging of masculinity from the taming influence of the domestic realm. Drawing on the "moral panic" model first developed by British sociologist Stanley Cohen, Estelle Freedman and George Chauncey convincingly argue that the first decade of the Cold War was marked by increased regulation and rigidity of sex and gender norms, and by the concomitant popularisation of the "sexual deviant," a character constructed from psychiatric and psychological ideas about sexual behaviour and who came to be widely perceived as a threat to both personal and political security and stability. But criminal sexual psychopath legislation represents the apex of the 20th-century marriage of psychiatry and law, the apogee of a century-long movement away from retribution and toward reformation, from classical to positivist criminology, from punishment to therapeutic confinement.[5] Seen across an extended historical trajectory, criminal sexual psychopath legislation—a legal, medical, and cultural phenomenon that dominated public safety concerns at mid-century—appears as more than the product of middle-class anxiety over disruptions to gender and familial configurations. It was equally part of a long-standing tradition of moral reform that, because of its social scientific emphasis on the consequences of bad parenting—a "sadly neglected childhood," for example—had an immediate appeal to parents of the baby boom generation. Viewed through this additional lens, we can better understand how it was that Canadian parliamentarians responded to widespread public concern over sex crimes by passing a law that gave psychiatrists unprecedented control over a segment of the federal prison population.

Most studies of the post-WWII sex crime panic and sexual psychopath laws focus on the US experience, but the 1948 passage of criminal sexual psychopath legislation in the House of Commons demonstrates that many Canadians were similarly preoccupied with sexual attacks against children, and that they too viewed psychiatric treatment as the solution. Canadian scholars Gary Kinsman and Mary Louise Adams have mapped out the post-WWII sexual landscape in Canada; the former is concerned largely with the implications of the post-war sex panic for sexual minorities, and the latter with the cultural contours of the emergence of heterosexual normativity.[6] This article makes a further contribution to our understanding of this period through an examination of medical ideas about sex and psychopathy in Canada. By understanding how this law came to be, we shall better understand how Canadians came to view sexual behaviour in mental health terms.

SEXUAL PSYCHOPATHY

Throughout the 19th century, psychiatrists maintained that there were some people who, though not insane, were compelled to commit a variety of crimes as a result of mental problems beyond their control. Turn-of-the-century moral reformers interested in new solutions to urban social problems embraced the concept of criminal "behaviour" as a medical (and thus treatable) problem, and helped to establish both public and private alternatives to traditional courts and prisons, especially for women and juveniles labelled "psychopathic." Originally termed "moral insanity" by early 19th-century English psychiatrist J. C. Pritchard, psychopathy was one of the five main categories of insanity elaborated upon by Canadian psychiatrist Joseph Workman.[7] By the early 20th century, psychopathy was generally applied to those whose inability to "conduct themselves with decency and propriety in the business of life" could not be medically accounted for by traditional measures of mental or intellectual impairment.[8]

In the early part of the 20th century, however, psychopathy came to be more frequently associated with sexual immorality. Historian Steven Maynard argues that as early as 1905 Ontario psychiatric testimony in gross indecency cases described male homosexual activity as the product of a "disease of the mind."[9] Women whose sexual activities violated social and moral standards were also likely to be labeled psychopathic.[10] But by the 1930s, the "sex psychopath" was more narrowly defined as a dangerous male sex pervert whose uncontrollable urges led him to commit increasingly violent crimes, and who would continue to commit crimes until his mental problems were resolved. Those early experiments with juvenile and family criminal courts, where the hard edge of the law was (theoretically, at least) mitigated by the soft edge of social and psychiatric services, paved the way for the creation of "criminal sexual psychopath" laws, a medico-legal experiment that typically imposed indefinite prison sentences on convicted perpetrators of sex crimes. The crimes covered by sex psychopath laws generally included the full spectrum of sex-related offences from sexual assaults against children to sex between two consenting male adults. Sexual assault against adult females was not often included under criminal sexual psychopath laws since the object of the perpetrator's desire—an adult female—was not abnormal or "deviant" and therefore was simply a violent assault and not the product of a mental defect. Although the legal penalty for a person charged as a criminal sexual psychopath varied across the American states that adopted it, many versions, including Canada's, allowed for their release from prison only after a psychiatric assessment declared the offender unlikely to commit a further sexual offence.[11]

Two major factors contributed to the medico-legal construction of the criminal sexual psychopath. First, Depression-era disruptions to traditional family arrangements triggered concerns about maintaining social order. Hoboes, groups of unemployed men riding the rails, and women left alone to provide for their children served to arouse public anxiety about the dangers of "men adrift" from the taming rewards of breadwinner masculinity and the feminizing influences of the nuclear family.[12] Secondly, the 1930s was a period of tremendous growth in the social scientific study of sexuality. New York psychiatrist George Henry penned the most comprehensive American study of sexual perversion in the interwar period. When New York City citizens demanded a political response to a perceived increase in sexual assaults, Henry and his colleagues were commissioned by Mayor Fiorello La Guardia to conduct a comprehensive study of sex crimes. Though the commission found no evidence to support the claim that sexual attacks were on the rise, their research contributed to the growing body of literature on the sexual practices of everyday people, of the sexual behaviour of "deviants" and "perverts," and of various treatment programs employed in European and Scandinavian countries, which together shaped a new scientific discourse about sex that would underwrite the sex crime panic of that decade.[13]

In fact, forensic psychiatry had long been the main source of "raw material" from which a science of sex evolved. The first major medical text in the field was Richard von Krafft-Ebing's *Psychopathia Sexualis: A Medico-Forensic Study*. Written as a courtroom guide, it lay the foundation upon which future sex researchers would sort, quantify, and organize a wide spectrum of sexual behaviours into "types."[14] For many medical experts, Krafft-Ebing's text was a tremendous advance. Sexual and moral regulations in the modern British, American and Canadian criminal codes were viewed by some as artefacts of an earlier age, many rooted in medieval ecclesiastical law which valued human reproduction within Church and state-sanctioned marriage.[15] Up until the late 19th century, for example, the Canadian *Criminal Code* made no distinction between different types of moral offences that sexologists had come to regard as categorically exclusive. Sodomy between two male adults and fornication between a human and an animal were the same offence. Similarly, the law drew clear distinctions between heterosexual intercourse with a female under fourteen, with a female between fourteen and sixteen, and with a female over sixteen, but homosexual sex between two consenting adult males was punishable under the same sections as were homosexual sexual assaults on a child or young adult.[16]

Inconsistencies such as these drove many early sexologists, Krafft-Ebing included, to become law reform advocates.[17] Some simply sought a clarification of existing laws, but others struggled to have certain laws repealed, particularly those relating to consensual homosexual acts, arguing that the state had no place imposing a fixed set of moral values on its citizens. Perhaps the most well-known in this respect were England's Havelock Ellis and Germany's Magnus Hirschfeld. Though there were no Canadian experts of comparable international stature, there were modest efforts to move in a similar direction. In 1933, the Toronto Psychiatric Hospital's senior assistant physician A. J. Kilgour noted that while the law allowed for harsh sentences for sex offences, "the magistrate, of his own accord or acting on advice, frequently refrains from carrying it out to the letter."[18] At least one other Ontario doctor took a dim view of incarcerating homosexuals, advocating instead that they be provided with out-patient treatment.[19]

Based on early 20th-century criminal trials involving sex between men and boys in Ontario, historian Steven Maynard has shown that psychiatrists in that province were among the earliest in North America and Europe to interpret sodomy, buggery, and gross indecency as symptoms of a mental disease.[20] However, the classificatory zeal that characterized psychiatry at the turn of the 19th century was not matched by advances in methods of treatment. Private "nerve" clinics such as those established by Krafft-Ebing in Austria and Germany, and the Homewood Retreat in Ontario, were the exception.[21] Most doctors specializing in mental disorders worked with acutely disturbed long-term patients in asylums or hospital. Only in 1925 did Ontario finally open the Toronto Psychiatric Hospital (TPH) where treatment was available for out- as well as in-patients, thus expanding its services to individuals suffering from more minor disorders.[22] The courts continued to serve as a primary source of new patients.

Between 1929 and 1933, almost half of the 3,622 people admitted to the TPH were court referrals.[23] Of those, 150 had been charged with sex-related offences. A. J. Kilgour thought the problem of sex offences significant enough to merit study, and his sample large enough to support the venture. Still a somewhat dubious field of medical inquiry, his 1933 article on sex delinquency opened with the self-legitimating assertion that the problem was greater than most people recognized. For example, while only 150 people were referred to the clinic, he argued they represented but a fraction of the total of 1,100 sex-related charges laid in Toronto in the same period. However, at the same time Kilgour reported that the number of court referrals was steadily increasing, indicating that local magistrates were more and more inclined to accept the argument that sex offences had important psychological aspects that merited medical examination. This was an important boost for psychiatry whose claim to authority beyond the realm of the mentally diseased and into the everyday lives of healthy but socially and morally delinquent citizens relied on the legitimation of the courts and other regulatory bodies.

Though perhaps something of a maverick in Canada, Kilgour was one among a growing number of experts inspired by new social sciences research into the sexual habits and behaviour of everyday people. Early 20th-century psychiatrists imagined themselves harbingers of a value-free scientific future. Casting off the false modesties and repressive tendencies of the Victorian era, the science of sex would liberate the masses from undue shame and stood to increase human happiness by releasing men and women from the restraints of myth and misconception propagated by religious dictum and social convention. Apprehending sex as a straightforward fact was a defiant strategy meant to align the profession with science and medicine and to "signal psychiatrists' and social workers' unflinching modernity."[24]

Kilgour's contribution to the growing body of international literature on sexuality was both defiant and self-avowedly modern. Based on physical examinations of his subjects, he refuted biological theories of heredity, commonly cited by European as well as North American medical experts as one of the more significant etiological factors that cause sexual abnormalities, particularly homosexuality.[25] In point-by-point fashion, Kilgour scrutinised his subjects for physical defects and other potentially meaningful signifiers, including nationality, place of birth, religion, and ancestry. No single feature emerged to explain any of the sexual deviations, he argued. There were no outward signs of physical degeneration; on the contrary many of his subjects were "athletic" and "robust." Indeed, the sample showed only that sex offenders represent a typical cross-section of society. Most of his subjects first engaged in "sexual misconduct" by introduction, not inclination, and for at least half of them, Kilgour attributed their crime to an unsatisfactory sex life caused by "(1) exaggerated sexual desire; (2) diminished sexual ability;

(3) interference with normal sexual activity because of moral, medical, and social restraint or marital dysharmony."[26]

Such assertions posed a direct challenge to mainstream psychiatry in Canada. Though C. K. Clarke, the highly influential Dean of Medicine and Professor of Psychiatry at the University of Toronto, died almost a decade before the article was published, his views on the primacy of biology and heredity in determining mental stability influenced a generation of Canadian psychiatrists trained under his tutelage. They also undermined the claims of Ontario's moral reformers—a decidedly pro-psychiatry constituency—of the day.[27]

Kilgour also raised provocative questions about some of the most deeply held beliefs concerning sexual morality. Many were given to believe, he argued, "that there is but one pattern of normal sex life and that any straying from that path was abnormal." New research, however, showed that "there are as many [paths] as there are individuals." Rather than use this as evidence of the erosion of morality and a threat to society, Kilgour drew on history to show that sexual and moral norms were in a constant state of change. Using homosexuality as an example, he claimed that earlier civilizations, upon which all of western civilization was built, accepted and even celebrated sexual activity between people of the same sex. Embracing sexual diversity, to use a modern term, was "not only a matter of justice to those who may vary from the conventional form in sex conduct, but also because it increases the stability of the whole moral system."[28] To suggest that it was unjust to persecute those whose sexual activities were unconventional and, furthermore, to propose that homosexuality was a stabilizing force was, in 1933, a radical proposition, especially given the lack of a visible intellectual or political community that might stand in support of his conclusions.

If the problem was not sexual practices but society's narrow definition of normalcy, Kilgour implored his readers to consider the extent to which the law should intervene in matters of sexual misbehaviour. However, little more than a decade after he posed the question, Canadians showed that they were more willing than ever to rely on Parliament to keep the country safe from the threat of sexual danger.

CANADA ADOPTS THE SEXUAL PSYCHOPATH

When Canada adopted its own criminal code in 1893, it was decided that Parliament, not the courts, would be the principal source of change in the criminal law, and using the law to regulate public morals was a process many politicians lauded.[29] "No higher functions rest upon the Government of a nation or of a people than to guard the morals and to promote the public welfare of the people in every way that it is possible to do so by legislation," declared MP John Charlton in 1893 when he introduced a bill prohibiting contraceptives and abortion.[30] Responding in part to the demands of their constituents, including women's groups, labour unions, and religious organizations, Parliament passed revisions in 1886, 1892, 1906, and 1927.[31] Changes to laws regulating morality and physical harm (for they were not organized into a single group of "sex laws" until the revisions of the mid-1950s) reflected changing ideas about women and about sexual activity between people of the same sex.

With Parliament the principal source of change in the criminal law, the *Criminal Code* was vulnerable to revision based on emotionally-charged public demands placed on elected politicians. It was precisely these factors at play during the 1947 House of Commons debate concerning a proposal to adopt criminal sexual psychopath legislation. On 3 July MP Howard C. Green introduced a resolution from the British Columbia Provincial Convention of Parent-Teacher Associations. "'Resolved,'" Green read,

> that representations be made to the federal government recommending that necessary legislation be enacted to provide for sentencing offenders against public morals where those offences are due to a psychopathic condition, to preventative treatment and detention in a separate institution provided for that purpose.[32]

When, an indignant Green demanded to know, will the Liberal government respond to the "alarming increase in Canada in moral offences against children"? British Columbia's Parent-Teacher Associations viewed the sex crime problem in the same light as had Mrs. Geraldine M. Sex offenders were mentally disturbed people in need of psychiatric treatment, and it was incumbent upon the government to ensure that they received it.

But it was the perceived threat of danger to the community rather than the potentially beneficial treatment to offenders that MP Green emphasized when endorsing the British Columbia Federation of Parent-Teacher Association's demand for criminal sexual psychopath legislation. [...] Green's support for criminal sexual psychopath laws similarly tapped into post-WWII social anxieties about sexual danger and child safety, and made "sex deviants" the folk devil of the day.[33] Support for criminal sexual psychopath legislation in Canada originated from parent-teacher and other women's voluntary organizations whose advocacy of treatment programs often was couched as a sympathetic rather than retributive response to the problems of the sex offender.[34] Green, however, exploited the fears of parents occupied with the task of raising the baby boom generation, and emphasized community protection over reformation.

Minister of Justice James L. Ilsley was fully prepared for Green's query. Earlier that spring Charles Stogdill, the Director of the Mental Health Division, and General Gibson, the Commissioner of Penitentiaries, embarked on a study of sex crime and the sexual psychopath statutes in the United States. Shortly thereafter, the Penitentiaries Branch of the Federal Department of Justice appointed psychiatrist Dr. L. P. Gendreau as Deputy Commissioner, indicating the department's long-awaited move toward applying the principles of reformation through therapeutic intervention.[35] [...] [T]here was no evidence that any treatment methods currently in use could be, or in some cases, should be, used to treat sexually deviated offenders.

Virtually every study undertaken by individual American states before, during, and in the case of New Jersey, after the passage of some form of sex psychopath legislation showed that the image of the sex psychopath—urban, recidivist, and prone to committing crimes of increasing violence—was more fiction than fact.[36] [...]

Minister of Justice Ilsley would have to wait more than a decade for Canada's statistical confirmation that there had not been a rise in sex crime rates in the years following WWII.[37] In the meantime, he argued against introducing sex crime laws similar to those in the United States. Citing a 1946 article from the British *Journal of Nervous and Mental Diseases*, Ilsley explained that the area of sex offender research "is a field in which there is much disagreement. . . . There are those who think psychiatry is not the whole answer." Indeed, Canadian psychiatrists were surprisingly forthright in their admission that no one had yet devised any cure.[38] In fact, by the late 1940s, those who had experience in the field were pessimistic that a cure would ever be found. Given the uncertainties of psychiatric treatment, Ilsley was reluctant to introduce an amendment to the *Criminal Code* "prescribing preventive detention for sex offenders for indefinite periods, when we are not prepared to state for sure that we can say when they should be released again."[39]

Minister of Justice Ilsley's reservations toward adopting criminal sexual psychopath legislation appear well founded, especially considering that sexuality was still one of the most underdeveloped areas of medical and psychiatric research. Large-scale studies were undertaken during the interwar period in the United States, but in Canada studies such as the one conducted by A. J. Kilgour at the Toronto Psychiatric Hospital were almost unheard of, due largely to the overwhelming influence of C. K. Clarke, who had rejected Freudian and other developmental theories of human sexuality.[40] Even in Canadian universities talking about sex could have severe consequences. In the 1920s Norman Jellinger Symons, the Chair of the Department of Psychology at Dalhousie University, taught a course in dynamic psychology. As part of his lectures Symons would solicit dreams from his students and "provide them with full-blown Freudian interpretations." The university administration was horrified and promptly demanded his resignation.[41] Concerned that this atmosphere still prevailed, in 1959 a prospective PhD student from Queen's University in Kingston was reassured by a member of Dalhousie's psychology department, "Young man, you may *describe* sex, you must never *advocate* it."[42]

THE COMMITTEE ON THE SEX OFFENDER

Keeping sex respectable may have been good for the national soul, but it meant that there was no intellectual foundation upon which to build a treatment program for sex offenders. When in 1947 sex assaults against children were made a matter of national concern, the Canadian Penal Association (CPA) [...] brought together a cross-section of Canadian experts in medicine, law and education to form the "Committee on the Sex Offender" (CSO). Representing government, academic, and professional volunteer organizations were Dr. L. E Gendreau, the newly-appointed deputy commissioner of Penitentiaries in the Department of Justice, Dr. J. D. M. Griffin, medical director of the National Committee for Mental Hygiene (soon to become the Canadian Mental Health Association), and lawyer J. Alex Edmison, president of the Canadian Penal Association. Joining this prestigious panel were a handful of Toronto-based experts, including members of the University of Toronto medicine and social work faculties; Toronto Chief Constable John Chisholm; Dr. Kenneth Rogers, executive secretary of the Big Brother Movement; and local Magistrates Robert Bigelow and Kenneth E Mackenzie. Three months after the committee was struck, the CSO issued an interim report. [...] Though the overall report did not provide a single solution or approach to the sex offender problem, it went a long way toward defining the parameters of the debate.

Gendreau and Griffin provided independent analyses of sex crime and its perpetrators. A study in contrasts, the two reports illustrate Canadian psychiatry's intellectual transition at mid-century from a mostly biological model to a developmental model. First, Gendreau illuminated his subject by providing a detailed depiction of a single case study, one of the oldest and most common tools of his trade.[43] Notably, he chose to reveal his assessment of a man who had recently been the object of media attention for a sex-related crime. Like most psychiatrists, Gendreau subscribed to no single theory of causality; instead, his analysis combined eugenic and degenerative as well as more modern environmental and behavioural theories. For example, he described his subjects' parents as "sexually delinquent and not likely to raise their children with moral standards above their own." They were "of low grade stock mentally and morally." The "morally deficient" father created a poisonous environment by carrying on an incestuous relationship with his twelve-year-old stepdaughter. The mother exacerbated the problem by being "overindulgent and overprotective"—a post-WWII descriptor that would increasingly come to be associated with developmental abnormalities, particularly male homosexuality.[44] In the interwar years mothers of delinquent and especially sexually "perverted" boys were more likely to be described in opposite terms, as uninvolved, negligent, and perhaps even "New Women," but here the failing mother was more likely to be "emotionally unstable." In this particular case, the mother "kept children home from school for no valid reason," which not only prevented them from receiving a proper education, but also kept them from the positive normalizing influence the school offered. For Gendreau it was clear that *"due to her own emotional deficiencies,"* the mother was unwilling to allow her children to be normal.[45]

Ensuring that children grew to be "normal" was, according to modern experts, the sole responsibility of parents, particularly mothers. These new parenting standards were widely promoted by Canada's federal government. [...] The post-WWII sex crime panic made sexual health a central component of modern parental responsibilities. Indeed, improper parenting techniques became one of the most ubiquitous and enduring explanations for social and sexual delinquency in the post-war era.

A careful reading of Dr. L. P. Gendreau's case study of a sex offender and his family illustrates how paradigm shifts are never sudden or complete, but that old and new ideas, even when they are seemingly incongruent, often overlap.[46] Specifically, he conjoined a germ disease model with newer developmental models of sexuality to explain sexually deviant behaviour. His subject was "initiated in early life, in sexual activities along homosexual lines," and had been in trouble with the law as a result of his sexual activities. The original contamination, left untreated, had led him to "become a confirmed sexual invert. This is confirmed by his inability to make heterosexual adjustment."[47] Unable to arrive at the heterosexual endpoint, the victim remained in a perpetual state of immaturity, his development into full manhood with all its attendant rights, privileges, and responsibilities thwarted.[48]

In his final analysis, Gendreau concluded, "There are numerous socioeconomic factors which work towards the development of such an individual emotionally conditioned to such behaviour." Unless he receives treatment in prison, he will most assuredly return to his "practices" and "be a menace, perhaps, to a greater extent than before and commit crimes of greater magnitude."[49] It was precisely these assumptions—that prison was not reformative, that sex offenders would re-offend and commit increasingly serious crimes, and that psychiatric treatment was the only possible method to rehabilitate (or perhaps more precisely re-educate) the deviated offender to the norms of society—upon which the criminal sexual psychopath as a clinico-legal construct rested. Even if there were no known treatment methods at the time, criminal sexual psychopath laws would provide experts like Gendreau with the opportunity to find one. It was an option that appeared much more appealing than the alternative: to return sexual psychopaths to the community untreated, unreformed, and unrepentant.

But what if treatment didn't work? It was a well-accepted truism that the better educated and more intelligent the individual, the more amenable to the most widely pursued form of therapeutic treatment: counselling, or, in modern terms, talk therapy.[50] Anticipating that his subject was not a good prospect for this very reason, Gendreau concluded, "Such an individual should not, for years to come, be given his freedom."[51] Thus the preventative sentence, originally intended to make the criminal justice system more pliable so that treatment programs would not be interrupted by the expiration of a prison sentence, could also now be conceived of as a means to ensure the long-term protection of society from a criminal deemed psychopathic and incurable. Sex psychopath legislation appealed to those who regarded the sex offender as more mentally disturbed than criminally-minded because it posited that psychotherapy and other forms of psychological and medical treatment, thought to be more humane and progressive, would be provided to those convicted as sex psychopaths. However, sexual psychopath legislation sated those who preferred to incarcerate sex offenders for life. The laws themselves guaranteed as much by ensuring that no one judged a sex psychopath would be released from custody until cured, or, as some American state laws held, judged by a psychiatrist to no longer be a threat to society.

While Gendreau reinforced the image of the sex fiend as the poor, unintelligent offspring of low-grade stock, Dr. J. D. M. Griffin joined a growing group of experts who challenged the most basic premise of sex research. Influenced by anthropologists like Ruth Benedict and Margaret Mead, a new generation of North American sex researchers set out to exorcise the moral assumptions embedded in popular ideas about sexuality.[52] "Ignorance, superstition, rigid taboos and violent prejudice" complicate our understanding of sexual disorders, Griffin complained. "So powerful have been the emotional and social repression concerning sex in our culture, that even scientific enquiry as to the actual facts has been hampered."[53] He and other experts argued that sexual practices viewed with hostility and contempt by most North Americans might be highly valued in other cultures. Moreover, he explained, sexual behaviour varied tremendously even within North America. Echoing A. J. Kilgour, Griffin argued that Canadians could no longer sustain the illusion that "normal" sex was static, stable, and definable. Any further advances in sex research required that we remove our sexual blinders and encourage more frank, open, and honest discussions about sex.

Griffin's report also diverged from Gendreau in method. By 1948 psychiatrists no longer had to rely on a handful of individual case studies to extrapolate some sort of understanding of sex crime and sexual deviancy. The interwar decades spawned a number of large-scale studies of the sexual habits and attitudes of Americans. [...] Griffin drew on the findings of LaGuardia's New York report on sex crime charges laid in that city. [...] As a result of these major surveys, including the just-released Alfred Kinsey report on male sexual behaviour, Griffin argued that sexual activities widely considered perverted and esoteric "are now known to occur with surprising frequency."[54] With the support of raw data collected from a cross-section of middle America, experts had the tools they needed to strip the study of sex of any moral embellishments, and sub-mit it to scientific scrutiny based not on obvious social norms and values, but on the innovative systems of measurement such as the one Kinsey created. His infamous scale, which challenged the notion of a sex "norm" by, for example, rejecting the categorization of humans as either heterosexual or homosexual in favour of a measure of "total sexual outlet" was a revolutionary new way to conceptualize human sexual behaviour.[55]

Kilgour, Kinsey, and Griffin all agreed there were no common features—physical or psycho-logical—that defined the "sex deviate." Griffin reported,

> Sex offenders have no particular or easily recognizable features or stigmata to distin-guish them from anyone else. They may be of any age, race, colour or creed. They may come from good homes or bad. They may live in wealthy or residential areas or in the slums. Their families may be criminals or respected pillars of the church.[56]

Indeed, Griffin continued, the sex psychopath scare was based on misinformation. According to the latest research findings, the vast majority of sex offenders were not mentally ill, and the mentally ill were not more likely to commit sex crimes. Neither were sex offenders more likely to be recidivists.[57] The sexual psychopath was a figment of the imagination of a zealous public, built on sketchy psychiatric profiles like the one offered up by Dr. Gendreau. Still, Griffin did not reject the "sexual psychopath" concept completely. Instead, he argued that even though recidivism rates are low, society still needed protection from those who committed "compulsive and repetitive" acts of sexual violence.[58]

Psychiatrists could not agree about whether there was such a thing as a sex psychopath, and when they did, there was little clarity about what one was, but on one point most everyone con-curred: the need for more sex knowledge. The education report, authored by Canadian Welfare Council member Kenneth Rogers, represented this position. Elaborating on the growing popular-ity of the socialization and behaviourism schools of thought, many leading experts agreed that the sex instinct needed to be properly guided lest a young child be misled by a corrupt friend or a perverted stranger.[59] But frank talk about sex was as controversial in the late 1940s as it had been in Jellinger's Dalhousie University psychology class of 1929, making Rogers' task a delicate one. Already Alfred Kinsey's path-breaking surveys were inciting angry and censorious responses in both Canada and the United States.[60] Many historians of the period have focused on the negative and controversial responses to his study, but in both countries Kinsey's reports were also greeted with cautious enthusiasm and tempered delight. [...] In 1946 Dr. D. Ewen Cameron invited Kinsey to McGill University to talk about the gap between socially acceptable sexual mores and actual sexual practices as part of the "Lectures on Living" series, a mental health education organized by the university but open to the entire community.[61] Kinsey received favourable publicity in the *Globe and Mail*, where journalist Lotta Dempsey covered his research activities and the publica-tion of his reports, and in 1953 the CBC invited him to record a nine-minute talk for the "In Search of Ourselves" mental health series. Though Kinsey's policy to never speak from written papers nor to appear on radio or television got in the way of his addressing a Canadian audience directly, there was a lively interest in his work on this side of the border.[62]

Not all who embraced the Kinsey report shared the author's desire to liberate sex from the shackles of cultural repression. For some, it only confirmed what they already suspected: sexual morality needed to be policed now more than ever. Contrary to Kilgour, Kinsey, Griffin, and others who argued that what social and moral convention deemed "normal" sexual practice did not reflect the wide range of sexual activity taking place, Kenneth Mackenzie's education report argued that the Kinsey data was proof positive of the urgent need for "greater moral restraints in family, community and national life."[63] If sexual perversion was psychogenic and not congenital, then sex education grounded in scientific principles was the key to guarding society against sexual danger and preserving sexual security. [...] For Rogers, the next and most important step in the battle against sex offenders was to offer "mass education for parenthood." This, he argued, would give a solid foundation for proper sex education in the home.[64]

With so little to recommend it, was criminal sexual psychopath legislation the answer? According to Kenneth Mackenzie, the legal expert, perhaps not. [...] [T]he *British North America Act* further complicated matters, and, Mackenzie pointed out, would impede any effort to fully implement the spirit of the legislation. Federal-provincial responsibility for prisoners was divided, the former obliged to care for those sentenced to two years or more, and the latter liable for those sentenced to anything less. Dangerous and repetitive sex offenders, the object of public concern and the intended target of sex psychopath legislation, would likely be sentenced to lengthy prison terms, and thus would be required to serve time in a federal institution. However, provincial governments were responsible for matters of health, including mental health. Criminal sexual psychopath legislation, Mackenzie rightly pointed out, would require first that the *Penitentiary Act* be amended to permit those convicted to be confined to a hospital for more than two years. Provincial governments would need to be persuaded to provide the facilities, the staff, and the treatment programs for them.

The CSO never had the opportunity to propose solutions to any of the problems the report raised. In 1950 all activity on the project was officially suspended due to a lack of funds. The committee was never revived, and no final report was ever published.[65] [...] Shortly before the *Interim Report* was publicly released to a large audience of citizens and journalists at a press conference held at Toronto's King Edward Hotel, Ilsley introduced a slightly modified version of Massachusetts' 1947 statute.[66] On June 14, 1948, Canada's Members of Parliament unanimously approved the passage of Section 1054A of the *Criminal Code*.

With the entire House standing firmly in favour of the new legislation, the Minister of Justice had little choice but to support it, remarking only that he hoped the passing of the law would be followed by the hiring of treatment staff in Canada's federal penitentiaries. There were no concomitant changes to the *British North America Act* enabling federal-provincial co-operation, meaning that despite repeated calls for freestanding research and treatment hospitals for sexual psychopaths, the only available option was to create treatment programs within existing prisons.[67] However, Ilsley's hopes were not realized. At the federal level, there were no treatment programs aimed at what were then called "dangerous sex offenders" until 1971.[68] Moreover, while judges frequently expressed support for some type of treatment alternative to prison, they were often reticent to accept the central principal behind criminal sexual psychopath legislation, that perpetrators of sex crimes were unable to control their sex impulses. In fact many were deeply concerned about sentencing convicted sex offenders to indefinite terms so that they might be "cured" when there were no treatment services in place. By 1952, the Canadian Welfare Council formally protested the government's failure to make provisions for treatment, and demanded that the government establish a Royal Commission to "study the whole matter of the sex offender."[69] In 1954 Prime Minister Louis St. Laurent finally agreed to establish a Royal Commission to investigate the matter.

From 1954 to 1958 the Royal Commission on the Criminal Law Relating to the Criminal Sexual Psychopath held hearings in every provincial capital as well as in Montreal and Vancouver. Medical experts, including psychiatrists, constituted the largest single group of witnesses, and they gave testimony on a full range of issues concerning human sexual behaviour, from masturbation to flagellation to homosexuality.[70] Though the hearings were removed from the everyday lives of Canadian citizens, local media provided coverage of the testimony as it unfolded, and assaults against women and especially children once again became headline news. By the mid-1950s journalists continued to seek the analysis of law enforcement agents when offering an explanation for why such horrendous crimes occur. Borrowing modern psychiatric terminology, urban police investigators claimed that hundreds of "sex deviates" roamed the city streets at any given time. Media reports such as these effectively heightened public anxiety, and ignited new demands for state intervention.[71]

A year after the Royal Commission concluded its public hearings, it presented the federal government with a remarkably conservative report recommending only minor changes to the existing law. Few of those were actually implemented, leading to neither an increase in convictions under what was renamed "dangerous sexual offender" legislation, nor to the creation of treatment programs, either within or outside of the prison.[72] However, in the ten years between the time criminal sexual psychopath legislation was first introduced and when the Royal Commission finally rested, the average Canadian citizen had been exposed to a great deal of information about the scientific approach to human sexuality. Though the law never functioned the way its supporters had hoped, by the end of the 1950s many Canadian citizens had come to accept sexual deviancy as a mental health problem.

CONCLUSION

Criminal sexual psychopath legislation in Canada was the product of a moral panic that took shape during a particular historical period, but it also must be seen as but one point along a century-old trajectory of psycho-medical thinking about criminality, sexuality, and the law. Beginning with simple "insanity" as a monolithic, homogeneous category in the early 19th century, the construction of the criminal sexual psychopath was part of an ongoing evolution of philosophical, legal, and medical ideas about regulating and assessing social behaviour and moral responsibility. The progeny of a marriage between the justice system and medicine, between social reformers and psychiatrists, sex psychopath laws were in part the product of an almost century-long effort to implement the principles of positivist criminology, spurred on by a moral panic over sex crime and inspired by new advances in the sexual sciences. Historians have rightfully emphasized the way criminal sexual psychopath legislation served as a literal and figurative expression of pre- and post-WWII ideas about containing and controlling male sexuality. However, it also must be regarded as part of a long tradition of social reform which took a dim view of punishment and repression, and instead sought new and innovative ways to solve intractable social problems.

Widespread support for what began as an American legal construct reveals something about Canada's changing location in the post-WWII political and cultural landscape. Though the Canadian legal system followed Britain's lead and rejected the concept of partial insanity at the turn of the 19th century, Canadian psychiatrists kept well abreast of the evolving relationship between psychiatrists, psychologists, social workers, and the courts and prisons in the United States, and even advocated for similar advances here.[73] For them, the border hardly existed. Canadian psychiatrists did not establish their own national professional organization until the mid-1950s, and even then retained their memberships in the American Psychiatric Association, attending their conferences, publishing in their journal, and sometimes even serving as president.[74] The post-war boom in university education further opened the doors of Canadian psychiatry, loosening the grip of the few dominant personalities that characterized the pre-WWII period and allowing greater circulation of the different schools of psychiatric thought. Given this environment, it is clear that Canadian psychiatrists were as much a part of the creation of the sexual psychopath as were their American colleagues.

Politically and culturally the war and the international re-organization of power that followed brought Canada even more firmly in line with American interests, and US cultural influence.[75] In the annals of legal history, the introduction of criminal sexual psychopath legislation illustrated Canada's growing intimacy with the United States. Everyday citizens had much more in common with the post-war reconstruction concerns in the United Sates than they did with war-torn Britain. The re-integration of military men, the removal of women from the paid labour market, the development of the suburbs, and the concomitant baby boom all helped contribute to the erosion of the border as a meaningful cultural divide. Cold War concerns about the preservation and protection of the family were no less poignant and pressing in the north, and the penetration of the mainstream US media helped to shape popular opinion here as effectively as it did in the 29 states that also passed some form of criminal sexual psychopath legislation.[76] But the Canadian media also participated, not by challenging the model of the criminal sexual psychopath, and not by "exposing" the fiction upon which it rested, but by perpetuating the construct through narrative accounts of sexual deviation and the victims of sex crimes and through interviews with psychiatrists and other "experts," and they used radio, print, and film to do so. Canada's early participation in the wave of criminal sexual psychopath laws that swept through America is not a portent of the rising dominance of the United States, but in this instance is an example of how the Canadian body politic drew many of its nutrients from the same cultural soil as the northeastern United States. In other words, Canadians did not merely follow the lead of their southern neighbours. They were full participants in the converging relationships between the science of sex, psychiatry, and the law.

Criminal sexual psychopath legislation is representative of an important shift in the way Canadians and Americans thought about sex. It was a decisive victory for forensic sexologists who, since the late 1800s, were determined to see "perverted" sex acts treated as a medical, not criminal, problem. However, theirs was not a liberation ideology. Like Mrs. Geraldine M., most citizens who supported sexual psychopath legislation were merely seeking to improve the way the justice and penal system handled sex crime. Though some might individually have supported the liberalization of sex in areas such as public education, sexual liberation was not what drove people like Mrs. M. to pen a letter to the Minister of Health. However, it would be equally erroneous to suggest treatment advocates were interested in greater sexual repression. What most citizens wanted was for the state to recognise that sex crimes should not be treated like other crimes. Like so many of her contemporaries, Mrs. M. was convinced that sexual deviants like the exhibitionists she and her daughter encountered needed help, not punishment. The "scientific" approach was the "intelligent" approach, and one that, at least on the surface, appeared more humane and less punitive. This epistemological shift was facilitated not only by the moral panic that characterized the age, but was also part of the overall triumph of "everyday psychiatry." In the years following WWII, Canadian citizens agreed that psychiatrists not only belonged in the bedroom, but also in the living room, the office, the factory floor, the courtroom, and even in the House of Commons and other political arenas.

NOTES

1 Archives of Ontario (AO), RG 10-107-0-224, Letter to the Minister of Health, 17 April 1947.

2 Committee on the Sex Offender, *Interim Report* (Toronto: Canadian Penal Association, 1948) in AO, RG 20-16-2-59.9, John Howard Society, 1951–52. The Vancouver story received national coverage after the Member of Parliament from Vancouver-South Howard C. Green raised it during a parliamentary debate. See: Canada, Parliament, *House of Commons* Debates, 6 (July 1947): 5031.

3 Philip Jenkins, *Moral Panic: Changing Concepts of the Child Molester in Modern America* (New Haven: Yale University Press, 1988), p. 82.

4 Late 19th- and 20th-century sex crime "panics" such as the one that unfolded at mid-century were based on a perceived rise in the number of violent sexual assaults. Some historians have argued that sex crime rates remained stable throughout the period under study, while others have argued that, in the United States at least, the rate of sex crime convictions during the post-WWII panic were actually lower than the rate of convictions during the war itself. See Jenkins, *Moral Panic,* p. 49–74; and Estelle Freedman, "'Uncontrolled Desires': The Response to the Sexual Psychopath, 1920–1960" in Kathy Peiss and Christina Simmons, eds., *Passion and Power: Sexuality in History* (Philadelphia: Temple University Press, 1989), p. 200, 218 n.3.

5 On criminal sexual psychopath and similar legislation as part of the rising therapeutic state, see Nicholas N. Kittrie, *The Right to Be Different: Deviance and Enforced Therapy* (Baltimore: Johns Hopkins University Press, 1971), p. 40–1. On therapeutic confinement in Canada, see Simon N. Verdun-Jones and Russell Smandych, "Catch-22 in the Nineteenth Century: The Evolution of Therapeutic Confinement for the Criminally Insane in Canada, 1840–1900," *Criminal Justice History,* 2 (1981): 85–108.

6 Gary Kinsman, *The Regulation of Desire: Homo and Hetero Sexualities,* 2d ed. (Montreal: Black Rose Books, 1996); and Mary Louise Adams, *The Trouble with Normal: Postwar Youth and the Making of Heterosexuality* (Toronto: University of Toronto Press, 1997). For an examination of representations of male homosexuality in one Canadian scandal sheet during this period, see Eric Setliff, "Sex Fiends or Swish Kids?: Gay Men in *Hush Free Press,* 1946–1956" in Kathryn McPherson, Cecilia Morgan and Nancy M. Forestell, eds., *Gendered Pasts: Historical Essays in Femininity and Masculinity in Canada*

(Don Mills: Oxford University Press, 1999), p. 158–78.

7 Paul Gebhard et al., *Sex Offenders: An Analysis of Types* (New York: Harper and Row, 1965), p. 845.

8 James Cowles Prichard, cited in Gebhard et al., *Sex Offenders*, p. 845; see also Elizabeth Lunbeck, *The Psychiatric Persuasion: Knowledge, Gender, and Power in Modern America* (Princeton, New Jersey: Princeton University Press, 1994), p. 65–71.

9 Steven Maynard, "On the Case of the Case: The Emergence of the Homosexual as a Case History in Early Twentieth-Century Canada," in Franca Iacovetta and Wendy Mitchinson, eds., *On the Case: Explorations in Social History* (Toronto: University of Toronto Press, 1998), p. 65.

10 Freedman, "Uncontrolled Desires," p. 203; Jenkins, *Moral Panic*, p. 39; see also Anne Meis Knupfer "'To Become Good, Self-supporting Women': The State Industrial School for Delinquent Girls at Geneva, Illinois, 1900–1935," *Journal of the History of Sexuality*, 9, 4 (2000): 420–46; Edith R. Spaulding, *An Experimental Study of Psychopathic Delinquent Women* (New York: Rand McNally, 1923); and A. J. Kilgour, "Sex Delinquency—A Review of 100 Court Cases Referred to the Toronto Psychiatric Hospital," *Ontario Journal of Neuro-Psychiatry* (September 1933): 34–50. I first learned of the last article in Steven Maynard's published work in this area.

11 Cyril Greenland, "Dangerous Sexual Offender Legislation: An Experiment That Failed," *Canadian Journal of Criminology*, 26, 1 (January 1984): 1–12; Group for the Advancement of Psychiatry (GAP), *Psychiatry and Sex Psychopath Legislation: The 30s to the 80s*, Vol. 9 (New York: Group for the Advancement of Psychiatry (GAP), April 1977).

12 "Men adrift" is a play on Joanne Meyerowitz's *Women Adrift: Independent Wage Earners in Chicago, 1880–1930* (Chicago: University of Chicago Press, 1988).

13 Freedman, "Uncontrolled Desires," p. 202–5; for a complete historical account and analysis of American studies in sexuality in the 1930s, see Jennifer Terry, *An American Obsession: Science, Medicine, and the Place of Homosexuality in Modern Society* (Chicago: University of Chicago Press, 1999), p. 120–267.

14 Originally published in German as *Psychopathia Sexualis, mit besonderer Berücksichtigung der konträren Sexualempfindung: Eine klinisch-forenisische Studie* (Stuttgart: Enke 1886). For a detailed study of Krafft-Ebing, see Harry Oosterhuis, *Stepchildren of Nature: Krafft-Ebing, Psychiatry and the Making of Sexual Identity* (Chicago: University of Chicago Press, 2000).

15 Alex Gigeroff, *Sexual Deviations in the Criminal Law: Homosexual, Exhibitionistic and Pedophilic Offences in Canada* (Toronto: University of Toronto Press, 1968), p. 3–36; GAP, *Psychiatry and Sex Psychopath Legislation*, p. 848–49.

16 Alex Gigeroff, "The Evolution of Canadian Law with Respect to Exhibitionism, Homosexuality and Pedophilia," *Research Conference on Delinquency and Criminology. Proceedings/4ᵉ Colloque de Recherche sur la Délinquance et la Criminalité, Montréal 1964* (Ottawa: Société de Criminologie du Québec, avec la collaboration de l'Institute Philippe Pinel, 1965), p. 299–308; Gigeroff, *Sexual Deviations*, p. 8–9; and GAP, *Psychiatry and Sex Psychopath Legislation*, p. 848–49.

17 Harry Oosterhuis, "Richard van Krafft-Ebing's 'Step-Children of Nature': Psychiatry and the Making of Homosexual Identity," in Vernon A Rosario, ed., *Science and Homosexualities* (New York: Routledge, 1997), p. 80.

18 Kilgour, "Sex Delinquency," p. 35.

19 Maynard, "On the Case of the Case," p. 77–78.

20 Maynard, "On the Case of the Case," p. 77–78.

21 On the Homewood Retreat see Cheryl Krasnick Warsh, *Moments of Unreason: The Practice of Canadian Psychiatry and the Homewood Retreat, 1883–1923* (Montreal and Kingston: McGill-Queen's University Press, 1989). On Krafft-Ebing's nervous clinics see Oosterhuis, *Stepchildren of Nature.*

22 Edward Shorter, ed., *TPH: History and Memories of the Toronto Psychiatric Hospital, 1925–1966* (Toronto: Wall & Emerson, 1996).

23 Kilgour, "Sex Delinquency," p. 34.

24 Lunbeck, *The Psychiatric Persuasion*, p. 49–54.

25 Terry, *An American Obsession*, p. 178–219. Henry L. Minton, *Departing from Deviance: A History of Homosexual Rights and Emancipatory Science in America* (Chicago: University of Chicago Press, 2001).

26 Kilgour, "Sex Delinquency," p. 49.

27 Angus McLaren, *Our Own Master Race: Eugenics in Canada* (Toronto: McClelland and Stewart, 1990); Terry L. Chapman, "Early Eugenics Movement in Western Canada," *Alberta History*, 25, 4 (1977): 9–17; and Catherine Annau, "Eager Eugenicists: A Reappraisal of the Birth Control Society of Hamilton," *Social History*, 27, 53 (1994): 111–133.

28 Kilgour, "Sex Delinquency."

29 James Snell, "The White Life for Two: The Defence of Marriage and Sexual Morality in Canada, 1890–1914," in Bettina Bradbury, ed., *Canadian Family History: Selected Readings* (Toronto: Copp Clarke Pittman, 1992), p. 386–87.

30 Cyril Greenland, "Is There a Future of Human Sexuality?" in Benjamin Schlesinger, ed., *Sexual Behaviour in Canada: Patterns and Problems* (Toronto: University of Toronto Press, 1977) p. 281. On Charlton, see Karen Dubinsky, *Improper Advances: Rape and Heterosexual Conflict in Ontario, 1880–1929* (Chicago: University of Chicago Press, 1993), p. 66–69.

31 Gigeroff, *Sexual Deviations*, p. 46–50.

32 Canada, Parliament, *House of Commons Debates*, 6 (3 July 1947): 5031.

33 See Jeffrey Weeks, *Sex, Politics and Society* (London: Longmans, 1991), p. 14.

34 Elise Chenier, "Stranger in Our Midst: 'Male Sexual Deviance' in Postwar Ontario," PhD thesis, Queen's University, 2001.

35 Providing adequate medical treatment to prisoners, including psychiatric services, was a key recommendation of the interwar investigation of the penal system. See Canada, *Report of the Royal Commission to Investigate the Penal System of Canada* (Ottawa: Queen's Press, 1938).

36 GAP, *Psychiatry and Sex Psychopath Legislation*.

37 Canada, Report of the Royal Commission on the Criminal Law Relating to the Sexual Psychopath (Ottawa: Queen's Printer, 1958), p. 75.

38 Osgoode Hall Law Library, transcripts of the hearings of the Royal Commission on the Criminal Law Relating to the Criminal Sexual Psychopath, 1954–58, Volumes 1–3.

39 *House of Commons Debates*, 6 (3 July 1947): 5033.

40 Terry Copp and Bill McAndrew, *Battle Exhaustion: Soldiers and Psychiatrists in the Canadian Army, 1939–1945* (Montreal and Kingston: McGill-Queen's University Press, 1990), p. 7–8.

41 Mary J. Wright and C. Roger Myers, eds., *The History of Academic Psychology* (Toronto: CJ Hogrefe; 1982), p. 26.

42 Wright and Myers, eds., *The History of Academic Psychology*, n. 15. Emphasis in original.

43 On the case file as a psychiatric tool, see Michel Foucault, *Discipline and Punish: The Birth of the Prison*, trans. Alan Sheridan (New York, Vintage Books, 1979), p. 184–94; Maynard, "On the Case of the Case," p. 65–87; and Lunbeck, *Psychiatric Persuasion*, p. 130–44.

44 Committee on the Sex Offender, *Interim Report*. Though it was psychiatrists and other mental health experts who propagated the idea, Cold War historians of women and the family have pointed to Philip Wylie's *Generation of Vipers* (New York: Rinehart, 1942) as one of the most egregious examples of this line of thinking. See Elaine Tyler May, *Homeward Bound: American Families in the Cold War Era* (New York: Basic Books, 1988), p. 74–75.

45 Committee on the Sex Offender, *Interim Report*.

46 On paradigm shifts see Thomas Kuhn, *The Structure of Scientific Revolutions*, 2nd ed. (Chicago: University of Chicago Press, 1970), esp. p. 43–51.

47 Committee on the Sex Offender, *Interim Report*, p. 5.

48 On the emergence of a developmental model see Stephen Robertson, "Separating the Men from the Boys: Masculinity, Psychosexual Development, and Sex Crime ithe United States, 1930s–1960s," *Journal of the History of Medicine and Allied Sciences* 56, 1 (January 2001): 3–35.

49 Committee on the Sex Offender, *Interim Report*, p. 6.

50 Even when other treatments were employed, including electro-convulsive and insulin-coma therapy, the formal purpose was to break down patient resistance to open, honest, and frank discussion with psychiatrists and psychologists. Aversion therapy did not come into usage in Canada until the 1960s. See Chenier, "Stranger in our Midst," p. 232–305.

51 Committee on the Sex Offender, *Interim Report*, p. 6.

52 Terry, *An American Obsession*, p. 163–68.

53 Committee on the Sex Offender, *Interim Report*, p. 9. This complaint was lodged in virtually every study in the field of sexuality until the 1960s. For a contemporary critique of that claim, see Johann Mohr, "The Contribution of Research to the Selection of Appropriate Alternatives for Sexual Offenders," *Criminal Law Quarterly*, 4 (January 1962): 317–28.

54 Committee on the Sex Offender, *Interim Report*, p. 9; Alfred Kinsey, Wardell B. Pomeroy, Clyde E. Martin, and Paul H. Gebhard, *Sexual Behaviour in the Human Male* (Philadelphia: W. B. Saunders, 1948).

55 This revolution was not limited to those who studied sex. At a 1962 conference in Colorado, the warden of the federal prison in Terre Haute, Indiana, reported that, after consulting with staff members at the Kinsey Institute, he approached the question of homosexuality in an entirely different manner. See Kinsey Institute Archives (hereafter KIA), Wardell Pomeroy, "Sex in Prison," audiotapes of a presentation to a meeting of the Federal Warden's Institute, University of Colorado, 26 June 1962.

56 Committee on the Sex Offender, *Interim Report*, p. 9–10.

57 National Archives of Canada (hereafter NAC) RG 29, Vol. 345, Department of National Health and Welfare, File 436-6-5, Mental Health, Diagnosis and Treatment of Sex Offenders, Letter from R. E. Curran, Legal Advisor, 19 November 1947.

58 Diagnosis and Treatment of Sex Offenders.

59 See also Canadian psychologist J. D. Ketchum, "Prude is Father to the Pervert," *Maclean's*, 15 (January 1948): 42–44.

60 For the impact of the Kinsey reports in Canada, see Mary Louise Adams, *The Trouble with Normal: Postwar Youth and the Making of Heterosexuality* (Toronto: University of Toronto Press, 1997), p. 35–38. There are many US historical accounts of the reports: one of the most recent is found in Terry, *An American Obsession,* p. 304–14.

61 KIA, Correspondence Files, D. Ewen Cameron to Alfred Kinsey, July–October 1947. Remarkably, after Kinsey agreed to address a Montreal audience in exchange for "histories," his usual required payment for any appearance, Cameron asked that Kinsey submit in advance a copy of the paper he would present so that it might be reproduced as part of the program material. Kinsey replied that he would be unable to furnish him with a written paper since his first priority was getting the report to press, and his second to control the publicity surrounding it. For that reason, Cameron politely thanked him for offering to participate but declined to have him included in the series. See: KIA, Correspondence Files, D. Ewen Cameron to Alfred Kinsey, 6 October 1947.

62 Actually, Kinsey did give a talk in Canada at least once. In 1949 he participated in a roundtable discussion on sex offenders at the American Psychiatric Association's Annual Meeting, which was held in Montreal, Quebec: KIA, Correspondence Files, Manfred Guttmacher to Alfred Kinsey, 1949.

63 Committee on the Sex Offender, *Interim Report,* p. 18.

64 Committee on the Sex Offender, *Interim Report,* p. 27.

65 "Resolutions from the 1950 Convention," *Canadian Home and School,* 10, 1 (September 1950): 24.

66 Philip Girard, "Gays and Lesbians and the Legal Process since 1945," 83; cited in Kinsman, *The Regulation of Desire,* p. 183, 209: 159. See also *House of Commons Debates,* 5 (14 June 1948): 5203.

67 Ewen Cameron of the Allan Memorial Institute in Montreal was an early advocate of a national research centre. See RG 29, Vol. 310, File 435-5-28, Mental Health Division: Interdepartmental Committee on Mental Health Research Centre, 1950; Memo, 29 March 1950, Re.: Dr. Ewen Cameron's proposal for a Mental Health Research Centre. The need to establish treatment programs was one of the findings of the Royal Commission. See Canada, *Report of the Royal Commission on the Criminal Law Relating to Criminal Sexual Psychopaths* (Ottawa: Queen's Printer, 1958).

68 Anthony Marcus, *Nothing Is My Number: An Exploratory Study With a Group of Dangerous Sexual Offenders In Canada* (Toronto: General, 1971).

69 NAC, RG 13, Department of Justice, Vol. 2837 File 155002: Revision of the Criminal Code, Summary of Objections and Representations Made to the Special Committee on Bill 93, clause 661.

70 Osgoode Hall Law Library, Transcripts of the hearings of the Royal Commission on the Criminal Law Relating to the Criminal Sexual Psychopath, Vol. 1–3, 1954–1958.

71 Elise Chenier, "Seeing Red: Immigrant Women and Sexual Danger in Cold War Canada," *Atlantis,* 24, 2 (Spring/Summer 2000): 51–60.

72 The one exception is the Toronto Psychiatric Hospital's Forensic Outpatient Clinic, which was a provincial program established as the result of lobbying by a local citizen action group. Its services were primarily aimed at treating minor sex offenders as an alternative to incarceration, or to parolees, although they did have voluntary patients as well. "Criminal sexual psychopaths" were sentenced to federal institutions and would never have come into contact with this clinic as a result of their conviction under that law.

73 On the rejection of partial insanity by the British courts, see Roy Porter's *The Greatest Benefit to Mankind: A Medical History of Humanity* (New York: Norton, 1991), p. 501. For the American situation,

see Kenneth Gray, "Hospital Examination of Adult Offenders," *American Journal of Psychiatry,* 108 (1952): 625.

74 I. Dickson, "Early History of the CPA: The Canadian Psychiatric Association, 1951–1958," *Canadian Journal of Psychiatry,* 25, 1(1980): 86–87.

75 Reg Whitaker and Gary Marcuse, *Cold War Canada: The Making of a National Insecurity State, 1945–1957* (Toronto: University of Toronto Press, 1994); Robert Bothwell, *The Big Chill: Canada and the Cold War* (Toronto: Irwin, 1998); and Douglas Owram, *Born at the Right time: A History of the Baby Boom Generation* (Toronto: University of Toronto Press, 1996).

76 Jenkins, *Moral Panic,* p. 82.

77 Psychiatrists would have two full decades to launch and expand a wide variety of experimental treatment programs before another generation would denounce their practices as cruel and inhumane.

CHAPTER 12

Continental Drift: The Imaging of AIDS

Richard Fung and Tim McCaskell

> We've got a desperate population here. This is the first time in history where the infected
> population is actually taking control of the epidemic.
>
> —Larry Kramer, ACT UP founder, *Testing the Limits*

Watching the 1987 AIDS activist documentary *Testing the Limits* 20 years after its release, what strikes us most is the confidence of the people on screen. It isn't that a cure seemed just around the corner or that the spread of the infection appeared manageable; the sense of barely controlled panic is palpable throughout. Nevertheless, speaker after speaker either echoes or illustrates Kramer's pronouncement. At a time when the cultural politics around identity fostered an acute sensitivity to questions of voice and representation, these activists exude the conviction and certitude that come from speaking in one's own interest when the stakes are high. "We are fighting for our lives," chant demonstrators in the one segment.

The year 1987 was a key year in the history of the epidemic. It saw the founding of the definitive AIDS activist group ACT UP (AIDS Coalition to Unleash Power), and the Silence=Death Project, which produced one of the iconic logos of the 20th century. These organizations, like the *Testing the Limits* project, were formed in New York City, which at the time had the highest number of reported AIDS cases in the world. In Toronto, where we live, AIDS Action Now!, roughly modeled on ACT UP, made its debut early in 1988 and soon grew into the leading AIDS activist organization in Canada. In 1989, a group of Canadian and American activists hijacked the opening ceremony of the international AIDS conference in Montreal to protest government inaction and the absence of people with AIDS in the conference program. When we look at the footage of Tim's unauthorized address from the occupied stage, captured in John Greyson's 1989 video *The World is Sick (Sic)* and recycled in Richard's *Sea in the Blood* (2000), we are similarly struck by his assurance: "On behalf of people living with AIDS in Canada and around the world, I would like to officially open the fifth International Conference on AIDS."

At the birth of AIDS activism, AIDS had only just stopped being referred to as GRID (Gay Related Immune Deficiency). The infected were seen to be gay men largely contained in the cores of cities like New York and Toronto, a location they shared with others under suspicion: Haitian immigrants, IV drug users, and sex workers.

The social contract that had traditionally allowed gay men continued access to gender, race, and/or class privilege was the closet—the original don't ask, don't tell. As long as homosexuality was private, everyone could pretend it wasn't there. Stonewall was the thunderclap that had announced the beginning of the renegotiation of that contract. The outcome of the subsequent gay rights strategy was to allow some gay men to be public about their homosexuality without losing social entitlements.

But AIDS blew the closet door open for many of those still content with the old arrangement. HIV did not discriminate, and people of status found themselves or their loved ones turned into pariahs and treated like the underclass. The dying bodies of some, like Rock Hudson and Liberace, slumped out of the closet in shame or ambiguity. Others were radicalized. For example, Brian Farlinger, one of AIDS Action Now!'s most prominent members, had been director of commercial affairs for the Canadian Bankers Association before coming out as both gay and HIV-infected. Unlike other grassroots movements, AIDS activism was able to draw on skills, information, and networks usually reserved for the elite. Looking back at the clip of the Montreal conference, we now see not only the desperation and righteous anger at people living with AIDS being overlooked at the opening ceremonies but also how privileges of class, race, gender, and geography came into play to enable the action.

The initial government and institutional response to AIDS, what little there was, fell within a purely public health paradigm. The goal was to stop the spread of the plague to "the public." Those who were already infected and sick and the communities they belonged to were ipso facto not part of that public. They were the "reservoir of infection," a danger, a swamp that needed to be mapped, put under surveillance, and, once delineated, its shores policed. If policing succeeded, if high enough walls could be erected, then the public would be safe, the epidemic would burn itself out. The reservoir would slowly evaporate.

So for the gay men who were the early core of ACT UP and AIDS Action Now!, being both "out" and part of "the public" took on a new life-and-death significance. To be part of the public was to claim rights—to medical care, treatment and research, and to be treated with dignity. To remain the other was to be isolated, quarantined, left to die. Activists on both sides of the border shredded the contract of silence with theatrical media-savvy tactics like staging mass die-ins on city streets, occupying drug company headquarters, and disrupting legislative proceedings.

But the struggle and the epidemic soon overflowed the confines of gay identity. More and more central to AIDS activism was the emergence of a new "poz" identity—a brotherhood (and soon sisterhood) of infection located within, but also outside, the gay communities. Activists demanded inclusion, and soon HIV-positive representatives were required for boards and advisory committees of AIDS service organizations—even gay ones—as well as government panels and advisory committees for pharmaceutical trials. Coming out as "poz" might be modeled on coming out as gay, but its soundscape was amplified. Positive people spoke, shouted, whistled, and chanted for themselves.

The insurgent liberating vision of this new identity claimed to reach beyond the divisions of race, gender, and class. At times it almost did. Impending common death tended to intensify the need for solidarity. The imperatives of prevention furthered this embrace of difference. Sex demanded talking about, in all its wild and wonderful permutations. Different races, body types, and practices required public eroticization if messages were to reach target audiences. It was a heady moment, expressing a defiant optimism as the epidemic continued to take its toll. Some of the most important artistic production and intellectual thought of the late 20th century was produced in response to the AIDS crisis.

Twenty years later, the map of AIDS has changed. The cities, once a place of danger, have become gentrified. In North America, most of the infected who survived the tsunami of the epidemic now float in a lifeboat constructed by pharmaceutical companies. In Canada, provincial drug programs, the ultimate victory by AIDS activists, make treatment accessible to all citizens, regardless of income.

But the demographics of infection have changed. The quintessential PWA is no longer a white, gay man in urban North America, but more likely to be a black, heterosexual woman in rural or township Africa, and as with the sinking *Titanic*, the lifeboats have not been distributed equitably. For the "new" person with AIDS, access to adequate nutrition and sanitary living conditions may be as crucial—and elusive—as medication. Dying has been outsourced, like manufacturing or telecommunications, to countries and peoples on the periphery.

While most people living with AIDS now reside in the third world, global political and economic disparity means that those who speak about and for them on the world stage are still based mainly in the first world: the scientists, policy makers, funders, even to some extent the activists. At the 16th International AIDS Conference held in Toronto in 2006, Bill and Melinda Gates advocated on behalf of poor women and sex workers. Stephen Lewis spoke out for African grandmothers. French and American activists protested the President's Emergency Plan for AIDS Relief (PEPFAR) and bilateral U.S. free trade agreements that limit access to generic AIDS medications. It isn't that there were no participants from Africa, Asia, or Latin America—Indonesian PWA Fricka Chia Iskandar addressed the opening ceremonies—but the media was more interested in celebrities like Richard Gere, Bill Clinton, and Alicia Keys. If the face of AIDS is increasingly coloured, its global public voice is still largely white, and increasingly heterosexual and HIV negative.

There is nothing wrong with actions of solidarity by the rich and famous or "ordinary" people, negative or positive, in the developed world. Philanthropic work is often effective and necessary, especially in the absence of support from impoverished or indifferent governments. However, altruism comes at a price. When American and Canadian PWAs are unhappy with policies or delivery of care that affect them, they can lobby, demonstrate, and confront decision makers. As part of the public and as citizens, they have rights, and officials can be held accountable. But if in Zambia or Cambodia the main source of support is not local, if it is based on charity and not a right, if priorities and delivery methods are not decided in the regional or national capital but in Seattle or Geneva, making demands, or even feeling one has the right to do so, is much more difficult.

Wealthy people and wealthy nations have always felt comfortable with the apparatus of charity. By giving, they garner praise, feel good about themselves, and stay in control. Philanthropy functions differently from taxes; indeed, it is often used to avoid paying taxes. Similarly, much foreign aid ends up subsidizing industry in the donor country. The West is perversely content to maintain African, Asian, and Latin American countries as recipients of benevolence. The ability to give—and the need to request—aid reinforces the neo-colonial status quo.

A crucial victory in the discursive war around the pandemic was the excision of the terms "AIDS victim" and "AIDS sufferer." "People Living with HIV and AIDS" insisted on their agency. But in the recent reporting on AIDS in Africa and elsewhere we see the reemergence of the AIDS victim, the suffering subject who stares motionless from the cot in a photogenic act of dying.

And it is not only in the popular media. In the first decade of the epidemic, artists and activists created a deluge of film and video that combined criticality, social urgency, aesthetic innovation, and novel approaches to building audiences. They deployed a variety of approaches in a range of genres, but common to all the work was the notion of personal investment by makers and intended viewers alike. Collectively the films and tapes posit a shared community of interest. By contrast, when Richard previewed work for the AIDS 2006 Film and Video Festival, held in conjunction with the International Conference, he was struck by a curious bifurcation among the submissions. Work about North American subjects tended to rehearse the genres of AIDS media established in the '80s and '90s, and were mute about the global context. Work about the rest of the world, often produced by Western filmmakers and/or Western-based international agencies, addressed the viewer as both HIV negative and foreign to the circumstances depicted on screen. There was little sense that makers, subjects, and viewers would constitute a common community of interest.

A startling exception was *Siyayinqoba Beat It*, a South African TV magazine program "for everyone living with HIV and AIDS, our partners, families, friends and colleagues." Because it is produced by South Africans for South Africans, and because all the presenters are HIV positive, the tone of *Siyayinqoba Beat It* is unlike anything that normally reaches North American audiences about AIDS in Africa. The program, which has run since 1999, does not shun the suffering endured by people with HIV and AIDS, not just resulting from the disease, but also because of the violence they face due to the fear and stigma. But *Siyayinqoba Beat It* documents the battles people go through to protect themselves and their loved ones. Upbeat and full of humour, it fearlessly challenges government policy while giving tips on nutrition or personal relationship management. *Siyaninqoba Beat It* also portrays the complexity of race and class in post-Apartheid South Africa, one segment featuring a spontaneous debate between two HIV positive people about whether yoga is just a middle-class option.

But while South Africa now has the highest number of people living with AIDS in the world, it is atypical of other countries in southern Africa because of its relative wealth, democratic stability, and developed infrastructure. It also has a tradition of mass struggle forged during the fight against Apartheid, which has inspired a highly developed and effective activist movement in the Treatment Action Campaign (TAC).

The emblematic TAC T-shirt defiantly and boldly announces its wearers as HIV POSITIVE. A "poz" identity has developed along with AIDS activism in South Africa. But what does this identity have in common with the one that emerged in America and Europe in the '80s and '90s? Given the relatively stable health that anti-virals offer, does Tim's "poz" status make him somehow closer than Richard to that African woman with AIDS with no access to treatment? Does she have more in common with him, or with her neighbour, HIV negative but fighting tuberculosis and malaria?

These questions have generated a crisis of legitimacy for the North American AIDS movements, already fatigued, depleted by the loss of comrades, and lulled because individual needs have been met. Kramer's assertion no longer rings true, as the epicenter of the pandemic has dispersed to other continents. Even those here most acutely affected by the disease lack the resources of the earlier generations of AIDS activists. In Canada, undocumented migrants and refugee claimants face major barriers to care, and the seroconversion rate is highest among youth, intravenous drug users, and Aboriginal people. While the desperation and anger survive, the confident voice of AIDS activists speaking from their own experience and in their own interest has been muted. The original AIDS activist organizations are now faced with the difficult task of reinventing themselves and struggling with questions of solidarity and voice unnecessary when they were at the centre of the holocaust.

CHAPTER 13

Emergence of a Poz Sexual Culture: Accounting for "Barebacking" among Gay Men

Barry D. Adam

B *arebacking* is a term that makes sense only in a particular social and historical context. Sex without a barrier did not need a name before the risks of Acquired Immune Deficiency Syndrome (AIDS) and other sexually transmitted infections became increasingly evident. Today it is an idea associated particularly with sex between men, as communities of gay men have been heavily impacted by Human Immunodeficiency Virus (HIV) and AIDS, but it has yet to gain much currency among other populations despite the rising prevalence of HIV disease around the world. *Barebacking* can be used to refer to any kind of unprotected sex, but more often it refers to *intentional* unprotected sex and not to various kinds of slips or accidents where unprotected sex is a consequence. In the context of elevated risk that characterizes communities of gay, bisexual, and other men who have sex with men, barebacking has at times been viewed as something of a scandal and its practitioners as deviants, rebels, or irrational and irresponsible individuals. Yet, closer examination reveals just how unsurprising and consistent it is with widespread rules of conduct circulating in advanced industrial countries.

This chapter delves into the history of the difficult relationship that gay and bisexual men have had with HIV and its prevention as they have sought pleasure and intimacy in an era marked by a life-threatening disease. The chapter examines a converging set of social, psychological, and physiological factors that created the conditions for the beginnings of a bareback microculture and identity. In doing so, it is important to keep in mind that in the first decade of the twenty-first century, *barebacking* remains an emergent, inchoate, and contested term and identity. Some men whose sexual practices might appear to an outside observer to fit the category reject the term. Others employ bareback language and participate in bareback circuits and scenes but limit their unprotected sex to particular partners and situations and often express a willingness to accept protected sex with partners who initiate condom use.

AIDS AND LGBT COMMUNITIES

Since the first identification of AIDS in 1981, public conceptions of the significance and danger of HIV and AIDS have shifted substantially. Faced at first by an unprecedented deadly threat, lesbian, gay, bisexual, and transgendered (LGBT) communities mobilized to support those struck by the disease and to find ways to limit its transmission. By the 1990s, the sexual practices of men having sex with men had changed profoundly and rates of transmission, as well as deaths from AIDS, had fallen sharply as a consequence. But in the first decade of the twenty-first century, HIV has changed yet again. Now it seems that the transmission of HIV has begun to edge upward among gay, bisexual, and other men who have sex with men, especially in the major cities of the advanced industrial world. The question is: Why? How has the face of HIV been transformed, and what are its consequences for the health of thousands of gay men now and in the decades to come?

When the first reports of an acquired immune deficiency surfaced through the Centers for Disease Control in 1981, AIDS was an unknown and unimagined affliction. At first, it was hard to believe that such a syndrome could really exist. In the early years, scientists, journalists, religious leaders, and politicians stepped into a conceptual chaos, with a range of motivations and agendas, to make sense of this new medical peril. AIDS was, at first, a blank slate on which a range of conflicting narratives were inscribed (Epstein, 1996). What was all too clear to LGBT communities was that many gay and bisexual men, their friends, and their partners were falling gravely ill, that public authorities were quick to either cast blame or refuse to acknowledge the problem, and that few were willing to provide support, research, or practical measures to face the new health menace. As it turns out, at the time of its identification, HIV had already infected a substantial number of gay, bisexual, and other men who have sex with men, resulting in a rapidly rising death toll through the mid-1980s. In the early years, the causal agent for AIDS was unknown, nor was it clear how to avoid it. The fact that epidemiology pointed to sexual transmission led to the first steps taken to develop an AIDS avoidance strategy through condom use. The New York Gay Men's Health Crisis (Kramer, 1989) issued a first guide on how to have sex in an epidemic, and soon gay men, lesbians, their families, and frontline professionals were pulling together community-based AIDS organizations in virtually every city to assist people living with HIV and to get the word out about how to avoid contracting the disease (Altman, 1986; Levine, Nardi & Gagnon, 1997; Patton, 1985, 1990).

AIDS arrived in an historical era when LGBT communities were making their first gains in abolishing laws that criminalized their sexual and affective relationships, as well as winning basic protection from discrimination through human rights laws. But in the 1980s, many jurisdictions, especially in the United States, continued to marginalize gay men as outlaws. Full citizenship rights and participation in the many spheres of life, whether in employment, residence, religion, recreation, government, or corporate services, could not be taken for granted and required struggle with social institutions, the courts, and legislatures. Public authorities were typically slow to respond to a medical syndrome that affected gay men and other populations such as injection drug users, hemophiliacs, and immigrants from Africa and the Caribbean—none of whom commanded much power or status in Western societies. Some 16,000 died of AIDS in the United States—most of them gay men—by the time a test for HIV was developed and made available in 1985 and 1986. This number turned out to be just a fraction of a global epidemic. With inadequate treatments, the prospect of testing positive was often perceived as a death sentence. With an average 10-year period of disease progression from the time of infection to the development of AIDS, many people faced an apparently relentless and deadly disease that they had unknowingly contracted before anyone had heard of it.

By the 1990s, gay men responded with a massive reorientation of their sexual practices by using condoms most or all of the time, and with this reorientation came a major decline in new HIV infections. In the same decade, with the 1996 world AIDS conference in Vancouver, came the announcement of a new class of anti-HIV drugs, the protease inhibitors, and with them, new hope for effective treatment of AIDS. The combination of protease inhibitors with other classes of antiretroviral drugs succeeded in stabilizing the health of many people living with HIV, but at the cost of a rigorous and expensive drug regimen that risked failure if the drugs were not taken consistently and on time every day. By the late 1990s infection rates had fallen steadily, though gay communities remain impacted by HIV much more than other communities in advanced industrial societies. Public discourses of panic and siege began to give way to more medicalized narratives of disease, and some speculated about a turn toward a "post-AIDS" era (Rofes, 1998) in which HIV was to become an enduring but less dominant concern of gay communities.

THE CONTEMPORARY CONTEXT OF HIV

In the early 2000s, the HIV epidemic appeared to be changing yet again. Rates of infection began to increase in more and more cities after having fallen to a plateau in the mid-1990s. A series of speculative theories arose to account for the apparent resurgence of HIV transmission. As media attention turned increasingly to the massive worldwide heterosexual epidemic, infection among gay men became old news, though male-to-male sexual transmission continued to be the leading risk factor for HIV transmission in the advanced industrialized nations of northern Europe, North America, and Australia and New Zealand. Popular narratives arose describing "condom fatigue" among gay men, whose supposedly greater confidence in the effectiveness of medication to control HIV was resulting in complacency about condom use and reduced personal vigilance against HIV transmission. A meta-analysis of 25 studies on treatment-related beliefs found evidence of a persistent statistical relationship between decreased concern and fear of HIV (compared to the preprotease era) and unprotected anal intercourse (Crepaz, Hart, & Marks, 2004). However, relatively small numbers of gay and bisexual men overall showed a willingness to consider HIV a diminished threat. Indeed, the enduring proliferation of the condom fatigue or treatment optimism narrative raises this question: To what degree is it an account so readily available in the public sphere that it supplies ready-made recipe statements that take on a life of their own and circulate through the media in a grand feedback loop? The degree to which it is a leading or persistent narrative among men speaking of the occasions on which they have had unprotected sex is quite another question.

Perhaps the most noteworthy finding to emerge from the large amount of research done on gay and bisexual men facing the threat of AIDS is that most men, most or all of the time, continue to take protective measures to guard against the transmission of HIV. This change in sexual practice is the largest behavioural change in sexuality found in any population. The underlying conditions and narratives influencing sexual practices in everyday life turn out to be much more complex than mediatized public discourses. Gay and bisexual men remain at high risk of acquiring HIV if they have unprotected anal intercourse, and a good deal of investigation has mapped out a range of vulnerabilities, situations, practices, and discourses that contribute to the heightened risk. These fall into a few broad categories: condoms and erectile difficulties, momentary lapses and trade-offs, personal turmoil and depression, alcohol and drug use, disclosure and intuiting safety, and relationship formation. There are, then, a number of push and pull factors associated with unprotected sex. The convergence of a critical mass of these factors creates the conditions for the emergence of a set of men whose sexual practices become more and more consistently unprotected. With these conditions in place come social networks and mutual communication and subsequently narratives that reflect on, encode, and justify these practices.

Condoms, Erectile Difficulties, and Momentary Lapses

Large numbers of men employ condoms without difficulty and make them a routine part of their sexual lives. Some prefer the hygienic qualities of condoms; others simply accept them as a necessity. Using condoms every time, rather than making a decision about risk and safety at each encounter, remains the most reliable method for HIV avoidance (Hart et al., 2005). But for some men—especially those who have difficulty maintaining an erection—condoms may be experienced as an impediment to satisfactory sex. Condom-avoidance rationales tend to fall into two major categories: *(1)* physiological (they are desensitizing), and *(2)* symbolic (they signify a barrier to intimacy and to its sexual expression through insemination) (Díaz & Ayala, 1999; Mansergh et al., 2002; Zwart, Kerkhof, & Sandfort, 1998). The statement of this man, drawn from a Toronto sample of men having difficulty with safe sex, is typical:

> It will not stay hard if I put one on, come hell or high water. Believe me, I've tried. So, you know, since I've started having sex, I've basically always had unsafe sex. (Adam, Husbands, Murray, & Maxwell, 2005a, p. 240)

In addition to the men who report their own erectile difficulties are those who report them in their partners.

Recent research in Sydney and Toronto has identified the practice of delayed condom use among some gay men. The Polaris study in Toronto found a strong association between this practice and becoming HIV-positive (Calzavara et al., 2003). Delayed use or episodic use during a sexual experience is usually due to difficulties in resolving the tension between condoms and erections.

> I find this more as I've gotten in my 30s. I find if I'm not into it, once I put the condom on, I can get soft.... We'd start with a condom and then if I got soft, I'd take the condom

off and I'd put my dick inside and get hard again and then we'd put the condom back on. But sometimes the condom just never came back on. (Adam et al., 2005a, p. 240)

In a number of instances, men report wrestling with a series of dilemmas about condom use: wanting to maintain an erection that refused to cooperate when sheathed, wanting to accommodate a partner experiencing similar difficulties, wanting to avoid exposure to the risk of infection, wanting to ensure that a partner does not become infected, attempting to keep up some degree of condom use even if inconsistent, and relying on a risk calculus that falls back on withdrawal, taking the top role, or avoiding tears to the rectal lining. For men who experience erectile difficulty with condom use, these are real dilemmas resolved through actions that may heighten the risk.

The urgency of passion and the opportunity to connect with a particularly desirable partner, sometimes facilitated by drugs or alcohol, account for some unsafe encounters. Heat-of-the-moment situations can be complicated by "trade-off" scenarios in which men who feel disadvantaged in some way—by age, ethnicity, or attractiveness—fear to offend a desirable partner and trade away safe sex lest it prove an obstacle to sexual interaction (Choi et al., 1999; Seal et al., 2000; Stokes & Peterson, 1998).

Personal Turmoil and Depression

A small but growing set of studies finds that men who report having experienced sexual abuse as children report higher rates of unprotected anal intercourse with casual partners when they become adults (Kalichman, Benotsch, & Rompa, 2001; Paul, Catania, Pollack, & Stall, 2001; Relf, 2001). Perhaps not surprisingly, then, men who are currently HIV-positive report having experienced childhood abuse at a higher rate than their HIV-negative counterparts (Greenwood et al., 2002; Kalichman, Gore-Felton, Benotsch, Cage, & Rompa, 2004; Paul et al., 2001).

Childhood sex abuse also appears to be a predisposing condition to a number of additional factors associated with unsafe sex, including drug use, higher numbers of sex partners, sex work, and sexual adventurism (Díaz & Ayala, 1999; Kalichman et al., 2001, 2004; Klitzman, Greenberg, Pollack, & Dolezal, 2002; Paul et al., 2001). Dorais' (2004) interviews with gay and bisexual men in Québec who had experienced sexual abuse in childhood concludes that they frequently suffer "depression, confusion and uneasiness about sex, and even loss of control over their love lives, mak[ing] meaningful self-protection more difficult" (p. 119) as they become adults.

Broad-based surveys of risk factors frequently identify depression as more common among those who have unprotected anal intercourse (Kalichman, Cherry, Cain, Pope, & Kalichman, 2005; Semple, Patterson, & Grant, 2000b). Qualitative studies give some insight into the way this everyday depression works (Adam et al., 2005a; Adam, Sears, & Schellenberg, 2000; Odets, 1995; Schwartz & Bailey, 2005). Episodes of unprotected anal intercourse may follow major stressful events such as job loss, financial crisis, moving to another city, homophobic victimization, breakup with a partner, or death of a partner (Boulton, Mclean, Fitzpatrick, & Hart, 1995; Vincke & Bolton, 1995). Personal disruption and depression can affect the sense of being in control of one's life and having the capacity to care for oneself. To be effective, then, the prevention message calls on an autobiographical narrative that life is worth living and that something done now makes sense because the future will be a desirable place. Yet, depression and personal turmoil can pull away the underpinnings of this belief. If life does not seem worth living now and the future appears bleak as well, then self-preserving actions no longer make much sense.

Alcohol and Drug Use

The relationship between drug and alcohol use with unprotected anal intercourse is one of the most developed areas of research. A plethora of studies reveal an association between rates of unprotected anal intercourse and the use of "club drugs" (Colfax et al., 2004; Klitzman et al., 2002; Parsons, Kutnick, Halkitis, Punzalan, & Carbonari, 2005) and the use of alcohol with or without other drugs (Hirshfield, Remien, Humberstone, Walavalkar, & Chiasson, 2004; Koblin et al., 2003; Vanable et al., 2004). Myers and colleagues (2004) conclude that

> the effects of substances varied not only by the type of substances used or the expectations of the participants who use them, but also by the context in which the same substance is used.... Risky sex does not result from the simple exposure to drugs or alcohol before or during sexual behaviours, but rather depends on mitigating factors such as the personal convictions of the individual, as well as the decision-making processes that occur well throughout the sexual act. (pp. 222, 225)

Observers of today's circuit parties and the "party and play" scene refer to the "tribalism," "esprit de corps," and sense of communion that attract a segment of the gay and bisexual population (Ghaziani & Cook, 2005; Green, 2001; Kurtz, 2009; Slavin, 2004; Westhaver, 2005). Club drugs have found a function that is not easily displaced, as they facilitate a sense of connection so desired by participants.

Disclosure and Intuiting Safety

Some HIV-positive men inform their partners of their HIV status and may then have unprotected sex on the presumption that the partner, having been duly warned, will take appropriate precautions where necessary. Settings with a reputation for quick sex such as baths, parks, sex clubs, sex parties, public washrooms, and some Web sites tend not to make disclosure of serostatus easy and operate more by the rules of the marketplace, namely, *caveat emptor* or buyer beware. In these situations, knowledge about a partner's serostatus may be more an assumption than a fact based on reliable information, and unprotected sex may be riskier than is initially understood.

Relationships

Anticipating that a relationship will occur, or identifying a new partner as "boyfriend material," is enough to motivate some men to drop condom use as a sign of the seriousness of the relationship. As long as condom use implicitly communicates distrust of a partner, dropping it can function as a tacit sign of trust and of the increasing seriousness of a relationship. Gay and bisexual men are scarcely unique in this practice, and research confirms its pervasiveness (Adam et al.,

2000; Carballo-Diéguez, Remien, Dolezal, & Wagner, 1997; Cusick & Rhodes, 2000; Díaz & Ayala, 1999; Flowers, Smith, Sheeran, & Beail, 1997; Mclean et al., 1994). Even among serodiscordant couples (where one partner is HIV-negative and one is HIV-positive), these meanings can exert a strong influence (Adam & Sears, 1996; Odets, 1995; Remien, Carballo-Diéguez, & Wagner, 1995). As Rhodes (1997) remarks:

> In the context of relationships where one partner is HIV positive, unprotected sex can be considered to communicate feelings of "love" and "commitment" in even more powerful ways than would be the case if both partners were negative. (p. 215)

EMERGENCE OF A POZ SEXUAL CULTURE

There is, then, a range of circumstances, assumptions, and vulnerabilities reported by men for whom unprotected sex is typically exceptional in a general pattern of consistent condom use. The uneven accumulation of these factors gives rise to conditions that increase the tendency for unprotected sex among particular individuals and microcultures. In recent years, a set of primarily HIV-positive men have given up on condom use most or all of the time, and their presence has now been well documented in major cities of the advanced industrialized countries. There are several conditions, incentives, and motivations that contribute to a bareback orientation, as well as an idea system to justify it. Yet, most gay men, especially HIV-negative men, and certainly nongay populations have little familiarity with the dynamics involved. This mutual misapprehension can result in sexual interactions where risk is indeed heightened, and these scenarios pose new challenges for effective HIV prevention messages in a context in which rates of HIV infection have begun to rise again among gay and bisexual men.

Certainly for most people who test HIV-positive the experience is disturbing—even devastating. But over time, as a sense of normalcy is restored and symptoms related to HIV disease may be resolved, some experience a sense of relief over not having to worry anymore about contracting HIV and indeed about sex with condoms. For many, the risk of infection with any other disease while being immunocompromised is incentive enough to maintain a policy of protection (Adam, Husbands, Murray, & Maxwell, 2005b). And for many other HIV-positive individuals, condom use remains the choice for sexual conduct with casual partners and any other partners who are not HIV-positive. For others, participation in support groups for HIV-positive people, getting used to seeing other positive people in the street, and developing friends and contacts among other positive people help contribute to a sense of living in a *poz* world where everyone "knows the score" and shares a number of assumptions about norms and expectations concerning sexual interaction. Combined with apprehension about having to explain their serostatus to naive outsiders or the prospect of rejection by fearful or uncomprehending prospective partners, some people also actively seek to restrict their romantic and sexual connections to other positive people (Adam & Sears, 1996; Stirratt, 2005). In this context of poz-on-poz sex, leaving condom use behind can seem reasonable and become a habit over time.

The rationale for condomless sex is readily at hand. The AIDS service organizations have long sought to educate the public that everyone must take responsibility for HIV prevention and that simply presuming that prospective sex partners are HIV-negative, then blaming them later if it turns out that they are not, is scarcely a reliable method of HIV prevention. It is advice that relies on sex partners being well-informed adults who calculate risk rationally and appropriately and enter knowingly into an implicit contract with each other when sex occurs. Those who employ the language of barebacking typically presume that prospective partners will be "in the know"— that is, they will be fully knowledgeable about the HIV risk, they will be adult men capable of making informed choices and of consenting after having weighed all relevant risks, and often they will be HIV-positive themselves. Few, if any, actually insist on unprotected sex; they are nearly always willing to respect partners who prefer to use protection, but if a condom is not produced by a new partner, there is a ready-made explanation applied to the sexual interaction that allows unsafe sex to occur. For the subset of men who have left safe sex behind, raw or bareback sex is justifiable by a rhetoric of individualism, personal responsibility, consenting adults, and contractual interaction. In other words, discourses of HIV prevention that postulate sexual actors as individuals acting defensively against potential threat converge with dominant narratives of consumption and competition in market societies in which they are to be responsible, contract-making individuals who must manage risk in a buyer-beware environment.

At a time when *serosorting* has become something of a buzz word in HIV prevention, many men who prefer barebacking consider that they are indeed serosorting—that is, selecting partners who share their HIV status. For those who go with a prospective partner for HIV testing and ascertain that they are in fact seroconcordant, reliable serosorting has been accomplished and, with a subsequent agreement about monogamy or shared risk prevention, they may not need to use condoms to avoid HIV infection (or reinfection). But few employ such a rigorous standard of verification. Some men rely on sometimes highly subtle clues to impute the seropositivity of a partner or to communicate to a partner that they are already seropositive (e.g., leaving pill bottles in view, mentioning having volunteered for an AIDS organization) (Adam, 2005; Serovich, Oliver, Smith, & Mason, 2005; Stirratt, 2005). Indeed, many HIV-positive men read the willingness of their partners to engage in unprotected sex as evidence that the partners are already HIV-positive (Adam, 2005; Gorbach et al., 2004; Larkins, Reback, Shoptaw, & Veniegas, 2005; O'Leary, 2005; Rhodes & Cusick, 2002; Richters, Hendry, & Kippax, 2003; Semple, Patterson, & Grant, 2000a; Stirratt, 2005). By contrast, HIV-negative men rarely make this assumption or they assume the opposite—that partners willing to engage in unprotected sex must be negative (Van de Ven et al., 2005).

The development of a bareback current among poz men may account for a cascade of recent evidence showing elevated and rising rates of unprotected anal intercourse among HIV-positive men with casual partners of unknown or negative HIV status (Frankis & Flowers, 2006; Grulich, Prestage, Kippax, Crawford, & Van de Ven, 1998; Mansergh et al., 2002; Morin et al., 2005; Rogers et al., 2003). Reback and associates (2004) typify the views of the men they interviewed as follows:

> Participants tacitly signed onto the social contract that states the primary responsibility to disclose HIV status is placed on the sexual partner. Many claimed to operate from the assumption that people are responsible for their own bodies, and that feelings of responsibility toward another are not obligatory. The participants referred to an

"unspoken rule" that men in public sex environments who did not initiate a discussion on disclosure were either HIV-infected or did not care about their health. (p. 94)

In many ways, these accounts of unsafe sex participate in the moral reasoning widely propagated by government and business today that constructs everyone as a self-interested individual who must take responsibility for himself in a marketplace of risks (Adam, 2005). The problem is that this moral reasoning works no better in the sexual realm than it does in government or business. Rational calculation of risk is just one possibility among many when unprotected sex is associated with condoms and erectile difficulties, momentary lapses and trade-offs, personal turmoil and depression, alcohol and drug use, disclosure and intuiting safety, and relationship formation. When one person presumes that his partner's failure to introduce a condom indicates HIV-positive status and the partner does not use a condom for any of the many unintentional reasons, a high-risk encounter may ensue.

CONCLUSION

Networks of gay, bisexual, and other men who have sex with men have been among the populations most heavily impacted by HIV transmission, and gay communities have been leaders in developing responses to the AIDS epidemic, both in terms of supporting people living with HIV and promoting HIV prevention techniques. In the decades since the discovery of AIDS the losses have been great, and gay men in advanced industrialized societies are still contracting HIV at a rate comparable to that of the most heavily afflicted communities in Africa. The sizable research literature that has developed to account for HIV vulnerability points to myriad social and psychological factors that reduce condom use. In the absence of any other effective HIV prevention techniques short of abstinence, HIV transmission continues to present a daunting challenge to the health of gay and bisexual men. Despite advances in treatment and management, HIV remains an onerous and life-threatening syndrome. Complicating this picture is the development of circuits or microcultures within gay communities acting on divergent norms and expectations concerning sexual conduct.

Narratives that call on individuals to act defensively and protect themselves against all others may collide with romantic scripts that prescribe how to show trust in relationships. The messages of AIDS service organizations intended to instill a sense of shared responsibility in sexual actors conflict with neoliberal discourses that posit citizens of contemporary societies as individual actors in a marketplace of risks. Disease-avoidance disclosures rely on particularly middle-class autobiographical narratives that presume a life trajectory with a bright future. Without a personal narrative on preserving oneself now for a better future, avoiding a long-term infection that could compromise that future stops making sense. While criminal justice systems seek to enforce an obligation to disclose one's serostatus in advance of sexual engagement, disclosure may be inhibited in everyday social interaction by fear of being stigmatized or rejected. Ultimately, the routine use of condoms with every sexual encounter is a safety technique that works without disclosure, and those who make decisions to have safe sex, encounter to encounter, depending on the disclosure of serostatus, have considerably higher odds of acquiring HIV than those who simply use condoms consistently. Gay, bisexual, and other men who have sex with men continue to face a series of dilemmas in preserving and promoting their health and the health of their communities. To some degree, the clash of narratives of the marketplace, law, biography, and romance increase the vulnerability to HIV transmission. Barebacking comes about at one intersection of these circulating narratives, further complicating the question of how viral circulation might be disrupted.

REFERENCES

Adam, B. D. (2005). Constructing the neoliberal sexual actor. *Culture, Health & Sexuality*, 7(4), 333–346.

Adam, B. D., Husbands, W., Murray, J., & Maxwell, J. (2005a). AIDS optimism, condom fatigue, or self esteem? *Journal of Sex Research*, 42(3), 238–248.

Adam, B. D., Husbands, W., Murray, J., & Maxwell, J. (2005b). Risk construction in reinfection discourses of HIV-positive men. *Health, Risk and Society*, 7(1), 63–71.

Adam, B. D., & Sears, A. (1996). *Experiencing HIV*. New York: Columbia University Press.

Adam, B. D., Sears, A., & Schellenberg, E. G. (2000). Accounting for unsafe sex. *Journal of Sex Research*, 37(1), 259–271.

Altman, D. (1986). *AIDS in the mind of America*. Garden City, NY: Doubleday.

Boulton, M., McLean, J., Fitzpatrick, R., & Hart, G. (1995). Gay men's accounts of unsafe sex. *AIDS Care*, 7(5), 619–630.

Calzavara, L., Burchell, A., Remis, R., Major, C., Corey, P., Myers, T., et al. (2003). Delayed application of condoms is a risk factor for human immunodeficiency virus infection among homosexual and bisexual men. *American Journal of Epidemiology*, 157(3), 210–217.

Carballo-Diéguez, A., Remien, R., Dolezal, C., & Wagner, G. (1997). Unsafe sex in the primary relationships of Puerto Rican men who have sex with men. *AIDS and Behavior*, 1(1), 9–17.

Choi, K. H., Kumekawa, E., Dang, Q., Kegeles, S., Hays, R., & Stall, R. (1999). Risk and protective factors affecting sexual behavior among young Asian and Pacific Islander men who have sex with men. *Journal of Sex Education and Therapy*, 24(1&2), 47–55.

Colfax, G., Vittinghoff, E., Husnik, M., McKirnan, D., Buchbinder, S., Koblin, B., et al. (2004). Substance use and sexual risk. *American Journal of Epidemiology*, 159(10), 1002–1012.

Crepaz, N., Hart, T., & Marks, G. (2004). Highly active antiretroviral therapy and sexual risk behavior. *Journal of the American Medical Association*, 292(2), 224–236.

Cusick, L., & Rhodes, T. (2000). Sustaining sexual safety in relationships. *Culture, Health & Sexuality*, 2(4), 473–487.

Díaz, R., & Ayala, G. (1999). Love, passion and rebellion. *Culture, Health & Sexuality*, 1(3), 277–293.

Dorais, M. (2004). Hazardous journey in intimacy. *Journal of Homosexuality*, 48(2), 103–124.

Epstein, S. (1996). *Impure science*. Berkeley: University of California Press.

Flowers, P., Smith, J., Sheeran, P., & Beail, N. (1997). Health and romance. *British Journal of Health Psychology*, 2, 73–86.

Frankis, J., & Flowers, P. (2006). Cruising for sex. *AIDS Care*, 18(1), 54–59.

Ghaziani, A., & Cook, T. (2005). Reducing HIV infections at circuit parties. *Journal of the International Association of Physicians in AIDS Care*, 4(2), 32–46.

Gorbach, P., Galea, J., Amani, B., Shin, A., Celum, C., Kerndt, P., et al. (2004). Don't ask, don't tell. *Sexually Transmitted Infections*, 80, 512–517.

Green, A. (2001). "Chem friendly." *Deviant Behavior*, 24, 427–447.

Greenwood, G., Relf, M., Huang, B., Pollack, L., Canchola, J., & Catania, J. (2002). Battering victimization among a probability-based sample of men who have sex with men. *American Journal of Public Health*, 92(12), 1964–1969.

Grulich, A., Prestage, G., Kippax, S., Crawford, J., & Van de Ven, P. (1998). HIV serostatus of sexual partners of HIV-positive and HIV-negative homosexual men in Sydney. *AIDS*, 12(18), 2508.

Hart, T., Wolitski, R., Purcell, D., Parsons, J., Gomez, C., & the Seropositive Urban Men's Study Team. (2005). Partner awareness of the serostatus of HIV-seropositive men who have sex with men. *AIDS and Behavior*, 9(2), 155–166.

Hirshfield, S., Remien, R., Humberstone, M., Walavalkar, I., & Chiasson, M. (2004). Substance use and high-risk sex among men who have sex with men. *AIDS Care*, 16(8), 1036–1047.

Kalichman, S., Benotsch, E., & Rompa, D. (2001). Unwanted sexual experiences and sexual risks in gay and bisexual men. *Journal of Sex Research*, 38(1), 1–9.

Kalichman, S., Cherry, C., Cain, D., Pope, H., & Kalichman, M. (2005). Psychosocial and behavioral correlates of seeking sex partners on the Internet among HIV-positive men. *Annals of Behavioral Medicine*, 30(3), 243–250.

Kalichman, S., Gore-Felton, C., Benotsch, E., Cage, M., & Rompa, D. (2004). Correlates of childhood sexual abuse and HIV risks among men who have sex with men. *Journal of Child Abuse*, 13(1), 1–15.

Klitzman, R., Greenberg, J., Pollack, L., & Dolezal, C. (2002). MDMA ("ecstasy") use, and its association with high risk behaviors, mental health, and other factors among gay/bisexual men in New York City. *Drug and Alcohol Dependence*, 66, 115–125.

Koblin. B., Chesney, M., Husnik, M., Bozeman, S., Celum, C., Buchbinder, S., et al. (2003). High-risk behaviors among men who have sex with men in 6 U.S. cities. *American Journal of Public Health*, 93(6), 926–932.

Kramer, L. (1989). *Reports from the Holocaust*. New York: St Martin's.

Larkins, S., Reback, C., Shoptaw, S., & Veniegas, R. (2005). Methamphetamine dependent gay men's disclosure of their HIV status to sexual partners. *AIDS Care*, 17(4), 521–532.

Kurtz, S. P. (2009). Between Kansas and Oz. In P. L. Hammack & B. J. Cohler (Eds.), *The story of sexual identity: Narrative perspectives on the gay and lesbian life course* (pp. 157–175). New York: Oxford University Press.

Levine. M., Nardi, P., & Gagnon, J. (1997). *In changing times*. Chicago: University of Chicago Press.

Mansergh, G., Marks, G., Colfax, G., Guzman, R., Rader, M., & Buchbinder, S. (2002). "Barebacking" in a diverse sample of men who have sex with men. *AIDS*, 16, 653–659.

Mclean, J., Boulton, M., Brookes, M., Lakhani, D., Fitzpatrick, R., Dawson, J., et al. (1994). Regular partners and risky behaviour. *AIDS Care*, 6(3), 331–341.

Morin, S., Steward, W., Charlebois, E., Remien, R., Pinkerton, S., Johnson, M., et al. (2005). Predicting HIV transmission risk among HIV-infected men who have sex with men. *Journal of Acquired Immune Deficiency Syndromes*, 40(2), 226–235.

Myers, T., Aguinaldo, J., Dakers, D., Fischer, B., Bullock, S., Millson, P., et al. (2004). How drug using men who have sex with men account for substance use during sexual behaviours. *Addiction Research and Theory*, 12(3), 213–229.

Odets, W. (1995). *In the shadow of the epidemic*. Durham, NC: Duke University Press.

O'Leary, A. (2005). Guessing games. In P. Halkitis, C. Gomez, & R. Wolitski (Eds.), *HIV + sex: The psychosocial and interpersonal dynamics of HIV-seropositive gay and bisexual men's relationships* (pp. 121–132). Washington, DC: American Psychological Association Press.

Parsons, J., Kutnick, A., Halkitis, P., Punzalan, J., & Carbonari, J. (2005). Sexual risk behaviors and substance use among alcohol abusing HIV-positive men who have sex with men. *Journal of Psychoactive Drugs*, 37(1), 37–36.

Patton, C. (1985). *Sex and germs*. Boston: South End.

Patton, C. (1990). *Inventing AIDS*. New York: Routledge.

Paul, J., Catania, J., Pollack, L., & Stall, R. (2001). Understanding childhood sexual abuse as a predictor of sexual risk-taking among men who have sex with men. *Child Abuse & Neglect*, 25, 557–584.

Reback, C., Larkins, S., & Shoptaw, S. (2004). Changes in the meaning of sexual risk behaviors among gay and bisexual male methamphetamine abusers before and after drug treatment. *AIDS and Behavior*, 8(1), 87–98.

Relf, M. (2001). Childhood sexual abuse in men who have sex with men. *Journal of the Association of Nurses in AIDS Care*, 12(5), 20–29.

Remien, R. H., Carballo-Diéguez, A., & Wagner, G. (1995). Intimacy and sexual risk behaviour in serodiscordant male couples. *AIDS Care*, 7(4), 429–438.

Rhodes, T. (1997). Risk theory in epidemic times. *Sociology of Health and Illness*, 19(2), 208–277.

Rhodes, T., & Cusick, L. (2002). Accounting for unprotected sex. *Social Science & Medicine*, 55, 211–226.

Richters, J., Hendry, O., & Kippax, S. (2003). When safe sex isn't safe. *Culture, Health & Sexuality*, 5(1), 37–52.

Rofes, E. (1998). *Dry bones breathe*. New York: Haworth.

Rogers, G., Curry, M., Oddy, J., Pratt, N., Beilby, J., & Wilkinson, D. (2003). Depressive disorders and unprotected casual anal sex among Australian homosexually active men in primary care. *HIV Medicine*, 4, 271–275.

Schwartz, D., & Bailey, C. (2005). Between the sheets and between the ears. In P. Halkitis, C. Gomez, & R. Wolitski (Eds.), *HIV + sex: The psychosocial and interpersonal dynamics of HIV-seropositive gay and bisexual men's relationships* (pp. 55–72). Washington, DC: American Psychological Association Press.

Seal, D., Kelly, J., Bloom, F., Stevenson, L., Coley, B., Broyles, L., et al. (2000). HIV prevention with young men who have sex with men. *AIDS Care*, 12(1), 5–26.

Semple, S., Patterson, T., & Grant, I. (2000a). Partner type and sexual risk behavior among HIV positive gay and bisexual men. *AIDS Education and Prevention*, 12(4), 340–356.

Semple, S., Patterson, T., & Grant, I. (2000b). Psychosocial predictors of unprotected anal intercourse in a sample of HIV positive gay men who volunteer for a sexual risk reduction intervention. *AIDS Education and Prevention*, 12(5), 416–430.

Serovich, J., Oliver, D., Smith, S., & Mason, T. (2005). Methods of HIV disclosure by men who have sex with men to casual sexual partners. *AIDS Patient Care and STDs*, 19(12), 823–832.

Slavin, S. (2004). Drugs, space, and sociality in a gay nightclub in Sydney. *Journal of Contemporary Ethnography*, 33(3), 265–295.

Stirratt, M. (2005). I have something to tell you. In P. Halkitis, C. Gomez, & R. Wolitski (Eds.), *HIV + sex: The psychosocial and interpersonal dynamics of HIV-seropositive gay and bisexual men's relationships* (pp. 101–119). Washington, DC: American Psychological Association Press.

Stokes, J., & Peterson, J. (1998). Homophobia, self-esteem, and risk for HIV among African American men who have sex with men. *AIDS Education and Prevention,* 10(3), 278–292.

Van de Ven, P., Mao, L., Fogarty, A., Rawstorne, P., Crawford, J., Prestage, G., et al. (2005). Undetectable viral load is associated with sexual risk taking in HIV serodiscordant gay couples in Sydney. *AIDS,* 19, 179–184.

Vanable, P., McKirnan, D., Buchbinder, S., Bartholow, B., Douglas, J., Judson, F., et al. (2004). Alcohol use and high-risk sexual behavior among men who have sex with men. *Health Psychology,* 23(5), 525–532.

Vincke, J., & Bolton, R. (1995). Social stress and risky sex among gay men. In H. ten Brummelhuis & G. Herdt (Eds.), *Culture and sexual risk* (pp. 183–203). Luxembourg: Gordon and Breach.

Westhaver, R. (2005). "Coming out of your skin." *Sexualities,* 8(3), 347–374.

Zwart, O. d., Kerkhof, M. v., & Sandfort, T. (1998). Anal sex and gay men. In B. S. R. Michael Wright & Onno de Zwart (Eds.), *New international directions in HIV prevention for gay and bisexual men* (pp. 89–102). New York: Harrington Park Press.

PART FIVE
Work

CHAPTER 14

From Modern Babylon to a City upon a Hill: The Toronto Social Survey Commission of 1915 and the Search for Sexual Order in the City

Carolyn Strange

At the beginning of the twentieth century, sexual vice and the city were virtually synonymous in the minds of most North Americans. The metropolis was more than a jumble of streets and stores and stones—to those who dubbed it "Modern Babylon," it was a mythical representation of cravings, temptations, and desires.[1] Sexual gratification and materialism were linked in the city's image as a "painted whore," the female personification of allurement. Progressive reformers vowed to transform "Babylon" into a modern "City upon a Hill"—the appropriate environment for a moral, industrial capitalist society. They believed it was possible to eliminate the deplorable side effects of material progress by intelligently managing economic and social change. The conventional image of Progressives—experts, dedicated volunteers, and professionals who tackled the trusts and lobbied for child welfare—has, however, marginalized the importance of sexual reform.[2] In fact, the search for sexual order was central in their attempts to bring about a moral urban society. When hemmed in by the conventions and intimacy of social relations in small towns, sex, like business, was a natural, vital force. In the amoral cities, however, small shops ballooned into monopolies and sex burst marital and procreative boundaries. Like a "painted whore," big cities reportedly lured innocents from the stability of their villages into the chaos of urban vice and depravity. [...] Accordingly, within the Progressives' campaign to rationalize urbanization, it was as important to reshape the urban sexual environment as it was to clear slums and purify water supplies. Indeed, they saw no contradiction between sexual reform and the bureaucratic management of urban society since industrial capitalist development depended in part upon a harmonious work force that could be counted on to produce a stable supply of workers and consumers. If big business was to be efficient, rational, and well-ordered, then sex would have to be as well.

The search for sexual order in Toronto inspired its urban reformers to launch a formal investigation of the state of immorality in their city. The record of their inquiry, the report of the Toronto Social Survey Commission of 1915, expressed a typically Progressive approach to urban sexual reform. Although the religious, civic, medical, legal, and philanthropic representatives who headed the commission presented themselves simply as "fact finders," they understood and portrayed vice as the tawdry underside of the "Queen City." Thus, they operated within a conceptual framework where women stood for the city's cheap allure. Sexual vice for these Progressives signified a serious breakdown in social organization generally, though they traced one of the greatest sources of immorality to Toronto's working women and their changing leisure patterns. The survey report presented "the working girl," not as a worker, but as an index of urban immorality; her leisure received more attention than her work because the commissioners believed that it was in leisure pursuits that moral choices were made. The findings of the report added a powerful voice to the rising chorus of alarm at the nature of women's pleasures. Along with others involved in the fight against vice, notably penologists and recreation proponents, they elevated working women's leisure to the status of an urban problem that could, they hoped, be solved by social and governmental supervision. Both the commissioners' recommendations and the programs instituted later by the prison and recreation reformers illustrate how the Progressives constructed vice as a gender- and class-related concept.[3]

In many ways, Toronto was hardly a typical city for a vice commission to investigate. Its population of over 200,000 at the turn of the century was dwarfed by the millions who crowded New York and Chicago, the sites of the two most famous vice surveys. [...] Known as the "City of Churches," Toronto was also labelled "Toronto the Good," as an affirmation of the Anglo-Protestant mores that set the city's tone. [...] The major areas of growth were in secondary manufacturing and in wholesale, retail, and financial sectors, so that Toronto could boast not only the highest productivity of any Canadian city (next to Montreal) but also the most diverse economic base.[4] [...]

There were those, however, at the religious, civic, and philanthropic helm of the city who were convinced that a lively trade in commercialized vice and "white slavery" flourished beneath Toronto's veneer of urban decorum. In the autumn of 1913, when a deputation from the Toronto Local Council of Women (TLCW) requested the civic board of control to appoint a "commission on social vice," they represented not only their more than sixty member organizations, but also a widely held conviction that Toronto was riddled with vice. [...] In Ottawa, the National Council of Women (NCW), the Women's Christian Temperance Union (WCTU), and newer figures on the moral landscape, such as Rev. Dr. Shearer of the Moral and Social Reform Council, urged the Dominion government to strengthen the criminal law as Canada's contribution to the "war on the white slave trade." Their efforts were rewarded in the Criminal Code Amendment Act of 1913, an expanded and more punitive version of existing legislation relating to prostitution.[5] Throughout North America, particularly in the cities, smaller local groups devoted exclusively to the promotion of individual and national purity sprang up in this climate of fear.[6] One local organizer—the Toronto Vigilance Committee—lobbied for the "prevention, by education and other means, of young girls entering into immoral careers," while its broader aim was "TO USHER IN A BETTER TORONTO."[7]

Protestant clergy were instrumental in gathering local support to combat vice, and the protestant churches provided the structure for organizing that support on a national basis. In 1913, the Board of Temperance and Moral Reform of the Methodist Church and the Board of Social Service and Evangelism of the Presbyterian Church combined their efforts to conduct social surveys of Canadian cities and rural districts. [...]

[...] Like many North American local governments in the 1910s, Toronto City Council was imbued with "a new spirit in social welfare, housing, land use planning and local government reform."[8] Local politicians began to promote social and economic welfare in the burgeoning city by expanding the range of physical and protective services, creating public utilities, and providing social, cultural, and recreational services.[9] As Mayor Horatio Hocken declared, municipal government could no longer confine itself to laying sidewalks and patching pot-holes as it had done in the days when ward bosses dominated city politics. "We have got a long way past that," he proudly stated.[10] [...] Progressive politicians in Toronto tried to link the existing voluntary social reform groups to the growing administrative arm of the city government; indeed they depended on both the energy and the expertise of those who had previously seen to the physical and spiritual welfare of Torontonians. The membership of the Toronto Social Survey Commission reflected city council's conception of the suitable blend of elected officials and other leaders who they assumed would "command the respect and confidence of the public at large." The City approved the survey proposal on October 27, 1913, and appointed as commissioners six clergymen, four representatives of social service agencies, four elected city officials, three doctors (including Medical Officer of Health, Dr. Charles Hastings), two lawyers, two businessmen, and an academic who acted as secretary and wrote the final report.[11]

With characteristic Progressive assurance, the investigators proclaimed that they were engaged in a fact-finding mission.[12] Like most Progressives, they considered themselves scientists who methodically explored social phenomena, and the regarded the city as their laboratory, full of troubling specimens of urban life. With the apparent detachment of anthropologists they gave accounts of their contact with the city's under classes as if they belonged to an exotic tribe. And finally, as social geographers, they undertook what the mayor of Toronto called a "moral survey of the city." [...]

It is apparent, though, that their pictures of Toronto resembled paintings more than photographs. Their distrust of the moral pitfalls of big city living, coupled with their association of women with urban allurement, washed over the canvas of the survey report. Just as they linked the city with sexual vice and likened urban temptations to feminine wiles, so they painted women's work and play in bold relief. In the background lay their interpretation of the broader economic and social changes that had transformed working women's lives in late nineteenth-century Toronto.

The debate on women's leisure in the Progressive period was an epilogue to earlier controversies about changes in women's work in the initial phases of industrial capitalism.[13] Women's work in manufacturing was unconventional because, unlike domestic labour, it entailed toiling for wages at relatively fixed hours. From the 1870s, when members of Toronto's female labour force first entered non-domestic wage labour, fearful observers predicted a breakdown in the prevailing standards of behaviour for working-class women. As long as these women worked behind closed doors in the "proper sphere" of either their parents' or masters' homes, they rarely attracted public notice. Domestics and daughters, however, proved equally eager to move out of their proper sphere once the diversification of secondary manufacturing multiplied the number of semi-skilled and unskilled jobs available in Toronto. Young women from working-class families were attracted to the small employment niches that opened up in the industrial sector as industrialists sought cheap labour in the persons of women and children. While male workers claimed most of the positions in Toronto's earliest factories, small groups of women could be found in paper box factories, shoe-making shops and cigar-rolling firms.[14] Though fewer than 10 per cent of the city's 5,500 women workers toiled in the nascent manufacturing firms in the 1880s, they attracted public attention that far outweighed their numbers.[15] It was clear to shop owners that women preferred factory work for they would accept as little as 30 to 60 per cent of men's wages,[16] while mistresses who had lost their domestics to alternative employment recognized that the rise of women's wage labour threatened to diminish the always inadequate pool of "good help." In 1887 a correspondent to the Toronto Bureau of Industry summarized this transition in women's work and sketched the economic and social reasons women gave for seeking wage labour:

> Many work through necessity that they may live, others that they may help their parents, while no inconsiderable number are daughters of country farmers who prefer city life and fixed hours of work, even at low wages, rather than remain at home, on the farm.[17]

The correspondent's observation suggests that women were attracted to the cities not just by waged labour but also by the prospect of freedom from family responsibilities and scrutiny. The workers who filled the city's growing number of non-domestic "women's jobs" led to the fear that patriarchal controls over daughters as well as employers' supervision over servants would be eroded. For those with an interest in maintaining those restraints, the female wage worker represented disorder.

The "women adrift" was the phrase that came to be used in the late nineteenth century to describe this novel type of worker.[18] YWCA spokeswomen were instrumental in drawing public attention to what they believed to be the moral danger when these young women "liv[ed] independently, unsupported and unsupervised by family, community and church."[19] Despite poverty wages and the health and safety hazards of manufacturing jobs (which might have caused public concern), it was women's time *off* more than their time *on* the job that members of the YWCA and other evangelical organizations found problematic. Mayor W.H. Howland portrayed the working girl of the 1880s as a lonely soldier in the battle for respectability, forced to dodge her way through the minefield of urban dangers. "Now that women are reaching out to take part with men in the labour of the world, some form of protection for them is necessary, particularly when young women gravitate toward the large cities."[20] He added that the "home influence" of the YWCA Boarding House would be the best protection for "women adrift" in Toronto. Under the scrutiny of her family, or the keen eye of a mistress, a young woman was assumed to be safely anchored, but under a foreman's control for a mere sixty or seventy hours per week, or even less in periods of unemployment, the female worker seemed to be adrift in a sea of urban dangers and temptations. Members of the YWCA feared that the lack of communal, religious, and family supervision of women's free time created a vacuum that drew working women directly to vice.

In the late nineteenth century, though, the waif-like figure of the "woman adrift" commanded less public attention than the male members of the "dangerous classes."[21] Whereas working women were pitied, working-class men were feared on account of their alleged taste for public gambling and carousing—activities that led all too often to crime and violence. Accordingly, such organizations as the WCTU emphasized *male* vice in their campaign against immorality. They stressed that it was but a short trip (literally only a few steps, in some drinking establishments) from the saloon to the brothel, and from there to family breakdown and crime. The election of W.H. Howland as a reform mayor in 1886 signalled the Toronto electorate's support for a crusade against dissolute pleasure. Shortly after taking office Howland created a morality branch, and its director, Staff Inspector David Archibald, diligently set about raiding Toronto's brothels, gambling dens, and saloons, the "most obvious threats to civic virtue" in their view. Complaints about the sweeping powers of the Morality Department show that disorderly drunks, vagrants, brothel "inmates," and young boys were the primary targets of Archibald's program to cleanse Toronto's blighted landscape.[22]

*****

By the second decade of the twentieth century, when efforts to re-establish order in the urban community included an attack on Toronto's growing commercial amusement industry, the subject of working women did come to dominate public discussions of immorality. Indeed, Progressive literature, including the social survey, discussed vice overwhelmingly in relation to working women's pleasures. Urban reformers attributed sexual meanings to the increasing visibility of women's work and play. By 1912 an estimated 40,000 women were working for as little as $5 a week. Yet the "problem of the working girl," as it came to be defined in mainstream newspaper columns, mass circulation magazines, and philanthropic organizations, was not a class issue but rather a moral dilemma. Women's entry en masse into an industrial work force dominated by unethical men seemed, to these self-appointed spokespersons for working women, to herald a "grave and generalized social crisis."[23] Jane Addams had expressed the Progressives' sense of crisis in a 1908 address on the amoral state of women workers in "the modern industrial city":

> Never before in civilization have such numbers of girls been suddenly released from the protection of home and permitted to walk unattended upon city streets and to work under alien roofs. For the first time in history they are being prized more for their labour power than for their innocence, their tender beauty, their ephemeral gaiety.[24]

The new forms of pleasure provided by the expanding commercial amusement industry only underlined the suspicion that the freedom of waged labour had led women astray as well as set them adrift. Fixed hours and wage labour made leisure possible for women in a way that other forms of women's work (notably the domestic labour of servants, young daughters, and married women) did not. Although working women remained constrained by their parents' expectations that they would contribute to the family economy, as well as not dishonour the family through promiscuous behaviour, the changing conditions of single, working-class women's labour did open up new possibilities for leisure pursuits. Unlike both bourgeois and working-class women who did not earn money, they were able to socialize with co-workers and participate in public amusements in ways that more closely resembled the leisure patterns of working-class men. And female wage earners who flaunted their working-class finery on downtown streets had a bold public style that asserted their intention to claim the same freedoms in their pursuits of pleasure that were traditionally granted only to men. Progressives challenged the legitimacy of these claims by expressing their fear that working women's taste for fun would divert them from their duties to their families, their employers, and later their husbands and children. For members of the Social Survey commission, an analysis of Toronto's vice problem necessarily entailed mapping out the contested terrain of women's leisure.

The survey report reflected the investigators' belief that the immorality of women's leisure pursuits outweighed the problems they were mandated to explore, namely, commercial vice and white slavery. With noteworthy lack of concern, they dismissed houses of ill-fame and resorts of assignation as reasonably discreet and few in number, and as for white slavery, they concluded that there was no evidence that an organized traffic in women operated in the city. The equanimity with which they regarded commercialized vice was based on their belief in the potency of the law as a remedy for social problems. The Toronto police were not as effective in stamping out the city's red light districts as the law permitted, but the commissioners suggested that with the greater vigilance and stiffer sentencing, the force's fight against commercialized vice would succeed. More troubling for them was the seriousness of a phenomenon they felt neither the law nor the police could attack directly, that of "occasional prostitution." The survey admitted that "out-and-out prostitutes, as a class, [were] known to have existed always, and in a large city their presence in considerable numbers [was] more or less to be expected." But this new form of vice seemed not to be containable within an easily defined class of fallen women, or even within the physical borders of the red light district. Illicit sex had long been associated with disorder (as "disorderly house," the legal synonym for "brothel" makes clear); yet segregated prostitution offered respectable citizens the sense that immorality could at least be confined to the "lower orders" within the physical borders of their urban dens.[25] "Occasional prostitution," however, unleashed sexual disorder upon the entire community. Surveying this scene of generalized vice prompted the investigators to predict:

> [When] more or less thoroughly commercialized immorality invades offices, shops and factories, takes up its abode in apartment and rooming houses, or even in the home, and lurks in amusement resorts, in such a form that those engaged in it are not a segregated and despised class, but outwardly respectable, and with a definite standing in the world of business and industry, there is a very much more serious situation.[26]

What did these moral surveyors mean by "occasional prostitution"? According to their definition, "women who, while living an immoral life, did not wholly depend on the proceeds of prostitution" could be labelled occasional prostitutes.[27] What constituted an immoral life, how-ever, was not as well defined. It appears that women who socialized with a variety of men out of desire for fun and not necessarily marriage conformed to the investigators' notion of prostitutes, though the lack of clear monetary payment for sexual favours made them hesitate to place them with the "out-and-outs."[28] The women they called "occasionals" or "semi-prostitutes" were sometimes married women or young daughters who still lived at home, but more often they were working women who either worked during the day to avoid suspicion about their night-time trade or who worked legitimately, and "in the phrase of their circle 'sported on the side.'" Occasionals admitted that they "sported" out of a desire "for fun" or "for a good time," phrases the investigators translated into young women's search for "sexual passion," plus the "suppers, shows and drinks their male associates provided" in exchange for sexual gratification.[29] Absent from this picture were the seduced innocent and the degraded fallen women: in their place was the coquettish working woman—the "good times" girl.

One explanation the Social Survey Commissioners considered to account for the rise of this figure on Toronto's social landscape was the possibility that low wages rendered working women dependent on men for money and material goods. The report in fact went to some length to consider whether poverty could be the prime motive for prostitution. Most women, it declared, earned between $6 and $9 a week. Those who boarded, of course, suffered the greatest hardships, and many reported that they were often forced to choose between food and a roof. "It is plain," the report stated, "that the pressure of poverty must be felt often very keenly by very many work-ing women and girls." Despite these telling observations, the investigators were convinced that working women's meager wages were neither the only reason nor the chief cause of professional and semi-professional prostitution. The temptation to supplement wages with gifts or money was great, they admitted, "but most girls in such positions successfully resist[ed] the pressure and retain[ed] their virtue."[30] The commissioners concluded that long periods of unemployment and the need to earn enough for food and lodging could hardly explain the extent of working women's immorality since such a high proportion of "occasional" and professional prostitutes were domestics—women assured of meals and a home. Their portrayal of women's work as a moral test rather than a class issue meant that poverty and alienation were never more than minor considerations in their explanations of vice.

In the social surveyors' search for the leading cause of urban immorality, they briefly con-sidered a number of alternative explanations. They had already dismissed white slavery and were relatively certain that, aside from a few Jewish and Italian pimps tucked away discreetly in the Ward, there were not many procurers in the city. As moral reformers who looked for environmental causes of social disorder, they turned their attention to the troubling features of city life that they believed had led to a breakdown in morality. The growth of Toronto's com-mercial leisure industry caused especial concern because it encouraged a degree of heterosexual familiarity that reformers did not connect to the established patterns of courtship.[31] Investiga-tors claimed that urban amusements were modern dens of iniquity disguised as pleasure resorts. Restaurants and ice cream parlours, where young men and women liked to meet over meals and treats, were actually "cloaks for the traffic of vice." Toronto's commercial amusement parks were equally suspect, since young women reportedly mingled with men who "picked them up and paid their way to various booths." In the winter, ice rinks contributed to the growth of vice since unescorted women were observed to allow "unknown men to accost and skate with them." But the worst offenders were the movie theatres and dance halls. In the dimly lit corners of nickel-odeons, undue familiarity seemed to be the object of the price of admission, the investigators concluded after they had seen some men "dancing with girls they did not know." Since there were no chaperons, the surveyors assumed that the patrons themselves appreciated the "prevalence of immorality" when they visited the city's dance halls.[32] The spectacular growth of the leisure industry, from nine places of amusement in 1900 to 112 in 1915,[33] gave Toronto's moral overseers reason to fear that working women's taste for good times would find an increasing number of outlets. Thus, there appeared to be a vicious cycle in which commercial amusements whetted young people's appetite for dubious pleasure and thereby created a demand for entrepreneurs to expand their facilities. Because the social surveyors believed that working women's familiarity with casual male acquaintances was tantamount to occasional prostitution, the city's leisure scene became a prime target in their war against vice. The mission in the years following the report was to restore the "unregulated sexual market place."[34]

Progressives had little faith that women themselves could be trusted to impose the limits necessary to channel heterosexual unfamiliarity into courtship and to confine sex within mar-riage. It was women's apparent freedom and independence in their leisure hours, more than anything else, that led the investigators to assume that intervention was necessary to re-estab-lish sexual order. They pronounced Toronto's moral atmosphere unsatisfactory because it has become fouled by "the free and promiscuous intercourse of the sexes in public dances, [and by] the readiness with which young girls enter[ed] into conversations with strangers at public rinks, and ma[d]e free with young men to whom they ha[d] not been introduced."[35] They believed that women's contact with the world through urban wage labour stripped them of the modesty that had supposedly preserved female chastity in the rural past. Since women's work had become essential to the growth of labour-intensive industries in the city, however, it was hardly feasible to send them back to the country; instead, the reformers tried to steer women away from "good times." One approach was to reinforce existing morals laws and to urge stricter policing on the streets and parks where women could easily make the acquaintance of strange men. Another was to channel women's search for fun away from commercialized amusements and into organ-ized recreation. These divergent approaches to the vice problem both stemmed from the larger attempt to establish order in the urban sexual environment.

The Progressives' most direct attack on the vice problem came in their calls for a more coher-ent criminal system that would emphasize reform rather than punishment. The Social Survey Commissioners were advocating such an approach when they recommended more arrests, longer sentences, and fewer options to pay fines, even in the case of juveniles, first offenders, and petty criminals.[36] The theory was that a strict system of reform at the first sign of criminal ten-dencies would ultimately benefit the individual offenders and the society to which they would be returned. In practice, however, Progressive penal theory weighed heavily on young, working-class women.[37] Often, it was not so much a young women's behaviour as her location and the time of day or night that left her vulnerable to apprehension by the police. This is evident in prison and police records. Arrest reports frequently mentioned that women were apprehended as morals offenders if they could not give a satisfactory justification for their presence at night on one of the city's streets without parental supervision or a respectable male escort. The assumption in virtually all cases of female juvenile delinquency or vagrancy was that a woman must have had an immoral purpose for appearing in public beyond normal work hours. The superintendent of the provincial woman's reformatory, Emma O'Sullivan, painted the entire inmate population (most of whom were serving sentences of a year or more for vagrancy or related moral offences) as "sex offenders," or what the social survey investigators might have called "occasionals."[38] With juveniles, it was enough to assume that a young woman had *probably* engaged in sexual misconduct. In 1917, for instance, a seventeen-year-old named Mary was apprehended in the company of another young woman at midnight on a downtown street. Though her companion was allowed to go home, Mary was sent to Toronto's Catholic training school for an indeterminate period of up to four years. When her parents engaged a lawyer to petition for her release after two years' detention, the head of Toronto Children's Aid Society replied that Mary could be detained for the full term of her sentence because "she admitted wrongdoing with a man the night prior to her arrest" and because a doctor had determined that she was "mentally weak."[39] The mother superior of this training school labelled another inmate "unusually depraved," stating, "she is somewhat proud of the fact that she has been 'going around' as she terms it, for more than a year." Eva, a sixteen-year-old arrested on a typically vague charge of "petty crime," was equally defiant in her defence of her leisure pursuits. In juvenile court, testimony was introduced to the effect that she liked to go out in "autos" with young men and with girls older than she was. Eva declared that after working as a waitress during the day, she enjoyed spending her evenings at the shows. A Children's Aid worker added that "she assumed a defiant attitude and used very bad language." Such damning evidence of inappropriate leisure activities and Eva's unfeminine defence of her right to her pleasures earned her an indefinite term of up to six years.[40]

The justification for such a long sentence for young women was the assumption that the purpose of the training school or reformatory was to re-educate moral offenders so that they would adopt the attitudes and behaviour deemed suitable to their class and gender. Both vagrancy and delinquency were *de facto* status offences in the eyes of keepers; to change the *status* of the offender—to re-form her—necessarily required extraordinarily long sentences. Reformatory records also suggest that penologists were influenced by a conservative impulse to resist economic and social changes that drew working-class women from domestic services into the world of wage labour and expose them to the temptations of urban amusements. One of Toronto's training school superintendents, for example, attributed what she believed to be an increase in female delinquency to working-class girls' inadequate training in sewing, cooking, and housework. Teaching "these most important lessons," she predicted, would help to keep them "off the streets."[41] Since most inmates were charged with offences that penologists connected to a lack of moral supervision, incarceration provided an opportunity for remedial lessons in domestic skills in addition to character reformation through the inculcation of proper attitudes. "It takes much longer to drive out bad habits," stated the reformatory matron, Emma O'Sullivan, "than to establish good ones."[42]

The good habits that she, like her colleagues, tried to develop in her charges were obedience, self-control, and diligence—all qualities highly desirable in a maid or wife. Preparing a young morals offender to take a situation as a domestic (often the only route to parole or early release) was doubly beneficial: not only did it replenish the dwindling ranks of women willing to work in service; in addition, it ensured that the released prisoner would have little free time. O'Sullivan recommended that one of her reformatory inmates be paroled into domestic service because "a mistress with sufficient time and patience and with the power of enforcing her commands could do quite as much or more perhaps than commitment."[43] If no situation was available, then requests for domestic help from a young woman's family were usually deemed sufficient to secure a release. The overriding goal of reformatory commitment, however, was to set the moral offender back on a path that would lead to marriage and a family. Instruction in domesticity was intended to make inmates "so devoted to and skillful at domestic chores" that they might attract prospective husbands on the lookout for dedicated housekeepers. If the prisoner did not marry upon release, she could still support herself by working in a respectable household.[44] In either case, reformatory officials could assure themselves that released inmates would lead home-centred lives under the supervision of guardians who had a vested interest in retaining the woman's domestic labour.

Penologists did concede that a strict regimen and domestic training might prove insufficient to the daunting task of character reformation. Prison superintendents were haunted by the knowledge that they could oversee women in prison and even provide careful supervision in parolees' own homes or in situations upon release, but, as O'Sullivan observed, "we surely cannot protect them in our own streets."[45] To counter this problem, several superintendents spearheaded a penal recreation movement that would pit "systematic and enlightened recreation" against the lure of commercial amusements. Disciplined exercise and organized play were presented as necessary antidotes to the dissolute tendencies of women who were "products of a poorly planned and badly organized social life."[46] Progressive educators and members of the playground movement voiced similar sentiment. "This stupid experiment of organizing work and failure to organize play," an exasperated Jane Addams complained, had turned the normal "love of pleasure ... into all sorts of malignant and vicious appetites."[47] Toronto's social survey was in tune with the Progressive program to rationalize the urban leisure scene and to instill a desire for respectable pleasure among the city's youth. The leisure problem would not be solved, the social survey commissioners warned, by simply suppressing the injurious commercial amusements, but also by providing a wider range of "beneficial and wholesome" diversions.[48] Recreation was a compromise between the fast-paced excitements and temptations of the city and the commissioners' idealized vision of home-based, family, and Church-oriented leisure pursuits.

[...] Recreation permitted none of the freedoms that commercial amusements allowed young women in their promiscuous mingling with men. In vigorous, outdoor exercise and well-supervised indoor sports, women and girls were to learn rules and respect for the authority of their leaders. Thus the well-ordered basketball or volleyball team could foster the ideal of a restored sexual order for recreational enthusiasts.

*****

Several voluntary social service and reformatory organizations concentrated on young working-class women in their campaign to reshape urban leisure patterns at the same time that juvenile authorities and the police were focusing on the same women in their crackdown against vice. Some groups failed because of their rigid, openly moralistic attempts at character reformation. Such was the case in 1912 when the WCTU advocated that Toronto's working women form clubs dedicated to the eradication of "undesirable dress, deportment and conversation."[49] Other groups were slightly more aware of their constituents' desire for fun, even if they were unwilling to provide fast-paced amusements. The women who helped found the Toronto branch of the Big Sisters' Movement in 1912 were committed to providing "friendly intervention and supervision" while they taught their charges "the art of having a good time in a wise and safe way."[50] One of the Big Sisters' brochures cautioned volunteers against adopting a superior attitude toward "her girl" while at the same time it underlined the social gulf that separated the respectable lady from the "good times" girl: "Don't patronize," it warned, "you may know more about virtue, but the girl is probably a better expert on temptation."[51] The Big Sisters fought an uphill battle in their attempt to compete in the city's leisure markets. Six years after they were founded, for instance, they decided that a "Little Sisters' Club House" would "offset the influence of unsupervised dance halls where far too many girls went to find doubtful forms of amusement." The club opened in 1918, featuring "safe, pleasant surroundings" to amuse more than 500 girls under their supervision. Despite a large expenditure of $3,000 for a tennis court and an ice rink, they could not attract enough girls to warrant the expense. "A few lost interest after a while," a Big Sister explained, "admitting frankly to a preference for the public dance halls, and the company of young men who possessed or were able to borrow automobiles."[52] [...] Working girls with a taste for good times continued to find the Big Sisters' diversions dull, while more serious-minded girls found their activities frivolous. In 1921, faced with large expenses and small victories, the Big Sisters abandoned their recreational schemes to concentrate on case work.

The YWCA proved to be more successful in its attempts to substitute recreation for commercial pleasures. The Y leaders were veterans in the crusade to improve working women's leisure activities, and by the early twentieth century they had begun to learn from previous failures. [...] By granting its members a degree of self-determination in their recreational pursuits, they attracted and sustained the interest of a large clientele of working women. [...]

By the 1920s, organizations like the YWCA had conferred a new legitimacy to working women's leisure. Ironically, the recreationists began to worry about the working girl who did *not* want to have fun, because she was a subject who was difficult to reach. Reformers feared that such women would fail to develop healthy bodies and healthy attitudes if they did not adopt a play discipline to supplement the work discipline demanded of them by their employers. Recreational leaders encouraged working-class women to be efficient employees and dutiful daughters while they were working; yet they never lost sight of their goal to prepare young women for their future roles as wives and mothers. Well-supervised recreation was designed to keep girls and women from sinking into dubious pleasures, while at the same time organized games and sports would permit them to satisfy their appetite for fun before settling down. And working-class marriage and motherhood had nothing to do with fun, as a training school superintendent reminded a recently married ex-inmate:

When a woman has a husband and child it is time for her to be very gentle and modest in all her ways. She can be cheerful and happy, but her days for fooling around ought to be over.... You can be friendly and pleasant, but never forget that you are a wife and mother now.[53]

As long as working-class women's leisure did not entail unsupervised heterosexual familiarity, it did not threaten to disrupt her path toward producing healthy children within the sanctity of marriage. And if having fun involved games that taught respect for authority and rules, it received enthusiastic support from those who considered the young working-class woman an important source of cheap labour and also a valuable tool for raising the moral standard of her class. Wholesome and clean recreation was therefore both an antidote to sexual disorder and a blueprint for the stabilization of gender and class relations.

In prisons and on playing fields, Toronto's Progressives sought solutions to the problems they had constructed out of the changing forms of women's work and leisure in the city. That the social survey commissioners' exploration of vice led them to Toronto's commercial amusements is evidence that they approached the leisure scene as contested moral terrain. The surveyors' emphasis on women's public leisure pursuits suggests, however, that they regarded working-class women's pastimes as an index of urban morality. If "working girls" flaunted their finery unreservedly on the city's downtown streets and made dates with strange men at dance halls, they expressed a brand of sexual autonomy that the investigators could only understand as "occasional prostitution." Women's spirited pursuit of commercial pleasure raised fears that the Queen City had turned into a "Modern Babylon" of materialism and sexual gratification. For Toronto to become a "City upon a Hill," working-class women would have to alter their taste for amusement. Some, like the young women sent to training schools for four or five years, learned the hard way that their right to find their own amusement was extremely limited, while those who participated in recreation programs received subtler lessons about the boundaries that circumscribed working women's fun. Whether guilty or innocent of moral transgressions, though, the "working girl" was a prime target in the Progressives' attempt to rationalize social organization by eliminating urban sexual disorder.

NOTES

1 References to modern cities as Babylon were common in this period, but the most famous reference comes from William Stead's series on vice in London, called "The Maiden Tribute of Modern Babylon." See R. Schults, *Crusader in Babylon: W.T. Stead and the Pall Mall Gazette* (Lincoln, Nebraska: University of Nebraska Press, 1972).

2 See Robert Wiebe, *The Search for Order, 1877–1920* (New York: Hill and Wang, 1967), for the classic assessment of Progressives as reformers who tried to establish order in "modern" life. For a somewhat darker view of the "search for order" in Canada, see Carol Bacchi, *Liberation Deferred: The Ideas of English Canadian Suffragists, 1877–1914* (Toronto: University of Toronto Press, 1983).

3 In this chapter, I will use "Progressivism" to label early twentieth-century Canadian as well as American urban reform. The term seems particularly appropriate for Toronto, where reformers looked to American cities (especially Chicago) for guidance on the improvement of urban living.

4 James Lemon, *Toronto Since 1918: An Illustrated History* (Toronto: James Lorimer, 1985), p. 13.

5 John P.S. McLaren, "Chasing the Social Evil: Moral Fervour and the Evolution of Canada's Prostitution Laws, 1867–1917," *Canadian Journal of Law and Society* (No. 1, 1986), 125–65, p. 149.

6 Mariana Valverde, "Constructing National and Sexual Purity—the 'White Slave' Panic in Canada, 1910–1925," paper presented at the Centre of Criminology, University of Toronto, Oct. 13, 1987.

7 Archives of Ontario (hereafter AO) Ontario, Attorney General of Ontario, Files, Criminal and Civil, 1912.

8 Lemon, *Toronto*, p. 17.

9 Roger Riendeau, "Servicing the Modern City, 1900–1930," in Victor Russell, ed., *Forging a Consensus: Historical Essays on Toronto* (Toronto: University of Toronto, 1984), 157–80, p. 159.

10 Horatio C. Hocken, "The New Spirit in Municipal Government," Canada Club, Ottawa, *Addresses* (1914–1915), 85.

11 Toronto, Social Survey Commission, *Report on the Social Survey Commission, Toronto, Presented to the City Council, October Fourth, 1915* (Toronto, Carswell, 1915), p. 3. The twenty-two member Commission included three women: TLCW President Mrs. Heustis; social worker Elizabeth Neufeld; and St. James (Anglican) Rectory representative Adelaide Plumptre.

12 The scientific language of the Progressives obscured their highly subjective interpretations of the social phenomena they explored. The Chicago commission, for instance, claimed that it would expose "conditions as they exist" and base its conclusions, not on preconceived notions, but on "incontrovertible facts" (The Vice Commission of Chicago, *The Social Evil in Chicago: A Study of Existing Conditions* (Chicago: Gunthrop-Warren, 1911), pp. 1, 32). The Progressives' extensive use of statistics has led some historians to assume that they were at least on the road to rationality. John McLaren, for instance, argues that the reformers turned what might have been "rational law reform" in regard to prostitution into a moral panic: "the predominance of rhetoric and [their] tendency to avoid the discussion of social data meant that the exact character and extent of the problem which the social purity crusaders were fighting for was typically obscured" (McLaren, "Chasing the Social Evil," pp. 153–4). Likewise, Lori Rotenberg uses the Toronto Social Survey Report's "social data" on vice uncritically in her description of prostitution at the turn of the century and never questions the report's use of ill-defined terms such as "occasional prostitution." See Lori Rotenberg, "The Wayward Worker: Toronto's Prostitution at the Turn of the Century," in Janice Acton, ed., *Women at Work, Ontario, 1850–1930* (Toronto: Canadian Women's Education Press, 1974), pp. 33–69.

13 Gareth Stedman Jones, "Class Expression versus Social Control? A Critique of Recent Trends in the Social History of 'Leisure,'" in Jones, *The Language of Class: Studies in English Working-Class History, 1832–1982* (Cambridge: Cambridge University Press, 1983), 76–89, p. 87.

14 Gregory S. Kealey, *Toronto Workers Respond to Industrial Capitalism, 1867–1892* (Toronto: University of Toronto Press, 1980).

15 Census of Canada, 1881, Vol. 2, pp. 292–303.

16 Ontario, Bureau of Industry, *Annual Report*, 1887, p. 28.

17 Ibid.

18 Lynn Weiner, *From Working Girl to Working Mother: The Female Labor Force in the U.S.* (Chapel Hill: University of North Carolina Press, 1895), chapter one, "Woman Adrift: The Era of the Working Girl."

19 Diana Pederson, "'A Building for Her:' The YWCA in the Canadian City," *Urban History Review*, 15 (No. 3, Feb. 1987), 225–41, p. 227.

20 AO, Toronto YWCA Minutes, May 1881.

21 See Paul S. Boyer, *Urban Masses and Moral Order in America, 1820–1920* (Cambridge: Cambridge University Press, 1978) for an analysis of changing conceptions of urban moral order in the United States.

22 Christopher Armstrong and H.V. Nelles, *The Revenge of the Methodist Bicycle Company: Sunday Streetcars and Municipal Reform in Toronto, 1888–1897*, (Toronto: Peter Martin, 1977), pp. 7–8, and C.S. Clark, *Of Toronto the Good* (Toronto: Coles, 1970 [1898]), pp. 19–27.

23 Alice Klein and Wayne Roberts, "Besieges Innocence: The 'Problem' and the Problems of Working Women, Toronto, 1896–1914," in Acton, ed., *Women at Work*, 211–59, pp. 211–12.

24 Jane Addams, "Address by Jane Addams," *The Playground*, 2 (No. 13, 1908), 25–8, p. 26.

25 Neil Shumsky, "Tacit Acceptance: Respectable Americans and Segregated Prostitution, 1870–1910," *Journal of Social History*, 19 (No. 4, 1986), 665–81.

26 Toronto, *Report*, p. 13.

27 Ibid., p. 12.

28 In New York such women were labelled "Charity Girls." See Kathy Peiss, *Cheap Amusements: Working Women and Leisure in Turn-of-the-Century New York* (Philadelphia: Temple University Press, 1986), Chap 4.

29 Toronto, *Report*, pp. 12–13.

30 Ibid., p. 36.

31 For an illustration of fears that young women were trading sexual favours for fun instead of marriage, see Mrs. Alice Kinney Wright's sermon, "Keep Thyself Pure," quoted in Clark, *Of Toronto*, pp. 185–87. She heaped praise upon the "sweet, pure girl who says, 'I do not believe in allowing my gentlemen friends those privileges which rightfully belong to the man I intend to marry. I have not met him yet, but he is going to be a good man, and I will reserve all right to myself for him,'" p. 186.

32 Toronto, *Report*, pp. 11, 50–51.

33 Figures tabulated from the listings under "Places of Amusement" in the Toronto City Directory, *Might's Greater Toronto City Directory*, 1900–1915.

34 Steven Schlossman and Stephanie Wallach, "The Crime of Precocious Sexuality: Female Juvenile Delinquency and the Progressive Era," in D. Kelly Weisberg, ed., *Women and the Law: A Social Historical Perspective*. Vol. 1, *Women and the Criminal Law* (Cambridge, Mass.: Schenkman, 1982), 45–84, p. 57.

35 Toronto, *Report*, p. 56.

36 See McLaren, "Chasing the Social Evil," pp. 149–50 for a summary of amendments to laws relating to prostitution in the Criminal Code Amendment Act (1913), 3 & 4 Geo. V, cap. 13.

37 Schlossman and Wallach, "The Crime," p. 47. Both the number of arrests and the periods of incarceration for crimes such as vagrancy jumped in the second decade of the century. Vagrancy was, and remains, an extremely ill defined offence. In practice, vagrancy was treated as a status offence, in that it reflected the arrestee's social and economic status rather than defined a specific crime. For an analysis of women charged with vagrancy in Ontario see Carolyn Strange, "The Velvet Glove: Maternalistic Reform at the Andrew Mercer Ontario Reformatory for Females, 1874–1927" (M.A. thesis, University of Ottawa, 1983).

38 Ontario, Andrew Mercer Ontario Reformatory for Females, "Annual Report," *Sessional Papers*, 1919.

39 AO, Ontario, Minister of Correctional Services, St. Mary's Training School, Case Files (reel 1, Feb. 13, 1913).

40 Ibid., July 28, 1924, and May 13, 1919.

41 Lucy Brooking quoted in Toronto, *Report*, p. 55.

42 AO, Ontario, Ministry of Correctional Services, Andrew Mercer Ontario Reformatory for Females, Case Files (no. 3683, April 12, 1907).

43 Ibid. (no. 3974, Apr. 15, 1913).

44 Schlossman and Wallach, "The Crime," p. 57.

45 "Committee on Reformatory Work and Parole," American Prison Association *Proceedings* 1910, p. 51.

46 Mrs. J.K. Codding, "Recreation for Women Prisoners," American Prison Association *Proceedings* 1912, 312–319, pp. 319 and 315.

47 Jane Addams, "Address by Miss Addams," p. 26.

48 Toronto, *Report*, p. 54.

49 Ibid , p. 39.

50 *Toronto Star*, May 1, 1912, p. 16.

51 Helen Robinson, *Decades of Caring: The Big Sister Story* (Toronto: Dundurn, 1979), p. 20. Settlement house organizer Dr. Ware felt the ladies of the leisure class were naturally endowed with the ability to teach sewing, cooking, and the "art of having a good time." He used this argument to explain the disproportionate number of women engaged in settlement house work. Wayne Roberts, "'Rocking the Cradle for the World': The New Woman and Maternal Feminism, Toronto, 1877–1914," in Linda Kealy, ed., *A Not Unreasonable Claim: Women and Reform in Canada, 1880s to 1920s* (Toronto: Women's Press, 1979), 15–45, p. 33.

52 Undated brochure quoted in Robinson, *Decades of Caring*, p. 34.

53 Ibid., pp. 38, 42.

CHAPTER 15

We Are Family:
Labour Responses to Gay, Lesbian, Bisexual, and Transgender Workers

Gerald Hunt and Jonathan Eaton

THE ROAD TO LIBERATION

[…] In 1971, […] more than 200 people rallied on Parliament Hill in the first significant 'gay pride' march ever held in Canada. Among the demands were an end to discrimination in housing and employment, the right to serve in the armed forces, and full equality for same-sex couples. Feeling empowered by activism such as this, and bolstered by equity challenges from other quarters, such as the civil rights movement, a few brave souls fought back publicly when they were fired or discriminated against for being openly gay or lesbian. One of the first was Doug Wilson, a teacher-in-training at the University of Saskatchewan. In 1975 he was barred from school placements because of his open gayness, a move that meant he would never be able to qualify as a teacher. His appeal to the Human Rights Commission, backed by a demonstration by more than 400 people, was unsuccessful. Barbara Thornborrow went public when she was fired from the armed forces in 1977. John Argue, a Toronto teacher and swim coach, came out at work in the late 1970s, and immediately had limits imposed on his interaction with male students as well as on the style of bathing suits he could wear. John Damien, an exemplary horse-racing jockey and steward, was immediately fired in 1975 once his sexuality became known. Although Damien was prepared to fight his case on the basis of wrongful dismissal, he died before his case could be heard by the courts.

These and other cases served to focus the burgeoning gay rights movement on the importance of fighting employment discrimination. Workplace issues began to move to the centre of activism, and this increased pressure on organized labour to acknowledge such discrimination and take seriously its duty to represent all workers, including gay, lesbian, and bisexual members.

Activists soon began to mobilize within the labour movement itself, challenging it not only to protect its own members, but also to fight for broader political and legislative change.

Women had been the first to challenge union orthodoxy, and activists concerned with sexuality issues were able to benefit from the changes in attitudes, policies, and structures that had been achieved by women. In many instances, lesbian and gay issues were first raised within women's committees, often by lesbians who felt their concerns warranted more attention both from women and within the broader union membership. These activists (using the skills and strategies they had learned within women's groups) then formed separate support groups and caucuses to deal specifically with issues related to sexuality. These separate caucuses subsequently became an organizing base for lesbians, gay men, bisexuals, and transgender people, a place where they could gain self-confidence, build political strength, and determine strategies, just as they had been for a previous generation of women activists.

One of the first of these caucuses was formed at the Canadian Union of Public Employees (CUPE), the largest union in the country. Gays and lesbians are reported to have 'found' each other at conferences as early as 1980, at first for social support and later as a political force pushing for change within their union. By the early 1990s, the group had been officially recognized by the union leadership as the Pink Triangle Committee, and had prepared a manual on sexual orientation issues covering topics such as homophobia and collective bargaining priorities. Gay, Lesbian, and Bisexual (GLB) caucuses also formed quite early at the Canadian Labour Congress (CLC), the Ontario Federation of Labour (OFL), the Public Service Alliance of Canada (PSAC), and the CAW [Canadian Auto Workers].

LABOUR RESPONDS TO THE RIGHTS OF GAYS AND LESBIANS

The first set of demands made by gay and lesbian activists who were working within the labour movement was to be included in human rights and anti-discrimination policies. In particular, they pushed their unions to bargain for the inclusion of sexual orientation in non-discrimination policies. These clauses were then used to help secure same-sex relationship recognition in benefit and pension programs, especially since they provided the basis for grievances and arbitration. Activists also sought to secure more inclusive and welcoming working environments, including formal representation in decision-making structures.

Policy Recognition, Inclusion, and Representation

From an early stage, activists targeted national and provincial labour federations and union headquarters, pressing them to take an active role in fighting sexual orientation discrimination. The Canadian Labour Congress along with the Ontario Federation of Labour were the first to accept this challenge, followed by federations in British Columbia, Saskatchewan, Manitoba, Quebec, and Nova Scotia. The CLC amended its constitution to prohibit discrimination on the grounds of sexual orientation in 1986, and at its 1990 convention passed a resolution to make same-sex benefit bargaining a priority for all Canadian unions. At its 1994 convention, the CLC passed a comprehensive policy statement on gay and lesbian rights, calling for workplace education concerning homophobic harassment, political action, public campaigning, and legal action. In 1997 the CLC organized Canada's first lesbian and gay labour conference, and in 2000, it created a vice-presidential seat to represent sexuality issues on its governing board. The OFL sanctioned a gay and lesbian issues committee in 1994, became the first labour organization in Canada (possibly in the world) to add a position on its executive board for a vice-president to represent the interests of its gay and lesbian membership in 1997, and in 1999 became the first provincial federation to sponsor a GLB labour conference. In Quebec, the three labour federations came together in 1997 and formed the 'forum des gais et lesbiennes syndiqués du Québec' to apply pressure on the government to amend discriminatory laws and regulations. Two years later, the group was victorious when 28 provincial statutes in areas such as family law, inheritance, and taxation were modified to ensure homosexuals and heterosexuals were treated the same way. By 2007, all of the major labour federations in Canada could be described as queer-positive, at least on paper. There remain, however, significant variations between regions of the country in how active the federations are prepared to be on GLB rights issues. Federations in the more populous regions are more likely to have caucuses and to have fought against discrimination on issues such as legalizing same-sex marriage.

Another early target for activists was union headquarters. Here, the objective was to convince union centrals to amend constitutions, manifestos, and policy statements to incorporate sexual orientation as a protected ground for non-discrimination. Once this was achieved, activists pressed their centrals to make collective bargaining on same-sex benefits a priority and to support the fight for the rights of GLB people inside and outside the labour movement. Larger public sector unions, such as CUPE, PSAC, those representing provincial government and health-care workers, as well as the CAW, were among the first to respond and take action.

Apart from formal commitments to equality, lesbian and gay activists from the beginning sought to make union cultures more inclusive and to be formally included in union decision-making. As a result, there has been increased emphasis over the years on expanding the number and mandate of GLB caucuses, developing educational activities such as seminars and conferences that highlight issues related to sexuality, and increasing the explicit representation of sexual minorities on governing boards and councils.

[By the year 2007], federations such as the CLC and OFL, and unions such as CUPE, PSAC, and CAW, continued to be at the forefront of broad-based support for GLB issues. These organizations now support caucuses and have equity officers with a focus on GLB issues. With the exception of the CAW, and more recently the Communication, Energy and Paperworkers Union of Canada (CEP) and the United Steel Workers of America (USWA), private sector unions have been less likely to respond to concerns raised by sexual minorities. Unions representing workers in the male-dominated trades and crafts, such as carpenters, plumbers, and transportation workers, and most of the American-based unions, have taken only limited action to make their organizations more welcoming for GLB members. One sign of change, however, has been the formation of a GLBT caucus in 2004, and a constitutional amendment in 2006 prohibiting discrimination on the basis of sexual orientation, by the Teamsters Union (affecting both its Canadian and American branches).

Collective Bargaining

Collective bargaining for better wages, benefits, and working conditions is the nucleus of union activity at the local level. The results of collective bargaining, as a result, are a tough and important guide to the seriousness of union engagement with an issue. Not surprisingly, the first target for activists was to have sexual orientation included in the non-discrimination provisions of collective agreements. Sue Genge (1983, 1998) undertook the first significant accounting of the status of gays and lesbians in the labour movement, and found that by 1980 'a few unions' had negotiated collective agreements that included a non-discrimination clause inclusive of sexual orientation. The number of collective agreements with such a provision continued to grow throughout the 1980s and 1990s. Collective agreements covering university professors, postal workers, librarians, health-care workers, and federal and provincial government workers, as well as teachers, nurses, and auto workers, were among the first to get these provisions. A 1999 study of 240 collective agreements, covering nearly half a million workers, found just over half had non-discrimination clauses specifically covering sexual orientation (Brown 2003). The same study found these provisions were much more likely in large membership and public sector bargaining units. As a result, the number of workers actually covered by such provisions is probably close to three-quarters of the unionized workforce.

The fact that provisions prohibiting discrimination on the basis of sexual orientation began to appear in collective agreements at a relatively early period in the gay and lesbian rights movement lent support to the fight to get similar provisions in broader human rights legislation. At the same time, collective bargaining itself was influenced by the fact that such provision started to be encoded in law. Quebec became the first province to add sexual orientation to its [Chartre des droits et libertés de la personne in 1976,] making it the first jurisdiction to formally protect gays and lesbians from workplace discrimination. This development provided ammunition for labour activists to use in convincing decision-makers to put similar non-discrimination provisions on the bargaining table and not fall behind legislators in protecting workers' rights. Similarly, gay and lesbian activists were able to argue, as a part of their strategy to achieve legislative change, that unions were beginning to take such actions. It is also important to note that many of the first collective agreements to add non-discrimination provisions for gays and lesbians were negotiated with public sector unions. This probably helped to make the idea of expanding coverage into human rights codes less alien to at least some legislators. It could also be argued that the fact that the amendment of some collective agreements to add anti-discrimination protection for gays and lesbians played a role in convincing non-unionized organizations to add similar provisions to their employment policies.

Given the level of legal protection that had emerged by 2007, one might argue that it is no longer necessary to formalize such provisions in collective agreements. But this is wrong. Non-discrimination clauses with specific reference to sexual orientation continue to be important because they provide workers with a local grievance mechanism, making redress quicker than through human rights appeals; they also provide an affirming statement to broader union membership.[1] (Unfortunately, it has become difficult to assess union progress in this area because in 2001 the Workplace Information Directorate, the main depository of collective agreements in Canada, decided to discontinue coding for anti-discrimination provisions—under the false impression that it no longer mattered.)

Beyond the inclusion of sexual orientation in non-discriminating language, the most important set of issues for activists centred on the recognition of same-sex relationships for benefit coverage. This became a priority from the late 1980s onward, and for many lesbian and gay activists it became a litmus test of union commitment. As with non-discrimination language, such coverage first began to appear in the collective agreements covering education, health care, and government workers, gradually fanning out to a wider range of organizations. By 1998, for example, unionized workers at General Motors, Ford, Chrysler, Northern Telecom, and Pinkerton had same-sex benefit coverage; and unionized workers at places as different as the University of Toronto and CAMI (the Suzuki auto subsidiary of General Motors) had negotiated same-sex pension benefits.

Unfortunately, there has not yet been a completely satisfactory study to determine how extensively same-sex relationships are recognized in collective agreements for benefit coverage. Eaton and Verma (2006) used a collective agreements database maintained by the Workplace Information Directorate of Human Resources Development Canada to track same-sex coverage for contracts negotiated in 2002. The database included information on same-sex coverage for the following provisions: short-term leave, long-term leave, and group insurance plans. Eaton and Verma (2006) found that of 780 collective agreements in four industry sectors (manufacturing, transportation, primary industries, and business and personal services) 94 (12 per cent) had same-sex coverage in at least one of these three provisions. Weighting by the size of the bargaining unit reveals that 16 per cent of workers were covered by a contract that included same-sex recognition. They were particularly interested in the CAW, and found it had better than average coverage, at 44 per cent overall, 44 per cent in manufacturing, 44 per cent in transportation, 49 per cent in business and personal services, and 65 per cent in primary industries.[2] [...]

Throughout the 1990s, court rulings were forcing more and more Canadian employers to provide equal benefits and pension packages to all employees regardless of sexual orientation. And, from 2000 onward, this principle was firmly embedded in law. This helps to explain why specific coverage in collective agreements is low, even though union support was growing, since it could be argued that fighting for such coverage at the bargaining table was made redundant. Nevertheless, activists continue to believe that explicitly providing equal benefit coverage in collective agreements is important because it provides a mechanism for local grievances, reinforces union commitment, and provides higher visibility on the issue.[3]

Grievance, Arbitration, and Legal Challenges[4]

Once sexual orientation was listed as grounds for non-discrimination in collective agreements, activists undertook to lodge grievance and arbitration proceedings based on such discrimination. In particular, these clauses became the basis for grievances when employers refused to recognize same-sex relationships for employment-based benefits and pension plans. Even if the overall union record on securing such benefits through collective bargaining may be mixed, the support of some unions for such benefits through grievance and court challenges was crucial to the universalization of these benefits in Canada.

[...] The first successful arbitration case occurred in 1993, lodged by PSAC on behalf of a member who had been declined family and bereavement leave provisions because it involved a same-sex relationship; the arbitration panel ruled that there had been discrimination on the basis of sexual orientation. Another landmark decision, in 1994, was lodged by the University of Lethbridge Faculty Association when a member was denied access to family benefits because of a same-sex relationship; the arbitration panel ruled that same-sex benefits coverage should be made available to academic staff. These cases initiated a pattern of success, and subsequent arbitration cases fought on the basis of discrimination in areas such as bereavement, marriage, and parental leave were all successful. An important policy grievance settlement occurred in 1998, when the CAW was successful in winning same-sex spousal and family benefits at Chrysler, an organization that had been intransigent on such issues in both Canada and the United States.

Unions were sometimes party to court cases on sexual orientation discrimination and same-sex recognition. [...] The first successful court challenge was undertaken in 1991 by the Hospital Employees' Union (HEU) of British Columbia. The court found that same-sex couples were included in the definition of spouse for the purposes of the Medical Services Act. Then, in 1992, an Ontario board of inquiry ordered that reference to 'persons of the opposite sex' be removed from Ontario's definition of marital status, in a case supported by the Ontario Public Service Employees Union (OPSEU). And, in 1998, CUPE won a groundbreaking case requiring an inclusive definition of *spouse* to be read into the Income Tax Act. Another important measure of union support for legal challenges took place in 2002, when the CAW offered its considerable resources to assist Marc Hall in his successful bid to take his same-sex partner to his graduation prom.

RESPONDING TO THE RIGHTS OF TRANSGENDER WORKERS

The term *transgender* is generally accepted as an umbrella term to encompass all people who do not fit into a binary conception of gender identity or expression.[5] It can include people who challenge stereotypes about gender in terms of dress, cosmetics, and 'acceptable' behaviour. This is a group that probably faces the sharpest edge of discrimination that society and the workplace has to offer. Transgender activism has been late to emerge as a social movement, building to a large degree on openings created by gay, lesbian, and bisexual activism—sometimes incorporated into this larger group, sometimes remaining apart from it as a separate movement. Labour's engagement with transgender issues was in a formative stage by the mid-1990s and began to take off in the early 2000s.

The Emergence of Transgender Activism

Until 1998, there had been just one human rights complaint by a transgender person in Canada in which a tribunal had issued a decision. In *Quebec v. Anglsberger*,[6] the Quebec Provincial Court held that transsexuals were protected under the category of 'civil status' under that province's Charter of Human Rights and Freedoms. The court found that a restaurant owner had illegally discriminated against a male-to-female transsexual by refusing to serve her and then throwing her out of the restaurant. While human rights commissions in other provinces had processed complaints from transgender individuals before, none had reached the tribunal stage.[7] Between 1998 and 2004 there were at least eight human rights tribunal decisions in Canada in response to complaints by transgender persons, and they were all successful. The best known of the cases,

Nixon v. Vancouver Rape Relief Society, dealt with a post-operative male-to-female transsexual who was denied the opportunity to be trained as a volunteer with the Vancouver Rape Relief Society because she had not been born a woman.[8] In a preliminary decision in this case, the British Columbia Supreme Court held that the ground of sex in the British Columbia Human Rights Code included a prohibition forbidding discrimination against transsexuals and transgender individuals.[9] A human rights tribunal subsequently found that Nixon had been the victim of discrimination; however, this decision was overturned by the Supreme Court of British Columbia in 2003. The court's decision, in this case, overturned the tribunal decision, but reaffirmed the principle that protection against discrimination based on sex in human rights legislation includes transsexuals. Nixon's appeal to the British Columbia Court of Appeal was dismissed in December 2005.

In 2000 the Ontario Human Rights Commission adopted a policy stating that a progressive understanding of the ground of sex in the Human Rights Code would be used by the commission to protect individuals who are subject to discrimination based on gender identity. All of the cases decided in Canada to date have followed this approach, reaffirming the principles that protection against discrimination based on sex in human rights legislation includes discrimination based on gender identity. Reports in both British Columbia and at the federal level have recommended that gender identity be included as a formal ground for protection in their jurisdiction's human rights law. In 2002, the Northwest Territories became the first jurisdiction in Canada to include this provision specifically in its human rights legislation.

Labour Responds

In recent years, transgender activists within the labour movement have pushed for greater recognition beyond just being the 'T' in GLBT, and some have succeeded in leveraging the power of the much larger GLB network within organized labour to achieve changes. Transgender activists have argued that they should be included in human rights policies, protected from harassment by co-workers, managers, and customers, and included in benefit coverage for procedures not covered by provincial health plans. Other issues for transgender workers include dress codes, washroom policies, and accommodations when transitioning.

*****

Policy Recognition and Inclusion

As with GLB issues, several of the federations have taken a leadership role in developing policies related to transgender discrimination. The Saskatchewan Federation of Labour, for example, provides a course called 'Inside and Out' at the popular Prairie School for Women, which includes transgender issues, and their 'Out Positive Space' campaign includes transgender on its campaign promotional material. Similarly, the OFL now includes gender identity as one of its grounds for non-discrimination and has called on the Ontario government to reinstate medical coverage for sex reassignment surgery.

At the 1997 CLC Solidarity and Pride conference, there was just one 'out' transgender delegate present, Gail Owen, a staff representative with PSAC. A forceful activist, Gail is credited—as one insider puts it—with 'bringing transgender issues out of the closet and into the union hall.' Through her efforts, a number of delegates at the conference argued that the CLC needed to take up the issue of equality rights for transgender workers. As a result, the CLC's Solidarity and Pride Working Group decided in early 1999 to include transgender issues in its mandate. After meeting with transgender activists in three provinces, the working group issued a discussion paper in 2001.[10] This paper recommended that unions negotiate collective agreement protections for transgender workers, lobby for rights, and expand education programs.

At the CLC's 2001 Solidarity and Pride conference, transgender issues were prominent throughout the conference, and delegates identified transgender rights as among the most pressing issues for the labour movement to confront. The impact of this activism could be seen the following year when the CLC constitution was amended to include 'gender identity' in the preamble, and at the 2005 Solidarity and Pride conference in Quebec City when a number of workshops were devoted to such issues.

Among Canadian unions, CUPE has taken the lead in raising transgender issues. In 2001, the national convention of CUPE amended the equality statement in the union's constitution to include transgender members. Delegates to the CUPE national convention also adopted resolutions calling on the union to develop educational resources concerning transgender issues; work to ensure that human rights protections for transgender persons are explicitly written into federal and provincial human rights legislation; work towards the decriminalization of sex work, since many transgender people are involved in the sex trade; and expand the mandate of CUPE's National Pink Triangle Committee to include up to three transgender members.[11] A CUPE policy statement entitled 'Transphobia: A Union Issue' states that 'Unions play an important role in supporting trans members and helping them fight for their rights. Member education, advocacy, and collective bargaining are all ways to advance these issues within a local.'[12] CUPE has developed a workshop called Pride in CUPE that is designed to provide members with the tools to recognize and tackle homophobia, heterosexism, and transphobia in the workplace, union, and larger society. At the national level the union has lobbied for restored funding for sex reassignment and related treatments.

In 2002, CUPW amended its anti-harassment policy, which is part of the union's constitution, to include transphobia. CUPW now integrates transgender issues in its human rights training, and transgender members of the union participate in CUPW's National Human Rights Committee. The USWA has not formally added 'gender identity' to its human rights policy, but the union includes transgender issues in its anti-harassment and human rights training for union officers and activists. Similarly, the CEP includes transgender issues in their Equality Action Bargaining Agenda education program. PSAC has also incorporated transgender issues into its human rights program, including its first ever national GLBT conference held in November 2003.

Collective Bargaining

Following the *Nixon* case, human rights policies and collective agreement provisions that refer to discrimination on grounds of sex can now be considered to include discrimination on the ground of gender identity. At the most basic level, an employer cannot simply fire an employee for being transgendered. Nevertheless, transgender activists argue that protections should be negotiated at the local level as an educational tool to ensure that specific rights (for example, leave related to sex reassignment surgery) are set out.

Similarly, the CLC policy paper on transgender issues advises unions to add gender identity as a prohibited ground of discrimination in their collective agreements. The paper notes that 'trans workers may be protected by language prohibiting discrimination on the basis of sex, or on the basis of disability. But, it is preferable to have clear language expressly prohibiting discrimination on the basis of gender identity.'[13] Few unions have yet achieved this goal. A search of the federal government's Negotech database identified only two Canadian collective agreements, out of exactly 5,000 in the database, that included the term *gender identity*. In addition, there have been no reported collective agreement arbitration decisions involving the assertion of transgender rights.[14]

The most comprehensive collective agreement language has been negotiated by a CUPE local representing teaching assistants and part-time faculty at York University. This collective agreement prohibits discrimination against transgender workers, and provides partially paid transition leave related to sex reassignment surgery.[15] The largest number of workers covered by protection based on gender-identity work is in the automobile sector. The CAW negotiated a letter of understanding with each of Ford, General Motors, and Daimler Chrysler in 2002 that recognizes gender identity as a prohibited ground of discrimination under their respective collective agreements.

A Shifting Target

[...] It is clear that significant movement has occurred within the labour movement on the issue of transgender rights within a relatively short amount of time, but there is still a long way to go. Of Canada's largest unions, only the United Food and Commercial Workers union (UFCW) had not adopted any policy or initiative related to transgender rights by 2004. Important to note is that changes seen in other unions have been initiated by activists rather than by the leadership. However, this has not been based on a broad membership mobilization. Instead, a small group of transgendered activists has been able to work through GLBT networks within the labour movement to gain leadership commitment on this issue. Once the change has been codified at the top (seen, for instance, in the constitutional amendment adopted by the CLC, and policies adopted by the CAW, CUPE, and CUPW), the trend reverses to a 'top down' pressure to diffuse these changes at the local level.

GLBT—LABOUR ALLIANCES MOVE FORWARD

Following on the pioneering work of a few unions and labour federations, more labour organizations are now active in the area of GLBT rights. Nearly all the provincial labour federations have GLBT-inclusive policies; those in British Columbia, Saskatchewan, Manitoba, Ontario, Quebec, and Nova Scotia have a formally recognized GLBT caucus. Unions such as CUPW, after a period of relative inactivity, now seem poised to re-engage more assertively. CEP [Communication, Energy and Paperworkers Union of Canada] offers an example of a union moving much more assertively on equity issues generally and GLBT issues in particular. Unions representing workers in the services, hotel, and restaurant sectors have also been nudged towards a more and more GLBT-positive position, in some instances limited to policy statements, but progress is being made.

Still, public sector unions (especially teachers, health-care workers, and government workers), large unions, and Canadian-based unions continue to stand out among those actively addressing the employment-based issues of concern to GLBT people. Unions representing workers in the traditional, male-dominated trades, such as plumbers, carpenters, and electricians, continue to be the group that has taken little action, opting merely to comply with changing legal requirements. International unions with headquarters in the United States, which still represent many of these trades, have tended to be the least active. The International Brotherhood of Teamsters, however, is one union that has recently undertaken a number of initiatives to support change in the area of GLBT rights.

*****

CONCLUSION

Canada's unions have demonstrated a commitment to fighting discrimination based on sexual orientation and gender identity. Labour's early support for grievances and arbitrations based on sexual orientation bias helped to set the stage for successful constitutional challenges that directly affected the working lives of unionized and non-unionized GLBT people. By the second half of the 2000s, unions could claim to have offered political support for equity in law, prohibited discrimination in their own operations, established GLBT caucuses, pushed locals to bargain for inclusive benefits programs in collective agreements, and attempted to confront prejudicial and hostile cultures in their own organizations. These kinds of initiatives were initially more pronounced in large, public sector unions and in the auto workers union, but a growing list of private sector unions are now active as well. Labour's commitment to sexual diversity issues does vary across employment sectors, regions of the country, and union categories. Some unions, especially those who represent craft and trade workers, and those unions headquartered outside of Canada, often acquiesce to broader political and legal changes rather than take a leadership or supporting role, and not all union members agree on the merits of tackling sexual diversity bias. The overall theme that emerges is that the good unions get better, the number of newer entrants grows, and a group of not so good unions stay about the same.

Early union activity was concerned with issues raised by gay men and lesbians. Initiatives designed to provide protection for individuals facing dismissal, demotion, and harassment on the basis of their sexuality resulted in inclusive non-discrimination clauses in collective agreements. These clauses provided the basis not only for addressing individual claims of discrimination, but also for grievance and arbitration cases based on same-sex relationship discrimination in pension and benefit programs. CUPE's successful legal challenge in 1998 to heterosexual bias in the Income Tax Act also represents an important milestone in labour's engagement and commitment to equality. Labour has continued to demonstrate its solidarity by supporting the extension of access to civil marriage for same-sex couples, and fighting for sexual orientation to be listed within hate-crime legislation.

Union response to discrimination based on gender identity has come later, and is still in a formative stage. There has been a major shift in the legal and social environment related to transgender rights in Canada, but this shift has not yet been reflected in collective agreement language. Only the CLC and a couple of unions have embedded transgender rights into anti-discrimination and harassment policies. Nor has there been much indication of a significant shift in social acceptance at the grass roots of the union movement. Nevertheless, transgender rights have become a significant issue within a growing number of decision-making circles.

Progress on transgender rights has been a direct result of earlier work on GLB rights, and in many ways has followed a similar trajectory. A small number of transgender activists within and external to the union movement have increasingly been able to leverage the power of the much larger network of GLB activists (again, inside and outside of unions) to get recognition and support for transgender issues. Where there has been change, it has been driven initially by transgendered activists, subsequently supported by GLB activists, and recognized at the leadership level.

All developments that have taken place have benefited from early activism by women. Feminists were the first to challenge union orthodoxy by raising post-materialist issues such as violence and harassment, suggesting that male-dominated union cultures were part of the problem. Women also developed the concept of separate committee and caucus organizing as forums to offer support, build confidence, and articulate demands. Women's caucuses were also settings where many of the first tentative demands for change related to GLB issues were raised and debated.

Too little research has been conducted at the local union level. While we do know that more and more unions have laudable policies to confront sexual orientation discrimination, little is known about the actual spread and depth of these initiatives. Too little is known about how thoroughly these policies have been implemented, and with what impact at the local level (one exception is Hunt and Haiven 2006). As a result, it is at the local level where further research is needed, and where unions might now concentrate their efforts for change.

NOTES

1 Note that arbitrators in Ontario have the power to enforce human rights legislation (affirmed by the Supreme Court of Canada in *Parry Sound (District) Social Services Administration Board v. O.P.S.E.U., Local 324,* [2003] S.C.R. 157). As a result, a union member who is the victim of discrimination would have a local grievance mechanism, even if his or her contract did not specifically refer to sexual orientation.

2 The study failed to take into account a number of important points. In some instances, same-sex benefit coverage is embedded in the general human resource policies of a given organization, rather than in a collective agreement, even if a union had been behind some of the pressure for change. Also, making an accurate assessment difficult is the fact that same-sex coverage may be contained in side documents, constitutional statements, memoranda of agreement, appendices, grievance decisions, or master agreements, and this makes electronic searching of collective agreements a less than reliable indicator of the extent of coverage. As a result, a reliable count of collective agreements (and their side documents) that contain specific language for same-sex benefits is not available.

3 See note 1 above.

4 We are indebted to the pioneering work of Petersen (1999) for some of the information in this section.

5 Some of the material in this section is based on Eaton (2004), and is used with permission.

6 (1982), 3 C.H.R.R. D/892 (C.P.Q.)

7 Ontario Human Rights Commission. 1999. *Toward a Commission Policy on Gender Identity: Discussion Paper* (October). OHRC.

8 [2002] BCHRTD No. 1 (B.C. Trib.).

9 *Vancouver Rape Relief Society v. British Columbia (Human Rights Commission)* (2000), 23 Admin. L.R. (3d) 91 (B.C.S.C.).

10 Canadian Labour Congress, Solidarity and Pride Working Group. (2001). *Transgender Discussion Paper*. CLC.

11 One transgender activist joined the union's National Pink Triangle Committee after this last resolution was passed. At the time of writing, the committee was seeking to recruit two additional transgender CUPE members. CUPE's Ontario Pink Triangle Committee also has one transgender member.

12 Canadian Union of Public Employees, *Transphobia: A Union Issue* (2 June 2002). www.cupe.ca/www/EqualityPride/4190/.

13 CLC, *Transgender Discussion Paper.*

14 There has been just a handful of reported arbitration decisions in which transgender workers are mentioned at all. In *Halkin Tool Ltd.* (2001), 100 L.A.C. (4th) 312 (Glass), the union challenged an employer's refusal to post a notice on a union bulletin board publicizing a 'Working With Pride' conference for 'CAW lesbian, gay, bisexual, and transgender activists and their allies.' Arbitrator Glass found that this refusal violated the collective agreement, and ordered the employer to post the notice. In *Royal Ottawa Health Care Group*, [2001] O.L.A.A. No. 35 (Keller), a social worker was suspended for two days, in part because he had jokingly introduced a female doctor to a relapse prevention group saying the doctor was 'not a transsexual.' Arbitrator Keller concluded that this comment was inappropriate, could cause embarrassment for the subject of the comment, and reflected bad judgment by the griever. However, the arbitrator found the penalty for this comment was too harsh, and substituted a written reprimand for the two-day suspension. In *Central Neighbourhood House* (2005), 137 L.A.C. (4th) 314 (Harris), the union grieved against the employer's practice of filling shift vacancies by gender rather than strictly adhering to the seniority provisions of the collective agreement. The employer (which operated shelters for the homeless) claimed that it was necessary to ensure that both genders were present on shift in order to provide appropriate services for its clients. In upholding the union's grievance, the arbitrator concluded that the policy of assigning specific sexes to relief shifts was 'mired in gender stereotypes.' In making this finding, the arbitrator was strongly influenced by the employer's own written standards 'Meeting the Needs of Transgendered/Transsexual/2-Spirited Residents,' which afforded clients the opportunity to define themselves in terms of their gender identity. In a fourth case, the Alberta District Court upheld the termination of a teacher/vice-principal who was dismissed after fifteen years of satisfactory service because of his 'abnormal behaviour' as a 'transvestite.' He had stolen minor items of women's clothing, and wore some of the items at school. He was convicted of possession of stolen goods and was given a conditional discharge. Based on the criminal offence alone, the court found that the school board had acted reasonably. See *Glass v. Warner County School Committee* (1979), 17 A.R. 313 (Alta. Dist. Ct.).

15 Collective agreement between York University and Canadian Union of Public Employees Local 3903, ratified 5 January 2001.

REFERENCES

Brown, Trevor. 2003. 'Sexual Orientation Provisions in Canadian Collective Agreements: Preliminary Results.' *Relations industrielles/Industrial Relations* 58(4): 644–66.

Eaton, Jonathan and Anil Verma. 2006. 'Does "Fighting Back" Make a Difference? The Case of the Canadian Auto Workers' Union.' *Journal of Labour Research* 27(2): 187–212.

Eaton, Jonathan. 2004. 'Transitions at Work: Industrial Relations Responses to the Emerging Rights of Trans gender Workers.' *Canadian Labour and Employment Law Journal* 11: 113–4.

Genge, Sue. 1983. 'Lesbians and Gays in the Union Movement.' In *Union Sisters: Women in the Labour Movement*, ed. Linda Briskin and Lynda Yanz. Toronto: Women's Press.

Genge, Sue. 1998. 'Solidarity and Pride.' *Canadian Women's Studies* 18(1): 97–9.

Hunt, Gerald and Judy Haiven. 2006. 'Building Democracy for Women and Sexual Minorities: Union Embrace of Diversity.' *Relations industrielle/Industrial Relations* 61(4): 666–83.

Petersen, Cynthia. 1999. 'Fighting it out in Canadian Courts.' In *Labouring for Rights: Unions and Sexual Diversity Across Nations*, ed. Gerald Hunt. Philadelphia: Temple University Press.

CHAPTER 16
Reframing Prostitution as Work

Deborah Brock

My research has examined not only how campaigns against prostitution are organized but how prostitution itself is organized at particular moments in history. [...] Prostitution was and continues to be relocated and reorganized through policing activities and through a range of regulatory practices. The trade has been shifted from relatively private indoor places of business to the markedly public sphere of the streets. It has been moved from street to street within neighbourhoods and cities. Its guise changes, from massage parlours to encounter studios to escort services, in an attempt to circumvent the law. [...]

*****

SEX, WORK, AND RIGHTS: SEX WORKERS ORGANIZE

As I undertook this research, the standpoint of women, men, and trans people working in prostitution was kept in mind, in order to describe the impact upon them as their work relations were continually reorganized. [...] [P]eople finding a source of income through prostitution have been prevented from entering into discourses which determine their work and construct their identities. The identification of prostitution as a social problem to be simply swept from the streets by police was increasingly challenged by these sex workers themselves in the aftermath of the Fraser Report release. Women who work in prostitution in particular have been brought into view as social subjects, rather than merely as social problems.

The standpoint of adult prostitutes [...] has revealed their practical consciousness about how their work is organized and their identities constructed, especially through the coercive powers of the state. Women working in prostitution have revealed themselves as often knowledgeable and savvy political subjects, more so because they come up against the state in a more direct and unpleasant way than most people experience in this country, on a daily basis. Through developing an activist voice, they are stating that they are not simply hapless dupes of patriarchal relations. They want more control over their working conditions and the same rights and responsibilities as other political subjects and citizens. The accomplishment of this end requires the decriminaliza-tion of prostitution. [...] Moreover, it indicates that any 'solution' to the 'problem' of prostitution cannot be achieved without the participation of sex-trade workers themselves.

Activists are demanding inclusion in the relations that organize their work and construct their public identities. This *resistance* [is] also being utilized to develop stronger alliances with feminist and lesbian and gay rights organizations to determine how sex (and sex work) is to be regulated. For example, sex workers in Canadian and U.S. cities worked with gay men to curb the scapegoating of both groups for HIV transmission. There have been recurrent attempts in the mainstream media to link prostitution to HIV transmission among the heterosexual population, which can potentially incite further campaigns against sex work as a threat to pub-lic health.[1] A critique of the scapegoating of sex workers for HIV transmission has led to the development of a broader social policy intervention by the Canadian AIDS/HIV Legal Network, which in 2005 released *Sex, Work, Rights: Reforming Canadian Criminal Laws on Prostitution*. This report provided compelling evidence in support of the decriminalization of prostitution.[2]

Moreover, throughout this period of study and since, sex worker service and activist organ-izations multiplied across the country and internationally. In Canada, these have included the Sex Workers Alliance of Vancouver, Maggies, the Canadian Organization for the Rights of Prostitutes (now Sex Professionals of Canada), the Erotic Labour Guild, and STELLA. These and other organizations have demanded inclusion in feminist organizations such as the National Action Committee on the Status of Women, Take Back the Night marches, and International Women's Day events. They have demanded the right to representation before municipal council meetings, local police commission meetings, and government commissions of inquiry. They have sought and gained an access, however modest, to mainstream media. They have sponsored or participated in international sex worker conferences, such as STELLA's 2005 eXXXpressions Conference in Montreal. And as we shall see, some organizations have launched legal challenges to Canada's prostitution-related laws. A central objective of these organizations is to accomplish the removal of prostitution-related legislation from the Canadian Criminal Code. And a key impetus for this demand is the desire to create safe working conditions for the sex trade.

VIOLENCE AGAINST SEX WORKERS

The criminalization of prostitution-related activities cannot eliminate or necessarily decrease the sex trade, because women (and men) have to work, and will continue to find new ways to do so. It cannot adequately address the 'crisis' of youth prostitution, because prostitution is not the source of young people's problems. It does not 'protect' women and young people from violence and coercion, but instead mandates regulatory strategies that may increase their vulnerability. Criminal legislation does more than make their profession difficult for these sex-trade workers, however. As Valerie Scott made clear, it profoundly affects their everyday lives; for example, through the silencing of prostitutes in relation to the regulation of their work, in interaction with family members, in opening a bank account, or in renting an apartment. Although the criminal label is not the only force at work in the creation of 'the prostitute' as a deviant identity and outcast status, the most difficult part of the prostitute identity may not be the use of one's body for sexual commerce but the stigma of the occupation, which criminal sanctions reinforce. Through regulatory procedures, the public identity of the prostitute is constructed. As Valerie Scott succinctly states, 'The government has told society that it's OK to treat us like shit because the government is treating us like shit.'[3] The murders of numerous women and transgendered people while working strolls in Canadian cities in recent years are therefore not simply the acts of the individuals who commit them.

*****

Statistics Canada has reported that between 1991 and 1995, sixty-three women *known* to be working in prostitution were murdered in Canada, and most of their murders have been attributed to 'customers' (generally men who find women working the streets easy prey), although more than half of the murders have not been solved. This figure represents 5 per cent of the women killed in Canada over the same period.[4]

*****

The most well known case of violence towards sex trade workers is now the case of British Columbia's so-called 'missing women.' But twenty-six of these women have their fates now known, as their DNA and body parts have been found on a farm outside of Vancouver. The police and the legal system are directly implicated in the deaths of many of the women, because for many years they refused to investigate growing concern among sex workers, and the families, friends, and social and legal service workers who knew the missing women, that there was a serial killer on the loose. Robert Pickton was finally arrested in February 2002 and tried and convicted of the second-degree murder of six of the women, with the jury reaching its decision in December 2007. He was sentenced to life imprisonment. At this time, it is unlikely that more of the charges laid against Pickton will be brought to trial, given the enormous expense of the legal proceedings, and the certainty that Pickton will never be released from prison.

Clearly numerous factors contributed to the deaths of these women, and law reform alone is not a panacea. That said, law reform is an essential component of any strategy to improve the lives of women working the streets of Canadian cities.

A CHALLENGE FOR FEMINISTS

During the Fraser Committee hearings, virtually every Canadian feminist organization supported the decriminalization of prostitution, arguing that the law further victimized women for work that they were compelled to do. However, an influential lobby of abolitionist feminists has now emerged, who argue that all prostitution is inherently violence against women, and prostitution therefore must be abolished. This is not so different than what earlier radical feminists argued, although early radical feminist were more likely to frame their politics as an act of political solidarity with their oppressed sisters. In contrast, abolitionists first pathologize women, and then attempt to rescue them.[5] However, the most significant shift is in the abolitionist feminist notion of legal remedy. They refuse to support the decriminalization of prostitution because they believe that criminalization is necessary in order to clearly demonstrate social condemnation, and as a necessary condition for rescuing women from prostitution.

As always, political struggles over law evoke political struggles over meaning. The struggle over the meaning of sex work has been nowhere more heated than within feminism. While there are a number of points that I could raise here, I will refer to just one contentious debate by way of an example: Can women who work in prostitution and other forms of sex work truly freely 'choose' to enter sex work? If choice is mitigated, is the ability to 'consent' to the sexual interactions typically entailed in prostitution also therefore illusory? And if consent is limited, is the existence of prostitution not also simultaneously an institutionalization of violence against women?

This kind of philosophical debate has taken precedence over a more practical approach to improving conditions in the sex trade, such as working with trade unions to organize sex workers into collective bargaining units. Instead, a simplistic and largely polarized formulation of philosophical positions has become a focus of debate. In this formulation, while some sex workers and sex-positive feminists argue that prostitution is a choice that women can make for themselves, abolitionist feminists argue that prostitutes are all inherently victimized, and there can be no real choice or consent involved under such conditions. This debate is not at all helpful.

It is clear that one cannot fully exercise 'choice' without creating the conditions for choice. [...] To quote Kara Gillies, a long-time board member of Maggie's (the first sex-worker-run education project in Canada, founded in 1986) and founder of the Erotic Labour Guild, the binary logic of

'free choice' vs. 'forced' prostitution is not only unconstructive but overly simplistic. The reality is that the issue of choice exists on a continuum—all of us have constraints on what we can and cannot do in our lives, and, of course, some of us face more limitations than others. However, the fact that some people make decisions based on a limited number of choices does not render those decisions any less valid—in fact, I have heard many women say that when a decision to work in the sex trade was a difficult or limited one, the more they expected others to recognize their agency and validate what for them may have been a tough decision. I find it ironic that people who claim to be concerned about women's limited economic options would see fit to limit those options further by attempting to eradicate or severely curtail employment in the sex trade.

In addition, the radical feminists (and others) have been incredibly expansive in what they label as 'force.' Examples include a lack of post-secondary education, poor relationships with parents(!) and other more global and reality-based issues such as economic disparity between the global South and North. It is notable, however, that workers migrating from the South to the North to work for poor wages under horrible conditions in sectors such as construction or the garment industry are not as facilely labeled 'forced' or 'trafficked.' Anyway, my point is that it has reached the stage where anything short of an idyllic set of personal, social and economic circumstances is being labeled 'force' in relation to sex work. This is not to deny that there are multiple systemic and personal issues that impact negatively in peoples' lives, nor that these have an effect on not only people's entry into sex work but also their experiences therein and the responses they encounter from the police, social services, etc. However, the denial of women's agency and the resultant push to limit choices even further is unhelpful and offensive.[6]

Kara Gillies has prioritized building links with organized labour as a necessary strategy in the fight for the decriminalization of prostitution. Having a labour rights framework in place means that, should decriminalization actually occur, there is an already existing mechanism for organizing sex work, thereby making sex workers less unprepared for and vulnerable to new forms of legal regulation.

I argue that a labour model for sex work renders the debate over choice largely irrelevant, as this debate takes place on the limiting terrain of liberal legalism. A labour model is based on a recognition of the need for broad *social* rights for all people. Moreover, it draws into the discussion the organization of work under capitalism, in which people are 'freely compelled' (to once again borrow this still relevant, after all of these years, phrase from Marx) to work under the conditions that are available to them. Moreover, given that a plethora of forms of sexual labour are offered in the contemporary marketplace, the provision of sexual services for monetary gain that has been denigrated as prostitution is not significantly different than what occurs throughout the entertainment and service sectors. Some people may object to this approach for moral and ethical reasons, but it is indeed an approach that addresses the reality in which people live and work.

MIGRANT SEX WORK/'THE TRAFFIC IN WOMEN'

Public and state attention to prostitution was once again revitalized in the late 1990s, and a key impetus this time around was the revival of an old discourse, reshaped and buttressed by some new ones. The 'traffic in women' has historical precedent in the late nineteenth century. This time, however, it was alleged to have a global character, entrapping women living in developing or politically and economically unstable countries in Europe, Asia, Africa, and Latin America, who were coerced by international organized criminal networks to work in brothels in foreign countries. Abolitionist feminists not coincidentally revived this discourse at precisely the time when sex workers in much of the West had become sufficiently organized to refuse to allow others to speak on their behalf.

There are a number of problems with this narrative. First, it conflates trafficking and prostitution, assuming that all prostitution is involuntary, and that therefore women moving across borders must be, by definition, being forcibly trafficked into prostitution. Second, it simplifies the range of means through which women move across borders in order to enter into sex work, identifying organized criminal gangs as the main culprits. I don't deny that these formal bureaucratic organizations play a role here, but they are only one means, and not necessarily the main means, through which women move across borders.[7] [...]

Some women may have indeed been recruited and misled about the work that they were to do. Others will have migrated knowing precisely what it was that they were being asked to do, and considered the potential economic rewards of sex work as reason enough. Rather than being duped from the outset about the work to be undertaken, Kara Gillies suggests that women are likely to have been unaware of the difficulty of the working conditions that they would face, navigating immigration law, criminal law, language barriers, and the demands of their employers.[8]

So how to address this divergent range of practices and experiences? It appears that the concept of trafficking is inadequate for framing a nuanced sociological account. What I prefer to do is to use the concept of 'migrant sex work' *and then to specify the conditions under which the migration occurs.* The concept of trafficking is historically and ideologically loaded, a concept that obscures much more than it illuminates. Yet it has become the dominant means of conceptualizing sexual labour as synonymous with forced labour. We need to talk instead about the working conditions that migrant sex workers face (in the context of conditions for migrant workers generally), and document how these conditions are worsened by criminal law, immigration law, and a lack of labour rights.[9]

A focus on trafficking, particularly through organized criminal networks, is a very state-organized means of understanding this issue. If we simply identify this phenomenon as strictly a *crime* problem, we avoid addressing this issue from *the standpoint of labour and from the standpoint of immigrant people.* We ignore the fact that people are now moving across borders globally in unprecedented numbers in order to find work, and that *they are indeed the flow of labour following, or anticipating, the flow of capital.* This holds for sex workers, just as it is the case for women who cross borders to work in other caregiving professions such as domestic labour, and just as people cross borders to pick fruit, etc. The focus on trafficking lends itself well to the, in effect, criminalization of immigration that has intensified in North America in the post–9/11 environment. It also avoids the question raised by the No Borders movement: If capital is free to move anywhere in the world, should not people/labour also be allowed to do the same? We need to shift the discourse in order to open the space for an alternative critical analysis. However, a simplistic trafficking narrative has now become hegemonic and increasingly difficult to challenge. We need to think about the implications of this. Whose interests are served? Whose interests are once again marginalized?

THE STRUGGLE FOR LAW REFORM: TAKING IT TO THE COURTS

In late 1989, following the completion of my research in its original form (a doctoral dissertation), a mandatory cross-country review of the 1985 communication law was completed and released. After two years of study, *Street Prostitution: Assessing the Impact of the Law* found that the new Section 195.1—communication for the purpose of prostitution—was not working, despite its more punitive character.[10] The report found that intensive enforcement of the law through a massive number of arrests merely spatially shifted prostitution. It also acknowledged that changes in land use in cities and communities had contributed to the problematization of prostitution.[11] This conclusion was repeated in the December 1998 *Report of the Federal/Provincial/Territorial Working Group on Prostitution.*[12]

Moreover, following yet another in-depth review, in December 2009 the all-party Subcommittee on Solicitation Laws of the Standing Committee on Justice and Human Rights delivered its own report, *The Challenge of Change.* In its response, *Not Up to the Challenge of Change*, the Canadian HIV/AIDS Legal Network found that the committee failed to identify the ways in which the regulation of sex work through the provisions of the Criminal Code increased the marginalization and stigmatization of the trade, thereby increasing the risk for sex workers.[13] [...]

In 1990 and 1992, the Supreme Court of Canada arrived at two long-awaited legal decisions, both disappointments to prostitutes' rights activists. First, in 1990 the court upheld both the communication law and the bawdy-house law, following a constitutional challenge on the grounds that Sections 195.1 and 193 offended the right to freedom of expression, as well as the right to liberty guaranteed by the Charter of Rights and Freedoms. In a four to two ruling split along gender lines, with the two women justices dissenting from the judgment, the court determined that whatever the infringements on Charter rights, there remained a greater social interest in restricting street solicitation. The majority ruling also stated that Charter rights were not applicable to the operation of bawdy-houses. As they stated of the communication legislation:

> First, there is a rational connection between the impugned legislation and the prevention of the social nuisance associated with the public display of the sale of sex. Second, s.195.1(1)(c) is not unduly intrusive. Although s.195.1(1)(c) is not confined to places where there will necessarily be many people who will be offended by street solicitation, the section is not overly broad because the objective of the provision is not restricted to the control of actual disturbances or nuisances but extends to the general curtailment of visible solicitation for the purposes of prostitution. Also, the definition of communication may be wide but the courts are capable of restricting the meaning of 'communication' in its context by reference to the purpose of the impugned legislation. Third, the effects of the legislation on freedom of expression are not so severe as to outweigh the government's pressing and substantial objective. The curtailment of street solicitation is in keeping with the interests of many in our society for whom the nuisance-related aspects of solicitation constitute serious problems. A legislative scheme aimed at street solicitation must be, in view of this Court's decision in *Westendrop,* of a criminal nature.[14]

As well, in 1993 the Supreme Court upheld the 'living on the avails of prostitution' statute in a four to three decision. The majority ruled that while the law presumes that people who live with or are habitually in the company of prostitutes are procurers, thereby infringing on people's constitutional right to be presumed innocent, this is justified in order to protect women and young people against a parasitical activity.[15]

Fourteen years later, sex worker activists were ready to try again. With a mounting death toll among street-level workers, and in the wake of the Subcommittee on Solicitation Laws report, having once again received indisputable evidence that the Canadian Parliament was unwilling to act, sex worker activists in Ontario and British Columbia reasserted that law reform was only possible through the courts.[16]

In March 2007, three sex workers in Ontario (including Terri Jean Bedford, who had been earlier convicted of keeping a common bawdy-house, and Valerie Scott, now Executive Director of Sex Professionals of Canada) announced their intention to once again challenge the constitutionality of Canada's prostitution-related legislation, beginning with the Ontario Superior Court. They argue that while the act of prostitution itself is legal in Canada, Section 210 (bawdy-house), Section 212(1)(j) (living on the avails), and Section 213(1)(c) (communicating for the purpose of prostitution) operate to deny sex workers safe legal options for the conducting of what is a legal business. They argue that 'the combined effect of these three provisions violates s.7 of the Charter of Rights and Freedoms by depriving sex workers of their right to liberty and security in a manner that is not in accordance with the principles of fundamental justice.'[17] They argue that there is a significant disproportionality between the harms caused by the law and any benefits gained from it. This is most clear in the functioning of the communication law. Indeed, there is now empirical data to support this argument, something that was not presented during the 1990 challenge, although it was already available through government-commissioned studies. Moreover, the December 1998 *Report of the Federal/Provincial/Territorial Working Group on Prostitution* confirmed that the law was largely ineffective [...]:

> The research results indicated that the law was not meeting its objectives as its main effect in most centres has been to move street prostitutes from one downtown area to another, thus merely displacing the problem. [...][18]

*****

Advocates for the decriminalization of prostitution believe that this is a necessary component for any strategy to reduce violence against women in the sex trade, and to provide them with the opportunity for greater control of their bodies and their working conditions. Accomplishing the elimination of all or part of the current legislation from the Criminal Code is, of course, only the first step in changing the conditions for sexual labour.

Sex-worker rights advocates recognize that the decriminalization of prostitution is not a perfect solution. First, decriminalization is unlikely to eliminate street solicitation entirely, even though the repeal of bawdy-house legislation would expand the options for working indoors (indeed, most prostitution already occurs in indoor locations). Some women and men will continue to work the street for the free advertising that a visible street presence provides, and for the mobility and lack of overhead costs entailed in street work. Activist prostitutes state that many of those who now work the streets would prefer the option of working indoors, and those who remain would shift out of residential areas into more advantageous locations. They assert that sex workers have a right to use public space, just as do the street vendors and restaurants that add sidewalk cafés to their premises.

Second, in order for decriminalization to be effectively implemented, it must be accompanied by the establishment of clear rights and responsibilities for sex workers, such as the right to form trade unions and professional associations. There is concern that the present model could be replaced by a legislative approach that is even more restrictive, exploitive, and dangerous. Should the federal government relinquish control of the right to regulate prostitution, the door will be open for provincial and local governments to develop their own regulatory strategies, and their effect may be as, or more, stringent. As well, there is nothing to prevent police from using bylaws, even those that are non-prostitution specific, against even the most unobtrusive prostitute. A reform of the law does not necessarily imply a reform of policing practices. Both are aspects of state regulation, but the state is not an organic unity, where a change in one part causes changes in the whole. This means that proactive strategic plans such as the model developed by the Pivot Legal Society are an essential component of the decriminalization approach, as are the building of alliances with labour organizations in order to foreground the labour rights of sex workers.[19]

*****

CONCLUSION

The preceding pages, I hope, draw attention to the necessity of reshaping the way in which social and legal 'rights' are allocated. The standpoint of those who are working in prostitution demonstrates the need for a participatory rather than a regulatory process in the allocation of rights; to develop a politics of rights that transcends regulation based upon state-defined public/private and adult/youth distinctions, and the present assignment of individual and property rights. This requires accounting for the origin and distribution of these rights, based on factors such as gender, class, age, and race, not to mention perceived 'moral' conduct (for example, sex-trade workers' relative degree of 'worthiness' before the law). It also necessitates changing the social conditions that give rise to rights, for example, by creating the conditions necessary for the autonomy of women and young people when they require independence from the family. In this task, feminism needs to be flexible enough to respond to the diversity of interests and experiences among women, in order to grasp the complexities of women's lived experience, including the experiences of prostitutes and other sex-trade workers. We might relinquish attempts to eliminate the sex trade and set ourselves to improving conditions for women, as well as men and trans people, within it, in order that sex workers gain more control over their working conditions. This will not eliminate the sex trade, but it will transform it.

NOTES

1 For a fuller discussion, see Brock, 'Prostitutes Are Scapegoats in the AIDS Panic.'

2 Canadian AIDS/ HIV Legal Network, *Sex, Work, Rights: Reforming Canadian Criminal Laws on Prostitution, 2005.* Available online at <http://www.aidslaw.ca/EN/issues/sex_workhtm>.

3 Gary Kinsman, 'Whores Fight Back: An Interview with Valerie Scott.' *Rites* 3, no. 1 (May 1986): 8.

4 Henry Hess, 'Sex-Trade Activity Up, Statscan Finds,' *Globe and Mail,* 14 February 1997, A3.

5 Control of women's sexuality and fertility, as prostitutes and as wives, was regarded as the cornerstone of patriarchal society. As Kate Millet put it, prostitutes were 'our political prisoners, in jail for cunt. Cunt the offence that we all commit in simply being female. That's sexual politics. The stone core of it.' Kate Millet, 'A Quartet for Female Voices,' in Vivian Gornick and Barbara Moran, *Women in Sexist Society* (New York: Basic Books, 1971), 120.

6 Kara Gillies, e-mail communication, 10 June 2005. Quoted with permission.

7 Diaz Barrero, 'Coming to Dance, Striving to Survive: A Study on Latin American Migrant Exotic Dancers.' Latin American Coalition to End Violence Against Women and Children (LACEV), Toronto, 2002. Available online at <http://reel.ulse.utoronto.ca/relac/library.php>.

8 Deborah Brock, Mook Sutdhibhasilip, Kara Gillies, and Chantelle Oliver, 'Migrant Sex Work: A Roundtable Analysis,' *Canadian Woman Studies* 20(2), Summer 2000: 84–90.

9 Ibid., where we first raised these points.

10 *Street Prostitution: Assessing the Impact of the Law.* A copy of the report was obtained by the *Toronto Star* under the Freedom of Information Act, prior to its public release. See David Dienneau, 'Soliciting Law Hasn't Reduced Street Prostitution, Study Shows,' *Toronto Star*, 1 August 1989, A3. Also see Michael Valpy, 'Different Faces of Street Prostitution,' *Globe and Mail*, 2 August 1989, A8.

11 *Street Prostitution: Assessing the Impact of the Law.*

12 Federal/Provincial/Territorial Working Group on Prostitution, *Report and Recommendations in Respect of Legislation, Policy and Practices Concerning Prostitution Related Activities* (Ottawa: Department of Justice, December 1998).

13 Canadian AIDS/HIV Legal Network, "Not Up to the Challenge of Change: An Analysis of the Report of the Subcommittee on Solicitation Law," 2007. Available online at: <http://www.aidslaw.ca/EN/issues/sex_work.htm>.

14 Canada, Supreme Court of Canada, *In the Matter of the Constitutional Questions Act, Being Chapter c-180*, 5.

15 'Top Court Endorses War against Pimps,' *Toronto Sun*, 22 May 1992, A15. Despite these decisions, in 1995 the City of Toronto Health Committee, comprising most of the city's councillors, voted in favour of the decriminalization of prostitution and for the investigation of alternative strategies for addressing the sex trade. Members were persuaded by the indisputable evidence that criminalization was ineffective. At least one residents' organization, the Toronto East Downtown Residents' Association, was also in favour of decriminalization at that time. Not surprisingly, Toronto police were not. The recommendation in favour of decriminalization was conveyed to the federal Department of Justice, where it was not well received. Still, the vote represented an important shift in regulatory strategy by these forces in social problem construction.

16 'The Prostitution Knot,' *Globe and Mail*, editorial, 18 December 2006, A14.

17 Federal/Provincial/Territorial Working Group on Prostitution, *Report*, 7.

18 Sex Professionals of Canada, press release, 21 March 2007. Available on the SPOC website: <http://www.spoc.ca/>.

19 Kara Gillies has been attempting to build these alliances through the formation of the Erotic Labour Guild. And the Canadian Union of Public Employees has engaged in internal debates about the inclusion of sex workers in its membership, although without agreement to date. See CUPE (Canadian Union of Public Employees), *Background Paper: Sex Work: Why It's a Union Issue*, 2005. Available online at <http://www.cupe.ca/lgbtt/samesexworkbackgroundpaper>.

REFERENCES

Brock, Deborah. 'Prostitutes Are Scapegoats in the AIDS Panic.' *Resources for Feminist Research* 18, no. 2 (June 1989): 13–17.

Brock, Deborah. *Making Work, Making Trouble: Prostitution as a Social Problem.* Toronto: University of Toronto Press, 1998.

Brock, Deborah, Mook Sutdhibhasilip, Kara Gillies, and Chantelle Oliver. 'Migrant Sex Work: A Roundtable Analysis.' *Canadian Woman Studies* 20(2), Summer 2000: 84–90.

Canada. *The Charter of Rights and Freedoms*. Ottawa: Ministry of Supply and Services, 1982.

Federal/Provincial/Territorial Working Group on Prostitution. *Report and Recommendations in Respect of Legislation, Policy and Practices Concerning Prostitution Related Activities*. Ottawa: Department of Justice, December 1998.

Globe and Mail. Editorial. 'The Prostitution Knot.' 18 December 2006, A14.

Kinsman, Gary. 'Whores Fight Back: An Interview with Valerie Scott.' *Rites* 3, no. 1 (May 1986): 8.

Millett, Kate. 'A Quartet for Female Voices,' in Vivian Gornick and Barbara Moran, *Women in Sexist Society*. New York: Basic Books, 1971.

Smart, Carol. 'Law and the Control of Women's Sexuality: The Case of the 1950's,' in *Controlling Women*, edited by Bridget Hutter and Gillian Williams, 40–59. London: Croom Helm, 1981.

Street Prostitution: Assessing the Impact of the Law, Synthesis report, Research Section. Ottawa: Department of Justice, 1989.

Supreme Court of Canada. *In the Matter of the Constitutional Questions Act, Being Chapter C-180*. C.C.S.M., May 1990.

CHAPTER 17
Working the Club

Chris Bruckert

Though it is frequently ignored in labour theory, sexuality does not operate outside of the labour market. Rather "sexuality is a structuring process of gender" (Adkins, 1992:208) and gender and sexuality are central "to *all* workplace power relations" (Pringle, 1988:84). Certainly women's interactive labour, the consumer-service sector where working-class women are clustered, explicitly or implicitly demands a feminine and attractive presentation-of-self. One of the skills women are traditionally required to bring to the labour market is the ability to present a pleasing "made-up" appearance so that "part of job for women consists of looking good" (Adkins, 1992:216). However, more than just a *good* appearance is required. There is a process of sexualization involved in women's working attire (Adkins, 1992:218); in fact, much of the publicly visible labour that women undertake has a sexual subtext. Sexualized presentation marks the labour process of much of working-class women's paid work in the main, and is also correlated to the application of moral stigma (e.g., the costume of cocktail waitresses). At times this sexualization may be made respectable by the terms though which it is described. For example, secretarial graduates are assessed in terms of their "femininity, defined in terms of appearance, fashion awareness, clothes and taste" (Pringle, 1988:132). Put this way, the erotic component of strippers' work situates them on a continuum of visible sexuality which frequently characterizes working-class women's labour force engagement. So while Susan Cole is right when she maintains that pornography is not mere representation but the documentation of real sexual events (1989:27), this sexuality does not locate the skin trades outside of the realm of labour, as Cole appears to assume. Rather, it provides an intriguing analytic point of entry.

Acknowledging the intersection between sexuality and labour does not negate the need to attend to subjectivity. The meanings ascribed to workplace sexuality that in turn shape how sexuality is integrated into everyday practices (Aronowitz, 1992:62) are always mediated by a range of other factors, including class culture. Perhaps working-class women are more prepared to assume authority over their sexuality and claim the erotic terrain as their own than their middle-class counterparts. Perhaps it speaks to resistance. At the same time, we must be wary of slipping into a liberalized celebration of the working-class hero by romanticizing their engagement with the instruments of capitalist and patriarchal oppression. Sexuality is never simply of our own making; the sexual, like the beautiful and the feminine, are culturally constructed. We are at some level constrained within the discourses of what is sexual, what is erotic, what is acceptable. Erotic presentations within already scripted discourses of sexuality are certainly not inherently emancipatory. In fact, the body in erotic labour, like the body in manual labour, must be disciplined.[1]

When we think about strippers' labour as a job, we can ask: What does the work entail? What skills, competencies and strategies do dancers employ to manage the labour site and the expectations of management and patrons? When we think about dancers' work in relation to erotic labour, leaving room for gender and social constraints and remembering subjectivity, new questions open up: What is the meaning of the erotic for workers and how does it shape their labour process? If a woman's site of discipline is the body, to what extent can she transcend her-self through the body? Will she reproduce sexuality without internalizing an alienating and oppressive regime of physical representation?

PUTTING ON A SHOW

A woman working in a strip club as a stripper has, first and foremost, to act like a *stripper*; whether she is on the stage or not, she is always *performing*. This involves both the ceremony common to employees of "playing [her] condition to realize it" (Goffman, 1959:76) and the fact that the dancer is allowed some creativity but is, like actors generally, required to assume a role that is neither her own nor of her making (Henry and Sims, 1970).

To entertain, she has to "do a stage." This public erotic labour involves the ability to perform for, but also interact with, the audience whose very presence legitimates the work. The dancer engages with the indicators of sexuality and these links to the erotic appear to define her job as a *stripper*. However, even this most explicitly erotic labour operates at the level of the visible body. It is not about sex, but about nudity and the visual presentation of the erotic: "You manipulate your body in a certain way and you throw a sexual aspect to it" (Debbie). Put another way, dancers engage in surface acting where "the body not the soul is the main tool of the trade. The actor's body evokes passion in the *audience*, but the actor is only *acting* as if he has the feeling" (Hochschild, 1983:37). The eroticized setting, available props and their own expectations may ensure that the audience defines the entertainers as sexual, but the experience of workers is markedly different:

> At the Blue Lagoon it's a lot easier because there [are] TVs. So I can't see anyone from the stage so I watch TV. I'll listen to music and I'll watch TV and I'll just dance. I've been doing it, you know when you do it so often you're looking straight at people's eyes but you're kinda looking over yonder, looking at the TV there. You're doing your little crawl and you're like giggling inside 'cause there's some show on. I mean I've lost it completely because I was doing a show and I was trying to talk to someone and *The Simpsons* came on TV and I started pissing myself laughing. I couldn't do it anymore. I walked off the stage. (Debbie)

In contrast to the idea prevalent in anti-pornography literature that women's erotic bodies are simply objectified (Cole, 1989, Dworkin, 1981), strippers have agency even as they are being constituted as an object of the male gaze. They establish the interaction with the audience and they determine the pace, the actions and the movement of the show. The audience's reading of her sexualized form does not erase her authorship. We see this clearly when a dancer enacts a fine parody as she plays with her own and her audience's sexuality—although she is usually quite careful, given the economic-power dynamic, not to let the audience in on the joke.

By definition, the stripper's act requires a degree of comfort with nudity and the willingness to expose herself physically (as distinct from exposing oneself intellectually, as do some other performers). In order to do her job, a self-assured and confident presentation-of-self is essential. An entertainer of any type who appears truly vulnerable, as opposed to assuming the role of a vulnerable female, is liable to experience a considerable number of disturbing encounters. Many strippers develop a strong stage presence and a number are competent dancers, proficient not only in the standard stripper "moves" but able to incorporate and execute (in very high heels) their own eclectic mix of ballet, jazz, acrobatics, aerobics and posing. On-stage a dancer must continue smiling, or at least assume the appropriate sexually vacant expression—"I think about doing laundry or watch the TV" (Debbie)—in the face of apathy and sometimes taunts. These kinds of verbal comments touch not only on her performance but, in light of the gendered appearance imperative, on her value as a woman. In short, she needs to develop the capacity to distance herself from the negative evaluation of the audience.

Although the difficulty of the dancer's work is overshadowed by the performance component and by her nudity, it is physically demanding manual labour, and like much other physical labour, it can be dangerous. On the one hand there is the threat of infectious disease. While many dancers take protective measures,[2] the dressing rooms, washrooms, stage, pole and chairs are not necessarily well maintained or hygienic. There is also the obvious potential harm of dancing in stiletto heels, and many other less immediately apparent dangers—"You wreck your knees when you do floor shows" (Kelly). Some dancers take steps to avoid harm by attempting to control the actions of other dancers:

> I've physically hurt myself. They're careless on-stage. They got, you know, oils and waters—shit like that. And they don't care about other people. So I do certain things on my stage, so the girl who's before me always gets told, "Use a blanket." They don't. (Debbie)

The work is also exhausting and technically difficult: "Pole work is a lot of hanging upside down, it's a lot of balance, muscle technique. It's hard to look sexy when you're upside down and all the blood's rushing to your head!" (Diane). Clearly, the "moves" can only be erotic if they appear effortless and natural, a feat that necessitates practice, skill and considerable muscle development. Constructing sexuality is hard work: the more effective the illusion, the more sexual the portrayal, the more the work is invisible to the audience. We are once again brought face to face with the problematic dichotomization of sexuality and labour: dancers are highly cognizant of the fact that being sexy is not natural or easy, but rather *work*.

This work also requires capital investment as well as countless hours in unacknowledged labour related to appearance, clothes, make-up and sometimes tanning salons or plastic surgeries—as well as such intangible capabilities as comfort with nudity and a sexualized presentation-of-self. Gender stereotypes including the whore complex mean that these competencies go largely unrecognized, dismissed as either normative female comportment in the case of the former or indicative of immorality in the case of the latter.

What does this public erotic labour mean for workers? Certainly "putting on a show" is *sometimes* exhilarating and ego-enhancing:

> You can feel kind of down or beat, having problems with a boyfriend or whatever, and, you go to work, and it kinda takes your mind off everything. And you have people looking at you and you have nice guys being nice to you. And they want you. And you think, Who cares about that guy.... Look, I have all these guys begging for more. (Diane)

For the most part, the rewards hardly compensate for "exposing myself for free" (Jamie). [...] [M]ost experienced dancers have become disillusioned: "[I was doing] the splits and working the poles and everything and then sometimes they wouldn't even clap" (Rachel).

Of course dancers recognize that the stage show "doesn't make any difference. Before we used to make it a really good dance and [we would have] everything timed, and the more it's going, the less we're giving, because money-wise it's the same. So why try hard?" (Tina). More importantly, the stage uses up the worker's time, and hence her ability to make money. During the time required to prepare and perform a show, no private dances can be solicited or performed. Furthermore, the stage is considered to potentially undermine earnings by offering nudity for "free." Accordingly, dancers frequently employ strategies to foil this exposure—for example, by demanding low lighting and mastering the illusion of nudity while really "they see nothing, I show them my breasts—that's it" (Tina). In short, while the stage physically dominates the club and is discursively central to the concept of stripping, it is peripheral for the women who work that stage.

Nudity and sexual presentations and interactions are normalized within the cultural environment of a strip club. It is perhaps not surprising then that the erotic nature of the labour is essentially a non-issue for the participants. "I found I liked being a sex object, because the context is appropriate. I resented being treated as a sex object on the street or at the office. But as an exotic dancer that is my job" (Sundahl, 1987:176). Moreover, unlike at other labour sites, in the club sexuality is explicit and monetarily compensated. "It [sexual harassment] was all over, in what I do, *no* that's the place" (Tina). In addition, out in the open, sexuality can be managed:

> Wouldn't you say in a restaurant, the owners, the cooks they're gonna grab you for free at their convenience? But in a bar, first of all they *don't* grab you, they're gonna be thrown out and whatever happens they're always forking out the bucks for it. (Kelly)

Soliciting: "Wanna Dance?"

As the stage has receded as the primary site of labour in a strip club, the "floor" has become central. Considerable energy is invested in selling (and of course providing) private erotic entertainment. Deriving little or no direct income from the club and carrying liability for bar and transportation costs, these workers are well aware that "if I don't work the club, I don't make money" (Josey). Approaches are constrained by specific house rules and shaped by club (and regional) practices:

> Working in Toronto is very different. There the girls hustle, going around in a circle asking, "Want a dance?" If I did that here I'd probably get punched out. Basically the dancers here are lazy. (Sarah)

For the most part, though, individual inclination and willingness to engage in particular labour practices determine whether a dancer adopts a passive, social or hustling approach to solicitation. Some dancers flatly refuse to approach customers: "I'll never ask a guy for a dance, 'cause I feel it's begging" (Rachel). In fact, there is a marked level of disdain for dancers who hustle: "Some girls go around and ask, 'Hi baby, how you doing' and start shaking their things in front of him. No! I don't like that at all. I just wait for them. If they want me bad enough, they'll come and get me, they'll signal me or tell the waitress" (Rachel).[3] The irony of this approach to work is not lost on some dancers:

> We would be sitting there thinking we're little prima donnas [laughing], going, "You want me to dance you can get off your ass and come ask." Or sitting and talking to each other and it's almost like, we act like sometimes we'll get in a conversation, the girls and we're huddling and we're "blah blah blah," having a drink of wine and the guys almost feel like they're interrupting or something to come ask us to dance. I mean it's hard. It's bad enough the guy has to get up to come over to ask us if he can give us some of his money for a job we're supposed to be doing—but then we look at him like, "*What!*" (Diane)

More frequently dancers "work the floor," socializing and engaging promising-looking customers in conversation.[4] Time spent at a customer's table is, of course, purposeful. Many customers are looking for company and are willing to compensate a dancer for her time whether she is providing a social or an erotic service. Although customers are undoubtedly cognizant of the commodified nature of their relations with dancers, they can be highly obtuse. This necessitates that the dancer simultaneously "play the game" and ensure that the customer appreciates that this is a financial and not social interaction. To carry out these two tasks with their contradictory demands is in itself a stressful endeavour. Failing to do so means that a dancer will "lose time talking for nothing" (Tina).

[...] The most aggressive hustlers greet all customers. At a minimum they "give them the eye, just like you would in a bar" (Debbie). Usually the approach is more blunt: "I play on them you know like 'Has anyone ever told you you're really cute na-na-na?' 'I'd really like to dance for you'" (Debbie). There is little point in being coy, since "everybody knows what they are there for" (Debbie). This approach is both the most labour-intensive and ego-defeating and the most profitable.[5] It would appear that a willingness to hustle and the possession of good interpersonal skills, rather than appearance, are the best indicators of income potential: [...] Unfortunately, aggressive hustling can also earn a dancer the disdain and animosity of her colleagues:

> I mean, how girls can walk to a table: "You wanna dance?" "No, okay," walk to another table, "Wanna dance?" "No, okay." They just keep going and going and that makes it harder for the rest of the girls that are trying to make money, with these ones hounding them you know. (Sally)

In some clubs, when business is slow dancers will resort to selling tickets. This is a lottery where dancers sell six tickets for a champagne-room dance at two dollars each. The disc jockey announces the winner, who is entitled to "enjoy a private champagne room dance with the lovely Pamela." The dancer keeps her usual fee of ten dollars and the disc jockey receives a two-dollar "cut" for his assistance. This practice, which not all dancers engage in, is labour-intensive but sometimes effective; it provides the worker with the opportunity to interact with customers without soliciting outright and—particularly on Friday nights when "the boys" monopolize the club—generate some income.

Regardless of a dancer's approach to making money and in spite of the fact that most dancers have good distancing skills because you "can't take it personal" (Ann),[6] the failure to make money can be perceived as rejection:

> If you're working and you've put a costume on, you can feel good about yourself, and you go out and sit for a few hours and you're not getting any dances. Then you go back in the change room and you put another costume on. And the longer you don't make money the more times you change [laughter]. And the more make-up, you keep fussing with yourself.... So then you're not smiling anymore. And then you look bitchy so you're not, so even more you're not going to make money. And it's just like a snowball effect. It just gets worse and worse. And you get feeling like you're fat, you start feeling like you are ugly. (Rachel)

The Private Show

In the late 1980s and early 1990s private dances moved from the floor (table-dances) to the champagne rooms, a shift welcomed by many dancers. One dancer described the problem of dancing naked in the middle of the bar:

> Didn't appeal at all! I hated it, hated it! I wouldn't dance on the box. No. I danced on the floor, because their face was at my flippin' crotch level, you know. I hated it. *I hated it*. But then when champagne rooms came in—when it was both of them and someone asked me to dance for them on the floor, "Ten bucks same as the champagne room," ya. Anybody, even now, they ask me for a dance on the floor, ten bucks. You might as well take it in the champagne room. (Sally)

In some ways the work remained essentially unchanged: private dances continue to be about the removal of clothing and sensuous movement. It is essentially about "how much sex can you give the guy on that little two feet by two feet square" (Marie). This is not necessarily easy:

> When I first started I had no idea how to go about it, but I finally discovered. It took me about a year to go from four hundred a week to over a thousand. I couldn't pin-point it, I couldn't pin-point it. It's the way you walk, the way you look at them, the way you move on the box. (Marie)

When clubs permit lap-dancing, some dancers engage in a different sort of erotic labour. As the name implies "You sit down on the guy ... with your panties on ... and he's allowed to touch you all over" (Tina). It "involves a lot of body rubbing ... kind of a seductive rub—from head to toe, sitting on their lap making sexual gestures" (Debbie).

Not only did the added privacy make some dancers feel more secure, since with table-dancing "there are too many people and I'm naked in the middle of the room" (Jamie), but it also changed the social and economic dynamics in the club, rendering the dancer both more vulnerable to aggression and pressure by customers and in a better position to increase her earnings by dirty dancing.

In order to make her money, the dancer has to first sell her service. To do this, she employs a range of strategies, including bartering:

> I'll charge them, like for the first song, because they're a little hesitant, I'll charge them half price. Make them think they're getting a really great deal. "But I'll only do it for you na-na-na." Well, I'll tell them that. They give me a ten and they don't see their change. So, "Ya ya, I'll bring it to you." Just give me the money. (Debbie)

She then seeks to maximize the spending of each of her customers using a variety of special skills. "Once they come and get me, they're screwed. They're stuck with me and I'm gonna keep them and siphon out every last dime I can get" (Rachel). In the champagne room, she carefully choreographs the interaction to her advantage and polices the boundaries she has established for herself:

> If it's gonna benefit my wallet, pardon me, I'll do it. Except I will draw the line. I will not step over the line. To me, I guess to me prostitution is actual penetration or ... holding his, ah, genitals with your hand, your mouth or, ah, there [your crotch]. That's the line! 'Cause I mean, I've had several people touch my chest. To me my chest is nothing. [But] you touch me *there* [my crotch], and we'll have words. That's the line. That's the only thing private to me. (Debbie)

The dancer needs to encourage the customer, retain his attention and goodwill and yet remain firmly in control of the situation:

It's not what you do, it's how you do it. That's where the experience comes in, you know. These girls think you have to touch all over every customer. It doesn't have to be that way at all. (Sally)

Because they are vulnerable in relation to both customers and—should the situation cross the obscure but very important line between dirty and straight—the bar, dancers employ a variety of tactics to protect themselves. Strategies are shaped by their intentions. If a dancer anticipates engaging in dirty dancing, she may take care in selecting the particular setting:

It's [the champagne rooms] like a cattle stall. When you go in they're all open booths and it's a row of them. And you have to walk by them to get to whatever one you choose. The further down you go the nastier the dancers are, 'cause the less people walk by. (Debbie)

She might also bribe the doorman:

If I'm gonna get really close to a customer because he's a good paying customer, he's got lots of money, I'll pay them to close an eye. [When?] You have to do it either before the dance or after the dance and you have to explain to him [pause]. He usually knows, but now, he'll only close his eyes to an extent. He'll only let you go so far. (Debbie)

More frequently, she will employ "straight" strategies to maximize her income:

I don't stop [dancing] until they tell me to stop and then I tell them how much. I don't do one dance and then sit.… I used to do that, one dance and that's it. Then you don't get another dance. So I just keep dancing. (Sally)

For dancers, making money also renders them vulnerable to physical or sexual aggression. As a result, they are attentive to clues and refuse customers they perceive to be potentially dangerous. For Sally this means favouring older patrons:

I find the older guys, they're there for communication. Really to communicate. They look at you, but they don't look at you with sex the way young guys do. Ya, like old guys *do*, but not that same way. You know what I mean? They're more with the look of admiring rather than the look of attacking sort of thing, pulling your clothes off, you know. It's different. Young guys are too rude … they got egos, they're the ones who are more likely to just reach out and touch someone.… [But] not all the old ones are good.

Sally's wry note that "not all the old ones are good" suggests that this tactic is not without limitations. In practice, dancers routinely rely on each other for protection—"In the champagne room we're all watching each other's back" (Debbie)—and most of the more experienced dancers have also perfected strategies that maximize their control of the interaction. One research participant described her atypically candid approach:

I stand [and] I make them open their legs like this. If they give me a problem, my knees are right here. Ya, I'm serious! Every guy has to sit with their legs open. I want full range. Some of them say, "Why?"— "'Cause if you get out of line I'll kick you right there." Fucking right, you hurt me I'll hurt you right back. These are the rules, you don't like them, you get the fuck out, don't ask me to dance. A lot of them [dancers] sit with their legs wide open—he's going to get his hands to your crotch before you get your feet to the floor 'cause he's got a hold of your legs. (Sally)

Without undermining the potential for sexual and physical aggression that dancers must contend with on a daily basis, we can nonetheless appreciate that unlike most female employees who are victimized by inappropriate sexual attention, strippers are positioned to effectively reverse the subtext and exploit their customer's vulnerability and/or investment in a non-deviant social identity:

A couple of weeks [ago] a guy bit me on the ass and I said to him, "I'm in here giving you pleasure and you fuckin' come in here and disrespect me like that. I'm doing you nice things and you bite my ass. Is that a normal thing in your life? You bend over and bite people on the ass?" I fuckin' belittled him something awful. How dare he? Drove him in the head with my elbow—he hit the wall. "What you do that for?" "What did I do that for?" Bite me again and I'll show you why I did it. I made him pay me fifty bucks! It was the first dance, I had my knees on his balls, I said, "That's fifty fuckin' dollars, ra ra ra." I said, "You pay it or I'm gonna break your balls," I wasn't gettin' off him either—*best defence*. (Sally)

During field work a similar incident unfolded. A customer exposed himself to a young but "wise" (Goffman, 1963) dancer. Not perceiving the situation to be threatening, she elected to manage the incident herself. As she explained to staff in comic detail after he had left, she had righteously advised him that his behaviour was inappropriate and criminal, but that she would be prepared to "forget it" if he compensated her for her trauma. He complied.

As the above incidents illustrate, strippers learn to assume control over situations and to assertively enforce their expectations. This competence, which is traditionally denied young women who continue to be socialized into "niceness," also facilitates an individual's assumption of agency in social interactions. As Debbie noted:

Ya, it's [stripping] given me self confidence. It's taught me a lot…. Because things happen and if I feel uncomfortable with it—I stop it. Whereas before I would have done it 'cause that's what I was expected to do. So I'm more confident…. It's what I say that goes. I am the boss. It's up to me. Before, I was very naive, I was a very, very naive girl, very gullible. Now I'm cold-hearted, a lot stronger emotionally, physically and mentally.

EMOTIONAL LABOUR, OR FRIENDSHIP AT TEN DOLLARS A SONG
Arlie Hochschild, in her groundbreaking study on airline stewardesses, argues that the boundaries of labour have expanded and new expectations are being imposed on workers. Capitalism

has colonized some emotions, so that within an increasing number of service industries, the "emotional style of offering the service is part of the service itself" (Hochschild, 1983:5). Rather than simply selling her mental and physical labour, the modern service worker must now engage in emotional labour. This requires the worker, in exchange for a wage, to "induce or suppress feeling in order to sustain the outward countenance that produces the proper state of mind in others" (Hochschild, 1983:7) and engage in "deep acting" by re-creating personal experiences in a commercial setting. Such a worker must manage her feelings not just for private social relations (which we all do), but as a commodity to benefit the corporation that pays her wage. The process, which requires her to transform her smile into a *sincere* smile, cannot avoid creating a sense of alienation from feelings (Hochschild, 1983:21). That is, as new areas of social and interpersonal life are transformed into services to be bought, the alienation inherent to the labour process in modern capitalist societies is extended into a new arena.

[…] The concept of emotional labour has resonance in the work of strip-club dancers. Since dancers are self-account service workers, all or most of a particular worker's income is directly paid by customers in a fee-for-service arrangement. Explicitly, the primary service is private dances or erotic entertainment. Equally prevalent, but largely unacknowledged, however, is another private interactional emotional service that necessitates a unique set of skills.

Many customers, particularly the "loners," are only marginally interested in nude entertainment whether it is on the public stage or in a private champagne room. Instead, these men "want someone to talk to" (Rachel). Perhaps they are socially isolated:

> They work, they have a normal life and maybe they don't know really where to go to meet some people, or girls or something, or too shy or something. So, they go there. And they spend a couple of hundred bucks and they sit there and talk to a girl that's nice to them and makes them feel good for a few hours. And that's it, y'know. And sometimes … you get ones that just go to see you all the time and get a little more attached and stuff like that. (Diane)

[…] These customers are the source of endless discussion by support staff, who regard them with a mix of pity and contempt: "When you have to pay ten dollars a song to talk to somebody, that's a lot of loneliness" (Brad, disc jockey); "Ah, customers, well, mostly I feel sorry for them" (Janet, waitress); "They're losers" (Kevin, doorman). While a market for social relations would appear to say a great deal about the alienation of social actors and commodification in modern society, the question remains: If an interactional service is being purchased, what does this mean for the labour experience of the service providers?

To be successful, the dancer has to master "playing the game." The "game" can be employed as a strategy to procure dances, but it can also be a compensated labour in its own right. It is a parody of social relations: "It's playing a game, of course it is. It depends on the guy, the drippier you are, the more money you'll make. The more you laugh at his jokes, the more money you'll make" (Sally). In essence, the dancer presents a "cynical performance" (Goffman, 1959:18), instrumentally and consciously playing to the expectations of an audience of one.

[…] The game analogy is particularly appropriate when we recognize that the audience is playing along in a fine parody of social interaction where the script is known—but never publicly acknowledged—by all participants. The client helps to maintain the fiction by "engaging in protective measures" (Goffman, 1959:212). Clients cooperate by never challenging the dancers' presentation-of-self and by focusing conversation on what defines her within the club—her appearance: "His conversation was like, 'Have you always had your hair that length?' 'Did you ever have it shorter or longer?'" (Judy). In the end, though, the dancer's livelihood depends upon her ability to maintain the fiction and "treat them like they're people. You don't just treat them like they're a ten-dollar bill" (Rachel).

For the dancer, the charade becomes routine as she re-enacts the game over and over again with her customers. In each interaction, she is required to create the fiction of a novel interaction with a "special" person. This constructed reality is fragile and susceptible to disruption at any time. With her regular clients, who might collude in the play but nonetheless expect narrative continuity, this is sometimes problematic:

> It's hard to keep your story straight. You tell different stories. I mean, you're one thing for one customer, you're one thing for another customer. And they come in and they start talking and you forget what you told them. [...] (Ann)

While the interaction between clients and dancers can be conceptualized as a game, it is, for the women, *work*. With the introduction of private table- and champagne-room dancing, workers have to sell not only their entertainment service but also a "social" service. To do so, they employ a range of highly specialized interpersonal skills, their presentation-of-self and a sales approach simultaneously. Maintaining the balance can be difficult:

> Some girls, they sit and talk to them three hours and expect to be paid three hundred dollars. And some guys are thinking in their head, "Well, she only danced, ah, ten songs, I only owe her a hundred and it's her own fault if she sat there for two extra hours to talk to me," y'know. He's only gonna pay the hundred that he owes and that's it. And she's freaking out 'cause she figures she should be getting two hundred more. I figure, well, if you don't tell a person at first that you're charging a hundred an hour then it's your own darn fault. (Rachel)

Dancers also engage in extensive emotional labour as they interact with clients and construct social relations. Most of the money that dancers make is from their "regulars." Getting and maintaining a regular clientele involves special relationship and boundary-maintenance skills:

> They [regulars] come to see you [pause]. Some of them get a little weird and you just gotta know when to back off I guess. It's different with table-dancing than just being onstage. Because now when you table-dance you sit with them, you're sitting with them for a few hours and you're talking one-on-one with the person a couple of hours every week. Plus you're going to start getting to know each other.... I mean, he's obviously physically attracted to you or he wouldn't have asked you to dance in the first place, and

then if he comes back to see you, then he likes your personality too. (Diane)

Of course, in spite of a time commitment that mirrors friendship, it remains an instrumental relationship. As Diane later noted, "They know nothing, nothing about you." Policing the boundaries can, at times, become a matter of survival:

> When I was working at the Copacabana there was this guy.... He'd come and see me and I'd knew him from before and stuff like that. And he kinda got a little excessive, y'know.... First he was really nice. And then and then he started being like, ah, weird.... So then I stopped talking to him. And then when I stopped talking to him he ended up being like, "Oh, why are you treating me like this?" Then one day he was outside my house so I had him barred from the bar and he got really upset with that. (Diane)

Not only are strippers continually playing the role of a stripper, they are also adopting other personas. In effect they play a number of roles within a particular spectrum of possibilities, consecutively and sometimes concurrently:

> I used to give every guy a different age depending on what they wanted. I also gave different stories, but that's complicated to keep track of. Sometimes I acted really young and walked around the club in a skirt being cutesy. You don't even have to look that young, just act young. It's really weird. Different guys want different things. (Sarah)

Most dancers use intuition to "read" the patron in order to determine the particular presentation-of-self they should conjure up. Others are more forthright. Debbie noted that "the first thing I ask my customers is 'what do you like?' 'What do you look for in a woman?' And I go with it.... They are there for the fantasy."

Thus, to be successful and to make money, dancers engage not only in the surface acting of cynical performance but also in "deep acting" (Hochschild, 1983). Deep acting goes beyond the *pretense* of emotion, requiring an individual to dredge up *actual* emotions to respond in an "appropriate" manner and to construct a self that is able to be (virtually simultaneously) assertive and coy but always pleasing and interested. It necessitates the management of all aspects of appearance; "My facial expressions, my body language, my vocabulary, I'm a [giggle], I'm a cold-hearted bitch." And, of course, "You make it look like it's fun.... If I'm not having a good time, then they're not going to want a table-dance" (Debbie).[7] Jamie, who used to work in the sex trades and was, at the time of the interview, frustrated with her job, was much more cynical:

> I'd rather be hooking. It's the same men you get in the champagne room. When [I] was lap-dancing it was easier, you didn't have to smile at them, pretend you're enjoying your dance in front of them. Now ... if they get ten dances, they blew a hundred bucks and they didn't get any [sex]. And you have to be pleasant, make them feel great. If you're hooking, you get a customer and you get it over with—like usually as fast as they can get it up. And you don't have to see them again.

Like other direct-service workers (such as airline stewardesses and waitresses), a stripper has to be able to manage her emotions and anger in the face of ignorant and trying customers. In light of the fact that the male clients define strippers as "other," as ersatz or real whores and since a whore (within the hierarchical gender dichotomy of the dominant discourse) has few rights and even less private space, she is likely subject to high levels of verbal and physical harassment. But there is more to it than this. The stripper participates in a financial interaction that masquerades as a social relationship, with a social relationship's sense of reciprocity: "I should probably have my Ph.D. in psychology by now for all the problems I've listened to and all the advice I've given" (Rachel). Social relationships are normally defined by mutual concern. In the strip club, however, the appearance of concern becomes a commodity that is purchased: "I feel guilty when they tell me things. Because personally I don't give a shit. But I have to pretend I do" (Jamie). Notably, unlike the professionals to whom Rachel compares herself, a dancer lacks the professional language and training that might guide her through the interaction; instead, she has to improvise by continually reinventing herself and adapting her performance.

While talking to customers may appear to be a rather innocuous activity, many dancers express exasperation about it: "You have to go sit down with the guy and blah blah blah blah blah blah blah blah. I hate that" (Tina). In fact, talking to customers, which is described as "hard on the head" (Diane), is dancers' greatest source of complaint. On reflection, this is not surprising. Strippers are alienated not just from their bodies or from their surface sexual self-presentation in a way that was normal in the burlesque theatres of the past. They are alienated from something more—their social selves:

> Temporarily you're someone you're not, just for this guy, just so you can get his money. If he wants to believe something then you just play right along with it. "Ya I'm from wherever," and make yourself up to be something you're not. (Sally)

The result is a disassociated sense of self; so that "I pretend I'm somebody else and I get all glamorous and I go into work. I'm a completely different person in the club, a completely different person" (Debbie). Workers are very explicit about the need to distance and separate their different selves: "I have a very distinct difference between my job and my life and I find if I mix the two of them that I can't keep it straight" (Ann). This assumption of separate identity is in part facilitated by the use of stage names so that "on-stage I'm Kim so it's not me either" (Alex). Still, the implications of this self-transformation can be very stressful. This breaking of boundaries suggests that it is not the naked body but the exposure of the self that is so difficult. We see the complex ways personal and social identities can be fractured when a job requires identity management of this magnitude:

> I have a hard time—you know—coming back, coming back to earth. I have a hard time remaining myself. When I get cornered, my defences always go up, whether it's needed or not. It's made me, it's made me a much harder person ... but I'm learning how to deal with it.... Who I play in the club [chuckling], is a completely different person from when I first started. When you learn how to play the game, I find myself playing the game with boyfriends, umm, not, umm, not consciously you know (Debbie).

Perhaps Jamie's comment is most revealing when she links her emotional labour with interpersonal relations: "I'm used to playing roles. I had a lot of bad relationships."

Erotic Labour? Emotional Labour?

The strip club is a business that self-consciously relies on women's bodies. While other service industries may use women's bodies to make a product or service more appealing (Adkins, 1992), here, the service and the body are conflated. This play on sexuality permeates the industry, so that while sexuality is a subtext in many jobs and an underlying dynamic of most (Hearn and Parkin, 1995), strippers' labour is explicitly erotic. The question now becomes: How does this shape the labour? Perhaps the most telling finding was how few comments were made by interviewees about sexuality; it appeared to be largely incidental. It would seem that financial success is contingent not on an outstanding appearance, but on finely tuned interpersonal skills and the presentation of friendly sexuality. Accordingly, the dress and body language of dancers reflect an eroticism that is as much social and emotional as it is visual and physical. Rather than engage fully with sexuality, they adopt a script and even on-stage play the roles in a half-hearted manner: "Y'know, I do little moves and stuff" (Diane).

Before the deprofessionalization of the industry, appearance was very important, because a stripper's success was contingent on her providing public erotic entertainment. In the late 1970s and early 1980s, "shop talk" centred on moves, costumes, the quality of the stage and audience response. There was considerable pride in doing a good show, and a sense of affirmation was realized when the audience responded enthusiastically. Today, though a dancer might be congratulated on her "set" by her co-workers, such conversations are largely absent. However, a sexualized self-image—so that "you feel good about yourself" (Sarah)—remains important. Put another way, self-sexualization, perceiving oneself to be sexually appealing and worthy of male adoration, is imperative for effectively engaging in the emotional work where a dancer can make money.

[...] For the most part, dancers are skilled at maintaining an ironic distance from their patrons' proclamations. At the same time, the sexual atmosphere and visible plays on the physical appear to have a positive impact on the workers' self-image. The acceptance of and open appreciation shown about women's bodies in the club seems to translate into a positive body image. I was continually struck by how dancers, unlike any other population of women I know, are content with and actually *like* their bodies. This acceptance and comfort frequently extend to the other naked bodies with which there is continual interaction. This can open up new spaces for sexual expression:

> I'm experimenting right now. So it's [stripping] opened my mind to different things. I mean, I would never ever ever in a million years would I ever think about touching another woman, when I was growing up. Now there are certain women I would love to go to bed with. I would. You know it's opened my mind to new ... it's expanded my way of thinking (Debbie).

In short, when we explore erotic labour from the perspective of its participants, nuances emerge that speak to the importance of moving beyond dichotomies. We can appreciate that sexuality is imposed, but it is also owned and manipulated as a source of power and pleasure (Pringle, 1988:102); we can furthermore recognize the ways that sexuality and its erotic manifestations can be destabilized and emerge as *contested* terrain. This being said, it is clear that strippers are involved in not only erotic labour but emotional labour as well. As capitalism expands and the service industry swells to include a supply of emotional and interpersonal services (for men) that contribute a commercial imitation of authentic social relationships,[8] the product is not just the service, but the servers themselves. For workers, engaging in this level of emotional labour in an erotic environment has significant ramifications.

NOT AN EASY JOB

As we have seen, strippers are part of the burgeoning service industry, and like other direct-service workers, they do a job that requires erotic and emotional labour. Yet, theirs is not simply a job like any other. So while dancers share many of the processes and practices of working-class women in the work force generally, such commonalties do not negate the need to attend to the specific hidden costs of participation in this marginal labour sphere.

Stripping can be a physically dangerous occupation. As already noted, there is the ever-present threat that customers will act aggressively. In spite of the strategies that all the research participants had developed to protect themselves, over half had stories of violence, often sexual, perpetrated against them.

[...] Like their working-class counterparts in the manufacturing industry, these workers receive little protection from their employers, who appear all too ready to blame the victim. Furthermore, there is a realistic fear that customers will contravene the established parameters (and criminal law) by attacking a dancer outside the club. "In danger? Quite a few times [pause]. Oh ya, sure. I'm working in this little place and there's three young guys.... [When I left] the three young punks they follow me" (Marie).[9] Sometimes the consequences are horrific: "My girlfriend was raped.... Ya, some guy I guess followed her home a couple of times. Y'know, knew where she lived and everything" (Diane).

Physical acts of aggression are not just committed by customers.[...] [T]he relations between dancers, which are shaped by an individualistic and competitive labour structure, are frequently antagonistic. Fights are certainly not the norm, but they do occur, and can be frightening in their intensity. [...]

In short, dancers labour in a highly volatile environment, where the potential for verbal or physical aggression is continually present. This possibility of aggression seems to exacerbate an already stressful environment.

[...] The danger of physical assault is compounded by the physical- and mental-health considerations of labouring in stressful environments (Shostak, 1980). A dancer might work eight hours and make no money, even losing bar and driver fees; or she might earn three hundred dollars during a four-hour period. This instability of income not only increases workplace tensions and conflicts, but increases the stress these workers experience in their day-to-day lives.

[...] For dancers, "role overload," identified as a key contributor to workplace stress (Levi et al., 1986:55), is normal. Dancers must continually negotiate two discrete and sometimes conflicting jobs during their workday. The quasi-contractual obligation of the stripper is to perform strip-tease shows and hang out "looking like a hooker" (Debbie)—tasks for which she receives not a paycheque but the opportunity to "make her money": that is, the chance to utilize the profitable skills of soliciting and playing the game. Her job requires that she fulfil a number of roles at the same time, and that she continually manage the emotional and sexual demands of patrons. She must try to maximize her income while engaging in boundary maintenance and the protection of her emotional and physical space. In addition, dancers are subject to the stress shared by other labourers engaged in emotional work (Adelmann, 1995:372) as well as the particular stressors shared by entertainers—performance anxiety and a fear of even minor physical injuries that could effectively curtail their careers (Sternbach, 1995): "I can't work with black eyes, I can't work with big scars across my face" (Jessie).

What does this mean for workers? Recent research suggests that stress is not simply the result of objective conditions; rather, "it is the interactive nature of the relationship between demands and the perception of the demands that is important" (Tattersall and Farmer, 1995:140). This highlights the importance of subjectivity. If autonomy and control over labour processes mediate against stress (Houtman and Kompier, 1995:210), perhaps the autonomy positively identified by workers in the industry is an important buffer. Seen this way, the definitions of self-as-entrepreneur [. . .] can potentially be understood as part of dancers' stress management strategy. This may be particularly important when we appreciate that some dancers are denied the supportive labour and home environments which are known to mediate against stress (Levi et al., 1986:55).

How individual workers cope with the stressors of their labour-force participation is diverse, and is necessarily shaped by the resources at their disposal and by their personalities. It would appear that humour may both serve as a tactic to mediate stress and affirm boundaries. The ironic distance that is evident throughout the dancers' narratives—in their stories, in their language and in their analogies—speaks to a sophisticated use of humour. By drawing attention to the absurd, not infrequently at their own expense, dancers signal not only their insightfulness and ability to assume distance, but their resistance to the capitalist appropriation of the self. Put another way, this working-class cultural-expressive form positions a dancer to illuminate power relations and insulate herself from their implications. She may be obliged to engage in erotic and emotional labour, but this need not touch her-self.

Of course, not all coping strategies are as benign as humour. Some are potentially problematic and may exacerbate the very dynamics that contribute to stress in the first place. Alcohol and illicit drugs provide readily available means for self-medication:[10] "The days that I can't do it and I need the money, ya, I'll probably smoke a joint—and then I'll go to work" (Debbie). We must appreciate that emotional labourers are particularly susceptible to the abuse of substances (Hochschild, 1983); furthermore, since the dancer's work site is also a leisure site for men, she is surrounded by the markers of social activity. For some women, alcohol and drugs become more than periodic aides. It is important that we acknowledge this potential cost of the occupation but remember that contrary to the dominant discourse, the immoderate use of drugs and alcohol is far from normative. During field work, I witnessed two cases where individuals started to "party" excessively at work. It is a disturbing process to watch and one that aroused a great deal of concern on the part of both dancers and support staff, who frequently attempted to intervene in what was clearly a destructive pattern. Discussing one such situation, Sally remarked:

Fuckin' right I told her. I said, "Look at yourself, you came in here wanting to get money for your baby and now your whole life is the bar. That's what you talk about. That's all you think about. You roll out of bed—you come to work." It's sad, you know.

RETHINKING SKILLS

Skills are generally assumed to be a legitimate barometer of a worker's contribution and thus of the economic and social rewards to which their holder is entitled (Gaskell, 1986:361). Labour stratification is assumed to be a function of degree of skill, so that the distinctions between skilled, semi-skilled and unskilled labour are largely unquestioned outside critical labour studies. In fact, skills are not neutral measures, but are embedded in ideological constructs that reflect gender and class bias, and in turn legitimate wage and status hierarchies (Cockburn, 1986).

The stripper's job, like that of non-unionized working-class women in general, involves hard work and offers limited job security and virtually no possibility of advancement. The job itself is physically exhausting, emotionally challenging and definitely stressful. Success is contingent on the development of complex skills and competencies. The very existence of these skills belies the customary focus on deviance (rather than work process) that is found in much of the literature on strip-club labour. Given that these skills are largely learned "on the job" through informal apprenticeships, the work can be classified as semi-skilled labour. However, the term is misleading, as it suggests that anyone can successfully undertake the tasks. In fact, during field work I observed many women who, enticed by the reported high earnings and relative autonomy associated with stripping, attempted the job but found themselves unable to master the necessary tasks successfully. That these skills are largely dismissed or rendered invisible is not unique to the skin trades, but characterizes many working-class women's jobs (Gaskell, 1986). It does, however, affirm once again the relative and subjective nature of the definition of "skills."

In the late 1970s and early 1980s, we could have argued that strippers received financial compensation consistent with the scarcity of their skills and other attributes brought by them to the marketplace—including the willingness and capacity to suspend traditional propriety, and the ability to transcend social norms regarding the appropriate location for nudity. In addition, they were presumably being compensated for the stigma their work incurred.[11]

With the industry shift towards service, the worker is now required to employ considerably more skill, face more danger and experience more stress than her counterpart twenty-five years ago. However, the work has been rhetorically deprofessionalized[12] and the labour redefined as not just semi-skilled, but essentially unskilled, so that the worker is someone "who can instantly be replaced by another if she or he doesn't smile enough" (Reiter, 1991:129). It would appear that a scarcity of jobs and the virtual absence of good jobs available to young working-class women through the 1980s and 1990s increased the labour pool and facilitated a construction of the dancer's labour as unskilled. When the skills necessary to stripping are scarce and when there is a shortage of labour, skills are recognized. Be that as it may, when the labour and job markets shift, the same (or even more complex) skills are rendered invisible. What we see as skill is always contextually defined and subject to reconceptualization when the labour becomes no less difficult, but labourers more available (Gaskell, 1986:373).

NOTES

1 Bartky's (1988) analysis suggests that in modern society all women are alienated from their physical reality. Compliance with standards of make-up, hair dressing and body clothing renders the woman an ornament. Perhaps the epitome of Foucault's internalized panopticon is the woman who perpetually checks (and fixes) her appearance, ever conscious of herself as an observed object of others' gaze (Bartky, 1988:81). A woman's discipline of the body is seen in body language, especially in her careful movements as she postures and positions her body/object to take up limited space.

2 These might include bringing their own towels to sit on or their own cleaning materials.

3 This approach is most effective with exceptionally attractive dancers whose eroticism is physical or visible. As a result, these women may use the stage as a self-promotion platform and tend to invest considerably more time and money in their appearance than other dancers: costumes, tanning and operations.

4 If a customer is not known to the dancer she will rely on either a tip from a member of the support staff (about cash or conversational clues) or her own reading of indicators including dress, demeanour and body language. Unless there is evidence to the contrary single men are assumed to be "looking" and are almost always targeted before those in groups. The most notable exception is, of course, members of stag parties.

5 Some customers appear to appreciate this approach. The role reversal absolves the patron of the need to approach a woman and positions him to refuse her sexual advances. This is an example of how complex and contradictory the dynamics can be. The woman is positioned as aggressor; the man is not only sought after but freed from the traditional expectation that men approach women.

6 Not "taking it personal" also requires dancers to distance themselves from the positive reactions of the audience. It is acknowledged within the industry that positive assessments must be similarly understood within the context of a scripted game.

7 "Fun" here must be understood in relation to Debbie's particular appreciation of the labour as providing, among other things, the opportunity to exploit men and realize "payback" for past injustices.

8 It is possible that capitalism is responding to the market and exploiting men's insecurity *vis-à-vis* the changing gender relations that have characterized the latter half of the twentieth century. With the erosion of male power that "is based on the compliance of women and the economic and emotional services which women provided" (Giddens, 1992:132), men struggle with the new expectations and their own need for intimacy (Giddens, 1992:180).

9 The driving service is also perceived as offering a level of protection when leaving the work site.

10 I am trying to distance the practice from deviance by pointing out commonality. Using drugs and alcohol in an environment where they are easily available can be compared to a nurse or intern getting colleagues to prescribe (or writing her prescription) for a desired mood-altering substance.

11 It would be misleading to construe the relationship between wages and labour processes as unmediated by exterior factors (Kessler-Harris, 1990:481). We need only reflect on the fact that danger, status, monotony and responsibility are all traditionally sites for labour negotiations.

12 This redefining of labour as semi-skilled is consistent with the trend towards de-skilling that Braverman (1974) identified as characteristic of twentieth-century capitalism. That de-skilling is ideologically and economically useful (for capitalists) is revealed when we realize that throughout the 1980s and 1990s, at the same time as skills were being denied, employers in mainstream sectors of the

labour market were establishing inordinate educational requirements (Rinehart, 1996:78). It would appear that labour-dependent personal-service industries capitalize on existing age, gender and racial stratifications by hiring marginal workers, and then justify their low wages through reference to their marginal status (Reiter, 1991:148).

REFERENCES

Adelmann, Pamela. 1995. "Emotional Labour as a Potential Source of Job Stress" in Sauter, Steven and L. Murphy, eds., *Organizational Risk Factors for Job Stress*. Washington: American Psychological Association.

Adkins, Lisa. 1992. "Sexual Work and the Employment of Women in the Service Industries" in Savage, Mike and A. Witz, eds., *Gender and Bureaucracy*. Oxford: Blackwell.

Aronowitz, Stanley. 1992. *Politics of Identity*. New York: Routledge.

Bartky, Sandra Lee. 1988. *Femininity and Domination: Studies in the Phenomenology of Oppression*. New York: Routledge.

Braverman, Harry. 1974. *Labour and Monopoly Capital: The Deregulation of Work in the Twentieth Century*. New York: Monthly Review Press.

Cockburn, Cynthia. 1986. "The Material of Male Power" in Feminist Review, ed., *Waged Work: A Reader*. London: Virago.

Cole, Susan. 1989. *Pornography and the Sex Crisis*. Toronto: Amanita.

Dworkin, Andrea and C. MacKinnon. 1988. *Pornography and Women's Equality*. Minneapolis: Organizing Against Pornography.

Gaskell, Jane. 1986. "Conceptions of Skill and Work of Women: Some Historical and Political Issues" in Hamilton, Roberta and M. Barrett, eds., *The Politics of Diversity: Feminism, Marxism and Nationalism*. London: Verso.

Giddens, Anthony. 1992. *The Transformation of Intimacy: Sexuality, Love and Eroticism in Modern Societies*. Stanford: Stanford University Press.

Goffman, Erving. 1959. *The Presentation of Self in Everyday Life*. New York: Doubleday.

Goffman, Erving. 1963. *Stigma*. Englewood Cliffs, N.J.: Prentice Hall.

Hearn, Jeff and W. Parkin. 1995. *Sex at Work: The Power and Paradox of Organization Sexuality,* revised edition. New York: St. Martin's Press.

Henry, William and J. Sims. 1970. "Actors' Search for a Self." *Trans-Action* 7, 11.

Hochschild, Arlie. 1983. *The Managed Heart: Commercialization of Human Feeling*. Berkeley: University of California Press.

Houtman, Irene and M. Kompier. 1995. "Risk Factors and Occupational Risk Groups for Work Stress in the Netherlands" in Sauter, Steven and L. Murphy, eds., *Organizational Risk Factors for Job Stress*. Washington: American Psychological Association.

Kessler-Harris, Alice. 1990. "The Just Price, the Free Market, and the Value of Women" in Karen Hansen and I. Philipson, eds., *Women, Class and the Feminist Imagination: A Socialist Feminist Reader*. Philadelphia: Temple University Press.

Levi, Lennart, M. Frankenhauser and B. Gardell. 1986. "The Characteristics of the Workplace and the Nature of Its Social Demands" in Wolf, Steward and A. Finestone, eds., *Occupational Stress: Health and Performance at Work*. Littleton, Massachusetts: PSG Publishing.

Pringle, Rosemary. 1988. *Secretaries Talk: Sexuality, Power and Work*. London: Verso.

Reiter, Ester. 1991. *Making Fast Food: From the Frying Pan into the Fryer*. Kingston: McGill-Queen's University Press.

Rinehart, James. 1996. *The Tyranny of Work: Alienation and the Labour Process*, third edition. Toronto: Harcourt Brace.

Shostak, Arthur. 1980. *Blue Collar Stress*. Menlo Park: Addison-Wesley Publishing Company.

Sternbach, David. 1995. "Musicians: A Neglected Working Population in Crisis" in Sauter, Steven and L. Murphy, eds., *Organizational Risk Factors for Job Stress*. Washington: American Psychological Association.

Sundahl, Debi. 1987. "Stripper" in Delacoste, Frédérique and P. Alexander, eds., *Sex Work: Writings by Women in the Sex Industry*. Pittsburgh: Cleis Press.

Tattersall, Andrew and E. Farmer. 1995. "The Regulation of Work Demands and Strain" in Sauter, Steven and L. Murphy, eds., *Organizational Risk Factors for Job Stress*. Washington: American Psychological Association.

PART SIX
Education

CHAPTER 18

Gay and Out in Secondary School: One Youth's Story

John Guiney Yallop

You made me believe that I could do anything that I set my mind to, and you made me self-confident. That certainly came in handy when I came out to all my friends and family over a year ago…

> —Donnee, an out gay secondary school student, in a letter to one of his
> elementary school teachers (quoted in Guiney, 2002, p. 114)

A PERSONAL JOURNEY

My Master of Education research project, "School Life for Gays: A Critical Study Through Story" (Guiney, 2002) used narrative inquiry to take a critical look at how gays experience school. "Narrative as research method … is less a matter of application of a scholarly technique to understanding phenomena than it is a matter of 'entering into' the phenomena and partaking of them" (Clandinin and Connelly, 1991, p. 260). The research became a personal journey for me as I reflected back on my own life in school as a closeted gay student and later as an out gay educator, a school life that spanned four decades. One participant was Donnee (a pseudonym), a 17-year-old gay male secondary school student who was out at school as well as in other areas of his life. This chapter focuses on Donnee's story as an out gay youth attending secondary school. In the original writing up of my research, I used **_bold italics_** to identify when I was quoting Donnee directly from the interview transcripts.[1] I have continued a similar practice in this chapter, using *italics* when quoting Donnee. In this way I hope to both honour Donnee's voice and allow the reader to share in Donnee's journey through his own words.

WHY STORIES?

Clandinin and Connelly (2000) explain that people "live stories, reaffirm them, modify them, and create new ones. Stories lived and told educate the self and others" (p. xxvi). This education happens through a process of engagement and identification with the stories. While the reader may not have had similar experiences in terms of detail to those presented in this chapter, the *qualities* of the experiences are still there to engage with, to identify with, and to be transformed by: "One of the purposes of narrative research is to have other readers raise questions about their practices, their ways of knowing ... The intent is to foster reflection, storying, and restorying for readers" (Clandinin and Connelly, 1991, p. 277). Dewey (1938) refers to this purpose when he says that the "most important attitude that can be formed is that of the desire to go on learning"(p. 48).[2] What this makes clear is that doing research or reading research texts, like life, is not neatly packaged and does not neatly unfold according to predetermined procedures. Reflection allows each of us to see with the stories of others. Donnee's stories can teach us about ourselves, how we live, and how we know. Reflection is essential in the educative process: "One learns about education from thinking about life, and one learns about life from thinking about education" (Clandinin and Connelly, 1991, p. 261).

METHODS

I contacted Donnee directly to request his participation.[3] While the methodologies for my research were narrative and critical inquiry, I used two specific methods to gather information: the interview and a *letter unsent*.[4]

LIMITATIONS

The story presented here is from one out gay male secondary student. This chapter is not intended to be representative of any population, including out gay male secondary school students. This study is one contribution to the telling of stories and the living of lives. Others may, however, find in the stories resonances with their own lived storied lives.[5]

AWARENESS

The school years are often a time when young gay males become aware of their sexual orientation and form an identity based on that awareness. D'Augelli ... (1998) states ... that the process of evolution of a same-sex sexual orientation may follow the same path as gender development. Because of societal attitudes toward sexuality, however, the former becomes repressed in childhood and does not fully assert itself until later, usually at puberty. The development from self-awareness to self-identity varies across individuals, societies, and time (Savin-Williams, 1995). Citing the two master's theses of Eric Dube and Lisa Diamond at Cornell University, Savin-Williams (1998) noted that younger groups of white gay males did not follow the same developmental path from self-awareness to self-identity that older, white gay males followed. Savin-Williams proposes "differential developmental trajectories" to help us understand the development of a sexual identity. This focus enables us to be more aware of the diversity of gay youth. A gay youth's family and social setting affect this development, as does the youth himself. This approach invites us away from simply looking at averages to looking at the life of each individual. The question "Are you gay or straight?" for Savin-Williams does not capture the complexities of sexuality.

An exclusive focus on mean ages may obscure (Savin-Williams, 1998), because some gay youth report never remembering a time when they were not aware of their same-sex attractions. Such statistics do refute some beliefs, such as the one that homosexuals do not exist in elementary school, a sentiment I frequently heard expressed throughout my career. D'Augelli (1996) points out that while no representative samples have focused on sexual orientation before puberty, the most recent studies indicate that erotic feelings occur before puberty and are later crystallized at or following puberty. Some studies found that the average age of awareness of their sexual orientation for gay youth was 10 years (D'Augelli and Hershberger, 1993; D'Augelli, Hershberger and Pilkington, 1998). Another study puts the age even lower (Savin-Williams, 1998). D'Augelli and Hershberger reported that over 90% of sexual minority youth were aware of their sexual orientation by age 15.

Donnee recalled no early memories of being gay:

> I really didn't think about being gay that young … to be completely truthful the thoughts or ideas never crossed in my head. I was just a regular, everyday kid. Woke up and went to school, had lunch, went outside and played in the playground for the lunch hour, then came in and did a few more classes. It was completely average for the 6 years I was there.

The response of youth to the realization that they have same-sex erotic attractions are varied from relief (that the issue is finally resolved) and joy to depression and self-destructive thoughts and actions (Savin-Williams, 1995). Anderson (1995) states that the realization is sudden because the cognitive development that happens at puberty enables a young person to make the connections that they previously could not. Others view it as a gradual progression. While the responses are diverse, many experience reactions of denial and internalized homophobia before they cross what Adnan (1998) calls the zone of half-denials and half-truths about oneself and one's affections. Lowenthal (1998) recalls being petrified as an adolescent by the vision of his future. Russell (1998) recalls himself from photos as looking like a kid destined to be a pervert. Mabry (1998) recalls the "sick urges." Many gay youth begin dating girls to prove to themselves and others that they are heterosexual (Savin-Williams, 1998). Some even engage in harassment of other gays (Anderson, 1995; Savin-Williams, 1998). The denial and self-hatred intensify at puberty (Chase, 1998; D'Augelli, 1996) and continue until the self reveals itself so strong that resistance becomes impossible (D'Augelli, 1996; Savin-Williams, 1998). It is a particularly painful time, a time when the feeling of difference becomes more acute because the reason becomes more obvious. This feeling of being different is very common among sexual minority youth (Isay, 1989, 1996; Savin-Williams, 1995, 1998). The realization that one will not be traveling the same life path as one's peers is so sad (Holleran, 1998) that some can only talk or write about it in retrospect, as do many of those in Chase's (1998) collection of writers who recall their years in junior high or middle school.

Awareness of same-sex attraction is not the same as adopting a gay identity. Self-identifying or self-labeling usually happens some time, even many years, after becoming aware of same-sex attractions. Particularly noteworthy, however, is that the age at which such milestones as first awareness of same-sex attractions, self-labeling, and coming out or disclosure to others, has been steadily declining since the 1970s. Savin-Williams (1998) presents the results of eight other studies, besides his own, which demonstrate this.

IDENTIFYING AS GAY

Some studies report gay youth self-identifying four years after self-awareness (D'Augelli and Hershberger, 1993; D'Augelli et al., 1998). Savin-Williams (1998) provides a range of experiences in his study of gay and bisexual male youth from self-identifying simultaneously with self-awareness to postponing self-labeling until later in adult life. Youth in Savin-Williams' study reported self-identifying as young as third or fourth grade up to being in graduate school when they reached this milestone.

The catalysts that lead to self-identification as gay vary. D'Augelli (1996) states that solitary and social sexual behaviours impact on how soon a same-sex sexual orientation is concretized. The youth in Savin-Williams' study reported that their first sexual experience with another male was not as significant a factor as falling in love with another male (Savin-Williams, 1998). Isay (1996) makes the same observation.

The belief that one has to be sexually active in order to credibly self-identify as gay is a double standard. This same measure is not used for heterosexuals because heterosexuality is assumed. In one study, adolescents who experienced same-sex attraction waited an average of four to five years after awareness before acting on that attraction (D'Augelli and Hershberger, 1993). Males waited longer than females. Another study revealed that half of the male participants acted on their same-sex attractions prior to puberty (Savin-Williams, 1998). Many youths, however, realize a same-sex identity without same-sex activity (Savin-Williams, 1995). As well, homosexual sex is not the sole domain of sexual minority individuals and, as noted above, heterosexual sexual activity is often engaged in by those of us who are not heterosexuals as *proof* of heterosexuality.

Whenever it happens, self-labeling as gay is a breaking away from heterosexual socialization (D'Augelli, 1996) and the creation of a new self. This journey brings its own challenges. If the individual has knowledge only of fragments of gay life, which is usually the case, he may not be able to identify with that life. Given some of the attitudes toward homosexuals, a youth may even fear identifying as gay (Lipkin, 1995). Once again, this process is not the same for everyone, and statistics may lead us away from individual realities.

Racial minority gay youth have more than one stigmatized identity to explore and claim (Savin-Williams, 1995). There may be a tension because the racial minority and sexual minority youth may feel more attached to, or more supported in, one community than the other. The youth may feel pulled in opposite directions by both communities. Savin-Williams also indicates that this can happen with gay youth who are members of religious communities. Religious restrictions can play a role in delaying self-identifying as gay.

While diverse in *when* they self-identify, gays seem to have similar feelings following their self-identification as gay. Many describe it as a relief (Savin-Williams, 1998). Looking back on his coming out, Chin (1998) said that it gave him back a sense of self and that it was an end to his feeling of worthlessness. Savin-Williams (1995) found a positive link between self-identification as gay and self-esteem. D'Augelli (1996) points out that for today's gay youth, unlike the experiences of many gay adults, coming out happens in a context of gay pride and greater social acceptance.

DONNEE'S AWARENESS AND SELF-IDENTIFICATION

Awareness requires language if one is to articulate that awareness to self and others, and claim an identity. Donnee recalls finding a language in elementary school:

It was probably in grade 8. I can even remember the exact class. It was in health class actually, because we did health all the way up until grade 9. But ... in health class there was a chapter in our book on homosexuality, and I can even remember the teacher being extremely tactful in how she taught that chapter, because she didn't want to impress the students to decide one way or the other ... I can remember her talking about that you might grow up and find that some of your friends are gay and that's okay. I guess that's when the idea of the possibility was put into my head. I guess somewhere deep down I always knew, but when we went through that chapter it kind of struck me. Then I started seriously thinking about it in the right terminology. I may have thought about it in grade 7 but just didn't have a word for it or a way to describe what I was thinking or feeling. But in grade 8 I was given that terminology, and I thought about it then right through grade 8 to grade 9, as well as in grade 10 in high school, and then I finally came out at the end of grade 10 because I had finally managed to make a decision.

Donnee also remembered this first experience of finding a language as being one where he encountered homophobia in school. In talking about the tact that his elementary school teacher exhibited when she spoke about the topic of homosexuality, Donnee recalled that "she even tried to make an effort to kill some of the homophobia that might have been in the room." Donnee added, "there were kids that laughed when that chapter was read and that kind of turned me off talking about it to anyone."

COMING OUT

Donnee related his experience of coming out to someone he knew:

The first person I ever came out to was my best friend at the time. We were up at his cabin. The entire day I kind of danced around it, and I think a lot of people were starting to question whether or not I was, at school. They kind of thought I was but weren't sure ... I kind of hinted towards it and I asked him how he felt, trying to feel him out, to see how he would react. He kind of looked at me strangely and then he answered in a positive fashion, and so that was good enough. I kind of left it. I had almost gotten up the guts to tell him then and there on the dock, but I let it go and kind of went through the rest of the day and the afternoon ... That night I decided that I was going to tell him, and I did tell him that night, and it went extremely well and he was extremely supportive. He thought it was completely fine that I was gay and he didn't have an issue with it and our friendship would never change. Subsequently he has pulled away a little bit in the past 2 years, and the friendship has kind of fizzled out. Now whether or not that's because he knows I'm gay now, I have no idea.

OUT IN SCHOOL

Donnee has not waited until adulthood to come out. After coming out to his best friend, Donnee began a very deliberate process of coming out to his peers:

I had originally decided that I would tell my direct circle of friends, that I would do it in a very paced-out manner and that I would do it in a very quiet manner, and I really had no intention of telling my ... mom right away. And so I worked on that for the next little while, for the next month or so ... We'd be in school and I'd pull someone aside and say to them ... Actually, to go back even further, when I first started coming out I came out as a bisexual, not as a gay man, because I think it was easier for me, and I think in my mind I thought if I came out as bisexual, people would be less shocked because there are still girls involved at times and it wouldn't have been a complete reversal. So, I think that's how I thought. And then eventually, after a while, I got so comfortable saying that I was, I thought about it even more, and I thought this is absolutely ridiculous ... I should just tell people that I'm gay because that's what I really am. So I went back and I changed it, and I talked to people, and that's how it went.

Donnee talks about his coming out experiences in very positive terms:

I never got a negative reaction when I came out to people, so I think that kind of helped me stepping forward and telling more people, and by the time 2 or 3 months had passed it had almost become general knowledge at school without me even trying hard, because it became so natural for me to say, and I think it was because of all the positive reactions that I got that allowed me to do that. And at this point I still hadn't planned on telling ... my mom.

When asked what he thought school was like for a gay person, Donnee spoke about his own reality:

I can really only talk from my perspective, because everybody is different. But I know I started thinking about it at the end of grade 7 and 8 ... the summer between 7 and 8 ... so 7, 8, 9, and 10, there was a 4-year span from the time I started to think about it until I definitely came out. Two and a half of those years it wasn't that big of an issue because I was only thinking about it. I could brush it off when I wanted to. But for the last year and a half to 2 years, personally it was very difficult for me and frustrating that I basically decided who I was and knew who I was and wanted to date people and wanted to talk about it but I couldn't because I was terrified of the reaction that my friends might have. You shouldn't be terrified like that. You shouldn't be terrified about the dating process. It's supposed to be a fun thing to do. The main feelings and sentiments are those of terror, confusion, and frustration. I think that's the main three feelings that people have. Because not only is there the worry about your friends' reactions ... of dating and that kind of thing, but I mean there is also the bullying aspect. As much as we don't want to admit it, there is still mean people out there like that. I've been fortunate enough never really to have encountered any of it, but they are still out there and I know that at schools, even in my city, and I wouldn't be able to be as out as I am.

COMING OUT: THE OTHER RESEARCH

Schneider (1997) points out that while the heterosexual assumption, the assumption that every-one is heterosexual, works well for heterosexuals, it injects considerable complication into the lives of sexual minority youth because, in order to live authentically, they must challenge this assumption. This coming out, Schneider emphasizes, is a developmental process that happens alongside other developmental processes of adolescence.

Coming out is both a personal and a political act (Henderson, 1998). Disclosing one's sexual orientation to others means an exiting from the assumed heterosexual identity and the lifelong expectations that come with it (D'Augelli, 1998). The new gay identity needs to be developed in a gay context (D'Augelli and Garnets, 1995). This cannot be done if the individual remains in the closet and cut off from gay life.

Young gay people come out at different time lapses following their self-awareness and self-identity. In some cases all three happen simultaneously, or the person is *outed,* meaning that their sexual orientation, or perceived sexual orientation, is disclosed by someone else. Sometimes this revelation is also a revelation to the youth. In those cases, the youth is most often a gender nonconforming youth. An average age of disclosure reported by some researchers is 16 years (D'Augelli and Hershberger, 1993; D'Augelli et al., 1998). This first disclosure to another person may be several years after becoming aware of one's sexual orientation and self-identifying as gay (D'Augelli, 1996). D'Augelli and Hershberger found that the average length of time between awareness and coming out to at least one other person was six years. Savin-Williams (1995) found that the most popular time for disclosing to another person was during the first year of college or university. The college experience is an opportunity for prolonged adolescence, which allows a gay person more time to work through internalized homophobia and come out to self and others (Anderson, 1995). The statistics, however, do not reveal the whole story. One youth in the Savin-Williams study disclosed to his parents when he entered junior high school. On the other end are those who are aware of their sexual orientation for many years before coming out. For some, their sexual orientation remains a lifelong secret.

While there is considerable diversity in when gays first disclose their sexual orientation, there is much similarity in whom they come out to. D'Augelli and Hershberger (1993) and D'Augelli et al. (1998) reported that over 75% of gay youth had told a friend first about their sexual orienta-tion. In most cases, this friend is a female (Savin-Williams, 1995). Savin-Williams reported that a considerably smaller percentage, 20%, first came out to a family member. This was usually a sibling rather than an extended family member.

It is significant to note that very few youth disclose first to the professionals in their lives, such as teachers or counselors (5%) and clergy (2%) (D'Augelli and Hershberger, 1993). Despite the fact that I have been an out gay and gay-positive elementary educator for many years, I have never had a student come out to me while they were in the school where I was teaching. Donnee did not come out to any of his elementary school teachers or even mention to them that he was considering that he was gay:

Things changed when I got to high school. I didn't tell any teachers in grade 10, because it was only that year that I had started to come out to my friends, and then I came out to friends, and then my mom, and then to family friends, and then my teachers. They were the last people that I came out to.

Donnee reported coming out to three of his teachers, and he feels that other teachers in the school know that he is gay: "No teachers have treated me any differently since I've told them."

The majority of gay youth do not come out in school. Those who do usually face the most difficult challenges (D'Augelli, 1996). D'Augelli points out that there will probably be more youths facing this experience, and professionals, including, or especially, teachers, need to be prepared to provide them with protection and support.

Two apparently opposing views summarize researchers' opinions about youth disclosing to others their same-sex sexual orientation. Savin-Williams (1998) holds that

> [a]dolescents who disclose to others are generally assumed to experience a diverse array of positive mental-health outcomes that are associated with openness, including identity synthesis and integration, healthy psychological adjustment, decreased feelings of loneliness and guilt, and positive self-esteem. Disclosure is thus assumed to reduce the stress that accrues to adolescents who actively hide or suppress their sexual orientation. (p. 142)

D'Augelli (1998), however, cautions that identifying earlier and coming out sooner may make today's gay youth "vulnerable to psychological risks unknown to earlier cohorts" (pp. 188–89). I do not believe D'Augelli (1998) is suggesting that youth stay in the closet, but that the responsibility for the supports those young people will need is a responsibility that belongs to the adults in their lives. Among those significant adults are educators.

Donnee speculated about why coming out seemed more of a possibility for him in his current educational environment:

> *I don't know if it's because of the school that I'm in, because of the people that are there now, or what it is. But I know that based on other schools' reputations ... if I came out and was as out as I am in the community, I would be uncomfortable with other people in school. I would be more afraid. Because there definitely are bullies in those schools that would probably take some form of action.*

The action that Donnee was talking about he clarified as "physical, violent action." He said that he would be worried about "making it home in the same condition" that he went to school in.

COMING OUT TO PARENTS

Home and *school* are considered *partners* in education. This can be a dilemma for the gay child who may experience both places as sites of homophobia and heterosexism. Even when the youth has a safe space at school, homophobic parents can jeopardize a young gay person, even at school. Disclosure to parents is a very emotionally charged stage of the coming out process, and can put the youth at considerable risk, especially if they are still living at home and going to school

(D'Augelli and Hershberger, 1993; D'Augelli et al., 1998; Henderson, 1998; Savin-Williams, 1998). D'Augelli et al. (1998) reported that the average age of first disclosure to a parent was 17 years. Mothers (65%) were preferred over fathers (9%) for coming out to. In that study, more males than females had disclosed to parents. Mothers (93%) were much more likely to have known or suspected in the case of their gay sons. Mothers were more accepting than fathers, but they were also reported to have been the most verbally abusive. Brothers of gay males were the most likely to be physically threatening and physically abusive. It is abuse, both verbal and physical, as well as the loss of emotional and financial support, up to complete ejection from the family home, that some sexual minority youth experience, and many fear, if they come out.

Pilkington and D'Augelli (1995) found that more persons of colour than white respondents described the prospect of family disclosure as extremely troubling (29% versus 20%). This highlights a major difference between members of other minority groups and individuals who identify as part of a sexual minority. The parents of gays are most often heterosexual, whatever their race, ethnicity, or religion. Heterosexuality is assumed within the family, and families are unprepared to deal with any reality other than heterosexuality. Racial, ethnic, or religious minorities, however, can usually find, within their families, solace and safety from the harassment and discrimination they may experience elsewhere. When gays come out to their families, however, that solace and safety are not always there.

COMING OUT TO MOM: FIRST STEPS

Donnee's story of coming out to his mother is a poignant story of trust, support, and love. It is also a story that contains pain and loss for both:

> One night … I thought, well, maybe I should start or I should tell her something. The night I told my mom I remember it like it was last night … She was in her room lying in bed … doing a crossword … and she was eating a tuna sandwich … I remember walking into her room and sitting down on the corner of her bed by her feet … At that point I knew that I was gay and I had been telling people that I was gay for the past 3 months, but I thought that I'd use the same tactic with her as I used with them … I decided that I would tell her that I was bi if I was going to tell her anything … I knew that when I told her, her immediate thought would be, "Oh my God, I'm not going to have any grandchildren." I knew that would be the first thought that she would have in her head … I had actually done research on coming out to your parents prior to telling her. I had gone on the net, and I had read books and I had asked people about it … I wanted to be able to answer those questions when she asked them … I wanted to be able to defend my thinking. Not to say that I would have to defend myself against my mother, but that I just wanted to make sure that I had the knowledge to tell her. I told her … the exact words that I used were … "I think I'm bisexual."
>
> She kind of laid down her sandwich and her mouth gaped open and that was kind of to be expected, and I wasn't shocked by the reaction I got. And all things considered I think that I have the greatest mom on earth, for the type of reception she gave me. We didn't talk about it much that night. She told me that, you know, if it was something I was thinking

about, then I had to be sure, that she would love me either way, no matter what I decided, but she thought I had to give it some time before I made my final decision. And she also told me that she thought I would have to experience both sides before I was able to make my decision. And by experiencing both sides, I mean have sex with a member of each sex. And of course, she promoted safe sex all the way through, as a mother would. And that was about it … I gave her a big hug and a kiss and left the room, and she went back to her crossword puzzle.

COMING OUT TO MOM AS GAY

Three or four months after coming out to his mother as bisexual, Donnee came home one night later than expected. The van belonging to the friend he was with had broken down. His mother had been extremely worried. As he walked in the door he met her anger, her joy, and her tears:

I asked her what's on the go, and she said that she was worried that I had gone out and gotten picked up by some guy and something, anything, could have happened to me and she was worried. And so that's when it all came out. I told her that, look, I would never do something like that, not without you knowing and without setting up safety guards. I wouldn't meet anyone off the internet unless I knew enough about that person to feel comfortable and unless I had safety nets put in place to know that if something did go wrong that I would be able to get out of the situation.

Donnee did eventually go on a date with someone he met on the internet. This date was with his mother's permission and with safety nets in place:

It had obviously been weighing on her mind. We stayed up the next hour and a half talking about college, my career, the family, absolutely everything under the sun, and I appreciate that. I appreciate that so much because I know that there are not a lot of kids out there who have mothers that would care that much or would be that support-ive. We also talked about dating, and we talked about bringing other guys home. We talked about sex. I was surprised about the amount she knew. She told me about gay friends that she had had in her 20s and she blew my mind by the amount of information she knew as well, because she went quite into depth. We also had a talk about safe sex.

Donnee related one painful part for him of his experience coming out to his mother. He also talked about what he believed his mother was facing:

The only bad feeling that I was left with that night was that one of the sentences that Mom told me that night, and I remember the sentence word for word exactly as she told me, "You realize that the family bloodline will end with you?" And hearing that line killed me. I didn't know what to think at first, and then the fact that she had said that in the open and the facial expression she had … when she told me that, and the tears that were streaming down her cheeks when she told me that, the only way to describe it was that it killed me, because although she was right ... I could certainly adopt ... I do have other relatives that will carry on. It just meant that my particular bloodline would probably end, and that's depressing to an extent. But at the same time, I don't believe that I should live my life in a lie for that one reason. I don't think that's enough.

She didn't say [this] to hurt me, and I know she didn't say the line to hurt me. I think she more or less said it to bring it out in the open and make sure that I realized, and I also think she said it because she was shocked as well. Her thoughts, her questioning of whether or not she had a gay son, had been confirmed that night, and she knew for sure, for 100% sure, that night that she was never going to have any grandchildren. And I think she said it for that reason. And it's fine, because we were both shocked that night ... Since then she has been completely supportive. I don't think I'd be wrong in saying that she is probably one of the most supportive parents I've ever encountered, and she's amazing for that reason. Since telling her that night that I was gay for sure was probably the most liberating experience that I had ever gone through in my life. While it was extremely difficult to go through emotionally, it completely changed my life, because I knew then that I would be able to date ... It felt like there was 20 tons coming off my shoulders, that I didn't have to hide anymore, and that I didn't have to not be who I was.

When Donnee's mother told him that she didn't want to see him "bringing home a guy next week" Donnee understood. "I understood that because I had a year and a half to think about this by now and she's had 3 months. So I understood that, and I didn't [bring home a guy the next week]." Subsequently, Donnee's mother has met some of his dates:

Since I've come out I've probably seriously dated seven other guys and the one I was with for 6 months and Mom knew him well ... She's met at least four of them ... One of them slept over one night, actually. She made the stipulation, when I asked her if he could sleep over, that he had to sleep in another room, but I was fine with that. I can respect that. Even parents of straight kids don't let their children sleep with the person they are seeing right off the bat.

Donnee's mother has also met members of the various gay community groups he is involved in.

THE INTERNET

Certain realities highlight the generational differences between some of Donnee's and my own experiences. The internet is one of them. When I was Donnee's age, the manner in which he now uses the internet as a gay youth was the stuff of my science fantasy. Donnee used the internet as a first avenue to explore gay culture. The use of the internet for this purpose began as research around grade 9:

I went to different sites about coming out and about being young and gay and this kind of thing ... Towards the middle of grade 9 and getting closer to the end, I started looking for visuals and looking at guys and saying to myself, "Well, he's good looking," and being able to say it to myself. And that's when I started to pin things down for sure. And then it was the summer between grade 9 and 10 ... when I started chatting ... and I have been chatting for 2 years.

The year before telling his mother that he was bisexual, Donnee had been chatting with other gay and bisexual males on the internet. Donnee said that there was danger with chatting on the internet, but he also felt that it was positive

because it gave me kind of a support group and people to fall back on ... I had been going there for quite some time and I had developed friendships. I had developed really strong friendships from the room, and there were people that I had wanted to meet, and mom probably knew that, but I continuously said no to them for the simple safety factor. For an entire year of my life I was going online, I was going to this room, and every time I got off my computer I was deleting the cache. I was deleting the history and I was doing computer cleanup and I was covering my tracks, for a year. And I think that's what finally pushed me to tell people and to tell Mom. It was because I got fed up with covering who I was, that I was covering my tracks, like I felt like I was a criminal in my own house and like I couldn't even do the things I wanted to do even on my own computer.

OUT, AND AN ACTIVIST AT SCHOOL

While many students still do not feel safe enough at school to come out, and many educators, whether queer or heterosexual, are oppressed into silence by homophobia and heterosexism, Donnee has found that he has a voice and he uses it to make a difference:

Health Canada put out a booklet for teenagers who are young and confused and trying to decide if they are gay or what their sexual orientation is ... I took one of them to school and I passed it to my guidance counselor and I told her that I felt our school should have some literature on that subject because there was nothing there for any student who was thinking about it, and she has taken the booklet and she has ordered a box of one thousand of them from Health Canada. So there's support within my school.

THE FUTURE

My sexual orientation became an issue for me as I was looking at career choices. While working as an educational assistant I became very attracted to teaching. I felt that it was a natural fit for me, but one day I recall saying to someone from whom I was seeking advice as I made my decision, "I want to find a career where I will not experience homophobia." His response was that my choices would be very limited. He encouraged me to not limit my choices and to do what I wanted to do. Once I had figured out what that was, I did. Despite the homophobia and heterosexism that I have encountered in the education community, I have remained grateful to him for that advice.

Donnee seems to have no such concerns about his future:

Well, career-wise, when I finish high school I am planning on going to our university here in the province and doing a Bachelor of Arts in English, and then I will be moving to Toronto when that's done and over with ... and I'll be doing a Bachelor of Journalism. As to how that relates to me being gay, I don't think it really changes much. I don't think the fact that I'm gay is going to change the career that I want to get into or how I go through the career. The other career choice that I'm planning on making is to go into politics for political office. Being gay may have a bit more impact there, but I don't plan on letting it ... You know, I wake up every morning and I put my pants on one leg at a time just like everybody else in the city, province and country. So the fact that I'm gay, I don't think it should make a difference and I won't let it make a difference in the career that I choose. That's how it relates to my career, that's how I've decided to let it relate to my career: I'm going to live my life, and if I run for a position or whatever, they bring their wives up on the stage, if I've got a husband he's coming up there with me. It's not something that I'm going to hide or make an effort to hide, but it's not something I'm going to flaunt either. The same way as I live my life.

A FINAL WORD OF THANKS

When I asked Donnee to write a *letter unsent* to one of his elementary school teachers, he responded with a touching letter to a teacher who had made a difference in his life. His letter, I feel, contains a message for all educators:

I wanted to write to you to tell you that I think I have become successful and part of it can be attributed to you and all the help that you gave me when I was going to school ... It makes a lot of difference when the teacher actually cares enough to sit down and get to know the students ... My life was probably drastically changed and my self-esteem boosted by all the encouragement and support that you gave me. You made me believe that I could do anything that I set my mind to, and you made me self-confident. That certainly came in handy when I came out to all my friends and family over a year ago ... That is definitely something I wouldn't have been able to do if you hadn't been there to make me feel like I was important ... I wanted you to know that you did make a difference in someone's life, and that is probably what makes teaching so worthwhile. Thanks a lot.

NOTES

1 This manner of honouring voice was used by Shields (1997) in her PhD thesis.

2 According to Packwood and Sikes (1996, p. 343) narrative also "attempts to recognize and capture the fragmentary, fractured, and chaotic reality of the research process for all of the individuals concerned. It embeds that process within the textual product. The voice of the researcher telling the story/stories of the research becomes part of the polyphony through which the text evolves. The dilemmas and tension are made explicit as a counterpoint to the harmony."

3 This contact was made following approval of my research by the Brock University Senate Research Ethics Board. An Information Letter and a copy of the Informed Consent form were given. Donnee selected his own pseudonym. As Donnee was under 18 years of age at the time of the study, it was necessary that

his mother also agree to his participation in the study and sign the Informed Consent form. Parental consent was received once Donnee had decided that he wanted to be a participant in the study.

4   Qualitative research interviews, unlike quantitative interviews, do not have as a goal the collection of *hard data* such as statistics or percentages. Qualitative interviews are open and do not have set techniques or rules (Kvale, 1996). Kvale calls the qualitative research interview "a construction site of knowledge" (p. 42). Both the researcher and the interviewee are engaged in that construction of knowledge. The reader of the final research text also constructs knowledge by engaging with the stories told. "The qualitative interview is theme oriented" (p. 29). The themes of the interview that I conducted with Donnee were themes from his experiences in school as a gay student. Oakley (1981) says that "the goal of finding out about people is best achieved when the relationship of interviewer and interviewee is non-hierarchical and when the interviewer is prepared to invest his or her own personal identity in the relationship" (p. 41). In the Information Letter, I identified as an "out gay elementary school teacher." I felt that it was important for Donnee to know that he was talking with another person who identified as gay. As well, prior to the interview, Donnee became familiar with some details of my life. The interview with Donnee was carried out by telephone from his home. Donnee lives in a Canadian city with a population of less than 200,000. The interview was tape recorded and transcribed. Donnee received a copy of the transcript of his interview for review and approval prior to the contents of the transcript being used for the study. The purpose of this exercise is to give the participant an opportunity to produce a reflective piece of writing subsequent to the interview. It was anticipated that the thoughts and feelings generated during the interview would need a vehicle for further exploration and expression. Donnee was asked to write a letter to one of his former elementary school teachers. This letter was given to me and formed part of the data for this study. Donnee's *letter unsent* was cited at the opening of this chapter.

5   Finally, the interview with Donnee was conducted at a specific time and place, and I write from a time and a place in my own life. If the times and the places were different, how Donnee would tell his stories might be different. Which stories I would write from those he told might also be different. Lives and the telling of stories of lives are not static. We change, and how we view our lives changes as we experience new events and situations across our lifespan (Dewey, 1938).

REFERENCES

Adnan, E. 1998. "First Passion." In C. Chase (ed.), *Queer 13: Lesbian and Gay Writers Recall Seventh Grade*. New York: Rob Weisbach Books.

Anderson, D.A. 1995. "Lesbian and Gay Adolescents: Social and Developmental Considerations." In G. Unks (ed.), *The Gay Teen: Educational Practice and Theory for Lesbian, Gay, and Bisexual Adolescents*. New York: Routledge.

Chase, C. 1998. "Introduction." In Chase (ed.), *Queer 13*.

Chin, J. 1998. "The Beginning of My Worthlessness." In Chase (ed.), *Queer 13*.

Clandinin, D.J. and F.M. Connelly. 1991. "Narrative and Story in Practice and Research." In D. Schon (ed.), *The Reflective Turn: Case Studies in Educational Practice*. New York: Teachers College Press.

Clandinin, D.J. and F.M. Connelly. 2000. *Narrative Inquiry: Experience and Story in Qualitative Research*. San Francisco: Jossey-Bass.

D'Augelli, A.R. 1996. "Lesbian, Gay, and Bisexual Development During Adolescence and Young Adulthood."

In R.P. Cabaj and T.S. Stein (eds.), *Textbook of Homosexuality and Mental Health*. Washington, DC: American Psychiatric Press.

D'Augelli, A.R. 1998. "Developmental Implications of Victimization of Lesbian, Gay, and Bisexual Youths." In G.M. Herek (ed.), *Stigma and Sexual Orientation: Understanding Prejudice Against Lesbians, Gay Men, and Bisexuals*. Thousand Oaks, CA: Sage.

D'Augelli, A.R. and L.D. Garnets. 1995. "Lesbian, Gay, and Bisexual Communities." In A.R. D'Augelli and C.J. Patterson (eds.), *Lesbian, Gay, and Bisexual Identities Over the Lifespan: Psychological Perspectives*. New York: Oxford University Press.

D'Augelli, A.R. and S. L. Hershberger. 1993. "Lesbian, Gay, and Bisexual Youth in Community Settings: Personal Challenges and Mental Health Problems." *American Journal of Community Psychology* 21, no. 4: 421–48.

D'Augelli, A.R., S.L. Hershberger and N.W. Pilkington. 1998. "Lesbian, Gay, and Bisexual Youth and Their Families: Disclosure of Sexual Orientation and Its Consequences." *American Journal of Orthopsychiatry* 68, no. 3: 361–71.

Dewey, J. 1938. *Experience and Education*. New York: Macmillan.

Guiney, J.J. 2002. "School Life for Gays: A Critical Study Through Story" (Master of Education Research Project, Brock University).

Henderson, M.G. (1998). "Disclosure of Sexual Orientation: Comments from a Parental Perspective." *American Journal of Orthopsychiatry* 68, no. 3: 372–75.

Holleran, A. 1998. "The Wind in the Louvers." In Chase (ed.), *Queer 13*.

Isay, R.A. 1989. *Being Homosexual: Gay Men and Their Development*. New York: Avon Books.

Isay, R.A. 1996. *Becoming Gay: The Journey to Self-acceptance*. New York: Henry Holt.

Kvale, S. 1996. *Interviews: An Introduction to Qualitative Research Interviewing*. Thousand Oaks, CA: Sage.

Lipkin, A. 1995. "The Case of a Gay and Lesbian Curriculum." In Unks (ed.), *The Gay Teen*.

Lowenthal, M. 1998. "Lost in Translation." In Chase (ed.), *Queer 13*.

Mabry, M. 1998. "Mud Pies and Medusa." In Chase (ed.), *Queer 13*.

Oakley, A. 1981. "Interviewing Women: A Contradiction in Terms." In H. Roberts (ed.), *Doing Feminist Research*. London: Routledge and Kegan Paul.

Packwood, A. and P. Sikes. 1996. "Adopting a Postmodern Approach to Research." *Qualitative Studies in Education* 9, no. 3: 335–45.

Pilkington, N.W. and A.R. D'Augelli. 1995. "Victimization of Lesbian, Gay, and Bisexual Youth in Community Settings." *Journal of Community Psychology* 23: 34–56.

Russell, P. 1998. "Underwater." In Chase (ed.), *Queer 13*.

Savin-Williams, R.C. 1995. "Lesbian, Gay Male, and Bisexual Adolescents." In D'Augelli and Patterson (eds.), *Lesbian, Gay, and Bisexual Identities*.

Savin-Williams, R.C. 1998. *And Then I Became Gay: Young Men's Stories*. New York: Routledge.

Schneider, M.S. 1997. "Pride, Prejudice and Lesbian, Gay and Bisexual Youth." In M.S. Schneider (ed.), *Pride & Prejudice: Working with Lesbian, Gay and Bisexual Youth*. Toronto: Central Toronto Youth Services.

Shields, C. 1997. "Behind Objective Description: Special Education and the Reality of Lived Experience" (PhD dissertation, University of Toronto).

CHAPTER 19
Canadian School Lethargy

David Rayside

T he 'take-off' pattern displayed in changes to relationship and parenting policies during the 1990s and early 2000s might anticipate widespread change in Canada's public schools. But it does not. Until recently, the activist challenge on schools issues in most of the country has been strikingly modest, and so has the response of educators and officials.[1] The stark truth is that, with only one important exception, Canadian school boards and provincial education ministries took almost no significant steps in developing policies and practices accepting of differences in sexual orientation and gender identity until the end of the 1990s. At the provincial level, no provincial government had taken serious steps to acknowledge sexual diversity before the mid-2000s. Even on the issue of harassment and bullying, around which so much evidence of harm was available, there is next to no evidence of concerted action beyond generic prohibitions on discrimination and harassment.

There is no obvious way in which mobilizing by religious conservatives could be blamed for this policy failure. Neither could a significant portion of the popular media be blamed for fomenting opposition to inclusive change, as it could be in the United States and Britain. Part of the reason must lie in the relatively low levels of activist pressure for change until the late 1990s; part, too, in the political caution that permeates the ranks of Canadian educators and policy makers when it comes to issues related to sexuality.

BEFORE THE MID-1980s: ALMOST UNBROKEN SILENCE

The oppressiveness of schools for sexual minorities received only sporadic attention within the lesbian and gay movement through the 1970s and early 1980s. Explicitly discriminatory treatment of educators Doug Wilson (in mid-1970s Saskatoon) and John Argue (in Toronto later in the same decade) briefly raised the profile of schooling. The refusal of Montreal's Catholic school board to rent facilities to a gay group also led to a successful court ruling in 1980. Some time would pass, however, before sustained activism focusing on schools was to emerge.

Toronto saw the beginnings of an activist network among educators in the early 1980s, supported by reform trustees on the city's public school board, though with little impact on policy. A proposal for a lesbian/ gay liaison committee was defeated in 1980.[2] A year later sexual orientation was removed from the board's anti-discrimination policy governing students, and a new policy set limits on discussion of homosexuality in schools and banned 'proselytization.'

1985–90: CAUTIOUS GAINS ON AIDS AND FORMAL EQUALITY RIGHTS

The rapid spread of AIDS, and the media dramatization of the epidemic in the mid-1980s, provided an opening in schools, as it did in other policy areas. The urgent need to reach adolescents with public education on the spread of HIV put pressure on schooling authorities to include AIDS education in the curriculum and, in the process, to acknowledge gay sex. AIDS policies were in fact widely developed across Canada, although only a minority required preventive action and, as Morgan Vanek points out, even fewer discuss even the basics of human sexuality.[3] The gains secured by activists in this period, in other words, were isolated and half-hearted. In 1987 Ontario's provincial government required AIDS education in all schools from the seventh grade on—the first large province to do so—but the fears associated with homosexuality remained strikingly in place. In 1988 provincial policy was changed to allow the inclusion of sexual orientation issues in the physical health education curriculum, but there is no evidence that this opportunity was widely taken up. Sexuality in general was still largely avoided in Canadian schools, and what passes for sex education remained sequestered in small curricular moments that were as antiseptic as teachers and administrators could make them.

[...] [T]he addition of sexual orientation to the province of Ontario's Human Rights Code provoked intense and prolonged debate in the legislature and the media. That debate seemed to re-energize activism within educator networks and among students and parents. [...]

Across the country, the inclusion of sexual orientation in provincial and territorial rights codes in the second half of the 1980s and the early 1990s extended formal protections to teachers, and potentially to students. By this time, some general anti-discrimination and harassment measures adopted by school boards included sexual orientation, but were accompanied by little or no discernable action. With rare exceptions, school officials ignored the subject, and teacher unions were generally not proactive in taking advantage of what openings there were, even if several unions in other sectors were. Informal networks of lesbian and gay teachers were forming, but with little visibility.

1990–99: SPREADING ACTIVISM, BACKLASH, ISOLATED SCHOOL RESPONSE

The 1990s saw continued incremental change in Toronto's public school system, and at decade's end encouraging signs of change in a few other boards across the country. In the late 1990s teachers in British Columbia developed a highly visible campaign to confront homophobia and heterosexism in schools. Yet there was still no cross-country take-off in activism among educators, nor was there an equivalent to the growing wave of student groups that was emerging in the United States. Provincial and territorial education ministries showed no signs of seizing the issues being raised by activists.

Toronto's Public School Board

In 1990 Toronto's public school board debated an equity policy that included a provision for an instructional unit on sexual diversity in senior high school health education.[4] This proposal grew out of pressure applied in earlier years to recognize sexual diversity in the student population and to the consequent 1987 creation of the human sexuality counselling program. Once again, religious conservatives mobilized against what they saw as the promotion of homosexuality, but pressure from progressive schooling networks and community supporters helped secure approval in principle.

One year later, local elections increased the number of progressives on the board, including an openly gay trustee, John Campey. Soon after, the board approved the creation of a new equity office responsible for curricular development related to the full range of diversity issues, including sexual orientation. In 1992 Campey pressed forward with motions to the board securing the staffing for the Human Sexuality Program, removing the prohibition on proselytizing homosexuality, adding sexual orientation to the board's harassment and anti-discrimination policies, and approving the fleshed-out curricular plan on sexual orientation. Religious-right opposition was mobilized once again, but the whole package of motions carried.

*****

In the fall of 1995, the board launched the Triangle Program, a form of alternative school modelled on the Harvey Milk School in New York, but different in that it was a fully academic program operated by the board. It provided up to twenty students at a time with a gay-positive curriculum and a counselling support system beyond what would be available in other schools.

These developments were just at the time that a new Conservative government of Ontario was threatening to cut school spending and return to basics. It was also forcing an urban amalgamation that would by decade's end combine the relatively progressive Toronto School Board with more traditional boards in neighbouring municipalities. In 1997, the year that measure was passed, the Toronto board approved its most expansive equity statement yet, aiming to set a new benchmark for the amalgamated board.

The first signals from the expanded board were not encouraging. In late 1998 and early 1999, a new equity policy draft covered only race issues. Only after pressure from both inside and outside the board was it broadened to include the full range of equity issues, sexual orientation among them. It covered each area comprehensively, addressing harassment, teacher training, support for student programs challenging homophobia, even curricular inclusiveness. This was the most expansive board policy yet developed in Canada, and it aimed at change in both elementary and secondary schools.

This policy provoked an intense debate within the school system and the local press, and encountered particularly virulent opposition from the very conservative Toronto District Muslim Educational Assembly and other right-wing religious groups. Late that year, however, the new policy was approved (with 'implementation' documentation approved the next year). By this time, there were signs of favourable change elsewhere in Canada, and particularly on the West Coast.

Gay and Lesbian Educators in British Columbia and the BC Teachers Federation

In British Columbia, Gay and Lesbian Educators (GALE-BC) had been working to address homophobic school climates from the beginning of the decade, but in small numbers and with little impact until the late 1990s.[5] In the fall of 1996, a GALE delegation met the New Democratic government's education minister Paul Ramsey, to press his department to take action. One of the teachers was James Chamberlain, an elementary school teacher in Surrey, a suburb south of Vancouver, where the school board was dominated by Christian conservatives. Soon after the meeting, the director of the ministry's curriculum branch sent a letter to the Surrey Teachers' Association indicating that a variety of families, including those with same-sex parents, should be included in discussions of family units in elementary classes.[6]

Early in 1997 Chamberlain asked his board if he could use three children's books for his kindergarten class: *Asha's Mums*, *Belinda's Bouquet*, and *One Dad, Two Dads, Brown Dads, Blue Dads*. He heard nothing for three months. In February, fellow GALE activist and teacher Murray Warren (with the backing of his local teachers association) proposed to no avail that the Coquitlam School Board establish a committee to study the challenges facing lesbian and gay students.

Both teachers, and the other members of GALE, also worked inside the province's teacher union. This bore fruit in March 1997, when the BC Teachers' Federation (BCTF) annual convention approved (with 96 per cent support) a resolution to create a program to eliminate homophobia and heterosexism in the BC public school system. The convention was picketed by conservatives brandishing signs that read 'No Homo Promo' and 'Stop Homosexual Recruitment in Schools.'[7] BCTF's offices were besieged by up to two thousand phone calls a day.

Right-wing opponents, dominated by the Christian right and spearheaded by a group calling itself the Citizen's Research Institute (CRI), were soon organizing across the province. Ten thousand copies of a 'Declaration of Family Rights' were distributed to encourage parents to pressure schools and school boards to reject any teaching or teaching materials that 'discusses or portrays the lifestyle of gays, lesbians, bisexuals and/or transgendered individuals as one which is normal, acceptable, or must be tolerated.' [...]

[...] [O]n 24 April, at a [Surrey] school board meeting packed with delegations and spectators, the board voted to ban the three books that James Chamberlain had asked about earlier in the year.[8]

BC premier Glen Clark condemned the action, and Education Minister Ramsey looked into whether the Surrey trustees had violated provincial curricular regulations. [...]

It was in this context, with the religious right as fully mobilized as it had ever been in BC, that the government introduced two new legislative bills aimed at recognizing same-sex relationships in family law. [...] Rallies organized by the CRI that fall attracted hundreds of supporters. The campaigns ultimately failed to obtain enough signatures, but they were effective enough to have scared the NDP government and education ministry officials. For example, a resource centre created as part of a 1997 Safe Schools initiative by the provincial government contained no materials on homophobia and heterosexism, at a time when the risks facing sexual minority students were widely known. In addition, rather than add gay-positive resources to a provincially approved reading list, which is what GALE had been demanding, the ministry eliminated the list altogether to leave such choices entirely in the hands of local boards.

The 1998 annual convention of the BCTF entrusted to GALE the development of a program to eliminate homophobia and heterosexism in schools. Workshops for teachers were developed by the summer, and before long several were mounted across the province. [...] These were encouraging grassroots developments, but there was still nothing in the provincially mandated curriculum that obliged or even induced schools, or boards, to take advantage of the resources now made available to them.

A large 1999 adolescent health survey across the province showed what had been found elsewhere, namely, that there was pervasive anti-gay harassment in schools, and widespread alienation among sexual minority youth.[9] In response, no one even pretended that any board in the province had made much progress in confronting the problem.

Developments Elsewhere

There were signs of activism in a few other Canadian centres, often first provoked by concerns over harassment and bullying. In 1993, Winnipeg school officials found widespread anti-gay sentiment in a student survey, and proposed action to confront it. When the possibility of board action became publicized, though, enough opposition was mobilized that trustees took no action.

Calgary's public school board added sexual orientation to its harassment policy in 1994, after the publication of evidence on the risk to sexual minority youth in the city. [...] Proposals for further action by the public board, however, were met by a wave of opposition, and resources required for effective implementation of new policy were dissipated.

*****

In Quebec, provincial curricular materials on homosexuality [...] had been prepared in the early 1990s. The regional health and social services coordinating agency in Montreal also provided training for teachers and school officials who wished to address issues related to homosexuality. But all this was optional, and through the 1990s only rarely taken up in any school system, especially in Catholic boards.

When Quebec's Human Rights Commission held hearings on sexual orientation in 1993, provoked by violence directed at homosexuals in Montreal, the issue of schooling was largely absent. [...] Activist attention to schooling was growing at mid-decade. In Montreal, the Groupe de Recherche et d'Intervention Sociale gaies et lesbiennes de Montréal (GRIS) was formed in 1994 by educators, community members, parents, and students. The group was focused on opening up opportunities to speak about sexual diversity in schools, and providing trained speakers to do just that. The youth help-line Gai Écoute was also aiming to publicize its service to schools, and in 1996 it sent letters to every French high school in Quebec, asking them to list the group's telephone number in school diaries issued routinely to students. But school response was tepid. Only 5 per cent of Catholic schools in the province responded positively to Gai Écoute's request.

Across Canada, only a few teacher unions had placed sexual diversity issues on the front burner. The Elementary Teachers' Federation of Ontario was active, building on the women's public teacher union that was one of its predecessors. The Saskatchewan Teachers' Federation was starting to take action at decade's end, as did the Alberta Teachers' Association, which approved (by overwhelming majority) a code of professional conduct that required teachers to instruct in a manner that respected sexual diversity. And the BCTF continued to be a leading advocate for change.

1999 AND AFTER: SLOWLY WIDENING LOCAL ENGAGEMENT

Activism in a few large-city school boards across Canada started bearing fruit at the end of the 1990s and the first years of the new decade, in Winnipeg, Vancouver, Victoria, and Montreal. A few other boards, for example in southern Ontario, were also taking up issues of sexual diversity. The inclusion of sexual orientation in school board non-discrimination and harassment policies was now routine across Canada. [...]

Provincial Lethargy until the Mid-2000s

School violence was in the headlines during 1999, the year of carnage at Columbine High School in Littleton, Colorado. Soon afterwards, a shooting occurred at a high school in Tabor, Alberta, increasing pressure on educational authorities to treat bullying and violence seriously. [...] Such events had some impact in Canada [...] but only modest.[10]

The Ontario legislature approved a Safe Schools Act in 2001, dramatically increasing penalties for bullying and violence. It was not tailored specifically to any one form of harassment, and its strategic focus on punishment came under attack for being used to target visible minority students. All this ensured that there was no focused debate on the specifics of homophobic violence, and little in the way of effective and widespread change in practice.

The pattern of provincial inaction prevailed in Quebec until the middle of the 2000s. Homophobic bullying became a front-burner issue early that decade in Montreal's French-language school board, and among unions representing the province's teachers; but the provincial education ministry remained unmoved by the mounting evidence that the province's schools were just as rife with prejudicial climates as schools in the rest of the country.[11]

British Columbia seemed it might be an exception. GALE activists had been pressuring provincial authorities for years on a variety of gay-related school issues. And then in 2000 a dramatic story unfolded. In March, Hamed Nastoh filled his knapsack with rocks and jumped off the Patullo Bridge over the Fraser River in Surrey. He left a suicide note that talked of being relentlessly picked on. He was called a variety of names, some just for being too good a student, but there was one part of the bullying that was especially difficult, as he recounted in his suicide note: 'I couldn't take it anymore. School is the main reason. It was horrible! Every day I was teased and teased. Everyone calling me Gay! Fag! Queer!, and I would always act like it didn't bug me and ignored them, but I was crying inside. It hurt me so bad! Please tell the people at school why I did this. I don't want somebody else to have to do what I did.'[12]

Pressure to act also came from the provincial auditor general who in 2000 recommended that the risks facing students use of anti-gay climates be addressed promptly and effectively.[13] [...]

*****

A right-wing Liberal provincial government, elected in 2001, seemed ill-inclined to take up sexual diversity initiatives, but they did establish a Safe School Task Force in 2002, which then heard substantial testimony about homophobic bullying. The task force delivered a report one year later, though, with no recommendations specific to anti-gay school climates. Later, in 2004, the provincial education ministry's guidelines on safety failed to specifically address harassment and violence based on sexual diversity. [...]

In 2006, the provincial education ministry agreed to the creation of an optional Grade 12 social justice course that would include attention to sexual diversity, in response to a human rights complaint against the limitations of the provincial curriculum, launched several years earlier by a Coquitlam teacher and his partner. If it is launched, it will probably be the first such course in Canada, and one that is provincially mandated, but it is hardly a breakthrough. By announcing that it would be optional, the ministry was once again planning to pass the buck to local school boards.[14]

Teacher Caution

In legal terms, public school teachers have been protected against discrimination based on sexual orientation for years, and by the end of the 1990s no denial of benefits to same-sex parteners could withstand constitutional scrutiny. Also, by the early years of the new decade, several provincial unions were taking up sexual diversity issues, most prominently in BC, Quebec, Alberta, and Ontario. The national LGBT rights group Egale was prioritizing schools and developing a network of educators, even if its tiny staff and broad mandate allowed for the allocation of no significant resources to the network.

Still, few teachers were out enough to take advantage of the formal supports available to them. In 2000–01, a survey of the Elementary Teachers' Federation of Ontario membership gave respondents an opportunity to self-identify as members of a variety of disadvantaged groups, and only 0.9 per cent flagged sexual minority status.[15] Teachers remain a cautious lot, and the great majority seem reluctant to rock the boat. Coming out, or talking freely about sexual orientation, is still considered controversial.

*****

Across Canada, there has been little teacher education on sexual diversity issues. Pioneering work was undertaken in the late 1990s at the University of Saskatchewan, and the University of Alberta's Faculty of Education has developed some prominence in teaching and research related to sexuality. The Ontario Institute for Studies in Education has several faculty interested in questions of sexual diversity, and early in the 2000s it created an in-service course on homophobia for teachers. As course instructor Tara Goldstein has pointed out, though, teachers are still worried about including the work on such a course in their teaching portfolios.[16]

Students Claiming Visibility

Pressure for change from students themselves has increased noticeably in the last few years. There are also, of course, more students than ever who are out at school, especially in urban areas. This obviously makes it hard to keep the issues that relate to them completely invisible. An important part of the story of American student activism has been the formation of Gay-Straight Alliances, and while the spread of such groups in several major urban centres in Canada has lagged behind the major U.S. surge in the late 1990s and early 2000s, the numbers are now becoming significant. In 2000 the BC Teachers' Federation approved a resolution supporting the formation of GSAs in the province's high schools and middle schools. GALE also produced guidelines and modest bursaries to stimulate their spread, so it is not surprising that BC saw the first significant cluster of such groups. By late 2004 about half of Vancouver's public high schools had them, and in total there were about thirty across the province.

In Alberta, the first GSA to form (in 2000) was in Red Deer, the centre of religious conservatism in an already relatively conservative province. Local schools had already confronted questions about racial prejudice, since the community was home to James Keegstra, one of Canada's most notorious purveyors of prejudice against religious and racial minorities. That seemed to arm schools with a willingness to take on other diversity issues. In 2004, interest in the formation of such groups spread rapidly in Edmonton, and by year's end there were five in that city (one in a Catholic school). There was evidence of similar expansion in Toronto's public schools and in some of the surrounding suburban areas.

In 2006 the Canadian Teachers' Federation issued a handbook on the development of GSAs, which may have helped spread the idea beyond the areas in which they are now prominent. By mid-decade, the 'Day of Silence,' an idea first developed by the U.S. Gay, Lesbian and Straight Education Network in 1996 to dramatize the silencing of sexual minorities in schools, and much facilitated by GSAs, was starting to spread in Canada.

In a growing number of schools across Canada, students were also claiming the right for same-sex partners to attend school social functions, and proms in particular. Many have secured that right without publicity, and with little opposition, so it is difficult to know how widespread this challenge to such bastions of heterosexism have been. One Ontario student's prom plans, though, did gain notoriety (see box).

Marc Hall and Monsignor John Pereyma Catholic Secondary School[17]

In early 2002, Oshawa's Marc Hall had never been to a Pride march, and he didn't see himself as a gay activist. He just wanted to take his boyfriend to the senior prom. But the principal told him that allowing a same-sex couple to attend would contradict school policy and Roman Catholic teaching. This was unsurprising in some ways. The leadership of the Roman Catholic archdiocese supported the Vatican's conservative line on homosexuality, and the Oshawa community was relatively traditional, with only modest gay visibility. On the other hand, a few other Catholic school boards in southern Ontario had allowed lesbians and gays to bring their dates.

Hall soon found backing from a variety of local groups, including PFLAG. He was also supported by the Canadian Auto Workers—one of the country's largest unions and a major force in this car-manufacturing city. In March, the CAW's nationally prominent president, Buzz Hargrove, wrote to the school principal, urging the acceptance of sexual diversity in the community and the student body: 'Today we spend a great deal of time in our educational programs working to dispel myths and stereotypes about gays and lesbians, and challenging our members to understand these issues as fundamental rights and freedoms. We call upon you as an educator to do the same.'

Hall's cause was supported by the leader of the generally cautious provincial Liberal Party. Dalton McGuinty was himself a practicing Catholic, and he headed a party that in the past was not reliably supportive of gay rights. But this time, his public appeal to the Durham Catholic School Board was unequivocal: 'By refusing to allow him to attend the prom with his companion, Marc Hall is being denied some of the most basic rights as a human being and as a Canadian. I cannot understand how the decision to invite his boyfriend to his high school prom poses a threat to Catholic education.'

But the board was unmoved, voting unanimously against changing their prom policy. Hall took the case to court in May, supported by a coalition of groups that included Egale. On 10 May, just hours before the prom, Justice Robert MacKinnon ruled in Hall's favour, clearing the way for Hall and his partner to attend.

Policy Change at the School Board Level

Bullying was often the wedge issue that students and other proponents of change could most effectively use to apply pressure on school boards. The power of stories of harassment, and sometimes violence, coupled with growing social science evidence on the prevalence of anti-gay behaviour, was not lost on advocates for change at the local level.

In Winnipeg, for example, the issue of anti-gay school climate had been first raised in 1993, though it would take another six years before concerted action was taken in the city's largest board (District Number One). A committee was created in April 1999 to look at gay bashing in high schools, a move recommended by lesbian trustee Kristine Barr, and supported by an openly gay city mayor, Glen Murray. At meetings on the subject in the same month, many students and parents spoke in support of the committee's mandate.

At the same time, anti-gay positions were staked out by many of the sixty delegations who appeared to speak before the board. The group Parents Against Heterophobia warned of the dangers of children becoming confused if they were to hear talk of homosexuality as an accepted lifestyle. [...] Two conservative radio show hosts then picked up the issue, and accused Barr of attempting to recruit children.

The board reacted by moving ahead cautiously, restricting the committee's mandate to high schools, but the policy deliberation process gained momentum. Once the storm of opposition had passed, the board put into place the most concerted awareness program of any school system in the country. Workshops were planned for the 2000–01 school year and made compulsory for all high school staff across the system.

In Ontario, a few school boards in the areas surrounding the metropolitan region of Toronto were beginning to address the issue. Beyond that, an initiative was being spawned in the relatively conservative southwestern Ontario city of London. [...]

*****

Elsewhere in Ontario, two cases of homophobic bullying were challenging school inattention to the issue. In 2002 high school student David Knight and his sister launched a legal suit after years of bullying directed at him and his sister in elementary and secondary school. His sister Katie had been harassed to the point of leaving school. In northwestern Ontario, the Ontario Human Rights Commission mediated a settlement in 2005 between the Lakehead District School Board and Gabriel Picard, with the board committing itself to the development and application of policies addressing sexual diversity. (Neither of these challenges produced the kind of large settlements that shocked many school authorities in the United States.)

Local Developments in BC

Even in the face of an unresponsive provincial government, schools issues retained a high profile in BC, and activist networks remained active. James Chamberlain launched a court challenge, with the support of GALE, the BC Teachers' Federation, and the BC Liberties Association, to the Surrey School Board 1997 ban on gay-themed books. In 2002, a 7–2 majority of the Supreme Court of Canada rejected the board's argument that these books were unsuitable for five- and six-year-olds, reasoning that children could not learn tolerance 'unless they are exposed to views that differ from those they are taught at home,' and that such teaching was always age-appropriate.[18] The court also cited the BC School Act in asserting that boards could not apply the religious views of one part of a community 'to exclude from consideration the values of other members of the community.' Writing for the majority, Chief Justice Beverley McLachlin of the Supreme Court of Canada then said, 'The requirement of secularism in s.76 of the School Act, the emphasis on tolerance in the Preamble, and the insistence of the curriculum on increasing awareness of a broad array of family types, all show, in my view, that parental concerns must be accommodated in a way that respects diversity. Parental views, however important, cannot override the imperative placed upon the British Columbia public schools to mirror the diversity of the community and teach tolerance and understanding of difference.'[19]

The Supreme Court's *Surrey* ruling could be cited across Canada in response to right-wing resistance to curricular change, even if it would not oblige any board to be more inclusive in its curriculum.

*****

In Vancouver, the 2002 local elections had produced reformist majorities in the city council and the public school board, for the first time in years. Not surprisingly, given the string of controversies over recent years, progressive school board candidates had raised the issue of school safety, and specified the importance of inclusiveness for sexual minority students and staff. Early in the following year, school trustees approved the creation of a Lesbian, Gay, Transgendered and Bisexual Issues Advisory Committee (later renamed the Pride Education Advisory Committee) with a very broad mandate to suggest changes to address sexual diversity. The committee had close working relationships with such groups as GALE, PFLAG, and Gay Youth Services, and so had lots of support in thinking expansively about what needed changing. In early 2004, the board approved a wide-ranging policy extending far beyond homophobic harassment, including curricular reform.

In 2003, the Greater Victoria School Board adopted recommendations aimed at fostering respect and safety for sexual minority students, including the transgendered, after being pressured hard by students in area schools. The code of conduct developed for schools included a prohibition of discrimination based on sexual orientation, gender identity, and gender expression, and educators were to take proactive steps to counter homophobic harassment. Support services were to be established; students groups taking up these issues were to be supported; and curricular resources were to reflect diversity. Elsewhere in BC, in Prince George, a site of so much controversy a few years earlier, the public school board approved recommendations on raising awareness of sexual diversity in 2004. The Gulf Islands and the North Vancouver school districts enacted anti-homophobic policies in 2006.

Quebec's Distinct Pattern

In Quebec significant uptake of sexual diversity issues in schools began only in 2002, but then spread quickly. During the 1990s, the Catholic school system had resisted any public acknowledgment of these issues. Secularization was more powerful in Quebec than anywhere else in Canada; however, the province's largest school board, the Conseil des écoles catholiques de Montréal, had been dominated by relatively conservative voices. (All publicly funded schools in the province were still formally Catholic or Protestant.) The rapid decline in the proportion of Montrealers with school-aged children, coupled with a pattern of lopsided municipal elections, contributed to electoral turnouts of as low as 20 per cent, creating opportunities for more highly motivated conservative Catholics to retain control over schooling. The city's Protestant school board had long had relatively secular leadership, though it too had never developed proactive policies on sexual diversity.

In 1998 the province's schools were reorganized on linguistic rather than denominational lines, resulting in a new French-language and secular Commission scolaire de Montréal. The new board had a progressive majority that included openly gay councillor Paul Trottier, though it would still take time to overcome fears associated with discussing sexuality in schools. Increased community activism and heightened attention to high rates of suicide among Quebec's gay and lesbian youth helped push the board towards more inclusive policy.[20] By 2002 sexual orientation and transsexualism were added to its harassment policy, and a resolution on initiatives to support sexual minority students was approved with virtually no vocal dissent.

There was no doubt that schools in the board's jurisdiction needed change. A 2002 study of teachers and administrators, commissioned by the board, showed widespread awareness of school-based homophobia, with three-quarters of respondents agreeing that they knew little about homosexuality and were in need of more information.[21] Another study showed, not surprisingly, that few teachers were out.[22] Faculties of education were giving virtually no attention to sexual diversity in the professional training they offered. Research published in 2003 and 2005 portrayed the province's schools as dramatically unfriendly to sexual minorities, using language indistinguishable from that used in studies of schools across most of North America over the previous decade.[23] A report issued by Quebec's Human Rights Commission in 2007 found little evidence of systematic school uptake of what resources were available to combat homophobia in schools in Montreal, let alone in other regions of the province.[24]

Quebec's unions representing teachers were now taking up the issue of homophobia. In late 2002 the Centrale des Syndicats du Québec (one of two unions to which Quebec's teachers belonged) launched a video entitled *Silence SVP* (Silence Please) on homophobia in school environments that was destined for students and educators across the province. In the meantime, student groups had been forming in several of the province's regions, joining together to form the Regroupement de jeunes allosexuelles du Québec (Queer Youth Coalition of Quebec). The Lesbian Mothers' Association, an influential force, was also engaging issues related to elementary schooling.

In Montreal, the Groupe de Recherche et d'Intervention Sociale gaies et lesbiennes de Montréal (Gay and Lesbian Research and Information Group, GRIS) was better resourced, and finding expanded opportunities to speak about sexual diversity in schools. It had two hundred volunteers by the mid-2000s, and a staff of three (largely through funding from the provincial ministries of health and justice). It was now visiting a few hundred schools a year, up from about thirty in the late 1990s, widely distributing resource guides for teachers, and recruiting well-known media personalities to publicize its work.[25]

Still, as recently as 2004, 40 per cent of Montreal's French-language schools, and 60 per cent province-wide, were still unwilling to list Gai Écoute's contact number in student diaries, and the group felt obliged to offer assurances in its materials that it was not trying to recruit students. At this late date, too, the provincial ministry of education appeared largely inactive. A day-long information workshop organized in 2002 by the Human Rights Commission on youth and homosexuality in schools, and attended by school officials, teachers, and agency representatives from across the province, was not attended by officials from the ministry. As one youth agency worker commented in 2004, 'At the Commission scolaire de Montréal, things are really changing; and on the ground in some schools, things are really changing. But when we go to the ministry of education, it's like a desert—nobody talks, nobody moves.'[26]

Since then, there are signs of significant movement, at last.[27] The provincial ministry has begun showing real interest in school homophobia. A 2007 Human Rights Commission report on homophobia in all sectors of society called for all schools (including religious ones) to engage in campaigns to combat homophobia, training for all school personnel on issues related to sexual diversity, and more inclusive curricula in faculties of education. What may result is a pattern reminiscent of policy change in the recognition of same-sex relationships—not particularly ahead of the curve by Canadian standards, but wide-ranging once it comes.

Policy Development and Implementation Gaps in the Toronto District School Board

Toronto District School Board's policy legacy provides an opportunity to explore questions of implementation. Recall that the year 2000 saw the passage of an equity implementation plan by the school board that had been first in the country to develop a comprehensive approach to sexual diversity, including gender identity. This plan—obligatory from kindergarten to grade twelve—stated that 'ideals related to anti-homophobia and sexual orientation equity be reflected in all aspects of organizational structures, policies, guidelines, procedures, classroom practices, day-to-day operations, and communication practices.' It specified that the curriculum should reflect these and other forms of diversity, and that all learning materials should be checked for bias.

Implementation was another matter. Radical cuts to provincial spending on schools during the second half of the 1990s and the early 2000s, and a prioritization of basic skills, effectively moved equity issues farther away from the core mission of schools. There were drastic cuts to the Toronto Board's Equity Department in 2003, and a reduction in counselling support provided to the Triangle Program. The absence of administrative support for diversity programming was destined to leave teachers relatively unpressured and unprepared to change. No doubt many of them were already using gay-positive resources in their classrooms, but most were not, either because they were personally uncomfortable with the issues, fearful of taking any steps beyond the provincial curriculum, or uneasy about parental reaction. Most teachers seem only dimly aware of their board's equity policies, and many of those who are more aware seem disinclined to act assertively on them.[28]

Attempts to teach inclusively were also still encountering vocal opposition from religious conservatives. The Campaign Life Coalition warned of the prospect of graphic sex education becoming ubiquitous in Canadian elementary schools, its president predicting that children would be provided with depictions of anal sex and other homosexual practices as appropriate alternatives.[29] In some parts of Toronto, conservative Muslims were among the most vocal of critics (see box).

Market Lane Public School, 2004

In 2004 a large group of parents, most of them Muslim, protested a workshop on sexual diversity held for staff and some students at their children's school.[30] A few parents talked about the school corrupting their children and insufficiently accommodating their faith. They were supported by the Toronto District Muslim Educational Assembly, which had intervened forcibly a few years earlier in opposition to the inclusion of sexual orientation and gender identity in the school board's equity policy. Its print materials accused the school board of indoctrination and the promotion of a homosexual lifestyle, and provided parents with forms requesting that their children be withdrawn from all discussions of moral corruption that were offensive to their faith.

The principal of Market Lane Public School convened a special information session for parents in November, though from the outset he made clear that board policy mandated the kind of workshop he had approved. At the meeting, school officials set out the board's equity policies, making clear that the recognition of religious differences could not extend to the infringement of other people's rights. After the formal presentations, various audience members raised objections to the workshop, more than one suggesting that it trampled on their religious rights. But a couple of the intervenors who identified as Muslim made clear that they were struggling with the issue and were open to the board's policy. One cited rulings of the Supreme Court of Canada that recognized lesbian and gay rights as human rights. Another talked of the need to live together, and to work on what he acknowledged was a sensitive issue for all religions. The meeting ended calmly, as it had begun.

Soon after, provincial premier Dalton McGuinty addressed Muslim parents concerned about their children being exposed to school discussions of homosexuality, arguing that teaching students to respect differences was important. Education Minister Gerard Kennedy spoke in similar terms when he said he did not think there was harm in exposing children 'to ideas that are different than the ones they teach at home,' perhaps coincidentally echoing the language of the Supreme Court of Canada in the Surrey School Board case.[31]

In some ways the Market Lane school story affirms the possibility of change even in a community of largely first-generation immigrants, from parts of the world where no recognition is accorded to sexual diversity. On the other hand, it demonstrates that taking up these issues requires clear-headed determination from school leaders on the ground. There is no doubt that few principals would have welcomed workshops on sexual diversity, or other forms of teaching about it, even in a board that technically obliged them to act inclusively.

Tim McCaskell, long a member of the equity staff at the Toronto School Board, has come to discouraging conclusions about the absence of effective means to implement the policies that are in place.[32] He tracks the gradual whittling away of resources devoted to equity initiatives of all sorts, hastened by provincial cuts to educational spending, just as formal board policies were developed for the full range of equity issues. Financial crises sharpened the focus on what was said to be the curricular core, and longer-term political shifts were highlighting the practical utility of public education. Faced with a new and more demanding provincial curriculum, few teachers and principals were rushing to fully incorporate equity principles into everything they taught.

The Toronto experience is a vivid illustration of an implementation gap that is inevitable in the translation of schools policy into practice. Try as they might, education departments and school boards cannot monitor everything that goes on in classrooms, and they would not even aspire to do so. Teachers and principals are professionals, and even if they are generally a cautious lot they are expected to exercise discretion every hour of the day. They are also expected to do far more than they are realistically able to, in the face of students with highly disparate learning skills. Schools are expected to respond to students with an extraordinary range of social and cultural circumstances. When a set of issues associated with sexuality gets added to the mandate of schools and teachers, even well-meaning educators will fail to respond proactively enough, or respond at all.

Implementation gaps work both ways, though, and we know that many teachers and principals have taken up the challenges of sexual diversity without the pressure or guidance of board policy. This would undoubtedly have been true before Toronto's school board developed inclusive policy. It is also true of many teachers in the Roman Catholic school system in Toronto, and undoubtedly of some school principals. These are not publicized, for school officials have a delicate path to follow between church doctrine and what they often know to be the needs of their students. But anecdotal evidence in Toronto and elsewhere indicates substantially more positive recognition of sexual diversity in Catholic schools than would be predicted by the stance taken on questions of sexual difference by the Vatican and the Canadian hierarchy.[33]

EXPLAINING LETHARGY

In Canadian schools, talking about sexual diversity in positive terms is still widely avoided. Until 2000 there was only sporadic talk of challenging homophobic school climates, and outside Toronto there was almost no policy development on the subject at either the local or the provincial level. Curricular change was almost entirely absent, even in that school system where most change in formal policy had occurred.

The slow start to the development of inclusive school policy, and the equally slow spread of practices that recognize sexual diversity in Canadian schools, are out of synch with developments on same-sex relationships and parenting. Why this should be so, especially in the face of overwhelming evidence that action is urgently needed, and in a political system with clear constitutional prohibitions on discrimination, is not altogether clear.

One institutional reason is that the substantial provincial leverage over schooling reduces the room for local innovation.[34] Canadian provincial and territorial governments tend to develop more detailed curricular guidelines than state authorities do in the United States, and across most of the country this regulatory detail is increasing.

School boards are also larger than they were, and more uniformly large than in the United States. This can act as a constraint on educational ideas coming from particularly progressive urban areas. This does, to be sure, reduce inequities between schools and districts, allows for economies of scale that are unavailable to very small boards, and in theory allows for a wider spread of inclusive policies once adopted. But it makes change more difficult to effect, and discourages many who might otherwise try.

Where questions of diversity have assumed high priorities in urban Canada, the very rapid growth in numbers of visible minority students has also given pride of place to race in recent years. This will sometimes push sexuality issues to the side, and may sustain nervousness about the controversy that might arise if such issues are raised. Such fear will often rest on unproven stereotypes of social conservatism among immigrant populations, though it is also reinforced by the opposition to public recognition of sexual difference by vocal representatives of visible minorities in such centres as Toronto and Vancouver.

Teachers, as we have seen, are generally cautious about pushing against boundaries. They are heavily circumscribed by curricular expectations, and by the rules and norms associated with a profession that is in the public limelight. The fact that their work brings them into close contact with young people, in a position of authority, increases the concern about being seen to step out of line. Until provincial curricular guidelines clearly direct educators to address questions of sexual diversity, and education faculties spend more time developing skills in addressing sexual diversity, most teachers will not fill in gaps.

Most activist teachers who seek change have only recently had support within their unions. And just at the time when those unions are taking up sexual diversity issues, they have also been confronted by provincial government retrenchment in a range of social policy sectors. Public schools have been under siege in several provinces, and this has often driven teachers and their unions towards a defence of what are seen to be core concerns.

Student activism has also not been as widespread in Canada as in the United States, at least not until very recently. At some level this is understandable, given the power of sexual and gender anxieties among young people. However, the same is true in the United States, and we shall find surprising levels of activism in schools there, and a preparedness to confront authorities even in very conservative areas.

One reason for modest levels of activism among educators and students is the weakness of organizational support for challenges to school complacency. The major national LGBT group, Egale Canada, has begun attending to schools issues only in the last few years. And even if it had begun earlier, it has nothing close to the scale of resources available to its American counter-parts. The kind of litigation that has been an important part of the American schools story is especially hard to sustain in the absence of substantial outside support. Unions have intervened on gay-related cases, but so far only rarely on schooling.[35]

Canadian complacency might be reinforced by the relative weakness of the religious right in Canada. Conservatives do raise alarms about schools, but their arguments have less and less credibility across most of Canada. And because they are less likely than their American counter-parts to resurrect the whole litany of reformist schools policies that they have fought against in the past, they arouse less activism among non-gay reform advocates. In any event, because Roman Catholics have their own school systems in much of Canada, the voices of Catholic conservatives are inactive on debates over public schooling, reducing the strength of claims by religious conservatives of other faiths.

Complacency, too, is reinforced by the extraordinary gains made in other policy realms. Most Canadians believe that the acceptance of same-sex relationships, up to and including mar-riage, speaks to overall policy inclusiveness, and they probably believe that schools have moved further than they have. LGBT activists without children, or whose own school experiences are far behind them, may also not be aware of how resilient past patterns are, especially in the absence of high-profile struggles over education.

CONCLUSION

The Canadian story on school inclusiveness is a late starter, and it has been moving at a slow and cautious pace in most of the country. In the late 2000s, across the country, great anxiety persists among educators when the subject of sex or sexuality gets raised. Proposals to address sexual diversity routinely confront patterns of hesitation and avoidance, and policy implementation meets the same barriers. Where policies have moved in adventurous and encouraging direc-tions, we do not yet have evidence of effective curricular change and of the kind of personal and principled commitment required among teachers, principals, and staff on the ground. Sig-nificant policy improvement has been effected in a few school districts and in a minority of schools. In many schools and classrooms, students, teachers, and school principals have made real changes to the classroom and extracurricular climate with the leverage of progressive board policy and sometimes independently of policy silence. But most of the story is riddled with complacency, with educators and politicians avoiding the subject.

NOTES

1 There are not many sources discussing the record of Canadian activism or its impact. Tom Warner, *Never Going Back,* provides useful information on activism. Various contributions to James McNinch and Mary Cronin, eds., *I Could Not Speak My Heart: Education and Social Justice for Gay and Lesbian Youth* (Regina: Canadian Plains Research Center, University of Regina, 2004) also address the current need for more schools' attention.

2 On early developments, see John Campey, Tim McCaskell, John Miller, and Vanessa Russell, 'Open-ing the Classroom Closet: Dealing with Sexual Orientation at the Toronto Board of Education,' in *Sex in Schools: Canadian Education and Sexual Regulation,* ed. Susan Prentice (Toronto: Our Schools/

Our Selves, 1994), 82–100, and Tim McCaskell, *Race to Equity: Disrupting Educational Inequality* (Toronto: Between the Lines, 2005).

3 Vanek was reporting, in personal correspondence, on a survey of school policies undertaken for Egale Canada, 2007.

4 This section relies partly on McCaskell's account in *Race to Equity* and on news stories over many years in *Xtra!* magazine and other local media.

5 Miriam Smith discusses BC educator activism in 'Questioning Heteronormativity: Lesbian and Gay Challenges to Educational Practice in British Columbia, Canada,' *Social Movement Studies* 3 (October 2004): 131–45.

6 Kim Bolan, 'Surrey School Teachers Fight Ban on Books about Same-Sex Families,' *Vancouver Sun,* 25 April 1997. See also Michael Valpy, 'Gay Books in the Classroom,' *Globe and Mail,* 9 November 1997.

7 See Raj Takhar, 'Queer Kids Want Support,' *Angles* (April 1997); Ian Austin, 'Gays Recall Abuse in B.C. Schools,' *Vancouver Province,* 17 March 1997; and Kim Bolan, 'Demonstrators Face Off over Homosexuality Issue,' *Vancouver Sun,* 17 March 1997.

8 Three days later, a meeting of Parent Advisory Groups from across the province approved resolutions proposed by a Surrey parents group opposing gay-positive materials in schools. One of the motions opposed curricular material dealing with same-sex couples or any material prepared by 'homosexual lifestyle advocacy groups,' and it passed 165–158. Stewart Bell, 'Ban Urged on Teaching about Homosexuality,' *Vancouver Sun,* 28 April 1997.

9 'Being Out: Lesbian, Gay, Bisexual and Transgender Youth in BC: An Adolescent Health Survey' (Vancouver: McCreary Centre Society, 1999).

10 The 2000 Alberta Schools Act required boards to establish a safe and caring environment for all students, and sexual orientation was not explicitly named.

11 A highly publicized study on LGBT youth at risk was published in 2002 by Michel Dorais, *Mort ou Fif* (Montreal: Editions de l'homme, 2001).

12 'Incessant Teasing by Schoolmates Drove B.C. Teen to Suicide,' *National Post,* 16 March 2000.

13 Auditor General of British Columbia, 'Fostering a Safe Learning Environment: How the British Columbia Public School System Is Doing' (2000), 61–2.

14 See Gary Mason, 'A Mother's Six-Year Saga of Sorrow,' *Globe and Mail,* 3 June 2006.

15 Equity and Women's Services, ETFO, Report to the Annual Meeting, August 2001. See also Noreen Shanahan, 'Safe at School: Gay and Lesbian Issues in the Classroom,' *Our Times* (February/March 2006): 30–5.

16 Presentation to 'Hearts and Minds,' a conference organized by the Sexual Diversity Studies Program, University of Toronto, 2003.

17 Drawn from Jan Prout, 'Canada: Student Fights for Gay Prom Date,' *PlanetOut* News, 28 March 2002, http://www.planetout.com/news; and CAW website, http://www.caw.ca/whatwedo/pride.

18 *Chamberlain v. Board of Trustees of School District No. 36 (Surrey).* For an analysis of the case, see Bruce MacDougall and Patti T. Clarke, 'Teaching Tolerance, Mirroring Diversity, Understanding Difference: The Effect and Implications of the Chamberlain Case,' in McNinch and Cronin, *I Could Not Speak My Heart,* 193–219.

19 Surrey trustees were still intent on discovering ways to secure the heterosexuality of school environments. In 2005, they cancelled a planned performance of the *Laramie Project* (based on Matthew

Shepard's 1998 murder in Wyoming). And then, in 2006, they turned down a request that the children's book *King and King* be used in its schools. In the meantime, however, they had acquiesced (in 2003) in the use of two books recognizing diversity in families.

20 Laval University Professor Michel Dorais was a key player in highlighting the risks of inattention to this issue, with work sponsored by Gai Écoute. As recently as 1998, sexual minorities were not identified as a risk group in a Health and Social Services report on suicide! 'Stratégie Québécoise d'action face au suicide' (1998), cited in the Quebec Commission des droits de la personne et des droits de la jeunesse (Human Rights Commission Report), *De l'égalité juridique à l'égalité sociale*, 39.

21 Daniel Martin and Alexandre Beaulieu, 'Besoins des jeunes homosexuelles et homosexuels et interventions en milieu scolaire pour contre l'homophobie' (Commission scolaire de Montréal, Service des ressources éducatives, May 2002).

22 Union research reported in Quebec, Commission des droits de la personne et des droits de la jeunesse, *De l'Égalité juridique à l'égalité sociale*, March 2007, 25–6.

23 See, for example, Irene Demczuk, 'Démystifier l'homosexualité, ça commence à l'école' (GRIS, Montréal, 2003); Alain Grenier et al., 'Résultat de l'enquête exploratoire sur l'homophobie dans les milieux jeunesse' (GRIS, Montréal, 2005).

24 Commission des droits de la personne et des droits de la jeunesse, *De l'égalité juridique à l'égalité sociale*, 27.

25 The resource guide is written by sociologist Irene Demczuk, 'Démystifier l'homosexualité.'

26 Interview conducted by author, June 2004.

27 This is based on an interview with Bill Ryan (McGill University), 9 May 2006.

28 I say this on the basis of an annual questioning of my undergraduate students (in a large course dealing with sexual diversity) on their school experience. Jordan DeCoste came to similarly discouraging conclusions about implementation in an unpublished paper, 'The Problem of Leftist Tokenism for High School Anti-Homophobia Initiatives' (January 2005). See also Ronnalee Gorman, 'An Exploration of TDSB Anti-Homophobia Equity: The Roles and Responsibilities of an Intermediate School Principal' (MSW research paper, York University, 2004); and Noreen Shanahan, 'Safe at School: Gay and Lesbian Issues in the Classroom,' *Our Times* (February/March 2006): 30–5.

29 See http://www.campaignlifecoalition.com/press, accessed on 8 December 2004.

30 The content of this box is based on personal observation.

31 *Gale Force* 15, no. 2 (March–April 2005), 4.

32 Tim McCaskell, *Race to Equity*.

33 Catholic school officials were concerned about anti-gay bullying in Calgary in the 1990s, at the same time or even earlier than officials in the public board. One of the GSAs formed in Edmonton high schools in the early 2000s was at a Catholic school. The Marc Hall school prom case revealed that some other Catholic high schools in the Greater Toronto Area had allowed same-sex partners to attend proms without incident. I also ask my own students (third-year undergraduate) about their schooling experience, and many who have come out of Catholic systems have reported positive experiences around sexual difference.

34 For a comparative treatment of Canadian public education, see Ron Manzer's excellent book *Educational Regimes and Anglo-American Democracy* (Toronto: University of Toronto Press, 2003).

35 Marc Hall was able to find help from the local CAW, but that kind of help is not yet routinized.

CHAPTER 20

Sexing the Teacher: Voyeuristic Pleasure in the Amy Gehring Sex Panic

Sheila L. Cavanagh

The deviant is not just the person who performs specific aberrant acts; the deviant is also the person through whom society communicates its beliefs and disciplines behavior into either normative or deviant categories through punishment, torture, ridicule, shame, exclusion, and voyeurism. These performances allow the "good" people of society to discuss, relish, pity, reconstruct, and narrate the deviant from a position outside.
— Kari Kessler, "The Plain-Clothes Whore: Agency, Marginalization, and the Unmarked Prostitute Body"

During a moral panic … the media become ablaze with indignation.
— Gail Rubin, "Thinking Sex: Notes for a Radical Theory of the Politics of Sexuality"

News headlines about the Amy Gehring sex panic read as follows: "Lusty Lessons: Ontario Teacher's Fate Now Lies in Hands of UK Jury"; "Boozy Teacher Had Alley Sex with Two Underage Boys and Bedded a Third"; "Teacher Too Drunk to Recall Having Sex with Boy"; "Amy's Pervy as Any Man"; "Sex Case Teacher 'in Row after Sex with Brothers'"; "A Jury in Guilford, England May Decide Today on the Fate of Canada's Lustiest Teaching Export"; "Boy Tells Jury of Drunken Encounter at Party: Night I Lost Virginity to Biology Mistress"; "Sex-Charges Teacher Labeled Risk by Police"; "Science Mistress Admits Kissing and Cuddling Boy, 15"; "Where Do Fallen or Flagrant Women Turn for Public Rehabilitation?"; "Canadian Teacher Cleared of Sex Charges"; "Amy's Caresses Were Wrong but Not Harmful."[1]

Feminist theoretical frameworks demand a critique of the sensationalist media coverage surrounding twenty-six-year-old former teacher Amy Gehring and allegations that she indecently assaulted two former students in the British school to which she was recruited in 2000 from her native Canada. Like most sex scandals involving female teachers in North America and the United Kingdom, the case has received a great deal of media fanfare; the former teacher has been morally condemned by school administrators, educational authorities, the mainstream press, concerned citizens, and so on.

Meanwhile, queer and psychoanalytic theory allow us to see that the Gehring case is scandalous not because it involves an instance of professional misconduct (although it does) but because it taps into a fear of who the feminine subject can be in sexualized power dynamics and what these dynamics do to heterosexual bifurcations of gender, intergenerational hierarchies in the school, and Oedipal resolutions to the troubling demands of the heterosexual matrix. Female teachers like Gehring seem to violate Western conventions of gender associated with the prototype of the younger, presumably passive female subject and the older, allegedly more aggressive male counterpart of the heterosexual encounter; intergenerational prohibitions on sex (with its associated refusal of ascetic motherly love imbued in the construction of the feminine teacher role); and the mythology of the "good girl" attributed to the sexual subjectivity of girls and young women in the school.

For feminists, the Gehring case begs the question of who the feminine subject of the feminist imagination can be and whether this vision is subject to mutation. Lisa Sigel, feminist and cultural porn historian, claims that "sexuality like pottery, changes over time and across cultures, and its representation reflects broader changes in the dynamics of power and vulnerability. My job is to expose the complex interaction between erotic fantasy and political reality."[2] Similarly, the media-induced scandal over Gehring reveals a change in what the public is able to think about the feminine subject as teacher and her sexual capacities. The case is appalling to conventional morality because it provides an instance in which the feminine subject is not a passive sexual object but allegedly an aggressive predatory object. It therefore provides an affront to societal conventions and understandings of the female subject in the realm of the sexual.

For queer theorists, the Gehring case enables us to understand gender, sex, and power as discursively produced (in the media reports). Female-teacher sexuality is read as queer and, consequently, subject to public debate and psychic anxiety. The heterosexual matrix is revealed to be unstable, and questions can now be asked about what active, allegedly predatory female-teacher sexuality does to traditional Western gender binaries governing the modern organization of heterosexuality.

*****

The Amy Gehring story made newspaper headlines in January 2002. It was one of the most controversial school sex scandals involving a Canadian-born female teacher in recent memory. Gehring had been accused of indecently assaulting two teenage boy students (aged fourteen and fifteen) in Guilford, England, where she was employed as a high-school supply teacher filling in for full-time teachers. The case was brought to court and testimonies were heard from complainants who told jurors that the female teacher seduced them. The Crown argued that Gehring was obsessed with the fifteen-year-old schoolboy and pursued him for sex. She was also accused of having sex with the boy's younger brother to make the older one jealous. Gehring denied the charges, and her lawyer insisted that the allegations were fabrications based on "too much testosterone on the part of two schoolboys supported by a complex web of rumor, speculation and insinuation."[3] The jury ruled that Gehring was innocent, but the voyeuristic interest in the case has yet to be understood by feminists concerned with the centrality of gender to sex-related moral panics.

The news coverage of the Gehring case was excessively lewd and voyeuristic. For example, the *Mirror* reported that Gehring wore "thin strapped tops, high boots and skirts so short her bum was hanging out" to school.[4] In the British press, the maligned teacher was said to have arrived to court in a "tailored pinstripe number that, along with shades, marked her out as ... [a] svelte supermodel."[5] Another reporter, quoting the testimony given by one boy student, wrote: "The way she talked and moved was always very sexual. Her tops were so low she didn't have to lean down to reveal herself and she wore lots of make-up."[6] As one journalist wrote: "Boy-hungry Amy Gehring dominated her impressionable pupils with her blatant sexual behavior both in school and out."[7]

Although Gehring was acquitted after ten hours of jury deliberation, she was placed on List 99, the British government blacklist that prohibited her from working with schoolchildren in the future. In Canada, the maligned teacher was subject to review by the Ontario College of Teachers (OCT), the professional body that regulates and disciplines teachers in the province, and designated unsuitable to teach because she was believed to be a risk to children. The OCT ruled that Gehring must wait ten years and pass a series of psychological tests to ensure that she understands the boundary violation she committed before she may apply for reinstatement. The OCT summoned her to appear before the tribunal for an official reprimand (which she did not do) and ordered her to pay $10,000 for the costs associated with the tribunal (despite the fact that Gehring agreed to have her teaching license revoked well before the tribunal was due to meet). This was the most severe sanction applied by the OCT to discipline a teacher having transgressed professional boundaries but not having committed an actual crime.[8]

The Gehring case is only one of a recent series of school-based sex scandals involving female teachers to receive notoriety and an unduly harsh reprimand by educational authorities. [...]

Such sex scandals are significant because they afford a means to think about female sexual subjectivity apart from conventional, heterosexually orchestrated gender binaries. Socially sanctioned feminine (and masculine) social scripts are reorganized, and, for a moment, it is possible to imagine the feminine subject as someone other than the passive recipient of a heterosexual overture. [...] In this way, a heterosexually oriented female can be queer in the way she may choose to refuse rigid gender binaries, the conventions of romantic love, monogamy, and dignified sexual propriety.

The Gehring story also queers heterosexuality by mutating feminine conventional scripts in the heterosexualized culture governing the school. On arriving at her teaching post in England, the twenty-six-year-old Gehring described herself to be a novelty with the boys, given her age, as part of her testimony in court. In an interview with BBC Radio Four's *Today* program, Gehring explained that the "boys were sexually rude towards me and the girls saw this and they were quite nasty to me."[9] As reported in one British newspaper, Gehring told the court that she had to put up with "incessant sexual innuendo [from her male students.] ... [The boys indulged in] grabbing, touching, gestures," which she "obviously didn't like."[10] She also said that the British boys were "more forward than those she grew up with in Canada and denied she had corrupted anyone."[11] Gehring also revealed that her detentions were famous: "The boys came to leer at me. In fact the boys at my second school were even more raunchy. They would pinch my backside and tell me they wanted sex. I lost count of the number of boys who scrawled their phone numbers on scraps of paper and threw them into my handbag."[12] Her testimony reveals the extent to which she was positioned as a sexual object for heterosexual, schoolboy, voyeuristic pleasure and the extent to which the details of her working environment can be read as emblematic of the "chilly climate" encountered by women in the public sphere of paid professional employment in the school.

What is interesting about the case is that Gehring does not fall prey to sexual harassment or to the prescribed gender norms governing the heterosexual ethos of the British school in any conventional way. Instead of allowing herself to be positioned as an object of schoolboy voyeuristic pleasure, Gehring assumes an active sexual orientation as desiring subject. She professes to be lustful and unapologetic about her sexual preference for young boys. "I don't go around intending to pick kids up off the streets. I look young and I like young men, that's all. I realize that I am every schoolboy's fantasy—their hormones are raging and they like older women … I was … lonely and foolish."[13] Insisting that she did not act on her desire for underage boys, Gehring maintains that legally sanctioned boundaries were not breached. The accused teacher claims that although her interpersonal relationships with underage students were professionally inappropriate, she never had sex with them.[14]

What is most exasperating about Gehring's conduct to middle-class, conventional morality is that she refused to align herself with common ideals of female teacher martyrdom in educational culture, "good-girl" sexuality, and ideologies of maternal passivity that shape the female teacher role. It is customary for the good girl to feel "shame and guilt and a compulsion toward incessant people pleasing. On the other hand, the bad girl is empowered to have desires and satisfy herself."[15] Veronica Monet argues that the epistemological standpoint of the female prostitute enables her to understand how our Western culture punishes the bad girl. Through her work in the sex industry she has come to understand how "central to feminism the liberation and the vindication of the bad girl must be."[16] Paula Webster similarly contends that the feminine subject experiences a "mix of desires for power and powerlessness, love and revenge, submission and control, monogamy and promiscuity, sadism, and masochism. Once we are able to acknowledge our own complete relationships to these feelings, we will be less likely to submit to pressures to punish our sisters who have dared to speak, act, and write about the taboos they have broken and the forbidden territories … they have entered."[17] Monet's notion of the bad girl is not confined to the prostitute but includes all feminine subjects who are unabashedly sexual, unapologetic about wanting, desiring, and seeking erotic pleasure in dynamics (and venues) that are anti-Oedipal.

*****

Amy Gehring is the bad girl because her desire cannot be reconciled with the Oedipal law of the father (which is often framed in terms of ethics, professionalism, and nationwide legalities).

The bad girl is bad not because she has an unacceptable desire but because she claims an identification with the desire and does not ask to be punished for it. Gehring is a bad girl in this way. She is shocking because she is unapologetic about her desire for young boys. The fact that Gehring does not act on these desires is a moot point because the heterosexual, patriarchal, cultural logic depends on a psychic struggle with culturally sanctioned taboos. The moral majority and the sexual deviant—Gehring in this case—are begotten and spurred on by the same sexual prohibition (around intergenerational desire and feminine gender transgression) but have different orientations to the illicit; the moral majority refuses it (on a manifest level) while the other—Amy Gehring—acts on it or claims an identity in relation to it.

As Freud argued in the infamous essay "A Child Is Being Beaten," the desire to punish (and to receive punishment) stems not only from "the forbidden genital relation [in the original, nuclear family forum], but also [from] the regressive substitute for it."[18] Those who take voyeuristic pleasure in reading about the ritualistic punishment of the estranged Canadian teacher are "good" not because they refuse to act on clandestine desires of their own but because they are morally outraged. The media-reading public are excited by the punishment given to Gehring, and, perversely, the punishment stands in as a substitute for the desire the moralistic subject cannot act on or claim an allegiance to. Freud argued that the desire for punishment is a displacement; it enables the subject to symbolically fulfill an illicit desire by being punished for it. The punishment is a socially sanctioned substitute.

*****

There is a masochistic desire involved in the moralistic demand that others be punished as stand-ins for the self. Refusing to understand the desire to witness punishment as sadism uncomplicated by masochism, Freud contended that the wish for punishment is an extension of the primary, masochistic yearning to satisfy a clandestine desire by submitting to punishment. Punishment can be understood more broadly, in this instance, to include the unspoken pleasure that comes from reading about the social castigation and ritualistic shunning of Gehring as licentious predator in the news press or by the OCT. "Oedipal conflict is managed by substituting punishment for love and is lived in the form of punishment *as* love."[19] It is also the case that morality is accomplished through a disavowal of the sexual. "Conscience and morality arose through overcoming, desexualizing, the Oedipus-complex."[20]

In fact, the law is the product of repressed desire.[21] Forgoing instinctual gratification enables the subject to develop a conscience. The strength of the Freudian superego (the moral conscience par excellence) develops on a par with the extent to which instinct has been renounced. As Gilles Deleuze summarizes: The law [acting on behalf of the moral majority] cannot specify its object without self-contradiction, nor can it define itself with reference to a content without removing the repression on which it rests.[22] It is, therefore, the moral majority who are most upset by the case because to be sexually moralistic they are forced to contend with what they must disavow.

*****

DESIRING FEMINISTS: PORNOGRAPHY, SADOMASOCHISM, AND THE PEDAGOGY OF THE FEMALE DOMINANT

A feminism of desire would fit me, I think, like a corset. Instead of wondering why I'm corseted in the first place, and whether others have to wear a corset, or what the corset means, or how I might remove it, I could instead focus on the intensity of sensation afforded by the constraint, becoming increasingly aware of the boundaries of my own body. A feminism of desire would hold me together, prop me up, cinch me in between thick pieces of social fabric, my gross-grain ribbons pulled taut. With it, I could get a better sense of where I begin and end, what I am up against and what is beyond my ability to change as a single body in the world.

—Jennifer Lutzenberger, "Cutting, Craving, and the Self I Was Saving"

Women, in other words, long identified as victims rather than perpetrators of violence, have much to gain from new and different configurations of violence, terror, and fantasy.

—Judith Halberstam, "Imagined Violence/Queer Violence: Representation, Rage, and Resistance"

The Gehring story captivated readers. People were engrossed by the details of Gehring's love life in Canada (and the melodramatic breakup with her long-term boyfriend in Otterville, Ontario); allegations that she slept with over fifty men (thereby demonstrating her sexual prowess outside of the marriage bed); her flirtations with schoolboys; her clothing; her positioning as temptress of boys and young men in the British school. Gehring's hometown of Otterville was also the subject of speculation and intrigue; sometimes described by reporters as a sedate horse-and-tobacco farming community and, at other times, "a hotbed of witchcraft and Satanism."[23]

Gail Rubin contends that for women, "virtually all erotic behavior is considered bad unless a specific reason to exempt it has been established. The most acceptable excuses are marriage, reproduction, and love. Sometimes ... a long-term intimate relationship may serve."[24] It is, therefore, not surprising that Gehring was compelled to assume an allegiance to a romance narrative intelligible to the heterosexual imaginary to buttress her own defense during the trial. In court, Gehring claimed that she was a quiet homebody, swept off her feet by her Canadian boyfriend (whom she expected to marry), and then devastated when he broke her heart by ending their relationship at Christmas. On the verge of tears, Gehring said that her "dream is to be happily married with children of her own. That is all I have ever wanted and all I still want."[25] Andrew Thompson, Gehring's lawyer, similarly described her as the daughter of a wealthy farmer and doting mother, saying also that she had been brought up with strict moral values. Not allowed makeup and given a strict curfew until she was fourteen, Gehring was certainly not permitted to mix with the wrong kind of boys and definitely ill prepared to deal with the sexually assertive boy students in her Guilford classroom. She was depicted as the typical "girl next door," a farmer's daughter who, through inexperience, found herself a victim of an unfortunate set of circumstances. Gehring's lawyer insisted that she was not a pedophile, only naive to have befriended her pupils, and that she was innocent of the charges against her. Heartbroken over the end of a long-term relationship with George Fulop (who later auctioned his version of the failed romance to the highest bidder), Gehring left for England to begin a new life.

Although Gehring attempted to present herself in court as a "traditional" farmer's daughter, brokenhearted after a breakup with her long-term boyfriend, she was repeatedly constructed by reporters as a lascivious predator with a sexual predilection for young boys. For example, the British tabloids suggested that Gehring's unusual interest in young boys directly resulted from the loss of her "hunky boy-friend," which "changed her from a shy homebody into a man-hungry seductress as she sought to blot out the pain."[26]

The Gehring trial was correctly described by one British reporter as resembling a "cross between a peepshow, a circus, an auction, and an invasion."[27] In a Canadian newspaper, one reporter described the court testimonies in the following way:

> Graphic descriptions of drunken sex in alleyways and on park benches [were given] … [She also confessed to] affixing herself to the group of fourteen and fifteen-year-old boys and girls, hanging out with them at pubs and McDonald's, buying them vodka ice coolers and Malibu rum, running up big cell-phone bills, sending text messages, and even sleeping at their homes on occasion.[28]

Another reporter for the *Times* agreed that the story had everything: "Wild stories of drunken orgies, schoolboys, saucy snaps, velvet handcuffs … and even that heart-quickening garment without which no British sex scandal is truly complete—a see-through blouse."[29] Another journalist described Gehring and her student entourage as "affluent, attractive, and hedonistic. They partied most nights, got riotously drunk and had lots of sex."[30] The sensational coverage reached a peak when "pictures of the drunken supply teacher simulating oral sex on a teen at a party and giving another teen an open-mouthed kiss had been entered into evidence" at the trial.[31]

After having been cleared of charges laid against her in court, Gehring overturned the good-girl persona she and her lawyer orchestrated to win the sympathies of jurors. She consented to an interview with the popular British newspaper, the *Sunday Mirror,* and the editors printed a story from her perspective that came equipped with images building on a cultural inscription of female erotic domination in sadomasochistic fantasy. In one such image, Gehring is seen in a dark evening gown, lounging across a plush sofa. In another shot, Gehring is shown wearing tight-fitting leather gloves, wielding what some reporters described as a whiplike riding crop; some thought it to be a cane, and still others believed it to be a rod. As one columnist for the *Globe and Mail* reported: "The four-page spread includes suggestive photos of Ms. Gehring including one where she holds a riding crop in her gloved hands. She is wearing low-slung jeans and a midriff-revealing blouse. In another pose, she is reclining on a couch, wearing a tight-fitting satin dress. The caption reads: 'The Scarlet Woman: Amy Gehring likes to show off her curves.'"[32] In this spread she confessed to having an affair with a sixteen-year-old boy virgin and revealed that the schoolboys in her class compared her to Britney Spears and Xena the Warrior Princess. One British reporter described Gehring as a "slit-skirted dominatrix."[33] Another British journalist wrote about one of the alleged victims: "He arrived at his biology lesson to find the busty brunette standing at the front of the classroom. [According to the boy] she was wearing black leather boots, a short skirt, and a tight jacket revealing her cleavage."[34]

Gehring built on (and took command of) the image of herself as a female dominant that had been circulating prior to her own public relations intervention. Gehring took the media-induced, sensationalized representation of her case (which was not consensual) and managed to alter the conditions of her engagement in the mass-public portrayal of her sexualized persona by taking control. "As a theater of signs, S-M grants temporary control over social risk. By scripting and controlling the *frame* of representation, in other words, the control frame [in this case the newspapers] … the player stages the delirious loss of control within a situation as extreme control."[35]

The feminist pornographer Marcelle Perks contends that the "right to consume and create our own pornography is essential if we are to emerge as full sexual beings,"[36] and Gehring adopted a similar political tactic to deal with her lewd and predatory sexual persona in the press. The former teacher attempted to take control of her already salacious image in the public eye and to profit from it. Gehring began by hiring a literary agent and reportedly sold her story to the tabloids for $80,000, which ensured that she would receive a monetary gain (along with the publishers that sold newspapers featuring her story without consent or financial compensation) for an image that should properly belong to her. The tabloids also reported that she was expected to receive £100,000 for newspaper interviews and that she could make even more by selling the rights to her story to a publisher or filmmaker.

The fact that Gehring used her story for economic gain led to public suspicion, and people doubted her credibility because she embraced her sexualized image. One British journalist felt that Gehring used a "prim and proper image … [in] court and then … [referring to her infamous interview with the *Sunday Mirror*] openly admitted to having had sex with a sixteen-year old virgin schoolboy,"[37] which, for him, raised questions about her credibility. "And nice girls don't pursue things like money or sex unless they have humanitarian or nurturing motives (e.g., supporting a child with money or loving a partner with sex)."[38] It has also been argued that feminine propriety makes it difficult for the good girl to negotiate desires—not just economic or sexual—with men,[39] and so feminine subjects, like Gehring, are, again, having to negotiate a restraining, gendered template.

Although Gehring's sexualized persona was publicly frowned on, the same persona of the sexually dominant female teacher is sought out in British and North American S-M dungeons, suggesting that the persona is central to culturally inscribed private fantasy. For example, in contemporary Western societies "older dominatrices are respected for their experience and authority and are in demand for fantasy roles such as mother or headmistress."[40] Professional female dominants and feminist pornographers regularly report that male clients request school-based scenes involving requests for punishment by an older, female, teacher-like figure.[41] Spankings and canings are particularly common requests in the contemporary British context. [...]

Gehring embraced the fantastical archetype of the sexually dominant female central to a masculine submissive fantasy sequence. Because this archetype is interwoven into the cultural ethos of the British school, it is instructive to examine the institution of adolescent, schoolboy, heterosexual fantasy sequences of female teachers as dominating forces as suggesting something about the permutations of gender, heterosexual instability, and intergenerational love, loss, and hate in school culture. Sadomasochistic scenes (real or imagined) enable "symbolic reenactments of the memory of violations to selfhood … [and not coincidentally] it is [most often the case that] the masochist's fantasies … are acted out … in fact it is the 'bottom' who is in control."[42] Much like the schoolboys in the Gehring case, it is the paying client (submissive) who normally sets the boundaries on an S-M scene choreographed by a female dominant. The schoolboys in the Gehring case controlled the representation of the sexualized scene (in the first instance) by officiating the allegations of abuse in court and in later interviews with the media. Unlike the scene orchestrated by the professional dominatrix, the media-induced fanfare was not consensual. Because the allegations were proven to be false, it is evident that Gehring stood in as a psychic marker of an earlier childhood trauma (castration anxiety, incestuous fantasies of the mother, unconscious memories of love, hate, and forbidden attachments in object relations, and so on) for the schoolboys.

The dominance and submission inherent to the sadomasochistic scene (which may involve the enactment of spanking, caning, discipline, or anything else that may be associated with school culture in the mind of the once boy, now adult, male/masculine-identified client) necessarily involve a safe reenactment of the original scene, image, or idea that provides the raw materials of fantasy. In other words, the boy students involved in the S-M-like portrayal of the Gehring case no longer have to be held captive to a troubling power relation (such as the ones taking shape in the school culture of chastisement and punishment) at the level of the psychic or to an illegitimate, Oedipal desire central to the dominant, heterosexual nuclear family structure. "As a theatre of conversion, S-M reverses and transforms the social meanings it borrows."[43] It also permutates institutional hierarchies, power relations between gendered subjects, and culturally sanctioned taboos in institutions like the school, the media, and the family. Sadomasochistic scenes exploit existing power relations, but they do so for pleasure as opposed to (nonconsensual) coercion. The ritualistic scenes test the limits of power, its potency, its ascendancy, its competency, and, finally, its ultimate undoing.[44]

The fantasy sequence choreographed by the professional dominant is dissident; it often depends on the rupture of conventional, heterosexual, middle-class sexual morality with its insistence on monogamy, intelligible gender positionings (with the masculine subject on top and the feminine subject on bottom), penile penetration, and formulaic erotic sequences in keeping with the missionary position. In fact, the professional dominatrix refuses to have sex with paying customers at all. Like Gehring, she takes command of a heterosexually masculine fantasy sequence composed of (but not determined by) the raw materials of the masculine imagination and does something other than consummate it. She queers the masculine imagination to undermine normative, masculine identifications with monogamous, missionary-like heterosexuality.

*****

CHILDHOOD INNOCENCE AND THE MYTHOLOGY OF FEMALE TEACHER SEDUCTION

Think of all the crazy barriers adults interpose between children and sexual experience: the breaking off of certain conversations when children appear (conspicuous enough to arouse the children's interest in the very things they were not supposed to hear); the whispering behind hands; the meaningful looks; the evasion of children's questions; the manufactured

lies; the inconsistency of their alibis; the frantic attempts to hide the genitals from the little ones' eyes; the horrified embarrassment when children ask the meaning of a forbidden
word; the panic when they pick up something new; the hysterical "where did you get that
from?"; the punishments threatening children who discover dark continents in the mutual
exploration of their bodies—all this, for the young boy, has the effect of making a monstrous secret of the opposite sex, of installing the notion of a "mystery woman," which does
anything but steer his instinctual desires away from women.

—Klaus Theweleit, *Male Fantasies, Volume 1: Women, Flood, Bodies, History*

As Michel Foucault points out, sexuality has a duplicitous history and so too does the child
trauma thesis. Reporters for the British and North American newspapers began to question the
trauma thesis and the representation of the lascivious teacher as pedophile. As the columnist
Margaret Wente of the *Globe and Mail* reported: "Despite the prosecutor's best efforts, the portrait of poor Ms. Gehring as a vicious pedophile began to fall apart when her victims took the
stand,"[45] and it became clear that the boys initiated the seductions alleged to have taken place.
The credibility of the schoolboys also began to wane as it was revealed that they sold their stories
to the press for monetary gain and stood to make more money if they won the lawsuit launched
against Gehring. As reported in the *Times,* a British newspaper: "Payments create a real risk of
encouraging witnesses to exaggerate their evidence in court so as to make it more newsworthy,
or to withhold relevant evidence from the court in order to give newspapers exclusive coverage
later."[46] It was also suggested in the British press that if the boys were, in fact, traumatized by
their allegedly sexual encounters with Gehring, it is curious that they so eagerly recounted the
graphic details of those supposedly horrendous events for "check-book" journalists.

Gehring's lawyer pointed out to the court that the "boys didn't appear traumatized when
they gave their evidence via a video link from another part of the courthouse, remembering that
they smiled during their testimony," seemingly enjoying the attention.[47] The British tabloids
continually referred to Gehring as every schoolboy's dream come true, and the lawyer representing Gehring similarly referred to the allegations as schoolboy fantasies. The columnist for
the *Guardian* proceeded to write that it "doesn't seem possible for a full-grown Englishman to
listen to the Tale of Amy without sighing and waxing poetic about Miss Sexy who taught him
in lower sixth, and who still comes back to him, all these years later, to perform unspeakable
acts in his dreams."[48] It was also noted that "some reporters doubt teenage boys are capable of
intercourse if the idea of it does not excite them … [and remarks were made to the effect that]
there was little shame attached to a schoolboy seduced by an older woman."[49]

Marilyn Ivy asks the critical question about child abuse: "Has its discursive construction—its
appearance and refinement as a category—enabled instances to become visible in ways that
weren't possible before?"[50] Might childhood sexual innocence and a flirtation (consummated
or not) by an older woman be only manifestly about the child? Could the anxiety reveal a latent
preoccupation with the sexual subjectivity of the adult female in the teaching (read mothering)
role? Underneath the obsessive condemnation of anything remotely connected to female adult–
childhood (especially boy) sexuality (consent aside) lies a more deeply entrenched cultural taboo
regarding female sexual agency and erotic domination as exemplified in the Gehring case.

Childhood sexuality has been a matter of public concern since the seventeenth century, when moralists constructed the child as both innocent and sexually ravenous and wanton at the same time.[51] The residual effects of this paradoxical construction become apparent in the Gehring case, well into the twenty-first century. The boy students were dually coded as in need of protection (as an underage girl student might be) and as hyperhormonal and lascivious at the same time. For example, in closing arguments in the Gehring case, the prosecutor maintained that just because sex with a female teacher is often thought to be "every schoolboy's dream," that should not detract from the seriousness of the charges launched against Gehring. British child protection groups argued in court that sexual acts between female teachers and boy students were harmful, just as harmful as those between male teachers and girl students. The boys—supposedly victims—giggled during testimony given by child protection advocates in order to express their sexual bravado and independence.[52]

The giggles raised doubt not only about the damage done to the complainants but about the boundary demarcating adulthood and childhood sexuality, the positioning of the lascivious female teacher in that divide, and the sanctity of the Oedipal prohibition. Foucault wrote that heterosexual intercourse was the dividing line between the adult and child. Boy children acting lasciviously toward an older, female, maternal stand-in threatens to collapse intergenerational boundaries along with the gendered subjectivities predicated on those boundaries. At the same time, the role (real or imagined) of the boys in the infraction hints at their capacities for independence, experience, and sophistication in matters relating to sex despite the cultural taboo surrounding childhood sexuality.

"The remarkable thing about the sex taboo is that it is fully seen in transgression ... The taboo is discovered directly by a furtive and at first partial exploration of the forbidden territory."[53] There is no incest taboo without incestuous desire, and an investigation (in court and in popular tabloid journalism) of the clandestine desire is what the transgression (real or imagined) in the Gehring case enables. What is remarkable about the Gehring case is that the incestuously coded infraction between female teacher and boy student is subject to exploration along with the taboo of female-teacher sexuality—and its permutations in the erotic pedagogical encounter. Judith Butler argues that the incest taboo functions to support the heterosexual matrix and bipolar gender positionalities. The taboo compels the preadolescent child to resolve the Oedipal complex that, for Freud, makes possible an adult heterosexual identification. Butler contends that "because [gender] identifications substitute for object relations, and identifications are the consequence of loss, gender identification is a kind of melancholia in which the sex of the prohibited object is internalized as a prohibition. This prohibition sanctions and regulates discrete gendered identity and the law of heterosexual desire ... Gender identity appears primarily to be the internalization of a prohibition that proves to be formative of identity."[54] The incest taboo is thus a prerequisite for heterosexuality. The rupture of the incest prohibition (real or imagined) in the Gehring case reveals the extent to which heterosexuality is predicated on a renunciation of same-sex (in this instance parental) desire.

But the rapturous entanglement between Gehring and the schoolboys also brings to light the ambiguous position of the maternal figure in the accomplishment of heterosexuality. Is the female teacher, strictly speaking, heterosexual when she defies the patriarchal law of the father, which demands the repudiation of intergenerational desire? Is she properly heterosexual when her own sexual orientation is for younger boys (even when those boys are of legal age to consent to sex)? Is she properly heterosexual when she is unabashedly sexual, wanton, and voracious about her sexual proclivities?

Freud challenged the idea of childhood sexual innocence in order to expose the inner workings of the Oedipal dynamic (and the requirements imposed on the child by Victorian culture), but he was less vocal about the (potentially transgressive) role of the mother in the Oedipal dyad. The Gehring story is shocking because it enables the public to consider the capacity of the female teacher, coded as maternal figure, to upset the institution of heterosexuality with its need for stable gender identifications along a stable masculine and feminine grid, by entering into the realm of masculine desire. "To desire someone younger than oneself, with less access to power than oneself, is certainly not an abnormal desire. It is the predominant construction of masculine desire in the contemporary form of heterosexuality."[55] If gender is an attempt to mediate object-loss (as in the case of the forbidden, same-sex parent through the heterosexual injunction) as Butler argues, then the accomplishment of schoolboy masculinity (not to mention female schoolteacher femininity) is under threat when the incest taboo is breached. The female teacher enters into the realm of masculine desire and the schoolboys are, by implication, feminized by their allegiance to sexual passivity. Nothing is as it would seem to the unexamined heterosexual imaginary.

Speaking about the human inclination toward polymorphously perverse sexual pleasures, [Sallie] Tisdale suggests that "to the unschooled body there are no good or bad sexual objects, no right or wrong responses. Sexual acts are one of the primary means by which we can act out our inarticulated lives."[56] One has to learn to fear the patriarchal, Oedipal father to domesticate desire. In the case of Guilford, England, something went terribly wrong. The female teacher refused an allegiance with the asexual mother role (necessitated by the heterosexual matrix proper), and the boy students refused to displace their original desire for the mother onto a socially sanctioned, age-appropriate substitute. The female teacher was no longer a heterosexually feminine, maternal-like figure encapsulated in the persona of state-appointed teacher; and the schoolboys, evidently, had not resolved their Oedipal complexes in accordance with the demands of British patriarchal society, which would enable them to move on to an adult, unequivocally masculine, heterosexual orientation. Schoolboy desire, in the Gehring case, was anti-Oedipal and hazardous to the heterosexual matrix.

According to Nancy Friday, "A fantasy is a map of desire, mastery, escape, and obscuration; the navigational path we invent to steer ourselves between the reefs and shoals of anxiety, guilt, and inhibition ... [each fantasy sequence] gives us a coherent and consistent picture of the personality— the unconscious— of the person who invented it."[57] Schoolboy erotic fantasies about older female teachers reveal anxieties associated with the maternal body (coded as lascivious teacher) in British (and North American) school culture. The schoolboys both desired and feared Gehring because she was associated with the mother, and the incest taboo demands that they expunge her from their psyche. The incest taboo produces the desire, and the associated cultural demand that she be abjected.

CONCLUSION

The feminine subject— whether mother, teacher, guardian, or governess— has been sexualized and, at the same time, held responsible for maintaining erotic boundaries that prohibit illicit sex in the domestic sphere (and let us not forget that the British school is culturally coded as a familial setting). As Anne McClintock contends in her discussion of sexuality and colonial conquest, such women have been "tasked with the purification and maintenance of boundaries; they were especially fetishized as dangerous, ambiguous, and contaminating."[58] This contention is predicated on the argument made by Julia Kristeva that social subjectivity is organized through the practice of expulsion. The need to abject the mother (which can occur through and results in fetishistic and sadomasochistic desires for authoritarian and dominating women) is crucial for the adolescent boy, who is called on to assume a normative adult, masculine, heterosexual identification.

The idea of the lascivious female teacher upsets the culturally inscribed emotional (and sexual) boundary between the boy student (coded as son) and female teacher (coded as mother) not only because she is a maternal stand-in but also because she poses an independent threat to the Oedipal complex (as theorized by Freud) and its resolution. [...]

I contend that the female teacher who is precariously positioned along the borders between the private and public is [...] implicated in the adolescent schoolboy's Oedipal resolutions. The power play is, in the case of the boy student and female teacher, mapped [...] onto British and North American professional school culture and the heterosexual bifurcations of gender inherent to that culture. The boy student overcomes his desire for domination (and possession of the mother) by submitting to a dominating maternal figure (female teacher) and uses the practice of submission to resolve the kaleidoscopically nuanced character of the Oedipal life drama.

The incestuously coded infraction is not subversive because it affords an alternative means to resolve the Oedipal complex (and thereby sidestep the heterosexual commandment, the law of the patriarchal father) but because it exposes the precariousness and the complications inherent to the resolution process. There are numerous points in which the resolution process may be upset, and it is not a given that adult, monogamous, age-appropriate heterosexuality is the inevitable outcome. Analyzing the voyeuristic pleasure in the Gehring case exposes the heterosexual matrix for what it is: an invention, a cultural logic, a psychic difficulty, and (sometimes in some moments) an impossibility.

NOTES

1 Rob Granatstein, "Lusty Lessons: Ontario Teacher's Fate Now Lies in Hands of UK Jury," *Toronto Sun*, 4 February 2002; Alexandra Williams and Fiona Cummins, "Boozy Teacher Had Alley Sex with Two Underage Boys and Bedded a Third," *Mirror* (London), 22 January 2002; Robert Westhead, "Teacher Too Drunk to Recall Having Sex with Boy," *Press Association* (London), 28 January 2002; Sue Carroll, "Amy's Pervy as Any Man," *Mirror* (London), 6 February 2002; Westhead, "Sex Case Teacher 'in Row after Sex with Brothers,'" *Press Association* (London), 24 January 2002; "A Jury in Guilford, England May Decide Today on the Fate of Canada's Lustiest Teaching Export," *London Free Press* (London, Canada), 4 February 2002; Adrian Lee, "Boy Tells Jury of Drunken Encounter at Party: Night I Lost Virginity to Biology Mistress," *Express* (London), 23 January 2002; Michael Horsnell, "Science Mistress

Admits Kissing and Cuddling Boy, 15," *Times* (London), 29 January 2002; "Where Do Fallen or Flagrant Women Turn for Public Rehabilitation?" *New Statesman* (London), 18 February 2002; "Canadian Teacher Cleared of Sex Charges," *Toronto Star,* 15 February 2002; Carol Sarler, "Amy's Caresses Were Wrong but Not Harmful," *Express* (London), 13 February 2002.

2 Lisa Sigel, "Autobiography of a Flea: Scrutiny and the Female Porn Scholar, " in *Jane Sexes It Up: True Confessions of Feminist Desire,* ed. Merri Lisa Johnson (New York: Four Walls Eight Windows, 2002), 245.

3 Chris Wattie, "Teacher Confesses to UK Paper," *National Post,* 11 February 2002.

4 Carroll, "Amy's Pervy as Any Man."

5 Nick Curtis, "Courtroom Drama Queens," *Evening Standard,* 13 February 2002.

6 Claire Collins, "Amy Loved Sex Talk in Lessons: Boy Victim of the Lusting Biology Teacher, " *People* (London), February 2002.

7 Ibid.

8 The college distinguishes between a sexual crime (which may include sexual assault or sexual harassment) and an unprofessional act (which may include fraternizing with students outside the school). Although Gehring was not convicted of a crime, she was found to have been unprofessional in her social interactions with students. It is far more common that teachers found to have been unprofessional receive a professional reprimand (as opposed to being excommunicated from the profession), and so the OCT's response was unusually harsh.

9 Sarah Montague, "Amy Gehring Interview," British Broadcasting Association, 11 February 2002.

10 Maureen Freely, "Real Lives: Sex Education," *Guardian,* 5 February 2002.

11 Duncan Roberts, "I Did Have Sex with Boy, 16, Says Teacher," *Evening News,* 11 February 2002.

12 Jane Johnson, "Time-Plan Boss Told Me: Lie to Police and the School; World Exclusive: Sex Case Amy's Story I am every schoolboy's fantasy," *Sunday Mirror,* 10 February 2002.

13 Ibid.

14 Gehring did, however, admit to at least one (and possibly a second) transgression involving schoolboys. She admitted that she may have had sex with a fifteen-year-old boy student at a New Year's Eve party, although she could not be certain because she was too drunk to remember for certain. After hearing rumors circulating throughout the school that she did have sex with this boy in a bathroom, Gehring took the morning-after pill. The schoolboy himself also could not remember having sex with the teacher, and so both were dependent on rumor, innuendo, and speculation to disentangle their fragmented memories.

Referring to the sexualized flirtations with schoolboys at one New Year's party, Gehring is quoted as saying that she was "too drunk. I wasn't myself. I was isolated. I was a kid really. They wanted it [sexual attention but not sex]. They initiated it. No one got hurt. It's all a bit embarrassing and that's all" ("Sex, Lies and Hopeless Excuses," *Independent,* 12 February 2002). The maligned teacher did, however, admit to having had sex with a sixteen-year-old boy registered as a student in her previous place of employment (which is legal in England because the boy was designated old enough to consent). This "confession" functioned to further ignite the media-induced panic.

15 Veronica Monet, "Sedition," in *Whores and Other Feminists,* ed. Jull Nagle (New York: Routledge, 1997), 220.

16 Ibid., 222.

17 Paula Webster, "The Forbidden: Eroticism and Taboo," in *Pleasure and Danger: Exploring Female Sexuality,* ed. Carole S. Vance (London: Routledge and Kegan Paul, 1984), 396.

18 Sigmund Freud, "A Child Is Being Beaten: A Contribution to the Study of the Origin of Sexual Perversions," trans. Alix Strachey and James Strachey, in *Sexuality and the Psychology of Love,* ed. Philip Rieff (New York: Collier, 1963), 49.

19 Wendy Brown, *Politics Out of History* (Princeton, NJ: Princeton University Press, 2001), 51.

20 Sigmund Freud, "The Economic Problem in Masochism," in *The Standard Edition of the Complete Psychological Works of Sigmund Freud,* vol. 19, trans. and ed. James Strachey (London: Hogarth, 1974).

21 Gilles Deleuze, *Masochism* (New York: Zone, 1991).

22 Ibid., 85.

23 Robbie Millen, "Gehring Says She Was Boy's Novelty," *Times,* 11 February 2002.

24 Gail Rubin, "Thinking Sex: Notes for a Radical Theory of the Politics of Sexuality," in Vance, *Pleasure and Danger,* 278.

25 "Headline: Dumped by My Darling on Xmas Day," *Sunday Mirror,* 10 February 2002.

26 Rachel Bletchly, "Miss Filth Tried to Bed My 13-Yr Old," *People* (London), 17 February 2002.

27 Bruce Wallace, "Teacher Admits She May Have Had Sex with UK Boy," *National Post,* 29 January 2002.

28 Ibid.

29 Richard Morrison, "Inappropriate Behavior," *Times,* 5 February 2002.

30 Harriet Arkell, "Broken-Hearted Teacher Who Fell in with Wrong Kind of Pupils," *Evening Standard* (London), 4 February 2002.

31 Granatstein, "Lusty Lessons." The interesting thing about the definition of pornography is that it must be subject to the threat of the censor to be, strictly speaking, pornographic. As Angela Carter writes: "When pornography serves—as with very rare exceptions it always does—to reinforce the prevailing system of values and ideas in a given society, it is tolerated; and when it does not, it is banned" (*The Sadeian Woman* [New York: Pantheon, 1978], 18). Despite the sexually graphic representation of the Gehring story in the tabloids, it is not considered crudely pornographic by the mainstream public because it insists on the condemnation of the sexually promiscuous, wanton, and voracious single female characterized by the former teacher.

32 Alan Freeman, "Gehring Tells Tabloid She Had Sex with Teen," *Globe and Mail,* 11 February 2002.

33 Curtis, "Courtroom Drama Queens."

34 Bletchly, "Miss Filth Tried to Bed My 13-Yr Old."

35 Anne McClintock, *Imperial Leather: Race, Gender, and Sexuality in the Colonial Contest* (New York: Routledge, 1995), 147.

36 Marcelle Perks, "DIY Pornography," in *Tales from the Clit: A Female Experience of Pornography,* ed. Cherie Matrix (Oakland, CA: AK Press, 1996), 66.

37 Jane Johnson, "Amy Gehring: I Did Sleep with a Virgin Age 16," *Sunday Mirror,* 2 February 2002.

38 Monet, "Sedition," 219.

39 Teri Goodson, "A Prostitute Joins NOW," in Nagle, *Whores and Other Feminists,* 248–51.

40 Liz Highleyman, "Professional Dominance: Power, Money, and Identity," in Nagle, *Whores and Other Feminists,* 150.

41 Roy Turner, ed., *You Beat People Up for a Living, Don't You, Mummy?* (Brighton: Absolute Elsewhere, 2001).

42 McClintock, *Imperial Leather,* 148.

43 Ibid., 143.

44 Not coincidentally, the sadomasochistic scenes inscribed by a professional dominatrix often involve the feminization (cross-dressing) of male clients (Highleyman, "Professional Dominance," 145). In her discussion of male fantasies, Nancy Friday explains, "One of the major themes in male fantasy is the abdication of activity in favor of passivity. Role reversal" (Men in Love: Men's Sexual Fantasies, the Triumph of Love over Rage [Durham, NC: Hutchinson, 1993], 268). The femme dominant uses leather and chain accoutrements and sets an erotic scene through stagelike scripts, costume, and theatrical performance, which enable gender transformations. Not unlike the mythology suggesting that the hermaphrodite had transcendent powers, the dominatrix wields a power that can effect a change in one's gender identity.

As Gilles Deleuze contends, in "sadism it becomes possible for the boy to play the role of a girl in relation to a projection of the father. We might say that the masochist is hermaphrodite and the sadist androgynous"(Masochism, 68). The boy student/adult male consents to a masochistic enactment in which the "feminine impulse is projected in the role of the mother; but in point of fact the two impulses constitute one single figure; femininity is posited as lacking in nothing and placed alongside a virility suspended in disavowal (just as the absence of a penis need not indicate lack of the phallus)" (ibid.). In the sadomasochistic scene, heterosexual bifurcations of gender (masculinity and femininity, organized along bipolar poles) cease to exist as fantasy becomes more exciting—or psychically meaningful—than the real. The penis does not matter, and the female possesses the phallus as she adopts an allegiance to female dominance.

45 Margaret Wente, "What If the Schoolmistress Were a Man," Globe and Mail, 4 February 2002.

46 Clare Dyer, "Plan to Make Media Payments to Witnesses a Criminal Offence," Guardian, 6 March 2002.

47 Kevin Ward, "Sex Tales Were Lies: Boys' Stories Contradictory," Hamilton Spectator, 1 February 2002. I wish to emphasize that it is possible for female teachers to sexually abuse and harm teenage boy students. It is also possible to understand the giggles as nervous reactions and the bravado as requirements of masculine social scripts. I do, however, contend that a distinction needs to be made between a consensual amorous flirtation (however unprofessional) and indecent sexual assault of minors.

48 Freely, "Real Lives."

49 Ruth Campbell, "Young Boys Need Protecting, Too," Northern Echo, 8 February 2002.

50 Ibid.

51 There is a long history of ideas about childhood innocence in British culture. For example, Marjorie Heins argues that the idea of childhood innocence was an invention of the seventeenth century and enabled a British moral appeal to child protectionism to take shape. Carnal knowledge was to be withheld from students in educational contexts. Paradoxically, by the nineteenth century, children were also thought to have the potential for sexually ravenous behaviours, an inherent wickedness, a vulnerability to temptations of the flesh demanding rigid control, censorship, and persecution for (real and imagined) infractions despite their alleged innocence (Not in Front of the Children: "Indecency," Censorship, and the Innocence of Youth [New York: Hill and Wang, 2001]).

52 Focusing on the "harm to minors" thesis, Heins demonstrates that "judges and school officials generally embraced the philosophy that students, even of high school age, must be shielded from the presumed shock or moral corruption of sexual subjects, or at least socialized to regard them as taboo"

(*Not in Front of the Children,* 134). The compulsion to protect children, to censor sexual material in the school, and the associated commitment to talk about sexually dangerous subjects (such as the pedophile) functioned not to protect children but to insert them into discourses about sexual danger by insisting on their vulnerability. In *Child-Loving: The Erotic Child and Victorian Culture* (New York: Routledge, 1992), James R. Kincaid summarizes: "By insisting so loudly on the innocence, purity, and asexuality of the child, we have created a subversive echo: experience, corruption, eroticism. More than that, by attributing to the child the central features of desirability in our culture—purity, innocence, emptiness, Otherness—we have made absolutely essential figures who would enact this desire" (4–5). The insistence on childhood sexual innocence produces the pedophile (and does not protect the child from intergenerational sexual scenes). "Defining the child as an object of desire, we create the pedophile as the one who desires, as a complex image of projection and denial: the pedophile acts out the range of attitudes and behaviors made compulsory by the role we have given the child" (ibid., 5). Ironically, moral sensibilities call for a stern disciplining (and censoring) of the pedophilic imagination when, at the same time, this very same moral sensibility is predicated on the existence of the pedophile and cannot survive without him (or her, as in the Gehring case).

53 Georges Bataille, *Eroticism: Death and Sensuality* (San Francisco: City Lights Books, 1957), 107.

54 Judith Butler, *Gender Trouble: Feminism and the Subversion of Identity* (New York: Routledge, 1990), 63.

55 Vikki Bell, *Interrogating Incest: Feminism, Foucault, and the Law* (London: Routledge, 1993), 158.

56 Sallie Tisdale, *Talk Dirty to Me: An Intimate Philosophy of Sex* (New York: Anchor, 1994), 4.

57 Friday, *Men in Love,* 1.

58 McClintock, *Imperial Leather,* 48.

PART SEVEN

Marriage, Parenting, and the Family

CHAPTER 21

'That Repulsive Abnormal Creature I Heard of in That Book': Lesbians and Families in Ontario, 1920–1965

Karen Duder

I n 1926 Helene Fraser remarked to her daughter, Frieda: 'It is pleasant for you to have Bud. I am glad the interns like her & I shall also be glad if she will like them & not concentrate all her affections on poor little you.'[1] She was commenting on a visit Frieda's partner was making to her while Frieda was working in New York as a doctor. Mrs Fraser's reactions to Bud were not always as 'beneficent' as they were on this occasion. Frieda conveyed her mother's words while writing to Bud in England, where she had been sent to get her away from Frieda. Their relationship continued through letters, sometimes several in a single day, as they successfully thwarted their families' attempts to keep them apart.

This chapter uses correspondence between and interviews with Ontario lesbians to examine the relationships between lesbians and their families of origin in Ontario between 1920 and 1965.[2] It might be assumed that lesbians in that period, because of their sexuality, usually had difficult relationships with their families. It would be tempting to view today's relatively 'liberal' attitudes towards lesbianism as contributing to higher-quality and longer-maintained family ties, and the attitudes of the past as deleterious to family relationships. In some cases a general improvement did occur, but many lesbians growing up and forming relationships between 1920 and 1965 remained close to their families, with sexuality forming a site of conflict but not of irrevocable division. This chapter argues that, in many instances, lesbians before 1965 had stronger ties to their families of origin than those who came out in the 1970s into the lesbian movement.

Lesbians, before the advent of the communes, the feminist movement, and the gay and lesbian rights movements of the late 1960s and 1970s, negotiated the boundaries of their sexuality in a situation that did not include the notions of 'alternative' family structure and lesbian 'community' which would later emerge with political activism and greater social tolerance of same-sex partners. What little community did exist was based on social connection rather than political agenda. Although many longer-term lesbian relationships were phrased in terms similar to those of heterosexual marriage, there was little theorizing of these relationships as representing alternative families. These ideas would come later in the century.

In the period 1920–65, Ontario was the site of considerable gay and lesbian community-building and, indeed, of regulatory and discursive reactions to it. Montreal also had a significant gay and lesbian population, but it was Toronto that became the destination for many a young lesbian seeking others of her kind, especially after the Second World War. Police and municipal authorities had increasingly to deal with the presence of larger numbers of lesbians on the streets, in clubs and bars, and in residential areas. Ontario was also the site of much mainstream and medical publishing on the subject of deviant sexualities in the postwar period. As Mary Louise Adams argues, Toronto was the centre of English-language publishing, broadcasting, and cultural production in Canada and was 'entwined with the definition of "national culture."'[3] Ontario is therefore an ideal geographical focus for a study of the tensions between lesbians and their families, acting as it did as a crucible of conflict between rebellious sexualities and hegemonic social norms in a rapidly changing nation.

In this essay, I suggest that Ontario lesbians before 1965, and especially before the 1950s, remained closer to their families of origin, even after becoming sexually active as lesbians, than did many later lesbians. The context of their lives was, in many ways, fundamentally different: not only were the ideological constructs of the lesbian community and the alternative family not yet in place, but earlier lesbians had less financial independence on the basis of which they could break their familial ties. Furthermore, while societal approval of close relationships between women began to wane as early as the turn of the century, and was all but gone by the 1930s,[4] Canadian society did not, until at least the mid-1950s, have a publicly available discourse of pathological homosexuality on which to base its reactions to women who transgressed heteronormativity. With the arrival of such a discourse, family reactions towards lesbians began to change.

It cannot be said that the 1950s and 1960s saw a sudden swing towards family intolerance of lesbians; nor did lesbians abruptly sever family ties once they became aware of their sexual orientation. In only some families were lesbians suddenly the target of rejection and isolation. What this small study of Ontario lesbians suggests is that, even within a context of increasing societal discussion of and hostility towards lesbians, many families remained very tolerant of their wayward daughters. Other factors militated against the tendency for lesbian sexuality to involve family condemnation. The mid-twentieth century was, however, a time at which a significant break occurred between lesbian and family life. The formation of urban lesbian communities, the structure of which would gradually replace many of the functions of the family, and from which would arise the alternative family structures of 1970s and 1980s lesbianism, was the key moment in the changing relationship between lesbian identity and the family.

Little is known about the lives of lesbians in Canada before the late 1960s. The dearth of information is hardly surprising, given the limited availability of lesbians' personal records and the equally limited purview of the state in the area of lesbian sexuality. What little scholarship does exist focuses largely on the public discourses concerning lesbian sexuality and the public lives of lesbians in Canadian cities. The Canadian public had few sources of information about lesbianism before the mid-twentieth century. By the 1920s, many authors were writing about homosexuality, and their works were being read by a broader section of the public. Those works were, however, primarily available to medical professionals. After the volumes of *Studies in the Psychology of Sex* were banned in Britain, Havelock Ellis published them in the United States, where they received wide distribution.[5] The extent of the availability of this and other such material to a Canadian lay readership is unknown, but there are indications that some sexological works were being read by heterosexual as well as homosexual people. Readers of the *Canadian Forum* would also have been aware of the furore caused by the publication and obscenity trial of Radclyffe Hall's *Well of Loneliness* in 1928.[6] Such information was most likely available to only a small proportion of the Canadian public and, before the Second World War, lesbians in particular remained virtually invisible in Canadian society.

*****

[…] The focus of legal authorities and urban policing was on sexual activity between men, and few beyond the walls of asylums and prisons considered lesbian sexuality a major threat to social order. There existed no law under which a woman could be convicted for specifically lesbian activity, unless she were arrested under a broader category such as gross indecency, fraud, vagrancy, or disorderly conduct. Moreover, even though women's mobility and independence increased as the century wore on, women had fewer opportunities to form the same kinds of sexual subcultures as did men. Lesbian sexuality was for the most part *ultra vires*. Even within the prison system, where lesbians formed a somewhat visible group, it would seem that lesbianism was largely ignored until at least the 1950s or 1960s. Robin Brownlie suggests that there was, until the mid-twentieth century, a 'continuing inclination to downplay and disregard prison lesbianism.'[7]

LESBIAN RELATIONSHIPS OF THE 1920s AND 1930s

From the 1920s to the 1950s, the level of acceptance of relationships between women gradually changed in Canada, as it did in the United States. Long gone were the halcyon days of the romantic friendship, although many middle-class lesbians still used the language of this type of relationship.[8] Only just emerging were the decades of psychotherapy and notions of family 'dysfunction.' Within this period of transition, lesbian relationships were disapproved of by the general public, but without the psychiatric and psychological discourses that were yet to become hegemonic within Canadian society. Family condemnation rested, therefore, on somewhat vague and unspecified grounds.

Frieda Fraser and Edith Bickerton (Bud) Williams, whose relationship lasted from the age of nineteen to Bud's death in 1979 at the age of eighty, had constantly to negotiate the waters of family disapproval. Bud left Ontario for Britain in 1925 to work in a bank. She was encouraged by her mother to stay there, but returned in 1927 to be with Frieda. Their letters during the time they were apart reveal the degree to which their families were opposed to their relationship and the strength with which they had to resist all attempts to keep them apart.[9]

*****

It was Frieda's mother who proved the more hostile to their relationship, and around whom Frieda and Bud most often had to plan their meetings. Frieda's father had died in 1916, and Frieda seemed to feel a great responsibility towards her mother, despite their ambivalent relationship. After a trip home for Christmas, Frieda wrote: 'By the way, when I was at home I took careful soundings as to your status in the home. Mother doesn't seem to mind your being talked of now—she did a bit when she was here—rather likes it up to a point.'[10] By the middle of 1926, when Frieda and Bud were planning their next meeting, the situation was tense once again. Frieda wrote to Bud: 'Either you arrive just before Mother & we greet her arm in arm, or Mother arrives just before you & will want me out of arm's [sic] way. I rather hope for the former. It would be a nightmare if it weren't so funny.'[11]

Both families posed problems. Bud wrote to Frieda: 'It seems such an appalling waste of time to have to go and see my family first and for most of the time. It isn't as if they wanted to see me particularly. They would bear up if I wanted to stay in any other place but N.Y. to see anyone else but you.'[12] [...]

*****

Frieda's mother was concerned about the relationship from its inception, but became especially concerned at the prospect of Bud returning to Canada on a permanent basis in 1927. She wrote to her friend Nettie for advice and, while her letter is not available, Nettie's response is revealing:

If I can *only* transfer to you, unbroken, my dear old friend, the vision which stands in my own mind with *increasingly persistent clearness and vigour* as a sure, safe, and upright method of meeting this rare problem—and, what is more, though God forbid that it should fail!—it seems to me looking at it in every way possible—it seems to me to be the *one and only* way which will bring everything around in the end!

As to Bud, the reaction that I have felt in realizing that she was not after all of the nature of that repulsive abnormal creature I heard of in that book, has resulted in a more tolerant leniency (perhaps that is expressing it a bit too strongly—as it might seem to you)—even you yourself could not help being conscious if you had read the thing!'[13]

It is unclear precisely to which book she was referring, but Nettie, in her guidance to Helene on how to deal with the relationship between Frieda and Bud, clearly reveals the availability in the 1920s of at least some works attesting to the existence of 'abnormal' sexualities. The degree to which Helene herself was familiar with such ideas is unknown, but it may be said that she held the relationship to be unhealthy and unnatural, even if she did not use any of the new sexological terminology with which to describe it.

Despite the obvious tensions involved in the relationships of Bud and Frieda with their respective families, the daughters maintained regular contact with family members and seemed to feel a duty to familial ties. During their separation and when they were able to live once again in Canada, their social worlds consisted primarily of women, some of whom were in same-sex relationships, yet these female social groups did not draw them away from their families.

Scholars suggest that lesbian communities, in which large numbers of women socialized together and even lived in close proximity to one another, based on their shared sexuality, formed in some areas of the United States as early as the 1920s and 1930s.[14] It is difficult to determine whether embryonic forms of lesbian community formed at this time in Canada. The evidence we do have suggests that the urban centres of entertainment, around which community often formed, did not begin as early in Canada as they did in the United States. How, then, were Canadian lesbians to recognize each other during these decades?

Frieda and Bud were both able to 'spot' other lesbians while they worked in the United States and Britain, but it is clear that they had an idea there were other women like themselves before they left Canada. Middle-class lesbian women were able to recognize each other within middle-class milieux. Precisely what 'signs' they looked for in other women is difficult to determine, however. For example, while travelling with her friend Bess on a cruise ship in Europe, Bud reported:

> Bess picked up the nicest women from the hospital on board—two nurses, Miss B and Miss S. They are head nurses at T.G.H. and quite old—about 45!!—They are *very* devoted to each other which is enough to make me interested in them even if they weren't such perfect lambs. We have been playing bridge with them a bit and this morning I had a long conversation with them when Bess was being professional. I was quite thrilled when they said that they had known each other for years and had always planned this trip, and had only managed it this year, and you could tell by the way they looked at each other, just *how* thrilled *they* were.[15]

How exactly Bess was 'spotted' by the Misses B. and S. is not known, but it would seem that they became reasonably friendly towards Bud, in whom they confided that 'their families had been awfully against their being together so much when they were young but after 20 years they are beginning to get used to it. It is an awfully difficult subject to chat about and it would never be approached if I had to do it, but they suddenly began to talk about it to-day.' Bud commented to Frieda that her new friends 'seem to agree with all we think about it, and also that there is no use trying to convince any other people about it—they simply can't see it.'[16]

During her stay in England in 1925, Bud wrote to Frieda about her aunt's cook and housemaid, revealing that her aunt

> told me that her cook and housemaid—who are by way of being ladies—had never had jobs before, but that their families had been rather disagreeable about their being awfully devoted and so they had up and left, and this was the only thing they could do. However, they loved it as it meant living together. So—there seems to be a fair amount of it about. And they were certainly the happiest looking creatures. I simply pined to talk to them about it. Aunt F. didn't like it much, but at the time she was ill and couldn't

get anyone else who could get on with her nurse and her companion, but she seems to be quite satisfied now. I asked her what her objection was and she said that is wasn't natural! Isn't it funny?[17]

Frieda discovered women who were 'devoted' to one another while she was working as an intern in New York during the late 1920s. She wrote to Bud concerning 'two middle-aged & very good looking females that spend all their week-ends together here.'[18] In the social milieux in which Frieda and Bud moved, it was likely that all of these same-sex couples were 'by way of being ladies' and were able to identify, in nuances of middle-class dress and language, others like themselves.

THE CHANGING DISCOURSE: LESBIANS AS ENEMIES OF THE FAMILY

It is difficult to determine the precise degree to which the increasingly medicalized discourse of sexuality infiltrated Ontario society beyond the medical profession and the educated elite. Emerging ideas about lesbianism, having their origin in the sexological and Freudian thinking of the early twentieth century, had both positive and negative effects for lesbians. Some women were able to frame their feelings within the new discourse without internalizing its more negative aspects. Bunny, writing passionately to her partner in Toronto, said:

> You have all the things that would, and did, hoist you almost beyond reach of my earthly eyes ... social poise, academic honours that are staggering in comparison to mine, achievement and prestige in the top drawer of social work ... teaching. Even those dizzy heights couldn't deter me, or send me ricocheting away from you as they might easily have ... Instead we reached out to each other from the ... to be analytical about this ... from *the libidinal level* ... the warm altogether pleasure of our emotional reaction to each other.[19]

Acknowledging that she and Elisabeth could not 'avoid the usual implications of the conservative school ... the biddies who frown upon close attachments between women,' Bunny commented: 'I faced the prospect of matrimony once, and decided with a cool sort of half logical knowledge that I would never be able to face the drudge, nor able to measure up to the usual expectations ... and once that was decided the rest has been easy ... lacking in conflict, I mean.'[20] The tide clearly was turning against lesbian relationships, yet Bunny and many other women of the 1940s were able to decide not to get married but to follow their passions, with only moderate public condemnation compared with that which would come later.

The Canadian public had to be trained slowly to view female relationships with an eye to lesbian content. Many parents remained ignorant of the possibility or saw it as something that could exist outside their family but not within it. Consequently, many lesbians were able to begin their sexual lives with other girls or women without fear of being caught. This may particularly have been the case for girls growing up lesbian in rural Ontario, which remained somewhat out of the reach of magazines and tabloid newspapers. Moreover, gender-bending was often more tolerated in rural settings, at least before the 1950s. Barb, a tomboyish young woman was active around the farm, helping with the manual work: 'Always known as a tomboy in the family … always like to wear my over-hauls, and my plaid shirts, and a straw hat. Oh boy. Spiffy!'[21] Her gender-bending behaviour was tolerated by her parents, who saw nothing unusual in it. She played most often with the boys, and did not care for the traditional pursuits of girls. She preferred the world of westerns, and would sometimes go into town to see a Roy Rogers or Gene Autry film.

*****

[…]Mary Louise Adams reveals that advice literature and films of the 1940s rarely explicitly linked 'sissy' and 'tomboy' behaviour with homosexuality because, she argues, to do so would have given credence to biological arguments about homosexuality and suggested the futility of the recent regulatory measures and sex education as a prophylaxis against social deviancy. Rather, gender-bending behaviour among children was portrayed as an adolescent condition, often the result of poor parenting, that could be reversed.[22] As Christabelle Sethna suggests, sex education was often conflated with gender instruction for girls. N. Rae Speirs, director of physical education for Toronto schools, argued in 1947 for the discouragement of antagonism towards the opposite sex; girls and boys 'needed to develop desirable attitudes toward each other.'[23] Barb began her first lesbian relationship with a friend while she was in high school in the late 1940s and recalls spending every available moment with her girlfriend, without her family, friends, or teachers being any the wiser. She states that after their first night together:

> I got more intimate with her … And then we used to go, back and forth, to our homes. She would come and stay a Saturday night and we'd be going to a show or something, and I'd go over to her house and stay. And then we got more intimate with touching the rest of our bodies … It'd be every weekend … and we'd have at least a night together, whether it would be a Friday or a Saturday night … so that went on for, oh, quite some time … probably two full summers and all the seasons through.[24]

When asked if she thought that her parents had figured out what was going on, Barb replied:

> No, or her parents, this girl's parents either. No, I'm sure they didn't. Or even the kids that we went to … school with in the classroom and stuff. I don't think, I don't know that anyone ever picked up anything. We were always trying, I was always trying to be close with her. Whenever we left school, we'd walk home together, or coming to school … so … I never heard anyone, no-one had ever said anything to me about 'What are you two together for all the time?' There was never anything of that said.[25]

It was not until Barb joined the armed services in 1952 that she heard much of lesbianism. She made friends with a group of five other lesbian women. In 1954 one of the women, under questioning, offered up the names of the rest of the group. Barb was hauled in to see a psychiatrist and, after an attempt to cover up her sexuality, was forced to admit that she was a lesbian. She was discharged. When asked how she had known what would be the consequences of telling the truth, Barb said that she could not remember specifically reading anything, but she had the distinct impression that, 'at that time, that was bad, bad, bad. Anybody caught you on your job, or any place, you know, that wasn't the right thing. In other words, you were queer, that was the whole thing, I think, you just weren't a normal person.'[26]

The armed services in the postwar period were the focus of much antagonism towards same-sex relationships. As representatives of the nation, of courage and honour, and of respectability, servicemen and servicewomen were subject to intense scrutiny of their sexual behaviour and gender performances. Any suspicion of a gay or lesbian relationship could provoke severe censure, if not immediate dismissal.[27] Fortunately, Barb was not asked to explain her military discharge to her family, as she had voluntarily left and received an honourable discharge, and she remained close to them throughout this period of her life.

'LESBIANS WHO FLAUNT THEMSELVES IN PUBLIC'

Although it is impossible to determine with certainty the proportion of the Canadian population that had heard of lesbian relationships in this period, it can be argued that, by the middle of the twentieth century, images of same-sex relationships and social worlds were increasingly available through mainstream media. This was particularly the case in Toronto, where a large gay and lesbian population congregated in the Yonge Street and Chinatown areas and was the cause of much comment. Lesbians became the subject of many a magazine or newspaper article. While some were vaguely sympathetic, many were lurid in their hyperbole about the 'homosexual lifestyle.' With the growth of the 'yellow press' in the 1950s, scare-mongering about homosexuality became *de rigueur*. The scandal sheets printed local and international material about lesbians and gay men. [...]

By 1964 homosexuality had become a more widespread concern. The *Telegram* published a series entitled 'Society and the Homosexual,' which aimed, after two months' research on the subject, to present 'accurate' information to the public. The first article in the series quoted the Toronto Forensic Clinic as believing that there were 15,000 active homosexual men in the metropolitan Toronto area, and a further 150,000 who were latent homosexuals or bisexuals. The article added: 'This deviate population is swelled by 6,000 Lesbians and 30,000 other women who live outwardly heterosexual lives but are sporadic or latent homosexuals.' The article went on to chronicle the torrid goings-on in a homosexual club on Yonge Street, where 'one pale, ethereal looking Lesbian danced with another who looked and moved like a sack of potatoes rolling downhill. To the homosexual, particularly, beauty is in the eye of the beholder.'[28] The newspaper reporter then tied the problem of homosexuality to the perceived breakdown in family life. Reporting that Toronto experts disagreed with rumours that the proportion of male homosexuals to heterosexuals had increased since the war, the paper nevertheless stated that the time was ripe for an increase. The cause? The author stated that 'the patriarchal society has become the matriarchal society and the lines of familial authority are blurring.'[29]

Such opinions echoed wartime fears of reversal in the 'natural' gender relationships of Canadian society. The presence of large numbers of women in the paid workforce during the war had produced considerable anxiety about the erosion of appropriate gender roles and, as Ruth

Roach Pierson indicates, had particularly aroused fears of the masculinzation of women. The Canadian military and the government had been at pains to emphasize the temporary nature and the femininity of the work involved.[30] The fears remained in the postwar period, however, and found their expression in an increasing range of regulatory and discursive measures aimed at controlling the behaviour of women and young people.[31]

While images of lesbians were becoming more widespread in Canada, the common assumptions about them were still largely negative, and many lesbians remained reticent about revealing their sexual orientation. This was particularly the case with middle-class and professional women, who kept their relationships out of public view and often condemned those lesbians who did not. [...]

Ross Higgins and Line Chamberland have shown that the yellow press of the 1950s and 1960s, while supporting and disseminating negative stereotypes of gays and lesbians, also helped to form the very communities they were describing. These papers, they say, not only described where the bars were but portrayed men and women of same-sex orientation, however strangely. Their study of Montreal scandal sheets shows that lesbians and gay men used the papers to give them access to personal contacts and to the bar scene, even while many papers were adopting a tone of moral outrage to sell more copies to a prurient heterosexual public.[32] The same dual function of the yellow press occurred in Toronto.[33]

Valerie Korinek's study of *Chatelaine* in the 1950s and 1960s has revealed that the magazine, unlike its American counterparts, published several articles on lesbians.[34] Many of these pieces perpetuated the psychological stereotypes of lesbians as neurotic and immature. Yet the few articles Korinek discovered which were directly related to lesbians avoided the turgid approach of the tabloid press in their attempt to provide an authoritative, scientific, and balanced viewpoint. The magazine interviewed lesbians to publicize their perspective. Korinek also argues that *Chatelaine* contained a number of stories, articles, and advertisements that were open to what she calls 'perverse readings,' in which 'lesbian readers could easily resist the preferred meanings of the material and opt for alternate interpretations which more aptly reflected their sense of themselves.'[35]

These media images, then, were available both to lesbians and to their families. But while open to the perverse readings of which Korinek writes, the new discourse of sexuality began to posit lesbians more forcefully as antagonists to the family, as both the result and the agents of family breakdown. Adams's *The Trouble with Normal* sets the increasing normalization of matrimonial heterosexuality within a framework of a postwar domestic 'revival,' in which deviance 'precluded the homogenization that was seen to be central to Canada's strength as a nation.'[36] Homogenization had to involve the protection of the young, who were believed to be particularly vulnerable to persuasion by popular images.[...]

Lesbians' relationship to family life began fundamentally to change in this new era of coercive heteronormativity. Whereas in earlier times the concept of family obligation and the lack of female financial independence (or, indeed, the family's need to rely on a daughter's income) might have militated against a family's wish to expel a daughter because of her sexuality, the new discourse allowed families to see their lesbian daughters increasingly as enemies, as threats to the further stability of the family home.

Lesbians themselves took advantage of the new employment opportunities and sought work and refuge from their families in the burgeoning metropolises of Toronto, Montreal, and Vancouver. Both middle- and working-class women sought new opportunities, which included the ability to live by themselves or with other women rather than with family. For the butch women, who most clearly transgressed the boundaries of gender, employment opportunities were few. In Toronto they were restricted to such jobs as driving trucks and labouring.[37] They were often supported financially by femmes or by other butch women in the community.

The most visible world of lesbians in postwar Canada was the predominantly working-class butch and femme bar culture of Toronto, Montreal, and Vancouver. There is little documentation of this culture in Canadian society. We know that there were many lesbian-friendly bars in Canadian cities in the 1960s, but fewer social outlets of this kind can be found for the previous decades.[38] Perhaps the most extensive study of a single Canadian butch and femme culture is Elise Chenier's examination of Toronto's public lesbian community from 1955 to 1965.[39] Chenier interviewed seven women in addition to examining the Lesbians Making History Project interviews also used in this chapter. She discusses the Continental Hotel, the main lesbian bar in the 1950s, and the lesbian community that used it. The Continental, like many other lesbian haunts, was in an area already associated in the minds of the police and the public with prostitution, drugs, and other illicit activities: Chinatown. Chenier argues that the lesbians involved in the bar culture in Toronto 'inadvertently helped to give shape to the postwar feminine ideal and provided medical experts with ammunition to launch an effective ideological war against women's social and economic emancipation.'[40] Despite these negative effects, however, the bar women also created for themselves a social environment based on their sexuality.

That the Ontario community was part of a wider trend is indicated by Chamberland's research into the Montreal lesbian community. Chamberland charts the bar scene of Montreal from 1955 to 1975 in an article that shows that the lesbian bar culture was structured along the same butch and femme lines as that of the United States.[41] She argues that Canadian butches and femmes, like their American counterparts, used their roles 'as a way of living [their] lesbian identity during an extremely repressive era by juggling gender categories and thus making visible or concealing lesbian existence, depending on the circumstances.'[42] Her research also indicates that butch and femme roles were strategies for securing and defending public space, in which she is in agreement with the Kennedy and Davis argument that butch/femme couples were the precursors to the lesbian-feminist movement of the 1970s in fighting for women's right to live openly and publically as lesbians.[43] As Chamberland states, 'exposure was needed in order to ensure that lesbian bars became known and accessible. Knowing that such places existed and discovering where they were was a problem. On the other hand, concealment was necessary in order to escape repression.'[44]

The mid-twentieth-century bar culture provided women with a sense of community: they knew where they could go to be with women like themselves; and they had a support group of women who trained them in the roles of the community, saw them through relationships and through struggles with the police and employers, and fought with them for public lesbian space. There was not necessarily a sense of community based on identity shared across class and other lines, however. Jerry, one of the women interviewed in the Lesbians Making History Project, argued that there was no lesbian community in the 1950s and 1960s. 'You survive, you survive,' she said.[45]

While their pre-war predecessors had been forced to deal with an emerging but still vague disapproval of their relationships, Ontario lesbians in the postwar era were faced with more hostile reactions from families informed by the new, public discourse of homosexuality and sexual pathology. In an examination of popular pscyhology in postwar Canada, Mona Gleason clearly demonstrates that psychologists, wishing to sustain the professional prestige established by their employment in the military, broadened their scope to take psychology into the innermost recesses of the public mind.[46] Via newspapers, magazines, and radio, psychologists gradually increased their hold on the Canadian psyche.

The new era made images of lesbians and their social worlds more available to young women coming to terms with their sexuality; it also meant that many families now had a name to put to their daughters' behaviours, and a socially approved framework within which to respond. That framework often involved psychiatric or psychological treatment. Jackie reported: 'They phoned my family up and they said, "Did you know that your sister's been seen in Toronto and she's dressing like a man?" My brother came looking for me, my older brother and my older sister. And I met them and they said, "We're going to put you in the fucking nuthouse: look at you!"'[47]

Pat came out to her family accidentally. Her mother's tone during a telephone conversation had suggested to Pat that she knew of her daughter's lesbianism, when in fact her mother had assumed that Pat was going out with a black man. Thinking that her mother had guessed her sexual orientation, Pat started talking about it. She had been a tomboy when she was growing up and later had been given a copy of *The Well of Loneliness* by her mother, a gift that might have suggested to Pat that her mother had some suspicions.[48] On revealing her sexual orientation, Pat was told to see a psychiatrist.

Jerry moved to Toronto at the age of fifteen, after receiving a hostile reaction to her sexuality. 'I was accused of being a lesbian at the age of 13 by my mother in the waiting room,' Jerry said. She continued: 'And this woman, her name was S. She had a pyjama party one night and there was 2 other, 3 other women I think. And S. and I got pretty heavy duty on the chesterfield.'[49] Jerry had known fully what lesbianism was, and had two books beneath her mattress at home about lesbian relationships, yet she was careful to deny knowledge when asked by her father and several doctors. After she left home, Jerry's father said to her sister: 'Your sister's a lesbian and I don't want her anywhere near my house. I don't want her anywhere near you.'[50] Jerry's father was in the airforce and might reasonably be expected to have had somewhat greater knowledge of homosexuality than many in the general public, given the high-profile purging of gay men and later of lesbians in the military.[51] He certainly was in command of a wider range of terminology for homosexuality than many others would have had, and he frequently lamented the fact that his daughter was 'queer.'[52]

Arlene discovered lesbians in the psychiatric hospital, after her mother had her committed at sixteen. She had been 'fooling around' with girls since the age of nine, but had not known what a lesbian was until she met several lesbian patients on the ward.[53] At nine, she and her best friend had started acting out the love scenes they saw at the movies. When she was ten, her friend's mother walked in on them making love, asked 'What are you doing?' and started to scream.

Arlene fled the house, went home, and overdosed on her mother's sleeping pills. Although it would appear that her friend's mother did not discuss the matter with Arlene's mother, her friend was put in another school and Arlene ceased most of her lesbian activity until her introduction to lesbians in the hospital.[54]

Arlene revealed that she was committed the same year that she came out to her family as a lesbian, but said the reason for the committal was that she was leaving home and her mother did not want her to go. Despite the fact that her mother abused her physically, Arlene described her family as a 'great one.' She was able to tell her whole family, including her grandparents, 'This is the way it is: I am a lesbian. I intend to stay one. You can either like me or not see me again.'[55] As Chenier comments, however, it is quite likely that her sexual preference was a factor in her mother's decision to have her committed.[56] Another Toronto lesbian, Alice, mentioned a friend who was kicked out of a convent when she was sixteen after she had been discovered in bed with another girl: 'And they threw her out because she wasn't Catholic. And her mother sent her to a psychiatrist and Betty lied to him.'[57]

Parents who regarded lesbianism negatively did not all send their wayward daughters to psychiatrists, however. Deborah, whose first relationship occurred in 1950, when she was sixteen years of age, had a very close relationship with her family. She had been told when she was growing up that homosexual men and lesbians were 'sick, depraved, mentally depraved.'[58] This comment had not deterred her from exploring a relationship with her teacher, who appeared regularly at the sports events Deborah was playing in. 'She made me feel whole—like I was the only person in the world and I was very special,' Deborah commented, though she knew that her relationship was risky: 'I used to think that if anybody ever knew that I was making love to a woman they would think I was crazy. They would think I was out of my mind. So we did everything we possibly could do to hide that, and we successfully did it, and I don't know how we did it. I really don't.' There were not even any close calls, 'because we always had a reason, and … I always had some backup … Although my family caught us lying in bed, looking through the crack of the door or something, you know, I found out that years and years later. But we were very cautious.'[59]

Veronica, who in 1956 began a relationship with a school friend, is sure that her girlfriend's mother knew of the relationship: 'There was her poor mother downstairs, you know, I'm sure. You know, we'd be up there … we're 16 years old. We were just so enraptured and so carried away, we could have carried on. And I'm sure her mother knew. And I'm sure her mother used to talk to her, Marilyn's aunt, whose daughter is [also a lesbian]. Maybe this was going on at the same time, you know, in her life, yeah. Yeah, so that was basically it, like in each other's homes. We never went anywhere and expressed anything.'[60]

These members of Ontario's lesbian culture reveal that even those lesbians who most clearly transgressed the boundaries of heteronormativity were not necessarily cast outside the family, but that attitudes towards lesbians had changed dramatically from the previous decades. Even though many women remained in touch with their families, concern about their sexuality could be explicit and overt. The new arguments of homosexual pathology were clearly available to parents and were part of their reactions to their daughters' behaviour.

For many lesbians, coming out meant giving up their own children. Jerry recalled that 90 per cent of women who were gay gave up their children. When asked why they did so, she replied:

'Because they figured they couldn't give them the proper life, the proper upbringing, give them what they needed while they were growing up or possibly the love and affection they needed because they were too fucked up in their own mind.'[61] Arlene confirmed that there were many lesbians who had children and had to give them up: 'I don't know any gay women at the time, that if the Children's Aid got hold of the kids, they ever got them back.'[62] In Ontario, all sexuality deemed 'deviant,' from unwed motherhood to homosexuality, was subject to moral regulation, which might take informal forms but was also policed by the province. Margaret Little clearly indicates that sexual morality was explicitly linked to deservedness in the case of the Ontario Mothers' Allowance in the postwar era.[63]

Because the discourse of the postwar era condemned lesbians as the products of dysfunctional families, it is axiomatic that they were held to be bad parents. It was therefore not possible for lesbians to maintain relationships with their children, since society held that exposure to the lesbian lifestyle would 'make' children homosexual. Even lesbian mothers themselves doubted their ability to be good parents to their children. It was not until the social movements of the late 1960s and the 1970s that a reverse discourse emerged. This discourse challenged the traditional, heterosexual family and welcomed new ways of interpreting 'family,' notions that would allow lesbians to conceptualize themselves as at least as fit as heterosexual parents.

Examining the period 1920 to 1965, one sees a gradual shift in the relationship between lesbians and their families. In the early twentieth century, several factors militated against families of origin rejecting outright their lesbian daughters. There existed perhaps a stronger sense of obligation within some families, although it would be difficult to assess the degree to which this comparison was true across class boundaries, given the paucity of records of working-class women for the years before the Second World War. This is not to suggest that there were not cases in which women were thrown out of the family home because of lesbianism. Doubtless there were, but this study of lesbian lives has revealed that family ties remained important for many lesbians even into the 1960s.

What is more important, however, is the impact of the postwar discourse about homosexuality. Whereas, before the war, families often condemned lesbian relationships with vague reasons for their views, the postwar era gave families a new terminology, and an extremely hostile one, with which to reject their daughters' sexuality. In addition, one might suggest that the expanding world of women's work allowed a diminishing of family obligation, in the sense that more women could be financially independent. For families, this made the expulsion of the lesbian daughter from the family home less objectionable. The rising standard of living in the postwar era might also have made it easier for some families to give up their daughters' incomes. For lesbians themselves, it meant the opening up of the possibility of living their own lives without the scrutiny of family members. Many working-class women in particular moved to Canada's cities both for employment opportunities and for the chance to live as lesbians within the emerging lesbian communities.

Ideologues of the postwar era in Canada tried to instil in family life an antagonism towards those who strayed from the path of heterosexual matrimony, yet they were only partially successful. Many lesbians suffered the consequences of the new, psychological arguments and were marginalized and institutionalized on the basis of their sexuality. Yet, as the sources for this essay indicate, family remained important in the lives of many lesbians. Few families absorbed the new discourse to the degree that they cut ties with their daughters absolutely.

With the advent of the social movements of the late 1960s, however, change occurred in lesbians' relationships with their families of origin. Society had come, over the preceding two decades, to see lesbians as antithetical to the family, and lesbians began to see the traditional family as heterosexist. By the 1970s lesbians could be singing 'Family of Woman.'[64] By the 1980s and 1990s one could speak of 'lesbian parenting' and 'lesbian families' as viable alternatives to the traditional normative family.[65] These ideas are a positive interpretation of lesbian life, in which lesbians are seen once again as capable of family life, albeit with a twist, and yet this positive development has its origin in the gradual separation of lesbians from the family unit in the postwar era. Born in antagonism, the alternative lesbian family is the result of a decades-old struggle between lesbian identity and notions of family life.

NOTES

1 University of Toronto Archives, Fraser Family Personal Records, Ace. No. B95-0044 (Fraser Records), sous-fonds III, box 036, file 8, Frieda Fraser to Edith Bickerton Williams, 5 March 1926. Frieda moved temporarily from Ontario between 1925 and late 1926 to gain her medical internship at the New York Infirmary for Women. She then moved to Philadelphia to complete her training and returned to Toronto in 1928.

2 This essay uses two archival collections of correspondence. Pseudonyms have been used in the case of one and its accession information is not included. Also used are interviews conducted by the author as well as several interviews conducted by the Lesbians Making History Project. Pseudonyms have been used to disguise the identities of the narrators. The author is indebted to Maureen FitzGerald for access to the Lesbians Making History Project interviews.

3 Mary Louise Adams, *The Trouble with Normal: Postwar Youth and the Making of Heterosexuality* (Toronto: University of Toronto Press, 1997), 5.

4 Lillian Faderman, *Odd Girls and Twilight Lovers: A History of Lesbian Life in Twentieth-Century America* (New York: Penguin, 1991), 93–4.

5 Jeffrey Weeks, *Sexuality and Its Discontents: Meanings, Myths, and Modern Sexualities* (London and New York: Routledge, 1985), 76.

6 Radclyffe Hall, *The Well of Loneliness* (London: Cape, 1928). The book was reviewed in the *Canadian Forum* 9, 103 (1929), 243–4. See also Steven Maynard, 'Radclyffe Hall in Canada,' *Centre/Fold* 6 (1994), 9.

7 Robin Brownlie, 'Crimes of Passion: Lesbians and Lesbianism in Canadian Prisons, 1960–1994,' paper delivered at the Canadian Historical Association Conference, Ottawa, 1998, 13.

8 Lillian Faderman argues that tolerance of romantic friendships between women began to erode at the beginning of the twentieth century with the gradual popularization of sexological theories. See, for example, Lillian Faderman, *Surpassing the Love of Men: Romantic Friendship and Love between Women from the Renaissance to the Present* (New York: William Morrow, 1981), and *Odd Girls and Twilight Lovers*. It can be shown, however, that the distinct vocabulary of the romantic friendship was still in use in the mid-twentieth century. The Elizabeth Govan/Bunny correspondence discussed in this paper and that between Ontario social welfare administrator and politician Charlotte Whitton

and Margaret Grier clearly indicate that the language of the romantic friendship was being used by Canadian women well into the twentieth century. Whitton's relationships with women are discussed in Patricia T. Rooke, 'Public Figure, Private Woman: Same-Sex Support Structures in the Life of Charlotte Whitton,' *International Journal of Women's Studies* 6, 5 (1983): 205–28, and in P.T. Rooke and R.L. Schnell, *No Bleeding Heart: Charlotte Whitton, A Feminist on the Right* (Vancouver: UBC Press, 1987).

9 This extremely large collection of letters is one of the most significant discoveries in Canadian lesbian history. The collection follows the entire course of their relationship, although the major part of the collection comprises the letters written between Frieda and Bud during their years apart in the 1920s. The author is indebted to Donald Fraser and Nancy Fraser Brooks, nephew and niece of Frieda Fraser and executors of her estate, whose assistance with this collection has been extremely helpful and whose realization of the historical importance of the letters has given to Canadian scholars the stories of two very interesting lives.

10 Fraser Records, sous-fonds III, box 036, file 7, Frieda Fraser to Edith Bickerton Williams, 1 January 1926.

11 Ibid., file 9, Frieda Fraser to Edith Bickerton Williams, 13 June 1926.

12 Ibid., box 010, file 4, Edith Bickerton Williams to Frieda Fraser, 11 June 1926.

13 Ibid., sous-fonds II, box 001, file 17, Nettie Bryant to Helene Fraser, 23 April 1927.

14 See, for example, Faderman, *Odd Girls and Twilight Lovers;* Elizabeth Lapovsky Kennedy and Madeline D. Davis, *Boots of Leather, Slippers of Gold: The History of a Lesbian Community* (New York and London: Routledge, 1993); and Esther Newton, *Cherry Grove, Fire Island: Sixty Years in America's First Gay and Lesbian Town* (Boston: Beacon Press, 1993). George Chauncey, although writing mainly of the gay male world, reveals lesbian social community in New York in this period in his excellent *Gay New York: Gender, Urban Culture, and the Making of the Gay Male World 1890–1940* (New York: Basic Books, 1994).

15 Fraser Records, sous-fonds II, box 010, file 3, Edith Bickerton Williams to Frieda Fraser, 30 June 1925.

16 Ibid., Edith Bickerton Williams to Frieda Fraser, 2 July 1925.

17 Ibid., 22 August 1925.

18 Ibid., sous-fonds III, box 036, file 11, Frieda Fraser to Edith Bickerton Williams, 5 March 1927.

19 University of Toronto Archives, Elisabeth Steel Govan Papers, Ace. No. 879-0027, box 003, file 4, 'Bunny' to Elisabeth Govan, nd., prob. 1945.

20 Bunny to Elisabeth Govan, nd.

21 Interview with Barb, 15 May 1998.

22 Adams, *The Trouble with Normal*, 95–8.

23 Christabelle Sethna, 'The Facts of Life: The Sex Instruction of Ontario Public School Children, 1900–1950' (PhD dissertation, University of Toronto, 1995), 253.

24 Interview with Barb, 15 May 1998.

25 Ibid.

26 Ibid.

27 Little work has yet been done on the experiences of lesbians in the Canadian military. Ruth Roach Pierson reveals, in *They're Still Women after All: The Second World War and Canadian Womanhood* (Toronto: McClelland & Stewart, 1986), 275 n. 83, that lesbians were forced to leave the military during the war. Much greater detail on the armed services during the war and the postwar period is

offered by Gary Kinsman, *The Regulation of Desire: Homo and Hetero Sexualities,* 2nd ed. (Montreal: Black Rose Books, 1996), 148–54, 181–3.

28 Ron Poulton, *The Telegram,* 11 April 1964, 7.

29 Ibid.

30 Pierson, *They're Still Women after All,* 129–68.

31 See, for example, those measures discussed in Mariana Valverde, 'Building Anti-delinquent Communities: Morality, Gender, and Generation in the City,' in Joy Parr, ed., *A Diversity of Women: Ontario, 1945–1980* (Toronto: University of Toronto Press, 1995), 19–45.

32 Ross Higgins and Line Chamberland, 'Mixed Messages: Gays and Lesbians in Montreal Yellow Papers in the 1950s,' in Ian McKay, ed., *The Challenge of Modernity: A Reader on Post-Confederation Canada* (Toronto: McGraw-Hill Ryerson, 1992), 428–30.

33 Kinsman, *The Regulation of Desire,* 168.

34 Valerie Korinek, '"Don't Let Your Girlfriends Ruin Your Marriage": Lesbian Imagery in *Chatelaine* Magazine, 1950–1969,' paper presented at the Canadian Historical Association Conference, 1998.

35 Ibid., 27.

36 Adams, *The Trouble with Normal,* 23.

37 Elise Chenier, 'Tough Ladies and Troublemakers: Toronto's Public Lesbian Community, 1955–1965' (MA thesis, Queen's University, 1995), 133–4.

38 Donald W. McLeod, *Lesbian and Gay Liberation in Canada: A Selected Annotated Chronology, 1964–1975* (Toronto: ECW Press/Homewood Books, 1996), 277–86.

39 Chenier, 'Tough Ladies and Troublemakers.'

40 Ibid., 229.

41 Line Chamberland, 'Remembering Lesbian Bars: Montreal, 1955–1975,' in Wendy Mitchinson et al., eds., *Canadian Women: A Reader* (Toronto: Harcourt Brace, 1996), 354–58.

42 Ibid., 361.

43 Kennedy and Davis, *Boots of Leather, Slippers of Gold,* 378–80.

44 Chamberland, 'Remembering Lesbian Bars,' 363.

45 Jerry, interview conducted by Elise Chenier, Lesbians Making History Project. Collection (LMH), 23 November 1992. Chenier donated this interview to the LMH Collection after completion of her MA thesis.

46 Mona Gleason, 'Psychology and the Construction of the "Normal" Family in Postwar Canada, 1945–60,' *Canadian Historical Review* 78, 3 (1997): 447.

47 Interview with Jackie, LMH, 19 October 1985.

48 Interview with Pat, LMH, 21 September 1986.

49 Jerry, interview conducted by Elise Chenier, LMH, 23 November 1992.

50 Ibid.

51 See Kinsman, *The Regulation of Desire,* 148–212; and Daniel J. Robinson and David Kimmel, 'The Queer Career of Homosexual Security Vetting in Cold War Canada,' *Canadian Historical Review* 75, 3 (1994): 319–45.

52 Jerry, interview conducted by Elise Chenier, LMH, 23 November 1992.

53 Interview with Arlene, LHM, 6 May 1987.

54 Ibid.

55 Ibid.

56 Chenier, 'Tough Ladies and Troublemakers,' 84.

57 Interview with Alice, LHM, 16 November 1985.

58 Deborah, e-mail interview, 10 June 1998.

59 Interview with Deborah, 29 September 1998.

60 Interview with Veronica, 27 September 1998.

61 Jerry, interview conducted by Elise Chenier, LMH, 23 November 1992.

62 Interview with Arlene, LHM, 6 May 1987.

63 Margaret Jane Hillyard Little, 'No Car, No Radio, No Liquor Permit': The Moral Regulation of Single Mothers in Ontario, 1920–1997 (Toronto: Oxford University Press, 1998), 130.

64 Title of a Linda Shear song, cited in Becki Ross, The House That Jill Built: A Lesbian Nation in Formation (Toronto: University of Toronto Press, 1995), 57, n. 258.

65 Katherine Arnup, ed., Lesbian Parenting: Living with Pride and Prejudice (Charlottetown: Gynergy Books, 1995), is the most recent Canadian work to explore the creation of alternative families on the basis of parenting by lesbians.

CHAPTER 22

Heterosexuality Goes Public: The Postwar Honeymoon

Karen Dubinsky

Leave It To Beaver was not a documentary.

—Stephanie Coontz, *The Way We Never Were: American Families and the Nostalgia Trap*

It is tempting to think of the 1950s as a time of conformity, conservatism, and silliness. One of the first feminist histories of that era, a book that helped to convince me I was fortunate not to have come of age then, was U.S. historian Elaine May's *Homeward Bound*, published in 1988. Beginning her study with a powerful 1959 *Life* magazine photograph of a newlywed couple who spent their honeymoon in a backyard bomb shelter, May tells the story of the domestic Cold War, which was based on the containment of threats to home and family. Lurking beyond this heavily fortified haven were not only the nefarious Russians but also a host of sinister home-grown dangers, spawned in what another historian has termed "the other Fifties"—tough butch lesbians, juvenile delinquents, rebellious "Beats," and pregnant teenagers.[1] The reds were under the bed, the queers were bunked down on top of it, and the normal people, so it seemed, were surrounded.

If we remember only those who obeyed the rules—the people of the white, suburban, middle-class fifties—we miss out on how the normal and the abnormal helped to create each other. To the normal went considerable spoils. Postwar North America was a place of prosperity and upward mobility, and a young married couple had good reason to expect a life of relative financial security. The abnormal—the sexual and gender non-conformists of the day such as homosexuals, promiscuous women, or disobedient teenagers—had an equally reasonable chance of ending up in a doctor's office, an unwed mothers' home, a psychiatric institution, or perhaps even a jail cell. But the creation of appropriate standards of social and sexual conduct invariably relies on a balance of consent and coercion; repression or punishment alone is not always effective (or necessary). The sexual politics of this era were shaped as much by the enthusiastic public emergence of the ideal—the happy heterosexual—as they were by the demonization of the pathological homosexual.

Homosexuality was relegated to the shadowy, unappealing margins of postwar culture. Certainly scenes like the ending of the 1962 film *The Children's Hour*, in which the self-loathing lesbian Shirley MacLaine moans about how dirty and perverted she is before hanging herself from the rafters, offered little in the way of positive advertising. Heterosexuality looked great when contrasted with this dreary Other. But heterosexuality was also transformed by postwar changes in the economy, leisure time, family life, and gender identities. Public, self-conscious, and thoroughly sexualized, heterosexuals became ubiquitous figures in the mid-twentieth century in part because they got around so much. "We are everywhere" remains a popular slogan of the modern gay movement, but in the 1950s it would have made more sense as a heterosexual maxim.

Getting everywhere started with the honeymoon. The travel boom after World War II was organized to take advantage of the disposable income and vacation time of the working class, as well as of the middle and upper classes. Like travel itself, the honeymoon became a popular and—along with the automobile and television set—accessible item of mass consumption. A great many more people could afford a honeymoon, but what was being purchased had also changed. Public discussions of the honeymoon expanded after the war, as did the promotion and advertising efforts of the tourist industry, especially at Niagara Falls.

Immediately after the war it seemed everyone was either getting married and having a honeymoon, or if not they were writing, joking, or singing about those events, advising others on how to plan them properly, or making films or television shows about them. Thus the honeymoon, and Niagara Falls as a honeymoon destination, acquired a much more overtly sexual meaning in the popular imagination. For the first time in history, massive numbers of people were invited to mark their entry into officially sanctioned public sexuality with a visit to an internationally renowned cultural icon, where they would be treated like honoured guests and showered with free gifts, roses, and complementary cocktails. With PR like this, who wouldn't want to be straight?

PERFORMANCE ANXIETIES: EXPERTS DEBATE THE HONEYMOON

A "real honeymoon" became a standard, routine, and familiar feature of postwar marriages. On one level, a real honeymoon was a simple undertaking. The more visible the honeymoon became, the more people understood what it was supposed to look like: it involved travel, privacy, and plenty of sex. But on another level, as more and more people participated and as the ritual attained wider cultural visibility, the meaning, purpose, and main features of the honeymoon came under serious scrutiny.

As before, doctors, psychiatrists, counsellors, and other marital experts led the debate. The huge growth of mass media determined that their messages would be carried far and wide. No longer did sex experts confine themselves to writing discreet, chastely titled advice manuals. After the war they spread their wisdom far and wide in newspapers and magazines, how-to films, radio shows, and even university courses.

Most postwar experts combined conservative views about gender roles with upbeat and optimistic predictions of heterosexual pleasure in marriage. Sexual compatibility was, as one Canadian manual put it, "the cement … that binds a home together." Others voiced the same sentiment in a gloomier manner, claiming, for example, that three-quarters of divorces were caused by sexual "maladjustments."[2] If sexual harmony "cemented" the marriage, the honeymoon was the foundation. A "bad" honeymoon might cause lifelong impotence for the male (particularly for "Mama's boys who fear women," latent homosexuals, or others with "doubts about their own virility"). For the woman, the experts diagnosed a new disease, "honeymoon shock"*(vaginismus),* which had potentially dire and similarly lifelong consequences. Bad honeymoons wrecked three out of five marriages, caused nervous and mental disorders, and, as Canadian sex expert Alfred Tyrer explained, "More psychological damage may be done on the honeymoon than the balance of life can correct."[3]

Here we see something of the dilemma of Cold War culture in North American culture generally: life was good, certainly superior to that of almost everyone else on the planet, but we had to guard what we had zealously, lest it go terribly wrong. This combination of optimism and anxiety was especially ironic when the topic was sex. For at the same time that the honeymoon—defined in explicitly sexual terms—was becoming a mass cultural phenomenon, North American society received some surprising news from Dr. Alfred Kinsey and his research staff. Apparently, about 50 per cent of American women and up to 90 per cent of American men came to their honeymoon as something other than blushing and virginal.

If premarital sex was as widespread as Kinsey's figures suggested, one might think that this news would have taken some of the spotlight off of the wedding night. The reverse was true, and medical experts and honeymoon promoters alike continued to assume that they were addressing the sexually innocent. Experts did begin to caution husbands against attaching too much importance to external signs of virginity, such as the condition of the hymen. According to one writer, this was an "unfortunate hangover from the past centuries of ignorance." But all concerned reminded old-fashioned husbands that hymens could be disrupted accidentally, through sports or doctors' examinations. In the world of advice-giving, rarely was the possibility—much less statistical probability—of premarital sexual activity raised. When it was, it was only to diminish its significance, for, as Maxine Davis declared in 1963, "Prior physical encounters, whatever their extent, are no preview of sexual love at its very best—within marriage."[4]

The honeymoon was not just popular, it was *important.* Like their predecessors in the 1920s and 1930s, postwar sex experts imagined a direct line that began at the honeymoon and extended to the health and well-being of the marriage and, hence, society itself. As historian Mary Louise Adams notes, the influence of psychoanalytic theories in postwar North America determined that heterosexuality meant something much more than relationships between women and men. Rather, "It came to be seen as essential to the expression of 'maturity.'" Yet, as always, heterosexual development was "a fragile process, one open to corruption."[5] Heterosexuality bore the weight of an increasing number of social, cultural, and political virtues: the well-being of the family and nation and the psychological fitness of the individual, to name just a few. A good send-off, in the form of a proper honeymoon, was crucial.

As in other eras, conformity to gender roles was part of the script. The notion that women and men had vastly differing sexual appetites was still widely held. Experts confidently asserted that women possessed a vastly slower libido (desiring sex approximately half as often as men did, one said), were slower to climax, and generally more "repressed" than men. [...] One team of Canadian writers explained that male physiology gave men both a stronger sex drive *and* a greater interest in their work, whereas women have only one "consuming interest" in life: home and family ("nature's purpose" for women, as another put it). Less crudely, perhaps, Maxine Davis explained that women "are equipped but not conditioned for sexual pleasure."[6]

The consequences of toying with gender boundaries were severe. Psychiatrist Harry Tashman related the sad tale of one couple, Laura and Ralph, who switched roles during their honeymoon. Ralph was seized by a bout of "surprising, shocking" insecurity, and so Laura took over and "attempted to make a success of their nuptial night." This effort proved a disaster. "They separated in bed, each taking a distant edge. Their brooding silence established an abyss between them. That abyss became a gulf they never really spanned" until, some ten years later, Ralph sought psychiatric help. The same logic determined that women should refuse sex only rarely, for "in this," Dr. Paul Scholten noted in 1958, "she is rejecting that which her spouse considers the most valuable and personal thing he has to offer her."[7]

The honeymoon was no picnic for men, either, though they were still clearly in charge. Francis Strain reminded husbands that they were "the leading man" and "this was his hour," and Margaret Sanger urged the husband to "dominate the whole situation." Women, she said, bear the burden of the engagement period, but the honeymoon "is essentially the responsibility of the bridegroom."[8] This was a responsibility men were not to take lightly. The old Victorian figure of the "brute"—rechristened "the caveman"—re-emerged, and postwar experts continued to deplore the "rape" of wives by insecure, overcompensating husbands.[9] [...]

But a greater problem than the emergence of the caveman was the updated, more medicalized version of the bumbling groom: the insecure, impotent husband. Men, argued one doctor, were under much more pressure than women: "She has not to do but merely to be, to exist." Little wonder that several experts cited "marital stage-fright" or "honeymoon impotence" as a serious wedding-night problem for men. They advised brides to "exercise extreme tact" should this situation arise, for "there is probably no subject about which the male is more sensitive." However, unless impotence had deeper psychological causes (such as repressed homosexuality), it could usually be dealt with by that modern panacea: consultation with experts such as doctors or psychiatrists.[10] Not surprisingly, no parallel alarm was raised over women's sexual dysfunctions, despite studies indicating that only 6 to 25 per cent of women achieved orgasm during their honeymoons.[11] [...]

The female wedding-night malady that did alarm physicians was the newly diagnosed condition "honeymoon shock" or *vaginismus*. The condition was first discussed in the 1950s, when doctors tended to blame it on husbands, whose failure to provide the "proper erotic atmosphere" caused their wives painful spasms of the vagina—also described as a "nervous reaction to a severe emotional shock." [...][12]

Such are some of the ways that the wedding night was, by mid-century, colonized by the helping professions. The premarital medical examination was taken for granted as part of wedding planning; almost everyone writing about the honeymoon recommended it. And lots of people, it seemed, were reading expert advice: according to a 1947 U.S. study, 70 per cent of men and

50 per cent of women had acquired a "book-knowledge of sex-life" and the "art of love" that helped their honeymoons considerably. Indeed, the proliferation of advice, and the ubiquity of the expert, spawned a backlash. As early as 1948 *Cosmopolitan* magazine wondered "Are Those Marriage Manuals Any Good?" and worried that the huge influx of "Baedekers to wedlock" was taking the mystery out of sex. In the late 1950s one pair of writers fashioned their claims to authority on a deft combination of anti-expert sentiment and heterosexuality, noting that they were "not physicians, but a married couple."[13]

In some quarters the backlash extended beyond the role of expertise to the honeymoon itself. There were those who believed the honeymoon craze had gone too far, that the ritual was out-dated, overdone, and a "barbaric" introduction to married life. The most outspoken critic was British psychiatrist and Member of Parliament Reginald Bennett, whose anti-honeymoon views made quite a splash in North America. The honeymoon, Bennett declared in 1955, was simply an "ordeal," and wedding-night sex was too often "a hopeless, fumbling effort." Like Victorian commentators before him, Bennett opposed the honeymoon because it was exhausting and embarrassing. He was especially perturbed by "the lore of the honeymoon, the vast repertory of awful jokes." Other commentators argued that, as a vacation, the honeymoon "constitutes an unreal introduction to life together." Still others adopted a more self-consciously "modern" perspective, maintaining that the ritual was simply out of step with the experience of the travel and sex-savvy postwar generation. Two such modern writers, the husband and wife team of Jerome and Julia Rainer, scorned the "doleful warnings" of other experts, arguing instead: "Only in the rarest instance is there a possibility of some deeply disturbing result from coital awkwardness during the honeymoon. Most modern couples are so keenly absorbed in the experience of total emotional surrender that they easily surmount even bungling and apprehension."[14]

A more breezy approach was taken by *Cosmopolitan* writer Caroline Bird, who praised "nature's merciful amnesia" for allowing most women to forget how horrible their honeymoons were. Fortunately for "the preservation of the race," she said, most women couldn't remember any more about their honeymoons than they could about "the pangs of childbirth."[15]

For it or against it, the honeymoon, it seemed, was everywhere. That the modern honeymoon had travelled far from the nineteenth-century wedding tour was clear from the story—which surfaced several different times in the 1940s and 1950s—of the mother-in-law who attempted to register in the same hotel as her honeymooning daughter and son-in-law.[16] That this situation was exactly what a honeymoon had been several generations earlier would have been lost on contemporary readers, who were expected to chuckle at the absurdity of the scenario.

HETEROSEXUALITY OFF-CAMERA: HOLLYWOOD DISCOVERS THE HONEYMOON

While the advice of medical and marital experts on the honeymoon—as on many other matters—cast a long shadow, those counsellors were certainly not alone in their depiction of the wedding night as a thoroughly reclusive, sexualized ritual. In the pop culture of the postwar era, the honeymoon quickly became a dirty joke—a sort of shorthand, indirect way of talking about what one was not supposed to talk about: sex. The only culturally permissible sex possible—between two married, adult heterosexuals—could be addressed *on-camera* only through innuendo, hints, and veiled, risqué humour, all reliant on social meanings and knowledge acquired *off-camera*.

The honeymoon could be used to say almost anything naughty, as long as it was said indirectly. The entire plot of RKO's 1940 film *Lucky Partners*, for example, turns on the impossibility of two people taking an "impersonal," non-romantic trip together to Niagara Falls. [...]

*****

Honeymoon humour generally turned on three sorts of jokes or scenarios: sexual potency, sexual anxieties, and disruptions to the traditional honeymoon script. Jokes about the honeymoon as the zenith of sexual passion were cheap and plentiful. [...]

*****

The flip side of potency is anxiety, and here too honeymoon humour played on some of the tensions identified by marital experts. Anxious brides were funnier. Ginger Rogers did a wonderful parody of a blushing bride in a hotel suite in Howard Hawks's 1952 film *Monkey Business*. [...] *The Long, Long Trailer*, starring Lucille Ball and Desi Arnaz, addressed the question of male anxieties. A virtual smorgasbord of popular Freudian sexual clichés, most of the humour in this film derives from Desi's fears of driving the "long, long trailer" they take on their honeymoon.[17] [...] Disruptions to the conventional honeymoon narrative were another popular storyline. When Eddy Cantor interviewed Hattie McDaniel on his 1941 radio show *A Time to Smile*, she had just been married. "Did you have a nice honeymoon?" inquired Cantor. In her most robust mammy voice, McDaniel replied, "I don't know. My husband ain't come back from it yet!" [...] Narrative disruptions were popular plot lines in honeymoon-themed fiction [...] and short stories and novels of this era abounded with ex-girlfriends, evil twins, children, or boorish friends tagging along with a newlywed couple. Travel mishaps were another narrative device that brought temporary catastrophe or, sometimes, adventure to newlyweds. Two genres, horror and pornography, have especially favoured this device.[18]

Pop culture, then, helped to establish the mass appeal of the honeymoon, as well as its particular features: travel, privacy, and sex. Niagara Falls was not the only place in which these stories unfolded, but it did come up often enough, especially in Hollywood films, to consolidate its reputation. Just as the honeymoon became a culturally acceptable, if risqué, metaphor for sex, so too did Niagara Falls itself. The connection between the two—Niagara and sex—was pretty obvious, as the imaginary geography of the place became a whole lot less imaginary. "To Niagara in a sleeper, there's no honeymoon that's cheaper, and the train goes slow" wrote Harry Warren and Al Dubin in the 1938 song "Shuffle off to Buffalo." [...]

Certainly *Niagara* is the most famous cinematic depiction of the Falls. That the movie was a tremendous boon to the local tourist industry was perhaps more a testament to its fabulous cinematography—it was, on one level, a two-hour travelogue chronicling the main attractions of the Niagara region—than its plot. Yet the film is not without its narrative charms, and it is especially striking how well it straddles two distinct eras of Niagara's sexual culture.

The story—of the awful power of female sexuality for men—echoes nineteenth-century depictions of Niagara as an alluring female icon, seducing and entrapping her male suitors.

Indeed, the advertising for the film featured Monroe reclining over the waterfall, her body and the water merging into each other; the caption: "Marilyn Monroe and Niagara—a raging torrent of emotion that even nature can't control!"

*****

Contemporary journalists adopted this same innuendo-laden, jocular script—the point of view so prevalent in Hollywood's honeymoon stories. Lurking between the lines of postwar newspaper and magazine commentary on the Niagara honeymoon was sex. Indeed, by all accounts postwar honeymooners were having so much sex that they forgot to tip their waiters, left their wedding rings in hotel bathrooms, did not emerge from their rooms for days on end, crossed busy streets on red lights, and generally wandered around the town dazed and disoriented.

This public recasting of the honeymoon as a specifically sexual ritual, geared solely to the newlywed couple, occurred at the same time as the postwar travel boom; and the two trends came together at Niagara Falls, the self-styled "Honeymoon Capital of the World." The expanded, reinvented, slightly lewd honeymoon found a congenial physical home in the expanded, reinvented, slightly lewd tourist industry at the Falls. It was a perfect match.

THE NIAGARA HONEYMOON: "MAGIC IN THE MIST"

[…] Few postwar tourism boosters were willing to leave their business success up to reputation, even one as powerful or enduring as Niagara's. Honeymoon advertising and promotion skyrocketed, and establishments outdid themselves trying to woo the honeymoon trade. Complementary cocktails, roses, breakfasts, and an array of other specials greeted honeymooners at local motels, hotels, and restaurants. Journalists were popping up everywhere wanting to interview or photograph newlyweds. City fathers on both sides of the river welcomed them warmly, and the entire tourist industry seemed to recognize them the moment they hit town. The attention may have been a bit embarrassing, but it also must have been flattering.

An early, and enduring, honeymoon promotional device was the "honeymoon certificate." The members of the Niagara Falls, Ontario, Chamber of Commerce lifted this idea from their counterparts across the river in June 1949, and they honoured the first winners, a cleverly chosen mixed-nation couple (he was from Ohio, she from Ontario) in a ceremony in the Oakes Garden Theatre.[19] […] The ensuing publicity was so great—stories and photos appeared in newspapers across North America and Warner Brothers even sent a cameraman to cover the event for Pathé Newsreels—that tourism entrepreneurs discussed making it an annual contest, a honeymooner's version of the Miss America pageant.

The contest didn't materialize, but the success of the certificates convinced local businessmen that the honeymoon trade was both lucrative and newsworthy. Milestones were quickly manufactured—the one-thousandth couple, the two-thousandth couple, couples on anniversary honeymoons—and "winners" were announced and celebrated. Dozens of local merchants contributed gifts to what the Chamber of Commerce called a "community shower" for the one-thousandth couple, and most winners (at least the white ones) could expect a night or two at the General Brock and, always, their pictures in the paper.[20] […]

*****

Journalists covering this oft-travelled Niagara honeymoon beat filled their pages with sly, but, for the most part, good-humoured insinuation. Writing for *Chatelaine,* Canadian journalist Lotta Dempsey noticed that most tourists at the Falls held hands and wandered around in a "dazed and daffy coma." June Callwood and Trent Frayne, sent by *Maclean's* magazine in 1950 as "undercover honeymooners" (at the time they had been married six years), were delighted to discover the tricks that Niagara residents used to spot the newlyweds: honeymooners sported new shoes and haircuts, held hands in public, and, especially, suffered acute embarrassment when registering at hotels.[21]

Others weighed in with a range of special honeymooner traits: they were poor tippers, they never ate breakfast, they constantly stared at each other. According to officers who patrolled Queen Victoria Park, "Love is conducive to forgetfulness," because jewellery, movie cameras, and full wallets were, apparently, regularly mislaid in the park. [...] A journalist from [...] *Esquire* magazine remarked that hotel staff kept track of newlywed sexual marathons, awarding the "unofficial record" to one couple who did not emerge from their room for nine days.[22]

*****

So closely were they identified with heterosexual passion, the Falls became, as they had in previous eras, an easy and obvious target for gay camp parody. This time, though, gay appropriations of the Falls went further than a few men giggling together over a beer. Now there were sequins. At the U.S. gay resort Fire Island, for example, drag shows featured a dance number that had a male/female couple dancing to "Shuffle Off to Buffalo" in front of a chorus line of six-foot-tall men draped in glittering strips of silver foil: Niagara Falls. The place was a popular location for self-styled "honeymoons" among working-class lesbians in Toronto in the early 1960s, and a gay male couple even registered for a honeymoon certificate later in the 1970s (which they received with "no giggles," according to the Chamber of Commerce).[23]

The Niagara region's local gay population might have had a less ironic perspective on the place. Regular police harassment was a staple feature of gay life in most North American centres in this era, and the Niagara area was no exception. When the scandal-mongering Toronto tabloid *Hush* reported a massive roundup of men at the Falls on gross indecency charges in 1962, the region's other important commodity, agriculture, inspired an attempt at metaphor: "Police admitted that Niagara Falls is in the Fruit Belt. And they are so right."[24]

As a metaphor for lost sexual innocence, an approved invitation into sexual adulthood, or gaining a "union card," the Niagara honeymoon was never discussed without a nudge, giggle, or wink. But while this cultural script rarely varied, real honeymoons were being taken by real people, who were not living their lives in film scripts or magazine articles. Some of these people have written their own versions of their honeymoons, in the form of responses to a contest held at the Falls in 1992. Over four hundred contestants from across North America accepted the invitation to "relive the magic moments" of their Niagara honeymoons by writing their honeymoon memoirs. A panel headed by Canadian historian Pierre Berton read the entries, and the winner and his or her spouse were flown back to the Falls for a lavish "second honeymoon" weekend.

According to the results of this contest, the popular honeymoon script matched people's experiences—or at least memories—of their Niagara honeymoons surprisingly well. A kind of playful modesty or knowing sense of embarrassment characterizes many of the accounts. Displacing sexual and emotional anxieties, many of them narrate their stories as triumphs over a variety of adversities: botched hotel reservations, missed train connections, automobile breakdowns. The refrain is always the same: the stories serve to highlight the anxiety and absurdity of potentially spending a wedding night in a hotel lobby, a train station, or a garage parking lot. Oblique and humorous sexual references also emerge, from those who recall their lack of interest in the waterfall when they first arrived or persistently missed the complementary breakfast in the mornings or never bothered to view the illuminated waterfall in the evening.

*****

Postwar stereotypes took their toll, as couples, especially brides, struggled with the public embarrassment of being a walking sexual cliché. Despite carefully removing corsages and shaking confetti from their hair, newlyweds felt as conspicuous as popular opinion held them to be. As one woman explained, "Everyone knew we were honeymooners, even the elevator boy, from the knowing glances that passed between the others." Yet others were quick to point out that visibility had its benefits. Several recalled noticing other honeymooners—in their hotel, on the dance floor at the Rainbow Room at the General Brock, on the *Maid of the Mist*—and, clearly, for many the presence of other newlyweds was both a comfort and a reassuring sign that they had made the right vacation choice. Adding to such anxieties were the travails of travel in general, especially for this first generation of newly enfranchised working-class and middle-class tourists. The Niagara honeymoon was, for many, a project that required considerable saving and sacrifice. Couples spent their recently acquired wedding money on the trip or compromised on the lavishness of the wedding to afford it—or even, as one woman recalled, chose the Falls over a new living-room set.

The contest responses show that the romantic lure of postwar Niagara was more than matched by what was, for many, a series of "firsts": the first time they travelled out of state or province, the first border crossing, the first train trip or hotel stay, and even, for some, the first restaurant meal, steak, or glass of wine. That all the correspondents expressed fond, even glowing, memories is perhaps not surprising; they were, after all, trying to win a contest. But despite the boosterish rhetoric, the responses reveal the significance of the Niagara experience.[25] [...]

When the Niagara Falls, Ontario, Chamber of Commerce celebrated honeymoon couple one thousand, local businessmen were, as always, thrilled with the ensuing publicity. The winning couple, declared the Chamber's president, were "naturals," and he congratulated his men on "the outstanding success of their carefully organized show."[26] Intensive honeymoon promotion, especially in the 1940s and 1950s, had made Niagara's tourist entrepreneurs hardened and cynical social constructionists. Several decades later, scholars of sexuality are busily investigating what Niagara's businessmen had figured out many years earlier: sexuality, like gender, is learned, acquired, ritualized, and performed.

They put on quite a show at the Falls, and it played to a packed house for decades. For millions of North Americans, married life after World War II began with travel, consumption, and plenty of sex. It was a vision of family life that most people, not surprisingly, found appealing, at least for awhile.

NOTES

1 Elaine May, *Homeward Bound: American Families in the Cold War Era* (New York: Basic Books, 1988); Winnie Brienes, *Young, White and Miserable: Growing up Female in the Fifties* (Boston: Beacon Press, 1992); Joanne Meyerowitz, *Not June Cleaver: Women and Gender in Postwar America 1945–1960* (Philadelphia: Temple University Press, 1994); Elizabeth Kennedy and Madeline Davis, *Boots of Leather, Slippers of Gold: The History of a Lesbian Community* (New York: Routledge, 1993); Mary Louise Adams, *The Trouble with Normal: Postwar Youth and the Making of Heterosexuality* (Toronto: University of Toronto Press, 1997); Joy Parr, *A Diversity of Women: Ontario, 1945–1980* (Toronto: University of Toronto Press, 1995).

2 Romar and Lee, eds., *The Canadian Male: A Manual of Personal Hygiene* (Vancouver, B.C.: A Modern Publication, 1961), p.4; Abraham Beacher, M.D., "Sex Problems of Newlyweds," *Sexology,* April 1957, p.558.

3 Henry Lee, "Should Honeymoons Be Banned?" *Pageant,* December 1955, p.7; Olivier Loras, "Honeymoon Shock," *Sexology,* August 1957, p.4; "Don't Let Your Honeymoon Be Hell!" *Fotorama,* December 1956, p.110; Alfred Tyrer, *Sex, Marriage and Birth Control* (Toronto: T.H. Best, 1943), p.157.

4 Salem Harrison, *Marriage Guide,* vol.1, no.1 (December 1956), p.17; Maxine Davis, *Sexual Responsibility in Marriage* (New York: Dial Press, 1963), p.161.

5 Adams, *Trouble with Normal,* p.10.

6 Theodore H. Van de Velde, *Ideal Marriage* (London: William Heinemann, 1942), pp.256–57; Romar and Lee, *Canadian Male,* p.4; Eustace Chesser, *Sexual Behavior* (London: Corgi Books, 1964), p.103; Davis, *Sexual Responsibility,* p.165.

7 Harry F. Tashman, *The Marriage Bed: An Analyst's Casebook* (New York: University Publishers Incorporated, 1959), pp.16–87; Paul Scholten, "The Premarital Examination," *Journal of the American Medical Association,* Nov. 1, 1958, p.1176.

8 Francis Bruce Strain, *Marriage Is for Two: A Forward Look at Marriage in Transition* (New York: Longmans, Green, 1955), p.86; Margaret Sanger, *Happiness in Marriage* (New York: Blue Ribbon Books, 1940), pp.85, 89.

9 Lois Pemberton, "Before the Wedding Night," *True Confessions*, June 1949, p. 12.

10 "Marital Stage-Fright," in *Illustrated Sex Quiz,* ed. Myron Jacoby (New York: Herald Publishing, 1943), p.3.

11 Clifford R. Adams, *Preparing for Marriage: A Guide to Marital and Sexual Adjustment* (New York: Dutton, 1951), p.141; Edward O'Rourke, *Marriage and Family Life* (Champaign, Ill.: The Newman Foundation, 1956), p.141.

12 Olivier Loras, "Honeymoon Shock," *Sexology,* August 1957, pp.4–5.

13 Stanley R. Brav, "Note on Honeymoons," *Marriage and Family Living: Journal of the National Conference on Family Relations,* February 1947, p.60; Jean Libman Block, "Are Those Marriage Manuals Any Good?" *Cosmopolitan,* October 1948; Jerome and Julia Rainer, *Sexual Pleasure in Marriage,* 2nd ed. (New York: Permabook, 1963), p.1.

14 "Honeymooners, Beware," *Time,* Aug. 15, 1955, p.7; Lee, "Should Honeymoons Be Banned?" p.7; Helen Colton, "When Honeymoons Are Dangerous," *Coronet,* June 1954, p.21; Jerome and Julia Rainer, *Sexual Pleasure in Marriage,* pp.168–69.

15 Caroline Bird, "Advice to Honeymooners," *Cosmopolitan,* July 1951.

16 See, for example, Jhan and June Robbins, "Honeymoon Business," *New York Herald Tribune This Week*

Magazine, June 6, 1948; June Callwood and Trent Frayne, "A Honeymoon at the Falls," *Maclean's,* Aug. 1, 1950; Bird, "Advice to Honeymooners."

17 *The Long, Long Trailer,* 1954, Vincente Minnelli, director.

18 Jennifer Ames, *Honeymoon Alone* (London: Hodder and Stoughton, 1940); Jerome Weidman, "Three Men on a Honeymoon," *Cosmopolitan,* March 1949; "Honeymoon for Three," *Cosmopolitan,* September 1946; Jack Woodford, *Savage Honeymoon* (New York: Woodford Press, 1949); Barbara Dickinson, "Separate Honeymoons," *Women's Home Companion,* October 1953; Robert H. Rimmer, *The X-Rated Videotape Guide,* vol.2 (Buffalo: Prometheus, 1991), p.251.

19 *Niagara Falls Review,* June 11, 1949; Chamber of Commerce minutes, Feb. 16, June 29, 1949.

20 See, for example, *NFR,* July 31, 1951; Jan. 24, 1952; June 15, 1955; Jan. 17, 1950.

21 Lotta Dempsey, "Honeymoon Town," *Chatelaine,* May 1947; Callwood and Frayne, "Honeymoon at the Falls."

22 Monroe Fry, "Cross-Section USA: Honeymoon Town," *Esquire,* June 1957.

23 Esther Newton, *Cherry Grove, Fire Island: Sixty Years in America's First Gay and Lesbian Town* (Boston: Beacon Press, 1993) p.89; Elise Chenier, "Tough Ladies and Trouble Makers: Toronto's Public Lesbian Community, 1995–1965," M.A. thesis, Queen's University, Kingston, Ont., 1995, p.157; Gordon Donaldson, *Niagara!: The Eternal Circus* (New York: Doubleday, 1979), p.229.

24 "Homosexual Scandal Rocks Niagara Falls," *Hush,* Oct. 27, 1962.

25 "Honeymoon Letters," McCaulay, 1945, Calvello, 1946, Coppinger, 1943, Hutton, 1946.

26 Chamber of Commerce minutes, Niagara Falls, Ont., Aug. 31, 1949.

CHAPTER 23
A New Entity in the History of Sexuality: The Respectable Same-Sex Couple

Mariana Valverde

n *The History of Sexuality: Volume I*, Michel Foucault argued that 'homosexuality' is a relatively recent invention, distinct from earlier forms of same-sex love and lust. 'Homosexuality' could only emerge when European scientific knowledges began to peer into—and construct—an inner 'self', a personal identity that the nineteenth century saw as a matter of physiology and that the twentieth century regarded as fundamentally psychological. Sexuality—in the West but not in the East—came to be regarded as that which is most secret and therefore most authentic about 'the self', the key, in other words, to personal identity.

Before the rise of modern scientific knowledges, law governed sexuality as a set of acts, mainly distinguishing the 'unnatural' from 'natural' acts. Many law codes still contain prohibitions against sodomy and other unnatural acts. And, exceptionally among advanced industrial democracies, the United States criminalized sodomy in many states until the very late date of 2003, when such laws were declared unconstitutional by the Supreme Court. Nevertheless, the persistence of 'sodomy' in legal codes owes more to the difficulties involved in changing and modernizing law than to any real belief that 'sodomy' is a useful category: it is highly doubtful that any of the men charged under sodomy laws in the waning years of US sodomy statutes thought of themselves as 'sodomites.' Of course some people, especially men, have sex with other men without thinking of themselves as 'gay.' But it is not inappropriate, when making a large-scale generalization, to say, in line with Foucault's famous thesis, that the regulation of the self has been increasingly dominated by the notion of 'identity.' What you did with various body parts came to be regarded, throughout the course of the twentieth century, mainly as a clue about what kind of person you were. And 'the homosexual' was probably the most successful of all deviant identities. It was invented at the same time as the hysteric, the nymphomaniac, and the kleptomaniac, but unlike these marginal entities/

identities, it ended up occupying a very central place in the constitution of twentieth-century human beings and social groups.

While subsequent research has shown that Foucault's contrast is far too sharp, nevertheless, the point about the shift from governing sexuality through acts to governing through identities has been generally accepted by historians and social scientists.

But what has happened since Foucault wrote the passage above, in the 1970s? Let me suggest, half jokingly but half seriously, that we have been witnesses to a historic event. This is the emergence, in the space occupied by 'homosexuality,' of a new sexual object/subject: the respectable same-sex couple. If the medieval soldier charged with sodomy was not 'a homosexual,' as Foucault argued, so too, we can argue that the respectable same-sex couple (RSSC) is not two homosexuals added together. Let me explain.

Almost twenty years ago, Jean Baudrillard wrote a little book, *Forget Foucault*, which, amidst much envy, contained a prescient passage:

> And what if Foucault spoke to us so well of sexuality … only because its form, this great production … of our culture was, like that of power, in the process of disappearing? Sex, like man, or the category of the social, may only last for a while. And what if sex's reality effect, which is at the horizon of the discourse on sexuality, also started to fade away radically …? Foucault's hypothesis itself suggests how mortal sex is, sooner or later.[1]

It certainly seems true that the particular form of the inner self that is 'sexuality'—the object of inquiries from 1890s sexology to sex-change clinics—may indeed be now fading.

Young people who would rather be 'queer' than 'gay' are leading the way. The term 'queer' blurs the boundaries of the homosexual self of tormented 1950s autobiographies and medico-legal inquiries. Queer is a purposefully vague name for a non-conformist lifestyle that is 'post-homosexual,' historically if not biographically. And AIDS discourse has also given rise to a new, post-homosexual object: the man who has sex with men. Contrary to Foucault's discussion of the disciplinary gaze, AIDS experts don't care one bit whether this personage is gay.

But the queer youth and the 'man who has sex with men' are marginal by comparison with the legally and culturally prominent figure of the 'respectable-same-sex-couple,' or RSSC. This is likely more apparent in Canada than south of the 49th parallel; but given the speed with which Americans rushed to San Francisco city hall during February of 2004, when gay/lesbian marriage was for a time provided in a more or less legal manner, perhaps the Canadian situation is relevant elsewhere, even in Bush's America.

The pictures that were used in the media are of particular importance for understanding how the RSSC is something new—rather than the addition of two homosexuals. As marriage for gays and lesbians approached legality, around 2003, Canadians were treated to an unprecedented visual display of respectable homosexuality—an extended series of photos displaying not the ashamed and effeminate homosexuals that used to be posed in dark corners in sixties reportage of seamy gay life, but rather an array of perfect 'same-sex' couples—usually shown in the full glare of sunlight, a lighting convention at odds with representations of the classic homosexual.

A look at the photographs that are still available, somewhat after the fact, proves enlightening. The first lesson in social semiotics is provided by an analysis focussing on that most important of all signs of marriage, notably, the wedding dress.

A number of the lesbian couples who got married in the San Francisco city hall actually wore wedding dresses. [...] And I can also attest to the presence of wedding dresses from personal experience. I happened to be in San Francisco in mid-February of 2004 (where my partner and I were constantly asked if we had come to get married by well-meaning ignorant Americans not aware of the fact we could have got married in Toronto quite easily, if that was our desire). My partner and I, used to the idea of gay/lesbian marriage but not to the flashier styles of American lesbians, were quite struck by seeing young lesbians in full wedding white waiting for the subway in the BART Berkeley station. It was very difficult to tell whether the wedding dresses were being worn in straight-up imitation of marriage or in playful parody. It is quite possible, given the mixed feelings gays and lesbians have about marriage, that the wearers were not themselves very clear about their intentions.

By contrast, the available photos of Canadian lesbian couples did not reveal a single wedding dress. All the couples depicted looked earnest and serious, sort of butch, and dressed in office attire. No wedding dresses; no playfulness; no parody—but also, no imitation of marriage. Perhaps Canada really is a more boring and earnest country; the lesbians do seem to just be wanting to get married, as opposed to wanting to dress up and have a really good time. But what about the male couples? The first thing that one notices is that in neither American nor Canadian pictures of gay male weddings do any of the guys wear white dresses. Drag queens seem to have vanished from view. Nearly all the men wore shirts and ties; nearly all were middle-class, middle-aged, and white. They all looked either like soft-spoken librarians or like beefy stockbrokers—not like [we expect] homosexuals [to look].

But perhaps pictures of actual weddings, or rather of that small sample of weddings that happened to be covered by the media, are not representative. I thus turned to another source. This was the *Toronto Star*'s Pride Day special section (June 19/04). This is significant, because the Pride Day celebration in Toronto draws around three quarters of a million people, many of them US gays and lesbians. The local press now covers this event in a boosterish manner, just like any other event that contributes to the local economy and to the local myth that Toronto is the mecca of multiculturalism and tolerance.

This special section of Canada's largest circulation daily had two main articles. One featured an elderly homosexual activist, George Hislop, 73, wistfully reminiscing about the days of illegality. This story was obviously meant to represent the ghost of gay lives past. The community's future, by contrast, was embodied not in a young queer person or a transsexual activist, but, predictably, in images of a respectable same-sex couple. Equally predictable, the couple in question was made up of two middle-class men. This couple is portrayed as totally immersed in the financial and logistical challenges of their upcoming wedding. It's as if there are two brides rather than just one, and, in what can only be described as a feminist nightmare vision, both are obsessing about the colour scheme, the food, the entertainment, and the guest list.

I looked in vain for something that the RSSC might have had in common with George Hislop. Sex, perhaps? Foucault would have said that in the end it is sex that holds the RSSC together and links it to both the homosexual of the 1960s and the eighteenth-century sodomite. But nothing was said or even faintly implied about sex in the article about the gay male couple about to wed. The two guys about to tie the knot seemed to be far too engrossed in the details of the wedding to even think about sex. The travel of relatives from Brazil to Toronto was one key logistical challenge discussed at length. Other practices of consumerism were also discussed in fine-grained voyeuristic detail. The readers aren't given even a distant hint that these two men might sometimes have sex with one another. Instead, the readership is excitedly told how much the flower arrangements and the rental of a pleasure boat on Lake Ontario are going to cost. The frisson experienced by the reader clearly has nothing to do with any sex that might be going on (though one suspects little time or energy will in fact be available for sex, for the marrying couple at any rate).

Other than the RSSC itself, the only people cited in the article are wedding professionals. These entrepreneurs offer up-to-date information about the new consumer niche and advise readers who operate small businesses to not neglect the gay marriage market (the gay male marriage market at any rate; lesbian weddings aren't mentioned). Readers (including business people) thus learn from authoritative sources that gay and lesbian couples always pay for their own wedding, with no parental involvement, which is apparently a key marketing point.

The Star's coverage of Pride Day certainly supports Jean Baudrillard's claim that if homosexuality did not die with Foucault in 1984, it will certainly die with old George Hislop. Hislop, who despite his advanced age likes to shock people by saying he likes boys, probably knows many florists; but he is otherwise wholly unconcerned with weddings, and indeed with consumption. In the days of homosexuality, activism meant poverty. Hislop, who is still fighting in the courts to get the Canadian government to retroactively include him in the same-sex pension arrangements that have been made available in recent years (his partner died a few years before the cut-off date for same-sex pensions), does not come across as a consumer at all.

But what about law? Putting away the newspaper, I turned to the relevant decisions of the Supreme Court of Canada, the decisions that were key in paving the way for gay/lesbian weddings, in pursuit of the vanishing homosexual. Instead of sexuality, homo or otherwise, I found two non-sexual themes. The two themes that run throughout the decisions are (1) family and (2) finance/consumption. Conjugality, family and impoverishment were the sole themes of the Court's descriptions of the retirement struggles of James Egan and his partner in the 1995 case *Egan v. Canada,* a landmark case that first declared that discrimination against gays and lesbians was in Canada just as illegal as discrimination on the basis of race or religion. Neither sex nor sexuality are mentioned in either the majority or the minority *Egan* decision. 'Sexual orientation' is the only sex-like term in the Court's text—but this is not a **sexual** identity. As I have argued elsewhere with much more evidence than can be presented here, 'sexual orientation' in Canadian law actually refers not so much to homosexuality as a sexual identity, but to an urban lifestyle, partly political and partly consumerist. Particularly in cases involving mayoral declarations about Pride Day, the 'gay community' is constructed as a quasi-ethnic group, a group that's entitled to rights because it has cultural and social solidity: it organizes bowling leagues, AIDS support groups, and all the other sort of community organizations that ethnic groups in Canada have long built. The Pride Day cases too are remarkably silent about sex; they are all about 'culture' and 'community,' the sort of entities that official Canadian multiculturalism can easily accommodate. But perhaps the desexualization of gay rights in this decision is due to the fact that the *Egan* case was about pension benefits. A couple who have been together 40 years are unlikely to have a sexy aura. Perhaps the Egans are not sexual, and hence not homosexuals, by virtue of the fact that they were challenging pension regulations.

So what about that other famous RSSC of Canadian law, then? The next most famous legal lesbian/gay couple is that known as 'M and H' (to preserve their privacy) and featured in a 2001 Supreme Court decision that, while not actually legalizing gay marriage, extended exactly the same recognition to lesbian and gay couples as is already available to heterosexual common-law couples, a recognition that involves compulsory support obligations after two years of living together. M and H are two women. They are not elderly. They weren't trying to get their pension. And they were undoubtedly presenting themselves as lesbians when they went to court. They could thus be sexual/homosexual. But their sexuality too is completely erased. Their issue was divorce, or rather, alimony. In a nutshell, M was unemployed or precariously employed, while H owned considerable property. When they split up, M claimed a right to alimony. The Supreme Court eventually ruled that H and others in similar positions did indeed have an obligation to support their ex-partners.

Not infrequently, people divorce for reasons related to sexuality; but this is not contemplated anywhere in the legal texts. The Court's recounting of their relationship is wholly devoted to financial matters. Of course, a claim for alimony is all about money; but nevertheless, some reference to the initial romance might have been found relevant, if only to explain the somewhat careless joining of finances that later caused discord. Let us turn to the Supreme Court text to see if there's any homosexuals.

> M and H are women who met while on vacation in 1980. It is agreed that in 1982 they started living together in a same-sex relationship that continued for at least five years.... During that time they occupied a home which H had owned since 1974. H paid for the upkeep of the home.... In 1983, M and H purchased a business property together. In 1986, they purchased as joint tenants a vacation property in the country. They later sold the business property and used the proceeds to finance the construction of a home on the country property.
>
> As a result of a dramatic downturn in the advertising business in the late 1980s, the parties' debt increased significantly. H took a job outside the firm and placed a mortgage on her home to pay for her expenses and those of M. M also tried to find employment but was unsuccessful.... By September of 1992, M and H's relationship had deteriorated.[2]

The sheer ordinariness of the details given here is no doubt intended: writing up 'the facts' in this dreary-details-of-domestic-life manner furthers the justices' project to normalize same-sex marriage. Amidst the property relations, sex is nowhere to be found; neither is homosexuality. Nobody even inquires whether they sleep together, much less what they do in bed: the famous disciplinary gaze has vanished.

The RSSC of the *Toronto Star* pre-wedding photos and the RSSC of M and H occupy opposite ends of the marital happiness spectrum. But neither entity is made up of two homosexuals. Nobody cares about their sexuality—including, apparently, the parties involved. The nonsexual transactions that make up the everyday fabric of coupledom are what the texts find worth recounting. In the *Star*, one finds that the happy Toronto couple is wholly made up of florists' bills and plane tickets for relatives. The divorcing couple of the M and H Supreme Court decision, on its part, is made up of joint tenancy agreements and bank loan documents.

The RSSC is still a very new object in the legal (and economic) horizon. It would thus be premature to make any grand claims about its 'essence.' But it is clear that George Hislop's reminiscences of homosexuality and its pleasures and dangers are precisely that—reminiscences. Bank loans, florists' bills, joint bank accounts, renovated gentrified downtown homes and worries about the relatives are the cogs that make up the new, post-homosexual entity that Canadian jurisprudence has helped to fabricate: the respectable 'same-sex' couple. Like other proper homosexuals, Foucault is no doubt turning over in his grave.

NOTES

1 J. Baudrillard, *Forget Foucault* (New York, Semiotexte, 1987), at 13.

2 Att. General for *Ontario v. M and H,* par. 9–13.

CHAPTER 24

Queer Parenting in Canada: Looking Backward, Looking Forward

Rachel Epstein

A SOCIAL HISTORY

The last thirty years in Canada have been marked by staggering social, legal, and political change in relation to LGBTQ families. The social and political climate has shifted from one that forced queer people to deny huge parts of themselves in order to keep their children, to one where we can increasingly claim our sexual and gender identities *and* our right to parent. And yet, our experiences in most institutions, including daycares, schools, health care facilities, and fertility clinics continue to be informed by profound hetero- and cis-normativity (the assumptions that heterosexuality is "normal" and that biological sex always matches gender identity). There are places in Canada (i.e., PEI) where non-biological parents are not allowed to legally adopt their own children through second parent adoption, and as recently as 2004, a Gallup poll found that only 52% of Canadians supported adoption rights for same-sex couples (Rayside, 2008: 47).

Despite unprecedented legal and social recognition, many LGBTQ parents still fear that their children will be taken away from them, struggle with questions about their own legitimacy as parents, and find that current family law does not adequately recognize or protect their families. These tensions underlie the lives of queer parents in Canada—the tensions between our history and current realities, between the enormous gains we have achieved and the ways our right to parent continues to be undermined. These tensions affect our daily lives, our consciousness, and the strength of our sense of entitlement to bring children into our lives. This chapter reviews some key developments in the social and legal recognition of LGBTQ families in Canada, exploring how this history links to and informs current realities, tensions, dilemmas, and debates in LGBTQ parenting communities.

The increasing visibility and social/legal recognition of LGBTQ parents and their children in Canada sometimes bolsters the false assumption that queer parenting is a new phenomena. In reality, there have always been queer people who were also parents. What *is* relatively new, however, is queer and trans people choosing to have children in the context of queer and trans identities. The oldest children of the "lesbian baby boom" are now in their twenties and thirties, the children of the "gayby boom" are close behind, and bisexual parents are becoming more visible and vocal. Recent years have seen an upsurge of trans activism and visibility, including an insistence on the right to parent.

The 1970s: Custody Denied

Thirty years ago, however, queer and trans parents were, for the most part, invisible. It was in the 1970s that lesbian mothers, a previously unrecognizable category, gained a degree of visibility. Women who had become parents in heterosexual relationships and then "came out" were in the courts fighting for custody of their children. Many, understanding the legal climate of the time, chose to relinquish custody in favour of liberal access (Rayside, 2008). In Canada, the climate was disheartening, with courts distinguishing between "good" and "bad" lesbian mothers (and gay fathers); the good ones being those who were not visible, militant, or sexual (Arnup, 1995). In 1977, Francie Wyland wrote, "Only once in Canada, and fewer than a dozen times in the United States, has a known lesbian mother been granted unconditional custody of her children" (Mackay, 1982: 16). Small, virtually unfunded groups such as the Lesbian Mothers' Defence Fund, based in Vancouver and Toronto, provided financial, emotional, and legal support to lesbian and gay parents fighting for custody of their children.

In these court battles, which involved enormous loss and heartbreak, lesbian and gay parents were pushed to present themselves and their children as "just the same as" and "just as good as" an ideologically based notion of the heterosexual nuclear family—itself an artificial construction that never in reality looked or worked like it was supposed to. Court decisions that denied lesbians and gay men custody of their children were based on a series of arguments that found lesbians and gay men to be "unfit parents" (Pollack, 1990). These arguments, originating in the custody battles of the 1970s and 1980s, have demonized lesbian/gay parents in popular culture and are now deeply embedded in mainstream consciousness. LGBTQ parents and their allies have spent decades rebutting them. They include assumptions that: lesbian/gay sexuality is immoral and that lesbians/gay men are promiscuous, sexually maladjusted, and likely to sexually harm children; children raised in lesbian/gay homes will develop inappropriate gender identities and gender role concepts and behaviours, and may themselves develop a homosexual orientation; healthy child development requires the presence and availability of biological fathers as "male role models" (or in the case of gay fathers, "female role models"); and children raised in lesbian/gay homes will be socially stigmatized and subjected to ridicule, teasing, and hostility from their peers.

When lesbian and gay parents (and their lawyers) were in court rebutting these arguments, they had to respond within the given framework. They had to prove that they were "fit" to be parents—that their kids would be "just like" kids growing up in heterosexual families. The research carried out during this period helped to bolster these arguments. (For a summary of this research, see Patterson, 2005.) There are now countless studies that prove that sexual abusers are not, for the most part, lesbians or gay men but are, in fact, heterosexually identified; that there is virtually no difference between the children of lesbians and those of heterosexual mothers with regard to gender identity, gender role behaviour, psychopathology, or homosexual orientation; that lesbian mothers are actually more concerned than heterosexual single mothers with providing opportunities for their children to develop ongoing relationships with men (Kirkpatrick, Smith & Roy, 1981), not to mention more complex arguments about the assumptions embedded in "male/female role model" arguments; and that it is a dangerous, bigotry-fueled argument to suggest that *any* group that experiences systemic oppression should not have children because of the potential emotional damage to the children.

Much as we would like to leave behind this framework that puts us on the defensive by requiring that we prove both our "fitness to parent" and our likeness to a non-existent heterosexual norm, the political and social context within which we parent does not fully allow us to do so.

Poster Families, Poster Children

Despite massive social change and the creation of new possibilities, queer parents and their children continue to feel pressured to conform in order to be accepted and to present as "poster families" and as "poster children." The sanitized version of their families they feel pressured to present does not include parents' struggling with depression, alcoholism, or domestic abuse, or those times when the kids don't like their parents, or feel ambivalent about their parents' sexual orientation, or long for a parent of the other gender. In this version, "Nobody is in trouble at school. Nobody throws tantrums or threatens to run away. Nobody is experimenting with drugs. Ever. Did I mention that the kids think their parents are the coolest?" (Garner, 2004: 22). There is a dearth of spaces where queer parents and their children can converse honestly about the full breadth of their realities.

Just as our children feel pressured to present sanitized versions of themselves, the attacks on our right to have families have sometimes led us as queer parents to desire "normal," to fit in and to be accepted "just like" everyone else. Some LGBTQ activists, myself included, have expressed fears about the potential dangers of this striving to be "normal," including the fear that we can end up denying parts of ourselves and our communities as we present an image of ourselves, our children, and our families that is non-threatening, recognizable and, sometimes, desexualized. (See Malone & Cleary, 2002; Epstein, 2005; Riggs, 2007) Many of us, and many of our children, are tired of this. We have been forced into a narrow conversation that insists that we prove our "sameness" and that we deny or ignore "difference," however difficult or interesting.

The 1980s: Seeds of the Lesbian Baby Boom

The 1980s were hardly a stellar time for queer parents, but the decade did nourish the seeds of what came to be known as the "lesbian baby boom." As part of a growing lesbian and gay activism, with links to feminism, the women's health movement, and other progressive social movements of the time, lesbians began to seek ways to bring children into their lives. But there were no places to go for information, no organized groups or programs. Those early days of lesbian conception were characterized by a feminist, self-help, empowerment model of women's health. The women's health care movement was premised on women taking control of their bodies and their reproductive lives; lesbians desiring children set out to do so. Many got pregnant at home, relying on knowledge of cervical mucous, known sperm donors or donors known to third parties, and syringes (not typically the mythical turkey baster, though it remains iconic). Small groups of women (e.g., the Lavender Conception Conspiracy in Vancouver) began to meet to share information, knowledge, and support. Women helped each other find men willing to be sperm donors, carried sperm for each other, shared knowledge about fertility and insemination, and supported each other through the roller coaster of conception, including the disappointments and heartbreak of miscarriages and infertility. The medical establishment, at this time, was not forthcoming in its support of other-than-heterosexual parenting. Some fertility clinics flatly refused to provide insemination service to lesbians, others acted as gatekeepers. A doctor in Toronto routinely required lesbians to write a "letter to the doctor" to convince him to provide access to services; others required lesbians to undergo psychiatric assessments before making decisions regarding service provision. In Quebec, clinics refused to give unmarried or lesbian couples access to donor insemination (Nicol, 2009).

And, while biological mothers who had children from heterosexual unions were fighting their male ex-partners for custody of their children, the female partners of women giving birth to children in the context of same-sex relationships had no legal rights to their children—non-biological parents were courageously committing themselves to children with no guarantees that they would be protected in their parenting roles. Gay fathers, in some instances, were choosing to stay in heterosexual marriages for fear of societal homophobia and the loss of their families. Those who were visible were struggling with disclosing their sexual orientation to children and spouses, with the consequences of a homophobic legal system, and with their own identities. Trans and bisexual parents were virtually invisible—and where trans people were visible as parents, they were subject to excruciating discrimination. The 1980s were marked by much discrimination and many barriers to parenting for queer and trans people, but also sowed the seeds for the significant and far-reaching changes to come.

The 1990s: Turning Points

The 1990s were marked by turning points for LGBTQ parents, including significant and hard-won gains in both visibility and recognition. In 1995 an Ontario family court judge granted non-biological parents the right to adopt their children, a historic decision, which, for the first time, recognized LGBTQ parents as "fit" to be parents *and* recognized non-biological parents as equally deserving of the title. This was followed by other major victories in LGBTQ family recognition. The decade also saw a shift from a self-help model of reproduction and family-building in LGBTQ communities to an approach that increasingly included the consumer-based, profit-oriented, highly-medicalized world of assisted reproduction. The existence of HIV/AIDS and fears about the medical and legal risks of involving known sperm donors led to what Mamo (2007: 129) refers to as the use of "hybrid technology" in lesbian reproductive practices—the coexistence of the feminist health ideals of the 1970s and 1980s with biomedical expertise and services (Mamo, 2007: 53). A brief review of the decade's developments illustrates their significance.

In 1994, Bob Rae, Ontario's NDP premier at the time, introduced Bill 167, a wide-reaching same-sex spousal rights bill, which initially included a clause allowing gay men and lesbians to adopt children. The vitriolic debate unleashed by the bill, particularly in response to the adoption clause, led the government to remove this clause. But the bill was defeated anyway in an open vote, sending a loud message to lesbian and gay communities, who, in anger, congregated en masse at the provincial legislature where they were met by latex-gloved police officers, pushing them away from the building.

A year later, the courts took a position that the politicians lacked the courage to take. In 1995 four lesbian couples went to Ontario family court, asking for legal recognition of non-biological lesbian parents. Judge Nevins, in an important and groundbreaking decision, recognized them as parents and granted the right to second parent adoption, a process which results in equal legal protection for both parents. Second parent adoption is now available to same-sex couples in most provinces and territories—with the exceptions of Nunavut and Prince Edward Island (Kelly, 2011).

While Judge Nevins' decision changed the landscape for LGBTQ parents in Canada by finding them "fit" to parent, he had to recognize the couples as "spouses" before he could declare the people involved "parents." So while the right to second parent adoption provided much-needed recognition and protection for non-biological parents, it also established that, at that moment in our history, the only legitimate legal way to parent was within a two-person spousal relationship. Also, second parent adoption, unless you are prepared to do hours of preparation and meticulous paperwork, requires a lawyer. Issues of class and access to financial resources become key when costly legal procedures are required in order to secure parenting status (Bogis, 2001). And, is it still a choice to not pursue state-sanctioned legal protections? For example, some lawyers have suggested that if a non-biological parent chooses to *not* pursue a second parent adoption, courts might interpret this as a lack of commitment to the child (Dalton, 2001). Each legal gain brings with it new questions and complexities.

While queer family recognition in most provinces came about largely due to individual legal challenges and court decisions, parenting rights in Quebec were won through grassroots organizing, coalition building, and legislative change. The Lesbian Mothers Association of Quebec (LMAQ), founded in 1998 in the living room of Mona Greenbaum and Nicole Pacquette, launched a focused and highly organized campaign for recognition of lesbian- and gay-led families. In coalition with organized labour and the women's movement, the LMAQ's campaign so influenced public opinion and the minds of legislators that, in June 2002, Bill C-84, a bill that revised the filiation provisions of the Civil Code of Quebec to extend equal parenting rights and recognition to same-sex couples, passed unanimously and without abstentions in the legislature (Nicol, 2009). Perhaps the grassroots approach assumed by activists in Quebec, and their insistence on the visibility of their families in their campaign for family recognition, is linked to the fact that Quebec is the only Canadian province that protects the integrity of lesbian primary parents, even when a known sperm donor is involved.

Dykes Planning Tykes: Toronto
With and beside the legal reforms of the 1990s came social programs for LGBTQ families. LGBTQ organizations began to recognize the need for queer families to gather to socialize, exchange information and support, and make sure their kids knew they were not alone. In 1997, Kathie Duncan, a Toronto-based midwife and I developed a course

for lesbian/bi/queer women considering parenthood. The course, which we called "Dykes Planning Tykes," was part of the Toronto-based Queer Exchange, a community education program sponsored by the Centre for Gay and Lesbian Studies.

Since 1997, more than 500 people have taken Dykes Planning Tykes (DPT) and it has spawned Daddies & Papas 2B (DP2B), a course for gay/bi/queer men considering parenting, the Trans-Masculine People Considering Pregnancy course, and a Queer and Trans Family Planning(s) course for those whose identities do not fit with the gender divide implied by DPT and DP2B. These courses are now affiliated with the LGBTQ Parenting Network, a multi-faceted program for LGBTQ parents, prospective parents, and families located at the Sherbourne Health Centre (see www.lgbtqparentingconnection.ca), in partnership with Queer Parenting Programs at The 519 Community Centre in Toronto. There are also many unfunded, grassroots queer/LGBTQ parenting groups across the country. In large cities, small towns, and rural communities, queer parents are connecting with one another to exchange information and support. In Montreal, the Lesbian Mothers' Association has merged with the Papa-Daddy Group to form the LGBT Family Coalition. It now has over 1,000 members, funding for a paid coordinator, provision for social and practical support to its members, and a focus on sensitizing schools to the realities of LGBTQ families. In Ottawa, the Family Service Association's Around the Rainbow program serves hundreds of queer families annually.

The 2000s: Queering the Family Tree

The new millennium brought with it continued and expanded legal and social recognition for LGBTQ families, as well as increasing visibility and access to parenthood for gay, bi, and trans people, and more social programs for parents across the LGBTQ spectrum and across the country. As well, and significantly, Canadian queer parenting activists have had the luxury of remaining removed from the struggle for same-sex marriage because in Canada, unlike many parts of the United States, parenting rights are not linked to marriage. (For a U.S.-Canada comparison, see Rayside, 2008). However, daycares, schools, and other institutions continue to be characterized by profound hetero- and cis-normativity, homophobia, and transphobia, and the law continues to lag significantly behind the structures of our families. Many of our families are still not adequately recognized or protected.

Legal and policy changes in the new millennium include adoption reforms that allow "out" same-sex couples access to public adoption in all Canadian provinces. Children's Aid Societies in most major Canadian cities are opening their doors to LGBTQ communities as prospective adoptive parents. Many have done internal educational work to make lesbian/gay adoption more possible, and are regularly placing children with same-sex couples. Some are also taking steps to process applications by transgender prospective adoptive parents.

While second parent adoption granted historic rights to co-parenting lesbian couples, many were frustrated by a system that required them to spend time and money in order to adopt the children they had been parenting since birth. Parents (and interested lawyers) started to seek other ways to gain parental recognition. A 2001 B.C. Human Rights Tribunal case (*Gill v. Murray*) was the first successful Canadian challenge to the exclusion of same-sex couples under vital statistics regimes. This was followed by a similar complaint in New Brunswick in 2004, and an Ontario Charter challenge in 2006 (*Rutherford v. Ontario,* 2006 CarswellOnt 3463, 81 O.R. (3d) 81, 270 D.L.R. (4th) 90, 30 R.F.L. (6th) 25 (S.C.J.)), which resulted in the striking down of the Ontario Vital Statistics Act as it was found to discriminate against same-sex couples in its birth registration procedures. This case eliminated the need for second parent adoption for those same-sex couples in Ontario who conceived via anonymous sperm donor—provided there was no sexual intercourse involved in conception. It is now possible for lesbian couples to enter both women's names on a birth registration in B.C., Alberta, Saskatchewan, Manitoba, Ontario, Quebec, and New Brunswick, conferring what is known as "presumptive proof of parentage." Birth registration reforms, however, continue to assume the two-parent family, and do not adequately address or recognize the more-than-two-parent family, a configuration not uncommon in LGBTQ communities.

The year 2007 saw a significant challenge to the conventional two-parent family model. In an Ontario case popularly referred to as AA/BB/CC, the courts, on appeal, recognized three people—a lesbian couple and the man they are parenting with—as a child's parents. (*A.A. v B.B.* (2007), 83 O.R. (3d) 561 (C.A.) [*A.A. v B.B.* (CA)]) This was particularly significant in that the courts did not require "spousal" status in order to recognize parental status, i.e., people outside of conjugal relationships were recognized as parenting the same child—a step forward from Judge Nevins' 1995 decision that required that spousal status precede parental status. In another Ontario case, a single gay man who became a father through a surrogacy arrangement with an egg donor and a gestational carrier successfully appealed to the courts to be the only parent named on the birth registration (Gulliver, 2006).

While each of these victories was hard-won and relied on passion, commitment, and untold hours of pro bono work from the lawyers who fought them, LGBTQ families in Canada continue to face much uncertainty within family law systems, particularly with regards to legal recognition of non-biological parents (at birth and post-separation), multiple parent families, and families created through assisted conception and third-party donors. The complexities of our families are, for the most part, not adequately reflected in the law.

Shifting Landscapes

As we achieve more visibility and social recognition, the framework that has had us defending ourselves against a non-existent heterosexual norm, proving how "normal" and "the same" we are, is shifting. Queer parents, and researchers of queer parenting, are starting to address some of the complexities of our lives, including the ways that LGBTQ families may differ in interesting (and, perhaps, not so interesting) ways from mainstream heterosexual experience. Stacey and Biblarz in their landmark 2001 article "(How) Does the Sexual Orientation of Parents Matter?" refuse the "we are the same" conversation and insist on exploring differences, drawing on fifteen years of research on children with lesbian moms. The differences they highlight in children growing up with lesbian/gay parents include less traditional gender-typing; higher self-esteem and better mental health; more egalitarian, shared parenting; more closeness and communication between parents and children; and increased awareness and empathy in children towards social diversity.

The most recently released study (Gartrell, Bos, and Goldberg, 2010) found that adolescents reared in lesbian families are less likely than their peers to be abused by a parent or caregiver, and that daughters of lesbian mothers are more likely to engage in same-sex behaviour and to identify as bisexual—a finding that will likely be used by some to promote the idea that LGBTQ parents "recruit" their children. While the differences both these studies point out are fascinating, the most exciting contribution they make is the shift from a limiting framework of defensiveness to one of exploration, curiosity, and possibility. This shift is made possible by the social and legal recognition and security that queer parents, in some places, have achieved.

QUESTIONS, DILEMMAS, CONTROVERSIES

There is much to celebrate on the queer parenting front in Canada. Lesbian, gay, bisexual, and trans parents enjoy unprecedented legal and social recognition. Our presence and our activism has spurred monumental change in the areas of law and policy; access to fertility clinics, sperm banks, and reproductive technologies; and social attitudes. Gay men, lesbians, bi, trans, and queer folk of all sorts are creating families and transforming the landscapes of their neighbour-hoods, schools, and communities. At the same time, in Canada, in 2010, we continue to grapple with the impact of our history, and to address new and emerging issues. I continue to be sur-prised when participants in our queer family planning courses arrive not knowing other queer parents, feeling isolated, lacking information, and still not confident that becoming parents as LGBTQ people is really okay. Each expansion of possibilities for LGBTQ families, whether in the area of reproductive technologies, legal protections, or social attitudes, has brought with it fresh opportunities, unique family configurations, and new questions, dilemmas, and controversies. A few of these are explored below.

Assisted Human Reproduction

Currently, some fertility clinics in large Canadian cities estimate that as much as 15–30% of their clients are from LGBTQ communities (statistic cited at joint session of DPT and DP2B, Toronto, 2007). Because of limited access to sperm in their daily lives, many lesbian/bi/queer women and trans men access anonymous or I.D. release donor sperm and/or donor conception with known sperm donors or co-parents to build their families. Some show up at clinics with donors and/or non-conjugal co-parents. Gay/bi/queer men and trans people visit clinics as gamete donors or to freeze gametes, as co-parents or sometimes as part of surrogacy arrangements involving egg donors and gestational surrogates. Trans reproductive practices have introduced a new social category—*the pregnant man*—a category poorly understood and subject to discrimination for challenging societal norms (Ware, 2009; Ryan, 2009).

While we welcome access to services that can assist us in our family-building, our increased use of reproductive technologies implicates us in the "techno-scientific practices and political-eco-nomic trends of global capitalism" (Mamo, 2007: 236). How do we negotiate the "fertility" clinic, a medicalized space primarily designed to "treat" infertility, as fertile (until determined otherwise) people, on the first step in our family planning process? How do we maintain control of this pro-cess when it is suggested that we take fertility drugs or undergo medical procedures to guarantee us a "better bang for our buck," or because it is standard procedure? Who is profiting from our use of reproductive technologies and what are the implications when some of the methods we use to create families are extremely costly and involve invasive medical procedures and physical risk? Who can access these services, and who is excluded? These are some of the questions we grapple with as LGBTQ people engage in increasing numbers with the world of assisted reproduction.

The *Assisted Human Reproduction Act*

In 2004, following two decades of debate and governmental process, the *Assisted Human Reproduction Act (AHRA)* became law in Canada. The intent of the Act is to regulate reproductive technologies. The Act prohibits and criminalizes certain activities, while regulating others. For example, commercial surrogacy and payment to sperm and egg donors are prohibited, while donor insemination and altruistic surrogacy are permissible, but regulated.[1] Queer communities were startled when the Act first became law because of its apparent criminalization of home insemination. We have since been assured countless times by the Assisted Human Reproduction Agency, with reference to Pierre Elliott Trudeau's trumpeted 1967 statement that "there is no place for the state in the bedrooms of the nation," that it is not the intent of the Act or the Agency to regulate or interfere with home insemination. A written declaration to this effect would go a long way to providing the reassurance queer communities are seeking.

In 2010 much of the *AHRA* was struck down as federal law, and key aspects of the regulation of AHR services were placed in the hands of the provinces (Reference re *Assisted Human Reproduction Act,* [2010] SCC 61). Aside from Quebec, no province has in place a comprehensive set of policies and regulations in this area and it remains unclear how regulation will unfold. What is clear is that LGBTQ communities are key and important stakeholders in the world of AHR, and it is critical that we be included in processes to establish provincial regulation.

The prohibitions of the *AHRA*, which remain in effect—including the ban on commercial surrogacy—mean that LGBTQ people are amongst the North Americans now complicit in a burgeoning system of transnational reproduction, including the increasingly common practice of hiring women in developing countries, such as India, to act as gestational surrogates for North American parents. Chris Veldhoven (2009: 59), facilitator of the Daddies & Papas 2B course, referring to discussions that take place in the course around the ethics of gestational and traditional surrogacy, notes "[t]here are many complexities. I've heard women say, 'It's my body, it's my choice, it's not up to the state to regulate what I do,' and I've talked to women who think surrogacy is always a form of economic slavery. How do you make an ethical decision? How do you go into a surrogacy arrangement where you know everybody is respected? For some there is no simple answer." It is nevertheless incumbent on queer communities, as participants in these practices, to continue to question the decisions we make regarding our reproductive lives and to carefully consider their political, social, and ethical implications.

Anonymous Sperm Donation

Also of critical concern to queer communities is the current worldwide debate about the ethics of anonymous sperm and egg donation. Unlike countries that have banned donor anonymity, which include the U.K., the Netherlands, Sweden, Norway, Finland, Switzerland, Austria, New Zealand, and Australia, Canada has maintained the possibility of donor anonymity. Those who argue for compulsory identity release of donors cite the experience of some donor-conceived children who describe a huge sense of loss at not having access to their genetic origins. Proponents of openness believe it to be a right of donor-conceived children to know their "parents," and to evaluate for themselves the relative importance of this information, with comparisons made to the opening up of adoption records (Johnston, 2002).

Those who raise questions about eliminating anonymity articulate concerns about the privacy rights of donors, the need to protect the integrity of chosen family structures, and about the genetic essentialism inherent in a focus on biology over recognition of the roles, rights, and responsibilities of "social parents"—those who commit themselves as parents outside of biological connections to their children. Those concerned about compulsory identity release also express worry that it could result in an overall shortage of donors, already, in some cases, a reality, particularly if one is seeking a donor from a particular racialized group, i.e., from a group that is not white and Anglo. Some queer people seeking donors from racialized groups, particularly those desiring I.D. release donors, are already being forced to seek donors outside of Canada.

In a recent landmark case in B.C., donor-conceived Olivia Pratten won a lawsuit against the provincial government seeking to amend the B.C. Adoption Act to require physicians to keep permanent records of all egg, sperm, or embryo donors and to allow offspring to access those records when they turn 19, if they so choose (*Pratten v. British Columbia* (Attorney General) 2011 BCSC 656). The case was based on the argument that it is discriminatory that donor-conceived children do not have the same rights to know their genetic origins as children who have been adopted. In June 2011, the B.C. government launched an appeal of the case to the Supreme Court of Canada. The results of the appeal are pending and could have national implications.

Interestingly, it has been lesbian communities who have historically pushed fertility clinics and sperm banks to provide more information about donors, including extensive health and social information, and to request that sperm banks set up identity release options for donors willing to someday be contacted by adult children (Vercollone, Moss & Moss, 1997). Perhaps this can be related to a history and culture in some queer communities of valuing and promoting honesty and truth-telling, particularly with regards to children and child-rearing. Many queer people have suffered as young people from secrets they were forced to keep and/or from silences that denied their experience. Many do not want to impose secrets and/or silences on their children (Epstein, 2008).

A major stumbling block to queer community support for an end to donor anonymity is the current legal ambiguity and uncertainty with regards to known sperm donors. The necessity, in many cases, of the use of donors in order to create families, means that extra care and protection is needed to protect the integrity of queer and trans family structures.

Square Peg, Round Hole? Thinking Outside the Box

Due to the relatively recent availability of identity-release donors in Canada and the relatively small numbers of these donors currently available, many queer and trans parents are choosing between the use of an anonymous donor through a sperm bank, and use of a sperm donor who is known to the prospective parents. The latter is risky, however, since current family law does not adequately protect primary parents from potential parental claims from donors. A second parent adoption, when a known donor is involved, requires that the donor consent to the relinquishment of his parental rights. Some donors are reluctant to give this consent for fear that in so doing, they may risk losing all connection to the child. Some primary parents, for fear of too much donor involvement, or of a potential parental claim from a donor, feel that they have no choice but to severely curtail his involvement, or to choose an anonymous donor. Birth registration schemes that allow two women to register a child's birth provide only presumptive proof of parentage and, in many provinces, are only applicable when an anonymous donor has been used. There is no allowance in the law for relationships with children that are significant, but not parental.

The symbolic weight historically attached to both biology and fatherhood, combined with recent moral panic about "fatherless families" and the activities of the father's rights movement, add fuel to the fear that "donors" will be granted the rights of "fathers" by the courts. In fact, in 2009 a judge in the Ontario Court of Justice chose to preserve the parental rights of a known sperm donor over those of the non-biological lesbian mother, basing his conclusions on the importance of the legal recognition of biological relationships to a child's self-identity (Bird, 2010: 7).

Queer people have a history of defining their families outside of traditional biological connections and family models, the concept of "families of choice" being a much-used and important concept in queer communities. Alison Bird (2010) argues that current family law in Canada continues to privilege the nuclear, heterosexual, one mother/one father family and has not kept up with changing family forms. As she puts it, "There is a disconnect between the law of legal parenthood and the societal reality in Canada. This must be addressed through legislative reform that uses a more inclusive and flexible family ideology to better reflect the fundamental shift in how individuals choose to structure their families" (p. 1).

Fiona Kelly (2011) tries to formulate a legal reform scheme involving automatic legal parental recognition of the person who gives birth and their conjugal partner (if desired), with an opportunity for others to opt-in either as legal parents *or* as non-parental adult caregivers. A scheme that clarifies and protects a range of parental and non-parental roles could potentially provide legal security and protection to all those involved in a child's life, eliminating the need for primary parents to guard against unwanted legal intrusions from known donors, perhaps resulting in increased comfort levels with proposals to eliminate donor anonymity.

Adoption

While public and private adoption within Canada has increasingly opened up to LGBTQ people, international adoption has become more difficult (i.e., almost impossible, as no country in the world, with the exception of some parts of the United States, will allow international adoption to openly lesbian or gay applicants). Some agencies are beginning a process of internal education with regards to lesbian, gay, bisexual, and trans adoption.

A Study of Ontario Adoption Licensees

A recent Ontario study (Ross, Epstein, Anderson, and Eady, 2009) surveyed adoption licensees in Ontario about their policies and practices with regards to LGBTQ adoption, and interviewed 43 LGBTQ adoptive parents about their experiences in the system. They found, not surprisingly, that public, urban, and non-affiliated (i.e., not religiously or culturally affiliated) agencies were, overall, more open to and comfortable with LGBTQ adoption. Several issues were particularly striking. It appears that lesbian and gay couples who come closest to resembling heterosexual couples have an easier time in the adoption system. Bisexual, trans, and single people, and those whose relationships do not resemble traditional "couples," encounter more barriers. Bisexual people, in both opposite- and same-sex relationships, often feel they have to "leave out" certain aspects of their identities in the home study process and generally encounter a lack of knowledge and understanding of their identities and experience. (Eady, Ross, Epstein, and Anderson, 2009)

The question of "male" and "female" role models also emerged as a complex issue. Frequently, as part of a home study process, LGBTQ prospective parents are asked about their ability to provide gender-based "role models" for their children. While children's individual needs for significant relationships with adults of different genders may vary, the questions as they are posed seem to be based on the assumption that children *require* male and female role models to develop normally, implying that families without a male and a female parent are in some way deficient compared to two-parent heterosexual families. Embedded too in these questions are assumptions about gender—for example, that there are only two genders (excluding trans people and others who fall outside of two-gender models) and that men and women, simply because of their biological sex, offer children fundamentally different things. Ignored in these arguments are a differentiation between sex and gender, and recognition of the diversity that exists amongst "men" and amongst "women." This study has facilitated some nuanced and complicated discussions with adoption and foster workers about the assumptions embedded in gender-based "role model" arguments.

While most child welfare agencies attempt to "match" an adopted child's race, ethnicity, and cultural background with those of the parents with whom they are placed, it is still the case that many adoptive parents, including LGBTQ people, are adopting across race. In many cases, white people are adopting racialized children. While experience of the stigmatization and discrimination that often comes with living as an LGBTQ person is sometimes viewed (often correctly) by adoption workers as solid preparation for becoming an adoptive parent and for assisting an adopted child in dealing with the social stigma they may encounter, LGBTQ people, like other adoptive parents, sometimes voice beliefs that a "colour blind" approach to racial difference will be best for their children. Informed by the voices and experiences of interracial adoptees, agencies are encouraging parents who are adopting interracially to recognize the complexities of their children's experience, to inform themselves about the daily and the institutional realities of racism, and to create communities for their children that will provide for them the knowledge and connections they require in order to feel secure in their own identities. While queerness offers a window into the experience of oppression, it does not necessarily ensure sensitivity to the complicated ways that issues of race, class, and family status often intersect in the lives of adopted children.

Gay/Bi/Queer Men as Parents

Inclusive adoption policies, access to reproductive technologies, and advances in the social and legal recognition of queer families have expanded parenting possibilities for gay/bi/queer men—a phenomena which further challenges traditional family models. As Schacher, Auerbach, and Silverstein (2005) argue, the fact that gay/bi/queer men are parenting, in many cases, without women and without mothers, is a radical challenge to notions of gender essentialism and the right to parent. Given culturally entrenched stereotypes of gay men as pedophiles and the iconic nature of motherhood, the expansion, in the last decade, of possibilities for gay men to become parents is one of the most exciting, interesting, and potentially radical developments in queer parenting. At the same time, parenting is perhaps the only area where men have historically been less privileged than women because the courts and social attitudes have favoured women as parents. What are the implications of these historical power dynamics when men in larger numbers become primary parents?

> A recent study of gay fathers in Toronto and Calgary (Epstein, Duggan, and Veldhoven, 2006) spoke with men who had become fathers both before and after "coming out," i.e., in the context of heterosexual identity and in the context of GBQ identity. Both groups spoke about the overall invisibility of GBQ men as fathers, and about the need for increased public awareness of their existence and experiences, as well as for inclusion of GBQ fathers in social programs and services. Both groups also identified issues of entitlement as key. Those who had children prior to identifying as GBQ were often fearful of the court system and reluctant to push for more or different time with their children—echoing the experience of lesbian mothers in the 1970s and 1980s. Those having children in the context of queer identities struggle against negative stereotypes about GBQ men as parents, and with the complexities involved in acquiring children through adoption, co-parenting, or surrogacy.

Chris Veldhoven (2009: 56) highlights some significant historical developments in GBQ men's relationship to parenting, and the barriers GBQ men continue to face: "I think some of the guys are still going through culture shock ... Historically men were generally taught not to be deeply involved in birthing and child rearing. Behind this was the tyranny of this being viewed as 'natural,' you know, 'naturally' men don't know how to do these things and women do."

Despite these barriers, GBQ men, in increasing numbers, are becoming parents. In so doing they challenge gender essentialist notions of who can be a parent and stereotypes and practices long associated with gay culture. Families led by GBQ men are transforming both straight and queer cultures and neighbourhoods. As Veldhoven puts it, "A few restaurants (in the gay village) are starting to say, 'Here's a high chair, here's a bottle warmer, here's a colouring book and some crayons.' ... Not everyone has to go through the pain that people in my fathers' generation went through. There are many more options now. It's about the evolution of possibilities" (2009: 64).

Trans Parents

There are no statistics regarding the number of trans people (or trans parents) in Canada, but it is generally assumed that numbers are significantly underestimated. The recent Trans PULSE survey found that 27% of Ontario trans people are parents (Bauer, Boyce, Coleman, Kaay, Scanlon, and Travers, 2010). Trans people in general face disproportionately high levels of discrimination in employment, housing, and service provision, as well as increased risk for violence. Clearly, these factors come to play in the lives of trans parents who, as a group, until very recently, have been largely invisible and dramatically under-served by both LGBTQ and mainstream services. Trans parents struggle with the transphobia entrenched in health care and social services as they attempt to get pregnant or adopt children. Service providers frequently lack the knowledge and information needed to effectively support trans-led families, and all trans parents and their children face the daily discrimination and exclusions that unfortunately mark contemporary trans experience.

Some who undertake a gender transition after having children become alienated from their children during a divorce or separation process involving angry, hurt, and transphobic spouses. Research has found that this alienation from children is not *inevitable*, but rather is *contingent* on various factors (Pyne, 2011). In a rare study entailing qualitative interviews with seven trans parents, Hines (2006) found that children responded to disclosure of a parent's trans identity in much the same way that children of gay and lesbian parents respond to disclosure of parental sexual orientation; that is, with initial shock and then gradual acceptance.

Like gay, lesbian, and bi parents, trans parents consistently confront a series of myths similar to those related to LGB parenting. Particular to trans parents are the ideas that children will be damaged by knowing that their parent is trans, that children need to be of a certain age before they can handle this information, and that trans parents must resolve all issues of gender identity before coming out to their children. As Brown and Rounsley note, these myths have been so powerful that at one point some mental health professionals instructed transitioning parents to move to another city and have their children told that they had died (1996: 187). Also particular to trans parents is the knowledge that they may or may not be welcomed within queer parenting communities, as transphobia can also persist amongst gay and lesbian people (Pyne, 2011). Trans parents are now in the unfortunate position of having to defend their rights and their adequacy as parents, calling on research, court cases, and their lived experience.

While trans parents in the United States are struggling to maintain legal relationships to their children, in Canada trans parents' custody rights are significantly less threatened. A landmark 2000 case in the Ontario Court of Justice awarded a trans woman custody of her child with a judicial statement at the outset that being trans would not be considered a negative factor in the determination of custody (*Forrester v. Saliba* (2000), 10 R.F.L. (5th) 34 (Ont. Ct. J.)). A 2004 case confirmed that gender identity, in and of itself, is not considered a parenting issue (*Boyce v. Boyce*, [2004] O.J. No. 2251 (Can. Ont. Sup. Ct. J. St. Thomas) (QL)). While trans parents in Canada continue to face painfully difficult custody cases, they at least have the benefit of several important legal decisions in their favour.

And, like the children of LGB parents, the children of trans parents are beginning to speak about their lives. Some describe the unique insights and experiences they encounter as a result of having a trans parent. Others describe the challenges they face, the impact of societal transphobia on their families, and the need for widespread education (Feakins, 2009; Canfield-Lenfest, 2008). Though no specific study has explored trans parenting strengths, trans parents and their children have begun to find a voice in the literature, highlighting the possibility of benefits to children, previously negated by cis-normative theoretical biases. A recurring theme is the benefits to children of a happier, healthier parent. Children of trans people talk about how transitioning increased their parent's happiness and well-being, leading to better parenting and improved parent-child relationships. Other benefits echo those articulated by children of lesbian and gay parents, including: open-mindedness and social awareness, understanding of oppression, and pride in their families (Hines, 2006; Garner, 2004; Canfield-Lenfest, 2008).

Trans parents, like GBQ men, profoundly challenge rigid and essentialist cultural links between gender and parenting. Adult children of trans parents who simultaneously refer to their fathers as "dad" and "she," and their mothers as "mom" and "he," offer a powerful critique of the assumption that fathers are always men and mothers are always women (Canfield-Lenfest, 2008: 16; Feakins, 2009: 363). As trans parenting communities grow in size, visibility, and power, broader LGBTQ communities stand to gain from the insights and perspectives on gender, family, and identity that trans parents offer.

Communities of Queer Spawn

Stefan Lynch, the first director of COLAGE (Children of Gays and Lesbians Everywhere) has coined the terms "queer spawn" and "culturally queer" to describe young people with queer parents. As our kids get older many of them seek a place in queer communities. They have grown up here, and yet do not always feel fully welcomed. One young woman interviewed by the LGBTQ Parenting Network's Culturally Queer Kids Project describes the ways that she recognizes queerness in others, but how they do not always recognize it in her:

> It's greatly influenced who I am because I feel a connection to the LGBT community in Toronto. It's weird because as a heterosexual female I am not recognized by that community … it's an odd kind of place to be. When I see a lesbian couple walking down the street, I feel like "Hi!" you know. If I'm with one of my moms they kind of acknowledge each other, but when I'm alone I never get that acknowledgement … it's kind of like a little secret I have with myself sometimes, that they can't see, but you know …

Our children are challenging us to create spaces in our communities that affirm and welcome them—particularly those who are, in Lynch's terms, erotically straight, but culturally queer. Abigail Garner (2004: 22) refers to the "bicultural identity of heterosexual children who are linked to queerness through their heritage." While not all children of LGBTQ parents identify as straight or cis-gendered, those that do sometimes find that it is not always clear where they fit in relation to queer or straight culture.

Anti-homophobia/transphobia initiatives in schools usually focus on queer and trans youth, often excluding queer spawn, who are uniquely positioned at school. The teasing or harassment of which they may be targets is not necessarily due to their own sexual orientation or gender identity but that of their parents. They may be straight-identified themselves, but find themselves identifying with and defending queer people and cultures (Epstein, Idems, and Schwartz, 2009). A study recently released by EGALE Canada found that 61% of students with LGBTQ parents reported that they feel unsafe at school.[2]

As more and more queer people have children, and as our children grow up, it is crucial that we do not, even inadvertently, exclude them from queer spaces. Our children can offer important and often unheard perspectives on personal, political, and social issues. For example, the debate about anonymous sperm donation, to date spearheaded by donor-conceived children raised in heterosexual families, would be enriched by the inclusion of queer spawn who have unique contributions to make based on their own experiences and understandings of the meanings and significance of blood, biology, genetics, gender, sexuality, parenting, and family.

LOOKING BACKWARD, LOOKING FORWARD

From early on and to the present, people writing about queer parenting have debated the radical nature of LGBTQ people becoming parents (Polikoff, 1987; Lorde, 1987; Copper, 1987; Weston, 1991; Lewin, 1993, 1995; Walters, 2001; Mamo, 2007). How do our families *challenge,* and how do they *recreate,* the conventional model of the heteronormative nuclear family and dominant constructions of gender, sexuality, family, biology, blood, and kinship? Is LGBTQ parenting a consequence of normalization and the pronatalism of dominant culture and to what degree does it mark a continued transgressiveness from feminisms and queer cultures (Mamo, 2007)? The answers to these questions are multidimensional and complex. We cannot parent outside of the cultural norms and discourses that shape our lives; and at the same time queer and trans families, in all our diversity, cannot help but disrupt the heterosexual/cis-gender matrix.

NOTES

1 For a full discussion of the *AHRA* and LGBTQ communities, and recommendations for fertility clinics working with LGBTQ clients, see Ross, Steele, and Epstein (2006), and a position paper written by the LGBTQ/AHRA Working Group, a Toronto-based group of service providers, researchers, and consumers of reproductive technologies (Epstein, 2008—available for download at www.lgbtqparentingconnection.ca). The LGBTQ Parenting Network (Sherbourne Health Centre) and the Re:searching for LGBTQ Health team at the Centre for Addiction and Mental Health have recently completed a Canadian Institutes of Health Research–funded study of LGBT experiences with fertility clinics in Ontario. For more info, go to: parentingnetwork@sherbourne.on.ca.

2 For more results of this study go to: http://www.mygsa.ca/YouthSpeakUp?show=wide.

REFERENCES

AHRA/LGBTQ Working Group. *The Assisted Human Reproduction Act and LGBTQ Communities.* Toronto: Sherbourne Health Centre, 2008. Available at: www.lgbtqparentingconnection.ca.

Arnup, K. *Lesbian Parenting: Living with Pride and Prejudice.* Charlottetown, PEI: Gynergy Books, 1995.

Bird, A. "Legal parenthood and the recognition of alternative family forms in Canada."*University of New Brunswick Law Journal.* Annual, 2010.

Bauer, G., M. Boyce, T. Coleman, M. Kaay, K. Scanlon, and R. Travers, *Who are trans people in Ontario?* Trans PULSE E-Bulletin, 1 (1), 2010. Retrieved November 25, 2010, from: http://transpulse.ca/documents/E1English.pdf.

Bogis, T. "Affording Our Families: Class Issues in Family Formation." In M. Bernstein and R. Reimann, eds., *Queer Families, Queer Politics: Challenging Culture and the State*. New York: Columbia University Press, 2001.

Brown, M., and C. A. Rounsley. *True selves: Understanding Transsexualism—For Families, Friends, Coworkers, and Helping Professionals*. San Francisco: Jossey-Bass Publishers, 1996.

Canfield-Lenfest, M. *Kids of Trans Resource Guide*. San Fransisco: COLAGE, 2008.

Copper, B. "The Radical Potential in Lesbian Mothering of Daughters." In S. Pollack and J. Vaughan, eds., *Politics of the Heart*. New York: Firebrand, 1987.

Dalton, S. "Protecting Our Parent–Child Relationships: Understanding the Strengths and Weaknesses of Second-Parent Adoption." In M. Bernstein and R. Reimann, eds., *Queer Families, Queer Politics: Challenging Culture and the State*. New York: Columbia University Press, 2001.

Eady, A., L. Ross, R. Epstein, and S. Anderson. "To Bi or Not to Bi: Bisexuality and Disclosure in the Adoption System." In R. Epstein, ed., *Who's Your Daddy? And Other Writings on Queer Parenting*. Toronto: Sumach Press, 2009.

Epstein, R. "The Assisted Human Reproduction Act and LGBTQ Communities," a paper submitted to the Assisted Human Reproduction Agency by AHRA/LGBTQ Working Group, LGBTQ Parenting Network, Sherbourne Health Centre, Toronto, Ontario, March 2008.

Epstein, R. "Queer Parenting in the New Millennium: Resisting Normal."*Canadian Woman Studies/les cahiers de la femme*, Special Issue, *Lesbian, Bisexual, Queer, Transsexual/Transgender Sexualities* 24 (2/3), 2005: 7–14.

Epstein, R., B. Idems, and A. Schwartz. "Reading, Writing, and Resilience: Queer Spawn Speak Out About School." In R. Epstein, ed., *Who's Your Daddy? And Other Writings on Queer Parenting*. Toronto: Sumach Press, 2009.

Epstein, R., ed. *Who's Your Daddy? And Other Writings on Queer Parenting*. Toronto: Sumach Press, 2009.

Epstein, R., S. Duggan, and C. Veldhoven. "Gay/Bi/Queer Fathers: Entitlement, Visibility, Pride." In Father Involvement Research Alliance e-bulletin, 1 (3), (2006).

Feakins, J. "I am My Father's Son." In R. Epstein, ed., *Who's Your Daddy?And Other Writings on Queer Parenting*. Toronto: Sumach Press, 2009.

Garner, A. *Families Like Mine: Children of Gay Parents Tell It Like It Is*. New York: Harper Collins, 2004.

Gartrell, N, H. Bos, and N. Goldberg. "Adolescents of the U.S. National Longitudinal Lesbian Family Study: Sexual Orientation, Sexual Behavior, and Sexual Risk Exposure." *Archives of Sexual Behavior*, 2010.

Gulliver, T. "Province ordered to recognize lesbian moms." Toronto: *Xtra!*, June 21, 2006.

Hines, S. "Intimate Transitions: Transgender Practices of Partnering and Parenting." *Sociology* 40 (2), 2006: 353–371.

Johnston, J. "Mum's the Word: Donor Anonymity in Assisted Reproduction." In *Health Law Review* 11 (1), 2002: 51–55.

Kelly, F. *Transforming Law's Family: The Legal Recognition of Planned Lesbian Motherhood*. Vancouver, BC: University of British Columbia Press, 2011.

Kirkpatrick, M., C. Smith, and R. Roy. "Lesbian Mothers and Their Children." *American Journal of Orthopsychiatry* 51, 1981: 545–551.

Lewin, E. *Lesbian Mothers: Accounts of Gender in American Culture*. Ithaca, NY: Cornell University Press, 1993.

Lewin, E. "On the Outside Looking In: The Politics of Lesbian Motherhood." In F. Ginsburg and R. Rapp, eds., *Conceiving the New World Order.* Berkeley: University of California Press, 1995.

Lorde, A. "Turning the Beat Around: Lesbian Parenting 1986." In S. Pollack and J. Vaughn, eds., *Politics of the Heart.* New York: Firebrand, 1987.

LGBTQ Parenting Network. "Culturally Queer Kids Project." 2004

MacKay, L. *Children and Feminism.* Vancouver: The Lesbian and Feminist Mothers Political Action Group, 1982.

Malone, K., and R. Cleary. "(De)sexing the Family: Theorizing the Social Science of Lesbian Families." *Feminist Theory* 3 (3), 2002: 271–293.

Mamo, L. *Queering Reproduction: Achieving Pregnancy in the Age of Technoscience.* Durham, NC: Duke University Press, 2007.

Nicol, N. "Politics of the Heart: Recognition of Homoparental Families in Quebec." In R. Epstein, ed., *Who's Your Daddy? And Other Writings on Queer Parenting.* Toronto: Sumach Press, 2009.

Patterson, C. "Lesbian and Gay Parents and Their Children: Summary of Research Findings." In *Lesbian and Gay Parenting: A Resource for Psychologists*, 2nd ed. Washington, DC: American Psychological Association, 2005.

Pollack, S. "Lesbian Parents: Claiming Our Visibility." In J.P. Knowles and E. Cole, eds., *Woman-Defined Motherhood.* New York: Haworth Press, 1990.

Polikoff, N. "Lesbians Choosing Children: The Personal Is Political." In S. Pollack and J. Vaughn, eds., *Politics of the Heart.* New York: Firebrand, 1987.

Pyne, J. "Erasure and Discrimination in the Lives of Transgender Parents: A Critical Review of the Literature." In press, 2012.

Rayside, D. *Queer Inclusions, Continental Divisions: Public Recognition of Sexual Diversity in Canada and the United States.* Toronto: University of Toronto Press, 2008.

Riggs, D.W. *Becoming Parent: Lesbians, Gay Men, and Family.* Teneriffe, QLD, AUS: Post Pressed, 2007.

Ross, L., L. Steele, and R. Epstein. "Lesbian and Bisexual Women's Recommendations for Improving the Provision of Assisted Reproductive Technology Services." *Fertility and Sterility* 86 (3), 2006: 735–738.

Ross, L., R. Epstein, S. Anderson, and A. Eady. "Policy, Practice, and Personal Narratives: Experiences of LGBTQ People with Adoption in Ontario, Canada." *Adoption Quarterly* 12, 2009: 272–293.

Ryan, M. "Beyond Thomas Beattie: Trans Men and the New Parenthood." In R. Epstein, ed., *Who's Your Daddy? And Other Writings on Queer Parenting.* Toronto: Sumach Press, 2009.

Schacher, S., C.F. Auerbach, and L.B. Silverstein. "Gay Fathers: Expanding the Possibilities for All of Us." *Journal of GLBT Family Studies* 1 (3), 2005: 31–52.

Stacey, J., and T.J. Biblarz. "(How) Does the Sexual Orientation of Parents Matter?" *American Sociological Review* 66, 2001: 159–183.

Taylor, C., and T. Peter, with T. L. McMinn, T. Elliott, S. Beldom, A. Ferry, Z. Gross, S. Paquin, and K. Schachter. *Every Class in Every School: The First National Climate Survey on Homophobia, Biphobia, and Transphobia in Canadian Schools.* Final report. Toronto, ON: Eagle Canada Human Rights Trust, 2011.

Veldhoven, C., and T. Vernon. (Interview.) "Daddies & Papas 2B: The Evolution of Possibilities." In R. Epstein, ed., *Who's Your Daddy? And Other Writings on Queer Parenting.* Toronto: Sumach Press, 2009.

Vercollone, C.F., H. Moss, and R. Moss. *Helping The Stork: The Choices and Challenges of Donor*

Insemination. New York, NY: Hungry Minds, 1997.

Walters, S.D. "Take My Domestic Partner, Please: Gays and Marriage in the Era of the Visible." In M. Bernstein and R. Reimann, eds., *Queer Families, Queer Politics: Challenging Culture and the State.* New York: Columbia University Press, 2001.

Ware, S.M. "Boldly Going Where Few Men Have Gone Before: One Trans Man's Experience." In R. Epstein, ed., *Who's Your Daddy? And Other Writings on Queer Parenting.* Toronto: Sumach Press, 2009.

Weston, K. *Families We Choose: Lesbian, Gays, Kinship.* New York: Columbia University Press, 1991.

Wyland, F. *Motherhood, Lesbianism and Child Custody.* Toronto: Wages Due Lesbians, 1977.

PART EIGHT
Sport

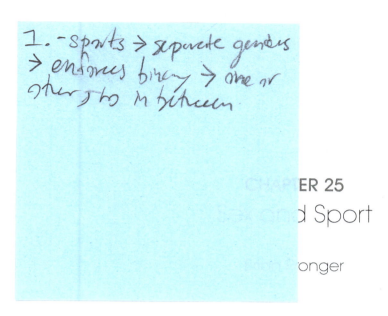

1. -sports → separate genders
→ endorses binary → one or
others to in between

... d Sport

... onger

He shoots! He scores!

—Foster Hewitt

SPORT AND THE HOMOEROTIC PARADOX

It's ironic that while sport is traditionally a sign of orthodox masculinity for men, emphasizing the conventional masculine values of power, muscular strength, competition, and so on, it is also a world that celebrates affinity among men, and therefore, paradoxical experience.

Women are excluded from most men's sports. Generally speaking, men don't want women on their hockey teams, in their rugby scrums, on their wrestling mats, in their locker rooms ... The fact is that there are very few sports that integrate men and women. Given that orthodox men are interested in women for the social and erotic production of mythic gender difference, one would think that they would make an effort to develop sports that include women. Instead, they have cultivated sporting styles, rules, and regulations that make it virtually impossible for women to participate. Rather than taking advantage of the many similarities of male and female physical capacities, sports have developed to emphasize the differences, thereby reproducing in that athletic/social sphere the mythic discourse of gender difference. The arguments about the physiological differences between men and women and their respective abilities to compete in various sports are legion. But since there is a more fundamental cultural and erotic dynamic at work here, one that precludes any mere physiological questions, one that may, in fact, construct the conceptual framework upon which scientific, physiological questions are asked in the first place, it's not necessary here to enter into the debate on the relative physical capacities of men and women.

Given that all sports are the products of social relations (that is, their origins are obviously social, not physiological), why do we have sports that segregate rather than integrate men and women? Why are men so anxious to perpetuate that segregation? What are men getting out of their sports that might be lost if women were to become involved?

The orthodox world of sports is a covert world of homoeroticism. I am not saying that men who like sports are necessarily gay, nor am I saying that their intuitions of themselves need be in some way fundamentally paradoxical. But lurking *mythically* beneath the ostensible orthodoxy of masculine sport is the ironic subtext of the paradox. [...] The irony of orthodox gender relations is that men become segregated from women; consequently, they develop a greater affinity for other men than they do for women. But is this the same gender affinity that [...] characterizes homosexuality?

Inherent in the structure of the gender myth is a strange slippage between orthodoxy and paradoxy, a slippage that is in itself paradoxical. Gender is in its essence a myth of difference. But that myth has so subjugated women that they are often not perceived by men as worthy. The intentionally segregated organization of sport, and the remarkable enthusiasm of men to keep it segregated rather than redesigning it so that integration is possible proves that women are not seen as the fellows of men. In the gender myth, women are tangential to the real world of men. We see this marginalization of women dramatized over and over again in segregated sports, both at the community level and in the prime-time television broadcasts of the NFL. So the paradox of orthodox masculinity is that the hierarchy of gender difference compels men to find satisfaction in one another. One of the ways they do so is in sports. It might seem that this is not erotic satisfaction in the usual sense; after all, it doesn't usually, or at least publicly, proceed to genital expression. Certainly, we don't see any of that in the television coverage of the NFL, or any other sporting event for that matter. But if one considers the wide range of experiences that one finds erotic, it becomes clear that for most of us, eroticism is not a strictly genital phenomenon.

Consider this popular, indeed legendary, scene that is played out time and again at high schools, universities, and community centres and is often featured on television, in newspapers, and magazines. A group of men get together in what are usually the rather close quarters of a locker room and take off their clothes. In various states of undress, they stand around talking to each other, preparing themselves for what is to follow. Ritual garments are donned. First of all, the jock strap. Then a coalition of pads and suspenders work together to dramatize and accentuate the masculine form. The men pull themselves into tight pants that closely adhere to the shapes of their buttocks. And not forgetting the twofold nature of Apollo, an elaborate set of laces frame the cupped and much-vaunted male genitals. The men then work themselves into a psychic frenzy of masculine unity and run out on the playing field ready to get the other team. One man bends over, while another, behind him, puts his hands between the inclined man's legs, grasps a ball that's shaped like a large testicle, and attempts to throw it to another man. Everybody wants the ball. Men along the line of scrimmage press themselves against each other enthusiastically. As a man out on the field runs with the ball, many others run after him, trying to grab him. Unless the ball goes out of bounds, each play climaxes with men lying on top of each other, the testicle-shaped ball forming the nucleus of this masculine clutch. The whistle blows and some variation of the same theme is played over and over. When time is up, the boys go back to the locker room, take their clothes off again, and shower together.

*****

Thematically, a satisfying sports competition is much the same as a satisfying homosexual, that is, paradoxical, fuck. The paradoxical play of masculinity is essential to both. In both well-matched sports and homoerotic fucking, masculine power meets masculine power; men play with each other's masculinity, paradoxically probing those places where masculinity can be undermined, painstakingly bringing each other to the edge of masculine dissolution. Crucial to fine athletic competition is the equality of the competitors. Likewise, fundamental equality in the gender myth is essential to a homoerotic encounter. Although they are often portrayed by the media as adversaries, competitive athletes are actually erotic accomplices. They are *accomplices* because the athletes must cooperate extensively with each other if the competitive struggle is going to take place at all. They are *erotic* accomplices because men's sport is a bodily, carnal experience in which the myth of masculine struggle is actualized. Just as in fucking there is an ecstatic meeting, a coalescence of equal bodies in the rapt oneness of the paradoxical project, so too in sports there is an exhilarating coalescence of equal bodies devoted to the carnal working out of manly struggle.

Ironically, men meeting men in sport, while pursuing an orthodox expression of their masculinity, also explore the paradoxical possibilities of their masculinity. Some are more aware of this than others. The paradox of homoerotic stimulation, the ecstasy of man-to-man struggle, disguised by the orthodox violence of sport, may be a deep secret whispered incomprehensibly in the grunts, groans, and moans of athletes straining their bodies against each other. And for those who are themselves unathletic but nevertheless fascinated by the play of masculine power, the excitement of the homoerotic paradox may be hidden deeply, indeed unconsciously, in the enthusiastic voyeurism of the dedicated sports fan, guzzling beer, cheering on the men who actually get to rub against each other on the playing field, wishing they were doing it themselves. For these men, televised sports spectacles are a deeply disguised form of homoerotic pornography. As Gore Vidal said, "The only time when heteros may openly enjoy what they secretly dream of is when watching handsome young men playing contact games."[1] For the orthodox sportsman, the sensibility of de-emphasis is paramount; it keeps the secret power of the paradox under wraps, even for themselves. For these men, the "orthodoxy" of sport exonerates the paradoxical subtext of exclusive, masculine, athletic struggle and the cult of manly contact, jock straps, and naked male bodies. The hidden erotic paradox of orthodox sport is terrifying for some men. Homophobia in sport is the fear of the inherent slippage between orthodoxy and paradoxy realized in sporting scenes. If the orthodox masculine world of athletics were to be known as a deeply hidden homoerotic world of paradox, the patriarchal power of athletics and of those men who pursue athletics for that power would be ironically undermined, making the entire edifice of orthodox athletic masculinity tremble at the very epicentre of patriarchal power itself. If deeply submerged in the orthodox pleasure of athletics, disguised by the "orthodoxy" of athletics, is the pleasure of the homoerotic paradox, then the masculine patriarchal significance of athletics will show itself as containing the seeds of its own paradoxical destruction. This is intolerable for men who truly desire the power that their orthodox relationship to patriarchy has so gratuitously afforded them. And so they homophobically deny that there is any homoerotic dimension in sport. The paradoxical erotic experience of sports can be concealed by the false consciousness of "orthodoxy." This alleviates the fear some men have of the concealed allure of the paradox, preserving for them their own orthodox patriarchal power. That de-emphasizing maneuver also sustains the patriarchal socio-cultural status quo.

For those who are more open to the paradox, however, whose intuitions of themselves in the gender myth motivate them to deliberately seek out the paradoxical eroticism of gender, the homoerotic dimensions of sport are full of promise. The more gay one is, that is, the more fully one has accepted the legitimacy of the paradoxical interpretation of gender, the more willing one is to draw out the homoerotic dimensions of sport. The intimate relationship between orthodoxy and paradox in contact sports is pursued by gay men both in the fantasies of pornography and the actual experience of sport. There are several gay pornography producers who are devoted to the homoeroticism of wrestling and boxing. These films make the implicit homoeroticism of mainstream sport spectacles explicit. [...]

One man told me that, as a boy, wrestling brought him to his first awareness of homoeroticism and has remained a source of erotic fascination for him. [...] As a legitimate activity for boys, wrestling allowed him the opportunity to explore, unwittingly, the homoerotic potential of masculine physical contact. He was fortunate enough to have a muscular uncle with whom he could encounter mature physical power. [...]

Boys and teenagers are intuitively aware of this kind of fun and wrestle with their friends. Some are content with the subtle, nongenital expression of the paradox; others use it as a mutual masculine ruse or prolegomenon to a more transparent homoerotic seduction. As Gregory Woods said, "Wrestling ... is the heterosexually acceptable form of homosexual foreplay."[2] Often boys will wrestle with each other hoping for a more explicit homosexual action. Describing an ultimately frustrating teenage relationship with another boy who turned out to be more interested in orthodoxy, one man told me that he and his friend, "were very physical, we were always wrestling, doing everything but having sex, and I think I just got tired of waiting for something to happen."

*****

A man I interviewed remembered the problems that competitive wrestling in high school caused him. He said he found wrestling

[v]ery sexual. I'd often get hard, I'd often come. It was difficult to deal with: "How did you get that hard-on off me." That became a problem in high school so that I ended up, grade twelve ... I stopped wrestling, I was too afraid that I was going to get hard and someone would notice. Actually, it rarely happens when you are really wrestling—it can't physiologically because the blood is going to the muscles and it's certainly not engorging your penis. So it has to be in a fooling-around sense, but still, it's happened to me, so you tend to become really cautious about coming out in grade ten in front of the gym class, it's not cool.

The homoerotic appeal of wrestling needn't always result in erections. As the wrestler above pointed out, when one wrestles intensely the muscles get precedence over the penis for the supply of blood. That physical economy, however, may have little to do with the erotic focus of the athletic activity. The lack of an erection does not signify a paucity of homoerotic attraction. As Neil Marks said, "There is a unique excitement in being aware of your physical attraction to a man and sublimating it into an athletic maneuver."[3] No doubt, there is also a *jouissance* in being *unaware* of your physical attraction to a man and sublimating it into an athletic maneuver. James Kirkup says that football is that game "Where players, colliding, shrink, / Yet with desired daring reach / Longingly at one another."[4] A gymnast I interviewed said, "I always enjoyed playing touch football; I remember in grades seven and eight we always played it during our lunch hour. It was great because it was a chance to jump on another guy." This is the concealed homoerotic appeal of contact sports.

Some of the masculine rituals that surround mainstream sport almost scream with homoerotic desire. Gary Shaw, a former University of Texas Longhorn football player, describes an after-dinner entertainment team members frequently enjoyed in the dorm.

> Probably the varsity's most popular game was "record races." Here they would strip several of us naked and divide us into two groups. Then they would bring out our "toy"—an old forty-five-rpm record. They placed the toy between the cracks of our asses. We had to carry it from one end of the hall to the other without using our hands. We would then have to—again without using our hands—place it in our teammate's ass. If he happened to drop it, his partner had to pick it up with his mouth, and put it back in place. These races were considered the highlight of the evening.[5]

A straight-identified university football player told me of a strangely homoerotic team initiation rite. Rookies would be stripped naked and then required to extract from the foreskins of their uncircumcised teammates, without using their hands or feet, olives, which they were then expected to swallow.

There are men who feel no need for these pretenses and happily admit the homoeroticism of sport.

> Wrestling and sex to me are the same thing; there's no difference. To get aroused, I need to wrestle, I need the physical contact, I need muscle, I need a response from someone else. If they just lie there and let you dominate them, that doesn't do a thing for me. It's the muscle, the meeting, the equal response, the body contact. That to me is synonymous with sex.

The homoerotic significance of masculine struggle can outweigh the importance of orgasm.

> The orgasm is almost incidental to the fact of the wrestling; that you come is almost like blowing your nose at the end. After you've had your bout, he's off getting a drink of water, and you sit there and you jerk off. It's not the most important part.

One needn't be a participant in sports to enjoy its homoerotic potential. A multimillion-dollar spectator-sports industry exploits that homoerotic appeal. Certainly, there are men who watch sports on television or go to games because they enjoy watching the skills of fine athletes. But [...] the world of sports is not *just* a world of athleticism. [...] One can't help but remark that many, if not the vast majority, of sports spectators are supremely unathletic themselves; the fat, beer-drinking baseball, football, or hockey fan is a legitimate cliché. Their lethargy leads one to suspect that *athletic* experience is not an important one to them. Those sports fans who are obsessed with the aura of athletes are known by professional athletes, quite pejoratively, as "jock sniffers."[6] Given what we know about the homoeroticism of jocks and jock straps, and also that hidden in the orthodoxy of sports is the homoerotic paradox, we can see that the interest male sports fans have in their athletic heroes probably involves the deeply submerged pleasures of homoerotic sniffing.

Although one may enjoy watching fine athletes accomplishing superb athletic feats in high-performance sports, the real appeal of sport lies in its exercise of masculinity. The orthodox appreciation of athletics as a masculine drama, involving the display of power, aggression, and violence, is well known to us all. The masculine combat of sport is thought to mirror the competitive, in fact war-like, relations between men. One need only consider the language typical of the sports pages to see the hostile nature of orthodox masculine relations as they are portrayed in sports: teams and athletes are routinely said to be walloped, bashed, thumped, crushed, slaughtered, and annihilated. The paradoxical appreciation of sports spectacles, on the other hand, views the games with ironic, homoerotic field glasses.

Typically, gay men are not inclined to be sports spectators. This is probably because the ostensible orthodoxy of that masculine world is incompatible with their personal reading of the gender myth. Most, however, are able to give that athletic masculinity a paradoxical interpretation and derive at least occasional pleasure from it.

> I don't watch [sports] on television. I've been to one major-league baseball game and one major-league hockey game in my life, and the one I went to because my lover at the time got free tickets, and the other I went to because my brother got me a couple of tickets and wanted me to take his son. I like some things to watch, like gymnastics on television. The bodies are nice.

A number of the men I interviewed said that although they were keen to play some sports, they were not interested in watching except for the athletic bodies. A swimmer told me: "I'd much rather participate than watch." [...]

A gay phys ed student said:

> I get bored very quickly watching any sport, unless there's somebody in it I know and I have a personal interest. I got a bit of a charge out of the pennant race a couple of years ago. I hadn't realized what an attractive bunch the Blue Jays were. I was surprised. I started watching ball games, and the next thing I knew there was a picture of Donald Sylveste in my desk I could pull out to look at. It was sexy watching Garcia slide.

A body builder I interviewed said he was very fond of watching sports for both orthodox and paradoxical reasons.

> [My lover] closes the door and I watch the NFL, track and field, I look at all of them. Eighty percent of my television watching is football, tennis, track and field, hockey, I don't watch boxing. [...] But I do watch these other sports and my rationalization is that's how I channel my competitive urges, I admit I have them, I'm just not prepared to act them out.

[Is there anything sexual in watching sports?]

> I'd like to say no, but I think I'd have to say yes. They played the 100m from Rome with Carl Lewis and Ben Johnson so many times. There's no question that I'm stimulated—although I don't get a hard-on—by seeing these beautiful masculine bodies doing what they do, and doing it very well. There is an element of sexuality there, maybe not consciously. I notice their cocks, but also the legs and the arms and how tight they are—all those things. When I watch tennis, yes, I'm watching the tennis, but whenever I get a shot of the front—I never noticed how cute the Australian, Pat Cash is, and then I think, I wonder what his basket is like, and it's all happening at the same time I'm noticing the score.... [The television cameras] give you crotch shots and bum shots. I'm sure they are subliminally seducing straights and overtly seducing gays. It does make me wonder sometimes who's behind those cameras.

*****

It's obvious that some sports producers choose to play on the homoerotic appeal of athletes. A poster from The Sports Network (TSN), a Canadian TV channel that gives twenty-four-hour sports coverage, is a case in point. It shows a sweaty, muscular young man pulling off his singlet. Beneath the picture in bold uppercase letters are the words: "WE DELIVER THE MALE." This picture presents a muscular, wet torso seductively arched, the head back (perhaps in ecstasy), with arms above the head in a pseudo–Athletic Model Guild pose. That hallmark "take me, do with me what you will, I can't resist you" pose is subtly reinforced by the seeming bondage of the muscular model, tied up in his own sweaty singlet. This provocative juxtaposition of power and vulnerability bespeaks an invitation to the homoerotic paradox, a fantastic enticement to the violation of masculinity. The Sports Network must realize this significance; the poster, after all, is directed at potential advertisers, people with a sophisticated sense of the commercial appeal of the not-so-subliminal seductiveness of the homoerotic athletic body.

*****

A homoerotic text can be gleaned from the common discourse of mainstream sport. Photos of athletes feigning homoerotic interest in each other regularly grace the pages of newspapers and sports magazines. For example, *Sports Illustrated* pictured basketball players Isaiah Thomas and Magic

Johnson kissing before a game. [...] The *Toronto Daily Star* pictured Wayne Gretzky seemingly kiss-ing the Philadelphia Flyers' goalie Ron Hextall. [...] *In Touch* and *Drummer*—gay magazines—have run humorous photo essays, highlighting this hidden erotic dynamic. [...] The vocabulary of sports can also betray hidden homoerotic significance. In collegiate wrestling there is a hold by which one immobilizes an opponent by pressing one's pelvis into his backside; the move is called "the Saturday night." Dennis Potvin, in *Power on Ice,* speaks of "the orgasmic delight of seeing the black hunk of vulcanized rubber penetrate the deepest recesses of the net." And regarding the importance of "assists" in a hockey player's career, Frank Rose says, "It pays to help your buddy get off his shot."[7]

Male athletes will often sell their homoerotic appeal to companies for advertising. The late Can-adian swimmer Victor Davis, who set a world record in the 200-meter breast stroke at the L.A. Olym-pics, lent his hard, shaved body to the Speedo swimsuit company as an image to help them sell bathing suits. Speedo then sold not only the bathing suits, but also the poster of Davis—a poster that made its way into the homes of numbers of gay men. Speedo, hypocritically exploiting the homoerotic appeal of Victor Davis, prefers to distance itself from homosexuality. I asked them for permission to repro-duce that poster here. When I spoke to the amiable general manager on the telephone, he said that he could foresee no difficulties in giving me permission; I should simply write to him explaining the context. The "context" turned everything around. I received a terse refusal. That the photographer and advertising directors who created the image the company now refuses to allow me to reproduce were unaware of its homoerotic appeal seems very unlikely to me. Advertisers put a great deal of thought into the nuances and implications of their work. So it would seem that the company prefers a covert association with homosexuality, making money from it without admitting it.

THE LOCKER ROOM
Looking
A gay phys ed student told me:

> It's an unusual situation in athletics, because in heterosexual society you don't have this contact. You can only suspect what may be underneath those clothes, but if you are gay, there are no surprises. My straight friends, they say it must be really tough, walking around the showers when you are gay. "I couldn't do it in a women's shower and try and be casual and talk with them."

A runner described the special experience of being gay in a locker room.

> When I was coming out and after I was out it was like, "Oh my God, all these gorgeous bodies." It was seeing all these terrific-looking men in one place. A "kid-in-a-candy-store" mentality—I want that one and that one!

But figuring out how one can get who one wants is not always that easy. He went on to say:

> When I was at college, just before I was out, I remember there was this one guy who I used to look at and I was worried that he would think I was staring at him. I only realize

now that I was staring at him because he had such a huge basket. Well, the reason he had such a huge basket was that he had an erection! I *knew,* or I sort of knew, but at the time, I didn't think it had anything to do with me looking at him.

A swimmer recalled an experience he had in the showers with his team, all of whom knew he was gay. Only a few of the showers were working and those that were, were right next to each other. He remarked how nice it was that the swim team was becoming so intimate. They laughed nervously since the comment "came as it did from the queer in the corner."

There I was and I was shampooing my hair, looking down, and Tom was talking to Frank and they were both about a foot away, and they both had about a foot each [the length of their penises]. Tom had this gorgeous bum. They were just chatting away in this terribly masculine sort of way, soaping up their dicks, and I was washing my hair and watching them; I know I had a grin on my face and I thought to myself, "Isn't this thoroughly pleasant." I had every right to be there—in fact, I was finished showering before them, I wasn't lingering and peering. I belonged there. It was like having chocolate sauce on your ice cream. It was a perfectly gratuitous, pleasant experience.

Finding it natural to look at men in the showers and locker room, a man told me: "I consider it perfectly normal. I am discreet about it. I do it and I feel fine about it."
Only one of the gay athletes I interviewed did not see erotic potential in the locker room.

That's something the gay pornographic film industry has been trying to tap into for some time now, but I'm afraid they're off the mark. There's nothing to me that's sexually attractive about a dirty locker room.

Several athletes told me that although they could see the erotic potential of the locker room, the fantasy about sex with teams and in locker rooms had little to do with real teams and locker rooms.

When you say that you play football, a lot of gay men who have never done that, they think about the locker-room scene from the porno thing. And nothing could be further from the actuality. Well, sorry to tell you, it's a lot more mundane than you think. You finish, you take a shower—if you win, everyone's patting each other's back and stuff— but essentially, you take a shower and everyone goes home. Not much happens. I can see where it would be a source of fantasy for people who [aren't athletes], but for people who are, you want to take your shower and go home, you're tired. For people who are fantasizing and are starting at that point, they still have all their energy, that's fine.

*****

For some gay men, being in the presence of other muscular men is an inspiration to their own athletic activity.

I can remember pacing myself behind some particularly nice man on that running track and that making it possible for me to run an extra half-mile or so. I'm not going to pass this man for anything.

A gymnast told me that working out and the erotic potential of athletic facilities are mutually enhancing:

Sometimes when I'd be lifting weights, I'd look out of the corner of my eye and see someone who has an amazing body and I would look at them and think, "Oh my god," and start pushing the weights harder and harder. It raises the motivation. It gives you a goal. Watching someone while working out hard is a lot like sex, minus the ejaculation.

In one's youth, locker rooms are often a source of erotic fantasy.

When I was age-group swimming, there were people from ten to twenty, I much preferred looking at the older boys. I remember doing that at swim meets. Now that I think of it, I have had fantasies of locker rooms and stuff. I don't have that kind of fantasy now, but I did then. [...]

Athletic settings in general and the locker room in particular feed the homoerotic imagination and provide homoerotic contact for boys. I asked a masters[8] swimmer if there was a sexual aspect to athletics when he was in high school.

There certainly was. There were boys flirting with each other the way boys do when they are fifteen or sixteen years old. Some of it is just playful mockery insinuating that everyone else is a fag. Some of it is curiosity. There were a few who really wanted to touch other boys or show themselves off in the locker rooms. I remember being in the locker room one day—everyone was naked and there was this one fellow who was about fifteen years old playing around and generally making an ass of himself. He was pretending that he wanted to fuck this other guy by thrusting his hips forward into the other naked boy. It was interesting because this boy was the most butch of all the boys around. He liked grabbing other guys' cocks. I think that he is probably straight; but he was awfully curious. [...]

*****

There are some men who get upset when the paradox is revealed by homoerotic voyeurism.

We all play voyeur, straights play voyeur all the time. I've seen just as much cruising from supposedly straight guys as I've seen from gay guys. Gay guys just make it more obvious. Straight guys do just as much comparison and cruising as anybody does. I've noticed that a lot of guys will not shower anymore in the gym, they refuse to. If you ask them why—"too many faggots around here." They towel off and off they go, they shower at home. Anybody who's that homophobic, I automatically question their sexuality. What are they worried about, "You've got twenty-inch biceps, fella!" It tells me they are really uptight about their sexuality and have problems dealing with it. Anyone who is sure about themselves isn't going to be concerned when someone is looking at them.... It doesn't have to be in the locker room or the shower, there's just as much voyeurism going on in the gym, people hanging around the big guys, watching as close as they can get, but not too close. It just never stops.

That the locker room can be an erotic environment is undeniable. Men who prefer to ignore that erotic potential are sometimes upset about the appreciative glances that they receive from the more homoerotically inclined. I interviewed a heterosexual man who had been a college football player and national track and field coach. Although homoerotic voyeurism did not bother him personally, he suspected that he knew why it was disturbing to some.

I think with some athletes, when somebody thinks somebody else is gay: "Boy, I feel dirty, somebody's staring at me." And I think that comes from equating it with what they do to women, that is that it's dirty, the sneaky peeks at women, and therefore it's what they would be doing and what they would be thinking about women. I think we tend to relate things to what *we* do, and so what they're thinking about women they realize somebody's thinking about them.

Another heterosexual coach agreed that the straight interpretation of the homoerotic voyeur's gaze is that the look mirrors the erotic interest that heterosexual men have in women. He told me that he disapproved of homoerotic voyeurism because it reminded him of the way he would look at women. As a result of having been cruised by men at a hotel, which turned out to be a primarily gay hotel in which he and his team had been unwittingly accommodated, he decided that he should no longer leer at women, but because the nature of homoerotic desire is fundamentally different from that of men's heteroerotic desire, the former being the eroticization of the paradoxical *violation* of mythic masculine power within a context of equality and the latter eroticizing the *affirmation* of that power within a context of inequality, it is incorrect to equate the meaning of a heterosexual man eyeing a woman with a homosexual man eyeing another man. The erotic intention of these two looks are, in fact, virtually opposite.

The combination of an intuitive understanding of the significance of homoeroticism as a violation of masculinity, along with the fragile status of their own mythic masculinity,[9] leads some men to homophobia. This fear is built into the masculine leitmotif of athletic culture, a culture that exists, after all, to celebrate and confer orthodox masculinity. The first of the previously quoted coaches said that growing up in sports, one grows up with homophobia.

You get taught those reactions too. "I was going to beat the shit out of a fag the other day, he was looking at me"—you hear that from the time you are really young in locker rooms. What does it mean? But you've been *told* that. Long before, and I mean eight years old, when you're eight years old on the hockey rink you hear that from the older guys, being twelve.... There's a real aversion to homosexuality around sport, and I really believe it's because people aren't sure of themselves. That's the bottom-line reason; certainly all the enculturation too, but it's an *aversion*—a "get-away-from-me" infection type of aversion, perhaps I might get it. It will *breed* like athlete's foot.

But there are many men who appreciate the attention of the homoerotic voyeur. Weight rooms are notorious as places where men and boys like to admire each other's bodies. They will spend a great deal of time admiring themselves—the notion that mirrors in weight rooms are aids to good weight-lifting technique is a macho conceit meant to disguise the narcissistic and homoerotic intrigue that surfaces as muscles flex and get bigger. Many of the men I interviewed said that there are seemingly straight men who appear to appreciate their adulations. And, of course, for gay men, being the recipients of the homoerotic voyeur's attention has its pleasures too.

One meets a whole range of people [in the locker room]. There are some who seem to be there a lot of the time. Some of them don't ever do anything, they just hang around and look. They are often quite good-looking. I think they just enjoy exchanging knowing glances and having people look at them—it is very flattering to have people admiring your body. A lot of that happens.

Hard-Ons

The erotic potential of the locker room can lead to an obvious physical sexual response: an erection. Such a prominent testament to one's desires can be embarrassing to men and boys who are trying to keep those desires a secret. Said a man who generally shied away from sports:

I didn't like going to the "Y" because you had to take your clothes off. [I was] scared to death of the locker room—it's partly frivolous but partly true—because you betray yourself, or might [that is, get an erection]. And all that towel flipping and so on might be just a little too attractive.

John Argue, a former varsity swimmer, told me, "By the time I was in university, I was getting a little more sexually frustrated, I would be acutely embarrassed about the possibility of getting an erection in the showers." He was in the uncomfortable situation of not yet having accepted his erotic attraction to men, yet while in the showers his body was giving him the all-too-obvious signal that he *was*. So, for him, there was a negative feeling associated with being in the showers; it forced him to confront something he would rather just repress. [...]

The fear of getting an erection can lead some boys to avoid showers after gym class; others avoid sports altogether because of that anxiety. Most learn to control their sexual response. Even so, a former gymnast told me that he still finds it difficult to restrain himself.

I have to get dressed and leave right away. If I've seen a guy in the gym and he starts getting undressed beside me, I'll have a strong sexual desire for him and I'll get an erection and there's nothing I can do about it. I have to get out right away because I've had the experience of being in the steam-room and if someone comes in and starts staring at me in the genital area, I'll get an erection. [...] It shouldn't be embarrassing because it happens; everyone gets erections, although some people can control it better than others; I'm just one of those people who can't. At least I let the guy know where he stands right away. If they want to laugh, fine, then I'll laugh too.

Not everyone is embarrassed about getting erections, in fact, it is often the prelude to more involved activities or at least a sign that the owner of the erection is keen. Some men are amazingly adept at controlling the exact amplitude of tumescence in their penises—they will signify their desire with varying states of erection—it goes up and down like a Geiger counter. A man said that in the university locker room

I had a guy flashing a hard-on at me, he was holding a towel over it so that he could expose it whenever he wished. I was in a real hurry that day. He was straddling the bench and lifted his towel for me to see his little pink erection. I remember the only thing I could think of was that I was in a hurry. [...]

The locker room sometimes becomes the place of sexual activities.

There is a surprising amount of cruising and sexual activity going on in the university locker room and showers. I've certainly had sex there. It's generally initiated in the sauna, it's just a look and then you go to the small shower room next door. I was in there one time masturbating this guy when someone pushed open the door and caught us in the act. He looked and said, "Oh, I'm sorry."

A swimmer told me that although he has been involved in sexual situations in the locker room, he finds the idea of it more comfortable than the actual activity.

I was in the shower and watching this guy who was obviously interested; he became visibly excited. The more I stared at him, the more excited he became. I found it kind of a thrill, there we were in the middle of [the athletic centre], and this guy is sporting an erection right in the open. So, we left the showers and went down to the end of the lockers and did a few things—we touched and stroked each other. He was a big guy, a bit goofy, it seemed like the only thing that interested him was sex and that was fine with me. When we weren't touching or stroking it was kind of exciting to think that we could be caught, but when we were actually touching each other it was too frightening and stressful. So I guess the thought of it was better than the actual act.

*****

Responding

A university physical education instructor told me:

> All these men with their clothes off. I really find the whole thing about walking around, straight or gay, in a room of twenty-five other people without anything on, is unnerving. And you find people walking around with towels around their waists, and then you have the studs strutting around without a towel, and these are the straight ones, and you wonder, "Are they flaunting it?" because they know there are only males in the locker room, they aren't flaunting for the women. They are strutting around in front of other men, are they gay? They are trying to do their peacock attracting number to other men. That blows me away.

Who is interested in whom in locker rooms? Life in the locker room illustrates the fluidity of homosexuality and the role of gay sensibilities. If we think of sexual orientation as the essence of one's being, as an identity, then the interest that "straight" men might have in men's bodies is problematic.[10] But because homoeroticism plays with desire in that slippery mythic world of orthodox and paradox, it may be that when confronted with naked men, homoerotic potential presents itself to all men. Some men, because of their attachment to orthodox power, either refuse to see or are blind to the paradox and its erotic promise; they exercise the sensibility of de-emphasis to the utmost. These are the men who seem the most straight in the showers. On the other hand, there are men who are keenly aware of every nuance and erotic possibility of the paradoxical understanding of gender; they seem the most gay. And there are those in the showers who arouse great curiosity among gay men because they show some awareness of the paradox and perhaps even a glimmer of interest in its erotic potential. They may seem to be straight, but their slightly lingering gaze and sometimes semierections suggest a sensitivity to the paradox of which they themselves may not be truly aware.

One gay man said:

> It can be quite fun to watch. The straight guys like to show off but then they get nervous when you watch too much. They like being looked at and they like looking. It's like a pot boiling of suppressed things, especially for straight men. There's a whole vocabulary of behaviours that are not clearly defined that are incredibly interesting in the locker room—exhibitionists who roam the locker room, whether gay or straight, they like the attention. Gay people playing with themselves, looking out for sex, straight people turned on by being with other men. There's a feeling of being with other guys, naked. I find it very sexual. A lot of guys like it. You see more than one man, and not all gay, with half-erect penises, taking their time, lounging around. Being naked with the boys, being part of the team.

Life in the locker room, and in sports in general, because of their exonerating orthodox jock associations, creates a safe place for the paradoxical imagination to feed itself. Here, there is a concentration of desirable masculinity in which men can immerse themselves and pretend that it's all orthodox masculinity. The degree of paradox and orthodox in the interpretations of these men is often a secret that only they know. It may be a secret kept even from them, deep in the subconscious. Athletic settings facilitate the potential of homoerotic paradox. Given that potential, various sensibilities go to work.

The sensibility of de-emphasis is at work for many men and for a variety of reasons. Men who take great pride in their orthodox masculinity, who feel they would be compromised by an erotic interest in men, de-emphasize the presence of the paradox in the locker room, ignore its potential, and claim not to be aware of it. Seeing the interest that other men may have in the paradox when confronted with naked men, they are disgusted.

Although heterosexual men generally do not get to shower and change with naked women as homosexual men have the privilege of showering and changing with other naked men, there are heterosexual arrangements that are similar. Consider life on the beach and around swimming pools where men and women wear as little as possible. Generally speaking, these arrangements for the stimulation of heteroerotic desire are not considered disgusting. But ethically, such arrangements should be a concern because they raise the spectre of the erotic consummation of orthodoxy in the gender myth, the erotic celebration of the power of men over women. The difference between hetero- and homosexual voyeurism is substantial. The power difference of the gender myth always puts women at risk in their relations with men; rape is an ever-present fear for women. Men, on the other hand, are virtually never raped by women, and very seldom by gay men (they are, however, often raped by straight men in prisons and other all-male environments). When a gay man looks at another man in the showers or locker room, it is never from the position of power that straight men have when they look at women at the beach or on the street. In fact, the erotic world that is invoked in homosexual voyeurism is one of equality in the gender myth and the paradoxical *violation* of masculine power rather than the orthodox, heterosexual *confirmation* of power difference that is fundamental to heterosexual desire. The homoerotic aura of locker room is disgusting to some, because it brings to the fore the potential for paradox, the violation of orthodox masculinity. Those who want to cling to their orthodox masculine power usually prefer to de-emphasize the homoeroticism of their athletic environments.

There are gay men who are happy to explore homoeroticism in other situations, but prefer to de-emphasize its potential in athletic settings. This is often the case with high-performance athletes. The athleticism of high-performance life can outweigh homoerotic possibilities—one's life is devoted to athletics. Immersed in the heterosexual athletic environment, the homosexual high-performance athlete will often ignore the homoeroticism of the locker room. [Rower] John Goodwin's experience [...] highlights the complex interactions between the fluidity of homosexuality and the sensibility of de-emphasis when a homosexual high-performance athlete is confronted with the homoerotic possibilities of the locker room.

> At that time, sports were a bit secluding—I trained hard from 1972 to '77. I don't remember anybody cruising me—I remember people looking at me and talking to me. I go there now and it's like night and day—I don't think there are any straight people there! Then, we were all on teams—we lived together, showered together, did everything together so that you learn to ignore everybody else and you purposely allow everybody their privacy in a very public place. I still do that—consciously not look at people so that I walk past people I know without seeing them. It's a way of behaving

in changing rooms.... I think I purposely kept my perceptions or involvement in the sexual thing very quiet. Getting into the boat, you're always close to everybody there. It was a very closely knit group that I just don't remember as being sexual.

He said he became so accustomed to ignoring the erotic implications of being with the other men on the team that it seemed to disappear as a dimension. The assumption of orthodoxy among the crew members made physical contact easy among them.

The guys I rowed with, I don't know whether any were gay or not, but they thought nothing about going up to someone they didn't even know and telling them how wonderful they looked and how great their legs were, and feeling their arms. It was very physical and complimentary, admiring, but nothing sexual. The people I rowed with I wasn't attracted to—there were other oarsmen, yes, but everyone was quite comfortable about talking about someone else's body. I didn't pay attention to what was going on, but now, in the last four years, I notice more of that going on—perhaps it always was and I didn't notice. If somebody admired the way I was doing bench presses and wanted to hold the bar for me I would have thought it perfectly normal, but today if somebody said that I'd interpret it as cruising. I can't remember anything ever happening to me with the team, when I was alone I was cruised a few times at the university but I only recognize that fact now.

For John Goodwin, understanding the homoerotic implications of his high-performance athletic life came only in retrospect. But as a young athlete, a combined lack of familiarity with the conventions of homosexual liaisons and his wish to avoid them, a wish based on his negative image of homosexuality, kept him from following through on desirable sexual possibilities.

There were some really gorgeous guys that I remember talking to and having these nothing conversations with but thinking all along how good-looking this guy was, and trying to interpret what he *really* meant. I know now if I was in that situation—somebody chatting with me and I thought he was very sexy—I'm sure I wouldn't have any difficulty in clearing the air.... Why didn't I do that? I don't know.

He said that although he felt very sexual at the time, the combination of a demanding training schedule and the seeming dearth of homosexual men made a sexual life impossible.

When you're in that kind of shape you're very sexual, you're like a high-performance vehicle, everything is finely tuned, but having sex with men, no, it just wasn't possible. I would have had to have gone to [the city] to have sex because I didn't know a soul [where I was]. Besides, in the whole rowing season we might have had one day off—and we didn't even want that, because if you take a day off, it throws you off, and it takes a week to get back to normal. Some of the guys had steady girlfriends and they would have sex. When women's rowing was brought in, a lot of men went out with those girls because they were always at the course at the same time.

Because heterosexuality is acceptable in sports, the advent of women in rowing introduced easy heterosexual relations in a busy athletic environment. John Goodwin remained "secluded." Now that he is out of his competitive career, he sees the erotic potential of the locker room. But he finds voyeurism unfulfilling. [...]

*****

Because one can disguise homoerotic desire in the orthodox masculine facade of the "straight" locker room—masculinity, as we have seen, has great homoerotic potential when it *seems* to be heterosexual—the locker room invites homoeroticism. The irony here is obvious. As one man I interviewed said: "The exciting part is that you think most of the people in there are straight and you're all walking around nude, and it's thought of as being very straight and masculine, and the excitement is to take it out of that context."

A heterosexual man asked a gay phys ed student what was different about being gay in physical education. The gay student asked the nongay man to imagine what it would be like to change and shower every day, several times a day, with the most physically fit women on campus. How would it feel to walk down his row of lockers and find sixty or seventy of those women pulling off their clothes? Imagine sitting on the bench between the lockers and engaging in conversation for twenty minutes at a time surrounded by naked women in various postures. Then try to imagine what it would be like for none of those women to know that he was a man and erotically interested in them.

*****

The showers can be the place in which double irony unfolds. It has happened that there has been more than one gay man in the shower room in the presence of other, probably straight men. The first irony becomes apparent to the gay men in the private realization that they are not alone in their ironic voyeuristic pursuits. However, rather than making this interior irony exterior and acknowledging each other as ironists, they suspend their recognition of each other as ironists, to build a second irony upon the first. Pretending not to recognize each other as gay voyeurs in a shower room surrounded by ostensibly straight men, they treat each other as though they were straight, thereby finding ironic voyeuristic pleasure in each other.

These gay men are manipulating appearance and reality. The appearance is that they are straight and simply taking showers. The reality is that they are gay and deriving voyeuristic pleasure. In the case of the first irony, ironic interpretation has been suspended, which allows for the experience of a second, richer, irony. They choose not to reject the original appearance, that is, that each other is straight. By choosing not to reject the original appearance, they have not opted to accept the appearance either, preferring to hold it in a kind of ironic limbo. Aware of the potential to reject and demolish the original appearance, leaving it intact, they proceed to the second irony. This will be an elegant voyeuristic pursuit of the homoerotic paradox. The second irony involves finding paradoxical pleasure in each other as "straight" men. The erotic voyeuristic appeal lies in the pretense that everyone involved in the encounter is straight. Eventually, they develop erections, which gives away their "straight" ruse, but offers them the alternative pleasure of knowing they are fellow erotic ironists.

They were gay, pretended to be straight, got "off" on the pretense, and through ironic destruction and reconstruction (signaled by the appearance of their erections), came to know the truth, which is that they are gay. The experience is satisfying because, as Wayne Booth says of irony, it's like moving to a better part of town: in this case, from seeming to be straight to being gay. In the creation and interpretation of irony, there is a special sense that one has accomplished something, and that the choice to reject appearance has led one to a better understanding. This voyeuristic encounter is a dramatization of a profound fact of gay life that involves the play of paradox and the manipulation of appearance and reality. It is the experience of things as they actually are, marbled through with the equal presence of things as they are not. Since irony brings with it a sense of superiority, a sense of looking at the world from a higher place, each gay ironic experience is a sublime reaffirmation of a gay world view. Such is the erotic and ironic joy of locker-room voyeurism.

While being in the locker room brings many pleasant erotic and ironic possibilities, it is important to be responsive to the sensibilities of others. Tactful honesty in the locker room is the best policy. A masters swimmer said:

> There are different kinds of voyeurs in the showers. My friend and I are different kinds of voyeurs. I don't like the kind that I am that much, which is to say, the discreet voyeur—although maybe I'm not as discreet as I think I am. But I do try to go for discretion, which my friend really doesn't go for unless he thinks he's about to get punched in the nose. I'm trying to train myself to either be brazen or not do it at all. The idea of covertness is so old-style homosexual, taking what you can get in little bits; it's not an attractive pose. The modern homosexual doesn't want to be seen to be doing that. On the other hand, it can go in the other direction, in which you are the other kind of homosexual, the kind who hangs around showers and leers.

Another fellow commented on the importance of tact when gay men are in the locker room.

> Locker-room voyeurism is a great opportunity to see a lot of men without their clothes on. I'm not always that subtle about it. It depends on who it is I'm looking at, whether he seems to like being watched, whether he seems to be gay, in which case I don't have to worry about it so much. Sometimes I'm quite blatant with people who I think are interested in my watching them. People should be allowed to look at other people. It's quite natural to be curious about what another person looks like. I'm sure that all the straight men look at each other. It is perfectly reasonable to expect that if you are anywhere where there are other people around, they are going to look at you whether you have your clothes on or not. If you're interested in sex, it's important to be sensitive to the person that you're trying to approach. I don't enjoy being stared at if I'm not interested; it makes me feel uncomfortable. I think that one should be aware of whether the person one's looking at appreciates the attention one's giving them.

The sensibility of change can also shape one's gay experience of the locker room. Given that there can be hostility from homophobically orthodox men when they find gay men in their midst, it is important for gay men to have a strategy, the most effective of which is to claim the high ground of legitimacy, which comes with being out of the closet.

When I decided to go into phys ed, I had to decide how to present myself; was I going to let the boys with whom I change, shower, play basketball, and wrestle know I was gay? I made it clear to everyone that I was gay and I think because of that I had absolutely no problems. I never heard homophobic comments and got along amiably with my classmates. When I asked one of my coaches what he thought of such a personal policy for gay athletes, he said:

> It sounds like the best course of action because I think you set yourself up for ridicule if you put the other person in the power position, in other words, "There's something wrong with me"—and then they jump on that because they smell fear. When we're talking about people who are not sure of themselves [which is how he described many straight male athletes earlier in the interview], and you come out strongly one way, what they tend to do is not say anything, at least not openly to you. They probably did behind your back, but they are not willing to confront; whereas had you showed some signs of being weak, you would have got many more comments because then people would have felt they could get away with it.

Another gay man agreed that it's best for the men in the locker room to know who is gay.

> I think that when straight men know that there are gay guys around them, they feel more comfortable. That's my experience in the locker rooms. They understand what the person is about so there is not the same fear of the unknown. I have never felt bad in the athletic centre. Confidence makes all the difference. Truman Capote was very effeminate but also very self-assured, and he went down to research *In Cold Blood* in a very rough part of America and he didn't have any problem. People can sense that you can be intimidated, and if you give that impression, then they will intimidate you. They never bother me.

NOTES

1 Woods, *Articulate Flesh*, p. 94.

2 Ibid., p.72.

3 Marks, "On the Underground Railroad to Cabbagetown," p.11.

4 Kirkup, "Football Action Shots," *The Descent into the Cave and Other Poems*, p.33.

5 Shaw, *Meat on the Hoof*, p.22.

6 Meggyesy, *Out of Their League*.

7 Rose, *Real Men*, p.79.

8 Masters sports are geared to mature athletes. Although competition is important to some masters athletes, it is not generally the major focus, which is participation for its own sake. Competition is organized in age categories. The masters movement started with swimming in the early 1960s and has spread to other sports and developed into an international sporting movement that culminates

in the World Masters Games, which are held quadrenially. They were held in Toronto in 1985 and in Denmark in 1989.

9 Masculinity is fragile because of the "intimate relationship," the all-too-easy slippage, between orthodoxy and paradoxy. Because it is fragile, some men feel compelled to reinforce their orthodox masculinity by playing football, or at least watching it (which we can now see is rather ironic), beating up women, fighting among themselves, and "beating the shit out of fags." Homophobia is the fear of the allure of the homoerotic paradox and its concomitant destruction of the orthodox myth of gender and the knowledge about oneself that that would bring.

10 It's often said that it's "normal," i.e., heterosexual, for men to look at other men's genitals and bodies; it's only a matter of comparing these masculine signs. While it may be a matter of comparison, there is also good reason to believe that the interest runs deeper. My own experience and that of a number of the men I interviewed suggests that the glances and the overt genital sexual response, i.e., erections, of some "straight" men while in the locker room indicates some degree of homoerotic imagination. The suggestion that this phenomenon is just a "comparison" is probably more of an alibi born of homophobia meant to disguise the awareness of homoerotic desire.

REFERENCES

Booth, Wayne. *A Rhetoric of Irony*. University of Chicago Press. 1975.

Kirkup, James. *The Descent into the Cave and other Poems*. Oxford University Press, First Impressions Edition. 1957.

Marks, Neil. "On the Underground Railroad to Cabbagetown." *Gaysweek* (21 Aug.): 11,19. 1978.

Meggyesy, Dave. *Out of Their League*. New York: Paperback Library. 1971.

Rose, F. *Real Men: Sex and Style in an Uncertain Age*. Garden City: Anchor. 1980.

Shaw, Gary. *Meat on the Hoof: The Hidden World of Texas Football*. Dell, first edition. 1973.

Woods, Gregory. *Male Homo-Eroticism and Modern Poetry*. New Haven, Conn.: Yale University Press. 1988.

CHAPTER 26

Transsexual Bodies at the Olympics: The International Olympic Committee's Policy on Transsexual Athletes at the 2004 Athens Summer Games

Sheila L. Cavanagh and Heather Sykes

Sport exists on the premise that males and females are radically different.

—Simon Barnes (2004)

Thus sex gradually became an object of great suspicion; the general and disquieting meaning that pervades our conduct and our existence, in spite of ourselves; the point of weakness where evil portents reach through to us; the fragment of darkness that we each carry with us: a general signification, a universal secret, an omnipresent cause, a fear that never ends.

—Michel Foucault (1978: 69)

In May 2004 the International Olympic Committee (IOC) implemented a policy enabling transsexual athletes to compete at the summer Olympic Games in Athens. The IOC Medical Commission proposed that transsexual athletes who had Sex Reassignment Surgery (SRS) before puberty shall be admitted to competition; that all other transsexuals must be post-operative (SRS including external genitalia and gonadectomy); must have legal and governmental recognition of their gender conferred by their country of citizenship; hormonal therapy administered by medical personnel to minimize 'gender-related advantages' in competition; and live for a minimum of two years in their newly assigned gender.[1] The guidelines proposed by the Medical Commission were accepted by the Executive Board of the IOC and it was also decided that individual cases would be assessed for eligibility. If the gender of an athlete is questioned the IOC reserves the right to carry out a sex-test. Although mandatory sex-testing of athletes was discontinued at the 2000 Olympic Games, the IOC is presently authorized to implement what has been called 'suspicion based testing' (Pilgrim et al., 2002–3: 511). In suspicious cases where the gender identity of an athlete is called into question an authorized medical delegate would be called upon to perform a sex-test.[2]

The new policy, referred to as the Stockholm Consensus, designed to admit transsexual athletes into elite sporting competition, has been controversial. Those who refuse to recognize the right to gender self-determination lament what they contend to be an unfair competitive advantage given to male-to-female transsexuals in women's competition. [...] In an editorial published in the *National Post*, a contributor wrote an inflammatory piece about Michelle Dumaresq, a Canadian male-to-female transsexual who represented Canada in the 2002 World Mountain Biking Championship in Austria:

> What we can't understand is how Ms. Dumaresq gets satisfaction from chalking up victories against natural-born female competitors. (In six races this year, she has twice finished first and twice finished second.) Though Ms. Dumaresq has not broken any rules, she reminds us of those able-bodied athletes who occasionally get caught feigning disabilities so they can compete in the Special Olympics—or parents who lie about their 14-year-old's age so he can be the leading goal-scorer in a hockey league for 10-year-olds. What's the point? Is there any glory in collecting a trophy when the people you're beating have been programmed by nature to lose? (*National Post*, 2002)

Some genetically born female athletes on Canada's mountain biking team also protested Dumaresq's position on the team and wore T-shirts which read 'biological women'. The petitioners believed that Dumaresq had an unfair advantage as a transsexual woman because she, allegedly, retained 'masculine' muscle mass.

The advantage thesis permeates public debate and discourse about transsexuality in sport and, due to the Stockholm Consensus, the IOC has become the official arbitrator of this debate. The Stockholm Consensus regulates access to binary gender identifications (male or female) when the IOC cannot agree—without equivocation and dispute—on what it is precisely that is being regulated. If male and female bodies are not natural (but social, culturally specific and thus mutable) the IOC is faced with the problematic of having to police (through medical and visual technologies) a categorical gender binary that cannot be shown to exist. In this article, we argue that the IOC policy—with its fluency in post-operative transsexuality—is a new disciplinary technique designed to manage binary gender designations. Using psychoanalytic theory, we contend that the almost obsessive attempt to manage gender and to cast a definitive mould onto the sex of bodies examined, in Olympic sporting competition, is indicative of a refusal to accept the changeability of bodies and to acknowledge the spectre of human mortality. Death and dying are precisely what Olympic bodies are supposed to countervail. We contend that muscular bodies in Olympic competition serve as fetishistic devices used to neutralize the otherwise overwhelming fear of annihilation.

The IOC policy on transsexuality is concerned with the medical creation of sex, the 'transition' if you will. Transitioning refers to the process through which one alters the sex of the body to bring it into alignment with an internal sense of what the sexed body should have been. In other words, a transsexual woman changes sex to make her body congruent with a psychically invested wish to be a woman. Jay Prosser (1998: 5) defines the transitioning process as involving the 'physical, social, and psychic transformations that constitute transsexuality'. The very notion of transitioning or changing sex has, historically, been regarded as a scientific, social, and phenomenological impossibility within the world of elite sport. Transsexuals and intersexed athletes—the groups most often subject to discrimination and disqualification—have always confounded a static and unchanging two sex model based on biology, and so their gendered subjectivities were erased (Namaste, 2000) and/or largely ignored in competitive sport prior to the 21st century.

While the Stockholm Consensus has been hailed as a progressive access policy designed to admit transsexual athletes (rather than bar them from Olympic competition as has been done in the past), we argue that it is more consistent with the original sex-tests used to police gender and to disqualify a significant number of female athletes. As Myron Genel, a Yale professor and member of the IOC committee, said: 'In a sense, this [Stockholm Consensus] was a continuation of that effort [to sex-test athletes]' (Hui, 2004: para. 17). The technology designed to test sex, which is now focused upon transsexuals, is a disciplinary regime only appearing to be based upon a spirit of inclusion. The Stockholm Consensus adopts a very narrow definition of transsexuality which, as we demonstrate later in the article, excludes a large segment of the international transsexual community. It also does nothing to admit intersexed athletes into Olympic competition. Transsexual men in sporting competition are rarely mentioned in conjunction with the IOC policy. Moreover, given that many transsexual men take testosterone injections, it is curious that the Olympic community does not consider that they may have an advantage over genetic men. We suggest that this omission is symptomatic of a refusal to see trans men as men and that it also provides an illustration of the popular compulsion to see gender as determined by nature, not culture (made men are, thus, not to be seen as legitimate competition).

The policy *appears* to be about the maintenance of a level playing field for genetic women. As Patrick Schamasch, Director of the IOC Medical Commission, said without apology, the Stockholm Consensus was designed 'more to protect the athlete who has not been sex reassigned than to help the person who is' (Marech, 2004: para. 5). The IOC's determination to provide access to fair, equitable competition for genetic women is, curiously, coming at a time when transsexuals and intersexed peoples are gaining access to basic civil rights. We suggest that the IOC commitment to neutralizing an alleged masculine competitive advantage in women's sport is only manifestly about the rights of genetic women. The latent anxiety is driven by a compulsive attempt to validate the age-old western, categorical gender binary. We argue that the policy functions to manage a categorical gender binary in the face of social, medical and legal uncertainty; gender identifications, anatomical, genital and chromosomal variations that aren't intelligible to those committed to a bio-centric two sex model; so-called gender 'purity' in women's sport; and to mask a fetishistic engagement with athletic bodies—as media spectacles—that are hyper-muscular, sculpted, highly toned, enervated, streamlined, and appear to be death defying.

The Stockholm Consensus is, also, symptomatic of a refusal to recognize self-identification with respect to gender. Priority is given to sex-testing regimes and narrow, medically governed, definitions of sexed bodies. The IOC policy reveals what Judith Butler (1990) refers to as 'gender trouble'. Bodies entered into Olympic competition have always seemed larger than life. Such idealized bodies seem to defy gravity, have immortal powers of concentration, and display superhuman strength, endurance, balance, coordination, speed and agility. The Olympic motto of *citius, altius, fortius* (faster, higher, stronger) is quintessentially about a metamorphosis into ever-increasing levels of bodily performance. Olympic bodies, as visual spectacles, transcend everyday conceptions of gender and exhibit physiques that cannot be easily seen as 'natural'. Much like the transsexual body, which is sometimes (though not always) surgically or hormonally induced, Olympic bodies are acquired through rigorous training and, in many instances, injections of steroids and other performance enhancing substances. While both transsexual and Olympic bodies have unique histories and vastly different experiences in the social and political realms, psychoanalysis helps us to see that the presence of transsexual bodies in sport reminds the IOC, and the Olympic community in general, that the fascination with athletic bodies is, in part, about a psychic investment in Olympians who already transcend the boundaries of binary gender categories, ideas about mortal human strength, aging and, finally, death.

To develop our argument we first discuss the history and politics of the Olympic sex-test and how it has been impossible to develop adequate testing mechanisms to measure a categorical gender binary that cannot be evidenced in biology. Sadly, the effect of decades of mandatory sex-testing (also known as the femininity test) was to discriminate against biological women and intersexed athletes identifying as women. The second section, 'Gender Troubles at the Olympics', reviews a number of high-profile female Olympic athletes who failed the sex-test (despite having lived their entire lives as women) in order to show how the policing of gender negatively impacts upon athletes who do not identify as transsexual. The article then introduces a psychoanalytic reading of the anxieties underpinning both the sex-test and the new sex-reassignment policy. We contend that as the sex of the body is, increasingly, seen to be unstable (or, at the very least, not determined by biology), new efforts to manage the gender of Olympic athletes comes into being. Focusing on female muscularity and the transitioning process for male-to-female transsexual athletes, we demonstrate how normative gender identifications—and the muscularities they depend upon—mask underlying fears about human mortality. In section three we offer a genealogy of the Stockholm Consensus and provide a context for its development by reference to well-publicized cases of transsexual discrimination in Olympic sport. These latter cases, involving transsexuals, are not unlike the earlier mentioned cases involving bio-women (some of whom later came to identify as intersexed) who failed the sex-test, but differences exist in terms of the way the two populations have been treated: both involve gender-based discrimination but transsexuals (unlike bio-women) have been subject to sex-testing motivated by transphobia. Third, we focus upon international panic about female muscularity in and out of Olympic competition to highlight psychic anxieties about gender indeterminacy. Using psychoanalytic theory, we argue that muscles are fetishistic objects used to manage a society-wide fear of death and dying in modern western, Christian nations and cultures.

THE IOC SEX-TEST

The gender of Olympic athletes has always been subject to question and anxiety. Dating back to ancient Greece male athletes engaged in competition without clothing to demonstrate that they were not female. As Laura Wackwitz (2003: 1) explains, it was believed that women would deplete the strength of a male warrior so they were rigorously barred from competing at Olympia (and could not even attend the festival as spectators). Wackwitz claims that the requirement for men to compete in the nude was the earliest manifestation of the Olympic sex-test. The modern incarnation of the sex-test focused not on genetic men, but on genetic women. Athletes entering into the women's Olympic competition were subject to mandatory sex-testing from 1968 to 1998. In both manifestations of the sex-test (in the Ancient Greek and the 20th-century Olympics) it is the genetic female body that is the site of anxiety. In Ancient Greece, the female body was thought to be a polluting body (capable of crippling male athletes) and in the 20th century the female Olympic body was the one that could be a genetic male in disguise.

*****

During the 1990s there was 'growing resentment and controversy amongst the athletes regarding having to submit to these tests' (CHANGE et al., 2000). The scientific technologies used to test sex were developed in the hope of clarifying the boundary between male and female bodies (although it was only female bodies that were subject to testing) and yet 'each advance in screening technology has failed to provide a definitive and undisputable marker of the category "woman"' (Wackwitz, 2003: 555). Using a range of sex-tests including the visual test,[3] the Barr Body test, and the Polymerase Chain Reaction test, the IOC could not ascertain beyond a shadow of doubt who was and was not genetically female. Some women had XY chromosomes typical of genetic men. For example, Spanish runner and hurdler Maria José Martinez Patino failed the sex-test because she was found to have XY chromosomes. Although her body did not produce testosterone on par with the average genetic man she was banned from competition in 1985 but reinstated in 1988 following the first successful petition of the IOC disqualification policy.[4] Each chromosomal variation could not be shown to lead to an anomalous muscle mass for either men or women.

The IOC tried to make a categorical gender binary self-evident through medical technologies but each version of the test revealed subtle differences between male and female genders, as opposed to clearly delineated 'opposite' sexes. [...] Increasingly, scientific and sporting technologies zoom in to categorize and reorganize chromosomes and genes (Miah, 2004) in order to shore up the fragile epistemological certainty offered by biological universalism and technological progress. [...] Sex-testing was designed to make the non-visible axiom of binary gender visible to the scientific eye and to sporting authorities, yet gender theorist Riki Wilchins (2004: 94) argues that the visual language of bodies isn't transparent: 'We learn to see things in a certain way, and by seeing them that way, we rely on our belief in that vision to inform us about what is ultimately real and out there.'[5]

The effect of the sex-test was to discriminate against intersexed and male-to-female transsexual athletes. Although the IOC claimed that the sex-test was not intended to 'differentiate between sexes but to prevent male imposters from participating in female competitions', the test banned athletes who had unusually high levels of androgen or testosterone from women's events because it was believed that they had an unfair competitive advantage (Simpson et al., 2000: 1569). In essence, intersexed peoples and those with atypical chromosome counts, testosterone levels, genital and skeletal configurations have been interrogated, scrutinized and, sometimes, disqualified from competition in order to protect the 'purity' of women's sport. Sex-testing was an attempt to pro-duce gender differentiation when it was not self-evident in the realm of biology.

GENDER TROUBLES AT THE OLYMPICS

*****

Gender trouble at the modern Olympic Games can be found throughout the 20th century. For example, in 1936, Helen Stephens, an American runner, was accused of being a man after win-ning the women's 100 meter run at the Olympics in Berlin. Stephens ran the 100 meters in 11.5 seconds in 1936 (a record that stood for over 19 years), which fuelled controversies about her gender. Few could believe that a genetic woman could run that fast. In response to accusations that Stephens was not a 'real' woman the runner was given a sex-test, which she passed. Tragic-ally, Stella Walsh, the Polish runner who came second in the same race in Berlin (who also accused Stephens of being a 'man') was shot dead by a stray bullet in 1980 (44 years after the infamous race) during a robbery in Cleveland. The Olympic community was startled to hear that the autopsy revealed that Walsh possessed male and female chromosomes, a tiny penis, testes and no female hormones. The second place runner was intersexed, Stephens was not. Walsh was an intersexual who would, by contemporary medical standards, be seen to have a congenital disposition called mosaicism (Diadiun, 1991). Her reputation as an Olympic athlete and supporter of women's sport was tarnished by sensational press refusing to attend to the complexities of her case with sensitivity. Headlines of the time read that 'Stella was a Fella'.[6]

Accusations abounded about men masquerading as women to win Olympic medals in the inter-national press throughout the 20th century. For example, in 1936, German high-jumper Hermann Ratjen was said to have masqueraded as a woman under coercion by the German government. The press reported that this athlete bound his penis and testes, assumed a false name (Dora) and, despite his 'masculine' advantage finished fourth in the women's high-jump (Beveridge, 2004). Kdena Koubkova, a Czechoslovakian high-jumper who won a world record in the women's event, was also accused of being a man because of her unprecedented athletic achievement. Ukrainian athletes Irina Press and Tamara Press (sisters) who won cumulatively five Olympic titles in the shot put and hurdles stopped competing in 1968, the year sex-testing at the Olympic Games in Mexico City was implemented. The disappearance of these women from Olympic competition in 1968 fuelled rumors that they had been men posing as women. It was believed that their power-ful physique was unfeminine and that without male hormones, a masculine physique and male muscular capacity their accomplishments were improbable. It is important to note that the panic about Eastern Bloc female athletes (and their—allegedly—'unnatural' feminine form) gestures to the extent to which gender was shaped by ideas about nation in the Cold War–era and how the

Olympics is a spectacle in which bodies are subject to western imperialist scrutiny.

Although it is possible that some genetic males did masquerade as female to gain what they believed to be a 'masculine' competitive advantage (under duress or by choice), the certainty through which the Olympic community appeals to their natural advantage as men is problematic. Feminist scholars of women's sport have argued that sex-testing was imposed not to even the playing field for women in the face of an unfair 'masculine' competitive advantage as IOC officials contended, but to manage the inconsistency between female athletic achievement and dominant beliefs about female athletic capacities (Kolata, 1992; Wackwitz, 2003). There is an incompatibility between conventional ideas about genetic women and femininity, and the idealized muscular Olympic body. Because muscles and muscularity (key ingredients of the most valorized Olympic bodies) have been gendered masculine, there is a psychic need to regulate female bodies entering into the masculinized arena of sport. Laura Wackwitz (2003: 556) argues that 'despite active measures taken to prevent women from participating in and excelling at athletic competition … the gap between elite male and elite female athletes is remarkably slight.' […]

Genetic women are encouraged to train their bodies to their maximum capacities but held accountable to strict gender prototypes and conventions. This is especially the case in female bodybuilding. For example, Marcia Ian (2001: 70) contends that bodybuilding plays a trick: while seeming to encourage men and women to exceed the norm and achieve heroic, outrageous physiques of increasingly 'monstrous' proportions, it actually uses these subjects to maintain, even more rigidly than does mainstream culture at large, reactionary norms, themselves 'ideals', of masculinity and femininity. Ian goes on to explain how female bodybuilders are subject to ridicule when their bodies develop on par with male bodybuilders, a form of ridicule that intersects with transphobia. In essence, their gender is called into question: 'Ann-Marie Crooks, a professional bodybuilder, reported … [that the] vice-president of the IFBB (the International Federation of Bodybuilders, the sport's governing body) … [said] he couldn't care less about female bodybuilding because "they're all he-she's"' (Ian, 2001: 73). Ian observes that female bodybuilders lose competitions (and corporate sponsorship) because they are seen to be too muscular, not feminine. […]

In female bodybuilding there is an attempt to re-femininize competitors in order to ensure that they are able to be positioned as both feminine and heterosexual for white, male, heterosexual viewing pleasure. [Cindy] Patton explains that in *Women's Physique World* the female bodybuilders are depicted as 'fresh-faced girls who seem to have accidentally produced their specialized shape' (2001: 127), and so there are no intentional transitions into masculinity or manhood. Patton contends that it is not coincidental that the female bodybuilders presented as 'the girl next door' look very much like the 'presumably male models who populate ads for transsexual phone sex lines in heterosexual male and gay male sex magazines' (2001: 127),[7] the implication being that heterosexuality cannot (or not without trouble) sustain itself in the face of transsexual subjects (or those who look very much like them). […]

The following section develops our psychoanalytic claim that elite sport evokes anxieties about gender instability, the changeability of the human body and, ultimately, death. Judith Butler (1995) argues that heteronormative gender identifications are responses to object loss. Due to cultural taboos (incest and homosexuality being the two primary taboos) the child cannot have the object of primary desire (usually the mother in psychoanalytic theorizing) and so at least two accommodations are made: the girl maps the gender of the mother onto her body as a way of incorporating that which she cannot have in the service of heterosexual identity formation; the boy, similarly, incorporates the father by assuming a masculine demeanour. Both accommodations are about the preservation of heterosexuality and binary gender (the staple ingredient of heterosexuality) and are accomplished by mapping the prohibited sex onto the body's surface. The compulsion through which athletes engage with one another (on the field, in the ring, or in the pool) is energized by something more primal than good-natured competition. Perhaps the impulse to win is about an attempt to move through the gendered imperatives imposed on bodies in the name of heterosexuality. If gender is a melancholic subject formation as Butler contends, then competitive sport might be an arena in which the despondency (defeatism) is felt most keenly.

In the sociology of sport, competitive play has been understood in terms of homophobia towards men (Pronger, 1999) but not transphobia. Similarly, gender has been theorized as an attempt to manage object loss (Butler, 1995) and to support normative heterosexualities (Patton, 2001) but not transphobia. This is a curious refusal; one that permeates sport theorizing and one that we suggest is precipitated by a white Judeo-Christian refusal to come to terms with the inevitability of death. In other words, the refusal to talk about transsexual transitions in sport sociology mirrors the difficulty we have in the West in acknowledging human mortality, death, aging and human frailty. This is not to say that transsexual subjectivity is linked to death but that sex changes (like gay outings) ignite what some have called the bereavement effect (Stockton, 2004: 285). Parents sometimes feel that their child has died after 'coming out'. It is also common to hear about parents grieving when they learn that their child is intersexed or transitioning into the so-called 'opposite' sex. Transsexuals are also, like those who depart from heterosexual mandates, subject to violent hate-crimes leading, sometimes, to death or to disability in the public sphere. The changeability of the body (along with the rupture of a heterosexual mandate) is psychically linked to human mortality and death in ways that queer theorists and those who study transsexuality are only beginning to understand.

Similarly, it is important to understand how Olympic competition and sport in general rallies against death and dying. As Pronger (2002) suggested, death has 'disappeared' in modernity but its power is felt because of the need to repudiate it.[8] We are keenly aware of the inevitability of death but distract ourselves so as to ease psychic anxieties surrounding it. [...]

The quest for sovereignty, along with a wish (however latent) to overcome or circumvent death is to be found in the refusal to admit or attend to human mortality in everyday life. Olympic competition is a more particular example in which the games are populated by bodies that are shockingly well-equipped to compete against the threat of death. The Olympian competes against death; the athlete lives by 'attempting to erase death' (Pronger, 2002: 171) and all that is associated with it (human disability, frailty, aging, infantility, obsolescence) and, most importantly, the failure to become a sovereign subject. Sovereignty, in this instance, is understood as the capacity to ascend from the earthly kingdom and to rise above the mundane cessation of life that plagues us all.

We contend that the hyperbolic discourse about muscles on Olympic athletes (transsexual and non-transsexual) is a ruse, a cover, a mask for a more insidious angst about human mortality. Although the Olympian (and the Olympic community) is invested in a symbolic victory over Thanatos (God of Death) he or she or he/she cannot contend with the latent content of the wish for transcendence,[9] immortality and mastery over nature.

[...] Muscles ward off death. But when muscles bulge or metastasize, appear in the wrong region or on the wrong body altogether (in the case of the genetic female Olympian who competes like a 'man' or the transsexual woman who shifts her muscle mass to accommodate a newly gendered physique, or the intersexed who cannot be—without contestation and confusion—designated 'male' or 'female' by existing genetic and chromosomal testing regimes) the Olympic community is reminded of the precariousness of the Olympic defense. [...] This is not to say that transsexuals, those who are intersexed or live with variegated chromosomal and genetic compositions are, essentially, associated with death but that they are metonymically associated with death (in the Olympic community) because they upset a defensive regime adopted in the white, western, Olympic, patriarchal and able-bodied psychic structure. The female Olympian, like the intersexed or the transsexual, brings to the surface a fear of death—well documented in modern western, Christian nations and cultures (here symbolized by a failure of Olympic mastery)—because their bodies appear to be malleable and not essential or statuesque (as the Olympian immortalized on the podium can appear to be). The malleable body is the one that populates the life-world; the idealized Olympic body is the mythological body that cannot, no matter what training regime is adopted, overcome the certainty of death.

THE STOCKHOLM CONSENSUS

What an Olympic Drag; These Queens will be Kings for a Day.

—*Canberra Times* (2000: 26)

But it's funny … the sight of women, who were once men, winning Olympic gold.

—Goff (2004: 7)

Unless the IOC establishes clear medical criteria for sex-change athletes, the new rules would make a mockery of sport.

—Hart (2004: para. 8)

[...] [In 2003] the IOC voted to admit transsexual athletes into Olympic competition (pending a medical review of the impact of hormone injection) and details regarding the policy were expected to be worked out in a matter of weeks. [...]

The Olympic community was caught off-guard when in February 2004 the IOC put the decision to admit transsexual athletes on hold. Discussions broke down because members of the IOC executive board failed to comprehend SRS and the hormonal injections accompanying the transition process for Olympic athletes. IOC president Jacques Rogge [...] claimed that the medical language used to explain the transitioning process (involving surgery and hormonal injection) was esoteric and too sophisticated for lay-persons. He explained that the proposal would be re-worked in non-medical language and again presented to the board at the next meeting scheduled to take place in Switzerland in May.

Strong indications were also given that the board was transphobic and so the committee defaulted into a defensive insistence upon the advantage thesis [...] [b]ut the IOC continued to support the proposal in principle. The outstanding issue was how to set up guidelines to govern the transition process and to ensure that transsexual athletes did not have an unfair competitive advantage.

After the Stockholm Consensus was adopted, Olivier Rabin, director of science for WADA (World Anti-Doping Agency), said that 'transgender athletes—like any other athletes requiring therapeutic treatment—will have to have their hormone substances approved by their respective sporting federations and national anti-doping organizations' (Willing, 2004: A1). Transsexuality is now recognized by WADA as a legitimate 'medical'[10] condition and so provisions regarding the use of hormones are allowed. Rabin explains that the 'hormone levels that appear in transgendered athletes' bodies will be compared and measured against what are designated as normal readings' (Willing, 2004).

The Stockholm Consensus is important because, until recently, most sport governing bodies either had no policy designed to admit transsexual or intersexed persons into competition or defaulted into a reactionary 'female at birth' policy. [...] The Stockholm Consensus stands to become the default policy for mainstream sport governing bodies yet, in the current moment, the range of policies being developed by sport organizations indicate different commitments to human rights protection for transgendered/transsexual/intersexed persons.[11]

*****

Some sport governing bodies have been forced to adapt their policies in response to individual transsexual athletes fighting for their right to compete. For example, in Canada the Canadian Cycling Association accepted Michelle Dumaresq's birth certificate—which she changed to indicate her newly assigned status as a woman—as a rationale to admit her into the women's competition (Hui, 2004). Sport governing bodies do not always accept birth certificates and it is, too often, the case that female-at-birth policies are implemented. [...]

Relatively few policies in sport protect transsexual athletes from discrimination over the 'fair play' policies (read advantage thesis) implemented to—allegedly—level the playing field for genetic women. Despite the gender-inclusiveness and attention to regional differences, even the Gay Games continues to be invested in the need to police gender through a gender policy (Gay Games Board, 2002). [...]

During the 2002 Sydney Gay Games, indigenous traditions regarding gender identifications were respected and testimony from indigenous community leaders (and organizations) were accepted as verification of an athlete's gender. By contrast, the 1st World Outgames in Montreal initially adopted the IOC policy. Due to mounting criticism of the Stockholm Consensus, World Outgames recently revised the policy which now distinguishes between 'transitioned athletes' and 'transgender athletes', and is accompanied by a statement expressing uncertainty about whether anti-doping rules will apply to transitioned male athletes (1st World Outgames, 2006).

THE GENDER OF MUSCLES AND OLYMPIC BODIES IN TRANSITION

> Bodybuilding has the potential to serve as an example of gender multiplicity and the
> potential to challenge dominant binaries of masculine-feminine and straight-gay.
>
> —Saltman (1998: 49)

The Stockholm Consensus is chiefly concerned with the psychic management of muscles. Sex-testing and the Stockholm Consensus are, in essence, attempts to manage muscularity and the illusions of binary gender in and between Olympic bodies, bodies that have already by definition transformed from the common non-Olympic body. The difficulty managing gender in bodies that swell and enlarge is not unrelated to transphobia (the irrational fear or hatred of the gendered subject in transition). Transsexual bodies are bodies that are in or have undergone transition. Sheila Cavanagh (2003) has argued that transphobia is, in part, incited by the threat posed to stable body boundaries and genital configurations governing (and giving shape to) two bi-polar, gender positionalities. [...] Both Olympic and transsexual bodies are made, not born. But the hyperbolic concern about muscle mass, testosterone and chromosome counts (indicative of the advantage thesis and drug testing) are not only about gender. As Ian contends, 'muscle does not have gender' (2001: 75) and it can thus undermine the psychic defenses employed to cultivate the fantasy of gender.

*****

Muscles are the site upon which gender territories are mapped and border crossings (extreme female muscularity being one example) incite anxiety. This is the result of what psychoanalysts call a fetishistic engagement with an anxious spectacle. Psychoanalysts have traditionally understood a fetish to be an object (or an allegedly 'non-erogenous' body part) that is endowed with sexual significance.[12] The fetish is invested with multiple meanings and stands in for something that is lacking, threatening or socially prohibited. Fetishes are, thus, ways of coping with anxiety (lack, threat, prohibition) by not admitting to them. Fetishism deals with ambivalence, that is, it reminds us that what is culturally desirable also covers over a cultural anxiety stemming from a lack, a fear or a need to protect the self from punishment. [...] Muscles are fetishized objects and as Heather Sykes (2001) argues in 'Of Gods, Money, and Muscle', they are also irresolute fixations giving way to fear and repulsion on the one hand, desire and adoration on the other. [...]

When the anxiety surrounding muscles is not recognized, it is disavowed and those muscles can be desired as fetish objects. When the threat of castration is recognized in the sight of muscles, the anxiety is acknowledged and those muscles become phobic objects. [...]

The Stockholm Consensus illustrates how, in a transphobic sporting imagination, the transsexual body occupies the phobic side of the fetishistic engagement and the phobia manifests itself in hyperbolic discourse about male-to-female transsexual muscularity (central to the advantage thesis) and paranoia about genetic men infiltrating 'women's' competition. The anxiety about muscles (including testosterone production, heart and lung capacity) permeated public debate and IOC discussions leading up to the formation of the Stockholm Consensus. For example, during their consultations with medical 'experts' on SRS, IOC officials were 'concerned that without genital reconstruction surgery, transsexual women may still enjoy the benefits of testosterone because they will still have testes that produce the hormone. The presence of testosterone may give those athletes a slight advantage over non-transsexual competitors' (Letellier, 2004), and the remaining muscle mass would, therefore, sustain the competitive advantage. [...] People also worry that the IOC policy on transsexuality would encourage genetic men to transition in order to pursue an Olympic medal. Transphobic imaginations envisioned hundreds of men donning dresses to compete in women's sporting competition.

We wish to make the seemingly obvious prediction that an athlete will not change sex in pursuit of an Olympic medal and even if he or she did the athlete would not have an advantage over genetic female competitors. Top IOC medical consultants agree that post-operative transsexual women do not have a muscular advantage over genetic women. [...] [A]n athlete who transitioned in pursuit of an Olympic win would experience gender dysphoria: a feeling of being at odds with the sex of the body and the mind's imagination of it, which would undermine balance, coordination, and agility (all of which are necessary for superior athletic performance). Many male-to-female athletes who have been accused of having a physiological advantage over bio-women explain how the process of adjusting to a new anatomical form alone is a disadvantage, not to mention balancing hormone injections, dealing with transphobia and other medical complications associated with surgery. Given the disadvantages associated with transsexuality in a transphobic culture; the paucity of transsexual athletes in Olympic competition; the impossibility of testing or determining sex; the long history of gender-based discrimination and exclusion in the Olympic Games; and because the Olympics should be accessible to all we contend that the IOC should respect an athlete's chosen gender and drop rigid and exclusionary policies regulating access to women's sport.

[...] Michelle Dumaresq [...] reported that after her SRS and hormone treatment 'her body was greatly weakened': 'I needed regular gym workouts just to build up enough strength to continue my job', and explained that her large legs (alleged masculine advantage) were a hindrance on the bike circuit. 'It actually made things harder because after the hormone treatment and operation I no longer had the muscle mass to support my bones. This so-called advantage I'm supposed to have doesn't exist' (cited in Goff, 2004: para. 19).

Much like the IOC insistence upon mandatory sex-testing to measure that which does not biologically speaking exist—a categorical and bio-centric gender binary—the IOC, and the sporting community in general, insist upon a transsexual advantage that does not exist. The anxiety about gender, muscles and transsexuality is, thus, suspicious. The anxiety that lies behind the fetishistic engagement with muscularity and the phobic response to genetic female, or transsexual female muscularity (not to mention intersexed competitors), is about a need to ward off a primal fear of annihilation.

CONCLUSION

Gender has always been subject to question and suspicion but in the 21st century the IOC has embraced a commitment to regulate gender and the processes through which transsexuals cross borders once believed to belong to the 'opposite' sex. Anxiety about gender in Olympic communities intersects with contemporary anxieties about immigration (illegal and otherwise) in a postcolonial context, and officials are increasingly determined to police borders (national, bodily and otherwise) in the name of equity, access and fair competition. Olympic athletes thought to be suspicious (meaning that they are rumored to be gender impersonators, illegal trespassers or otherwise genetically 'anomalous') are vulnerable to sex-testing. In fact, the IOC had a team of medical experts on staff at the Sydney Olympics to test individual athletes subject to gender-based suspicion. It is not known if any athletes at the Athens 2004 Summer Olympic Games were subject to testing but a working group on transsexual people's issues believes that the Buccal Smear test was to be used if an individual deemed suspicious was to be investigated (CHANGE et al., 2000).

Ian contends that gender shields the subject from a fear of death and we suggest that the fetishization of muscles is, similarly, based upon a fear of human frailty, injury, sickness, incontinence and decay, the inescapable, yet endlessly disavowed, fate of bodies entered into Olympic competition. [...]

*****

The absence of any meaningful reference to human mortality in Olympic coverage of athletic prowess, curiously, mirrors the refusal to engage with the realities of transphobia and bio-centrism in the Olympic community. The disavowal of transphobia keeps at bay the recognition of gender as an achievement and Olympic prowess as an ephemeral, fragile attempt at corporeal mastery (immortality). We conclude that Olympic prowess (and spectator pleasure) is associated with the refusal to accept the passing of life and human frailties. As in the case of female bodybuilding, sex-changes reveal the essential mutability of the body; the social, cultural, medical and legal negotiations at play in the making of gendered bodies. There is in the western, Olympic, imperial white imagination a desire for corporeal homogeneity, bio-centric gender demarcation and stable corporeal body boundaries. Heterosexual orifices and muscular permutations administered by traditional training regimes are not only upset by the presence of trans/intersexed/hyper-musculine women in sport but exposed as a wish for something else. The something else is a desire for immortality and corporeal mastery.

NOTES

1 Sportswriter Simon Barnes recounted how the original proposal for the 2004 UK government law on the Gender Recognition Bill required legislators to 'forget about hard and fast distinctions between the sexes and accept that there is a border area, and those who live there are entitled to certain rights in all respects, including sport. But it is clear that sport depends for its very existence on more traditional, reactionary classifications' (Barnes, 2004: para. 20). The IOC opted for an exclusionary and rigid policy in adopting the Stockholm Consensus (with its narrow definition of gender and refusal to address the nuances and complexities of transgendered and transsexual subjectivities).

2 The International Association of Athletic Federations (IAAF), the international track and field governing body, discontinued mandatory sex-testing of all female athletes through the Barr Body test in 1991 but adopted a suspicion-based model in its place. The IAAF developed protocol allowing a medical designate to administer a sex-test at his/her discretion. In 1992 the IOC refused to follow suit and continued

to use the PCR test until 2000 (Pilgrim et al., 2002–3: 511), the year in which they abolished mandatory sex-testing of female Olympic athletes. Like the IAAF, the IOC now maintains the right to investigate what they call 'suspicious cases' where athletes are rumored to be 'masquerading' as women.

3 The visual sex-test was also accompanied by a genetic sex-test in Olympic competition and, sometimes, the results were contradictory. For example, Ewa Klobukowska, a Polish sprinter, was the first to fail the genetic sex-test in 1967 during the European Cup in Kiev despite having lived her entire life as a woman (later giving birth to a child). She passed the visual test in 1966 but failed the genetic test in 1967. Klobukowska was said to have chromosomal 'irregularities'. The fact that Klobukowska passed the visual verification test the year before did not mitigate the decision to ban her from competition in 1967 (Pilgrim et al., 2002–3). She was, consequently, stripped of her Olympic medals won in 1964 and banned from international competition entirely (*Toronto Star*, 1989).

4 Maria José Martinez Patino was the first Olympic athlete to successfully overturn the results of an IOC genetic sex-test. Patino was fully reinstated in 1988, three years after being banned from Olympic competition in 1985. The sex-test revealed that she had XY chromosomes (usually found in genetic men). Because her body could not register testosterone she developed female genitalia and a female anatomical form (no masculine 'advantage'). The runner and hurdler refused to fake a 'career-ending injury' (as instructed by her government) and with legal support challenged the IOC ruling. Patino was subject to humiliating press coverage and, as Laura Wackwitz contends, her case 'serves as a reminder of the capriciousness of power, the fragility of the category "woman," and the problems with applying a base 2 system of classification to base 10 reality' (2003: 557).

5 There is evidence to suggest that drug testing is now being used, also, as a means to sex-test athletes. For example, the IAAF 'endorsed a policy that used the conditions created through drug testing to visually inspect genitals' (Cole, 2000: 332). Effectively this means that sex-testing has been given refuge in the drug-testing procedures which enable officials to visually inspect the genitals of athletes during urine collection. The UK Government (2005) guidelines for drug testing transsexuals in sport mandates that a Doping Control Officer (DCO) must 'observe the urine sample leave the athlete's body' although 'when providing a sample, only the athlete and the DCO will be in the toilet, thereby providing the athlete with the optimum amount of privacy' (p. 14). In addition, the guidelines obliquely warn that 'no *written* record disclosing a variance between the athlete's gender and their genitalia will be made' (p. 14, emphasis in original). Cole argues that because drug testing is less controversial than sex-testing it shores up support for an investigation (and policing) of bodies that would otherwise be seen as intrusive (and discriminatory) in the domain of gender. Because the condemnation of performance-enhancing drug use routinely invokes a logic of bodily essence defined, in part, by sex, we might guess that the rhetoric around drugs secures the conditions for less controversial but strikingly similar public debates over gender. Drugs are now seen to create gendered bodies, whereas in the 20th century gender was seen as a biologically determined phenomenon (an essence) above and beyond medical, legal, and social gender construction.

6 Roxanne Atkins Anderson, a 79-year-old who coached Mildred Fizzel (the athlete who finished second to Walsh in the 1934 Los Angeles Olympics), unsuccessfully petitioned the Athletics Congress (TAC), the American governing body for track and field, to take Walsh's title away and give the gold medal to Fizzel, whom she now believed to be entitled to an Olympic win. Speaking of the autopsy performed on Walsh, Anderson said, 'If that coroner was correct, and I have no reason to doubt it,

then our history reads that a man won all these women's championships' (cited in Diadiun, 1991: para. 12). Lynn Cannon, chair of the women's committee affiliated with TAC said that the 'issue of gender identity is more complex than it might seem and that statements that Stella Walsh masqueraded as a woman or that Walsh was definitely a man are unfair' (Wilson, 1991: para. 3).

7 Cindy Patton situates the fear of masculine women in relation to a postcolonial 'xenophobic discourse about which women [on the international scene] are real' (2001: 131). Questions are regularly asked in the bodybuilding community about which women are pumped full of hormones, 'artificially' masculinized through drug injections and, thus, in their minds, un-American.

8 Soon after publishing *Body Fascism: Salvation in the Technology of Physical Fitness,* Brian Pronger experienced a viral brain infection that radically changed his physical and cognitive ways of being in the world. Some of his ideas in the book about confronting and transcending socially abjected states of bodily change, health, and death now seem prophetic. At the time of writing we continue to wish him transcendence on his terms, peace, and recovery.

9 For a discussion of transcendence in Olympic sport see Synthia Sydnor (2004).

10 For a discussion of the politics surrounding the medicalization of transsexuality see Pat Califia (1997), Dwight Billings and Thomas Urban (1996), Judith Butler (2004), Dave King (1996) and Viviane Namaste (2000, 2005).

11 A small number of organizations decided that the IOC's suspension of the sex-test meant that there was no mechanism to exclude transsexual women. For instance the world chess organization (FIDE) and the US Chess Federation decided not to contest Angela Alston's right to play in 'women only' chess tournaments to follow the IOC's suspension of sex-testing simply because there was no mechanism in place to test gender/sex.

12 For a discussion of the racialized fetish, see Bhabha (1994), Eng (2001) and McClintock (1996).

REFERENCES

1st World Outgames (2006) 'Gender Identity Policy', May 12. URL (consulted 26/07/06): http://www.montreal2006.org/en_gender_identitypolicy.html

Barnes, Simon (2004) 'Welcome to Sport's Twilight World, where Tina Henman Wins Wimbledon', *The Times,* 23 January.

Beveridge, Ann (2004) 'How Stella the Fella Stole Hitler's Heart', *Daily Telegraph,* 27 August.

Bhabha, Homi (1994) *The Location of Culture.* London: Routledge.

Billings, Dwight B. and Thomas Urban (1996) 'The Socio-Medical Construction of Transsexualism: An Interpretation and Critique', pp. 99–117 in R. Ekins and D. King (eds) *Blending Genders: Social Aspects of Cross-dressing and Sex-changing.* London and New York: Routledge.

Butler, Judith (1990) *Gender Trouble: Feminism and the Subversion of Identity.* New York: Routledge.

Butler, Judith (1995) 'Melancholy Gender/Refused Identification', pp. 21-36 in M. Berger, B. Wallis and S. Watson (eds) *Constructing Masculinity.* New York and London: Routledge.

Butler, Judith (2004) *Undoing Gender.* New York and London: Routledge.

Califia, Pat (1997) *Sex Changes: The Politics of Transgenderism.* San Francisco, CA: Cleis Press. *Canberra Times* (2000) 'What an Olympic Drag; These Queens will be Kings for a Day', 25 August.

Cavanagh, Sheila (2003) 'Teacher Transsexuality: The Illusion of Sexual Difference and the Idea of Adolescent Trauma in the Dana Rivers Case', *Sexualities: Studies in Culture and Society* 6(3–4): 361–3.

CHANGE, The FTM network, G & SA, The Gender Trust, GIRES, Liberty and Press for Change (2000) 'Gender Confirmation Certificates: The Implications for Sport and the Provision of Changing Facilities', a Consultation Paper to the Interdepartmental Working Group on Transsexual People's Issues. URL (consulted 26/07/06): http://www. pfc.org.uk

Cole, C.L. (2000) 'Testing for Sex or Drugs', *Journal of Sport & Social Issues* 24(4): 331–3.

Diadiun, Ted (1991) 'Walsh's Dignity Assaulted', *The Plain Dealer,* 9 June.

Eng, David (2001) *Racial Castration: Managing Masculinity in Asian America.* Durham, NC: Duke University Press.

Foucault, Michel (1978) *The History of Sexuality: Volume 1,* trans. R. Hurley. New York: Vintage Books.

Gay Games Board (2002) 'Gay Games Gender Policy', 20 December. URL (consulted 26/07/06): http://www.gendercentre.org.au/48article3.htm

Goff, Peter (2004) 'Transsexual; Issue Remains; Olympics Poser', *South China Morning Post,* 21 March.

Hart, Simon (2004) 'IOC's Rules of Competition', The Age.com, 25 February. URL (consulted 26/07 /06): http://www.theage.com.au/text/articles/2004/02/24/1077594826637.html

Hui, Stephen (2004) 'Transsexuals Headed for Athens', *Rabble News,* 10 August. URL (consulted 26/07/06): http://www.rabble.ca

Ian, Marcia (2001) 'The Primitive Subject of Female Bodybuilding: Transgression and Other Postmodern Myths', *Differences: A Journal of Feminist Cultural Studies* 12(3): 69–100.

King, Dave (1996) 'Gender Blending: Medical Perspectives and Technology', pp. 79–98 in R. Ekins and D. King (eds) *Blending Genders: Social Aspects of Cross-dressing and Sex-changing.* London and New York: Routledge.

Kolata, Gina (1992) 'Ideas and Trends: Who is Female? Science Can't Say', *The New York Times,* 16 February: 6 (late edition), sec. 4.

Kristeva, Julia (1982) *Powers of Horror: An Essay on Abjection.* New York: Columbia University Press.

Letellier, Patrick (2004) 'Olympics to let Transsexuals Compete', UKGay.com, 19 May. URL (consulted 26/07/06): http://uk.gay.com/headlines

McClintock, Ann (1996) *Imperial Leather.* New York: Routledge.

Marech, Rona (2004) 'Olympics' Transgender Quandary: Debate on the Fairness of New Inclusion Rule', *San Francisco Chronicle,* 14 June. URL (consulted 26/07/06): http://wwwSFGate.com

Miah, Andy (2004) *Genetically Modified Athletes: Biomedical Ethics, Gene Doping and Sport.* London: Routledge.

Namaste, Viviane K. (2000) *Invisible Lives: The Erasure of Transsexual and Transgendered People.* Chicago, IL and London: The University of Chicago Press.

Namaste, Viviane K. (2005) *Sex Change, Social Change: Reflections on Identity, Institutions and Imperialism.* Toronto: Women's Press.

National Post (2002) 'Dump Dumaresq', 10 August. URL (consulted 26/07/06): http://80-global.factiva.com.ezproxy.library.yorku.ca/en/archdisplay.asp

Patton, Cindy (2001) 'Rock Hard: Judging the Female Physique', *Journal of Sport and Social Issues* 25(2): 118–40.

Pilgrim, Jill, David Martin and Will Binder (2002–3) 'Far from the Finish Line: Transsexualism and Athletic Compeition', *Fordham Intellectual Property Media and Entertainment Law Journal* 13: 495–550.

Pronger, Brian (1999) 'Outta my Endzone: Sport and the Territorial Anus', *Journal of Sport and Social Issues* 23(4): 373–89.

Pronger, Brian (2002) *Body Fascism: Salvation in the Technology of Physical Fitness.* Toronto: University of Toronto Press.

Prosser, Jay (1998) *Second Skins: The Body Narratives of Transsexuality.* New York: Columbia University Press.

Saltman, Ken (1998) 'Men with Breasts', *Journal of the Philosophy of Sport* 25: 48–60.

Simpson, Joe Leigh, Arne Ljungqvist, Malcolm Ferguson-Smith and Albert de Ia Chapelle (2000) 'Gender Verification at the Olympics', *Journal of the American Medical Association* 284(12): 15, 68–9.

Stockton, Kathryn Bond (2004) *Curiouser: On the Queerness of Children.* Minneapolis, MN: University of Minnesota Press.

Sydnor, Synthia (2004) 'Essence of Post-Olympism: A Prolegomena of Study', pp. 165–76 in J. Bale and M.K. Christensen (eds) *Post-Olympism? Questioning Sport in the Twenty-first Century.* Oxford and New York: Berg.

Sykes, Heather (2001) 'Of Gods, Money, and Muscle: Resurgent Homophobias and the Narcissism of Minor Differences in Sport', *Psychoanalysis and Contemporary Thought: A Quarterly of Integrative and Interdisciplinary Studies* 24(2): 203–25.

UK Government (2005) 'Transsexual People and Sport: Guidance for Sporting Bodies', Department for Culture, Media and Sport. URL (consulted 26/07/06): http://www.uksport.gov.uk/images/uploaded/transsexuals.pdf

Wackwitz, Laura A. (2003) 'Verifying the Myth: Olympic Sex Testing and the Category "Woman"', *Women's Studies International Forum* 26(6): 553–60.

Wilchins, Riki (2004) *Queer Theory, Gender Theory: An Instant Primer.* Los Angeles, CA: Alyson Books.

Willing, Jon (2004) 'Decision Balances Rights, Fairness: Olympics Body Outlines Rules for Transgender Competitors', *Guelph Mercury,* 22 May. URL (consulted 26/07/06): pqasb.pqarchiver.com/guelphmercury/640600021.html

Wilson, Austin (1991) 'TAC Refuses to Discuss Gender Issue', *Capital City Press,* 7 December.

CHAPTER 27

Consuming Compassion:
AIDS, Figure Skating, and Canadian Identity

Samantha King

> They still sometimes wear sparkling costumes. They take ballet. They flutter their arms
> in rhythm with soft music. They are men trapped in a woman's sport.
>
> —Christine Brennan (1997: 58)

I n these days of tabloid media, we are accustomed to hearing spectacularized tales about the
lives of transsexual and transgendered people who, we are told, find themselves with bodies
in which they feel alien. In her best-selling book on the world of figure skating, *Inside Edge,*
Christine Brennan (1997) plays on this cliché to introduce her readers to what she calls "Skating's Tragic Secret"; namely, that many male figure skaters are gay (and that those who are not
merely tolerate the sequins and the makeup) and that a high number of skaters, coaches, chor-
eographers, and officials have died from AIDS-related illnesses in the past decade. In Brennan's
mind, AIDS is inherent to gayness and gayness is inherent to figure skating. For Brennan, these
relationships are so embedded that she goes so far to imply that heterosexual skaters live in fear
of sexual predation and even death. [...]

[...] This chapter examines public discourse about what has become known as "the AIDS crisis
in figure skating." More specifically, it explores how this story has played out in the Canadian
media, how it is implicated in struggles over Canadian AIDS policy, and how it is articulated to
the ever-present crisis of Canadian identity.

My version of this story begins on November 17, 1992, when an article appeared in the *New
York Times* telling of the recent AIDS-related deaths of three world-class Canadian figure skaters: Brian Pockar, Rob McCall, and Shaun McGill (Bondy, 1992a).[1] Published in the run-up to
Skate the Dream, a star-studded Toronto AIDS benefit, this report signaled the beginning of a
wave of similar media stories. As the *New York Times* attempted to assess the prevalence of the

virus in the top ranks of the sport, Tracy Wilson declared, "You can safely assume that there are more out there who have the disease and aren't talking about it" (Bondy, 1992b, p. D13). Four weeks later, following a slow trickle of reviews and editorials, the *Calgary Herald* expanded the focus of public attention with a report that announced the recent AIDS-related deaths of at least 40 male skaters and coaches in the top ranks of North American figure skating (Clarkson, 1992). This was released on syndication to most of the major Canadian newspapers as well as the *New York Times*, bringing widespread national and international attention to the issue.

Although the last 2 months of 1992 brought a flood of stories about "AIDS and figure skating," the actual content of these stories varied little, with the respective narratives revolving around three main themes; namely, that HIV is a problem specific to figure skating and a new occupational hazard for participants in the sport; that the skaters did not make their HIV status public both because of the strictures of U.S. immigration law vis-à-vis HIV and for fear of loss of endorsements; and that their deaths and the courageous responses of their friends and families provided an opportunity to educate the Canadian public and the figure skating community about HIV and AIDS. Deployed through careful, sympathetic language, these themes were framed as concerns of an anxious and compassionate Canadian public. Conspicuously absent from the narrative were the familiar, hysterical, and often hate-inflected stories about the lives of gay men, sex workers, drug users, Haitians, and "Africans" so ubiquitous in the Canadian media at this time.[2]

My argument is organized around two broad claims. First, I suggest that the story of AIDS and figure skating tells us more about the relationship of AIDS and sexuality to the formation of Canadian identity and the constitution of Canadian citizenship in the present moment than it does about the reality of HIV and AIDS, figure skating, compassion, charity, or death. But as Treichler (1993) argues, the ways in which we construct narratives about AIDS helps shape the epidemic—in all its realness. [...] Taking her argument seriously, I explore, first, how knowledge about HIV/AIDS is constituted; second, how this knowledge operates in the formation and deployment of Canadian national identity and citizenship; and, third, the extremely real effects of this formation and articulation. I argue that the positive images and performances of kindness and compassion played out in the figure skating story are not evidence of the superior moral nature of Canadian citizens, as public discourse frequently suggests, but rather serve to illustrate the ways in which the struggle to define a distinct and unifying Canadian national identity relies, in part, on narratives that imagine Canada as more compassionate and tolerant than the United States.[3] Although I contend that the figure skating story specifically, and the AIDS crisis in general, is a product of this fiction, I contend that the story functions, at the same time, to reinscribe the United States as the economically domineering, culturally expanding, illiberal, and intolerant neighborhood bully. Finally, I suggest that Canada's assumption of a minority subject position in relation to the United States works as a strategy by which Canada can deny responsibility for its own disenfranchised subjects—subjects who share more in common with their similarly disenfranchised sisters and brothers over the border than they do with the abstractions embodied in the "Canadian people."

My second broad claim is that the weight of the history of AIDS is such that the adoption of well-intentioned narratives brings with it new silences, different elisions, and alternative modes of making deviance visible.[4] To this end, Cole (1997) argues,

Despite the apparent distinction between the narrative of compassion and the narratives that pathologize and police deviance, both narratives are implicated in and bound
by the same normalizing logic that structures the discursive formation around AIDS.
(p. 283)[5]

Thus, the careful, sympathetic language deployed in the framing of the figure skating story is
remarkable precisely because of the rigidity of categories on which it relies, the stereotypes it
perpetuates, and the everyday violences and histories of violence that it denies. The framing of
the story in this manner worked to elicit public compassion through its focus on the heroism of
the skaters' friends and families, its celebration of individual, private activism and fund-raising,
and its presentation of "evidence" to reassure the Canadian general public that they were not at
risk for AIDS. Finally, I suggest that the positive public and corporate response to fund-raising
efforts prompted by the skating crisis is evidence of the commodification of AIDS in an era in
which a product's salability frequently rests on its ability to cultivate national self-esteem.

CLEAN, COLD FUN? FIGURE SKATING, CANADIAN IDENTITY, AND THE "CRISIS" OF MASCULINITY

Canadians of all ages, from all walks of life have found common ground on frozen
ground.

—ABC coverage of the Calgary Olympics

The significance of skating as a national pastime and core element in Canadian national identity
is persistently touted by the media, popular authors, and academics. This claim often is framed in
terms that suggest that skating represents an "organic connection" with the Canadian landscape
or national psyche (Gruneau & Whitson, 1993). [...] Beardsley [1987] draws on a long tradition
in Canadian writing that emphasizes the nation's frigid vastness, its cold, white landscape with
which Canadians must make common cause. In such writing, in the words of George Elliot
Clarke (1998), "The primeval frontier and the white body become one" (p. 107).

In a slightly different vein, and in response to the International Skating Union's decision to
drop compulsory figures, columnist Charles Gordon (1988) wrote,

The ... decision could cut to the heart of Canada's identity as a nation ... for figure
skating is the quintessential Canadian sport, more than hockey, more than baseball,
more than lacrosse, perhaps more, even, than shopping. (p. 30)[6]

Such romantic formulations arise from Anglocentric notions of Canadianness that serve to
homogenize the diversity of populations and cultures within Canada and erase the implication
of ice sports in the global economy, culture, politics, and history. However, these interpretations
also represent the very means by which Canadian national identity is constituted and performed
and are therefore key to understanding the "AIDS crisis in figure skating."[7]

Figure skating has long been a popular sport in Canada, in terms both of participation and spectating. During the 1980s, as a result of the intensely hyped rivalries between Katarina Witt of East Germany, America's Debi Thomas, and Canada's Elizabeth Manley, and between Brian Boitano of the United States and Canada's Brian Orser, television viewing figures for skating received a significant boost (Milton, 1990). Indeed, by 1990, the figure skating world championships ranked only third in importance behind the National Hockey League's Stanley Cup playoffs and the Canadian Football League's Grey Cup on the CBC's sports schedule (Milton, 1990). This popularity was reflected in participation rates as enrollment in figure skating clubs jumped by nearly 30% between 1988 and 1995 (Deacon, 1995).

The Calgary Winter Olympics of 1988 were instrumental in increasing the sport's popularity during this period. Earlier that year, Orser had won the World Figure Skating Championship, making him the first Canadian to capture a world championship medal in any sport in 1988 and the first Canadian man in 24 years to win a medal at these championships (Jenish, 1987). His victory was met with extensive media attention and became central to the patriotic and nationalistic buildup to the Olympics, in which skating was rated as the host nation's most promising source of medals (Jenish, 1987).[8] Orser eventually placed second to Brian Boitano, and Rob McCall and Tracy Wilson won the bronze medal in the ice dancing competition. Over the next 4 years, the Canadian media built on the momentum generated at Calgary, so that the 1992 Albertville Olympics attracted considerable public attention and even bigger audiences ("Indelible Memories," 1991).[9] The media buildup to the "battle of the Brians"; the enormous success of the marketing blitz around skating events at Calgary; the creation of new stars such as Kurt Browning (the skater most often positioned as Orser's successor) and, more recently, Elvis Stojko; the introduction of star-studded professional tours; and the consistent attention paid to the sport in the media combined to make skating a central point of identification in the contemporary Canada's national imaginary.

These events coincided with a concerted effort on the part of officials in the Canadian figure skating world to reform the sport's image to make it more appealing to Canadian consumers. In a chapter on male figure skating and the ideology of gender, Adams (1993) describes the resulting reforms as "the most radical change in the history of the sport" (p. 71). Of particular importance, according to Adams, was the elimination of school figures (a move designed to increase audience appeal) and the decision to allow professional and amateur skaters to compete together at international championships. However, Adams also argues that any analysis of changes designed to increase the credibility of skating as a sport must take into consideration the question of gender. Specifically, she argues that the failure of male figure skaters to fulfill cultural expectations of athletic masculinity can account for an effort on the part of endorsers, agents, journalists, and skating officials to promote individual skaters who are more macho and to masculinize the image of skating more generally. As evidence of both cultural anxieties about the sexuality and masculinity of male skaters and of unofficial or unspoken changes to the image of men's figure skating, Adams cites media interest in the sexuality of male skaters, strategies employed by officials, journalists, and commentators to entrench sexual difference and heterosexuality in the sport, and the aggressive marketing of apparently more masculine, athletic, jocklike skaters such as Kurt Browning.[10]

Given this [...] history, what are we to make of the positive public response to *Skate the Dream* and the extensive lineup of well-known brand names that chose to sponsor the event? If Canadian figure skating was already embroiled in a masculinity crisis, would the revelation that several of its finest talents had died from AIDS, an illness inseparable from sexual identity in the national imaginary, not scare endorsers and audiences away?

SKATE THE DREAM

> Many people in skating and the arts are very personable and friendly towards one another, and in some cases it has led to their deaths. It's like a Greek tragedy.
> —Gary Beacom (Clarkson, 1992, p. B1)

Skate the Dream: A Tribute to Rob McCall took place at Varsity Arena, Toronto, on November 21, 1992.[11] A total of 5,000 people attended two performances of the sold-out fund-raiser for the Toronto General Hospital, Canada's leading AIDS research and treatment facility. Organized by McCall (prior to his death), his mother Evelyn, his skating partner Tracy Wilson, and his best friend Brian Orser, the event brought together the world's leading amateur and professional skaters, including Kurt Browning, Brian Boitano, Katarina Witt, Kristi Yamaguchi, Toller Cranston, Robin Cousins, Isabelle Brasseur and Lloyd Eisler, Barbara Underhill and Paul Martini, and Ekaterina Gordeeva and Sergei Grinkov. The performances attracted coverage from *People* magazine and *Entertainment Tonight* and were televised on the CTV (Canadian Television) network twice on December 19. A pledge line set up during the broadcasts raised more than $500,000.

Presented by CTV sportscaster Rod Black and skating correspondent Debbi Wilkes, the broadcast comprised a sentimental collage of interviews with McCall's mother and friends, photographs of McCall from childhood through to his years as an amateur and professional skater, footage of his most well-known performances, excerpts from the show at Varsity Arena, and inspirational epigraphs from an array of sources including Garth Brooks, Franklin D. Roosevelt, and the *Wizard of Oz*.[12]

*****

By inviting the public to hear testimony from McCall's mother and share in the intimacy and nostalgia of the McCall family photo album, the show immediately embarked on a narrative about the safety, security, and love promised by the nuclear family. The displays of black-and-white photographs and references to the hope and happiness of bygone years (which appear throughout the broadcast) conveyed a sense of nostalgia and yearning for a better past, a mythic time when the family, and particularly children, were not under constant threat from an imagined amoral and antifamily world outside.

*****

[...] Given that AIDS threatens to expose the contingency and fragility of categories of identity and naturalized bodily boundaries, it is not surprising that the nature/nurture debates reemerged as the AIDS crisis entered its second decade and that they have been played out in public discourse about the "AIDS crisis in figure skating." In the early days of AIDS, as scientists worked under the assumption that homosexuality or "gay sex" caused HIV, HIV was known as "gay cancer" and the Gay Related Immune Deficiency (GRID) (Ordover, 1996). The plausibility of both these categorizations relies on a notion of biologized homosexuality derived from the belief that gay men share some specific physical abnormality not found in heterosexuals. At the same time, other scientists (most prominently Peter Duesberg), journalists, and politicians sought to blame "the gay lifestyle" for transmission of, and susceptibility to, HIV.[13] Again, both sides of the debate work to pathologize gay identity while leaving straight identity uninterrogated. Debbi Wilkes's interview with Brian Orser toward the end of the show, in which she asked him (with a sigh) if McCall should be blamed for his own death, exemplifies the violence embedded and mobilized through the nature/nurture question and makes explicit the underlying and unspoken logic of the *Skate the Dream* narrative.

> It's a tough question to ask, but I'm going to ask it. A lot of the public, maybe a lot of people who don't know better, criticize Rob for his lifestyle. Do you think what happened was fair to him?

*****

Although McCall's sexual identity was never explicitly mentioned in the broadcast, and although talk of transmission routes and identity categories were, in general, strikingly absent from the show, scenes such as these illustrate the ways in which the assumption that he was "gay," and that his gayness was the cause of his death, was carefully and politely re-enacted through—and indeed drove—the narrative. In other words, the family photo album and the CTV commentary and interviews functioned as a form of retroactive surveillance and a means of warning the public about the "inevitable consequences" of "being gay" in the era of AIDS. Thus, as the audience was asked to cast its mind back to McCall's childhood, it was also being asked to consider how things might have been different. This narrative makes sense, because, by the 1990s, the AIDS–gay association was firmly entrenched in public discourse, and the heterosexualized general public was so clearly marked as "not at risk." A brief look at the press coverage of the figure skating deaths and *Skate the Dream* will illustrate this point.

Is AIDS a "figure skating problem" or one of "wider society"? Do figure skaters constitute "a high risk group"? Asked in tones thick with care and concern, these questions occupied a pivotal position in the Canadian coverage of "the AIDS crisis in figure skating."[14] The most detailed and widely circulated example (the piece was released on syndication to newspapers across Canada) of the media's preoccupation with this question appeared in the *Calgary Herald* on December 13, 1992 (Clarkson, 1992). Building on the extensive copy devoted to *Skate the Dream* and assuming the role of journalistic epidemiologist extraordinaire, the *Calgary Herald* published the lengthy findings of a survey designed to measure the extent of AIDS in the figure skating world. Under the headline "Skating's Spectre. The toll: 40 male skaters and coaches in North America lost to AIDS. The future: The grim statistics can only darken with time," Peter Dunfield, a coach who has lost five colleagues to AIDS, told the *Calgary Herald*, "I continue to be surprised at the number of people we're losing" (Clarkson, 1992, p. B1). On a similar note, Toller Cranston said, "I've always thought that skating should not be singled out for AIDS attention, but it's becoming more and more disturbing" (Clarkson, 1992, p. B1). These sound bites from the sport's insiders suggest that AIDS is indeed a (growing) problem peculiar to figure skating and hence work [is needed] to contain the possibility of infection within the apparently self-contained and discrete community of figure skating, leaving the general public free from risk and blame. [...] In this way, the narrative is thoroughly embedded in the popular understanding that HIV has reached epidemic proportions only in certain, apparently contained, populations such as the gay community and "Africa" and stands as a stark reminder of the inability of the straight, White general public to consider itself at risk despite the fact that risk for HIV depends on practices, not identities.[15] The danger of this denial becomes apparent when membership in a low-risk group and a "1 in 10,000 chance" of contracting HIV deem safe sex and clean needles superfluous. My point here is not to deny that many figure skaters have died of AIDS-related illnesses. Rather, my intention is to draw attention to the way that this conceptualization of the problem, albeit in tones of compassion and concern, functions to cast the Canadian general public as not at risk for AIDS and, moreover, to disseminate publicly acceptable knowledge about AIDS in which the syndrome continues to function as evidence of secret and inner immorality, deviant bodily acts, and corresponding identities (the homosexual, the drug user, and the prostitute), rather than a possible outcome of bodily acts (unprotected sex, needle sharing).

Although *Skate the Dream* implicitly posits McCall's death as a lesson about forms of sexuality that are dangerous and deviant, the broadcast also works to desexualize and infantilize McCall. Debbi Wilkes's visit to "Rob's Room" ("a place for Rob to come home to"), typifies this strategy. With a Calgary Olympic Games flag superimposed on a huge Canadian flag draped along the back wall, the room houses a locker packed with McCall's personal possessions: items of "immeasurable sentimental value" that he willed to his family and friends. As Wilkes draws attention to McCall's frog collection, postcards of Ginger Rogers, various items of clothing, and drawings he did for his mother prior to his death, McCall is desexualized and infantilized, reduced to the figure of a child. This theme is sustained throughout the length of the broadcast with references to McCall's favourite pastimes—eating pizza, watching nature films, and playing cards—through to the closing sequence in which a black-and-white 8mm home movie shows McCall as a toddler playing with a puppy.

Whereas the appearance of McCall's mother and brother (who is interviewed later in the show) functions to make visible McCall's nuclear family, Wilson and Orser are quickly introduced as McCall's closest friends, his "skating family."[16] Wilson's and Orser's recollections and tributes are accompanied by photographs of the trio, in various poses, faces animated, always smiling, eyes sparkling, arms wrapped tightly around one another:

> Inseparable as dancers may seem, Wilson and McCall always made room for Brian Orser. (Cut to photo of the trio and sound bite from Orser): "He touched our lives, mine, Tracy's and anyone else who's fortunate enough to know him."

In Western AIDS narratives of the 1980s, gay men often were portrayed as lacking a family (biological or nonbiological). If they did appear with someone, it was usually a partner or lone friend. In either case, the figure of the gay man with AIDS was inevitably depicted as antithetical, and indeed threatening to, the heteronormative nuclear family. In the appearance of Evelyn and in the friendship of McCall, Wilson, and Orser however, the Canadian public is offered a new model for dealing with AIDS, a model in which friendship, respect, and love for gay men and people with AIDS are acceptable and even to be admired.[17, 18] Moreover, *Skate the Dream* also gives Canadians the opportunity to enact this new model of citizenship through frequent invitations to "make a friend in Rob." Take Black's words at the beginning of the show:

> As Rob McCall's legacy comes to life tonight, you are going to travel on a journey to times gone by: good times and sad times too, times of laughter and joy, and times of tears and sorrow. But most of all, you will savor the values of life and love, and I promise you that tonight, you will make a friend that you will never forget.

[...] These invitations ask Canadians to feel close to McCall—a person who had AIDS—and to participate in a simultaneously national and intimate performance of compassion and charity. The effect is to transform the story of McCall's life and death into a narrative about the heroism and compassion of the Canada public. The public's intimacy with McCall is mobilized and sustained through the prominence accorded to McCall's family and friends both in the broadcast and in the press coverage that surrounded it. Under headlines such as "Mom takes up AIDS crusade" (Guy, 1994) and "Helping buddies through bad times" (Smith, 1992), Evelyn McCall and Wilson were celebrated and admired for the care they showed their loved ones and for their efforts to promote public awareness about HIV/AIDS and to raise money for the cause.[19, 20] Evelyn, in particular, was the subject of numerous interviews and profiles as journalists recounted her battle to come to terms with Rob's illness and death, and her determination to devote herself to the struggle to find a cure for HIV. As Greg Guy (1994) of the *Chronicle Herald* put it,

> Two years ago, Evelyn McCall found it hard to say the word AIDS. Today, she considers herself a crusader in helping find a cure for the disease that killed her son almost three years ago. (p. A1)

Patton (1996) argues that the figure of the compassionate citizen also serves to reinforce the gap between the dangerous bodies of the sick, or those who have died, and the "safe," "general population." Thus, by asking the public to identify with the friends and families of the skaters, not the skaters themselves, the skaters remain the objects of others' compassion, and the public is able to maintain its difference and safety from people with HIV/AIDS and to sustain the image of themselves as not at risk.

At the same time that *Skate the Dream* shores up the distinction between so-called at-risk populations and the general public, it also works to reinscribe difference among people with AIDS/HIV. Like North America's mediated friendships with other people with HIV/AIDS— Magic Johnson, Greg Louganis, Ryan White, and Arthur Ashe—the compassion shown for McCall is dependent on his status as, in the words of Black, an "exceptional human being" loved through Canada and beyond, and on his apparent difference from and definition against other "deeply obscene bodies" (Cindy Patton's term) with HIV/AIDS. It is this distinction that undergirds Debbi Wilkes's claim that McCall's death, which in her account remains at the level of an individual tragedy, has given AIDS meaning for the first time:

> The figure skating community is a family, and like any family, to lose a member is a painful and traumatic ordeal. Unless you have been part of this pain, you might find it difficult to relate to this level of tragedy. I know the sadness, and I know the loss, because Bobby was a friend of mine too. For me, now AIDS has a face.

[...] AIDS has always had a face, a plethora of faces. Wilkes's claim might be read, then, as a means of distinguishing McCall, a less threatening, more palatable "face with AIDS" from those other, more familiar, unincorporated, dangerous, and addicted bodies of gay men, drug injectors, people of color, and sex workers. Moreover, at a time when activism through conflict and dissent are typically portrayed by the mainstream media as passions that are dangerous and destabilizing, these particular gestures of citizenship function as proof that their very claims are illegitimate; in contrast, talk shows and other forms of gossip media have helped make personal witnessing about trauma or injury highly valued political testimony (Berlant, 1997). Thus, the stories of McCall's life and the accompanying tales of individual triumph put a face on or concretize, in a more accessible form, what are otherwise abstract issues. As a strategy of journalistic commonsense, the "face" uses sentimentality to elicit personal identification with a difficult issue.

Although the success of *Skate the Dream* was already dependent on McCall's status as a national celebrity, McCall's popularity and significance to Canada was tirelessly invoked and reinforced throughout the broadcast. Of McCall and Wilson's bronze medal performance at Calgary, which is played in full at the start of the show, Black declares, "It wasn't gold, but it was an unprecedented victory and one that Canada embraced. Wilson and McCall had danced their way into the history books and into the hearts of people everywhere they went." Together with testimonies and tributes from McCall's international skating colleagues, such sound bites work to position McCall as a representative of the Canadian body politic, an international ambassador of whom Canada is proud. With McCall infantilized and desexualized, and the general public reassured of its nonsusceptibility to HIV, *Skate the Dream* became a performance of (Canadian) national compassion, a way to make visible and celebrate the lukewarm liberal diversity so central to Canada's self-esteem and national identity.

ERASING COMMUNITY/RAISING MONEY: THE COMMODIFICATION OF AIDS IN AN ERA OF (CORPORATE) COMPASSION

> With all of the skaters whose lives McCall touched jumping on board, so did the sponsors.
> —Smith (1992, p. D5)

In an image-dominated consumer culture, a scandal in the sports world usually prompts public debate about the effect that this scandal might have on the marketing potential of the athlete, team, or sport in question. This was one of the first issues raised by the media when Magic Johnson made his HIV status public, and not surprisingly, this same question figured prominently in the news coverage of the deaths of Dennis Coi, Shawn McGill, Brian Pockar, and McCall. Bondy's (1992b) response for the *Vancouver Sun* was typical: "Now figure skating is left with the task of educating its anxious athletes and avoiding the publicity that might damage this theatrical, marketing driven sport" (p. D13). Judging by the long list of high-profile corporations who sponsored the event—Campbell Soup Co. Ltd., Canadian Airlines International Ltd., Canadian Tire Corp. Ltd., Sunlife, Honda Canada Inc., Nestle Foods Corp., and President's Choice—Bondy and co. need not have worried. By 1992, AIDS publicity was, it seems, no longer, necessarily, bad publicity.

Rose (1999) has argued that at the present time in history, self-gratification is no longer defined in opposition to civility, as in the ethical codes of puritan sects that Weber considered so important in the early moments of capitalism; that is, consumers can—and do—build civic identity and virtue through their consumption practices. But in the 1990s, corporations do the same. They produce goods for profit and promote these goods by aligning themselves with virtuous causes and by performing a variety of civic acts (by, for example, donating money, equipment, or paid time off for employees to do volunteer work). Indeed, corporations and consumers rely on each other for the constitution of their respective ethical identities. Commodities such as the *Skate the Dream* appear to illuminate or reveal the virtuosity of those who pay for them, to transform spectators and audiences into certain kinds of people living certain kinds of lives. A corporation's sponsorship of *Skate the Dream* performs a similar function by forging a respectable, ethical, and responsible identity for that corporation. Thus, *Skate the Dream* was a site for the production of both consumer citizens and corporate citizens and as such exemplifies the ways in which citizenship advances through consumption (and spectacle) in the present moment.[21]

The red ribbon, conceived by a group called Visual AIDS to raise awareness of AIDS through celebrity events in the United States, is the most visible and well-known symbol of both the AIDS epidemic and the extent to which AIDS empathy has become a multinational industry (Sturken, 1997). [...] The success of *Skate the Dream* built on, and cannot be understood apart from, the history of the red ribbon and other cultural products designed to make people feel good about themselves. Both the ubiquity of the red ribbon and the public response to *Skate the Dream* are testament not only to the importance of public displays of compassion in the 1990s but also to the public's willingness to associate themselves, through the donation of money, with publicly acceptable forms of knowledge about HIV and AIDS.

Although there is a difference between corporations increasing profit margins by associating themselves with HIV/AIDS and nonprofit organizations raising money through the sale of goods, the form of politics and activism promoted and legitimized through both these channels and epitomized in events such as *Skate the Dream* is deeply problematic. *Skate the Dream* celebrates the promise of passive, individual action, social change through consumption, private fund-raising over state-sponsored research, and uncontroversial aims and strategies. According to this model of politics, citizens display concern and are deemed active simply by attending a show or watching a television broadcast and (perhaps) donating money.

The "politics through consumption" model of activism combined with the nostalgic tone of *Skate the Dream* (Kammen, 1991, fittingly describes nostalgia as "history without guilt") also serve to promote national amnesia about the AIDS crisis. The following excerpt from Rod Black's commentary is instructive here:

> Incredible but not invincible. The spotlight would fade. The journey continues to a place where dreams never die and friends never forget. On November 15th, 1991, Rob McCall walked into the light (Black, with his back to the camera, moves toward a dim light struggling to shine through the thick mist). Leaving behind a battle against insurmountable odds, there were dreams that were unfulfilled, dances incomplete, symphonies unfinished. But through the adversity, Rob McCall embraced a dream that someday, somehow, this disease that had stolen his life would be beaten.

Although these glowing tributes to McCall are far removed from the hate-inflected, punitive, and pathologizing mass media treatment of gay men with AIDS in the 1980s, the euphemistic and fairy tale qualities of the narrative prohibit consideration of the widespread devastation wrought by AIDS. In other words, *Skate the Dream* asks the Canadian public to consider AIDS as an individual tragedy alone, rather than an individual and collective tragedy, exacerbated by public neglect, in which we are all implicated.[22] Indeed, during the broadcast, there were conspicuously few references to HIV/AIDS. The exceptions were a 2-minute compilation of sound bites of the "anyone can get AIDS" variety delivered by McCall's friends and family, and the following plea from Toller Cranston:

> The motivation behind our performances goes far beyond the self. It even goes, for me, far beyond Robert McCall. Because I feel that what the skaters are doing here is skating for people that have become infected with AIDS, anybody in the world that has this disease, and also for the awareness, public awareness, of AIDS and with the money that's made, which I've heard is like half a million dollars that it's for, you know, trying to find a cure.

Moreover, although the event was billed as a fund-raiser for AIDS research, the only clue that this was its purpose came prior to each intermission when a pledge line number, accompanied by the words "Support AIDS Research at the Toronto Hospital," flashed on the screen. No information about why the money was needed or how it would be spent was offered.

Although *Skate the Dream* minimized and individualized the tragedy of HIV/AIDS, it also worked to erase the atrocious record of official responses to the epidemic in Canada and to rewrite the history of crisis *without* the gay community. The monumental violence of this erasure becomes apparent when one considers that Canada's response to AIDS, for at least the first eight years, stemmed almost entirely from local community activist groups. To examine the history of Canadian government and community responses to AIDS, I want to turn to the question of Canadian identity and, specifically, to interrogate this history in the context of Canada's image of itself as a compassionate, tolerant, and liberal nation committed to difference and diversity. How is Canada's image of itself implicated in the neglect and marginalization of people living with AIDS (PLWA)/HIV and other minoritized subjects? To what extent does the AIDS crisis reveal both the absolute fragility and contingency of Canada's claim to embrace difference and the remarkable similarities between the situation of Canada's minoritized subjects and the minoritized inhabitants of other Western nations?

CONSTANT CRAVING: AIDS AND THE PERMANENT CRISIS OF CANADIAN NATIONAL IDENTITY

> Canadians: "Caring, sharing, patient, mostly tolerant and a bit boring."
> —Wilson-Smith (1997)

Canada appears to be in a constant identity crisis. Canadian popular culture, academia, government, and business have been consumed with the question of Canadianness since at least the 1920s.[23] Both Canada's size (and hence geographic and climatic variety) and its racial, ethnic, linguistic, and sexual diversity ensures that this question is not easily resolved and that the intensity of national concern over this question remains high. For similar reasons, attempts to define Canadianness in the past three decades have rarely begun with the notion of a unitary, distinct identity (as is the case in many modern Western nation states) but instead with a state-sanctioned recognition of difference, contradiction, and tension—most obviously illustrated in its policies of official bilingualism and multiculturalism, and fondly known as the Canadian "mosaic." The mosaic was born in the 1960s and 1970s during a period in which the Canadian government undertook widespread social reform designed to facilitate cultural expression, forge a strong national identity, and project an image of Canada as a model liberal democracy. The problem with the mosaic, particularly for aboriginal peoples, Quebec sovereignists, recent non-Anglo immigrants, and gays, is that this recognition of difference frequently fails to translate into economic, political, or cultural autonomy, and indeed often translates into state-sanctioned oppression and violence.[24] Thus, for marginalized populations in Canada, the struggle for Canadian national identity is not the most pressing issue on the political agenda (as saturation-point media coverage of this question suggests) and, indeed, the national preoccupation with the search for the meaning of Canada often works as a tool to make invisible the relations of power and privilege that work to constitute such populations as marginal.

The success of the Canadian mosaic as a point of national pride relies primarily on its difference from what is understood as an inferior approach to national assimilation: the melting pot of the United States. A sense of urgency around the struggle for national identity is most often mobilized through reference to Canada's proximity to the United States and the image of a fragile Canadian multiculture gradually being swallowed up by a homogeneous American commerce, media, and culture. Thus, Canadian identity, such as it is, defines itself primarily in opposition to the United States. According to this national fantasy, Canada defines itself as the peaceful, pristine, liberal, and minoritized subject in a relationship dominated by a trigger-happy, urban, illiberal, economically domineering, and culturally expanding neighbor to the south. The point here is not to deny the significance of the difference between the histories of the two countries, their political cultures, labour laws, health care systems, and social security networks, but rather to consider the implications of Canada's image of itself as a model of liberal tolerance.[25]

This issue is of particular importance in the context of the 1990s, a period in which the moral and political difference (read, superiority) of Canada has consistently been brought into question both on the international stage and within its national borders. Internationally, Canada has garnered much critical attention around its treatment of Native people and over the "Somalia Affair."[26] Internally, Canada's "model" liberal democracy and welfare state is being torn apart, as many doctors and politicians on the right campaign for a two-tier health care service (the wretched state of health care provision in the United States is the dominant point of reference for opponents of reform), as the Reform Party (with their anti-Native, anti-immigrant, anti-feminist, anti-gay stance) comprises the official national opposition and the major force in provincial politics in the west of Canada and as Conservative governments in Alberta and Ontario rush to dismantle welfare and social security provisions in their provinces.

These tensions are nowhere more obvious than in the history of sexuality and HIV/AIDS in Canada. Although Canada has some of the most progressive "gay rights" legislation in the world, the focus of this legislation is primarily in areas of housing and employment and varies greatly from province to province. Moreover, the focus on equality and rights carries with it all the limitations and problems associated with liberal politics in general: A minority group is identified as in need of protection, but when legislation is accordingly introduced, the group is inscribed in law as a fixed minority, whereas systemic inequalities and violence usually remain. Moreover, the national, public face of Canada's approach to sexuality (diverse, tolerant, even enabling) is not consistent with its record on so-called private issues (sodomy, sex between men, and queer media). For instance, whereas the age of consent for women and men having sex is 14, men younger than 18 are prohibited from engaging in anal sex.[27] The perceived threat posed by gay men to children was also behind the defeat, in 1994, of Bill 167 that would have given same-sex benefits and family relationship rights to lesbians and gays in Ontario. Although the bill itself was embedded in and representative of liberal imperatives, its successful passing would have represented a significant victory for gays and lesbians in Canada, who in the moral conservative campaign against this legislation—which centred on a clause that would have granted adoption rights to same-sex couples—were persistently labeled as a threat to children and the (heterosexual) nuclear family. Moreover, despite Canada's claims to tolerance and diversity, the Canadian police have continued, through the 1990s, to survey and prosecute men engaging in consensual sex in public washrooms and parks, to raid gay bars, and to refuse to respond adequately to violence against gay men.[28] In addition, perhaps the most highly publicized and symbolically weighted example of Canada's failure to live up to its imagined national character in the realm of sexuality lies in Canada Customs' censorship campaign against lesbian and gay books, magazines, and films coming into the country from the United States (mainly).

CANADIAN AIDS ACTIVISM AND POLICY

> Jean Chrétien, you can't hide, we charge you with genocide!
> —Activist slogan for the 11th International Conference on AIDS in Vancouver[29]

The emergence of the AIDS crisis in Canada coincided with the tenure of a neoconservative federal government led by Brian Mulroney, and the rise of the Canadian profamily movement and the anti-gay, anti-immigrant, anti-feminist, monetarist Reform Party, which made considerable electoral gains during the 1980s (Erwin, 1988). The federal response to AIDS in Canada was tardy and uneven on a number of levels, not the least because it failed to act, in its usual capacity, as coordinator of federal-provincial strategies (Rayside & Linquist, 1992).[30] For most of the 1980s, federal efforts were driven by a desire to protect the general public from people with HIV and AIDS, who were understood to be irresponsible, rather than funding research and treatment programs and taking action to assist people with HIV/AIDS (Kinsman, 1996; Rayside & Linquist, 1992).[31] Moreover, the Laboratory Centre for Disease Control (1998), a body that worked according to coercive and regulatory public health ideology, was responsible for running the federal agenda during this time. In addition, during this period, pharmaceutical companies were left with almost sole responsibility for drug testing, and the government refused to budge on its overly cautious procedures for testing drugs. Finally, because it was also assumed that all PLWA would die quickly, research efforts toward treatment were neglected. Thus, for the Canadian government, doctors, researchers, and epidemiologists were to be the main players in the national response to the epidemic, while community groups and activists were virtually ignored until much later.

Whereas the federal government sat on its laurels in Ottawa for most of the 1980s, community activists "out in the provinces" were quick to respond to the crisis and, from the beginning, called for candid education for the whole population, adequate funding for community groups and medical facilities, widespread distribution of condoms and needles, recognition of and responses to discrimination based on HIV/AIDS status, increased research, and government consultation with community activists (Rayside & Linquist, 1992). Although the concentration of PLWA and people with HIV in large metropolitan centres (Toronto, Vancouver, and Montreal) and the vast differences between the political scenes and health care services of the provinces was reflected in the varied and uneven community response to AIDS, it is fair to say that without community groups there would have been nothing that could be recognized as an organized response in Canada.[32]

According to some critics, the May 1988 burning of an effigy of federal Health Minister Jake Epp by members of AIDS Action Now! to protest the lack of a national AIDS strategy marked a turning point in the Canadian government's response to the AIDS crisis (Kinsman, 1996).[33] Whether the government's turnaround was as impressive as these critics claim, and whether this shift was also prompted by the increasing visibility of White, straight people with AIDS, things did begin to change shortly thereafter, when 2 months later Epp announced a $116 million federal government commitment to AIDS. In November, the morally conservative Epp was replaced by the more liberal Perrin Beatty, who, in the face of a strong showing by ACT UP and AIDS Action Now! announced at the fifth International Conference on AIDS that a national AIDS strategy was in the works; 1 year later, it was officially announced (Kinsman, 1996). The strategy met two of the activists' major demands in its promise to establish a national treatment registry (which did not get off the ground until 1995 due to resistance from medical professionals and academics) and to fund a clinical trials network. Treatment-based activism in Canada was also responsible for the release and approval of aerosolized pentamidine (AP), a preventative treatment for pneumocystis carinii pneumonia (the largely preventable yet major cause of death among PLWA in North America in the 1980s), the limited release of ddI (an antiviral drug), and an end to the use of double-blind trials. Unfortunately, government and corporate apathy and inefficiency meant that many of these strategies and policies did not get off the ground until long after they were approved (Kinsman, 1996).[34]

At the turn of the century, despite the much heralded introduction of protease inhibitors and combination therapies—HIV treatments that are successfully decreasing the viral load in up to 50% of users—and the frequent media declarations that the worst of the AIDS epidemic is over, the crisis continues. For instance, the number of Native people with AIDS in Canada is growing every year (Laboratory Centre for Disease Control, 1999). Activists cite lack of federal money for First Nations AIDS/HIV programs and poor access to condoms and clean needles as factors that need to be addressed (Laforest, 1999). Moreover, a study conducted on behalf of the federal government found that between 1992 and 1997, the annual number of new infections soared by 50%, with injecting drug users, Native people, women, and young gay men disproportionately affected (Archibald et al., 1997). Activists have cited this study as evidence of the government's neglect of preventative strategies (Prentice, 1997). In addition, the price of new therapies can reach up to $15,000 per year, a price out of the reach of most people not covered under private insurance or government drug plans and absolutely unaffordable to the vast majority of people in the Third World, who are unable to afford even the older generation of drugs.

CONCLUSION

As a commodified performance of national compassion, *Skate the Dream* captured, as it also established, the preferred version of Canadian character and citizenship. Canada's image of itself as a tolerant and caring national community that is essentially and fundamentally differ-ent from its neighbour to the south works to both erase alternative versions of its history and character and to administer and configure its minoritized subjects in ways that make it hard to see that their interests and experiences may indeed have more in common with minoritized subjects across national boundaries than with the rest of Canada.

Perhaps the most poignant illustration of this point lies in the claim, made repeatedly in Can-adian press coverage, that the skaters did not make their HIV status public because of the strictures of U.S. immigration law. Although there is no mandatory screening of applicants for non-immi-grant visas, those discovered to be HIV positive are refused admission, and people planning to visit the United States for business, medical treatment, or family visits may apply for a waiver. Although Canada, as yet, does not have immigration law pertaining specifically to HIV, politicians on the right have been campaigning for such a law since the early 1990s.[35] Moreover, although there is no routine testing of potential immigrants for HIV, an applicant who tests positive for HIV is medic-ally inadmissible on grounds of excessive demands.[36] If the person is only visiting Canada, the decision is made at the discretion of the immigration officer. The tremendous discretionary power of immigration officials in Canada means that there have been incidents in which individuals have been harassed and refused entry.[37] In addition, until spring of 1997, Canadian immigration authorities were authorized to refuse entry to short-term visitors with HIV/AIDS.

Although this claim effaces Canada's own problematic immigration policies, it also implies that people with HIV/AIDS in Canada are able to live fully safe, fully public, full national lives. Given the history of AIDS in Canada and given the glaring absence in the figure skating narrative of a frank, accurate discussion of HIV transmission, of safe and unsafe practices, of discrimination, and of what it might mean to be living with AIDS in Canada, it would appear that this most certainly is not the case.

NOTES

1 McCall was a bronze medallist (with his partner, Tracy Wilson) at the Calgary Olympics in 1988, the winner of a bronze medal in the 1986 and 1987 world championships, and a successful professional skater. Pockar, from Calgary, Alberta, was the winner of three Canadian figure skating championships and a bronze medal in the 1982 world championships. At the end of his amateur career, Pockar joined the professional circuit. He also worked as a commentator on CTV (the Canadian Television network). McGill was the winner of the 1988 world professional silver medal and enjoyed a successful career as a producer and choreographer.

2 See Miller (1992), Kinsman (1996), and Klusáček and Morrison (1992) for cultural analyses of AIDS and AIDS activism in Canada. For examples of explicitly homophobic AIDS discourse in Canada, see the Canadian AIDS Society's *Homophobia, Heterosexism and AIDS* (1991). For an analysis of Canadian media coverage, see Emke (1991), "Speaking of AIDS in Canada: The Texts and Contexts of Official, Counter-Cultural and Mass Media Discourses Surrounding AIDS."

3 Clarke (1998) makes a similar argument in his article, "White Like Canada."

4 Of course, there is a significant variation in the way that people living with AIDS (PLWA) are understood in public culture, understandings that usually vary according to the imputed mode of transmission.

5 Similarly, in *Fatal Advice,* Patton (1996) argues that the AIDS epidemic in the United States prompted the formation of a new paradigm for citizenship: Americans were to be compassionate and tolerant toward people with HIV but as part of this approach were never required or expected to think of themselves as susceptible to HIV.

6 Compulsory figures are variations on the figure 8, where a skater attempts to skate a perfectly round circle on a perfectly clean edge, and then do the same on the other foot. Compulsory figures used to be worth 60% of the score, but after 1968, they were progressively devalued and finally eliminated completely from the international competition after the 1990 season. In the United States, figures competitions were held as separate events between 1991 and 1999, but those, too, have now been phased out because few skaters take the time to learn figures any more; it is hard to find rinks that will give them their own patch of ice on which to practice; and most importantly, skaters slowly carving barely visible ice tracings did not, in the minds of producers anyway, make good television viewing.

7 For a useful analysis of sport and contemporary Canadian identity, see Jackson (1994).

8 For Canadian skating coverage before, during, and after the Olympics, see Jenish (1987), Howse (1987), O'Hara (1988a, 1988b), and Walmsley (1988).

9 In an article charting the boom in the market for professional figure skating, Deacon (1995) claims that enrollment in figure skating clubs has jumped by nearly 30% since 1988.

10 An example of media interest (albeit covert) in McCall's sexuality and masculinity appeared in a *Maclean's* magazine preview of the Calgary Olympics. In the middle of a discussion about McCall's

experience skating in the newly built $100 million Saddledome, reporter John Howse (1987) writes, "McCall ... dismisses the hoary argument over whether the elegant figure skaters, in rhinestones and makeup, belong in the company of athletes" (p. 51). Howse then moves swiftly along to a discussion about Canadian medal hopefuls.

11 A second *Skate the Dream,* held in McCall's hometown, Halifax, took place on October 27, 1994 (Guy, 1994). This event raised money for the McCall Centre for HIV Research at the Victoria General Hospital, Halifax.

12 Examples of epigraphs include "Life is better left to chance.... We could have missed the pain, but then we'd have missed the dance" (Garth Brooks).

13 Duesberg (1992) is a researcher in molecular and cell biology at the University of California, Berkeley. He is most well known for his contention that HIV does not cause AIDS. Instead, he claims that AIDS is caused by lifestyle factors: in the United States, by the use of recreational drugs, which he claims is so prevalent among gay men, and in Africa, by protein malnutrition, poor sanitation, and subsequent parasitic infections.

14 Even prior to the media frenzy of late 1992, 2 days after McCall's death and 10 days after Magic Johnson's announcement that he was HIV positive, the *Toronto Star* published a piece headlined, "McCall's death shouldn't set off alarms." The article featured extracts from an interview with Toller Cranston, a well-known Canadian skater, who told the *Star,* "I knew nothing about Rob McCall's personal life but in the skating world, as far as I know, (AIDS) is not rampant" (Zwolinksi, 1991, p. B1). Cranston also said that Canadian figure skating had suffered only one other AIDS-related death—Dennis Coy, "a successful junior skater, who had died two years ago" (Zwolinksi, 1991, p. B1). Cranston's (1997) autobiography devotes a chapter, "Three Funerals," to the deaths of Rob McCall and Brian Pockar.

15 Patton (1996) argues that cases in which a person with AIDS does not fit neatly into any of the pathologized identity categories are treated as aberrations and exceptions, rather than as part of a worldwide, cross-cultural epidemic.

16 Orser was a double Olympic silver medallist, world champion, and Canada's most well-known skater in the 1980s.

17 See Watney (1987, 1989) and Crimp (1987).

18 The desexualization of McCall, however, is enacted through a heterosexual lens. The figure of Wilson is particularly significant in this respect, as her centrality to the McCall-Orser-Wilson friendship is identified and emphasized repeatedly.

19 See Bondy (1992a, 1992b), Guy (1994), Smith (1992), and Toneguzzi (1993) for examples of media coverage that focuses on the skaters' friends and families.

20 Coverage of Brian Pockar's death was similar, with his sister, Leanne Pockar, at the centre of media attention. See "Skater's sister rallies back" (Toneguzzi, 1993).

21 Other examples of corporations selling products through images of social responsibility include, among many others, athletic apparel manufacturers such as Reebok and Nike who present themselves as profeminist and actively involved in improving the quality of life for the inhabitants of America's inner cities; the Body Shop, which sells its products through campaigns to "save" the indigenous peoples and rain forests of South America; and a whole array of oil companies and car manufacturers who present themselves as the protectors of the environment (see Cole & Hribar, 1996; Sturken, 1997).

22 Indeed, the broadcast was so drained of social context that it even failed to include any mention of other skaters who were sick (Britain's John Curry for example) or who had died by this time.

23 See Berland (1995) for a discussion of this observation with reference to cultural studies in Canada.

24 The much lauded landmark Royal Commission on Bilingualism and Biculturalism, launched in 1963, stands as a striking example of exclusivity on an official level, when in an attempt to recognize the two founding nations of Canada, the government instituted French-English bilingualism and biculturalism as national policy, to the exclusion of the people of the First Nations and the millions of Canadian citizens of non-Anglo and non-French origin. Moreover, one of the most well-remembered and often-cited examples of state-sanctioned violence in the name of the Canadian nation occurred during the same period, in 1970, when Trudeau imposed the War Measures Act and sent the military into Quebec.

25 Clarke (1998) argues that, in the mind of Canada, the most significant difference between Canada and the United States is that America has a race problem. He cites numerous examples of this belief at work, including a 1995 poll that found that 83% of Canadian adults did not know slavery was practiced in pre-Confederation Canada.

26 In 1993, a suicide attempt by six Innu children of Davis Inlet, a tiny community on an isolated Labrador Island, 275 kilometres north of Goose Bay, brought worldwide media attention to Canada's treatment of aboriginal people. The horrific nature of their bid to end their lives—they were found high on gasoline and shrieking that they wanted to die—became the focal point in the chorus of international condemnation for a government that had forcibly ended the Innu's nomadic life, resettled them on this desolate piece of land, and forgot them (28 years later, the Innu were still living without the promised running water and electricity). Also in 1993, Canadian soldiers on United Nations "peacekeeping" duty in Somalia tortured a 16-year-old Somalian boy to death. The government launched an inquiry into his death; however, before the inquiry even heard evidence relating to this atrocity, the government curtailed the proceedings because it was "taking too long." It turns out that the proceedings may have been curtailed to suppress information about the shooting by Canadian troops of two unarmed Somali citizens prior to the murder of the teenager, a murder that may not have happened had the military not covered up the first shootings. The Somalia "affair" did not receive quite the same level of attention as Davis Inlet in the international media, perhaps because almost every Western "peacekeeping" force in Somalia wound up committing its own atrocities. It is, however, the ongoing source of Canadian media headlines.

27 Although the law does not target anal sex between men specifically, Kinsman (1996) argues that it has been used by the police to target mainly young male prostitutes with male clients.

28 See Kinsman (1996).

29 Activists were angry at the possibility that Chrétien might not renew Canada's national AIDS strategy. Other concerns addressed by activists at the conference included the high price of antiviral drugs and the government's refusal to release new drugs swiftly.

30 For this section of the article, I am indebted to the work of Rayside and Linquist (1992) and Kinsman (1996), as well as the resources of numerous activist organizations including the AIDS Committee of Toronto, the Canadian HIV/AIDS legal network, and AIDS Action Now!

31 In the light of the several comparisons already made between the United States and Canada, I should point out that this work reflects a tension peculiar to any project concerned with Canadian culture: on one hand, it takes seriously the specificities of the political, cultural, economic, and historical context in which the AIDS crisis has been articulated and experienced in Canada; on the other hand, because,

like it or not, Canadian identity is largely dependent on the way Canada imagines itself in relation to the United States, this article cannot but help participate in this discourse.

32 Toronto was home to successful community organizing in the form of the AIDS Committee of Toronto (established in 1983), the People with AIDS Coalition (established in 1987), the Safe Sex Corps (Canadian Organization for the Rights of Prostitutes, established in 1987), and the more radical AIDS Action Now! (also in 1987) (Kinsman, 1996). Toronto's municipal government was among the first to fund community organizations and also cooperated with activists in establishing a needle-exchange program and installing condom dispensers in high schools in 1989. Ontario's provincial government, once it changed to Liberal hands in 1985, established the Ontario Public Education Advisory Panel (OPEPA) in 1985, was the first to mandate AIDS education in schools (1987), and passed provincial legislation in 1986 that barred discrimination against PLWA. In contrast, for much of the 1980s, British Columbia was in the hands of the right-wing Social Credit party who refused to respond to the crisis and was unwilling to work with or show support for, what was for them, a problem of the gay community (although free testing and counseling was made available throughout the province in 1985). In Vancouver, health administrators and community activists were able to institute discrimination protection, and the Vancouver People With AIDS Coalition led the successful effort to force the federal government to release AZT in 1986 (although by 1991, AZT was still only free to those on welfare). In 1991, the New Democratic Party government in British Columbia, under constant pressure from activists, introduced a provincial AIDS strategy and legislation to make all approved AIDS drugs free of charge. In Quebec, the provincial government introduced progressive legislation early on to establish anonymous testing and ban discrimination, and established a highly successful needle-exchange program. Unfortunately, government spending in Quebec lagged way behind other provinces, due in part to a Conservative health minister and the organization of the health care system in Quebec (Rayside & Linquist, 1992).

33 Kinsman (1996) makes this argument in *The Regulation of Desire*.

34 For an outstanding exploration of AIDS research and activism, and particularly the politics of clinical trials and drug approval schedules, see Epstein (1996).

35 In 1994, in the run-up to the International Conference on AIDS to be held in Vancouver, however, Canadian politicians were debating legislation on mandatory HIV testing for all immigrants. Reform Party MP Art Hanger proposed the legislation, claiming that immigrants with HIV are a threat to "health, safety, and people" and a burden on the health care system. In addition, he claimed that Sergio Marchi, the Canadian Immigration Minister, could not guarantee that "some conference delegates won't illegally overstay their visas or apply for refugee status" (Bryden, 1994, p. B4). In response to these claims, Marchi agreed to review Canada's policy. Fortunately, for the time being, the law remains unchanged.

36 This rule does not apply to refugee claimants.

37 Canadian Immigration lawyer Rob Hughes has written about the case of David Rowe, a gay, African American, U.S. citizen with HIV, who was removed from a cross-border train bound for Montreal on the "discovery" of HIV medication in his luggage. Immigration officers told him that he was medically inadmissible to Canada and that if he wished to appeal the decision, he would have to spend up to 3 weeks in a regular jail cell while the assessment was done. Mr. Rowe understandably "chose" to return to New York (R. Hughes, personal communication; http://www.smith-hughes.com.border.htm).

REFERENCES

Adams, M. L. (1993). To be an ordinary hero: Male figure skaters and the ideology of gender. In T. Haddock (Ed.), *Men and masculinities: A critical anthology* (pp. 163–181). Toronto: Canadian Scholars' Press.

Archibald, C., Remis, R., Williams, G., Farley, J., Albert, T., Yan, P., Cloutier, E., & Sutherland, D. (1997, May). *Estimating current prevalence and incidence of HIV in Canada.* Plenary Presentation at sixth Annual Canadian Conference on HIV/AIDS Research, Ottawa.

Beardsley, D. (1987). *Country on ice.* Winlaw, BC: Polestar.

Berland, J. (1995). Marginal notes on cultural studies in Canada. *University of Toronto Quarterly, 64,* 514–525.

Berlant, L. (1997). *The queen of America goes to Washington City: Essays on sex and citizenship.* Durham, NC: Duke University Press.

Bondy, F. (1992a, November 17). "AIDS deaths are tearing at figure skating world." *The New York Times,* pp. A1, B16.

Bondy, F. (1992b, November 18). "Figure skating fraternity shocked by Canadian AIDS deaths." *The Vancouver Sun,* p. D13.

Brennan, C. (1997). *Inside edge: A revealing journey into the secret world of figure skating.* New York: Anchor, Doubleday.

Bryden, J. (1994, April 26). "Marchi considers AIDS tests for immigrants." *The Montreal Gazette,* p. B4.

Canadian AIDS Society. (1991). *Homophobia, heterosexism and AIDS.* Ottawa, Canada: Author.

Clarke, G. E. (1998). White like Canada. *Transition,* 7(1), 98–119.

Clarkson, M. (1992, December 13). "Skating's spectre." *Calgary Herald,* pp. B1–B2.

Cole, C. L. (1997). Containing AIDS: Magic Johnson and post[Reagan] America. In S. Seidman (Ed.), *Queer theory/sociology* (pp. 280–310). Cambridge, MA: Blackwell.

Cole, C. L., & Hribar, A. (1996). Celebrity feminism: Nike style, post-Fordism, transcendence and consumer power. *Sociology of Sport Journal,* 12, 347–369.

Cranston, T. (1997). *Zero tolerance: An intimate memoir by the man who revolutionized figure skating.* Toronto: McClelland and Stewart.

Crimp, D. (1987). *AIDS cultural analysis/cultural activism.* Cambridge, MA: MIT Press.

Deacon, J. (1995, April 10). "Ice time." *Maclean's,* pp. 34–36.

Duesberg, P. (1992). AIDS acquired by drug consumption and other noncontagious risk factors. *Pharmacology & Therapeutics,* 55, 201–277.

Emke, I. (1991). *Speaking of AIDS in Canada: The texts and contexts of official, counter-cultural and mass media discourses surrounding AIDS.* Unpublished doctoral dissertation, Carleton University, Ottawa, Ontario.

Epstein, S. (1996). *Impure science: AIDS, activism, and the politics of knowledge.* Berkeley: University of California Press.

Erwin, L. (1988). What feminists should know about the pro-family movement in Canada: A report on a recent survey of rank and file members. In P. T. Shaerif (Ed.), *Feminist perspectives: Prospect and retrospect.* Montreal and Kingston, Canada: McGill-Queen's University Press.

Gordon, C. (1988, June 27). "Skating away with our identity." *Maclean's,* p. 30.

Gruneau, R., & Whitson, D. (1993). *Hockey Night in Canada: Sport, Identities and Cultural Politics.* Toronto: Garamond.

Guy, G. (1994, October 27). "Holding on to McCall's dream." *The Chronicle-Herald*, pp. A1–A2.

Howse, J. (1987, November 9). "Previewing the games." *Maclean's*, pp. 50–51.

"Indelible Memories." (1991, December 2). *Maclean's*, p. 28.

Jackson, S. (1994). *1988: Sport and a year of crisis in Canadian identity*. Unpublished doctoral dissertation, University of Illinois, Urbana-Champaign.

Jenish, D. (1987, March 23). "Sweet victory." *Maclean's*, p. 31.

Kammen, M. (1991). *Mystic chords of memory: The transformation of tradition in American culture*. New York: Knopf.

Kinsman, G. (1996). *The regulation of desire: Homo and hetero sexualities*. Montreal: Black Rose.

Klusáček, A., & Morrison, K. (1992). *A leap in the dark: AIDS, art and contemporary cultures*. Montreal: Vehicule.

Laboratory Centre for Disease Control. (1999, May). HIV/AIDS epidemiology among aboriginal people in Canada. In *Bureau of HIV/AIDS, STD, and TB Update Series* [Online]. Web.

Laforest, M. (1999, January 17). "HIV on rise among aboriginals." *Calgary Herald*, p. A3.

Miller, J. (Ed.). (1992). *Fluid exchanges*. Toronto: University of Toronto Press.

Milton, S. (1990). "TV and skating made for each other." *Today's Skater*, 86.

O'Hara, J. (1988a, February 29). "Looking golden but missing the ring." *Maclean's*, pp. 14–16.

O'Hara, J. (1988b, February). "Superman on skates" [Special Issue]. *Maclean's*, pp. 36–36.

Ordover, N. (1996). Eugenics, the gay gene, and the science of backlash. *Socialist Review*, 26, 125–146.

Patton, C. (1996). *Fatal advice: How safe sex education went wrong*. Durham, NC: Duke University Press.

Prentice. M. (1997, November 19). "Canada 'has lost control over AIDS': Study shows treatment costs soar to $26.4 billion, while epidemic grows." *Ottawa Citizen*, p. A3.

Rayside, D. M., & Linquist, E. A. (1992). Canada: Community activism, federalism, and the new politics of disease. In D. Kirp & R. Bayer (Eds.), *AIDS in the industrialized democracies: Passions, politics and policies* (pp. 49–48). New Brunswick, NJ: Rutgers University Press.

Rose, N. (1999). *Powers of freedom: Reframing political thought*. New York: Cambridge University Press.

Smith, B. (1992, November 23). "Helping buddies through bad times." *The Globe and Mail*, p. D5.

Sturken, M. (1997). *Tangled memories: The Vietnam War, the AIDS epidemic, and the politics of remembering*. Berkeley: University of California Press.

Toneguzzi, M. (1993, October 4). "Skater's sister rallies back." *Calgary Herald*, p. B1.

Toneguzzi, M. "Top figure skater McCall dies at 33." (1991, November 16). *The Toronto Star*, p. Bl.

Treichler, P. (1993). AIDS, gender, and biomedical discourse. In L. Kauffman (Ed.), *American feminist thought at century's end: A reader* (pp. 281–354). Cambridge, MA: Blackwell.

Walmsley, A. (1988, February). "A magical pair: Two Canadian ice dancers are closing in on the reigning Soviets" [Special Issue]. *Maclean's*, pp. 43–44.

Watney, S. (1987). *Policing desire: AIDS, pornography, and the media*. London: Methuen.

Watney, S. (1989). Introduction. In E. Carter & S. Watney (Eds.), *Taking liberties* (pp. 11–58). London: Serpant's Tail.

Wilson-Smith, A. (1997). "Canada and the world: A new poll finds that Canadians are envied and happy" [Online] (*Maclean's* Special Report). Available: http://www. canoe.ca/Macleans/keepers

Zwolinski, M. (1991, November 17). "McCall's death shouldn't set off alarms." *The Toronto Star*, p. Bl.

PART NINE

Media, Popular Culture, and Youth Culture

CHAPTER 28

The "Blood Libel" and the Spectator's Eye in Norwich and Toronto

David Townsend

A gregarious, plucky twelve-year-old boy appears regularly on the streets, working as he can to supplement the resources of his poor but loving family. His routine puts him in contact with unsavoury elements, against whom his innocence and naïveté are a poor match. A stranger meets him and shortly thereafter lures him to a private place with promises of money to be earned. There the ensnarer and his confederates abuse the boy horribly and eventually kill him in an obsessive, orgiastic frenzy. They dispose of the body, but with insufficient stealth. The corpse is subsequently discovered, and the full horrors of what happened are reconstructed with the assistance of a witness to the tortures the boy endured. Clear traces on the victim's body supplement that testimony to his sufferings. Testimony and deduction meet in a narrative that synthesizes the available details, but which also bears, in its repetitions and its speculative tone, the marks of its piecemeal and reconstructive origins. Despite its gaps, the tale apprises an appalled public of the outrage perpetrated by outsiders in their midst. The demands of popular opinion for just retribution are ultimately both heeded and contained by the apparatus of the state. But the child's memory lives on and alerts the public to the dangers of moral contagion presented by the class of social parasites who, if not the boy's actual murderers, are certainly by their very presence the fomenters of all such crimes against the innocent young. The awful but ultimately saving truth is recognized: the boy's death has galvanized the social body into a necessary state of vigilance. His innocent life, it can now be observed, is the price paid to cleanse the social and spiritual life of the community. The child's interment offers a focus in shared ritual for the cleansing recognition of the purity he preserved even unto death, but at the same time it consolidates the memory of the unspeakable and unavenged act that society must never forget.

I have been describing the July 1977 murder of Emanuel Jaques, a shoeshine boy in downtown Toronto, and its aftermath, much as it was described in the voluminous newspaper coverage it received in the weeks after his death and again during the February 1978 trial of four men charged with and subsequently convicted of the crime. But I have also been describing the martyrdom of little William of Norwich in 1144, much as it was described by Thomas of Monmouth, who, beginning in 1149, five years after the boy's death, recorded for posterity the story of his alleged murder at the hands of the Norwich Jews (Jessop and James).

Thomas's biography of William stands not only as the most substantial single hagiographical source of the "blood libel"—the repeated charge that Jews ritually murdered Christian children around Passover—but as its actual point of origin in the West, as Gavin Langmuir has shown (1984). Langmuir and others have intensively scrutinized the text for its witness to conditions in Norwich at the time of its writing, between 1149 and 1172–73.[1] Langmuir, as a historian, demonstrates great concern not so much to establish what actually happened, and did not happen, to William, as to determine who first invented the charge of ritual murder by crucifixion. His conclusion is that it is the invention of the hagiographer Thomas himself. Langmuir acknowledges the deadly power the myth has had in subsequent European culture, at the same time that he points out that Thomas was himself not primarily motivated by hatred of Jews. Mercifully, the text of Thomas of Monmouth exists only in a single copy. But the blood libel narrative that he created spread throughout Europe, staining the lips of Chaucer's Prioress along its path; over the centuries it has cost thousands, if not millions, of lives. Similarly, it is the use to which the dead Emanuel Jaques was put by the political and journalistic establishment of Ontario that concerns me here.

As I wrote the précis of the opening paragraph, I found myself running a rapid relay of memory between Thomas's text and a file of clippings on the murder trial.[2] How many narrative elements could I include in my initial summary of events without reducing one story to a trope of the other? Could I cast a sentence representing the murder(s) that ventriloquized the lurid sensationalism of both accounts and at the same time did not tip the reference in the exclusive direction of either sociopathic sexual license (the Jaques murder) or imputed religious fanaticism (William's martyrdom)? Could I allude to the funeral of Emanuel Jaques at a Portuguese Catholic church in Toronto in language that did not distort the circumstances of the translation of William's body from the woods outside Norwich, where it was first discovered, to the monks' cemetery at the cathedral? Or distort, for that matter, the fact that in William's case I'm not dealing with a single interment, but with an almost ghoulish obsession, even by medieval Christian standards, with repeated translation ceremonies (four in a decade)? Could I mimic the platitudinous metamorphosis of innocent suffering into salvific necessity, without falling off the line into the secularized moralism of WASP Toronto journalism, on the one hand, or into the more narrowly hagiographical tropes of *imitatio Christi*, on the other? Could I, in short, evoke representations of the "degeneracy" of both gay men and Jews, without collapsing one into the other?

And moreover, why would I want to indulge in this exercise? Part of the answer to that is, inevitably, a matter of personal history. I first moved to Toronto in 1977, a few weeks after the Jaques murder, when, in my early twenties, I was still far from entirely out of the closet. A few months earlier, Anita Bryant had "saved" the children of Dade County, Florida, from the prospect of growing up in a society which accorded equal protection under the law on grounds of sexual orientation.[3] In Toronto, the first major city in which I had ever lived, the daily press coverage of the killing and trial offered the murderers of Emanuel Jaques as the most pervasively and powerfully represented of all homosexual men. At the time, I perceived the discourse of those representations as almost seamlessly monologic.

Such perceptions were of course skewed by the terror that discourse held for me. Going back to review the documents a generation later, I remember the terror and despair, but it is also clear that the presentation was as characterized by rupture and internal dissent as is any such apparatus of ideology: it is due to those ruptures and their later valorizations that much has changed in the Canadian politics of sexual orientation over the last two decades (Rayside 105–211). At the time of the murder, the Ontario Human Rights Commission was in fact recommending that Ontario incorporate sexual orientation as a protected category under its human rights code. (The actual passage of that amendment would wait until the mid 1980s, when a Liberal minority government was pushed toward the legislation by the New Democrat opposition with which the government had entered into a coalitional agreement [Rayside 142–43].) But the reportage of dissenting voices to the side, the press's obsessive repetitions of the details of the boy's multiple rape, and of his assailants' repeated botched attempts to kill him, imparted a naturalized energy to a plethora of outraged voices. Those voices called for a clean sweep of the human trash downtown (Grass) and rejected the statutory protection of lifestyles that led to such crimes (Davidson; Hoy; Ross; Shulman; Worthington; "Not so 'Gay'"). The totalizing objectifications of homosexuality and of homosexuals made it clear that I was part of the human trash that needed sweeping up.

The fact is that for the past twenty years, my reading of the blood libel "saints' lives" of murdered little Christian boys has necessarily been a polyphonic one, imbued with intertextual associations not because of the allure of their postmodern vogue, but because those associations are burned into my consciousness. I read the text of Thomas of Monmouth, that opportunistic scum of the twelfth century, much as I read the 1977 and 1978 *Toronto Sun* columns of Claire Hoy.[4] I am not particularly interested in doing justice to the *Weltanschauung* of either.

Of course, I am not the only gay man to make such connections between anti-Semitism and homophobia. In bathhouse raids one Thursday night in Toronto in early February 1981, 150 Toronto police officers swooped down simultaneously with crowbars and sledgehammers on five establishments and arrested some 286 gay men. Immediately thereafter, a local gay activist compared the operation to the *Kristallnacht*.[5] I clearly recall a placard at one of the demonstrations after the raid, though I cannot find any documentation of it now, that read "We are the new Jews." The connection is hardly surprising, given the adoption of the pink triangle from the Nazi death camps as probably the most widespread symbol of the queer liberation movement. To be sure, there are substantial dangers in an untheorized assertion of such connections. Pragmatically, such aphorisms can easily trigger—have repeatedly triggered—divisive games of "More oppressed than thou."[6] And the elision of profound historical differences between the oppressions of Jews and of gay men does nothing to further a politically and culturally useful analysis of either.

The fact of my hermeneutic predicament remains, however, and it is clear from the connections drawn by other gay men between their oppression and anti-Semitism that I am not alone at my peculiar interpretive intersection.[7] That my intersection is large enough to accommodate others as well is what I wished to demonstrate with my initial fence-sitting simultaneous paraphrase of the two murder stories. And my project in this chapter has to do, if not with faith seeking understanding, then with the intuitions of lived experience seeking theory. That search involves two overlapping movements. The first might be thought of as the "what" of the two narratives' rhetoric—a delineation of the unsettling structural resemblances between them. The second might be seen as the "how" and "why" of their rhetoric—a consideration of the cultural work, in radically different milieus, that those parallel narrative trajectories appear to perform.

In pursuing the first of those movements, I confine myself, unlike Langmuir, to issues of discursive formations. Somebody murdered a boy named William and left the body in Thorpe Wood just before Easter of 1144. The four men accused and convicted of Emanuel's murder certainly killed him above a body-rub parlor on Yonge Street in the summer of 1977. But I want to steer clear of the events themselves and their status as facts. I want to focus, rather, on the cultural power of the narratives constructed around the putative givens of the events. That power has been as substantial as it is insidious.

In pursuing the second of my aims, I spend more time than does Langmuir on the "how" as opposed to the "what" of the narrative qua narrative. Langmuir adumbrates this question, when he remarks on the unusually scopic quality of the medieval text's rhetoric: "We observe William's disappearance with a stranger who takes him to a Jew's house, we watch him being tortured and crucified by Jews, we listen to the murderers talking among themselves about how to dispose of the body, and we are told how they did dispose of it and how it was found" (1984, 828). But this comment aside, Langmuir passes fairly lightly over the pragmatics of Thomas of Monmouth's rhetoric. It is with such considerations in mind that I read Thomas's text against the newspaper coverage of the Jaques trial. How does each text situate the reader in relation to the chimerical perpetrators of the murder? What relation does the all-seeing eye that witnesses William's, or Emanuel's, torture behind closed doors bear toward the violence the text represents? Is that relation one of passive observation, or of active though vicarious participation in the violence that the text ostensibly deplores? And how, moreover, do the public rituals recounted in, and as, the history of the cult's development provide mechanisms whereby such vicarious experiences can be articulated in a socially visible form?

Some readers might entertain doubts about the commensurability of a medieval saint's life and a file of newspaper clippings. I read the collected coverage of the Jaques trial as a single and very vaguely bounded whole, a text that bled out into the Toronto communities that consumed it and absorbed again the discursive energies those communities fed back into it. If reading such a ragtag file of fragments as a whole is problematic, one should keep in mind that the wholeness of Thomas of Monmouth's text, for its part, is also problematic. Thomas composed it over a period of more than twenty years. The first book is datable to 1149, Books 2–6 to 1154–55, and Book 7 to 1172–73. Book 2 is largely a pointed response to unnamed opponents of William's claims to sanctity. Much of the energy that feeds Thomas's vivid imaginings of childhood innocence and Jewish guilt must surely have been absorbed into the text from the oral circulations of Norwich in the years before Thomas's arrival there in the late 1140s. The impetus for the central five books is clearly drawn in large part from the reception of the text's first book. The intertextual vagaries that blur the boundaries of Thomas's text are more submerged, but no less problematic, than those surrounding the coverage of the Jaques murder and trial, and it is with this in mind that I read the two narratives as comparable documents.

The two stories' shared elements begin with the memories of characteristic good cheer projected back onto the lives of both boys. News of the discovery of Emanuel Jaques's body first broke on August 1, 1977, four days after the boy's disappearance from the Yonge Street "sin strip" opposite a vast, newly erected downtown shopping concourse, the Eaton Centre. The boy had last been seen, the front page story in the *Toronto Star* said, "walking away from Yonge St. with a man who offered to pay him $35 an hour to help move camera equipment. He had been polishing shoes on the strip for about a month with his brother ... and a friend ... The brothers used to hand over their $35-a-night earnings to their parents. About 5:30 p.m. last Thursday a man dressed in overalls talked to the boys, bought them hamburgers and asked Manuel *(sic)* if he would like to work with him ... 'let me earn the money, let me earn the money,' Manuel cried" (Thomas).

Several interesting parallels emerge with the story of William even at this early stage in the ongoing construction of the Jaques narrative. Emanuel's innocence, soon to become a trope of explicitly hagiographical force, is already adumbrated in the explanation that the enterprising young brothers hand their earnings over to their parents every night: Emanuel's rovings in the heart of the downtown core are thus drawn into the cohesive circle of his family life. The trope of Emanuel's innocence builds rapidly in the coverage of the case. The next day in the *Star*, a page 2 article begins, "Emanuel Jaques was an outgoing 12-year-old who loved to make friends and who trusted everyone—and that led him to his death" (Bullock, Dalby, and Norris). The same piece adds later that everyone interviewed agreed that the boy's lack of street smarts had rendered him vulnerable. This innocence was extended, moreover, to Emanuel's entire Portuguese immigrant family: the article suggests they remained unaware—after several years of living in a downtown public housing project—of the true nature of the place they by all accounts allowed a twelve-year-old to roam unsupervised for hours at a time. An interview with the mother of Emanuel's friend and fellow shoeshine boy Shane McLean was reported as follows:

> Mrs. McLean asked the Jaques' 17-year-old daughter, Valdemira, if her mother understood about homosexuals and the possible danger her missing son might be in.
>
> "She tried to tell her mother about it in Portuguese, and she didn't understand. She'd never heard of it, didn't know what the daughter was saying. That explains how Emanuel knew so little. One of the first things Shane said to me when he explained about the man taking Emanuel away was: 'Mom, the guy was queer.'" (Bullock et al.)

The same article records testimonies by family and neighbours to the cheerful obedience of a child who did "all kinds of chores, but never asked for money." The same day, the tabloid *Toronto Sun* began its article with a further paean to his cheerful and family-centred obedience (Scanlon).

The parallels with the representations of little William's precocious virtues are clear: they amount to a shared hagiographical topos. Though of course more secularized—unlike William, for example, Emanuel does not fast Mondays, Wednesdays, and Fridays—Emanuel's virtues are equally in line with contemporary expectation and serve to heighten the pathos of his death. At the same time, accompanying an innocence that leads directly to vulnerability is the understated but clearly visible issue of economic pressure in both stories. Dynamics of wealth and poverty in each case justify the innocent's traffic with unsavoury elements, resisted though these associations are by his family. In William's case, his apprenticeship as a tanner brings him into repeated contacts with Norwich Jews, who favour him and subsequently mark him out for his death of ritualized anti-Christian mockery. (The stench and proximity to dead flesh involved in the work of tanners adds to the general sense that William belongs to the working poor, much as Emanuel works in conditions his family finds undesirable.) William terminates these transactions with Jews under orders from his uncle Godwin and from one Wulward, with whom the boy resides in Norwich (Jessop and James, I. iii). Emanuel, likewise, at least as reported a day or two later in the press coverage, shines shoes on Yonge Street despite familial resistance: the *Globe and Mail*, tradition- ally the most staid and ostensibly the most respectable of the Toronto dailies, offers the observation on August 2 that "[h]is parents did not entirely approve, but peer pressure encouraged Manuel to spend his summer holidays shining shoes on Yonge Street" (York and Lipovenko). Emanuel's mother is quoted at the beginning of a *Star* article the next day as saying, "I didn't realize how bad a place it was. Close it down for all mothers to protect their sons" (Dalby).

In William's story, but not in Emanuel's, we observe a direct confrontation between the boy's family and the stranger who lures him to his death. William is taken off by a man who claims to be in the employ of the archdeacon's cook. William's mother resists the man's requests and Wil- liam's own entreaties—"Let me earn the money, let me earn the money," we might well imagine him saying at this point—but she subsequently capitulates, conquered if not convinced both by the boy's entreaties and by the three shillings the ensnarer pays to her (Jessop and James, I. iv). William's aunt subsequently meets the ensnarer in William's company when they reach Nor- wich; she dispatches her daughter to follow them from afar. The daughter sees them turn into a Jew's house. By contrast, Emanuel's brother and friend last see him leave the restaurant where all three have met the ensnarer, after all three have hoped to get in on the lucrative prospect of a few hours' work that he offers.

Compensating for this gap in the Jaques narrative is the increasing emphasis on Emanuel's mother's altogether intelligible regrets. The August 3 *Star* article cited above reports, "'My chil- dren have been told not to go anywhere far from home,' she said. 'I feel terrible. I made a mistake, a terrible mistake,' she said quietly. She said her husband Valdemiro was literally 'sick with grief in his bedroom'" (Dalby).

The dynamics of familial grief are likewise bound up with the communal pity and rage that follow the discoveries of both murders. In both instances, the excessive quality of feminine reac- tions figures largely. Upon hearing of William's death, his aunt recalls a dream she had had the week before Palm Sunday, in which the Jews tore off her right leg. She then collapses in a swoon, from which she recovers only to fall into protracted, unrestrainable lamentations. William's mother weeps and wails in the streets like a mad woman, denouncing the guilt of the Jews in public places, until the populace at large begins to cry out unanimously that "the Jews ought to be utterly destroyed as constant enemies of the Christian name and the Christian religion" (Jessop and James, I. xiv–xv).

A particularly striking image in this regard from the Jaques coverage is the photograph pub- lished by the *Sun* in its coverage of Emanuel's funeral (Cosway). The caption reads, "A cousin of Emanuel's, Dianna Correira, is carried from graveside after fainting." In the photograph, a young woman is held chest-high by a sober-faced young man in three-quarters view. She is wearing a dark dress; her head, shown in profile, hangs back limp from his arm, which supports her shoulders; his right hand curves over her breast just under her right arm. Her left shoulder is slightly higher, making of the modest neckline of her dress a dramatic V that focuses our attention back onto the grim expression of the dark, long-haired, photogenic man who carries her. The background is filled with out-of-focus foliage and the faces of other mourners. Under an accompanying photo on the same page, we are told, "Weeping mother Maria Jaques is helped from the church by family friends." She is viewed from above, her darkened eyes visible under her veil; her left hand is grasped by a man in a plaid jacket. On her right, an older, soberly dressed woman in glasses holds her hand. Each of her supporters has an arm around her shoulder. The gaze of all three is directed at a single object (the coffin?) to their right.

The cries for vengeance against the Jews that are taken up at women's instigation by the people of Norwich are echoed in the protests and petitions organized before and after the Jaques funeral. A photo in the August 4 *Globe and Mail,* the day of the funeral and the day before its coverage, shows protesters from Regent Park, the public housing project where the Jaques family lived, carrying signs that read "Kill Sex Perverts. Jail's Too Good," and less prominently in the background, "Capital Punishment Again! Down with Body Rub Joints!" (Porambo, 4 Aug.). The next day, in the *Globe's* coverage of the funeral, columnist Dick Beddoes reports a petition being handed around the funeral at St. Agnes's Church by Austin Raymond Miller of the Regent Park Community Improvement Association. "The petition was headed 'STAMP OUT GAYS AND BODY RUBS' and Miller said he had 1,000 names on it. 'I'll get more', he said, 'and send it to Mayor Crombie.'"

Beddoes's same column is worth further attention. It contains an uncanny echo of the dream of William's aunt: "Lose a child you've loved and it's like amputating a limb," Beddoes observes with a level of journalistic detachment characteristic of much of the coverage. "You keep going, but there is less of you." Beddoes's column furthermore ends with one of the earliest, and probably the most explicit, assertions of Emanuel's canonization: "So young—12. Saint Agnes was also young—13 when she was murdered in Rome in 304 A.D. for rejecting a suitor. Martyrs in death before they knew very much about life." Ron Porambo's *Globe* coverage, carried as well by the *Vancouver Sun* on August 9, ended its account of the funeral with a roster of collapsing mourners including Emanuel's father, his sister, and finally his mother. Porambo concludes, "Then the funeral that had turned into a virtual public passion play was finally over and done with" (Porambo, 9 Aug.). These point-blank assertions of canonization in fact summed up the impulse toward redemptive teleology that had already been indulged in a statement by Alderman Joseph Piccininni in the August 2 *Star* that "Emanuel's death is a 'terrible price' to have to pay to show that the strip needs cleaning up" (McNenley and Barnes 3). Such impulses had also already informed suggestions by Premier William Davis, Ontario Attorney General Roy McMurtry, and Toronto Mayor David Crombie that Emanuel's death was providing the impetus to deal with the long-standing problem of the Yonge Street strip ("Boy's death prompts government action"; "Toronto boy homosexual orgy victim").

Finally, all coverage of the Jaques murder and trial, virtually without exception, places one man first among the four perpetrators—Saul David Betesh. Betesh was in fact the man who went to the police and shortly thereafter confessed to the murder. He is also the only one among them whose given names distinctly suggest the possibility that he is a Jew, and whose surname sounds distinctly other than Anglo-Germanic.[8]

What to make of these and other narrative parallels between Thomas of Monmouth's text and the Jaques coverage? How conscious can such correspondences have been? Was the Jaques coverage in fact shaped by the broadly diffuse intertextual valences of the blood libel? If it was, did the coverage itself contrive such correspondences, or were the behaviours of the principals themselves shaped in real life by those intertexts? (As a specific example, did Ron Porambo gratuitously construct the funeral as a "virtual public passion play," or was it so lived by those who attended—Emanuel's photogenically fainting cousin and the rest of his family, the Toronto Portuguese community, Auxiliary Bishop Aloysius Ambrozic [now, incidentally, Cardinal Archbishop of Toronto], whom Dick Beddoes quotes praying over the body?) And if one can make a case for the construction of Emanuel as a blood libel saint, can one go even further and establish specific intentional parallels with the life of William? The answer to this latter question is far more likely to be negative—though William's biography is the source of all later blood libel narratives, it exists in only one copy: the breadth of its influence is itself a testimony to the power of texts to proliferate beyond their ostensible boundaries into their cultures at large (Langmuir 1984; Dundes; Hsia). But even so, I do find interesting parallels not only in the narrative sub-stance of the William and Emanuel stories, but in what I can only call the rhetorical pragmatics of the gaze in the two texts. Here I shift to engage principally the second of my inquiry's two movements, the rhetorical "how" and "why" of the texts.

I have already touched on one example of these pragmatics, the narrative importance of women's grief in the two accounts. Thomas of Monmouth is particularly striking in this regard. He describes the feminine weakness of William's mother and aunt in terms that the conventions of monastic antifeminism would normally lead us to take as straightforwardly repudiative. In fact, we might be somewhat surprised, coming to the end of his account of William's mother's very publicly displayed grief, that the author is not preparing us for a final comment of cen-sure upon such excesses. Instead, the rage against the Jews incited by her intuitive accusations becomes the horizon of naturalized expectation: it pervades the entire account of how the Jews escaped with relative impunity from the consequences of their crime. Thomas, in other words, maintains the disembodied distance of his own gaze from the feminized excess of mourning. Yet at the same time he incorporates the energy of that irrational and feminized surfeit of emo-tion into the anti-Semitic ideological apparatus he constructs.[9] No ordinary practitioner of mis-ogyny, Thomas manages both to objectify women as hysterics and to appropriate that hysteria into his own ostensibly gender-neutral worldview.

The gaze of the Jaques coverage deploys its representations of grief according to analogous patterns. The familial sorrow and anger described by Dick Beddoes and Ron Porambo is the pathetic object of journalistic scrutiny. Representations of the behaviour of an enraged com-munity are likewise held at writerly distance. In a demonstration by 10,000 to 15,000 people covered in the *Star* on August 9, reportage takes the homophobia of the crowd as its object without absorbing that homophobia directly into the writerly voice. Victoria Stevens's article quotes, among others, a woman who demands, "Are the queers and prostitutes more important than these people? Are the perverts running Yonge St.?" But precisely the same sentiments emerge naturalized as they spread from news items to the editorial columns and investigative reporting of all three Toronto dailies. Claire Hoy's *Sun* column of August 10 was particularly noteworthy for its homophobic virulence, as would be his later pieces in the ensuing months, but the two more comfortably middle-brow dailies voiced similar sentiments, albeit in more moderate language—sentiments Upper Canadian respectability might view as more foreign if displayed by fainting, shouting Portuguese mourners or protesters. In the *Star* on August 5, Dennis Braithwaite delivered a lengthy jeremiad, justifying his remarks as a response to an editorial published in the journal *Content*. As a furious Braithwaite summarized, "what is agitating the editor of *Content,* and what he devotes most of the magazine's limited space to, is an outraged attack on Toronto newspapers for their alleged denial of the rights of homosexuals. Virtue itself of vice must pardon beg." Braithwaite goes on to praise Anita Bryant for her crusade against gay rights: "Anita thought she had God on her side, forgetting that liberals long ago buried God and dethroned His teachings with a simple dictum: Every evil to excess." A somewhat more restrained but still clearly exasperated Scott Young began an editorial in the *Globe* on August 8 by reporting a conversation which "tacked around from consideration of last Monday's horror, the shoeshine boy murder, to distantly related subjects—such as whether decloseted gays (publicly declared homosexuals) should be allowed to teach school." He concluded, "The gays should tell the nuts among them—the ones who want to teach their branchline sex to children or youths—to shut up. They will never get the human rights they do deserve, if they insist on the one about taking it into the schools like a bunch of gay Billy Grahams."

It is the comfortable liberalism of Young's piece that in fact strikes me as in some sense closest to the rhetorical double play of Thomas's deployment of reported hysteria. Young casts himself as the exasperated holder of the middle ground, graciously conceding the eventual appropriateness of gay rights, while deferring any positive move toward the justice of immediate enfranchisement. His deferral of justice is implicitly rationalized on the grounds of precisely those connections to Emanuel's murder which he superficially claims are of the most distant sort: it would be immoderate, after all, to ban discrimination in the face of the level of furor surrounding the murder, particularly since militant homosexuals have no better sense than to rub salt into the social wound.

The gaze that operates in the Jaques coverage and in William's biography is most powerfully focused, perhaps, in the central events of the narratives that I leapt over in my comparative reading. I need to backtrack to the accounts of the murders themselves.

William is lodged comfortably with the Jews for a day after his arrival in their company. The next day he is bound and tortured with a teazle placed in his mouth and a knotted cord wrapped around his head and neck. Later his head is shaved and punctured with numerous thorns. Then the Jews crucify him in a peculiarly unstraightforward fashion. This they do, Thomas of Monmouth tells us, in order to leave marks on the body that would point to Christians rather than Jews as the perpetrators. Finally, a deep wound to his heart from the left side kills him. His murderers pour boiling water over the body to cleanse and close the wounds. The Jews decide that disposing of the body near their own lodgings is dangerous and agree to carry him outside the city to Thorpe Wood. En route, they meet one Aelward Ded, whose suspicions are aroused and who, upon examining the bag they carry over one of their horses, discovers that it contains a human body. The Jews flee into the wood, and Aelward returns home, saying nothing due to the injunctions of the Sheriff, who silences him in order to protect the Jews. (Only on his deathbed, five years later, will he reveal that he had encountered the murderers as they were transporting the little saint's body.) By a complex series of miraculously aided discoveries and rediscoveries, burials and exhumations, William is recovered and a month after his death translated to the monks' cemetery at the cathedral.

For the full details of Emanuel's death, we have to leap from the initial coverage of the murder investigation in August 1977 to the coverage of the trial of Saul David Betesh, Robert Wayne Kribs, Josef Woods, and Werner Gruener in February 1978. Emanuel is taken to an apartment above a body rub parlor. There his ensnarer Betesh and the other three take photographs of Emanuel for about an hour. At first the boy is clothed. He is persuaded gradually to remove his clothing. The men then tell him they want sexually explicit "action shots." According to the testimony reported in some of the accounts (O'Hara), Emanuel is at first reluctant but cooperates for a while after being offered an extra $20. (In most repetitions of the testimony this last detail is omitted.) Later the boy is repeatedly raped, in an orgy that lasts about twelve hours. The men decide that it is impossible to let the boy go and the decision is made to kill him. Betesh tries for several minutes to strangle him with a length of plastic stretch cord. Woods then suggests he place a pillow over his face so that Betesh doesn't have to look at him. Finally, Betesh and Kribs drown Emanuel in a sink. The murderers go out to purchase a shovel and bury the boy, but the ground behind the building is too hard to dig and the corpse is left in a garbage bag on the roof. Several days later, Betesh goes to the police with a story that at first suggests his own innocence. In the course of the interrogation, however, he soon confesses his central role in the murder.

What distinguishes the life of William of Norwich from most later blood libel accounts is the graphic detail to which the reader is subjected. We do not merely learn that the boy is murdered. We are privy to every detail, with a gruesomeness that puts off a great many modern readers who can by contrast read Chaucer's Prioress's Tale with relatively unruffled sensibilities. And we are privy to the sight of the murder not only in the extended chapter of Book 1 which describes it, but again in its rehearsal in Book 2, where Thomas obsessively accumulates proofs of the guilt of the Jews. Most spectacularly, we are told that a Christian woman serving the Jews beheld through a half-closed door the body of William strung up between beams in the room where he died; but she dared not report the sign to anyone (Jessop and James, II.ix). The repetitive detail with which William's ordeal is described is recapitulated as by a kind of extended montage, in the proofs of his martyrdom in Book 2, and less palpably by memorial association in the repeated translations with which the body is brought out into the sight of men, four times in a decade.

The Jaques coverage is even more obsessive in its repetition of the gory details, both after the murder and during the trial the next winter. One might well expect this, given the commercial exigencies of journalism. I am nevertheless inclined to see the horrified fascination by which the Jaques coverage binds its reader to the text as deploying the abject pleasures of its gaze more insidiously than, say, the coverage of the Jeffrey Dahmer murders.[10] The journalistic rehearsal of Emanuel's multiple rape, his botched strangulation and eventual drowning in a sink are like the "money shots" of film and video pornography, repeated from different angles, sometimes at real speed, sometimes in slow motion. As with pornography, what drives the viewer's fascination is the fact that the visual sequence somehow stands in for an unconscious but altogether crucial narrative pattern.

I propose that the urgency driving these representations is the ability of both Thomas's text and the Jacques coverage to stand as "faultline narratives," to use Alan Sinfeld's term—stories that can elide the contradictions in the cultural dispositions they purport to represent (3–5). Here, finally, I focus more on the "why" than on the "what" and "how" of comparative rhetoric. As to the ideological contradictions that made the blood libel legends culturally useful in the high and late Middle Ages, I find useful the work of Kathleen Biddick and, once again, of Gavin Langmuir.

Biddick has traced some of the cultural predicaments at the heart of medieval Christian piety that may have displaced themselves into accusations of ritual murder against the Jews. Specifically, she suggests that the central importance of the Eucharist for medieval Christendom, and consequent upon that importance, the affective pieties of medieval women around the consumption and refusal of food, and around Christ's body and blood as food, dangerously juxtaposed the normative body with the excessive, in a way that threatened to break down the constitutive distinctions between Self and Other upon which the culture relied. As she puts it:

> The Eucharist was good to think with, and it guaranteed the symbolic order of medieval Europe. It was both a "classical" body in the Bakhtinian sense, elevated, static, and monumental, and a "grotesque" body, broken, bleeding, excessive, maternal, paternal, a body that upset any fixed gender binary, a fluid body that troubled any container. It was a body that was distributed across different—and noncommensurate—textual, material, and visual realms. Christians fantasized intensely both the pollution and the purification of the Eucharist because of its ambivalent position as a border phenomenon. (153)

Biddick argues that the desecration of the bodies of Christian children represented in blood libel narratives constitutes an abjection of precisely those cultural predicaments created by the dominant discourses on the body of Christ in iconography, sacrament, and affective piety. She adduces in support of her argument the fact that noteworthy excrescences of Eucharistic piety frequently cropped up in the same times and places as blood libel accusations and rumors of Jewish desecrations of the Host (147-52).

Langmuir (1990) also addresses the kinds of pressures that lead people to adopt irrational hatred of the other in their midst as an alleviation of unbearable tension, but in contrast with Biddick's work, his argument proceeds in broader categories of the phenomenology of religion. Langmuir is at pains to establish a taxonomy for the representation of Jewish abjection. He argues for a threefold distinction between confessional opposition to Jewish beliefs, acceptance of negative representations of Jewish practice and identity due to inadequate empirical data, and irrational hostility in discourse and practice as a defence against rational objections to a belief system (or dominant cultural praxis) that one hypothetically could entertain but instead represses: "It can be argued that anti-Judaism is a nonrational reaction to overcome nonrational doubts, while anti-Semitism is an irrational reaction to repressed rational doubts" (276). By a different path, Langmuir arrives at territory also explored by Biddick:

> "The Jews" had become the great symbol of hidden menaces of all kinds within Christendom. In a rapidly changing Europe suffering from economic depression, social discontent, ecclesiastical divisions, bubonic plague, and endemic and devastating wars, many Europeans were prey to lurking doubts that sapped their self-confidence. They struggled to repress them but remained anxious, and many gave expression to their unease by attributing to Jews evil characteristics that made the goodness of Christians obvious by contrast and attributed their problems to an external source. (303)

As Langmuir suggests, the deployments of the blood libel from the twelfth to the twentieth centuries have embraced and attempted to contain a wide range of tensions. What Langmuir says of the need to expel doubts that might well occur about the cultural and economic dynamics of a society can serve as a starting point for comparing the cultural logic of the Norwich and Toronto narratives.

Among the pressing realities that the canonization of Emanuel Jaques elided was the economic deterioration of downtown Yonge Street in the heart of Toronto during the 1970s. The district had earlier functioned as a viable commercial neighbourhood of local businesses selling a range of ordinary wares and servicing residential streets not far distant. Yvonne Chi-Ying Ng has documented the pressures placed on this local community. Yonge Street's emergence as the sex strip decried in the Jaques coverage had been proceeding for some years. Chief among the economic pressures that destroyed the viability of the street's earlier culture was the speculative rise in land values and rents from 1972 through 1974, as land parcels were assembled for the construction of a hulking shopping mall, the Eaton Centre, in the midst of the city (77–78).

For all the representations of Emanuel's loving family, of the cohesive working-class multiculturalism of his neighbourhood, and of the wider but close-knit Portuguese community of Toronto, all those social configurations stood in jeopardy, as did the economic base on which 1970s Toronto had relied. At the same time, Emanuel's work as a shoeshine boy was, ironically, itself an index of the economic shifts that the cooption of the neighborhood for large-scale economic development had effected. He was himself one of those marginalized denizens of the street whose presence representatives of "respectable" businesses in the area found objectionable. Ng's study traces the deployment of the Jaques coverage as a mechanism to produce public consent in support of a cleanup campaign that such figures, supported by the mayor of Toronto, had periodically advocated for several years.

If homosexual murderers of little boys, and by synecdochic extension all queers, became a widely adopted object of enraged denunciation in late-1970s Toronto, the dynamics of that hatred were surely various. But the Eaton Centre stood—stands—as a palpable coordinate of the social pressures that energized a significant share of that hatred.[11] With that, I come full circle to the shamelessly personal set of associations with which I began, by connecting the landscape of downtown Toronto with that of twelfth-century Norwich. The Norwich Jewry lay in the so-called New Burg, the twelfth-century settlement beyond the Norman castle at the southwest limit cf the original Saxon town (Jessop and James, xlv–xlix). Norwich Castle thus stood in the midst of a vastly transformed and bustling twelfth-century city, perhaps the most palpable coordinate of the pressures that shaped life in that economically and culturally tumultuous time. Anti-Semitism offered Thomas's contemporary readers a way to expel a plethora of intolerable contradictions in their lives. In the twelfth as in the twentieth century, hatred, oppression, and murder were part of the practice of everyday life. But against the vagaries of texts, and their uses, some monuments to power stand as givens above our lives, mute and guiltless, beyond the rage of those who read the world as its text is transmitted to them.[12]

NOTES

1 See Langmuir for his revision of M. R. James's earlier dating of the entire text to 1172–73 (1984, 838–40).

2 All citations from periodicals are drawn from the holdings of daily press clippings in the Canadian Lesbian and Gay Archives in Toronto, whose staff I wish to thank for their help.

3 The referendum, held on June 7, 1977, repealed by a margin of 69 to 31 per cent a Dade County ordinance which had prohibited discrimination on the basis of "affectional or sexual preference" in the areas of housing, public accommodations, and employment (Hamburg 1).

4 Some of the choicest examples of Hoy's homophobic vitriol were in fact generated not by the story of the Jaques murder, but by the December 1977 raids on the offices of *The Body Politic,* a radical gay liberation journal published in Toronto. But in the peroration of the August 10, 1977, editorial already cited. Hoy can be seen moving toward a wholesale appropriation of homophobia as the substance of his professional output: "They complain they haven't been getting the press they deserve, I agree. Until recently, the coverage they got was far too soft, accepting their line about how wonderful gay life is when in fact it's not. It's unnatural and sick. Period. They want to institutionalize it, to have it taught in the schools, and thanks to lunkhead organizations like the Ontario Human Rights Commission they appeared to be making progress. But not now. Not with public sentiment swinging against them. There's no way [Ontario premier] Billy Davis and his bunch are going to touch the OHRC recommendations giving gays all sorts of rights and privileges they think they deserve."

5 The raids took place on February 5 and were followed immediately by protests, which continued with mounting attendance and escalating possibilities of violence through the summer. The protests focused on the trials of the men charged as "found-ins" and "keepers," and on the anniversary of the raids. Coverage of the first of the demonstrations and retrospective coverage of the raids themselves was carried by various regional editions of the *Globe and Mail* on February 7, 1981 (Mulgrew). The comparison to the *Kristallnacht* was reported elsewhere in the *Globe and Mail* on the same day as it was being made by George Hislop, a Toronto gay activist (and bathhouse proprietor). One sign carried in the February 7 protest read "Liars, bigots, Nazis: Toronto cops" (Mulgrew, "1,500 demonstrators," Toronto edition). Comprehensive coverage of the raids and their aftermath appeared in *The Body Politic,* beginning with the March 1981 issue. That coverage included a more direct quotation of George Hislop's remarks: "It was midnight, February 6—just 24 hours after what George Hislop has called the gay equivalent of the 'Crystal Night in Nazi Germany—when the Jews found out where they were really at'" (Hannon 9). (*Kristallnacht*—usually translated as "The Night of Broken Glass"—is the name given to the anti-Jewish pogrom organized by the Nazis in Germany and Austria on the night

of November 9–10, 1938. For specifics, see the Museum of Tolerance's informative webpage at <http://www.wiesenthal.com/mot/moths.htm#kristalnacht>.)

6 Hislop's comment, for example, produced an outraged refutation of any similarities between the circumstances of German Jews and Canadian gays (Jonas).

7 In a more directly academic context, John Boswell alludes to the historical parallels between the social status of gays and of Jews and immediately qualifies those parallels (16–17). Boswell's observation leaves me with the impression that he, too, grasped the connection as both palpable and strangely protean—in short, as a matter of intuition.

8 Betesh was the adopted son of Lillian and James Betesh of Toronto. "The Beteshes ... at the time ran a highly successful linen-importing business ... When a physician they knew and trusted approached them with a Jewish male child who had, he said, a very healthy background, they didn't hesitate [to adopt the child]" (Williams).

9 I use the term anti-Semitism here, despite the historical gap between the medieval blood libel and the modern secular anti-Semitism of the nineteenth and twentieth centuries, as Langmuir has defined it, as a scapegoating of Jews to compensate for the intolerable contradictions in a dominant belief system (Langmuir 1990, esp. ch. 14). My understanding of ideology draws on current appropriations and critiques of Althusser's model as outlined in "Ideology and Ideological State Apparatuses," notably those by Silverman and Sinfeld. Silverman assimilates Althusser's model to post-Lacanian feminist conceptions of the constitution of the subject. Sinfeld, following Raymond Williams over Althusser, is concerned to allow for a literary reading practice that both critiques the ideological imbrication of literature and allows for the possibility of resistant readings: such readings generate potentially counterhegemonic discourses out of the ruptures and gaps in the text's ideological surface.

10 Jeffrey Dahmer was the Milwaukee man charged and convicted in 1992 for the killing and mutilation of seventeen young—mainly Asian and African-American—men.

11 The contrast between the Eaton Centre and its surrounding streetscape, incidentally, has not diminished in the past two decades. Complaints about the seediness of the street continue, and a redevelopment project currently underway aims to create a more open (and sanitized) space—dubbed Dundas Square—more or less exactly on the site of the Jaques murder.

12 Robin Metcalfe's play *The Civilization of a Shoeshine Boy* treats the connections between the Jaques murder and the pressures of urban redevelopment. It was produced by Buddies in Bad Times Theatre in Toronto in June of 1993. It remains unpublished.

REFERENCES

Beddoes, Dick. "In Sorrow and Anger." Toronto *Globe and Mail* 5 Aug. 1977: 8.

Biddick, Kathleen. "Genders, Bodies, Borders: Technologies of the Visible." *The Shock of Medievalism*. Durham: Duke University Press, 1998. 135–62. Reprinted from *Speculum* 68 (1993): 389–418.

Boswell, John. *Christianity, Social Tolerance, and Homosexuality: Gay People in Western Europe from the Beginning of the Christian Era to the Fourteenth Century*. Chicago: University of Chicago Press, 1980.

"Boy's Death Prompts Government Action." *Montreal Star* 3 Aug. 1977: A2.

Braithwaite, Dennis. "Was Puritan Repression Really so Bad?" *Toronto Star* 5 Aug. 1977: E5.

Bullock, Helen, Paul Dalby, and Dave Norris. "Emanuel's Trust Led to his Death Neighbors Say." *Toronto Star* 2 Aug. 1977: 2.

Cosway, John. "A Farewell to Slain Boy." Photos by Jac Holland. *Toronto Sun* 5 Aug. 1977: 32.

Dalby, Paul. "Rip Down 'Evil' Yonge Sin Strip Boy's Mom Says." *Toronto Star* 3 Aug. 1977: 1.

Davidson, True. "Guy-wires." *Toronto Sun* 11 Aug. 1977: n pag.

Dundes, Alan, ed. *The Blood Libel Legend: A Casebook in Anti-Semitic Folklore.* Madison: University of Wisconsin Press, 1991.

Grass, Jennifer. "'Close the Trash' on Yonge Strip Woman, 74, Urges." *Toronto Star* 2 Aug. 1977: 2.

Hamburg, Harvey. "Anita Takes Miami; Gays Fight On." *The Body Politic* 35 (July/Aug. 1977): 1 & 12.

Hannon, Gerald. "Taking it to the Streets." *The Body Politic* 71 (Mar. 1981): 9, 12, & 16.

Hsia, R. Po-Chia. *The Myth of Ritual Murder: Jews and Magic in Reformation Germany.* New Haven: Yale University Press, 1988.

Hoy, Claire. "Gay Whining Falls on Deaf Ears." *Toronto Sun* 10 Aug. 1977: 16.

Jessop, Augustus and M. R. James, eds. *The Life and Miracles of St. William of Norwich.* Cambridge: Cambridge University Press, 1896.

Jonas, George. "Operation Bathhouse." *Toronto Life* May 1981: 35.

Langmuir, Gavin. "Thomas of Monmouth: Detector of Ritual Murder." *Speculum* 59 (1984): 820–46.

Langmuir, Gavin. *History, Religion, and Antisemitism.* Berkeley: University of California Press, 1990.

McNenley, Pat and Alan Barnes. "'Terrible Tragedy', Davis Says." *Toronto Star* 2 Aug. 1977: 1 & 3.

Mulgrew, Ian. "1,500 Demonstrators in March to Protest Police Raids on Baths." *Globe and Mail* 7 Feb. 1981, Toronto ed.: 1; "Homosexuals, Lawyers Claiming Harassment over Bathhouse Raids." British Columbia ed.: 2.

Ng, Yvonne Chi-Ying. "Ideology, Media, and Moral Panics: An Analysis of the Jaques Murder." M.A. Thesis. University of Toronto (Centre of Criminology), 1981.

"Not so 'Gay.'" *Toronto Sun* 11 Aug. 1977: 10.

O'Hara, Jane. "Boy Ravaged for 2 Hours: 'We Couldn't Let Him Go.'" *Toronto Sun* 14 Feb. 1978: 3.

Porambo, Ron. "The Neighbours March for Manuel." Toronto *Globe and Mail* 4 Aug. 1977: 4.

Porambo, Ron "The Day They Buried Emanuel." *Vancouver Sun* 9 Aug. 1977: 5.

Rayside, David. *On the Fringe: Gays and Lesbians in Politics.* Ithaca: Cornell University Press, 1998.

Ross, M. "Sacrificed on Altar of Civil Rights." *Toronto Star* 9 Aug. 1977: B5.

Scanlon, Kevin. "Portraits—TRAGEDY ... AND SLEAZE." *Toronto Sun* 2 Aug. 1977: 34–35.

Shulman, Morton. "Never One to Stay out of a Fight." *Toronto Sun* 9 Aug. 1977: 11.

Silverman, Kaja. *Male Subjectivity at the Margins.* New York: Routledge, 1992.

Sinfeld, Alan. *Cultural Politics—Queer Reading.* Philadelphia: University of Pennsylvania Press, 1994.

Stevens, Victoria. "Angry Crowd Seeks Revenge for Emanuel." *Toronto Star* 9 Aug. 1977: 1.

Thomas, Gwyn (Jocko). "Shoeshine Boy Found Slain Suspect Held." *Toronto Star* 1 Aug. 1977: 1.

"Toronto Boy Homosexual Orgy Victim." *The Province* (Vancouver), 3 Aug. 1977: 5.

Williams, Stephen. "Sympathy for the Devil." *Toronto Life* Sept. 1979: 182–83.

Worthington, Peter. "Government Subsidized Trash." *Toronto Sun* 16 Aug. 1977: 11.

York, Marty and Dorothy Lipovenko. "4 Men Charged with Murder After Body of Boy Discovered," Toronto *Globe and Mail* 2 Aug. 1977: 1.

Young, Scott. "Gays Should Learn When to Hush Up." Toronto *Globe and Mail* 8 Aug. 1977: 8.

CHAPTER 29

Queering "Pervert City": A Queer Reading of the Swift Current Hockey Scandal

Debra Shogan

In 1997, junior hockey coach Graham James was sentenced to three-and-a-half years in prison for abusing Sheldon Kennedy and another unnamed player whom James coached as junior players. Sheldon Kennedy was well known as a National Hockey League (NHL) player and this, together with the fact that hockey is considered by some to be Canada's national pastime, created great interest in the incident not only among the people involved in the scandal but in the places where the abuse was reported to have happened. One of these places, Swift Current, Saskatchewan, received most of the media attention because it was here that James, Kennedy, and Kennedy's teammates achieved their greatest success, winning the Memorial Cup for junior hockey supremacy and producing a number of stars for the NHL.

While much can be written about this episode in Canadian sporting history, including how sexual abuse in sport emerged as an ethical issue worthy of attention,[1] in this chapter I am interested in how representations of the James scandal by the popular media relied on a dominant cultural story (Hall; Kincaid) about sexual abuse of children and youth in dysfunctional families. I focus on how newspaper representations constructed meaning about the events, people, and place associated with the scandal from a pervasive cultural narrative that gave "form to ... our ways of seeing children, sexuality, and transgression" (Kincaid 5). Demonstrating how the scandal was represented in the media is not intended as a denial of events that took place in Swift Current. Rather, it is an attempt to make apparent how newspaper representations of these events invoked a dominant cultural story about sexual abuse in dysfunctional families and, in this particular case, represented Swift Current as a dysfunctional family, a complicit yet innocent bystander in the sexual abuse of junior hockey players coached by James.

Once the story broke that James had been charged with assaulting junior hockey players, and particularly once Sheldon Kennedy, by then an NHL player, came forward to talk publicly about what had happened, news media across North America became interested in Swift Current. *The Globe and Mail,* for example, described Swift Current this way:

> To understand why the James affair has hit Swift Current so hard, you first need to understand how small the city is and how big the sport.
>
> Swift Current is the sort of place where people are excited that Tommy Hunter is coming this month to perform ... It's the sort of place where people are still known by what church they belong to, where you could drive down the fiendishly cold main street last week and see a whole row of cars left running and unlocked.
>
> ... In such a climate, those who play for the Broncos are local heroes who stand a chance of living the Canadian dream of playing in the NHL, feted guests of honour at fowl suppers, and community leaders with a stature far beyond their years. (Mitchell A6)

Swift Current was also described by the media as angry and betrayed (Brownridge, "Assault" A2); characterized as a town of deep shame (Gillis, "Sex Assaults" A1); and called "pervert city" by one of my colleagues, when I indicated that that was where I was born. Swift Current was reduced simultaneously to a city of perversion and bucolic innocence: a place with "its heart broken, its shoulders slumping, every bone in its body aching as it searches within itself for answers" (Drinnan B1). As I explain, these contradictory representations can coexist within a cultural narrative about sexual abuse in dysfunctional families.

In what follows, I first read newspaper representations of Swift Current as a dysfunctional family through a familiar cultural story about sexual abuse that highlights notions of complicity, duplicity, and innocence. However, in order to confound representations of Swift Current as a place fixed by this cultural story, I intervene with my own understanding of this place. As a queer youth living in Swift Current in the 1950s and 1960s, I was often smitten by adults who were my mentors. By interjecting some of my experiences, I hope to disrupt the cultural story of Swift Current as a dysfunctional family, as well as open up notions of authority, innocence, and sexual abuse to other possibilities. I offer my experiences not to assert the truth of this place, thus applying a different but still singular set of meanings to Swift Current and the relationships of the people who live and have lived there (Scott; Sedgwick). Rather, this is a deconstructive move.

Referring to writing about her experiences with the diagnosis and medical treatment of breast cancer, Eve Kosofsky Sedgwick indicates that "it's hard not to think of this ... experience as ... an adventure in applied deconstruction" (12). Sedgwick's experiences call into question neatly packaged oppositions between safety and danger, fear and hope, past and future, thought and act, and the natural and the technological and, in doing so, disrupt precise definitions of identity, gender, and sexuality (12, 13). Likewise, recounting some of my experiences of sexuality as a youth living in Swift Current, including my pursuit of my coach, has the potential to call into question oppositions between innocence and dysfunction, the normal and the perverted, and insiders and outsiders and, in so doing, disrupt the tidy stories told about sexual abuse of innocent youth in dysfunctional families (or places). I intend the intervention of my experiences to be a queer reading of this place called "pervert city," where queer suggests that "meanings ... can be at loose ends with each other" (Sedgwick 6). In turn, I hope to show that Swift Current exceeds its representations as a healthy, family town *and* its representations as a town of perversion or dysfunction.

But before proceeding with the popular media and my own reading of Swift Current, I present a brief chronology of the scandal involving James and Kennedy.

THE SCANDAL

Graham James began his coaching career in Manitoba in the late 1970s and by the beginning of the 1980s he had become a Junior A hockey coach. He first encountered Sheldon Kennedy at a hockey school in 1982 when Kennedy was thirteen years old. In 1984, James recruited Kennedy to his Winnipeg team and, when this team was moved to Moose Jaw, James managed to have Kennedy move with him. According to Kennedy, James began sexual contact with him not long after his arrival in Winnipeg. While in Moose Jaw, the expectation that Kennedy would go to James's apartment every Tuesday and Thursday began and continued until Kennedy was nineteen years old.

James was dismissed from the Moose Jaw team for suspected improprieties that were only revealed once the abuse story broke. He moved Kennedy with him to Winnipeg for a short time and then in 1986 he became the head coach of the Swift Current Broncos. He ensured that Kennedy joined him there. In 1986, a bus accident killed four of the Bronco players and James was credited with helping the surviving players through the ordeal (Robinson 160). In 1989, the Swift Current Broncos won the Memorial Cup with the most successful record ever in the Canadian Hockey League. Sheldon Kennedy had outstanding seasons both in 1988 and in 1989 and was named to the national junior team in 1988.

Kennedy was drafted by the Detroit Red Wings in 1989 and acquired a reputation as someone emotionally out of control. He was convicted of reckless driving and charged with drug possession, and he was traded a number of times. Meanwhile in Swift Current, James continued his success as a winning coach and gained popularity as a colourful personality. However, at the end of the 1993–94 season, James's contract was not renewed. He subsequently appeared in Calgary where he became part-owner, general manager, and head coach of the Calgary Hitmen (Robinson 164). In 1997, while Kennedy was a player for the Boston Bruins, he went public with his story.

In 1997, Graham James was sentenced to three-and-a-half years in prison. He was released from prison in July 2000 and, to the consternation of the Canadian Hockey Association and of many in the sporting public, James became a coach with the Spanish national team.

READING REPRESENTATIONS OF SWIFT CURRENT THROUGH STORIES OF SEXUAL ABUSE

Experts in psychology, social work, and other human sciences have played a prominent role in producing a story about sexual abuse in dysfunctional families that has become familiar in Western culture (see Armstrong; Crewsdon; La Fontaine; Miller; Rush). This is a story of sexual abuse in a "'family system' gone wrong [where] each family member own[s] a piece of the problem" (Dinsmore 15). According to Pat Gilmartin, family pathology is not regarded as an "idiosyncratic behavior of a single member of that unit; rather, the family system is implicated as causing and perpetuating whatever problem that exists" (82). Family members are all implicated in the abuse as victims, perpetrators, gullible innocents, or complicit third parties (Butler).

As I have said, newspaper reporters' attempts to understand what happened in Swift Current were cast in terms of the familiar cultural story about sexual abuse in dysfunctional families. Official City information sources and outside media represent Swift Current as valuing families. The city website, for example, indicates that "Swift Current is a city of families and friends. Our continuing efforts to maintain a high quality of life and opportunity for our neighbours is only rivalled by our desire to welcome new families to Swift Current and make new friends" ("Swift Current"). Swift Current not only values family, it is a family, according to some. For example, Joe Arling, a hotel owner and member of the board of directors of the Broncos, was reported in 1997 to say:

> This is a community with very strong morals and beliefs. It has very strong family values and in a way, it's a family itself. To me, what Graham did was a violation of trust and position, just like priests and teachers have abused their positions. Hockey just happened to be the venue, in this case. But like anywhere, there'll be significant hurt here. No one would have expected it to happen in this community (qtd. in Gillis, "Hockeytown" H2)

Swift Current is a family, but a dysfunctional one. Moreover, people in Swift Current were represented as recognizing the dysfunction of the community: "One thing's certain, this farming, railway and oil community—a well-spring of dedicated, sometimes brilliant hockey players—will never feel the same about itself. Or its and Canada's favourite game" (Gillis, "James Incident" A2).

As a dysfunctional family, Swift Current was represented as complicit in the sexual abuse of the junior hockey players who lived there. In some accounts James was cast as a member of the dysfunctional family that made possible the abuse of Kennedy and other junior hockey players: "while preying on boys for his confessed sexual gratification, James could not operate alone. He had help and lots of it. Passive, blind, hopelessly naive help from those who most trusted the junior hockey coach: parents, billets, league and team administrators, and teammates" (Ormsby D3).

Many reporters and some residents of the city were reported to have thought it was impossible that no one knew that the sexual abuse was happening in Swift Current. Two residents of the Saskatchewan city were quoted as saying: "I just can't imagine how somebody could live with these players and not try to figure out why they were spending so much time with the coach"; "What do you mean nobody knew? I'm sure people knew, but they just didn't do anything" (qtd. in Gillis, "Sex Assaults" A4). Another account went so far as to surmise that the team organization refused therapy for team players after the tragic bus accident in 1986 left four players dead, because they were afraid that "the terrible truth about James' sexual shenanigans [would] surface" (McConachie B1). In these representations, Swift Current assumed the role of the mother within the dysfunctional family: the "invisible third partner," "colluding" in the sexual interaction between the abuser and the child or abandoning the child to the abuser (see Butler 102, 113). It is assumed in this conventional story about sexual abuse that abuse would not have occurred if the mother, in this case Swift Current, had not created a particular emotional climate through "commission and omission" (Butler 114).

Central to the story of sexual abuse in dysfunctional families is the gullibility of at least some family members. Reporters represented Swift Current as innocently caught up in and bewildered by the events:

> Meanwhile, the citizens of Swift Current will never understand how or why all of them came to be victims, too. But that's what happens when sexual abuse, society's dirty little secret, rears its ugly head in your community. There are good people in Swift Current, good people, salt-of-the-earth people, who are torturing themselves, trying to understand what it is that went on behind closed doors in their community and why they weren't able to recognize the signs. (Drinnan B1)

The trainer of the Broncos was reported to have said, "I've been lying awake every night thinking, 'Did I miss something? Were there signs I didn't see?' But there just weren't any hints" (qtd. in Gillis, "James Incident" A2).

The familiar cultural story of sexual abuse in dysfunctional families includes accounts of loyalty of members to the abuser (see esp. Butler 121). The loyalty of some Swift Current residents to James was central to some media depictions. When faced with the allegations about James, team president, John Rittinger, was reported to have said that "the Graham I know was always a pleasant, humorous fellow. It's impossible for me to believe that a man of his intelligence would get involved in something like this. I couldn't be more devastated by this if Graham had died. I couldn't feel worse by this if it was my own family" (qtd. in Todd G2). There were many letters of support submitted at James's trial by former players and administrators of the Broncos' organization (Robinson 168). This loyalty to James was interpreted as just another indication of the dysfunction of the city.

Gilmartin indicates that social-psychological explanations of sexual abuse of children in families "keeps the focus on individual families as the problem and ignores the societal power imbalances which many families mimic" (87). Much of the reporting about the James case, while differing about whether Swift Current was complicit, innocent, or both, nevertheless represented this place as an aberration among Canadian cities. Administrators of hockey sport governing bodies were also keen to make the point that what happened in Swift Current was not representative of hockey culture. Hockey authorities were quick to represent the James case as an isolated incident and not reflective of junior hockey (see Todd G2). However, accounts such as Laura Robinson's in *Crossing the Line: Violence and Sexual Assault in Canada's National Sport* document how abuse of and by hockey players may be central to hockey culture. Robinson argues that abuse in hockey is institutionalized and that abuse takes many forms, including pressure on young players to excel and conform, hazing rituals, and sexual abuse.

A common representation by the media of the James affair was that James duped Swift Current by fooling them with his charm and knowledge of hockey.

> This was a man of contradictions … James was a pillar of the community. He was a role model. He was on the Broncos' bus that ugly night 10 years ago and he helped the community mend its broken heart, the same heart he would smash to smithereens. He

picked that team up by the skate laces and took it to a Memorial Cup championship just three years later. It was a miracle that put Swift Current on the map. Now it turns out he was the devil in disguise. (Drinnan B1)

In this representation, James is not one of the family. He is an outsider, described by one of the players' billets as "an import to the community" (qtd. in Gillis, "James Incident" A2). The mayor of the city at the time also distanced the community from James by indicating that "this is an isolated event by perhaps a deranged person. Certainly, it doesn't reflect the community" (qtd. in Vanstone A1).

While, for the most part, the mainstream media did not link the charges of abuse to James's homosexuality, they did portray him as "a very private man, rarely seen socially" (Brownridge, "Feeling" A1). The *Alberta Report,* a right-wing, Christian fundamentalist news weekly accused other media of downplaying James's homosexuality and ignoring what they portrayed as "the known link between homosexuality and pedophilia" (Sillars 34). Albert Howlett, a Bronco supporter, shared the indignation: "You pretty near have to put him down near the lowest class of person you can be. What he did with those boys was terrible" (qtd. in Vanstone A1).

Many in the city were reported to have known about James's homosexuality, with the effect that reporters did not take seriously the representation of the city by one of its citizens as a naive Bible-belt town (Mitchell A6). A former Bronco director was reported to have said: "There were rumors about Graham's sexual orientation, but never any suggestion he was sexually abusing players ... Innuendo, suspicion and rumour was all there was, and until someone comes forward, there's really nothing you can do. If you decided to end a coaching contract on something like that, human rights would be all over you" (qtd. in Gillis, "James Incident" A2). In another report, the director was attributed with the following remark: "Some of the club's inner circle suspected that Mr. James was a homosexual but they were broad-minded enough not to assume that a gay man also had a taste for the youths under his control" (Mitchell A6). That the "homophobic world of junior hockey" (Todd G2) would be so open to homosexuality stretched the limits of credulity for most reporters. One asked rhetorically, "Could it be that as long as you're winning and developing NHL stars, people look the other way? Could it be that James would have been found out long ago if he was a losing coach?" (Todd G2).

A flurry of articles identifying other "homosexual" coaches who had been "known" to prey on players (see Houston and Campbell A1; Spector, "Scars" A1; Stock and Crowley A1) belied the representation of James as an exception. Many of these coaches were dead and not in a position to defend themselves. Most attention was paid to Brian Shaw, former coach, general manager, and owner of the Edmonton Oil Kings and Portland Winter Hawks. The *Edmonton Journal* also carried a front-page story with pictures about Peter Spear, who died in 1988, and who allegedly abused at least one of his players (Spector, "Scars" A1). None of these accounts of homosexuality in hockey, including the disingenuous reference to looking the other way, acknowledged what many of the reporters must have witnessed: the homoeroticism of the locker room. As Brian Pronger indicates, "locker rooms are places where orthodox men like to hang around naked, talking and joking with each other" (76). In response to the revelation that James regularly showered with his players after practices, Western Hockey League coach Mike Babcock reported that, in the aftermath of the scandal, he and his assistant coaches had talked about whether they should continue to shower with players when the team was on the road ("Stars" E2). If there were indications of James's sexual interest in Bronco players, they may have been indistinguishable from homoerotic interactions taken for granted on male sporting teams.

The story about sexual abuse in families and family-like settings is unable to account for homoerotic behaviour on male athletic teams nor can it contain Kennedy's or James's understanding of what happened between them. When asked about his willingness to go to where James was coaching after the first sexual encounter, Kennedy responded, "Well yeah … I was scared sh—less … I knew right after, but there was nothing I could do because I wanted to play" ("Player's Self-Esteem" D10). Jimmy Devellano, who drafted Kennedy from Swift Current, was one of many people surprised by Kennedy's accusations because, according to Devellano, Kennedy "always talked about Graham so sincerely" (Simmons B1). A former Bronco vice-president said he was told that James was "doing it" with Kennedy: "I figured that if they were doing it, they were doing it with consent" (qtd. in Vanstone A5). Kennedy later said that he believed that James was in love with him. He also indicated that James knew what he was doing and "he should have known that it wasn't accepted, because I had mentioned many times that I hated it" (qtd. in Board D1). Kennedy said that he could not tell anybody because "I was so scared to come out and admit it happened to me. I was scared to say I was with another man" ("Learning" A12). James commented after his trial that he realized that Kennedy was not comfortable with the sex but he tolerated it because "he legitimately cared. Not about THAT (the sex) obviously. He cared. He knew I was lonely and you know, that sort of registered as desperation" (qtd. in Spector, "Kennedy Disclosure" D6). When asked in an interview from prison whether he realized that what he was doing was wrong, James responded, "[W]hen you're attracted to somebody, you're blinded, and you try to justify things, and you figure if you can do enough for somebody then somehow that makes up for it" (qtd. in "'Caring'" K2); "I suppose you don't think these things … will be brought out into the general public. It's like anybody's sex life—it goes out in the general public [and] it doesn't look too flattering" (qtd. in "James Says" E2).

Irrespective of the homoeroticism of the locker room or what James or Kennedy had to say, media representations of Swift Current and the people who live there sustained an understanding of sexual abuse consistent with conventional stories of abuse in dysfunctional families. This is a story of innocence, collusion, duplicity, and gullibility. Yet Swift Current and the events that took place there are open for other readings.

ANOTHER READING OF SWIFT CURRENT

As it turns out, many of the places where the events that implicated James and Kennedy occurred were places I had inhabited under different conditions, twenty years earlier. During high school, I lived in a house on Jubilee Drive in the northeast side of the city. This house was later sold to Colleen and Frank McBean who billeted Bronco players through the 1990s. Kennedy was one of these players.

Kennedy would have left the side door into the car park every Tuesday and Thursday evening to go to James's house. Was his room the southeast bedroom where I had spent so much time as a fifteen-year-old thinking about my first girlfriend? This girlfriend was eighteen, and under today's laws would be considered an adult. As I found out later, she was two-timing me with her female college coach.

Many reporters have wondered how the people of Swift Current, especially those billeting players, could not have known that a player was sexually involved with the coach. They surmised that people must have known or were too simple or naive to have guessed. I often went to my basketball coach's apartment, usually unannounced, hoping to seduce her. I was oblivious to whether the neighbours knew. My coach's careful closing of the curtains upon my arrival was reason for me to be hopeful of what might happen but, as I think about it now, she was likely very aware that some would think that a player should not be in her coach's home unsupervised at night. Only she and I were aware that the seventeen-year-old girl was pursuing the twenty-five-year-old coach. Applied to me, the story of innocence and dysfunction would have shrunk a "smart and active older adolescent … into a child, a generic 'essence-of-child'" (Kincaid 31).

My mother did not ask me questions about spending time with my coach. Instead, my mother often helped me buy chocolate bars for her. Nor did she have much to say about the black eye my coach accidentally gave me when we were wrestling in the locker room. This black eye would have been very difficult for my coach to explain if someone had chosen to cast my relationship with her as inappropriate. In some accounts, James was accused of threatening Kennedy with a gun. James had this to say about the gun: "There was a gun in a sense of a Clouseau-Kato type thing. He'd chase me until I could find something to stop him, and vice versa. Then we'd laugh about it. That's all there was to it" (qtd. in Spector, "Kennedy Disclosure" D6).

Was my mother complicit in my sexual encounters with girls my own age? Was she implicated in my active pursuit of a young woman in authority who, arguably, in sexual terms was more innocent than I was? My mother told me much later that she did not have the language to broach my sexuality with me. According to the "familiar story," this inability to talk about what may have appeared as an unusual relationship with my coach is evidence of the dysfunction of my family. As the titles of books telling this story reflect, silence is considered to be central to dysfunction (Butler; Miller; Rush). I had a sense then, however, that by helping me buy small presents for my coach my mother communicated her tacit approval of me.

Agonizing about what the adults should or should not have known or done cannot account for the complications of people's lives. Colleen and Frank McBean, for example, began billeting Bronco players, including Kennedy, after losing two of their sons in a tragic vehicle accident. Whether and how this tragic event affected the decisions that were made in relation to the boys in their care cannot be captured by implying that they somehow colluded in what was later understood as Kennedy's abuse. They may have been unable to make explicit what was later construed as a terrible abuse of authority by a coach whose "victim" left his home twice a week, every week, for four years to visit the coach.

Swift Current and its people cannot be captured by stories about dysfunction and innocence, nor can the relationships between the adults and youth who live and have lived there. Many of my memories of living as a child and teenager in Swift Current reproduce this as a time and place marked by innocence, exuberance, creativity, and fun. But I know that these memories make sense to me in contrast to the heaviness that often accompanies adulthood. With little effort, however, I can also remember the stranger in the car who persisted in trying to give me a ride home when I was five; the woman who did some sewing for my mother who was found dead in the Swift Current creek; the rape of one of my sister's friends; the way the kids at school treated the children of one family because they were poor and Arab and lived in the valley; the man who turned out to be a woman who drove the "honey wagon" (the name given for the horse drawn wagon that carried the excrement from the outdoor toilets used by the people in the valley); children throwing rocks at the man with cerebral palsy who dared to try to walk in his neighbourhood; what I now understand to be the racism that invaded the speech of the adults around me; or the awesome wrath of one of my teachers when I was ten because I persisted in playing hockey with the boys.

Years later, my mother apologized for not doing something more to ease what she thought must have been a horrible time for me living in Swift Current. But it was not a horrible time. Rather it was then and there that I found other girls like me and we engaged in sexual lives not remotely imagined in representations of Swift Current as a quaint, quiet family town or as a dysfunctional city complicit in the sexual abuse of its young people. Still, I am surprised by the apparent casual-ness to homosexuality expressed by at least some in the community during the James scandal. In the 1960s, I would have sworn that, except for those of us engaged in these thrilling subterranean practices, no one had a clue that people did these things. But at least some people did know about these activities when I lived there, including my mother, as did some during the time James and Kennedy were living in Swift Current. Yet, dominant cultural stories about families, sexuality, relationships, and innocence still circulate, making it difficult to understand events, people, and places in anything but the terms of these stories. What has changed, however, is that queer stories are being told about the relationships between people that occurred in these places. These queer stories situate dysfunction not in individuals or places but in a cultural story that simplifies com-plicated lives. The dysfunction of the cultural story is that it permits only two main roles, "monster and victim … along with supporting parts for police, judges, juries, therapists, parents, friends, journalists, and lawyers" (Kincaid 30).

I want to emphasize that I am not saying that my experiences in Swift Current prove somehow that Kennedy was not traumatized by the sexual encounters he had with James. Rather, I want to show that the stories about dysfunctional families and the innocence of youth are too simple to capture the complexity of relationships, events, and people. In their simplicity, they have the effect of fixing what we can know about a place, the people who live there, and certain events in a way that is "intolerant and relentless" (Kincaid 30). My queer reading of "pervert city" renders the meaning of this place and of the events that happened there a little less tidy.

NOTES

1 While little attention was paid to this issue before, despite frequent concerns expressed by female ath-letes in relation to their male coaches, it took NHL player Sheldon Kennedy's story to produce policy, handbooks, websites, hot lines, skateathons, TV movies, and other ways of dealing with these issues.

REFERENCES

Armstrong, Louise. *Home Front: Notes on the Family War Zone*. New York: McGraw-Hill, 1984.

Board, Mike. "Kennedy Describes His Life as a Lonely Hell." *Gazette* [Montreal] 7 Jan. 1997: D1.

Brownridge, David. "A Feeling of Betrayal." *Leader Post* [Regina] 4 Jan. 1997: A1.

Brownridge, David. "Assault Charges Stun Swift Current." *Star Phoenix* [Saskatoon] 4 Jan. 1997: A2.

Butler, Sandra. *Conspiracy of Silence*. Volcano, CA: Volcano, 1985.

"'Caring' Coach Tells His Story." *Edmonton Sun* 7 Jan. 1997: 12.

Crewsdon, John. *By Silence Betrayed: Sexual Abuse of Children in America*. New York: Little Brown, 1988.

Dinsmore, Christine. *From Surviving to Thriving: Incest, Feminism, and Recovery*. New York: State University of New York Press, 1991.

Drinnan, Gregg. "Swift Current Tries to Heal Its Wounds." *Leader Post* [Regina] 9 Jan 1997: B1.

Gillis, Charlie. "Hockeytown, Canada Searches Its Soul." *Edmonton Journal* 11 Jan. 1997: H1–H2.

Gillis, Charlie. "James Incident Steals City of Its Innocence." *Star Phoenix* [Saskatoon] 14 Jan. 1997: A2.

Gillis, Charlie. "Sex Assaults Shock Prairie Town." *Gazette* [Montreal] 12 Jan. 1997: A1, A4.

Gilmartin, Pat. *Rape, Incest, and Child Sexual Abuse*. New York: Garland, 1994.

Hall, Stuart, ed. *Representation: Cultural Representations and Signifying Practices*. London: Open University, 1997.

Houston, William and Neil Campbell. "Ex-WHL Boss Abused Players." *Globe and Mail* [Toronto) 9 Jan. 1997: A1.

"James Says He Feels Betrayed by Kennedy." *Vancouver Sun* 8 Jan. 1997: E2.

Kincaid, James R. *Erotic Innocence: The Culture of Child Molesting*. Durham: Duke University Press, 1998.

La Fontaine, Jean. *Child Sexual Abuse*. Cambridge, UK: Polity, 1990.

"Learning to Live Again." *Leader Post* [Regina] 7 Jan. 1997: A1, A12.

McConachie, Doug. "Independent Investigation Needed by WHL." *Star Phoenix* [Saskatoon] 15 Jan. 1997: B1.

Miller, Alice. *Thou Shalt Not Be Aware*. New York: Farrar, Straus & Giroux, 1983.

Mitchell, Alana. "Swift Current's Hockey Pride Left in Tatters." *Globe and Mail* [Toronto] 14 Jan. 1997: A6.

Ormsby, Mary. "Be Vigilant to Protect Vulnerable Youngsters." *Toronto Star* 4 Jan. 1997: D3.

"Player's Self-Esteem Sank after Years of Abuse." *Vancouver Sun* 7 Jan. 1997: D10.

Pronger, Brian. *The Arena of Masculinity: Sports, Homosexuality and the Meaning of Sex*. Toronto: University of Toronto Press, 1992.

Robinson, Laura. *Crossing the Line: Violence and Sexual Assault in Canada's National Sport*. Toronto: McClelland and Stewart, 1998.

Rush, Florence. *The Best Kept Secret: Sexual Abuse of Children*. Englewood Cliffs, NJ: Prentice-Hall, 1980.

Scott, Joan. "Experience." *Feminists Theorize the Political*. Eds. Judith Butler and Joan Scott. New York: Routledge, 1992. 22–40.

Sedgwick, Eve Kosofsky. *Tendencies*. Durham: Duke University Press, 1993.

Sillars, Les. "Hockey Pays the Price for Gay Tolerance." *Alberta Report* 20 Jan. 1997: 30–34.

Simmons, Steve. "Many Tried to Help a Troubled Kennedy." *Star Phoenix* [Saskatoon] 8 Jan. 1997: B1.

Spector, Marie. "Scars That Last a Lifetime." *Edmonton Journal* 9 Jan. 1997: A1, A9.

Spector, Marie. "Kennedy Disclosure a Betrayal: James." *Star Phoenix* [Saskatoon] 9 Jan. 1997: D6.

"Stars Looking to Shine over Hockey Scandal." *Leader Post* [Regina] 22 Jan. 1997: E2.

Stock, Curtis and Norm Cowley. "The Saddest Power Play." *Edmonton Journal* 7 Jan. 1997: A12.

"Swift Current Community Information." 1 Dec. 2001 <http://www.city.swift-current.sk.ca/info/index/htm>.

Todd, Jack. "Junior Hockey Looks Other Way." *Gazette* [Montreal] 4 Jan. 1997: G2.

Vanstone, Rob. "Shadow over a Hockey Town." *Leader Post* [Regina] 11 Jan. 1997: A1

CHAPTER 30
Beyond Image Content: Examining Transsexuals' Access to the Media

Viviane Namaste

They cannot represent themselves, they must be represented. Their representative must at the same time appear as their master, as an authority over them, as an unlimited governmental power that protects them against the other classes and sends them rain and sunshine from above. The political influence of the small-holding peasants, therefore, finds its final expression in the executive power subordinating society to itself.

—Karl Marx[1]

In recent years, English-speaking contexts have witnessed a proliferation of images and representations with transsexual or transvestite content. These documents take different forms, from films such as *Priscilla, Queen of the Desert*; *All About My Mother*; *Ma Vie en Rose*; and *Boys Don't Cry*, to academic studies such as *Gender Trouble* and *Female Masculinity,* to popular books such as *Stone Butch Blues, Gender Outlaw,* and *Read My Lips.*[2] Photography has also played an important role in recent years, notably with the works of Del LaGrace Volcano, Loren Cameron, and Dean Kotula.[3]

This explosion of images related to transsexuals and transvestites has encouraged everyone to talk about gender. Whether it be on the talk-show circuit or in the university classroom, everyone is fascinated with, in the words of Marjorie Garber, "looking at" transsexuals and transvestites.[4]

Now, the reasons for such "looking at" may differ. The American host Maury Povich, for example, may present a talk show purely for entertainment purposes: audience members and the spectators at home are invited to "guess" if the guests are biologically male or female. American humanities-based academics such as Garber and Butler, however, are fond of putting images of transsexuals and transvestites alongside their readings of French theory. They are primarily motivated by their institutional location: they are less interested in understanding the everyday lived experience of transsexuals and transvestites, and deeply invested in making their theoretical point. Butler, for instance, makes casual references to drag queens on stage in order to make broad claims about the sex/gender system. In this view, transsexuals and transvestites are a pawn of knowledge, propped up on display only to be erased in the complicated fabric of their struggles. And activists such as Cameron and Kotula want to make transsexuals visible for a different reason altogether. They want to offer the crucial information about transsexualism and sex change to other transsexuals and those who support them. They take photographs to make visible the erasure of transsexual men in culture.

Now, with all this talk about transsexuals and transvestites, it is perhaps especially difficult to think about some of the images of the people we do *not* see. Furthermore, in such a context it becomes increasingly challenging to make adequate sense of the conditions that govern what gets put on display. That is the subject of this chapter. I want to explore some of the institutional ways in which transsexuals and transvestites can be represented (whether that representation be proffered by a non-transsexual or a transsexual individual). I will consider how it is that certain kinds of speech about transsexuals are not allowed, while others can only occur in select contexts. Let me put it another way: everyone else is talking about transsexual and transvestites, limiting their discussion to image content. I shift the focus by looking at the institutional elements of representation. [...]

*****

THE AUTOBIOGRAPHICAL IMPERATIVE

An important limit to contain transsexual self-representation is the autobiographical imperative, a logical result of the limit in which non-transsexuals have the final word on transsexual lives. Transsexuals may be allowed to speak, but only insofar as they offer their personal autobiographies, and only as long as they respond to the questions posed by a non-transsexual interviewer.[5] Another example from my work as a project coordinator of a community-based transsexual health project drives this point home.

I was approached by the French-language Radio Canada television program *Enjeux*. *Enjeux* has a reputation of being serious journalism, dealing with contemporary social and political issues in a sensitive, thought-provoking, and in-depth manner. It is akin to the American program *20/20*, or the English-Canadian *Witness*. (Indeed, the final program produced by Radio Canada on transsexuals also aired on *Witness* on the English airwaves of CBC.) This is no sensationalized show just for the ratings, then, no *Métier Policier* here. *Enjeux* is serious investigative reporting.

Journalists for the program telephoned me in my role as project coordinator in order to contact transsexuals to be interviewed for the show they were planning on the subject. Given the high profile of the show, I asked to meet with them to learn more about their request and to provide them with some relevant information on the situation of transsexuals in Québec.

Having had some experience with the media and the silencing of transsexual voices, I made it clear to the journalists and producers that my participation—even in a preliminary interview so they could gather information—was conditional on publishing the phone number of the community group I coordinated. I was conscious that transsexuals all over Québec (and elsewhere) would watch the show, and they would need information, resources, and support immediately. I was assured that the contact information would be communicated.

Our meeting was most pleasant, and I spent a great deal of time situating the lives of transsexuals in Québec within their proper judicial, political, and economic contexts. For instance, I explained how sex-reassignment surgery was not paid for through provincial health insurance. I outlined how the law with respect to the change of name and the change of sex in Québec states that transsexuals can only change their names after they have had a genital operation. This situation causes incredible stress and hardship for people, and prevents them from adequately integrating into Québec society. At the medical clinic or the hospital, transsexuals are often ridiculed or stared at incredulously because of their unchanged papers, while getting a job or going to school are remote possibilities indeed. And because of this legal situation, many transsexuals live in extreme poverty, with all that entails: inadequate nutrition and substandard housing. We spoke about these issues in great length, and I provided them with appropriate documentation.[6] I stated quite clearly that it was important to address these issues in the show, since they determine how transsexuals in Québec live and since they constitute the fabric of our daily lives.

The journalists were most interested in the possibility of conducting a formal interview with me for their show. Yet they limited their questions to those about my personal history. How long had I lived as a woman? When did I have my surgery? Was I happy with the results? How did my family accept my transformation? I informed the journalists and producers that I was not interested in telling my personal story. I did specify, however, that I was open to granting an interview as an expert in the field: I laid out my credentials, with several research projects on transsexual health care, many years of community experience in the field, and (at that time) a book contract. Perhaps not surprisingly, however, the journalists continued to try to persuade me to accept the terms of an autobiography. I was so articulate, they noted. (How shocking that people can change sex and still maintain their linguistic capabilities! Imagine how impressed the journalists would have been if we had spoken in English; I was, after all, conversing with them in French, my second language!)

The situation made me both uncomfortable and angry. I carefully pointed out that they were reducing me to only a transsexual. Were they to do a show on vaginal cancer and interview community health activists in the field, they would not demand that the women health activists speak of their own personal vaginas. Yet transsexuals are not accorded the same respect: we can only tell our stories and respond to their questions. We cannot be positioned as experts in the field, and we cannot set the agenda for discussion.

Since I did not agree to the terms of autobiography set out by the *Enjeux* team, the journalists did not interview me. Sadly, they also neglected to include in the broadcast the contact information for the community group I coordinated, despite their assurances to do so and their stated understanding of the needs of transsexual viewers. The interviewees chosen for the *Enjeux* show—a male-to-female Canadian soldier transitioning in mid-life, a male-to-female police officer transitioning after retirement, and an American female-to-male transsexual—all preempted a critical analysis of health care and universal access to services for transsexuals. The soldier was able to have her surgery paid for through the military, since they have an internal policy that guarantees the provision of health services available to the Canadian population at large. Since some provinces pay for sex-reassignment surgery (though not Québec), this individual did not have to pay for surgery. The police officer, from Ontario, was planning to pay for surgery privately, as did the FTM from the United States. In all of these instances, then, the issue of privatization of health care for transsexuals remained unaddressed. This absence underlines the severe limitations of an autobiographical framework. An exclusive focus on the *what* and the *why* of transsexuality ("Can you orgasm?" "How did your family take the news?") forecloses a critical analysis of the institutional, economic, and political contexts in which sex change occurs.

The autobiographical imperative requires that transsexuals tell our stories of sex change on demand, that we speak about our bodies, our sexualities, our desires, our genitals, and our deep pain at the whim of a curious non-transsexual person. It requires that we recount all this—whether in a public café, in a university classroom, or on the set of a television studio—on command. And by extension it ensures that we will not have the time, space, or authorization to address the underlying political and institutional issues that make our lives so difficult: the legal context of name change, or the administrative policies governing the universal health insurance of sex change surgery and other services related to transsexualism. The autobiographical imperative is a natural progression of a social relation in which non-transsexuals determine when and where transsexuals can speak.

PROFESSIONAL TRANSSEXUALS ONLY, PLEASE

My experience with the *Enjeux* show provokes a reflection on the kinds of transsexual people often portrayed in the mass media, notably within print and television. There are several common characteristics of the individuals profiled. (I am speaking here in generalities, recognizing of course that exceptions are possible and do exist.) In the first instance, most of the transsexuals are male-to-female. Furthermore, they are usually at the beginning of their transition: it is extraordinarily rare for us to see a documentary in mainstream media about a transsexual woman who has lived as a woman for 25 years. Most of the interviewees are white, and they almost always have some professional career. Finally, they have generally begun their transition late in life, somewhere in their forties or fifties. The case from *Enjeux* illustrates well this portrait: two MTFs are portrayed, one a soldier in the Canadian army and the other a police officer.

While these individuals certainly are able to speak about their own experiences of transition, they are not necessarily able to speak about the process of sex change for younger transsexuals, or for those who are poor. And it seems to me important to question the generalizability of these women, the fact that through the media they stand in for all transsexual people. This point was made most clear to me in my meetings with the staff of *Enjeux*. In seeking my assistance to contact potential interviewees, the journalists and producers informed me that it was important to find someone who was well-spoken and articulate, who would present the issues well on air. I raised the question of the inclusion of prostitutes. Since most transsexual youth work as prostitutes, and since most of these individuals are from ethnocultural communities, I felt it important that the research team work to have a diversity of transsexual experiences included in the show. The idea was not well received; they justified their position by explaining that they wanted to offer education on transsexuals to the everyday viewer ("Monsieur et Madame Tout le Monde"), and that if the individuals presented had stable jobs, this would facilitate acceptance.

Sadly, this discourse is often repeated within transsexual communities, as when non-prostitute transsexuals lament the fact that there is an implicit link between transsexuality and prostitution. Such individuals happily accept invitations from the media with the argument that they are going to show everyone that transsexuals are "normal."[7] How sad that the hatred of prostitutes has been so internalized by these people that they do not see prostitutes, transsexual or otherwise, as "normal." The justification of the *Enjeux* team for the exclusion of prostitutes raises some important questions. Are we to accept transsexuals based on their jobs and professional status? Do poor people have the right to change sex? Furthermore, given problems transsexuals experience in changing their papers before sex change surgery, and the subsequent difficulties in finding employment, what does it mean when there is a systematic silencing of the people who live in the margins of society as a direct result of these policies? Does the critical journalist not have a moral and an ethical obligation to discuss the very social policies and institutional practices that force transsexuals into abject poverty and profound social isolation?

Professional and middle-class norms determine not only what transsexuals can say and in what spaces, they also confer the right to speak to those transsexuals who will abide by the codes of a middle-class discourse. These codes, then, proclaim who has the right to speak. In this light, the behind-the-scenes decisions of the *Enjeux* team tell us a great deal about the professional and class biases of the mainstream media. The media want nice, middle-class professionals to speak about the marginal transsexual position, presumably so that the imagined middle-class viewers at home will identify with them. Such a position is offensive both to poor transsexuals and to the viewers of programs like *Enjeux* who do not share middle-class values.

Herein lies the ultimate irony: non-transsexual people working in the media make calculated decisions about which transsexuals can speak, what they can say, and when they can say it.

"WE LOVE TRANSSEXUALS … ESPECIALLY THE LESBIAN AND GAY ONES!"

Transsexuals are further limited in gaining access to the media to the extent that they do not present themselves in a lesbian/gay discourse. Indeed, careful reflection on the transsexuals who do manage to distribute their work and ideas widely in English-speaking contexts reveals that they almost all advocate an alliance between lesbian/gay and transsexual/transvestite communities. Consider, for example, the work of Leslie Feinberg, Kate Bornstein, or Riki Ann Wilchins. All of these authors are cited and discussed within lesbian/gay activist and academic circles. Their names come up again and again in conference presentations, community-based education workshops, and on the syllabi of college and university courses dealing with issues of sexuality and gender. All three elaborate at great length on the value of a coalition between lesbians/gays and the transsexual/transvestite movement.

Now, the issue here is not that they propose a coalition. The matter at hand, rather, is that these three writers come to stand in for an entire transsexual community. This representation is further ironic when we consider that most transsexuals do not want to have any formal association with the lesbian/gay communities. (I make this statement based on my observations within transsexual communities for 10 years, as well as extensive research on the health care needs of transsexual and transvestites.) Yet the position of transsexuals who want no association with the lesbian/gay communities is never heard in most English-speaking discussions of transsexual ("transgendered") identity and politics. The situation is a curious contradiction. It is claimed that there is a coalition to be made between transsexuals and the lesbian/gay movement, and the evidence cited to support the position is the words of the transsexuals who advocate this program and who designate themselves as representatives of the transsexual community. We must ask: Why is this so? And how did it come to be that the knowledge we have of transsexuals is so circular? Margaret Deirdre O'Hartigan, in an insightful and damning critique of the relations between lesbians and transsexuals, offers an important contribution in this regard. O'Hartigan goes beyond talking about these political issues in the abstract. She provides an analysis of some of the unseen institutional relations that determine who gets to speak in public forums on transsexual issues. O'Hartigan says,

> Leslie Feinberg, Kate Bornstein, and Riki Anne Wilchins all share the same lesbian publicist—Gail Leondar—and are repeatedly booked by Leondar for paid speaking engagements before lesbian audiences.
>
> Imagine the righteous anger amongst Blacks if mainstream, white-owned media proclaimed as "leaders" a handful of collaborators publicized by a white PR firm while ignoring true Black leaders like Jesse Jackson and Louis Farrakhan. That is the situation occurring with the proclamation by the lesbian press that Feinberg, Bornstein, and Wilchins are transsexual leaders.[8]

O'Hartigan's intervention is so worthwhile because she rips us out of the abstract world of political utopias and plunges us into the seen but unnoticed workings of institutions. She exposes how the infrastructure of lesbian organizing serves to propel the visibility of lesbian-identified transsexuals. Within these institutional relations, transsexuals who do not adopt the party line (when it comes to the relations between lesbian/gay and transsexual communities) cannot speak.[9]

O'Hartigan's point is confirmed in considering the reception of the work of female-to-male transsexual Max Wolf Valerio. Valerio is well known within English-speaking transsexual communities. He was featured in Monica Treut's film *Female Misbehaviors*, in Loren Cameron's book *Body Alchemy*, and in the documentary about FTMs *You Don't Know Dick*. Despite this wide exposure, a lesbian reception of Valerio frequently misunderstands his life. Valerio is often portrayed as a "controversial" figure within the transsexual scene, notably in reinforcing sexist stereotypes of men and masculinity. In an open e-mail and fax sent to supporters and allies on the issue of transsexuality, Mirha-Soleil Ross outlines this attitude:

> The idea that transsexuals (and especially transsexual men) are reinforcing sex/gender stereotypes is one of the most damaging pieces of propaganda we are dealing with on a regular basis in our relationship with non-transsexual lesbians and gays here in Toronto....
> I recently gave a course for the Queer Exchange (a series of courses of lesbian/gay/bi/

43434

transsexual/transgender interest) about transsexual/transgender activism and that was one of the major issues that came up. During one of the seminars, I presented *You Don't Know Dick*. Several of the non-transsexual participants (many of whom were lesbian-identified) said they found the men [in the film] to be very sexist and misogynist. The non-transsexual women were particularly disturbed when transsexual men talked about the effects of testosterone on their sex drive and the way they see and live in the world. I also showed the film *Max* (an excerpt of *Female Misbehaviors*) by Monika Treut featuring Max Wolf Valerio who also appears in *You Don't Know Dick*. I had Max on speakerphone live from San Francisco for a question/answer/discussion period afterward. There is a moment in Monika's film where he is goofing around pretending to shadow-box in the air. So one participant asked if he was forced into or manipulated into performing that scene and if not, why he needed to reproduce such stereotypically masculinist behaviours. Max responded that he was not "forced" into it and that interestingly, if he had performed the same scene when living as a woman and a lesbian, he would have been held as a heroine, breaking gender stereotypes.... He also said, "Now that I have transitioned, what do you want me to do? Start knitting?"[10]

This particular reception of Valerio tells us a great deal about the accommodation of transsexuals within lesbian and gay communities. As long as transsexuals present ourselves with the language, gestures, clothes, and political-speak familiar and comfortable to English-speaking lesbian and gay activists, we are accepted. We may even be celebrated, as the lesbian enthusiasm over Leslie Feinberg attests. But if we dare to present ourselves as we are—if those darned FTMs have the audacity to beat up the air like that, if those MTFs have the temerity to wear perfume to the conference, even when they know it's a scent-free event—our gestures, clothing, "experience," political commitment, and thoughts are sure to be questioned.

Within English-speaking contexts, transsexuals are silenced to the extent that we do not speak the language of lesbian/gay politics.

CP2: AN INTERVENTION IN THE INSTITUTIONAL DIMENSIONS OF ART AND CULTURE

The innovative and groundbreaking nature of Counting Past 2 (CP2) needs to be situated in relation to the institutional exclusion of transsexuals from self-representation as outlined above. Indeed, CP2 offers much more than a variety of images of transsexual and transvestites in all our diversity. More important, CP2 intervenes in the ways in which a silencing of transsexuals is institutionally organized. In this regard, the festival offers an important contribution not only to transsexual politics, but also to the politics of art and culture more generally. Given this contribution, it is useful to briefly examine the different ways in which CP2 intervenes in the forms of institutional exclusion outlined above.

The very organization of the CP2 festival is a direct result of outright refusal of access and a continued dismissal of transsexuals who contact the media. The festival offers a forum in which transsexuals and transvestites can articulate their own lives and bodies on their own terms. It encourages people to submit creative cultural and political work, even if it does not follow the "accepted" aesthetic or production standards of the artistic world. Numerous examples from the festivals throughout the years offer compelling evidence of the importance of this strategy. CP2 has presented many student films, as well as videos produced by people who are not film- or video-makers. Some of it is not very polished on a technical level. Some of it is rough: the sound is a bit off, the editing was done on two VCRs and it shows, or the camera is out of focus. CP2 accepts this kind of work as a way to encourage transsexuals to represent themselves. Were the festival to impose professional standards of the art world on all its submission entries, the result would be one that excludes most transsexual voices. The third manner in which trans-sexuals are silenced has been characterized as representations that satisfy the curiosity of the non-transsexual viewer. CP2 offers an important departure from this framework, by creating a social context in which transsexuality is assumed. In this regard, transsexuals are not bound to respond to the questions posed by a non-transsexual journalist. They can create work that asks and answers the questions they deem relevant for their lives.

CP2 also challenges the autobiographical imperative. To be sure, the festival provides an occasion for transsexuals to recount their personal narratives. Yet interestingly, much of the work departs from this perspective. In several instances, transsexuals have used the opportun-ity created by CP2 to question the very terms and conditions of the autobiographical impera-tive. In its first year (1997), for instance, activist Xanthra Phillippa MacKay presented an audio performance that questioned the representation of transsexuals on talk shows. On the level of content, MacKay's piece provided incisive critique of the stereotypical ways in which talk shows frame transsexual lives. And on the level of form, MacKay's piece offered a brilliant critique of the autobiographical imperative: here was an audio piece about the visual representation of transsexuals! Transsexuals were nowhere to be seen. That is, of course, precisely the point MacKay wanted the listeners to understand. Aside from questioning how the autobiograph-ical imperative functions, CP2 allows transsexuals to just simply bypass their personal stories. Indeed, it is possible to see work created by a transsexual whose subject matter has nothing whatsoever to do with transsexuality! How refreshing.

CP2 also intervenes in the requirement that professional transsexuals offer the only public face of transsexual and transvestites. The festival's flexibility with regard to film and video style ensures that more than professional artists get to have their say. Moreover, CP2 has since 1998 incorporated a cabaret evening into its festivities. This forum has allowed for the participation of broad and diverse segments of the transsexual and transvestite communities, notably people of colour and prostitutes. The cabaret has featured spoken-work artists, dancers, performance artists, drag kings, drag queens, and female impersonators. Interestingly, the cabaret showcases a much more ethnically diverse group of people than that comprising the filmmakers, who are predominantly white. In the past, for instance, Mister Cool presented an energetic Soca dance from Trinidad, while Maury Mariana delighted participants with a flamenco dance.

Importantly, the cabaret also creates a context in which transsexual prostitutes are both comfortable and willing to participate. Within the local Toronto transsexual community, there is a great deal of crossover between prostitutes and show queens. In some instances, these are the same persons: an individual who sometimes does female impersonation shows, and sometimes works as a prostitute. In other cases, the link is one of physical space: the prostitutes work out of a bar, and so come to know the female impersonators. And in still other contexts, the prostitutes and the female impersonators are friends, socializing both inside and outside of transsexual/ transvestite spaces such as bars. What all of this means, in the concrete terms of transsexual/ transvestite community and politics, is that it is important to create a context in which transsexual prostitutes are at ease. By involving some show queens in the cabaret, and by having it in a bar, CP2 organizes itself to ensure the active participation of transsexual and transvestite prostitutes. Whereas the media and many non-prostitute transsexuals work to exclude transsexual prostitutes, CP2 allows them to be full and active participants in the festivities. CP2 isn't a designated "scent-free" event, because the organizers know that prostitutes like to wear perfume and hair spray. And they reapply all night long! CP2 teaches us that "inclusivity" and attention to "diversity" is more complicated than a formula learned in a self-designated feminist activist arena.[1]

Finally, CP2 challenges the assumption, taken for granted in most English-speaking contexts, that transsexuals automatically endorse a coalition with lesbians and gays and that they express themselves in these terms. The choice of invited guests is insightful in this light. CP2 has brought in a variety of transsexual individuals to promote their ideas and their work, including Max Valerio. Now, the festival certainly would have been able to garner more media attention if it had invited Leslie Feinberg, Riki Ann Wilchins, or even well-known San Francisco FTM activist James Green. Yet CP2 has refused such an easy solution, and instead has invited people who do not necessarily endorse a coalition with lesbians and gays. Invited guest Valerio, for instance, read from a section of his upcoming work when he presented at the festival in 1998. Among other material, Valerio read from a very charged segment that speaks about the powerful, almost uncontrollable, effects of testosterone on his sex drive and his daily life. He writes about feeling an uncontrollable, biological urge to rape. Valerio's work is challenging. He offers no easy solutions, and asks us to think. He doesn't provide a succinct recipe, or a passionate speech to motivate his listeners. He confronts us with the very raw material of our lives as transsexuals: we know, experientially, what it is to have testosterone rage through our bodies, to feel out of control, to want to do anything just to get off. It's not an argument that sits easily with feminists. And it's not one you will hear articulated by Leslie Feinberg or Kate Bornstein.

The choice of Valerio as a featured guest, then, challenges the requirement that transsexuals present ourselves in terms acceptable to English-speaking lesbians and gays.

CONCLUSION

*****

The CP2 festival is so important given the general silencing of transsexual voices in the mainstream and alternative media. It is a festival, to be sure, with images about transsexuals. And it is also a festival with images about transsexuals created by transsexuals. As such, CP2 intervenes in the actual institutional relations that determine what kinds of images get created, seen, and discussed. CP2 provides an engaging opportunity for an institutional analysis of culture.

At the beginning of this paper, I stated that everyone is talking about transsexuals. CP2 is crucial in this regard. More than just allowing us to note a recent visibility of transsexuals, CP2 asks us to think through the conditions that have rendered transsexuals invisible.

NOTES

1 Karl Marx, *The Eighteenth Brumaire of Louis Bonaparte* (Moscow: Progess Publishers, 1972): 106.

2 Judith Butler, *Gender Trouble: Feminism and the Subversion of Identity* (New York: Routledge, 1990); Judith Halberstam, *Female Masculinity* (Durham, NC: Duke University Press, 1998); Leslie Feinberg, *Stone Butch Blues* (Ithaca, NY: Firebrand, 1993); Kate Bornstein, *Gender Outlaw: On Men, Women, and the Rest of Us* (New York: Routledge, 1994); Riki Ann Wilchins, *Read My Lips: Sexual Subversion and the End of Gender* (Ithaca, NY: Firebrand Books, 1997).

3 Del LaGrace Volcano and Judith Halberstam, *The Drag King Book* (London: Serpent's Tail, 1999); Loren Cameron, *Body Alchemy* (San Francisco: Cleis Press, 1996); Dean Kotula, *The Phallus Palace: Female to Male Transsexuals* (Boston: Alyson, 2002).

4 Marjorie Garber, *Vested Interests: Cross-Dressing and Cultural Anxiety* (New York: Routledge, 1993), *passim*.

5 For a compelling analysis of the ways in which media interviews contain public representations of the private, pre-empting any political representation of the private, see Friederike Herrman, *Medien, Privatheit und Geschlecht: Bisexualität in Daily Talks* (Opladen: Leske und Budrich, 2002).

6 For more on the juridical dimensions of name change in Québec, see Viviane Namaste, *Invisible Lives: The Erasure of Transsexual and Transgendered People* (Chicago: University of Chicago Press, 2000).

7 An exposure of the discrimination against prostitutes within transsexual communities is available in Monica Forrester, Jamie-Lee Hamilton, Viviane Namaste, and Mirha-Soleil Ross, "Statement for Social Service Agencies and Transsexual/Transgendered Organizations on Service Delivery to Transsexual and Transvestite Prostitutes," *ConStellation* 7.1 (Spring 2002): 22–25.

8 Margaret Deirdre O'Hartigan, *Our Bodies, Your Lies: The Lesbian Colonization of Transsexualism* (Portland, Oregon: 1997). A copy of O'Hartigan's pamphlet can be obtained by writing her c/o P.O. Box 82447, Portland, Oregon, USA, 97282.

9 For more on the ways in which transsexuals must present themselves within the terms of lesbian and gay politics, see my *Invisible Lives: The Erasure of Transsexual and Transgendered People* (Chicago: University of Chicago Press, 2000): especially pp. 60–9.

10 Mirha-Soleil Ross, open letter, April 7, 1998.

11 Lessons from non-prostitute feminists working with prostitutes are instructive here. In the organization of a conference on prostitution, designed to bring together both prostitutes and feminists, the organizers met regularly for planning meetings. However, the meeting was held in a smoke-free house: a compromise was reached wherein one room was designated for non-smokers. All of the prostitutes were smokers, and so much of the concrete organizing was accomplished in that room. Here, politics that are friendly to non-smokers exclude, de facto, most prostitutes. See Laurie Bell, *Good Girls/Bad Girls: Feminists and Other Sex Trade Workers Face to Face* (Toronto: Women's Press, 1987): "Introduction," 13–14.

CHAPTER 31
Queer as Citizens

Brenda Cossman

In *Kissing Jessica Stein,* two 20-something straight girls—one curious, the other frustrated with the dating scene in New York—decide to give lesbian love a shot. And it works, at least for a while: they date, fall in love, and move in together; even Jessica's mother accepts her daughter's choice. The film is a story about exploring sexuality and accepting yourself for what you are or what you choose to become. It is a story about acceptance—self-acceptance, family acceptance, and community acceptance. And it is, in part, a story about normalizing lesbian sexuality—if not the erasure of difference, then at least its reduction to a matter of personal taste.

By contrast, the American version of the television show *Queer as Folk* follows the sexual exploits of a group of gay men who are unapologetically eroticized. They have sex—lots of it— with many sexual partners. They are pleasure seekers—sex and drugs and the throbbing beat of techno-pop. At least initially, they have no time for monogamy, marriage, or military service. The show openly mocks assimilation—disparaging everything from gay marriage to gay designer reality shows—for their heterosexual normativity. It is a story about sexual difference, about bodies saturated with sex, and about the difference that this sex makes.

Both of these cultural productions tell stories about sexual citizenship. *Kissing Jessica Stein* can be told as a story about citizenship as normalization. It is a story of assimilation in which the heterosexual requirement of membership is relaxed, but in which individuals can still live happily—if not ever after—in monogamous couplings, surrounded by loving families. By contrast, *Queer as Folk* can be told as a story about sexual citizenship that refuses normalization and assimilation. These are gay men who celebrate their sexual difference and their outlaw status. These are the contrasting stories, the fault lines of contemporary debates about sexual citizenship for gay men and lesbians: stories about assimilation versus subalternity, about the privileges of inclusion versus its normalizing costs.

Some tell the story as a progress narrative in which gay men and lesbians are in the process of becoming full and equal members of the polity, with increasing access to the panoply of rights and obligations of citizenship. Others tell a darker narrative about the costs of membership, with citizenship coming at the expense of transgression.

It is a debate that is all too well rehearsed in the context of gay marriage. Advocates of same-sex marriage argue that inclusion in this important social and legal institution is fundamental to the full citizenship of gay men and lesbians. It provides access to legal rights and responsibilities as well as to broader cultural discourses and practices of belonging. Opponents from within gay and lesbian communities argue that same-sex marriage will be normalizing and domesticating, undermining and excluding the more subversive dimensions of queer identities (Warner 1999). The debate performs an either/or of being for or against same-sex marriage, and for or against inclusion in citizenship as it is currently constituted. It is a debate that can be mapped rather neatly on *Kissing Jessica Stein* and *Queer as Folk*: assimilation versus transgression, monogamous loving relationships versus multiple libertine sex.

But, it is a debate that misses the messiness, ambivalence, and multiplicity of the inclusions and exclusions of citizenship. As performed, the debate utterly fails to capture the multiple readings that need to be brought to bear to the stories of inclusion and exclusion. *Kissing Jessica Stein* may be told in the register of assimilation. But, it can also be told as a story about the fluidity of sexuality. In an exchange with her two gay best friends, one accuses Helen of trying on lesbianism like a new fashion and reprimands Helen for the idea that she can just choose her sexuality. But, the other friend is more open-minded, encouraging Helen in her new pursuits. The vision of sexuality that infuses the film is one of the fluidity of sexuality, in which attraction and intimacy are not reducible to stable identity categories. *Kissing Jessica Stein* is then also a story of the socially constructed nature of sexuality, a story that challenges the more essentialist approaches that posit sexuality as a fixed category of identity. Jessica and Helen have a fluid sexuality, and their identities are not derived from these sexualities. The sexual politics of the film has a "more queer" sensibility, destabilizing the lines between heterosexual and homosexual, suggesting those lines are more porous and less important than those policing the borders would suggest. The private intimacies of Jessica and Helen are morphed into a more public transgression of stable sexual categories.

Similarly, *Queer as Folk* can be told as a "less queer" story. As Michael explains in the opening narration of the pilot, "The thing you need to know is, it's all about sex." Gay male identity is conflated with sex—public, anonymous, excessive sex. Straight folks are discussed with derision, representing all that these queer boys are not. Despite its name, *Queer as Folk* runs contrary to a queer politics. It does not challenge gay and lesbian identity categories, nor does it attempt to displace the hetero/homo binary. It posits an essentialized gay identity, a fixed identity constituted in and through sex, constructing itself in opposition to heterosexuality.

Nor is *Queer as Folk* unapologetically transgressive of established borders. The gay men in *Queer as Folk* are consumers. Brian's apartment is exquisitely modern, adorned with all the accoutrements of stylish living. His car, his clothes, his cell phone are always the best, the latest, the most beautiful. While the others in the posse are not as rich, they are no less consumption oriented. Indeed, these gay men inhabit a universe of private enterprise: from the glitzy bars to the small comic shop to the online live sex site, the gay counter public is a deeply marketized space. In *Queer as Folk,* the gay male subject comes into being as a privatized consumer of these sexualized spaces and services. Over the show's five seasons, many of its characters come to embrace the very issues that they initially mocked, like monogamy and marriage. *Kissing Jessica Stein* turns out to be open to a more queer reading, and *Queer as Folk* to a rather less one.

These rereadings suggest that struggles for sexual citizenship are more ambivalent than the fault lines of the debate would suggest. Some scholars have tried to make this point, arguing that inclusion within citizenship contains elements of both normalization and subversion (Stychin 2003; Weeks 1997, 1999). Others have suggested that the fault lines of the debate are themselves foreclosing. Judith Butler, for example, has argued that to be for or against gay marriage, gay rights, or inclusion within citizenship is to engage the framework of normalcy and deviance, of legitimacy and illegitimacy, that forecloses other ways of thinking about the sexual field (Butler 2004). In its dichotomized performance, the fault lines of the citizenship debate, particularly as it plays out in the context of same-sex marriage, fails to interrogate the transformations occurring in the process of becoming. Gay and lesbian subjects are in the process of becoming citizens. This process may be incomplete and uneven. But, it is a process that is underway. The sides of the debate fail to capture the multiplicities and contradictions of this process of becoming.

In attempting to move beyond the stultifying binaries of the same-sex marriage debate, Butler suggests that there are "middle zones and hybrid formations" between legitimacy and illegitimacy: "nonplaces ... are not sites of enunciation, but shifts in the topography from which a questionably audible claim emerges: the claim of the not-yet-subject and the nearly recognizable" (Butler 2004, 108). [...] I use the ambivalence of border crossing as an entry point into the same-sex marriage debate, in an attempt to displace the dichotomous performance of either/or. I approach same-sex marriage as a zone of ambivalence and multiplicity, arguing that as same-sex marriage becomes part of the present, the marriage debate is no longer productive. Same-sex marriage needs to be approached through the temporality of the present, as a new moment in the process of becoming, constituting new modalities of citizenship and new borders.

Rather than arguing for or against citizenship for gay and lesbian subjects, I explore some of the discursive and material realities and ambiguities of the process of becoming citizens. What happens at the borders of citizenship? As some gay and lesbian subjects cross the border into legitimate citizenship, how are those subjects transformed? In what ways are gay men and lesbians becoming subject to new forms of self-governance as they come inside marriage? How is citizenship transformed? And how is the border itself transformed? How porous is the border, and what anxieties are produced by such fluidity? How do these anxieties produce a desire for more intense border patrol? What is opened and what is closed at these border crossings?

SAME-SEX MARRIAGE AND THE ZONES OF AMBIVALENCE

Same-sex marriage has not been produced as a zone of ambivalence. Indeed, it may be among the least ambivalent zones in the public sphere. There are two positions: for or against. Social conservatives are against it. Progressive liberals are for it. In a parallel debate, gay and lesbian mainstream rights advocates are for it. Queer activists are against it. The debate has raged, and the dichotomies have been performed over and again. As Judith Butler has argued, it is a debate that forces a foreclosure of the spaces in between, of the questions that cannot be asked, because if one is not for it, one is against it (Butler 2004).

Further, it is a debate with a temporal dislocation: It assumes same-sex marriage as the future and debates the desirability of this future. But, same-sex marriage is no longer only of the future; it inhabits the present. Same-sex marriage now is—uneven, ambivalent, fragile—but it is.[1] Gay and lesbian subjects are getting married in the here and now. Indeed, gay and lesbian marriages are now in the past—as the ceremony fades into the day-to-day realities of marital practices, or further, into the shadows of divorce. The marriage debate must accordingly shift its focus from the future to the present, from what will be to what is starting to become. Same-sex marriage is not what it once was, as gay and lesbian subjects cross the borders into marriage and into citizenship. No longer the antithesis of gay and lesbian, what has marriage become? What have gay and lesbian become?

This process of becoming the present is found in the transformations within *Queer as Folk*. The representation of the gay and lesbian subjects is not static. While it may have begun as a performance of radical gay sexuality, in favour of sexual multiplicity and against sexual monogamy and marriage, its characters have changed over time. Michael—the one who brought us the foundational narrative "The thing you need to know is, it's all about sex"—enters into a monogamous relationship with Ben. Michael and Ben begin to displace Melanie and Lindsay, the lesbian couple, as the models of familial domesticity. They are not only monogamous, but they assume all of the trappings of a privatized, self-disciplining domesticity. Michael and Ben become the foster parents of a troubled teenager, Hunter. In the process, they must transform themselves into the folds of respectability, ever ready for the visit of the social worker. Their apartment, although small, is impeccably tidy. Theirs is not the average family—Ben and foster son Hunter are HIV positive. Their worries traverse the gay/straight spectrum, with self-discipline extending from domestic aesthetics to getting Hunter to school on time, to ensuring the diets, exercise, and mentality to keep the disease at bay.

In a dramatic shift from the show's earlier performance of gay politics, the fourth season ends with Michael and Ben getting married. They travel to Toronto, Canada, along with the gang, for the purpose of cycling back to Pittsburgh as part of the Liberty Ride, a fundraiser for a local hospice. En route to Toronto, Ben proposes and Michael—initially ambivalent—accepts. They go to City Hall, and in front of friends and family (Michael's mother Debbie is ever-present), exchange their wedding vows. But, not without the performance of the marriage debate. During his moment of doubt, Michael tells Brian that Ben has proposed, and the two argue.

> BRIAN: We're queer. We don't need marriage. We don't need the sanction of dickless politicians and pederast priests. We fuck who we want to, when we want to. That is our God-given right.
> MICHAEL: But it's also our God-given right to have everything that straight people have. Because we're every bit as much human as they are.

Not only does Michael overcome his doubt, but Brian puts his politics aside to make sure that the newlyweds are given a proper celebration. The marriage debate is performed, and although Brian does not change his views, he does respect and embrace his best friend's choice.

Their debate reveals something of the transformations that occur in the process of becoming citizens. As the gay subject comes to be incorporated into some of the institutions and practices of citizenship, a new range of choices confront this subject:

> BRIAN: ... And since when did you ever have the least interest in getting married?
> MICHAEL: I didn't. But not because I didn't want to, but because I never thought I could. It wasn't a story I told myself like straight kids did—you know, that someday I'd meet that special person and we'd fall in love and have a big wedding. It was never real for me. And all the stuff started happening in Massachusetts and California and here....

For Michael, law enters into the cultural realm, creating a narrative that was not possible before. The process of becoming brings into existence a range of possibilities and choices that were previously unthinkable: Now, marriage is thinkable, if not entirely legally accessible. With these new choices comes a further transformation of identity: Michael embraces an identity antithetical to his identity but a few years earlier. Crossing borders begets new borders.

The episode performs a multiplicity of border crossings, including a literal one. As the Liberty Ride comes to the Canada/U.S. border, Ben and Michael have their first newlywed encounter with the U.S. state as they attempt to cross the border as a married couple. The U.S. federal government does not recognize same-sex marriage and therefore refuses to allow them to submit a single customs card. The process of crossing the territorial border is simultaneously a recrossing of the social citizenship border; they are cast back into noncitizens, or less than full citizens, as they are reconstituted as unmarried. As the subjects cross the territorial border, their marriage is effectively annulled. Yet, the cultural reality of their marriage does cross the border—the couple wears their wedding rings, they made their commitment, they know in their hearts that their marriage is real.

While the territorial border survives intact, the cultural border between gay/straight, married/not married undergoes its own transformation. Ben and Michael live in a cultural space somewhere in between married and not married. They imagine and make audible a new identity—the gay married citizen—and a new practice of citizenship—two men performing marriage. It is an identity and practice that can be viewed through Brian's assimilationist lens: queers mimicking the most normalizing dimensions of heteronormativity. But, it can also be viewed through a lens of the multiple changes that accompany the process of becoming. Ben and Michael may be highly domesticated subjects, but they refuse to be de-eroticized. The final scene of the marriage episode closes on newlyweds Michael and Ben having sex with a lingering shot of the wedding bands on their fingers. A jarring punk version of "Over the Rainbow" plays in the background. On one hand, the scene can be read as the most normalized gay sex ever represented—it is not only marital sex, it is the scene of consummation, the very thing that makes a marriage real, transforming it from contract to status.

Yet, in an extraordinary transformation of the representation of gay sex as promiscuous, threatening, disrupting the social order here, in a double reversal, gay sex makes gay marriage real. In this scene, the gay subject/citizen refuses its de-eroticized modality. Not unlike the transformation of sodomite to citizen in the film *Wilde* and [U.S.] Supreme Court ruling in *Lawrence v. Texas,* citizenship is accomplished not through an erasure of the act of sodomy but, rather, in and through it. This performance of sodomy—sodomy as consummation—pushes at the edges of domesti-cated citizenship. Gay marriage is no longer sexually anesthetized; rather, in this representation, it includes sexual desire. One of the producers, Daniel Lipman, says of this scene:

> What happened was the music forced you to hear the song that you've heard a zillion times in a new way. The lyrics, what they're saying, is "somewhere over the rainbow, birds can fly, why can't I?" and what you see are the two men who are married, who have rings. Basically, they are saying "we are here, gay marriage is here, and whatever happens, ultimately, you're going to have to recognize it, world." And you look at that in a new way with the song.

Alongside the jarring music, the viewer is asked to reimagine a world in which gay marriage simply is. The music also forces the viewer to reimagine a world in which gay marriage includes sex. It is a new look not only at gay marriage, but also at gay sex: gay sex as domesticated within mar-riage but not erased, and gay sex as a site of celebration, erotic desire, and relational commitment.

This consummation scene represents another in-between space, a middle zone between mar-riage and non-marriage, between legitimate and illegitimate citizenship. Gay sex is domesticat-ed, yet the heterosexual core of marital sex is displaced. Gay marital sex is performed publicly, as it simultaneously privatizes that desire. The subjects are transformed, the border is transformed, the practices of citizenship are transformed in ways both more and less radical than a dichotom-ized same-sex marriage debate can capture.

The marriage episodes also witness a series of border crossings in the underlying gender politics of the show. The gay/lesbian opposition played out in earlier seasons of *Queer as Folk* is now further complicated. It is no longer simply the heteronormativized lesbians who embrace familial domesticity, but it becomes part of the potential identity of the gay male citizen. Yet, there is arguably still an underlying opposition: Just as the gay men do weddings better (recall that they saved Mel and Lindsay's wedding), so too do the gay men do familial domesticity better. The domestication of Ben and Michael within the bonds of sexual matrimony occurs at precisely the same time as Melanie and Lindsay—once the models of a much disparaged familialized domesticity—are coming undone. The season ends with Mel and Lindsay separating because of Lindsay's affair with a man. Becoming citizens sets them up for citizenship failure. Mel and Lindsay have stumbled on the terrain of citizenship. They are bad citizens—not by being outside of marriage, but by failing within its terms.

These marriage episodes at the fourth season of *Queer as Folk* mark a moment in the process of becoming in which gay and lesbian subjects have crossed a particular set of borders into legitimate citizenship and begun to engage, in ways both aspirational and oppositional, with the terrain of marriage. Marriage is no longer represented as the antithesis of gay identity but as a possible choice of citizenship.

It is also represented as involving a range of risks of citizenship once reserved for heterosexuals. Same-sex marriage is no longer simply aspirational or, conversely, something to be against. As it becomes part of the sexual field, part of the terrain of sexual citizenship, gay and lesbian subjects will now have to negotiate its multiple normativities and regulatory practices. Consummation and adultery, once exclusively heterosexual terms, will themselves be transformed by the entrance of these new citizens and so, too, will these new citizens be transformed by their entry into a world that includes consummation and adultery, in ways that remain as yet unknown.

REAL MARRIAGE IN REAL TIME

*****

The idea of marriage as commitment is a redefinition consistent with what Anthony Giddens and others have called the "transformation of intimacy" (Beck 1999; Giddens 1992). Marriage has changed from a lifelong status to an individualized and voluntary relationship intended to promote the emotional well-being of its parties (Giddens 1992). It is based on individual choice and individual fulfillment; entry and exit is governed by individual choice rather than lifelong commitment. In this transformation, marriage is no longer a lifelong commitment for reproduction, childrearing, and social stability but rather a relationship of emotional intimacy. Giddens describes it as a "pure relationship"—a relationship that is "entered into for its own sake, for what can be derived by each person from a sustained association with another; and which is continued only insofar as it is thought by both parties to deliver enough satisfactions for each individual to stay within it" (Giddens 1992, 58). It is based on the idea of confluent love or an "opening oneself out to the other"; its continuation depends on the ability to sustain intimacy (Giddens 1992, 61). As Giddens further argues, pure relationships and confluent love have "no specific connection to heterosexuality" (63).

This transformation of intimacy is evident in the pro same-sex marriage cases where marriage is redefined as no longer about procreation and channelling sexuality but rather about voluntary commitment and emotional intimacy. The incorporation of same-sex couples into the institution has precipitated a transformation in the articulated definition of the institution. Admittedly, these changes to the definition of marriage have not been caused by same-sex marriage, but reflect broader social transformations in the relationships of intimacy through the latter part of the twentieth century. It's these broader transformations of intimacy that produce same-sex marriage as imaginable, as a meaningful idea. Nonetheless, it is in these constitutional challenges that many of these inchoate changes to social understandings of marriage are being legally articulated. It is in the moment of border crossing, of same-sex couples being included in the institution of marriage, that marriage must be explicitly redefined.

*****

This is not, however, to suggest a winner in the same-sex marriage debates. While same-sex marriage does seem to have a transformative dimension, it is not unambivalently so. If marriage is being redefined as commitment, it is important to ask, Commitment to what? At an obvious level, it is commitment of two people to each other. But, what is the nature of this commitment? What is its purpose, and what is its effect? […]

In the pro same-sex marriage decisions, marriage is all about social stability through the orderly distribution of rights and responsibilities, the privatization of dependency, and raising children. Commitment involves the commitment not simply of two people to each other, but a commitment of those two people to live with each other and the world around them in a particular way. It is an economic commitment to assume mutual rights and responsibilities, to financially support each other and their children. It is a sexual and emotional commitment to monogamy and fidelity, a commitment to each other to the exclusion of all others. It is a commitment that is, at least in principle, lifelong. Despite the rejection of marriage as in essence about procreation, this emphasis on stability, monogamy, and fidelity has a strikingly similar effect; marriage is produced as including stable and responsible procreation in monogamous relationships. Unpacking the commitment suggests that it is a vision of marriage that is not that different from the one articulated in the anti same-sex marriage decisions. It is a commitment to having and raising children in a stable, two-parent, monogamous family, admittedly with a nonheterosexual twist. It is a commitment to the very vision of marriage that queer scholars have critiqued, that is, a highly privatized, domesticated, normalized vision of human relationships.

While same-sex marriage forces the articulation of a significant transformation in marriage, it is simultaneously performed through the rearticulation of many of its more conventional dimensions. [...]

*****

[The] two sides of the same-sex marriage debate have more in common than may initially meet the eye. Both are encountering the constitutive tension of citizenship and border control. Citizenship requires borders; it demands an inside and an outside, with clear lines of demarcation between the two. Porous borders cannot be protected, so border crossings—the inclusion of the previously excluded into citizenship—must necessarily be accompanied by a propping up of the crossed borders. While one side seeks to maintain heterosexuality as a thick border, the other seeks to maintain the borders of marriage by redefining it in the language of intimacy and solidarity. Further, both sides increasingly share a language of the citizenship of gay and lesbian subjects. As gay and lesbian subjects become citizens—or at least unbecome outlaws—they can no longer be vilified in the moral discourse that only a few years ago was still politically viable. And it is this process of becoming that creates the very anxiety of border control. Both sides are producing and responding to anxieties about border control, which in turn reconstitute the borders and the citizens who cross them.

GOVERNANCE INSIDE MARRIAGE

As same-sex couples come inside marriage, they will become—or will seek to become—subject to its regulatory practices. The inside of marriage is a site of multiple forms of legal regulation and self-governance. It involves not only a set of legal rights and responsibilities, but also a broad set of societal expectations and practices of self-conduct. As they cross the border into marriage, same-sex couples will begin to face a new set of citizenship norms. They, too, now face societal judgment for practices unbecoming of a citizen. Like Melanie and Lindsay, the lesbian couple in *Queer as Folk,* or Bette and Tina on *The L Word,* these same-sex couples now face a new set of risks of citizenship failure: adultery, relationship breakdown, divorce.

*****

[...] [U]nlike the constitutional challenges, the plaintiffs in these cases [of marriage failure] are no longer heroic citizens, performing the virtues of stable, privatized citizenship, but rather are now failed citizens. They are forced to relitigate their marriages at the moment of marriage failure. Their failure is held up for a kind of public viewing.

*****

Some social conservatives have been quick to jump on the bandwagon of these divorce cases, not only as a way of relitigating the invalidity of the initial border crossing, but also as a way of performatively ridiculing the very idea of same-sex commitment and stability. [...]

[...]Same-sex couples will be increasingly subject to the same set of cultural norms and practices as opposite-sex couples, including the mandate to make their relationships a project of self-governance and to take all reasonable steps to minimize the risk of relationship breakdown. They, too, will be called upon to become responsible risk managers, who recognize the fragility of relationships and will take all reasonable steps to minimize the risk of relationship breakdown, including immunizing their relationship from the epidemic of adultery.

Some of these messages of self-regulation have begun to appear in the cultural domain of same-sex marriage. In the marriage episodes of *Queer as Folk,* where the marriage of Ben and Michael is accompanied by the separation of Melanie and Lindsay, we begin to see this idea that entrance into marriage includes exposure to a new set of relational risks including infidelity and divorce. Mel and Lindsay have stumbled on the new citizenship terrain. Having become sexual citizens, they now represent a rather unbecoming facet of it: infidelity, failure to work on their relationship before and after it, and separation notwithstanding the presence of very young children. Theirs is a failed sexual citizenship, within the new politics of adultery and the pushback on divorce.

Lindsay's affair plays out many of the fears of the new politics of adultery. It is a woman choosing to have an affair; she has the affair at work; she fails to resist at the moment when she could have just said no; and, contrary to the therapeutic model of deliverance, she is not sufficiently contrite and apologetic in its aftermath to allow for treatment. Mel too, however, is unable to commit herself to the course of treatment; she is unable to forgive Lindsay and unwilling to do the work on the path of forgiveness. Lindsay's affair is made all the worse by its timing. Melanie is pregnant with what was supposed to be the couple's second child. Lindsay has not only jeopardized her relationship, she has jeopardized the well-being of her family and her family-to-be. She has callously put her sexual self-interest in front of the interests of their children—born and unborn. While in the new politics of adultery, sexual infidelity always represents a citizenship failure, the familial circumstances of the couple heightens the nature of the infraction.

There is a further twist in Lindsay's infidelity, insofar as her affair is with a man. This makes her infidelity both more and less transgressive. On the one hand, she has engaged in heterosexual sexual intercourse and has therefore committed adultery by the strictest of legal definitions. On the other hand, her affair with a man raises questions about her sexuality. After all these years, is Lindsay really a heterosexual, a reading that would fit within the show's performance of a fairly rigid gay/straight dichotomy? Or, does her sexual desire begin to displace that dichotomous sexuality, creating the possibility of a more fluid sexuality? To what extent are Mel and Lindsay separating because Lindsay has had sex with a man or because Lindsay has had sex with another person? Is the violation a specifically lesbian one? Or is it simply a marital exclusivity one?

This sexual ambivalence plays back into the new politics of adultery. If the violation is that Lindsay had sex with a man, then there are several interpretive possibilities. One reading is that Lindsay is a heterosexual woman. Although she has failed in her relationship, it was untrue from the beginning. Lindsay would be analogous to the *Oprah* and *Dr. Phil* stories of husbands who realize that they are gay or transsexuals. In *Oprah's* "My Husband Is Gay" or *Dr. Phil's* "Extreme Marriages," the infidel husband is treated differently from those who have heterosexual affairs. The infidelity is condemned, but the dissolution of the relationship is treated with a kind of inevitability. The major mistake that these husbands made was a failure of self-discovery: They failed themselves and their families by not recognizing their gay essence before they married. The infidelity is not the major story but a kind of subplot leading to an inevitable conclusion.[2]

In a second reading, Lindsay is bisexual. This is a much more complicated terrain, in which the risk of infidelity is exponentially higher. Bisexuality, in popular discourse, is often associated with non-monogamy; bisexuals are only really bisexual if they have relationships with women and men at the same time (Klesse 2005). It is associated with a kind of failure in self-discipline; bisexuals are individuals who cannot even commit themselves to a single gender, not to mention a single person. If Lindsay is bisexual, her relationship then faces a heightened risk of infidelity and a diminished capacity for self-discipline. In order to protect her relationship and her children from the chaos of adultery, Lindsay will have to work at least twice as hard as a straight woman to ensure that she does not fall prey to the seductions of adulterous desire. On the flip side, the problem for Mel is that she must be able to work to forgive Lindsay. But, unlike the more run-of-the-mill heterosexual victim of adultery, she must be able to forgive the fact that Lindsay had sex with a man. She must now recognize and embrace the possibility of bisexual adultery: The risk is higher, and the ability to forgive potentially more difficult. The generic risks and harms of violating marital exclusivity are thereby heightened, making the possibility of treatment even more challenging.

In a third reading, Lindsay is a lesbian who has sex with men. After Lindsay's sexual encounter with the artist Sam, Melanie becomes suspicious and confronts Lindsay. Lindsay does not deny the affair, but instead insists that it "reconfirmed for me that this is who I am. That my life is with you and Gus. And the baby. That I still choose you." Melanie, unable to forgive Lindsay, continues to focus on the fact that she had sex with a man and that she cannot be a lesbian.

> MELANIE: I know which team I play on. It's not a choice or a preference. It's who I am. It's who I've always been. A rug muncher, a muff diver, a cunt lapper, a bull, a lezzie, a dyke.
> LINDSAY: What do you think I am?

MELANIE: Don't ask me to make up your mind for you. You have to do that all by yourself.

LINDSAY: I'm a lesbian.

MELANIE: Not if you're having sex with a man, honey.

Lindsay insists on her identity as a lesbian, while Melanie denies her qualifications. Lesbian becomes a site of contestation. Is it defined exclusively in terms of sexual desire and sexual practice? Is it a category foreclosed by one sexual encounter to the contrary? Lindsay acted out her desire for Sam but argues that it only reconfirmed her identity as a lesbian. It is an acknowledgment and simultaneous denial of a category of lesbians: lesbians who have sex with men.

The category of lesbians who have sex with men is one that begins to confuse the gay/straight dichotomy, while remaining framed within it. It still insists on the identity of lesbian, yet it refuses to define it exclusively in terms of sexual desire and practice. It also raises the possibilities of a more fluid notion of sexuality—one defined in less absolutist terms. Lindsay's affair is, in one reading, reminiscent of the sexuality of *Kissing Jessica Stein* in which attraction and intimacy are not reducible to stable identity categories. Yet, even with this reading, with its more fluid and contested notions of sexuality, there is no narrative ambivalence over the infidelity: Lindsay cheated. She violated the terms of their marriage. She put her relationship at risk, and she seriously compromised the best interests of the children of the marriage.

In the final season, Melanie and Lindsay reconcile. They looked over the edge of their relationship abyss and, against the odds, they came back. They become part of the mysterious 35 percent of couples who survive infidelity (although there are no known statistics about same-sex couples and infidelity). Melanie is able to forgive Lindsay; she recommits herself to the relationship and to the process of rebuilding trust and intimacy. It is part of the complicated story of treatment and relationship redemption in the new politics of adultery. It is not enough for the guilty party to simply seek forgiveness; the other party must be prepared to engage in the equally difficult work of forgiveness and reconstruction.

Despite these ambivalences and the fairy tale ending, the message is consistent with the new politics of adultery: Extramarital sex is dangerous, corrosive, destructive. It will ruin your relationship. Gay or straight, don't do it. It is a story that runs counter to the nonmonogamous narrative that characterized some of the other gay relationships in *Queer as Folk*. Brian, in particular, long insisted that monogamy is for heterosexuals. Yet, even Brian and Justin have their rules: no kissing on the mouth, no repeat partners. They, too, have their lines for protecting the emotional intimacy of their relationship. It may be a far cry from the new politics of adultery, which condemns any and all forms of sexual interaction with another. But, they have their own version of fidelity. Brian and Justin are juxtaposed with Michael and Ben, who are more traditionally monogamous. In one of the episodes of the fourth season, Ben is shown facing down an adulterous seduction, and in keeping with his promise of sexual and emotional exclusivity to Michael, just says no. Ben performs the ethical moment of the new politics of adultery, the moment where resistance is possible. In contrast, Lindsay did not. While Brian may still be opposing the normativity of this new sexual citizenship, Ben is becoming a good citizen within its discursive frame. Lindsay is not. The ideas of the new politics of adultery can thus be found creeping into the show's narratives, despite the ambivalent performance of the citizenship debates.

Queer as Folk is not alone in these representations. *The L Word,* Showtime's lesbian version of *Queer as Folk,* explores the romantic and sexual exploits of a group of rather fashionable lesbian friends living in Los Angeles. Amongst the many characters are Bette and Tina, who in the first season are the long-term lesbian couple trying to have a baby. But, before the season is over, the not-so-stable-after-all couple is rocked by infidelity: Bette has a passionate affair with Candace, the sexy carpenter helping her with her gallery's art installation. Tina discovers the affair through an intimate touch exchanged between Bette and Candace. The couple has an emotional confrontation, ending in tearful sex. But, the damage is done, and the season ends with Tina leaving. She takes refuge at her friend Alice's apartment, where she is shown in tears, her wedding ring removed.

Much of the second season focuses on their separation. Tina and Bette are shown with their lawyers, arguing over the terms of their "divorce" and their division of property. Yet, throughout the legal conflicts, Bette desperately wants to get back together. She tries to apologize, privately and publicly, in hope of reconciliation. But, her efforts are rebuffed by Tina, who becomes involved with another woman, Helena. The plot is further complicated by the fact that Tina is now pregnant, with a baby that she and Bette had planned to have together. Eventually, after much work on Bette's part, the couple reconciles, and Tina moves back home for the birth of their child.

Bette's infidelity is loaded with many of the messages of the new politics of adultery. It is costly and destructive. It could have been resisted but it isn't. It is with a woman who works for her. It is a woman having the affair. Moreover, it is a manifestation of an underlying crisis of intimacy: The couple has been drifting apart for several months. But, it is the infidelity itself—the ultimate act of betrayal—that pushes the couple over the edge into relationship breakdown. While treatment may be possible, it is never guaranteed, and in this case, Tina is initially unable and unwilling to forgive Bette. Bette is devastated by the breakup, all the more so by the fact that she is ultimately responsible for it. She replays the affair in her mind, trying in her words, to figure out "the moment that I could have said no" (episode 203). Resistance is possible and would have been the better option. But, ultimately, she does the hard work of contrition and apology, and Tina eventually forgives her. In the third season, it becomes clear that Bette has learned her lesson. When confronted with the possible seduction of a beautiful senator, to whom she is obviously attracted, Bette walks away.

Queer as Folk and *The L Word* are illustrative of the kind of self-governance to which same-sex couples may be increasingly subject. Being inside marriage means being subject to its regime of responsibilization. It means taking responsibility for one's marriage and taking all necessary precautions against its failure. [...] [T]his is a kind of governance that may be increasingly performed on a cultural rather than a legal terrain. While it may be a while before same-sex couples begin to appear on *Dr. Phil,* self-help guides for same-sex couples are beginning to appear, some of which specifically highlight the challenges of sexual exclusivity for a culture that has at times self-consciously celebrated nonmonogamy. For example, in an article posted on the National Center for Lesbian Rights website, lesbians are advised on how to survive infidelity (Huntington). Some of the advice is lesbian-specific, noting for example that lesbians are more likely to have affairs than straight couples: "Well, whereas straight men and women have best friends, comrades and confidants of the same sex who they are not attracted to, lesbians are almost always best friends with a potential mate." The treatment advice directly parallels that directed at heterosexual married couples in the new politics of adultery: "complete honesty," severing any and all contact with the third party, taking responsibility, and getting "to work and fix[ing] your relationship" (Huntington). Such self-help guides are likely only the beginning of a multiplicity of cultural representations that will subject gay and lesbian subjects to these new citizenship norms.

*****

The politics of adultery is but one example of how the inside of marriage will subject gay and lesbian subjects to a new form of governance. It is an example of how inclusion within citizenship transforms the subjects, and in the language of its critics, subjects them to a regime of normalization.

When same-sex relationships are recognized—legally or culturally—same-sex couples become subject to the demands of responsibilization. They, too, will be called upon to take responsibility for their relationships, to make their relationships a project, and to work hard on them to make them work. Citizenship success within this new-found recognition lies in the choices of individuals. Good citizens will choose to work hard to manage the risks to their relationships. If the going gets tough, they will choose to work harder, calling in the experts if necessary. And if they fail, they will be subject to the regime's normative judgments of unbecoming citizenship.

QUEER EYE BEYOND THE GAY/STRAIGHT GUY

In *Queer Eye for the Straight Guy*, five gay men come to the rescue of a disheveled straight man. They descend upon his house like an aesthetic swat team and engage in "a playful deconstruction of the subject's current lifestyle" (QueerEye.com). Carson, the fashion stylist, savages his clothes closet—making fun of his style and throwing out clothes by the pound. Thom, the interior designer, disparages the décor or lack thereof and begins the process of purging furniture, lamps, and other sundry items that have seen better days. Ted, the food and wine guy, tackles the kitchen and parodies the food in the fridge. Kyan, the beauty guru, zeros in on the obscenities of the bathroom, focusing on the filth and the lack of grooming products. And Jai, the culture guy, tries to figure out their straight guy's cultural edge, anxiety, or aspirations.

Having established his multiple fashion and aesthetic crimes, the Fab Five set out to "build a better straight man." They take him shopping and begin a makeover. All the while, the banter is playful—simultaneously teasing and supportive. The Fab Five try to get a sense of their straight man—his likes and dislikes, his comforts and aspirations. They listen to him. While they make him over, they try to do so in a way that respects his inner sense of self. And they listen in particular to his romantic goals: he wants to be a better boyfriend or husband; he wants to change for the love in his life; or if he is single, he wants to bring love into his life. Throughout the show, both his inner self and his romantic aspirations are the referent points for the Fab Five's transformation.

*****

The show is a shopping fest, highlighting the newest trends and brand names in fashion, home design, grooming, food, and culture. It is a performance in marketized citizenship, where status and identity is produced through consumption. The goal of the Fab Five is to increase their straight man's cultural capital, by teaching him to make better consumer choices, all the while remaining true to his social origins (Bordieu 1984). But, the show is about more than consumer citizenship and its brand names. It works because of the synergy between the Fab Five—the constant witty repartee, the mild sexual banter, all with a gay twist. And it works because of the synergy between the Fab Five and their straight man. While they engage in relentless teasing, it is done with a kind of earnest sensitivity; they care about their straight guy, they want to make him a better straight man, they want him to succeed. They are experts in the arts of self-transformation and self-governance, and they only succeed if he succeeds, if he learns to take better care of his domestic life.

Some have criticized the show for playing into gay stereotypes (Sawyer 2003). Others suggest that the show transcends those stereotypes. It is a debate not unlike same-sex marriage with positions for or against; is it assimilation or transgression. And not unlike the marriage debate, it is a debate that misses the broader discursive significance of the Fab Five as the new models of citizenship. As media critic Jack Myers has observed, "*Queer Eye* takes the stereotypical gay character and elevates him to iconic status" (Myers 2003). *Queer Eye* is not simply illustrative of gay men crossing the borders into legitimate citizenship; rather these five gay men have become heroic citizens. They come to the rescue of domesticity, heterosexuality, and masculinity.

*****

While *Queer Eye* is not alone in its attention to the aesthetics of domestic consumption and self-conduct, it does so in a rather unique way. *Queer Eye* is all about the role of gay men as experts in this resuscitation. As some of its detractors have pointed out, gay men have long been associated with the domestic arts—they are the decorators, the fashionistas, the stylists—now, these gay men are specifically coming to the rescue of the straight guy in this domestic sphere. With changing gender relationships, heterosexual men can no longer simply rely on women—as mothers or wives—to maintain the domestic sphere.

These men sometimes live alone—never married, newly divorced, or widowed. Or they live with women who themselves seem to have lost the art of the domestic. With this once invisible work of the domestic sphere—decorating, cooking, dressing, and grooming—no longer being performed by women, the domestic is collapsing into utter disarray, at precisely the same time as greater emphasis is being placed on the domestic as a site of cultural capital and aesthetic self-governance. These men are desperately in need of training in the lost arts of the domestic.

[…]These are heterosexual men whose failure in the domestic sphere is threatening their ability to attract, marry, and/or keep a partner. The masculinity that these straight men have been performing is failed one: It is operating to repel—or at least not sexually excite—the very women that they want to attract. As one commentator has observed, beneath all of its queerness, *Queer Eye* embraces the very traditional ideal of heterosexual romance: "In its best moments, it's about rekindling romance for the person who makes us want to be better people—it's about understanding and empathy, and the Fab Five are the guiding spirits to that ideal" (Shimes 2003).

The Fab Five do their work by privileging heterosexual masculinity, while simultaneously remaking it. [...] [T]hey are not out to destroy masculinity, but to perfect it. They are, in their own words, "building a better straight man." It is by placing heterosexual masculinity in this privileged position—as that which is in need of rescue—and by positioning the Fab Five as the knights in shining armour, that *Queer Eye* is able to accomplish a reversal in the terms of citizenship success and failure. [...] It is this positioning that allows for a reconfiguration in the relationship between them. The gay men become the experts in performing heterosexual masculinity, as they teach the straight guy to perform it better.

Ironically, this rescue is accomplished through a ritualized performance of the gay/straight dichotomy. [...] The show's tension works because of its reversal of the traditional antipathy of straight men to homosexuality. Straight men must displace their discomfort with gay men in favour of trust. And the Fab Five are as gay as gay can be. [...] While Carson, the fashion guy, may be the most screamingly effeminate, each of them perform their sexuality. The straight guys are similarly confidently—if ineffectually—heterosexual. They play poker or collect baseball paraphernalia; they wear rock and roll t-shirts or NASCAR hats. There is no mistaking the differences between gay and straight.

Yet, the gay/straight opposition is simultaneously reconfigured. Not only are gay men cast as the heroes of straight men, but the very border dividing them is destabilized. The straight men must be prepared to accept the sexuality of the Fab Five, to be the focus of its attention albeit for a few brief days with considerable pecuniary benefit, but nonetheless in a kind of public spotlight where the presence of their sexuality cannot be avoided. The very difference capable of producing cataclysmic violence is here downgraded and reconfigured as a kind of ironic, playful cleavage. United in the pursuit of a better masculinity, the erotic is both more and less important. The gay/straight relationship is reconstituted, with gay men as experts in all things male, and with straight men as the willing receptacles of their knowledge.

The mainstreaming of gay characters on prime-time television, and the queering of cultural citizenship, is, paradoxically, performed through a simultaneous deconstruction of the very categories that bring gay/straight into being. Becoming citizens means becoming both more and less gay, as the category of gay becomes less stable. Gay/straight required clear borders. But as gay crosses into citizenship, the borders become more porous and more ambiguous.

Queer Eye bears more than a slight resemblance to same-sex marriage. It delivers a message about the importance of marriage. It tells us that good citizens must make their marriage—or their relationship or their relationship in prospect—a project. They must learn to work hard on their relationship by working first on themselves. The queer boys of *Queer Eye* are the heroic citizens who will lead this renewal of the domestic and help save heterosexuality from imminent collapse, just as same-sex couples are cast as heroic citizens who are committed to the fundamental importance of the institution of marriage. *Queer Eye* and same-sex marriage are both arguments for marriage and the intimate sphere: these are important, indeed absolutely crucial, sites for our personal happiness and self-fulfillment.

In both *Queer Eye* and same-sex marriage, the queering of citizenship begins to blur the boundaries that produced gay and straight, citizen and non-citizen, hero and outlaw. They both help reveal the extent to which the transformations in the modalities of sexual citizenship require an analysis that moves beyond a focus on the multiple instantiations of heteronormativity. The sexing, privatizing, and self-disciplining of citizenship is occurring in many ways not captured by a focus on a gay/straight divide, in the multiple contestations of sexual citizenship between and among straight citizens, and in the ways in which these same contestations and forms of governance are extending to the gay citizen.

The debates about both *Queer Eye* and same-sex marriage also raise questions about who is policing the borders of citizenship. We have seen the extent to which social conservatives are attempting to resurrect heterosexuality as a thick border. We have also seen the extent to which many courts entrusted with border patrol allow border crossings only by reinforcing the idea of clearly delineated borders. But, there are also ways in which those inside gay or queer politics are engaged in varying forms of border patrol. For example, the debate about *Queer Eye* involves the question of representability: who gets to be represented and what qualifies as a gay stereotype. Its critics suggest that the Fab Five are simply gay caricatures, reinforcing negative stereotypes of gay identity as queens, designers, and decorators. Underlying this critique is the idea that these gay stereotypes hark back to a day of exclusion (or at best, limited inclusion as decorating consultations) and that they are best left behind as gay and lesbian subjects cross the borders into citizenship. There is an implicit policing of the borders of citizenship here, with only some gay and lesbian subjects entitled to cross, lest the other less respectable subjects undermine the legitimacy of those newly inscribed citizens. It may encourage border crossing (for some); it nevertheless seeks to police that border.

The queer critique of same-sex marriage is one that arguably engages in its own form of border control. In asserting that same-sex marriage is normalizing of gay and lesbian identity, there is a way in which this queer critique has the paradoxical effect of propping up the very gay/straight dichotomy that it so often seeks to deconstruct. The very identity of queer seems to be predicated on its exclusion; its radical and subversive nature is dependent on remaining on the outside. The idea here is that if gay and lesbian subjects cross the borders into citizenship, and become assimilated into its many norms and practices, they will lose their radical edge.

While queer theory is extremely critical of the essentialist notions of identity that inform much gay and lesbian politics, including the movement toward same-sex marriage, there is a way in which their defense of the outside, the outlaw, the beyond has the effect of reinforcing a gay/straight opposition, with gays/queers on the outside and straights on the inside of citizenship. The queer side of the same-sex marriage debate appears to be oddly vested in the very border and its underlying dichotomies that it asserts to be an artifice. In a reversal of the claim that marriage excludes the queer, this critique can be read as insisting on its own exclusion.

QUEER AFTER GAY

Six Feet Under, HBO's award-winning offbeat drama, tells the story of the lives, loves, and losses of the Fisher family, who own and operate a funeral home in Los Angeles. The show begins with the death of the patriarch, Nathaniel Fisher, which sets the stage for his two sons, Nate and David, to take over the family business. Among the cast of characters are their mother, Ruth, their teenage sister, Claire, and a revolving door of their girlfriends, boyfriends, and spouses. The dysfunctionality of the Fisher family is set against the arbitrary nature of death, with the regular cast supplemented in each show by corpses, grieving families, and visiting ghosts. The show's sardonic humour explores the emotional melodrama and repressed desires of each of the characters, as they fumble through their daily existence, surrounded by death.

David, like the other main characters of *Six Feet Under*, is on an emotional journey, trying to come to terms with his internal demons. But, David's particular struggle begins, and ends, with the fact that he is gay. Throughout the first season, David struggles with his closeted sexual identity and his on-again off-again relationship with boyfriend Keith. He eventually comes out to his family, but his self-loathing continues, with recurrent relationship crises and confrontations. Along the way, the show explores the ups and clowns of David and Keith's same-sex relationship, from negotiating monogamy to adopting children.

David's brother Nate—heterosexual to his core—struggles with his own demons—an inability to commit to a relationship, wavering between Brenda and Lisa (he marries each one in due course). Nate never conquers his demons; his first wife dies, and he is about to leave his pregnant second wife when he suddenly dies. Nor does he find solace in death, coming back to taunt Brenda. It is David who triumphs. It is David and Keith whose relationship survives, who adopt children, who buy the funeral home, redecorate it, and live happily, if not "ever after," in it. It is the same-sex couple who overcome their adversities, their demons in themselves and each other, and who negotiate the treacherous terrain of a marriage-like relationship.

Six Feet Under is not a gay show in the style of *Queer as Folk*, *The L Word*, or even *Queer Eye for the Straight Guy*. It is a quirky family drama, which has a gay man as one of the central characters. It is a kind of post–identity politics cultural representation, where gay characters begin to be mainstreamed into a broader narrative. It is a new kind of mainstreaming, in which gay characters have crossed the borders into representation in a way that begins to explore their multidimensionality rather than simply their gayness. While their gayness [is] an important part of their emotional and relational struggles, it [is] not their whole story.

David and Keith's relationship is tumultuous. They fight and bicker. At times, it is simply a representation of the daily discord of intimacy; other times, it is a manifestation of deeper psychic wounds. They go to couples therapy to work on their relationship and to work on themselves. As self-disciplining selves, they seek to manage the risks of their relationship. Their relationship is also sexual. From the beginning to the end, David and Keith—like all the characters—have sex. Despite their move toward, and episodic repulsion from, domesticity, David and Keith are deeply sexual beings. They watch porn. They have hot passionate sex together. Sometimes, they have sex with other men. But, even as they move toward monogamy, their conjugal lives affirm the sexual. Their citizenship is not achieved at the expense of sex, but rather, is affirmed on the terrain of the sexual, alongside the familial and the domestic.

Six Feet Under represents a reversal in the heterosexual conventions of sexual citizenship. After six seasons it is the same-sex couple that emerges triumphant in life, even if unable to avoid the vicissitudes of death. It is the same-sex couple that embraces domesticity, that seriously undertakes couples counseling to work on their relationship, and that buys and manages the family business. It is the same-sex couple that succeeds in all the markers of good citizenship—domesticated sexual citizenship, market citizenship, and self-disciplining citizenship.

They are not alone; the Fab Five too have emerged as new model citizens. But unlike the gay

men of *Queer Eye,* David and Keith are avowedly sexual. Their citizenship may have circumscribed sex to the domestic sphere, but in that sphere, the sex is represented and affirmed. In
many ways, David and Keith evoke the zeitgeist of the present. As same-sex marriage becomes
a reality, as gay and lesbian couples cross the border into this dimension of citizenship, new
realities are produced; new things are happening that are simply not captured by a debate that
argues for or against. Borders are being crossed, moved, defended, and reconstituted. Citizens
are being made, contested, and remade. It is a process within which some gay men can even
emerge as heroic citizens—their avowedly sexual citizenship coupled with domesticity, markets, and self-discipline. And as they cross the borders, so too are the borders transformed. To
the extent that queer citizenship is beginning to disrupt and unsettle the borders between gay
and straight, queer critique needs to move beyond its focus on the heteronormative if it is to
capture the emerging modalities and ambivalence of inclusion and exclusion. Just like in *Six Feet
Under,* gay/straight is coming undone.

NOTES

1 This is not to suggest that the battles over same-sex marriage have been won. Clearly, they have not,
as legal defeats in constitutional challenges to the opposite-sex definition of marriage and state constitutional amendments protecting traditional marriage continue to pile up. In July 2006 the New
York Court of Appeals and the Washington State Supreme Court reversed lower court rulings and
upheld the opposite-sex definition of marriage; the Georgia Supreme Court reinstated a constitutional
amendment banning gay marriage; a federal appeals court reinstated a Nebraska voter-approved ban
on same-sex marriage; and the Tennessee Supreme Court dismissed an effort to keep a proposed
ban on same-sex marriage off the November ballot. Forty-five states have banned same-sex marriage
through statute or constitutional amendment. But, despite the ongoing struggles and setbacks, gay
men and lesbians are getting married and entering civil unions in the United States and beyond.
Same-sex marriage may be contested, but it has also become part of the present.

2 Dr. Phil in "Extreme Marriages," for example, tells a married couple who have tried to remain married
despite the husband's attraction to and affairs with men: "However you define marriage, for sure it's
about commitment, it's about fidelity, it's about being there for one another and in a way that is based
on trust.... Now just take out that it's men that he's involved with. If marriage is just what I said—it's
commitment, it's fidelity ... that's not happening here, right?" Dr. Phil concludes that this marriage is
"not going to work."

These stories of gay or transsexual husbands (and occasionally lesbian wives) often tell a rather
sympathetic, even heroic story. After the wife overcomes her emotional devastation at the loss of her
marriage and seemingly goes through multiple stages of grief, she sometimes articulates not only
an acceptance of her husband but respect for the difficult choice that he made. In a television show
on Lifetime entitled "My Husband is Gay," one of the four women interviewed stated "I've not only
forgiven him—I'm actually proud of him. By coming out, he did the right thing, which is a lesson we
both want to teach our children." A similar sympathetic affirmation is sometimes found in the shows
chronicling the struggles of couples where the husband undergoes a sex change. In several *Oprah*
shows ("The Husband Who Became a Woman," "More Husbands Who Became Women"), the narrative is one of self-realization: The husband must self-realize by becoming a woman. And sometimes,

their wives choose to stay with them after the operation, affirming their difficult journey toward self-realization. While raising its own unique challenges, the transsexual husbands—as highlighted in these shows—do not raise the same infidelity issues, and therefore they are not seen to have engaged in the same kind of violation of the marital relationship. Self-realization can be affirmed without running into the problems of infidelity.

REFERENCES

Beck-Gernsheim, Elizabeth. "On the Way to a Post-Familial Family: From a Community of Need to Elective Affinity." In Mike Featherstone (ed.), *Love and Eroticism* (pp. 53–70). London: Sage, 1999.

Bordieu, Pierre. *Distinctions: A Social Critique of the Judgement of Taste.* Cambridge, MA: Harvard University Press, 1984.

Butler, Judith. *Undoing Gender.* New York: Routledge, 2004.

Giddens, Anthony. *The Transformation of Intimacy: Sexuality, Love and Eroticism.* Cambridge: Polity Press, 1992.

Huntington, Keston. "How to Survive Infidelity." n.d. <http://www.lezbeout.com/howtosurviveinfidelity.htm>.

Klesse, Christian. "Bisexual Women, Non-Monogamy, and Differentialist Anti-Promiscuity Discourse." Sexualities 8 (4) (2005): 445.

Myers, Jack. "Gays are America's New Role Model." (2003). <www.jackmyers.com/JMER_Archive/08-06-03E.pdf>.

Sawyer, Terry. "Blind Leading the Bland." PopMatters. (2003). <http://www.popmatters.com/tv/reviews/queer-eye-for-the-straight-guy.shtml>.

Shimes, Stephen. "Building Bridges, One Manicure at a Time." (2003). <http://www.filmsnobs.com/www/shimes/queereye.htm>.

Stychin, Carl. *Governing Sexuality: The Changing Politics of Citizenship and Law Reform.* Oxford: Halt Publishing, 2003.

Warner, Michael. *The Trouble with Normal: Sex, Politics, and the Ethics of Queer Life.* New York: Free Press, 1999.

Weeks, Jeffrey. "The Delicate Web of Subversion, Community, Friendship, and Love: In Conversation with Sue Golding." In Sue Golding (ed.), *The Eight Technologies of Otherness* (pp. 320–32). London: Routledge, 1997.

Weeks, Jeffrey. "The Sexual Citizen." *Theory, Culture and Society* 15 (3–4) (1999): 35–52.

CHAPTER 32

FOBs, Banana Boy, and the Gay Pretenders: Queer Youth Navigate Sex, "Race," and Nation in Toronto, Canada

Andil Gosine

Queer youth are strangely configured in nations, placed somewhere between nationalist proclamations that celebrate young people as (or burden them with responsibility for) "the future of the nation" and discourses framing queer sex as an urgent threat to nations' sustainability. These positions are woven around, into, and from discourses of gender, "race," class, and (dis)ability—and the material conditions they produce—through which queer youth navigate senses of and sensibilities about themselves and the spaces they occupy and cross. Recently, queer and feminist scholars have argued that desires expressed for or participation in homosexual acts would necessarily place queer youth outside their "home" nations. M. Jacqui Alexander innovated this position in her essays on the criminalization of homosexuality in the Caribbean. She suggests:

> The state has always conceived of the nation as heterosexual in that it places reproduction at the heart of its impulse. The citizenship machinery is also located here, for the prerequisites of good citizenship and loyalty to the nation are simultaneously housed within the state apparatus. They are sexualized and ranked into a class of good, loyal, reproducing heterosexual citizens, and a subordinated, marginalized class of non-citizens, who by virtue of choice and perversion, choose not to do so. (46)

Legal codes and social-cultural norms across contemporary geographies compel heterosexual citizenship, denying, denunciating, and/or punishing any expressions of nonheterosexual desire. Gayatri Gopinath characterizes queers as "impossible subjects" in national imaginaries. Writing about South Asian lesbians living in the United States, Gopinath observes:

> Within patriarchal diasporic logic, the "lesbian" can only exist outside the "home" (as house-hold, community, and nation of origin) […] the "lesbian" is seen as "foreign," as a product of "being too long in the West," and is therefore annexed to the "host" nation where she is further elided—particularly if undocumented—as a nonwhite immigrant within both a mainstream (white) lesbian and gay movement and the larger body of the nation-state. (263)

The situation of the *young* diasporic queer is further complicated: an outsider to her "home" ethnicized/racialized nation, and a marginal, racialized figure in the white-centred gay and lesbian community and heterosexual public space of her adopted "host" nation, her "youthful-ness" offers the possibility of being shaped to fit nationalist objectives of either (or both). She is recognized as a subject still in formation; her ills may yet be remedied, her outsider status, revised. A young queer is a deviant body but, still, a recuperable citizen.

This chapter engages transnational feminist analysis to explore the configuration(s) of immigrant queer youth in and across nations. I read two cultural works produced by queer youth to discern some of the appeals made to and negotiations undertaken by them in their encounters with nationalism(s), in Western metropoles: *Fresh Off the Boat (FOB)* (2004), a deliberately named zine that collects stories, poems, and images created by queer-identified, young immigrants working with the social support group Supporting Our Youth-EXPRESS (SOY-EXPRESS) in Toronto, Canada,[1] and *Banana Boy* (2003), a digital video made by (then) twenty-three-year-old filmmaker Samuel Chow about his experience of migrating from Hong Kong to Toronto. As anticipated in feminist literature, both texts demonstrate the incompatibility of queer sexual desire with "good citizenship," and their creators' struggles against marginalization in "home" and "host" nations. But the texts also present challenges to this analysis, and suggest a more complex operation of sexuality in some nation-building projects. They provide evidence of ways in which nonheterosexual desires are being racially maneuvered as cultural capital, presenting some nonwhite queer youth with a strange proposition, among others: of *potentially* crossing "nation" through queer sexual identification and simultaneous invocations of colonial-imperialist narratives about "race." The contemporary resonance of this logic, I suggest, is exemplified in the emergence of, and expression of anxieties about, "gay pretenders"—would-be migrants who adopt "queer" sexual identities as a strategy to access residency and citizenship in Western metropoles.

IN THE SPACE OF IMPOSSIBILITY

Queer, immigrant youth, it appears, occupy—to borrow Gopinath's expression—"a space of impossibility" (265). They are perpetually cast outside the nations they cross: bad ethnic citizens who betray the reproductive prerogatives of the "home," and racialized bodies read as abnormal, incompetent, and/or inferior in the "host," including in its principal gay and lesbian venues. *FOB* and *Banana Boy* provide several examples of the disavowal and derision of queer sexuality in some nation-building spaces, including the family, and the perseverance of racism and/or homophobia in others.

Banana Boy puts pictures to the "space of impossibility." In the video, images of Toronto and China are interspersed with those of Chow submerged underwater, as the filmmaker describes several tensions that shape his experiences of moving from Hong Kong to Canada in 1989. He discusses his parents' active refusal of Chinese culture ("the first thing my mother decided to do [...] was to move as far away from Chinatown as possible," he reports, "my mother didn't want me watching Chinese television"), and his confrontations with racism within Canada ("I got teased at school [...] I didn't do things the Canadian way") even as he yearned to "fit in [...] to be Canadian." Chow tells about his longing to belong and his attempts to move between or in opposition to competing cultural hegemonies. The video's title references his experience of struggling against being read as a banana boy, "white on the inside, yellow on the outside," even as he feels compelled to assimilate into whiteness, to assume rights as a Canadian. Near the close of the story, Chow emerges out of the water as he turns his attention to how his homosexual desires impact these negotiations. He reports encountering resistance from his mother after he comes out as gay, and uncomfortable silence from his father. "Every time the topic came up over dinner," Chow says, his father remarked "it's unnatural." In gay spaces, readings of his body oscillate between racialized exoticism and rejection, recalling one "cute boy who looked at me and ran off screaming, 'Chinese boys are supposed to be smooth!'" and another "who never looked at me because I am Chinese." By the time the video's closing credits appear, audiences have been exposed to multiple ways in which gendered, racialized, and sexualized inscriptions of Chow's body have aggressively situated him outside the territories to which he is attached, and a persuasive case has been made for characterizing Chow as "an impossible subject."

Similar practices of exclusion are described in *FOB*. In the zine's longest and most prominently featured essay, "personal story," a young lesbian recalls how her subversion of prescribed gender roles and expression of queer desires exposed her to various forms of violence in her country of birth, Iran. As a young girl, she remembers being so uncomfortable "acting like a girl" that she hoped divine intervention would change her sex:

> Every night before I go to bed I was praying to my god "God everybody saying that your powerful and generous ... Can you look at this human of yours down here and grant her wish?? I wish that tomorrow morning when I wake up I won't be a girl anymore. Thank you god, amen" next [day] as soon as I wake up the first thing I would check was if I am still a girl!!! Well god disappointed me every single time I asked him. (6)

She says she longed "to become free, to tell my parents that I like girls," but "[t]hat was not a good idea, they would kill me if they would know I am gay." "Thinking about it," years later, in Toronto, still makes her "shiver from my head to toe. Stoning you, dying alive under stones," she says, "that is scary" (6).

When she is found out to be involved with another girl—after police uncover love letters at her lover's house—she is forced to flee to another country, with her family, to escape a possible death sentence. In Canada, she finds some respite from forms of extreme violence, but the young woman still remains excluded from her new, adopted nation. Describing her family's first experiences of the Canadian state, she recalls:

> The immigration people were very rude and impolite. They asked us where are we from and with the little English I learnt in school I told them Iran and the guy started swearing

at us "fucking Iranians why you come to Canada?" he was saying stuff but I couldn't understand only from the way of his language I knew he is not saying good stuff. They told us we have to wait until morning till they get somebody to translate to us.

    After the interview and making papers and stuff they told us to go, but where???? We didn't have anybody here, didn't know anywhere. (8)

Eventually, the family moves into a shelter, and, two months later, a more permanent home. But when she later comes out as lesbian to her mother, she is expelled from her family. "My mom couldn't stand me being gay and all the things that she went through because of me so she kicked me out of the house," she says, "I didn't have anywhere."

No mention is made by this writer or by any of the other contributors to *FOB* of the persistence of racism in Toronto's gay and lesbian public spaces, but SOY-EXPRESS staff coordinator Suhail AbualSameed suggests that this is a chief concern among participants. He recalls one example of an experience shared by many of them:

    This young guy went to a queer youth group in the community and [...] he went a couple of times there and said it was the worst experience of his life, because everybody was making fun of him. He couldn't speak English very well. He dressed modestly [...]. Nobody would engage him in the conversation [...]. He felt totally alienated. He didn't go back. (Personal Interview)[2]

Asked to identify the main problems faced by SOY-EXPRESS clients, AbualSameed also easily references a list of priorities, which include: "isolation, language and communication challenges, unemployment, legal issues, and racism," he says, "especially in the gay community."

"QUEER CANADA" POSSIBILITIES

The very existence of SOY-EXPRESS provides evidence of the perpetuation of hetero-racism in Canada, since the organization was conceived as a response to state deficiencies in attending to the welfare of young, immigrant queers. However, criticism of the Canadian state's failings is framed in an important and telling way in the introduction to *FOB*, written by AbualSameed. "Young queer people who move into this city from other parts of the world," his note reads, *"seeking freedom and acceptance in a more open and tolerant environment* find no guidance or support from any of the existing institutions in Canada" (my emphasis, 1). It is not just that young queer immigrants "find no guidance or support" from the Canadian state, but that there is an expectation that they would.

In the *FOB* scripts, Canada plays the part of invitational "host" to sexual outsiders expelled from their "home" nations. The young men and women writing in the zine describe their experiences of migration to Canada as flights to freedom; one participant writes:

                i always wanted to fly out of the country where every day
                        was night
                i wanted freedom ...
                respect for who I am

> YES I AM GAY
> i wanted to say it loud without any fear of getting stoned
>   for who I was
> Travelling
> from THERE to HERE
> from NIGHT to SUNRISE was hard
> i can taste f r e e d o m
> i can be myself and enjoy being myself …
> all i want is happiness to come to me. (Anonymous 11)

Echoing this perspective, the poem "There is a place for me and my friends" describes the author's "trip" from a place of oppression to one of liberation:

> It's been a trip
> A trip with no ending
> A trip with no wishes
> A way to dream and wake
> Far away from my place
>
> [to a]
>
> A place of freedom
> A place of wishes
> A place to find myself
> In the way I never found before …
> And before … (Gotz 7)

A similarly themed testimonial written by Morlon appears at rocktheboat.ca, a companion website to *FOB*. Morlon migrated to Toronto from Jamaica in December of 2002, "seeking a better life as a young gay male from the Caribbean." Of his experiences in Canada, Marlon says, "I love living and working in Toronto as I can be myself and enjoy my life without having to hide who I am and lying to myself."

These affirmative celebrations of Canada as "a place of freedom," "a place of wishes," and a place that allows gay and lesbian men and women to "find" and "be" themselves reveal much more than the optimism of their authors; they also suggest the tenacity of nationalist narratives celebrating Canada as a queer or "queer-friendly" state. The introduction of a Multiculturalism Policy in 1971, a Human Rights Act in 1977, and Charter of Rights and Freedoms in 1982, and former prime minister Pierre Trudeau's widely circulated public assertion that "the state has no business in the bedrooms of the nation" have driven local and global imaginations of Canada as a welcoming place, more respectful of individual choices and cultural and sexual diversity than other countries. More recently, necessary comparisons with our closest neighbor have reinforced the notion that Canada is a site of liberation, especially for gays and lesbians. In the United States, social conservatives seized upon political opportunities made available to them post 9/11 to pursue an agenda that includes new controls on civil liberties, tightened censorship regulations, aggressive militarism, and the repudiation of gay rights advances, including legislated prohibition of same-sex marriage in several states. Over the same period in Canada (1999–2006), successful court challenges resulting in the revision of immigration, labor, and pension laws to accommodate same-sex relationships, gestures toward the legalization of marijuana, and the refusal of the Canadian government to join the U.S.-British invasion of Iraq earned its celebration or condemnation as "Hippie Nation" or "Soviet Canuckistan" (Klein).[3]

Consequently, Canada has been declared, as American syndicated columnist Dan Savage put it, a "morally superior" destination for gays and lesbians fleeing repressive regimes (2). In the days following George W. Bush's election to a second term in office, the website marryanamerican.ca elicited thousands of personal ads from Americans looking for Canadian partners (and, through marriage, citizenship). "Forget the brain drain," announced one headline in Canada's most widely circulated gay publication, *Xtra!*, "it's all about the gay gain" (Gnutel). Canada has fast become "a country to call homo," declared another (Garro). Since the mid-1990s, in fact, over three thousand immigration permits have been issued to self-identified gays and lesbians seeking refugee status in Canada, more than any other market in the world, including the United States (Jiminez A3). Claimants' successes in immigration and refugee tribunals have permitted such self-adulatory pronouncements as the *Globe and Mail* headline for a story about Al-Hussein, a forty-seven-year-old man who successfully applied for refugee status: "Gay Jordanian Now Gloriously Free in Canada" (Jiminez A3). The title also references Al-Hussein's participation in *Gloriously Free,* a documentary about the experiences of queer men who sought refuge in Canada. The publicity brief for *Gloriously Free* describes it as "the first documentary ever to explore the world of gay immigration and the desperate search of five young men to find welcoming arms outside their countries of birth, where persecution and hatred of alternative lifestyles may lead to torture or death." It goes on to praise Canada as "a vast country that now leads the world as the safest haven for persecuted international gays and lesbians" and that it "is fast becoming the world's unspoken symbol of sexual freedom."

For many who have taken these flights to freedom, immigration to Canada has been a much more ambivalent experience than the promotional rhetoric suggests. Against depictions of Canada as an egalitarian, multicultural Mecca are its historical truths: the origins of the Canadian state in colonialism, the violent displacement and systemic oppression of Aboriginal peoples, internment of its ethnicized Japanese nationals during wartime, and immigration, education, and housing policies that at various times included legislated discrimination against African, Afro-American/black, Chinese, South Asian, and Jewish peoples. Contemporary scholarship by Himani Bannerji, Frances Henry, Rinaldo Walcott, and Sherene Razack details the multiple ways in which racism, patriarchy, and heterosexism shape Canada's economy and its social, cultural, and legal codes; and novels, films, and music by Dionne Brand, Richard Fung, Faith Nolan, and many others expose the work of "race," gender, class, and sexuality in determining accessibility to the full privileges of Canadian citizenship and to resources of the Canadian state. Nevertheless, characterization of Canada as a liberating space has persisted.

This mythology is so powerfully wielded that it tends to subsume any potentially oppositional or challenging narratives. In the *FOB* texts, for instance, few examples of the situations that AbualSameed describes of young queer immigrants not being able to access work, encountering hostility and/or indifference in the gay community, and being ridiculed or humiliated for their aesthetic choices are represented. Most often, despite their own struggles finding jobs and homes, accessing comfortable social space, and developing connections within various communities, the works' creators consistently characterize Canada as a refuge. Even the young Iranian-born woman whose essay is quoted at length in the preceding section counters her criticism of racist practices at immigration with positive affirmations about Toronto and Canada, characterizing her and her family's experiences as exceptional situations, not the rule. Following elaboration about one difficult experience in Toronto that brings her to the conclusion that "[c]oming to Canada was the worst experience of my life," she adds the caveat, "Not that it's a bad city no." She also concludes her essay with another statement professing her loyalty to Canada: "Nowhere *is* like home but I am trying to make Canada my home, the land that I can be who I am and I can live as who I am and I don't have to pretend being somebody else, lots of freedom. Great country a little cold but that's ok!" (8).

Her and other *FOB* contributors' adoption of the rhetoric of state multiculturalism also demonstrates how marginalization comes to be explained in the context of "Queer Canada" narratives. As expressed in their artwork, young queer immigrants appear to feel compelled to explain their experiences of isolation and marginalization as a consequence of their "freshness" to Canadian society (and not of socioeconomic relations in Canada) and, furthermore, to couch their reflections and analysis within a nationalist framework that maintains its celebratory demeanour—to insist that they *will be* "gloriously free" even as *they are not.* This position is reinforced by the organization of SOY-EXPRESS as a response to the "difficulties" faced by "newcomer" immigrant youth, which focuses attention on young queers' "inexperience in Canada" and not on the country's social and economic policies or its investments in racism or hetero-patriarchy.

"RACE," SEX, AND NATION-CROSSING

The persistence of "Queer Canada" mythologies troubles queer and feminist approaches that emphasize the heterosexual basis of nation-building; it forces us to ask, for example: What [are we] to make of nationalisms that are, at least partly and in theory, premised on the inclusion of and recognition of rights for homosexuals? How do we understand emerging situations where expression of queer desires do not simply dictate the exclusion of their holders but may in fact function to include them, in certain ways, in particular national imaginaries (e.g., in Toronto, Canada)? What is being negotiated when queers' admission into "host" nations is premised on sexual deviance in their "home" nations—and what is being said about "race," culture, sex, and difference in the execution of these negotiations? How do we understand *homosexual* "race"—crossing through sex, when racial anxieties about sex (e.g., about interracial sex) obsessively privilege reproduction?

Transnational feminist and queer scholarship about relationships between heterosexual and gay capital (e.g., Alexander), the sexualized, racialized, and gendered imperative of colonization and nation-building projects (e.g., McClintock, Stoler, Gopinath, Bhaskaran) which problematize the universal-imperialist production of sexual identities (e.g., Manalansan, Sinfield, Patton) have laid the groundwork for fuller pursuit of these interrogations. Here, I draw upon some insights expressed in this work to call attention to some of the ways in which strategic wielding of sexual identities in the particular production of (metropolitan) Canadian nationalism, as represented in *FOB* and *Banana Boy,* are articulated through colonial-imperialist narratives about "race."

In the opening sequence of *Banana Boy*, three images locate Chow in a "space of impossibility." The second of these images is of the narrator himself, unclothed and submerged, face up, underwater. His eyes are closed, his expression, tense. This image is sandwiched by two others: that of a fisherman, standing and gently rowing what appears to be a small, wooden boat, his head covered by a round, broad "peasant" straw hat—a familiar, iconic figure that has often stood in for East Asia or "Asian-ness" in many Orientalist texts. The third image is of Toronto's landscape marker, the CN Tower. It is an unstable image, likely filmed by a handheld camera, by someone passing over the city on an airplane. Both images reference the points of departure and arrival for Chow—Hong Kong/China and Toronto/Canada. Chow's use of these two images in this sequence seems to play into and reproduce a racializing developmental narrative that characterizes non-Western countries as primitive/premodern (the "traditional" fisher representing Hong Kong/China) and Western countries as progressive/modern (a tower—"the World's tallest tower" representing Toronto/Canada). As Chow's story unfolds, this juxtaposition of primitive/premodern Hong Kong/China against modern Toronto/Canada is reinforced in visuals and his narration. For example, even though his family is from Hong Kong, not the Chinese mainland, images from the 1989 Tiananmen Square prodemocracy protests form the backdrop of Chow's discussion of their departure to Canada. When the next scene cuts to his arrival in Toronto, the image of the CN tower gives way to a bird flying—perhaps, like the *FOB* contributors, to freedom.

Queer sexuality, in Chow's narrative as well as in many of the *FOB* texts, is the trope that enables his transition from a premodern/primitive Chinese to the modern/progressive Canadian nation. In the third act of *Banana Boy*, Chow emerges from underwater as he explains, "I came out a few years ago. One night, my mum asked me straight out if I was gay. I told her the truth […]." Images of the army tanks that attacked protestors at Tiananmen Square appear next on screen, as Chow completes the description of his "coming out" to his mother: "[…] there was no turning back." The appearance of the tank at the moment of this announcement collapses Hong Kong/China with Chow's own "pre-outed," premodern past—the corollary being that Toronto/Canada is his "liberated," modern, gay future. The Tiananmen massacre tanks appear again, when Chow announces, "[S]he still thinks my being gay is a phase." After his emergence from the water—at which point audiences see that he was lying in a bathtub—Chow gets up and moves to the bedroom, where he joins a young, white man in bed. Chow embraces and kisses him. "Now that I'm out," he says, "the banana boy phrase has taken on a whole new meaning."

Chow doesn't develop this idea except in the statements that next follow it with which the story closes: "My father never spoke about my sexuality ever since I came out. He went on his usual ways. Sometimes, I wonder if he is proud of me. Is he proud of his *banana boy*?"

The question is gently posed, but given Chow's earlier references to his parents' determined efforts to put distance between their new lives in Canada and their experiences of "Chinese-ness" in Hong Kong, and to rid Chow of his Chinese accent and consumption of Chinese culture, one wonders whether it is meant as a provocation; is his father "proud" of him becoming such a model "banana boy," of "betraying" his "home" nation so profoundly that he has also become gay—a possibility not available to a "real" Chinese boy? When Chow says "the banana boy phrase has taken on a whole new meaning" since he has come out, does he mean that his adoption of a "gay" identity has provided a final rupture from his Chinese-ness, whereby though he looks "yellow on the outside," he has become "white on the inside" through his declaration of homosexuality? Since this comment comes after we see Chow in bed with a young, white male, is "the whole new meaning" of "banana boy" that his assimilation into white Canadian culture now includes a sexual valorization of white bodies? Does he offer the term as a partner to "Rice Queen" (reserved for white men sexually attracted to East Asian men) to suggest that a "banana boy" seeks white men for sex? Does he mean that he has become a more palatable object in white culture?

Whatever the explanation inferred from his comment, it is always inscribed in "race." Colonial-imperialist narratives of "race" underlie not just Chow's representation of his navigation through competing and/or collaborating discourses of nation in *Banana Boy,* but also those of the *FOB* contributors, through the framing of their experiences of migration that privileges characterization of Canada as a site of liberation. There are four collaborating strategies through which nation-crossing into "Queer Canada" is configured around "race": through (1) the conflation of varied sets of cultural and sexual practices with instruments of the state that results in the racialized characterization of nonwhite people as "natural" homophobes; (2) the invocation and affirmation of modernist discourses predicated on racial hierarchy; (3) the privileging of white Western ways of knowing and speaking about sex and sexuality; and (4) the neutering of colonial anxieties about the reproductive potential of nonwhite peoples.

In the production of "Queer Canada" narratives, legislated protections for sexuality rights in Canada have come to be understood as the cultural beliefs of the whole nation, which is certainly not the case—even the current prime minister of Canada, Stephen Harper, has declared his opposition to same-sex marriage and other queer sexuality rights. The corollary to this is that the repressive laws of states with punitive consequences for homosexuals also cast whole cultures as homophobic. Thus, Jamaican criminal codes that define imprisonment terms for acts of sodomy become racially reinterpreted as: "Jamaicans are homophobic" or "Jamaican culture is homophobic." In the case of Jamaica, these laws do not merely stand in for public opinion, and emerge out of a particular history of colonialism and directly out of colonial texts. This collapsing of culture with legislative codes also makes little or no accommodation for the ambivalent ways in which they are experienced, including by those who are marginalized and who consequently resist them. In this gesture, no recognition is made of nonwhite peoples' subjectivities.

As so clearly demonstrated in *Banana Boy*'s and *FOB*'s stories of young queers leaving oppressive pasts for freer futures, the "Queer Canada" narrative is a modernization discourse. Alexander points out:

> Modernization discourses and practices it infuses … collapse divergent histories and temporalities into these apparently irreconcilable binaries of tradition and modernity […]. In doing so, they also territorialize their own difference, ultimately placing their claims within an ideological universe, whose analytic and material boundaries dovetail with imperatives that are most closely allied with those of colonization. (189)

The comparisons of cultures and nations articulated in the characterization of Canada as a site of liberation—and those of Third World nations as sites of repression—work to reify perceived ideological differences generated out of this tradition-modernity binary. They necessarily invoke a racial hierarchy that privileges and valorizes whiteness as a marker of progress, civility, and authority and that works to colonize the articulation of sexual identities and practices.

FOB and *Banana Boy* represent nation-crossing into "Queer Canada" as a teleological transition, moving from a regressive to a progressive site of sexual politics, but the experience might be better characterized as becoming familiar with a different set of cultural codes. Sometimes, young, queer immigrants do not experience "Queer Canada" as a "freeing" experience. For example, "Rolondo," an eighteen-year-old Jamaican, bisexual-identified immigrant, found that he encountered less rigid demands made about gender roles in his home country than in Canada:

> In Jamaica [I'm] living with people who were used to me acting like this, so it was not a big deal for them—from the day that I was born, so it was not a big deal for them. They understood "that's just the type of person [I am]." My mom was the coolest person about it, because I can remember, from age nine or ten, I was washing dishes and cleaning the house and doing stuff that you see mostly women doing. You know, sweeping the room, mopping stuff. (qtd. in Lord 42)

Similarly, "Ahmed," a twenty-three-year-old Somali man who migrated to Toronto with his family, also found that he had to adapt to more strict gender behaviours:

> I remember being in grade 6 and being all effeminate, being told "you walk like a girl" ... it didn't make any sense to me ... [I had] to learn to walk like a guy by using the cracks in the sidewalk to measure how far my feet were apart ... I'd walk with my wrists held all high and my hand all dangling and people would smack it like, "Put that down. Don't do that all the time." I always knew that it showed a bit and I didn't like that either. I tried to hide it myself and the whole thing was to hide it from other people. (qtd. in Lord 43)

Twenty-year-old "Nellie," whose family emigrated from Nigeria, also found that even queer traditions that are normalized in Canada presented new difficulties:

> That's another big difference between Nigeria and here [Canada]; it was like you had a duty—it was necessary to come out—but back home it was like they knew what you were, it was known ... and it was hidden so there was no need to come out. Like it wasn't assumed that I was only attracted to men in the first place. That's what having to come out does—I'm not coming out, cause don't assume I am straight in the first place. (qtd. in Lord 42)

Citation of these passages is not meant to suggest that Canada is a more repressive place for queers than the home countries of Nellie, Ahmed, and Rolondo. Instead, it compels reconsideration of assumptions about the easy "welcome" Canada is said to offer queers, and it also calls for more critical appreciation of the complex cultural contexts in countries that are generally dismissed as inferior—including ones that may well offer more affirmative views of same-sex sexual practices; Nellie's grandmother, for example, used to tell her stories with "goddesses" who were "pure lesbians," including narratives about women who rescued their daughters from marriages to men (Lord 44). They also challenge the insistence that non–Euro-American queerness be articulated through frameworks of sexuality generated in white-Western/metropolitan culture to access political consciousness, subjectivity, and liberation.

Nation-crossing into "Queer Canada," finally, also raises the ugly proposition that queer sexual identification by nonwhite youth may work to allay white racial anxieties about the reproductive potential of nonwhite people that have circulated since the dawn of European colonization. Nineteenth-century theories of "race," like those posited by Count Gobineau in *Essay on the Equality of Races,* focused on reproductive sex, "or rather its consequence, namely the degree of fertility of the union between the different-races" (Young 101). Such racial theory, Robert Young argues, "projected a phantasmagoria of the desiring machine [of colonialism] as a people factory." There were great fears about "uncontrollable, frenetic fornication producing the countless motley varieties of interbreeding, with the miscegenated offspring themselves then generating an ever increasing mélange, 'mongrelity,' of self-propagating endlessly diversifying hybrid progeny [...]" (181). Although all kinds of "illicit" sexual practices disturbed colonial officials, anxieties about *reproductive* sex have been consistently reiterated in contemporary sites, such as the fears about burgeoning Third World populations that guide family planning and environmental policies of global institutions (cf. Bookchin; Hartmann; Gosine, "Dying Planet"). Even responses to the global AIDS crisis appear most anxious about reproductive sex; homosexual sex might have "caused" the disease, in their analysis, but it is heterosexual sex between MSM (men who have sex with men) and their female partners that has gotten the bulk of attention from global institutions, nongovernmental organizations, and aid agencies (cf. Gosine, "Sex for Pleasure"). Queer identification by Third World youth would, in this context, appear to neuter worries about the threat posed by nonwhites' reproductive sex to the "purity" and cultural dominance of the white race.

CONCLUSION: THE GAY PRETENDERS

By way of conclusion to the discussion introduced here, I want to leap from the cultural texts to briefly bring attention to a curious contemporary phenomenon that demonstrates the analysis of "race," sex, and nation. [...] In 2006, stories about "gay pretenders" seeking refuge in Western states started to circulate in national and community newspapers. On May 6, the *Hindustan Times* ran a story entitled "For Greener Pastures—Turning Gay to Chase British Dream" about "people of Punjab aspiring to immigrate to the United Kingdom [who] have found a new alibi—that of being homosexual" (Jalandhar). According to the article, legalization of same-sex marriages in the UK last year has resulted in immigration consultancy offices in India "being flooded with queries from youths in search of a greener pasture." Immigration consultant Kamal Bhumbla reported that he has received "at least 15 to 20 queries in the recent times inquiring about the UK law. A number of Punjabi youths are willing to pose as homosexuals, if that helps in moving to the UK." Among the young "pretenders" vying for status was twenty-two-year-old Sukhwinder Singh (alias) of Noormahal, who admitted that he wished to apply for a visa under this category. In the article, Singh explains: "I got hold of one of my friends after I came to know about this law. He too was desperate to go abroad and readily agreed to the plan. My girlfriend knows about it. I have assured her that once I immigrate, I will marry her in the UK." Another hopeful emigrant said it was his father who gave him the idea. "I have been trying to go abroad for the last many years but nothing clicked," says Vikas Dhir, "I know it is simply not acceptable in Punjab, but I don't have any other option to achieve prosperity in life."

Representation of this event in the *Times* (and its similarly framed repetition in other diasporic presses) affirms feminist readings of nation and nationalism that mark homosexuality as threatening. The story reassures Indian nationalist anxieties about homosexuality by suggesting that young men "claiming" to be "gay" really are *not* homosexual, and are even attached to heterosexual partners; queer identification is merely a strategy toward a loftier, and respectable, goal. (In this analysis, physically leaving the nation through migration is seen to be less threatening than declaring a public homosexual identity). The act of "turning gay" as a means to access more desirable citizenships, on the other hand, reconfigures the space occupied by young diasporic queers as one of possibilities; queer identification offers new residences, new citizenship, "prosperity." As I have argued here, these offers are mired in racial discourse; but they are nevertheless meaningful to and valued by subjects who pursue their realization.

The article's observation that it is "young" Indian nationals who are willing to "turn gay" in their efforts to migrate to the UK, furthermore, reveals how "youth" is specifically rendered in national contestations—as both an object to be regulated and a source of disruption. The figure of the "gay pretender" is a strategic response to the ideological xenophobic and homophobic anxieties of "home" and "host" nations that strives to undermine their material objectives. It speaks not only about the tightly reined and powerfully wielded narratives of "race," sex, and gender through which queer-identified diasporic youth must navigate their futures but also to young people's creative potential to subvert their intentions.

Special thanks to the Social Sciences and Humanities Research Council of Canada and to Alexandre Beliaev and Suhail AbualSameed.

NOTES

1 As explained on the group's website, SOY-EXPRESS works to "provide newcomer and immigrant queer youth with a safer space where they can meet others who share their experiences and feel comfortable expressing themselves and making friends, as well as gain more knowledge about Canada and Toronto that will help them build their life in the city" <http://www.soytoronto.org/current/express.html>.

Around sixty people participated in the program from the start. Weekly drop-in meetings have regularly attracted eight to twelve young men and women aged between sixteen and twenty-seven, while many youth keep in touch or request services by telephone and/or email. Most participants have been young men from South America and South Asia, with some participants from Africa, the Middle East, and East Asia. Cultural production has been a major feature of SOY-EXPRESS since its inception. *FOB* was its first group project. The group's coordinator, Suhail AbualSameed, explains the title of the zine: "The members wanted to reclaim a term that was often used against immigrants in a derogatory way, in rejection and humiliation. They wanted to say "yes we ARE newcomers ... we ARE immigrants ... we ARE "fresh off the boat," and it doesn't take any of our humanity or pride away from us" (AbualSameed).

Other cultural production projects followed the publication of *FOB*. In 2003, one of the project's participants proposed production of a video and, with the group and the assistance of a local filmmaker, created a short video, *My Name Is Javier,* and a website, rocktheboat.ca.

2 In Ruthann Lee's "'Coming Out' as Queer Asian Youth in Canada: Examining Cultural Narratives of Identity and Community," interviewee Mark describes his experience at the largest youth organization in the city in similar terms: "The first organization that I connected with—went to LGBYT [Lesbian, Gay, Bisexual Youth of Toronto] which is very clique-y, mostly white males, but some people of colour [...] and they all fitted stereotypes, I think, when I was there. Some of them didn't but those who didn't weren't there for very long. And stereotypes of flaming gay male or the preppy white boy who's into the gay community type thing. It was very clique-y and they were already friends so it was really a horrible space" (67). Mark added, "If I am around a lot of white gay males, for example, who are very 'in' with the community, I just feel like I'm not even there" (69).

3 All of these measures are under review by the Conservative minority federal government elected in 2006.

REFERENCES

AbualSameed, Suhail. Personal Interview. Toronto: May 2005.

AbualSameed, Suhail. "Introduction." *Fresh Off the Boat.* Toronto: Supporting Our Youth, 2004.

Alexander, M. Jacqui. *Pedagogies of Crossing.* Durham: Duke University Press, 2005.

Anonymous. "Personal Story." *Fresh Off the Boat.* Toronto: Supporting Our Youth, 2004.

Banana Boy. Dir. Samuel Chow. Inside Out Video, 2003.

Bannerji, Himani. *The Dark Side of the Nation: Essays on Multiculturalism, Nationalism and Gender.* Toronto: Canadian Scholars' Press, 2000.

Bhaskaran, Suparna. *Made in India: Decolonizations, Queer Sexualities, Trans/National Projects.* New York: Palgrave Macmillan, 2004.

Bookchin, M. *Which Way for the Ecology Movement?* San Francisco: AK Press, 1994.

Brand, Dionne. "A Working Paper on Black Women in Toronto: Gender, Race, and Class." In *Returning the Gaze: Essays on Racism, Feminism and Politics,* ed. Himani Bannerji. Toronto, ON: Sister Vision Press, 1993.

Brand, Dionne. *In Another Place, Not Here.* Toronto, ON: Vintage Canada, 1997.

Brand, Dionne. *A Map to the Door of No Return: Notes to Belonging.* Toronto: Doubleday Canada, 2001.

Dirty Laundry. Dir. Richard Fung. Toronto: V Tape, 1996.

Fresh Off the Boat. Toronto: Supporting Our Youth, 2004.

Garro, Julia. "A Country to Call Homo: How Welcoming Is Canada of Queer Immigrants and Refugees?" *Xtra!* (Toronto) 10 June 2004.

Gloriously Free. Dir. Naomi Weis. OMNITV 10 June 2005.

Gnutel, Shawna. "Forget the Brain Drain, It's all About the Gay Gain." *Xtra!* (Toronto) 22 July 2004.

Gopinath, Gayatri. "Nostalgia, Desire, Diaspora: South Asian Sexualities in Motion." In *Theorizing Diaspora: A Reader,* eds. Jana Evans Braziel and Anita Mannur. New York: Blackwell, 2003.

Gosine, Andil. "Sex for Pleasure, Rights to Participation and Alternatives to AIDS: Placing Sexual Dissidents/Minorities in International Development." *IDS Working Paper #228.* Brighton: Institute of Development Studies, 2004.

Gosine, Andil. "Dying Planet, Deadly People: 'Race'—Sex Anxieties and Alternative Globalizations." *Social Justice* 32, 4 (2006).

Gotz, Andre. "There Is a Place for Me and My Friends." *Fresh Off the Boat.* Toronto: Supporting Our Youth, 2004.

Hartmann, B. *Reproductive Rights and Wrongs.* Boston: South End Press, 1995.

Henry, Frances, and Carol Tator, eds. *The Colour of Democracy: Racism in Canadian Society,* 3rd ed. Toronto: Harcourt Brace Canada, 2006.

Jalandhar, Manpreet Ranshawa. "For Greener Pastures—Turning Gay to Chase British Dream." *Hindustan Times* 6 May 2006.

Jimenez, Maria. "Gay Jordanian Now 'Gloriously Free' in Canada." *Globe and Mail* 20 May 2004, A3.

Klein, Naomi. "Canada: Hippie Nation?" *The Nation.* 21 July 2003.

Lee, Ruthann. "'Coming Out' as Queer Asian Youth in Canada: Examining Cultural Narratives of Identity and Community." Master's thesis. University of Toronto, 2003. *ProQuest Digital Dissertations.* 1 June 2005.

Lord, Cassandra. "Making the Invisible/Visible: Creating a Discourse on Black Queer Youth." Master's thesis, Ontario Institute for the Studies in Education, University of Toronto, 2005.

Manalansan IV, Martin F. "In the Shadows of Stonewall: Examining Gay Transnational Politics and the Diasporic Dilemma." In *Theorizing Diaspora: A Reader,* eds. Jana Evans Braziel and Anita Mannur. New York: Blackwell, 2003.

McClintock, Anne. *Imperial Leather: Race, Gender and Sexuality in Colonial Context.* New York: Routledge, 1995.

Nolan, Faith. "Long Time Comin'." Faith Nolan, 1993.

Out of the Blue. Dir. Richard Fung. Toronto: Fungus Productions, 1991.

Patton, Cindy. "Stealth Bombers of Desire: The Globalization of 'Alterity' in Emerging Democracies." In *Queer Globalizations,* ed. Arnaldo Cruz-Malave and Martin F. Manalansan. New York: New York University Press, 2002.

Razack, Sherene. *Race, Space, and the Law: Unmapping a White Settler Society.* Toronto: Between the Lines, 2002.

Savage, Dan. "'Oh Canada!'" *The Stranger* 21 October 2004, 2.

Sea in the Blood. Dir. Richard Fung. Toronto: Fungus Productions, 2000.

Sinfield, Alan. "The Production of Gay and the Return to Power." In *Decentering Sexualities: Politics and Representations beyond the Metropolis,* ed. Richard Phillips, David E Shuttleton, and Diane Watt. London: Routledge, 2000.

Stoler, Ann Laura. *Race and the Education of the Desire.* Durham: Duke University Press, 1995.

Stychin, Carl F. *Law's Desire: Sexuality and the Limits of Justice.* London, New York: Routledge, 1995.

Walcott, Rinaldo. *Black Like Who? Writing Black Canada.* 2nd rev. ed. Toronto: Insomniac Press, 2003.

PART TEN
Visual Cultures

CHAPTER 33

The "Hottentot Venus" in Canada: Modernism, Censorship, and the Racial Limits of Female Sexuality

Charmaine A. Nelson

There is an indelible mark in my memories of my undergraduate education as a student of Western art history in Canada.[1] If I had been given a penny for every time a professor had lectured on Edouard Manet's *Olympia* (1863), only to refuse to discuss the conspicuous presence of the black maid, I would be quite a wealthy woman today. Noting the historical compulsion to erase her presence, Lorraine O'Grady has argued that:

> She is the chaos that must be excised, and it is her excision that stabilizes the West's construct of the female body, for the "femininity" of the white female body is ensured by assigning the not-white to a chaos safely removed from sight.[2]

While my claim may seem like an extraordinary exaggeration, when art historical discursivity, especially its Modernist permutations,[3] are scrutinized for their ability or willingness to accommodate race, my point as a comment on the dominating Eurocentrism of art historical disciplinarity becomes painfully clear. Modernism refers to a cultural movement and an historical moment but, more important for art history, to a specific artistic practice generally designated by a dominating, often formalistic interest in issues of style and aesthetic concerns. Modernism, however, must also be acknowledged as a specific art historical discourse that dictates the limits of art production and interpretation. Historically, Western Modernism has privileged painting above all other media and has further privileged aesthetic practices that reinforced and celebrated the two dimensionality of painting. This explicit focus upon materiality has often elided social, historical and political issues from the discourse. The Modernism of visual culture has also historically been the exclusive domain of white-male artistic production centred around notions of urbanity, voyeurism and bohemianism. Ironically, Modernism's obvious dependence upon the bodies of transgressive female subjects (often prostitutes or courtesans) and the appropriation of African, Native and Oceanic arts has only recently been given critical attention. Manet's *Olympia* is not an arbitrary choice on my part.[4] The utter disavowal of race as a valid issue of art historical inquiry is evidenced in T.J. Clark's otherwise archivally exhaustive chapter on this painting, "Olympia's Choice". Clark's social art historical analysis of the painting is fundamentally based upon class identity. Griselda Pollock has noted his unwillingness to deal with the obvious gender and sex issues that are latent within the painting.[5] However, my concern is with his almost complete disregard for the racially "other" subject of the painting—the black maid who is clearly visible. [...]

Although Manet's name and the basic formalistic and stylistic concerns of the art object as a seminal painting that marked the celebrated beginnings of Western Modernism need not be restated, I would argue that what has been consistently disavowed, and what needs now to be urgently examined and retrieved, is the body of the black female maid, her colonial context and the psycho-social constraints that have facilitated the erasure of her obvious presence and significance in the first instance. [...]

We need to ask what art historical discourse, especially its Modernist permutations, makes possible and suppresses and through what logic and apparatus its borders are policed.[6] In other words, we need to examine the historical suppression of issues of race, colour and colonialism within art historical discursivity, and create a space for post-colonial interventions within cultural practice and analysis. Just as feminist interventions have made it possible to discuss gender and sex issues within the context of patriarchy, a post-colonial intervention within art history would privilege discussions of race, colour and culture within a colonial context. A post-colonial art history also creates a space for the discussion of the production of Native, black, Asian and other traditionally marginalized artists. This intervention would also fundamentally take up representation as a process of identification and, therefore, position visual culture as colonial discourse, a site where racial identities are produced and deployed.

Critical theory, especially feminist interventions, have provided clear and effective strategies for cultural transformation of the traditionally patriarchal disciplinarity of art history.[7] However, recent criticisms of white feminist practice have contested the extent to which the deployment of an essentializing category of Woman, coupled with the silence around race/colour, have re-entrenched the colonial privilege of the white female body. Post-colonial scholarship, particularly its manifestations within Cultural Studies, is helping to provide the theoretical and material structure for a racial intervention within art history, one that acknowledges culture as a site of colonial discourse and, thus, a generative source of racialized identities and racism.[8]

Post-colonial scholarship has also informed the recent racial interventions within the overwhelmingly colonial discourses of anthropology, ethnography and museology. Recent critical contributions to the study of culture have interrogated Western colonial histories of exhibition and human display.[9] Within the institutionalized museum practices of ethnographic display, human anatomical and skeletal remains often served as "primitivizing" markers of the racial identification of colonial subjects: evidence of the supposed evolutionary inferiority of colonized populations. Exceeding museum practices in their mass appeal to broad middle- and lower-class populations, the more socially accessible spectacles of fairs, circuses and open-air exhibitions often replaced skeletal remains with the living bodies of colonized subjects.[10] As Rosemary Wiss has argued, "European discourse on the perception of difference was partially informed by exhibits of indigenous people brought back to Europe by colonial scientists and entrepreneurs during the eighteenth and especially nineteenth centuries."[11] Colonial subjects framed within the Eurocentrically biased and artificially imposed boundaries of reconstructed and anthropologically "authentic," "primitive" villages were made to perform their cultures and also, significantly, their races, for the entertainment of white audiences.

The colonial practice of human display distanced the white observer, both literally and figuratively, from the primitivized bodies of colonial subjects. Safely behind the carefully demarcated boundaries of the exhibitions and fairgrounds, the space of the colonial "other" was clearly separated from the privileged space of the white viewer/"self". The deliberately cultivated material and psychic distance was a part of the colonial apparatus that visually objectified the exhibited human subjects and racialized the bodies of the exhibited and spectators alike within colonial binaries.

COLONIAL EXHIBITION PRACTICES

It is within the colonial space of the West that the "Hottentot Venus" emerged, an iconic sexual and racial identity that resulted from the transatlantic imperialist regimes of global colonization.[12] The term "Hottentot" is present within nineteenth-century Western human sciences as a name for a group of people or tribe and, sometimes, even for a distinct race. Whereas Hottentots were often considered a subcategory of the Negro/Negroid race, the nineteenth-century human scientist James Cowles Prichard went so far as to distinguish them as a separate and inferior race to Negroes. To append Venus to this term has both general implications in its referencing of ancient mythology and more specific implications in its referencing of nineteenth-century cultural and social ideals of female sexuality and beauty. Since Venus, which has most frequently in Western art been represented as white female subjects, has widely been read as an idealization of female beauty, to affix the term "Hottentot" is an ironic or cruelly "humorous" gesture that substitutes a racially "othered" body—the grotesque—for the expected beautiful white female body. Saat-Jee/Saartje/Saartjie, or Sarah Baartman, as she was named by her Dutch owner/agent, was one of several South African women who were displayed naked throughout Europe for the sexual titillation of white audiences.[13] It is important to note that although the legal status of these women as slaves is in dispute, the nature of their interaction and relationships as African women with European men during a colonial period where slavery and scientific racism were prolific makes it easy to assume at the very least a fundamentally inequitable and exploitative engagement based upon dominant ideals of racial and sex/gender difference. Taken from South Africa in 1810 by Hendrick Cezar (the brother of her Dutch "master") and the Englishman Alexander Dunlop (a ship's surgeon and trader in "museum specimens"),[14] Saat-Jee was exhibited in London, toured throughout England and, finally, taken to Paris.[15] The colonial regime that transfigured Saat-Jee into the "Hottentot Venus" relied upon the dissolution not only of her individuality, but also of her humanity since, as part of an animal act, Saat-Jee's humanness was fundamentally questioned through her constant juxtaposition with animals.[16] The "Hottentot Venus" was a colonial stereotype that attempted to homogenize representations of black female sexuality as "primitive" and pathological.

Within the practices of colonial ethnographic exhibition, the living Saat-Jee was publicly displayed to curiosity seekers who were "… amazed and affrighted by the sight of her naked body with its enlarged buttocks and elongated genital flap."[17] It is critically important to note that it was these corporeal signs, the buttocks and the flap, that were seized upon and reified as intrinsic signs of a deviant sexuality. As such, these signs of corporeal excess became fundamentally connected not only with blackness but also with the pornographic. It is the visibility of these signs, and their legibility as racially specific, that provoked the cultural censorship that I will discuss in detail below.

Other Hottentot women suffered fates similar to that of Saat-Jee. As the entertainment at dinner parties of the social elite, their naked bodies became a sexual spectacle for the titillation and curiosity of white viewers. The sexual exploitation of black women within Western exhibition practices worked to dichotomize the Hottentot body with the ideals of white bourgeois womanhood. This coerced public performance was an integral part of the racial and sexual othering of the black female body within the cultural imagination of the modern West. The sexual and racial objectification of Hottentot women was a matter of life and death. Besides being exhibited as scientific specimens, subhuman examples of racial and sexual difference, Hottentot women had autopsies performed on them by Western scientists in a deliberate search for a source of pathology that would confirm colonial theories of sexual and racial identity as biologically based and, thereby, fixed and essential.[18] Saat-Jee died in 1815 of an inflammation. Her body was subsequently autopsied by the revered comparative anatomist Cuvier and, post-dissection, ceded to the Musée de l'Homme in Paris, where its scientific efficacy as a racial and sexual specimen became institutionally sanctioned. The museum displayed her skeleton, genitalia and brain until 1974. Saat-Jee's remains were finally repatriated 186 years after her death in Paris. Indigenous leaders of the Khoisan people, or "Bushmen" (widely believed to be the original inhabitants of the southern tip of Africa), heralded her repatriation as a symbolic act that could aid in the reclamation of Khoisan identity.

THE "HOTTENTOT VENUS" IN CANADA

Although Hottentot women were never (to my knowledge) "imported" to Canada, the Hottentot Venus did make a significant appearance within early twentieth-century Canadian culture—an appearance that, despite the vast geographical distance between Canada and Europe, clearly indexes the prolific circulation and normalcy of colonial ideals of blackness and their saturation of Western consciousness. The Hottentot's representation and legibility in Canada is significant not only for the way this identifiably iconic anatomical type indexed racialized and sexualized conceptions of the body, but also for the way it speaks to the social and psychic constitution of difference within the colonial politics of identity. It is the hierarchization of racialized bodies and their cultural policing that must be interrogated if Modernism's investment in coloniality and, indeed, blackness is to be understood.

Within a conservative cultural milieu, Canadians embraced censorship as a means of enforcing the arbitrary social boundaries of artistic production. However, this censorship was not universally applied. Rather, it was practised within historically Eurocentric hierarchies that racialized concepts of beauty and sexuality. In April 1927, Max Weber's *Contemplation* (ca. 1923) and *Retirement* (ca. 1921) and Alexandre Archipenko's *The Bather* (date unknown) were secretly removed from the walls of the *International Exhibition of Modern Art* hosted by the Art Gallery of Toronto.[19] To acknowledge this censorship as a racially motivated action within a colonial cultural framework calls for an understanding of the conservatism of early twentieth-century Canadian figure painting, the simultaneous politics of representation and censorship, and the historical pathologization of blackness and black female sexuality. But since colonial stereotypes are not only polarized but also parasitic, we must hold these factors in tension with the white female body and its liminality—its proximity to the so-called primitiveness of the black body and the subsequent threat to white male identity. It is within this colonial matrix that the "Hottentot Venus" made an appearance within the Canadian cultural landscape.

ADHERENCE TO TRADITIONS

In 1931 the Canadian artist and critic Bertram Brooker called the Canadian art community puritanical, and over 15 years later the Montreal-based painter Louis Muhlstock deemed the lack of artistic freedom to be the result of an "excess of prudery."[20] Although these established Canadian artists were more directly concerned with the state of figure painting in Canada, their opinions appropriately surmised the conservative climate of Canadian artistic production in general.

Early Canadian artists commonly emulated European models to validate their art within the youthful colony. However, this emulation did not extend itself to Modern European trends. Rather, twentieth-century Canadian artists embraced established historical styles of recognized European artistic schools. This colonial dependence was fostered by art patronage and art education that celebrated and rewarded artists who patterned their work after canonized Western art. The resulting lack of innovation was evidenced, to varying degrees, within the different genres of painting.[21] This traditionalism was partially maintained through the practice of museum censorship that was used to eliminate potentially offensive representations of the human (particularly female) body. Within this realm, the "offensive" paintings were usually those that broke from such traditional and idealized visions of the white female body as the nude.[22] "The nude" and "the naked" are two specific art historical terms that have most often been applied to representations of the female body in Western art. The nude, which dominated French nineteenth-century academic tradition, has historically needed a *raison d'être*. Generally pandering to a heterosexual male gaze, it has been the more conventional of the two categories, and is associated with the Beautiful and "high art." The naked is aligned with limitlessness, sexuality and impropriety, while the nude is often allegorical, or a body that is *always already* unclothed. The naked often points up the process of undressing, the social and biological body and, therefore, is generally aligned with the Sublime and the pornographic.

Lack of allegory, of contrived womanly innocence, or of nature's canopy generally provoked controversy and, inevitably, censorship. Paintings that represented naked, as opposed to nude, women were said to pose moral threats to the viewing public. Censorship was used in an effort to monitor and carefully delimit the boundaries of female sexuality. However, this practice was not arbitrary but directed specifically at representations of the white female body in an effort to protect the idealization of white womanhood through a policing of the arbitrary divide between art and pornography.

Representations of the black female body in Canadian culture have historically received no such paternalistic concern. Overtly sexualized images of black women were condoned, even praised, while comparatively innocuous paintings of white women were actively censored.[23] Within this colonial practice, the Canadian museum community was enforcing deterministic ideals of race and sexuality by participating in the construction and perpetuation of a Euro-centric womanhood. As such, black women were constituted as "other" by the white artistic community at the centre.

The Canadian museum community, whether sanctioning or censoring female nudes, partici-pated in the construction of whiteness. As Ruth Frankenberg has illustrated:

> … whiteness refers to a set of locations that are historically, socially, politically, and culturally produced and, moreover, are intrinsically linked to unfolding relations of domination.[24]

The paradigmatic nature of whiteness within colonial discourse provided, and continues to provide, a protection to white women not historically extended to black women. But within any dichotomous relationship there is an interdependence and, thus, the identity of the white woman is constructed not only in her presence, but in her absence; her "other"—that is, Black Woman. It is crucial, then, to examine not only what was representable at any given moment, but also what was beyond representation.

CONTROVERSY, CENSORSHIP, AND WHITE FEMALE NUDES IN CANADIAN PAINTING
During the late 1920s and early 1930s, white female nudes regularly incited controversy and provoked censorship within the Canadian art milieu. Censorship was generally enacted under the guise of a "public service" imposed by museum officials, who, as the purveyors of an authori-tarian knowledge, acted for the greater benefit and protection of the community. Serving two main agendas, the censorship of white female nudes functioned simultaneously to protect the museum audience from the social threat of pornography and to preserve the ideals of white womanhood and the definitions of femininity and sexuality at its core. Yet, censorship was not limited solely to Canadian art works, but extended to art works exhibited in Canada.

Non-Canadian artists were targeted by censors during the first Canadian exhibition of international Modern art at the AGT. Three paintings of female nudes were removed from the *International Exhibition of Modern Art*: Max Weber's *Contemplation* (ca. 1923) and *Retirement* (ca. 1921) and Alexandre Archipenko's *The Bather*. The exhibition (also known as the Brooklyn Exhibition for its original site) was assembled by the Société Anonyme, largely owing to the efforts of Katherine Dreier. As president of the society, Dreier was a vigorous supporter of Mod-ern art and had earlier founded the society with the assistance of Marcel Duchamp and Man Ray.[25] According to Ruth Bohan:

...[t]he Brooklyn Exhibition was both the largest and most comprehensive exhibition
of modern art shown in this country [United States of America] in the 1920s and the
Société Anonyme's grandest achievement.[26]

American audiences had been better prepared than their Canadian neighbours to consume
these Modern art works. As Bohan has noted, the occurrence of several other exhibitions of
Modern art had laid the foundation for the *International Exhibition*. The *Armory Show,* the
Forum Exhibition, and the several other smaller exhibitions of Modern art held at Alfred Stieg-
litz's gallery at 291 Fifth Avenue had injected Modernism into the consciousness of the American
audiences, even if those audiences had not yet been ready to embrace it.[27]

Contrarily, the *International Exhibition of Modern Art* marked the first direct exposure of
Canadian audiences to the international Modernism of twentieth-century artists. To all but
those intimately acquainted with current European artistic trends, these Modernist art works,
many of which had begun to embrace abstracting principles, would have seemed "alien" to the
conservative Canadian audience. That the exhibition opened in Canada at all is due in large
part to the diligent individual efforts of a Canadian familiar with artistic developments in the
international art arena, Lawren Harris.[28] After much determined negotiation with officials at
the AGT, Lawren Harris' relentless efforts resulted in the exhibition's showing in Toronto. A successful Canadian artist and patron, Lawren Harris' nationalist ideology embraced Modernist
art as a vehicle for the articulation of a uniquely Canadian cultural identity. As a member of the
Canadian Group of Seven, Harris' painting, though considerably more conservative than that
of his counterparts in the *International Exhibition,* reflected his belief in the need for Canadian
artists to embrace the possibilities of Modernism.

Toronto was the final venue of the *International Exhibition*. The show had opened at the
Brooklyn Museum on November 18, 1926. From there it had travelled to the Anderson Galleries,
New York, and the Albright Art Gallery, Buffalo, before concluding its journey in Toronto.[29] The
presence of the Weber and Archipenko nudes in the original AGT catalogue is evidence of the
original intention to include the pieces and the hastiness of their withdrawal once in Toronto.

According to a first-hand account, the exhibition organizer, Miss Dreier, had overseen the
hanging of the exhibition, but upon returning to the gallery the same evening for the private
opening, she found that works by Weber and Archipenko had been removed in the interim.[30]
Though a local report noted that "... the exclusion of these nudes may not be an instance of
prudery,"[31] another explanation located the nexus of sexual and racial motivations that had
provoked their censorship. The report stated:

> These that the censor has consigned to the coal regions are physical.... They are readily
> identifiable as women.... One of Weber's nudes, "Contemplation," might win a prize in
> a Hottentot beauty contest.[32]

The reference to the Hottentot bodies as the catalyst for censorship situated the network of
racialized anatomical codes that governed the representational practices of the body at this
historical moment.

NEGROPHILIA AND MODERNISM: BLACK WOMAN AS SUBJECT

Throughout the 1920s and 1930s, both Weber's and Archipenko's female nudes possessed the so-called fleshy, excessive, spectacular Hottentot anatomy described by this Canadian newspaper reporter. Both artists were active within European Modernism, the undisputed capital of which was Paris, at a moment when *les choses africain* dominated the consciousness of Western cultural production. The colonial origins of Modernism must be examined within the context of negrophilia, the social and cultural phenomenon of white fear/desire for the black body. Beyond recognizing negrophilia as a phenomenon through which blackness, as supposedly primitive, was revealed and celebrated, we must scrutinize it as a generative force and interrogate it as the very process through which Africanness and blackness were othered, and the white body/ self located as "civilized", beautiful, rational and intelligent. As Petrine Archer-Straw has commented upon the avant-garde cultural scene of 1920s Paris:

> The negrophiles who fraternized with blacks cultivated a shadowy world of nightclubs and bohemianism; their interests were in conflict with mainstream, "traditional" values. "Blackness" was a sign of their modernity....[33]

James Clifford situates this Modernist preoccupation with African art and peoples within the framework of the colonial power structure that facilitated the appropriation and fetishization of the colonial subject as "other":

> Picasso, Leger, Appollinaire, and many others came to recognize the elemental, "magical" power of African sculptures in a period of growing *negrophilie*, a context that would see the irruption onto the European scene of other evocative black figures: the jazzman, the boxer (AJ Brown), the *sauvage* Josephine Baker. To tell the history of modernism's recognition of African "art" in this broader context would raise ambiguous and disturbing questions about aesthetic appropriation and non-Western others, issues of race, gender, and power.[34]

Modernist practice, then, was as much about the West's colonial fascination with African cultural production as it was the racist surveillance, representation and consumption of African bodies as "primitive" objects themselves.

Early in his career, Max Weber spent three formative years in Paris, then the centre of Western artistic activity. While studying at the Academie Julian, Weber became active in Parisienne contemporary life, socializing with other avant-garde artists, among them Henri Matisse, Robert Delaunay, Henri Rousseau and Pablo Picasso.[35] The artistic community within which Weber circulated was full of young, white, male Modernists who actively appropriated so-called primitive art forms, African and otherwise. It was within this context that Weber, as William Gerdts has noted, "...[a]lso became acquainted with African Negro sculpture, then newly discovered and highly popular with young moderns in Paris."[36]

Alexandre Archipenko's experience with the "primitive" art of Africa parallels that of Max Weber's. Arriving in Paris from Russia in 1908, Archipenko quickly became associated with the

Parisienne artistic vanguard.[37] By 1910 Archipenko was exhibiting with the Cubist painters at the *Salon des Independants*. Although Archipenko did not embrace all of the Cubist idioms, a kinship was forged through a mutual fascination with African art. The following year, Archipenko's debt to the "primitive" was directly revealed in the title of his bronze sculpture *Negro Dancer*.[38]

The preoccupation of Modern European artists with African art has been historically rationalized as a purely superficial interest based mainly upon formal aesthetic concerns. This narrow assessment has been perpetuated throughout art historical discourse, attributing the overwhelming influence of African art on twentieth-century Western culture to a mere formal reactionism to dominant artistic styles. It is the Eurocentric exclusivity of art historical discourse and its inability to accommodate questions of race, colour and colonialism that have effectively suppressed the colonial context of Western Modernism within the discipline. Contemporary art historians have continued to replicate these beliefs. According to Katherine Janszky Michaelsen:

> In their search for alternatives to impressionism, painters and sculptors alike employed these "primitive" sources to arrive at the new vocabulary of clear massive forms that became the point of departure for cubism. With a new emphasis on formal and structural problems ... subject matter began to lose the importance it had in the nineteenth century, as is demonstrated by the many generically titled works by Archipenko and others.[39]

This statement not only frames Modernism as a superficial search for a new aesthetic vocabulary, it blatantly refuses the obvious colonial context of Modernism's preoccupation, appropriation and exploitation of African cultures and peoples. Weber, Archipenko and their contemporaries shared not only a fascination with African art and objects, but with Africanness and blackness as they had been defined in terms of white contact with "primitive" peoples of African descent. This fascination, fuelled by white male artists' interaction with African art and their experiences with the "primitive" presence of black people (primarily as artistic performers in nineteenth- and twentieth-century Paris) was largely played out through representations of black women. That Weber and Archipenko were participants within this negrophilia reveals itself in their construction of the female body as Hottentot.

Both Weber's *Contemplation* (ca. 1923) and *Retirement* (ca. 1921) are compositions that incorporate several female forms represented with thick limbs; rounded stomachs; wide hips; heavy, circular breasts; and large buttocks. Similarly, Archipenko's female bathers of this period exhibit sturdy proportions and fleshy bodies that were categorically opposed to more traditional Western notions of female beauty. Weber clearly represented the "Hottentot" bodies of his women as white.

While the presence of the four male figures in Weber's *Retirement* (ca. 1921) may also be located as a source for the disturbing reception of this painting, the Hottentot anatomy of the women must be understood as a device that could mediate this otherwise unacceptable presence. The bodies of Weber's women mark them as possessing a "primitive" black sexuality and, through this inscription, normalized the otherwise problematic presence of the men. Weber's painting recalls Manet's *Déjeuner sur l'herbe* (1863), whose representation of a naked white woman with two fully clothed white men can be read as a commentary on the role of class in the social construction of female sexuality within the social structures of nineteenth-century Paris. When Manet painted

Déjeuner sur l'herbe, Paris was erupting with controversial debates about prostitution, and the human "sciences" were actively engaged in a search for a visual vocabulary of the body that would identify and fix the body of the white prostitute as an essential site of sexual deviance. Class, then, as race, would be revealed as a predetermined physical marker of sexual behaviour and deviance.

Manet's juxtaposition of the black body of the maid with the white body of the prostitute in *Olympia* (1863) located the conflation of race and sexual deviance within the nineteenth-century discourses of female sexuality. As two separate bodies, the maid and the prostitute reflect two different sides of the same coin. They were both viewed as sexually deviant in an essential way that implicated their very biology. But whereas the white woman's sexual deviance allowed for the possibility (however slim) of transcendence or redemption, the black woman, physically marked by the stain/colour (and other anatomical and physiognomical signs) of her racial difference, could never transcend her "primitive" sexuality. Part of the problem of *Olympia's* reception was her elusiveness to class categorization, a commentary by Manet on the increased social confusion of prostitutes and "proper" women by men in Paris. The hysteria around the (in)visibility of the prostitute indexed concern for the spread of syphilis and its problematic and sexist alignment with the female bodies of prostitutes as opposed to the male bodies of their clients. But the cool reception of this painting must also be examined in terms of Manet's rupturing of the fantasy of the prostitute as Desire for a heterosexual male gaze, a fantasy dependent upon the subsumption of the economic exchange of money for sex, a fact revealed by the placement of Olympia's hand securely over her genitals and the fixing of her ambiguous gaze outward to the implied John whose position we (the viewer) now occupy.

Through the proximity of the two bodies, Manet clearly referred to a significant trope within the annals of Western figure painting through which a "black sexuality" was transferred onto the body of a white female subject, or the black female subject acted as a surface to reinforce the unquestioned beauty and racial superiority of the white female subject.[40] As Deborah Willis and Carla Williams have described:

> Exotic but rarely exalted, the black female image frequently functioned as an iconographic device to illustrate some subject believed to be worthier of depiction, often a white female. When she appeared at all, she was a servant in the seraglio, a savage in the landscape, "Sarah" on the display stage, but always merely an adjunct.[41]

However, I would argue that part of the overwhelming rejection of Manet's *Olympia* was based precisely upon its refusal to reinforce this colonial dichotomization of black and white female identity and sexuality. It was the white female body within *Olympia* that was read as naked, dirty, dead, and sexually uncontrollable.[42] Juxtaposed with the fully clothed demure presence of the black maid, Manet effectively reversed and problematized the stereotypical racial positions to which these two bodies were generally assigned. The rejection of Weber and Archipenko at the AGT in Canada was based on a similar refusal—the destabilization of a presumed colonial racing of female sexuality.

For Picasso, the bodies of the black woman and the white prostitute became conflated into a single iconic Hottentot anatomy in his drawing *Olympia* (1901), after the earlier painting.[43]

Unclothed on a bed, she is ready to service not one (as Manet's *Olympia* implied), but two white men (one of them, arguably, Picasso himself). Black Woman, always already sexually promiscuous, uncontrollable, feral, is represented as a prostitute.[44] The grave irony here is, of course, that within the colonial history of slavery, black women did not have the privilege of exchanging their sexuality for personal economic benefit, as such an exchange was premised upon the legal and material ownership and control of one's body. Disenfranchised by colonial legal discourse, black female slaves were property, and the rights to economic benefit from their labour and procreative capacities were invested with their white owners.

The iconic stature of the Hottentot body as a marker of black sexual deviance and availability was evidenced in Matisse's *Blue Nude (Souvenir of Biskra)* (1907), a work whose inspiration Archer-Straw traces to the artist's North African trip the previous year.[45] Although the artist chose non-flesh colours to represent the body of the female subject, the arbitrary nature of this selection is undermined by the geometric and Africanized mask-like face that refutes the otherwise indiscriminate palette by signifying a black body. The thick limbs and full circular breasts are accompanied by deliberately enlarged, overemphasized buttocks that manage to reveal themselves to the viewer despite the fact that this blue woman is positioned with her body frontally aligned with the viewer in a reclining pose.

This is the same point at which Weber's and Archipenko's representations of women are inserted into the Modernist dialogue. Unlike Manet's *Olympia,* with the separate bodies of the black and white women, or Picasso's *Olympia,* which still constituted the represented female body as black, the works of Matisse, Weber and Archipenko share a moment in which the signification of race at the level of skin colour was unnecessary to establish the race of the represented body. The woman could be white, as in the images of Weber, or even blue, as with Matisse's *Blue Nude (Souvenir of Biskra),* yet the viewer was able to read race into these bodies despite the ambivalence of skin. It is clear, then, that anatomical and physiognomical signs of the body were as important as colour in the identification of race. It is also clear that race was not only visual but also, crucially, what was visible when taken as a sign of what was beyond vision—since, regardless of skin colour, the Hottentot anatomy signaled that deep down within the body, in the biology and the "essence" of these women, they were all black. And blackness was not just a racial position, but also a sexual one.

CONCLUSION

Weber's and Archipenko's representations of the Hottentot body locate the colonial fascination of Western artists with blackness and Africanness, particularly as it has been manifested within representations of black women. By the twentieth century, the Hottentot body type was intimately connected with a Western artistic consciousness that perceived black women as sexual "primitives". The iconic nature of the Hottentot body provided a concrete visual language for this perception, which could then be constituted in a specific, representable, physical body.

The censorship of Max Weber's and Alexandre Archipenko's female nudes from the *International Exhibition of Modern Art* at the AGT was a reaction that perpetuated the dichotomous perception of black and white female sexuality within colonial discourse. The representation of the "Hottentot" body type of itself was not enough to seal the fate of Weber's and Archipenko's final subjects. The represented female bodies were offensive not because they depicted the so-called anatomical irregularity of the Hottentot anatomy but because they dared to construct this body for women who were not definitively identifiable as black. This ambiguity recalled the Freudian preoccupation with white women as the "weak evolutionary link" and their constant danger of backsliding into the "primitive" state of black sexuality, a threat that a patriarchal logic registered mainly in terms of the inevitable danger to the white male body. Although idealized as the paradigm of beauty and sexual purity, within the phallocentric West, the impossibility of female sexual difference as anything but black led to white women's precarious and liminal position, which was further destabilized by associations with the "primitive."

Within Freudian psychoanalysis, white female sexuality has been located as a site of "primitive" fear/desire. The inscription of female sexuality as danger has aligned white female sexuality with colonial representations of blackness. Accordingly, white women were seen as the most immediate threat to the imagined "purity" of white men and the heterosocial sanctity of Western civilization. It is the liminality of the female body that Weber and Archipenko works recalled, breaching the racialized standards of social propriety as they marked the tenuous boundaries between art and pornography.

The Weber and Archipenko works, in representing the iconic Hottentot body, recalled the "primitive" site of a black sexuality. But also, as a white or racially unfixed body, they recalled the instability of white female sexuality, and threatened the idealization of white womanhood. While the marks and assigned meanings of the Hottentot body seemed essentially appropriate for the representation of "black sexuality," when applied to the white female subject they became foreign, offensive, potentially pornographic and worthy of cultural policing.

NOTES

1 I am using the term "Western" to indicate original European traditions and their colonial permutations in countries such as Canada, the United States and Australia.

2 O'Grady, 1991, p. 153.

3 For an understanding of Modernism within the visual arts *see* Greenberg, 1994. For a feminist critique of this tradition *see* Pollock, 1988.

4 T.J. Clark quotes a nineteenth-century source that perverts the black maid's representation as that of a "hideous negress," uncritically used the Hottentot Venus as a barometer of the grotesque, and included contemporaneous "humourous" engravings of *Olympia* that radically burlesqued and mammified Manet's demure, even pretty, black maid. However, he fails to address the core issues of race and racialized sexuality as an obvious theme compelled by the deliberate juxtaposition of the white and the black female bodies (Clark, 1984, pp. 92, 93, 96, 97).

5 *See* Pollock, 1998.

6 A significant tactic used in the policing of traditional art historical hegemony is to control which questions may or may not be formulated in the face of an art work. A fitting recent and personal example occurred in a review of my art exhibition *Through An-Other's Eyes: White Canadian Artists—Black Female Subjects* (1998), in which I employed a post-colonial feminist perspective to explore the three century-long fascination of white Canadian artists with black female subjects. In a review by Henry Lehman in *The Gazette,* rather than critique the exhibition within its own stated thesis and discourse,

Lehman belittled the very premise of the show by demonstrating its difference, and implied inferiority and exteriority, to the discourse of Modernist art history and its singular and supposedly universal concerns with formal analysis and "pure" aesthetics. In so doing, Lehman also effectively dismissed the possibility and legitimacy of anything other than a white male viewing body (*See* Lehman, 2000; *see also* Nelson, 1998 and 2000).

7 Pollock & Parker, 1981, and Pollock, 1999.

8 Two recent and excellent examples of a post-colonial art history are Pollock's *Differencing the Canon* (1999), and Wood's *Blind Memory* (2000). In the Canadian context, Gagnon's *Other Conundrums* (2000) and Acland's "Elitekey" (1998) have set a high standard.

9 *See,* for example, Clifford 1988; Lavine & Karp, 1991; and Coombes, 1988.

10 Hinsley, 1991.

11 Wiss, 1994, p. 12.

12 *See* Prichard, 1851, p. 109.

13 Wallace, 1990, p. 45.

14 Wiss, 1994, p. 13.

15 Jounnais, 1994; Wiss, 1994, pp. 11, 13.

16 Within the scientific discourse of the body, the Hottentot's increasing viability as a "missing link" between the animal kingdom and human beings is consistent with Saat-Jee's bestialization and display as part of a stable of animals.

17 Gould, 1982.

18 *See* Allie, 2002; Jounnais, 1994; Wiss, 1944, p. 11.

19 The Art Gallery of Toronto is today known as the Art Gallery of Ontario. I will henceforth refer to this institution by the abbreviation "AGT."

20 Brooker, 1931; Muhlstock, 1947.

21 Twentieth-century Canadian landscape painting, although heavily dependent upon Dutch art, was decidedly more progressive than figure painting. While many landscape artists, including the acclaimed Canadian Group of Seven, aggressively pursued a Modern vision of the vast Canadian wilderness, figure painters adhered more rigidly to nineteenth-century European prototypes.

22 *See* Clark, 1972; and Nead, 1994.

23 Nelson, 1995.

24 Frankenberg, 1991, p. 6.

25 Bohan, 1980, p. iii.

26 Ibid., p. ii.

27 Ibid.

28 Ibid., 1980, p. 140.

29 Pfaff, 1984, p. 80.

30 Brooker, 1931, p. 94.

31 Ibid.

32 "Paintings of Nudes", 1927.

33 Archer-Straw, 2000, p. 19.

34 "Histories of the Tribal and the Modern" in Clifford, 1988, p. 197.

35 Gerdts, 1959, p. 7.

36 Ibid.

37 Michaelsen, 1986, p. 19.

38 The bronze sculpture *Negro Dancer* (1911) is in the Schueler Collection, Stockholm, Sweden.

39 Michaelsen, 1986, p. 20.

40 See, for example, Dante Gabriel Rossetti, *The Bride* or *The Beloved* (1865–66); Jean Léon Gérôme, *Moorish Bath* (ca. 1870); Lilly Martin Spencer, *Dixie Land* (1862); John Lyman, *Sun Bathing 1* (1955).

41 Willis & Williams, 2002, p. 1.

42 Clark, 1984.

43 Pablo Picasso, *Olympia* (1901), pen and coloured crayon, private collection, Paris, France.

44 The institutionalization of breeding practices that effectively encouraged the rape of black female slaves for the economic benefit of the white plantocracy must be scrutinized with regard to the de-/regendering of black bodies within slavery.

45 Archer-Straw, 2000, p. 56.

REFERENCES

Acland, Joan. (1998). Elitekey: The artistic production of Mi'Kmaq women. *Canadian Art Review,* 25(1–2), 3–11.

Allie, Mohammed. (2002, May 6). Return of 'Hottentot Venus' unites bushmen. *BBC News.* Retrieved October 25, 2003, from http://news.bbc.co.uk/1/hi/world/africa/1971103. stem

Archer-Straw, Petrine. (2000). *Negrophilia: Avant-garde Paris and black culture in the 1920's.* New York: Thames & Hudson.

Bohan, Ruth Louise. (1980). The Société Anonyme's Brooklyn Exhibition, 1926–1927: Katherine Sophie Dreier and the promotion of modern art in America. Unpublished Ph.D. dissertation, University of Maryland, College Park, Maryland.

Brooker, Bertram. (1931). Nudes and prudes. *Open House.* Ottawa: Graphic Publishers Limited.

Clark, Kenneth. (1972). *The nude: A study in ideal form.* Princeton: Princeton University Press.

Clark T.J. (1984). Olympia's Choice. *The painting of modern life: Paris in the art of Manet and his followers.* London: Thames & Hudson.

Clifford, James. (1988). *Predicament of culture: Twentieth-century ethnography, literature and art.* Cambridge: Harvard University Press.

Coombes, Annie. (1988). Museums and the formation of national and cultural identities. *The Oxford Art Journal,* 11(2), 58–68.

Frankenberg, Ruth. (1991). *White women, race matters: The social construction of whiteness.* Minneapolis: University of Minnesota Press.

Gagnon, Monika Kin. (2000). *Other conundrums: Race, culture, and Canadian Art.* Vancouver: Arsenal Pulp Press.

Gerdts, William H., Jr. (1959). *Max Weber: Retrospective exhibition October 1st–November 15th, 1959.* Newark: The Newark Museum.

Gould, Stephen. (1982). The Hottentot Venus. *Natural History,* 91, 20–27.

Greenberg, Clement. (1994). Modernist painting. *Art in theory 1900–1990: An anthology of changing ideas.* Oxford: Blackwell.

Hinsley, Curtis M. (1991). The world as marketplace: Commodification of the exotic at the world's

Columbian exposition, Chicago, 1893. In Ivan Karp & Steven D. Lavine (Eds.), *Exhibiting cultures: The poetics and politics of museum display* (pp. 344–365). Washington: Smithsonian Institution Press.

Jounnais, Jean-Yves. (1994, May). The Hottentot Venus. *Art Press, 191,* 34.

Lavine, Steven D., & Karp, Ivan (Eds.). (1991). *Exhibiting cultures: The poetics and politics of museum display.* Washington: Smithsonian Institution Press.

Lehman, Henry. (2000, March 4). Artists' vision coloured by prejudice? *The Gazette,* p. J2.

Michaelsen, Katherine Janszky. (1986). *Alexander Archipenko: A centennial tribute.* Washington: National Gallery of Washington and Tel Aviv Museum.

Muhlstock, Louis. (1947). An excess in prudery. In Robert Ayre & Donald W. Buchanan (Eds.), *Canadian art: Christmas-New Year, 1947–48* (Vol. 5, No. 2). Ottawa: Canadian Art.

Nead, Lynda. (1994). *The female nude: Art, obscenity and sexuality.* London: Routledge.

Nelson, Charmaine. (1995). Coloured nude: Fetishization, disguise, dichotomy. *Canadian Art Review,* 22(1–2), 97–107.

Nelson, Charmaine. (1998). *Through an-other's eyes: White Canadian artists—black female subjects.* Oshawa: Robert McLaughlin Gallery.

Nelson, Charmaine. (2000, March 11). Art critic called misinformed. *The Gazette,* p. J5.

O'Grady, Lorraine. (1991). Olympia's maid: Reclaiming black female subjectivity. In Joanna Frueh, Cassandra L. Langer & Arlene Raven (Eds.), *New feminist criticism: Art, identity, action.* New York: Harper Collins Publishers (Icon Editions).

Paintings of nudes consigned to cellar. (1927, April 4). *The Toronto Daily Star,* p. 22.

Pfaff, L.R. (1984). Lawren Harris and the international exhibition of modern art: Rectifications to the Toronto catalogue (1927), and some critical comments. *Canadian Art Review,* 11(1–2).

Pollock, Griselda. (1988). Modernity and the spaces of femininity. *Vision and difference: Femininity, feminism and the histories of art.* London: Routledge.

Pollock, Griselda (1999). *Differencing the canon: Feminist desire and the writing of art's histories.* London: Routledge.

Pollock, Griselda, & Parker, Roszika. (1981). *Old mistresses: Women, art and ideology.* London: Pandora.

Prichard, James Cowles. (1851). *Researches into the physical history of mankind* (4th ed., 3 vols.). London: Roulston and Stoneman.

Wallace, Michelle. (1990). Modernism, postmodernism and the problem of the visual in Afro-American culture. In Russell Ferguson, Martha Gever, Trinh T. Minh-ha & Cornel West (Eds.), *Out there: Marginalization and contemporary cultures.* New York: The New Museum of Contemporary Art.

Willis, Deborah, & Williams, Carla. (2002). *The black female body: A photographic history.* Philadelphia: Temple University Press.

Wiss, Rosemary. (1994) Lipreading: Remembering Saartjie Baartman. *Australian Journal of Anthropology,* 5(1–2), 11–40.

Wood, Marcus. (2000). *Blind memory: Visual representations of slavery in England and America.* London: Routledge.

CHAPTER 34
Porn Wars and Other Hysteries

Kiss & Tell

We experience the contradiction. We understand the seduction. We understand the contradiction. We experience the seduction.

—Sur Mehat[1]

NOTE ON LANGUAGE

These days, many people seem to use the word "pornography" to mean sexual images that they don't like and "erotica" to mean sexual images that they do like. This is confusing, since we all have such different opinions. It also makes invisible the class biases intertwined with those words. In this [chapter], we use the words pornography, erotica, and sexual imagery interchangeably.

SURVIVING THE SEVENTIES

SUSAN: I remember clearly the moment when I first held Monique Wittig's book *The Lesbian Body*[2] in my hands. It was the seventies, in Calgary, and it was as if I was seeing that title from some far distant place, through some kind of mental and emotional fog. The Lesbian Body; the sheer boldness of those words was stunning. Who would be brave enough to keep this book on the coffee table? I was, because I didn't have anything to lose. I was straight. A straight radical feminist artist. Books with dangerous sounding titles had a lot of currency in my crowd. Yet this book was having a marked and decidedly different effect on me, and I hadn't even got past the title.

With some premonition I sensed that this text had an edge on all the other radical texts I had come across. Somehow I knew, even then, that to comprehend the meaning of this text, to approach this unknown world where a lesbian body existed, would require a definite separation from the world I knew. Witness the faint tremor in the hands, the thin veil of sweat starting to cover my body, my rapidly beating heart. Surely these symptoms were telling me something, something I can say now but couldn't say then. That the very hands that held those texts were lesbian hands, that those legs, arms, breasts, cunt, feet, hips were lesbian, that the mind attached to that body was a lesbian mind, thinking lesbian thoughts, seditious and rebellious lesbian thoughts.

This was a truth impossible to acknowledge. This internal outing, this epiphany of the spirit was happening to a heterosexual woman whose childhood had been one of thorough indoctrination in both Christian morality and institutionalized familial responsibility. An indoctrination so complete that the mere idea of refusing that role, of living without a man brought intense thoughts of fear, retribution, and unmitigated peril. There was no way on earth that I could verbally articulate this insurrection that was brewing at the depths of my being. Mere speech felt far too hazardous. The way I and the women I worked with found to describe this and other contradictions in our lives was by making pictures, photographs.

PERSIMMON: Back in the seventies, anti-porn analysis reigned supreme in the feminist movement, and I was a for sure feminist. Feminism had broken me out of a long, hard breakdown and I was never going to feel that bad again. I was saved. I was a new convert to the adventure of feminism, full of passionate ideas and unexamined arrogance; a born-again lesbian, making right-on art about right-on sex: pure theory.

If what we don't like is man-made images of subservient women in lacy underwear, then what we do like must be perfectly naked lesbians, with equal haircuts. If this one's touching that one's cunt, then that one better be touching this one's cunt, at the same time, in the same way, or else it's not True Equality.

I made a lot of sculptures of women floating in the air, because perfect mutuality was otherwise anatomically impossible.

But nothing is ever that simple. At the same time as I was making theoretical art, my sex life was more complicated. My lover at the time was a retired sex worker who had come out in the sixties, in a bar scene where drag queens, dykes, and prostitutes hung out together and watched each others' backs. What was *she* doing with *me*? I guess despite my naiveté, we did have some things in common. Neither of us had ever identified as heterosexual. Both of us had been through the psychiatric system, her as an inmate and me as an outpatient. We were both artists, and both alcoholics.

Sex between us was sweet, terrifying, and wild.

The feeling of our sex was *not* what I was calling up when I made those sculptures. Why didn't I notice that the sex I was having and the sex I was portraying were so different? Why didn't I pay attention to how sex *really felt* when I was making those flying fucks? Shame, I guess. Shame so deep I couldn't look it in the face. *Sometimes even the softest of sex scared me. Other times rape fantasies turned me on. Sometimes I pretended my lover was a guy.*

Let's be clear about this: it wasn't feminists who taught me sexual shame. I learned it long before, under harder hands. By the time I was a teenager I had already learned to disconnect from my body. How I felt didn't matter. Sex wasn't about how I felt. It was about doing what I was told. Trying not to gag when my gentle boyfriend came in my mouth; pretending I was turned on when I wasn't or pretending I wasn't when I was; pretending I didn't see the tied-up girl in the porn mag; pretending I didn't know her, want her, want to be her. *Because if you want that (they say), you will be telling men that rape is fun (they say), you will be asking for it (they say). Good Girls look the other way.*

The feminist movement gave me far more than its faults. It gave me hope, pride, work, a place to stand. But sometimes it seemed no different from where I grew up. You had to pretend and not notice you were pretending. You had to shut up and swallow it.

So I went to those meetings and kept my mouth shut when some of the bad pictures in the anti-porn slide shows turned me on. I learned the lines, but they didn't fit my life. And I hadn't learned my sexuality from porn. I had learned it from cartoons, commercials, and comic books. I had learned it from the everyday violence of childhood. I wasn't Good, I was a complex mixture of rebellion, analysis, and internalized sexism.

These were things you couldn't talk about, back then, without fear of losing your feminist membership card. The best I ever got was a condescending lecture from some nouveau dyke about not giving in to my male-identified conditioning. It was years before I found a place where I could admit to my sexual contradictions.

LIZARD: In the seventies, while many of my friends were already wrestling with feminism, I was in high school, wrestling with sex. It turned out the feminist community was a lot like high school in some ways. With some high school friends, it was assumed you knew what a blow job was; with other friends you wouldn't think of using the words. But who could you ask? Later, among feminists, there were groups where you couldn't admit you had never been tied up, and groups where reviling bondage constituted small talk. No one agreed, but everyone seemed sure their own position was right. It was a tricky time for the curious.

I came into the women's movement in 1982, at a time when feminists my age (twenty) were rebelling against what was perceived as impossible dogma on the part of older (in their thirties by this time) feminists. I wore miniskirts to work at the feminist newspaper and this was a sign of my rebellion. I scoffed at square lesbians, separatist lesbians, flaky lesbians. I listened to The Slits, The Clash, Marianne Faithfull, and Patti Smith instead of Holly Near and Meg Christian. I read lesbian sex magazines.

At the same time I was trying to get men in anarchist/peace/anti-prison groups to recognize that sexism existed in their groups too. Often this took the form of getting the group to take a stand against pornography. It was the most visible feminist issue of the time. It challenged the media. And we were all against it, weren't we? I see now that part of why it was accepted as an issue was that men could be against porn and still have sexist relationships, worksites, and meetings. All they had to do was not have the magazines. Politics made easy.

I thought lesbian magazines were different, but just like I knew to keep *Playboy* hidden from my parents, I knew to keep *On Our Backs* out of the women's centre, and out of the peace march. It felt like the same fears were at work, even though the situations were supposedly so different. And my lover, and my friends, kept disagreeing with me about everything.

Lots happened in the eighties. For one thing, women with more courage and sexual confidence than me took their *On Our Backs* to feminist places and began talking. Feminist debates about porn became more and more entrenched. I gave up on the men of the fringe left and focussed on lesbian issues and lesbian concerns.

But I was still silenced, now because I was a fence-sitter, and there was no room for fence-sitters in our movement. By the late eighties, the split was there, the sex radicals vs. the feminists, the male-identified vs. the prudes.

IN THE TRENCHES

KISS & TELL: Part of our community is fighting *for* state censorship of sexual imagery, in the form of anti-porn legislation, and part of our community is struggling *against* homophobic suppression of gay and lesbian sex. Sometimes both parts are in the same person.

Kiss & Tell's roots are in the anti-pornography movement. We were all three anti-porn activists at one time or another. We picketed porn shops by day, and spray-painted them with anti-porn slogans by night. We organized events, did door-to-door education, and made posters for various groups. We knew where we stood (or pretended to). Porn was bad and we were good and people who were worried about censorship were labelled as old-fashioned liberal free speechers or selfish, sexist gay men.

So what happened? How did we lose our answers and end up with endless questions?

All of our lives, we three (and perhaps some of you, also) have lived in this strange culture where we are taught to see the world in a very linear, binary fashion. True and false, yes and no, right and wrong, good girls and bad girls. But life comes at us from a hundred different directions at once. Points of view collide, separate truths contradict each other.

If we look at our sexuality from one point of view, we feel that sex is empowering. We affirm our sexuality, we celebrate it. From another point of view, we recognize that we have been victims of sexism and sexual violence. We want to be protected from sexual images.

Sometimes in debates about pornography and censorship we are acknowledged only as victims, or only as self-affirming sexual subjects. Other times, everything that is painful is defined as male and everything that is joyous is defined as female, and we are urged to reclaim our "natural" female sexuality, as if it existed untouched under the layers of pain, shame, and fear. As if our sexist conditioning were a T-shirt with a slogan we were tired of, that we could just whip off, and feel the sun and wind on our naked breasts.

But if it's a T-shirt, it was put on long ago, over open wounds. Our flesh has healed around it, only to be wounded again and again. It is part of us, grown into our scars. And yet we have joy. It all comes at us at once, not neatly separated out. Sexual abuse, male violence, repression, pleasure, sexism, friendship, love, racism, state control of our bodies and our art, political disagreements, television … all these things are part of our sexuality.

In this strange culture, being nice girls has been our safety and our trap. Women are taught to smile, to placate, to take care of other people and not talk back. We are taught that if we do this well enough we may be safe from male violence. It's not true, of course, but that's the message. We've grown up with images of women "getting what they deserve." For being bitches and ballbreakers and sluts. Being nice is a survival strategy for some of us. Others of us take our chances as "bad girls." Nice girls have to distance themselves from bad girls, though, and show the boys that they're "not that kind of girl." Or (we are told) they may be at risk too.

For lesbians, invisibility has been our safety and our trap. Being in the closet may be stifling, but it could save you from losing your job, your children, your life. It's frightening to leave that trap. When other lesbians do it, it can feel like they're endangering all of us, giving all of us a bad name. Sometimes we are quicker to punish each other than the outside world is.

Making lesbian sex art isn't safe. It's not invisible, and it's not always nice. Why does Kiss & Tell deliberately set out to do things that make a lot of people angry? Why did we walk into the middle of the porn wars when we could have been safe at home in bed? None of us loves conflict. Susan grew up in a conservative Christian family. She was punished for being a bad girl. Lizard learned to be silent before she even learned how to talk. Persimmon grew up with learning disabilities. She was punished for doing it wrong. We really just want to be good and quiet and do it right. We have such fine-honed fear. Why do we keep doing things that are bound to get us into trouble?

COMING TOGETHER

KISS & TELL: The group that later evolved into Kiss & Tell started in 1984 as a big meeting of feminists who came together to talk about sexual representation—the whole "what is pornography, what is erotica" thing. It settled into a group of eight or so who met once a week. It turned out all of us were artists, which made sense, because as artists we had an extra stake in thinking about images. We were all artists and we were all confused. Our need to work through our confusion was the thing that held us together. It was bigger than anyone's need to show off how tough and cool she was, or how politically pure. We weren't pure, we were halfway desperate. It was time to stop pretending and look at where we really were.

We met for a couple of years. We had weekly updates on each other's sex and art lives. We each took hours telling our complete sexual histories. We learned to trust each other, to know that we could ask each other hard questions, to know that we could tell the truth and not be rejected.

We made art together. We had a "desire diary" that we passed around from week to week, where we each did collages about the current state of our sex lives. We made strange lingerie. Sometimes we would each start a piece of art about sex and give it to someone else in the group to work on, and someone else, and someone else, until we had all worked on each piece. Our group was a place where we could take chances, make art that frightened us, art that we sometimes decided to throw away and sometimes used as the basis for new directions in our individual art practices.

We never worked through our confusion, but we learned to stop pretending. We learned to make confused art. For a while, the group stopped meeting. Then a few years later, the porn wars were heating up and there was a lot of anger flying, and we again needed a place to ask hard questions and tell the truth. So we started up again, and eventually it was Lizard, Persimmon, and Susan, talking sex and making art.

SUSAN: My real reasons for turning up at that first meeting back in '84 didn't emerge right away. Like everyone else, I was confused. I had just finished several years of political work around issues of violence against women and I carried a secret that was aching to be told. It took a while, but I finally found the courage and safety I needed, within this group, to disclose the terrible truth: not only did I like looking at porn but I also made it.

At the same time as I was out there organizing Take Back the Night marches and leading discussions on the evils of pornography, I was leading a kind of double life in my studio, photographing my friends and myself in constructed scenarios that implied uninhibited and sexualized narratives of passion, lust, and betrayal. Images that I never showed. Images that would have disclosed another impossible truth, that I was queer.

Photographs have a wonderful ability to traverse the edge between what is commonly known as *reality* and *the invented,* making it unclear which is which. For myself and my friends these early images constructed themselves: we didn't know what we were doing or even why, we just knew that to make the pictures was to describe something that couldn't be put into words. Our pictures felt like proof that our reality could be altered, that the world we lived in and were part of was not the only world, and that within our imaginations dwelt another reality that was mysterious and potent.

For me this reality included the possibility of women together, and signified that beneath the outer trappings of our everyday masks and costumes there existed a body that hungered and thirsted for freedom. That beneath the artifice there existed another "self," another, more authentic body—in my case, a lesbian body that was struggling to name itself by imagining and then imaging its own unspeakable yearnings.

Those early representations were like canaries brought into a mine to test the toxicity of the environment, to see if it was fit for human use. If the photographs survived scrutiny, if the soft pseudo-lesbian content passed, then perhaps it would be possible to be what the pictures suggested one could be, to be a lesbian in the full sense of that word.

Looking at those pictures now, they don't seem to be saying much. They feel oddly out of place, yet it is in these images that the seeds of discontent took root and a means toward sexual liberation was first formulated. The magic and the power of representation rests in its ability to take the raw stuff of life, both conscious and unconscious, and shift meanings to create new ways of being in the world. Or so it seemed to me as I navigated the treacherous boundaries between the straight world I knew and the queer world I aspired to.

So it is with some irony that I realize that the first images I made of the lesbian body weren't of lesbians. They were fictions, designed to suggest a lesbian body. This point highlights another powerful and mischievous aspect of the photograph, its chameleon-like ability to suggest completely different things to different people. What is truth in the face of such a representation?

It wasn't until more than ten years later, in the decade in which I finally came out, that I was presented with the opportunity to make photographs with real live lesbian bodies, and it was as if a dam had burst open.

BETWEEN THE LINES

KISS & TELL: In 1988, we started work on what was to be our first collaborative work made for a public audience, DRAWING THE LINE. The catalyst for our project was a series of lesbian sex photographs by artist Li Yuen that were printed as an International Lesbian Week poster in Vancouver's gay, lesbian, and bisexual paper, *Angles.*[3]

This poster caused an uproar in our communities. *Angles* was flooded with letters, pro and con, for weeks after. There were organized meetings, spontaneous debates, contradictory commentaries:

"This doesn't represent my sexuality."

"How wonderful to see such a variety of lesbian sex."

"The pictures that are fragmented instead of showing the whole woman are implicitly violent."

"The fragmented shots are what you actually see when you're lying next to someone—the close up view."

"This one is so playful."

"This one is posed and stilted."

It was an amazing event in our community, because for the first time, the debate about imagery was focussed on a particular set of images, produced by and for lesbians, that had been widely viewed and circulated. We were looking at the same pictures, and our reactions were incredibly diverse. One photo reminded a woman of the feeling of making love, when she could no longer tell whose body was whose, the feeling of dissolving into a tangle of arms, legs, mouths, moving together. The same photo reminded another woman of a picture she had once seen of a tangle of dead bodies.

Which woman was "right" about the meaning of the photo? Is it possible to honour both the one woman's joy and the other woman's fear? Is it possible to admit the mutability of images without retreating to a position that says all images are neutral?

Kiss & Tell decided to make a piece that would continue the exploration started in Li Yuen's work. DRAWING THE LINE is a series of 100 photographs, set literally within the context of the debate about sexual representation. Susan was the photographer and Lizard and Persimmon were the models. The overall concept and all decisions along the way were arrived at collectively. The photos cover a range of lesbian sexual practices, and are deliberately constructed to cover a range of problematic issues. At the exhibits, women viewers write their reactions directly on the walls around the photographs. Men write their comments in a book.

DRAWING THE LINE has been shown 16 times in 15 cities since 1988. The show still travels, and in every place women respond. Those polite and pristine gallery walls are soon scrawled over with writing. The photos float in a sea of text; not "fine art objects" but part of a loud, rowdy community argument and celebration. We want everyone to feel that they have a right to their reaction, and that they can speak out about it, even if it doesn't make perfect political sense, or upsets their best friend, or whatever. Some people write long, thoughtful analysis. Others react very directly and succinctly, saying things like "great," "stupid," "nice," "fuck me," etc. Viewers have their own dialogue with the anonymous commentators, and on it goes.

DRAWING THE LINE was created within a lesbian context that included responsibility, col-laboration, safety, community, and the wild, intoxicating freedom that came from uninhibited representation of our own lesbian bodies. We learned many things from this project, not the least of which was that the two bodies we represented over and over, Lizard's and Persimmon's, took on multiple and widely divergent meanings for other lesbians. No two responses to any single image were ever the same. Before long it became very clear that the notion of any single, unified account of what a lesbian body was or could be was an utter impossibility. The most we could do for our work was to provide it with a lesbian context. The "body" in that work was an untamed and unpredictable creature open to interpretation by whoever viewed it.

TRUANT VIRGINS

PERSIMMON: In 1992, Kiss & Tell produced the multi-media performance and video TRUE INVERSIONS. It was a monster. It ate our lives for months. Three performers, one singer, four scenes, three video tapes, four audio tapes, and over 200 slides. And three technicians. At first

Joelene Clarke was the only technician, and Suzo Hickey and Ali McIlwaine were just girlfriends who were going to come with us to Boston and Northampton for a romantic vacation. And maybe they would help out a little bit when we did our show. Ha! It was soon obvious that we couldn't do it without all three of them busting butt throughout the six-hour set-up, and then running the simultaneous tapes, slides, and lights during the show.

Girlfriends. Kiss & Tell is run on the exploited labour of girlfriends. Some of them don't think that's such a funny joke. The reason TRUE INVERSIONS has three videos (two used as background to other action, and one that plays by itself while we change costumes) is because one of my girlfriends, Lorna Boschman, is a video maker. We got the idea to make a two- or three-minute video segment and asked Lorna if she'd help us. She said yes. Then we gave her the script and she said, "[T]his is not a three-minute video." In the end it was 30 minutes. Oh well.

It was shot in two days, by Lorna's ace video crew along with a couple of reinforcements from our side. Lorna had directed explicit sex scenes before and she was really comfortable, but some of the crew seemed to find it a little strange that my girlfriend was directing me having sex with Lizard. My other girlfriend brought us lunch. Life in Kiss & Tell.

And that was just the video. We still had to do four audio tapes, shoot the slides, build the set, etc. And we had to create a performance piece. Rehearsing, rewriting, reworking ... We were still changing our script right up to the day of our first show. Actually, now that I think of it, we've changed our script on the day of every show we've ever done. Why would anyone want to be a performance artist? You can't ask for a week's extension if you're not ready to perform. You've got to be ready. You've got to get up and do it, and if you fuck up it's right out there in front of a whole bunch of people. Jesus. Why did I let them talk me into it? I hate it, I hate it, I hate it.

But I love the piece—I love the interwoven sex stories in the first section, where Susan and I have these mad back-and-forths building to a wild climax that Lizard grabs out of our hands. And then the part with Emily Faryna, the singer whose music is used in TRUE INVERSIONS, who eventually started performing live with us. Emily looking tough in a leather coat and pig snout, singing about surveillance, state control, and everyday working life. I can feel her voice rip through the audience while we're changing our clothes on stage behind her, and Ali up in the tech booth cruises us with a spotlight that moves like a police searchlight. And then the part where our slides are projected on top of a commercial porn video and they just float there like ghost images while fake lesbians have fake sex around, behind, and through them.

And I love sitting in the dressing room while the long video is on, gauging the audience by when they laugh, trying not to think of all the ways I could still blow it. And then we go back on for the part where we read letters to our mothers, explaining to them why we're doing this public sex thing. I have to stand up there alone on stage and talk to my mother about sex. Why did I let Susan talk me into this? How many people in the audience could possibly relate to growing up like me, in a left-wing family where your mother takes you on picket lines, and then in later years brags about your lesbian exploits to her friends? But it doesn't matter, I can feel the audience with me. I can feel them listening, and it's a rush like nothing else.

After that, it's easy—keeping count in my head in the dark so I can be there frozen when the spotlight hits—move—freeze—move. And Emily is doing Marlene Dietrich and I don't think about fucking up. I love that song.

KISS & TELL: Our first audience was a crowd of 400 lesbians at the York Theatre in Vancouver. To feel the excitement in that room was to understand the power of live theatre and its activist potential to move both performer and spectator in unexpected ways.

Informal lesbian performance occurs constantly, on the street, in the bars, and in our bedrooms. As lesbians we continuously perform for each other. It can be as simple as a discrete triangle worn at the ear, the cut of a jacket, a way of walking, or as flagrant as the live sex shows we organize in our bars. We are consummate actors. Some of us have been practicing stagecraft from our earliest years. We've learned to perform *lesbian* to find and attract each other and we've learned to perform *straight* when disguise is our best defense for survival.

Staging lesbian performance in a theatrical context implies theatre within theatre. The lesbian subject is performing herself performing herself. Taking our spontaneous theatre and putting it on a stage ritualizes and distances it, while at the same time acknowledging it, and, paradoxically, bringing it closer to home. Theatre offers a space where audience and artists can look each other square in the face. Whatever exchange happens does so immediately and irrevocably. There is power in this, not unlike the power people create when they consent to sex. There is seduction, anticipation, desire, gratification (or not), intense sharing, and sometimes pain, sometimes love. A volatile and reactive mix.

Given the potential of live performance, the question becomes what would make it most effective as a tool for resistance? What strategies would be most useful for the spectator *and* the performer, to counter the oppressiveness of social rejection and political discrimination? How can we use theatre and performance to empower ourselves and tackle the contradictions in our lives? And how can we have *fun* while doing these things?

SUSAN: Theatre heals. It can also hurt.

Standing on stage at the Academy of Music in Lesbianville, USA,[4] I noticed that several women walked out during part of our performance. Now this can be a very discouraging thing for a performer. An *"Oh no, that bad!"* type of feeling can quickly ensue, but I had a hunch that wasn't happening here. These women didn't go far, just to the front of the house, to the lobby. They stood in the open doorway, still listening, but they were smoking too and the outside exit was a comfortable distance away. The part of our show that prompted this mini-exodus wasn't the explicit sex, nor was it our experimentally formatted video. It was the letters we read aloud to our mothers.

Queer, lezzie, dyke, pervert, monster. I am your daughter, your beloved. I want you to know me— who I am, not what I am called.

It is hard to talk to you after so long. You were two years older than I am now when you died. The child I was then died with you, torn in two from grief. I dreamed you in a thousand dreams, and waking, your presence would linger like the scent of a forgotten perfume. How dare you leave me and turn out all the lights in your passing?

Now, you are back—here on stage, alive in memory, the recipient of this letter.

How will I explain myself to you, what sense would you make of this distance, this difference?

What sense would you make of this lesbian daughter, your own daughter, this unthinkable choice? How did we get from the ordered days of the family—clothespins, baking, church suppers, school meetings, regular appointments at the beauty parlor—to pornography, censorship, lesbian sex, and radical art? What strange path was it, from you to me, mother to daughter?

The word lesbian didn't exist in our world because lesbians didn't exist. The concept was unthinkable, impossible, unspeakable … repulsive. Yet the sheer weight of that silence was not enough to extinguish imagination. Friendships. Deep, passionate, engrossing friendships between women. I followed your example in this. I thrived in the love of friendship—and I crossed the line. The line that had no description, no form, no word—the line that separates our worlds—the line that gave me my name—lesbian.

—SUSAN (from TRUE INVERSIONS)

It made sense that some of our audience could have been affected by these letters, since we had been, too. When the idea first came up, when we realized that this was indeed an idea we could explore, an idea that stuck in the gut, it was initially greeted with absolute silence. For me the word "abject" suddenly took on the force of meaning. Miserable and wretched, it means, and so I felt as I attempted to bring my mother into our work. Lesbian sex and mom didn't quite fit, or else they did fit in ways that were impossibly confusing and painful. Each of our stories about our relationship with our mother was very different, yet the anxiety and grief and coming to terms with the past were things we shared.

There is the temptation to generalize, to try to figure out if there is a universal lesbian/mother experience, but I suspect this would be a mistake. There are far too many variables, too many stories, too many different ways of being. I can only speak for myself and I know that I have the need to discover some kind of coherency in this pain and to give it broader meaning.

I grew up with a societal understanding of what a mother is, of her precise location and function within this system called the family, within a culture that privileges heterosexually pre-scribed roles for women to the exclusion of any alternative choices. If a woman's self-definition is formed by a role, if her very existence is defined by that role, what possible relationship is she likely to have with a daughter who rejects that role for the risk and freedom of a lesbian alterna-tive? For many lesbians the mother-daughter relationship is characterized by painful rejection and separation that is culturally reinforced by discrimination and rage wherever we turn.

It is one of those things some of us have a hard time talking about. Our silences speak volumes.

LIZARD: I have nightmares. There is one where we have forgotten our costumes for the second part and are fighting in the dressing room, about whether to go home and get them or to go ahead in the wrong outfits. Or the dream where Persimmon chats with her friends in the audience while the video is showing, and forgets her cue. Or the real life nightmare when we stood on stage realizing a prop was missing, Susan and I watching slack-jawed as Persimmon improvised. Dreams are important. The first sex story I ever wrote was for TRUE INVERSIONS, and it came to me in a dream. All I had to do was describe it. I was paralyzed by fiction writing (of any kind, and especially sex stories), went to bed knowing I was going to miss *another* Kiss & Tell deadline, and woke up with a story. Phew.

Looking back on it now I realize that our minds have their own ways of circumventing our fears. It is really scary to write a sex story, because if no one else likes it it feels like a personal blow. Essays can be good or bad, clear or unclear, without a lot of personal pain, but if you try to write something that turns you on, and everyone else hates it, what does that say about you? Even in Kiss & Tell it can feel like your desires are weird.

But my story came to me unbidden, in a dream. It wasn't *my* story, really, so I could let them see it.

The other thing about my story is that it's pretty goofy. I mean, my life is pretty goofy, which is probably why that happened, but why a goofy sex story? (I can talk about this objectively because I didn't really write the story. It came to me in a dream, remember?) I think the goofiness works like the dream. It works like a spoonful of sugar. It works like a safety valve.

My story is all about a shy and nervous gal with a monster crush. She doesn't know how to come on to anybody in any kind of suave way. She's overwhelmed by lust. She makes a fool of herself. But she gets what she wants. You can laugh at her or with her. You can laugh because you've been there, or because you're anxious that Persimmon's character just slapped her girlfriend, or because Susan's character is turning you on, or because the images are from your fantasies, or because you've got some hot date with you, or your ex is in the next row, or whatever. You can laugh and it's a release and it's allowed. It brings you close.

I am convinced that people hear more through a joke than a lecture, and learn more from friends than enemies. However, I am also convinced that lying and pretending not to be angry do not serve the purposes of hearing or learning. This means that different audiences have profoundly different reactions to our show. Perhaps barriers are inevitable in political art-making. Maybe the difference is just that sometimes we erect the walls to enclose, instead of to divide. Sometimes we are united with our audience. Sometimes they feel like an adversary. The pact between audience and performer is tenuous. When things don't work, it is brittle as ice. When things go well, it is steel cable, flexible and strong. It is sex without the contact, all images and words. Take me, says the audience, but do it right.

There are orgasms to be had.

The trick becomes how to weave this dynamic with the anger, pain, fear, and joy of our lives and politics. How to get the audience to figure it out along with us, to be right there, to talk beside us.

When I think about making a performance piece, I think about that old story about the Sun and the Wind. You know the one, where the Sun and Wind have a bet about who can get a man to take off his coat first. And the Wind tries to blow it off, and the man just clutches his coat tighter. But the Sun makes it so hot that the man takes off his coat himself.

That's what we are trying to do, make it so hot that you take off your coat yourself.

NOTES

1 Sur Mehat, Artist's statement for "sixbooks for public and private usage," exhibited at Women in Focus Gallery, Vancouver, B.C., 1992.

2 Monique Wittig, *The Lesbian Body* (New York: Avon Books, 1975).

3 *Angles*, September 1987.

4 "Lesbianville, USA," was the tag given to Northampton, Massachusetts, by the front-page story in that week's issue of *National Enquirer*.

CHAPTER 35

Forbidden Love, or Queering the National Film Board of Canada

Thomas Waugh

[…] to interpret Canada to Canadians.

— Mandate of the National Film Board of Canada

BURSTING SUITCASE, OR THE ELEPHANT AS AUTEUR

[…] [N]o institution has had more impact on shaping Canadian cinematic cultures historically, whether in English or in French, than the National Film Board of Canada. Even more than other excluded and silenced constituencies, GLBTQ Canadians have had a rollercoaster love-hate relationship with John Grierson's studio, founded in 1939 to construct our national imaginary, as per my oft-invoked epigraph above. Many of us have watched very carefully the innovative documentary and animation studio of the forties, fifties, and sixties as it became the stodgy old uncle of later decades. Today the board is a miniature version of the behemoth it became during the Trudeau era, having barely survived the ferocious downsizing imposed by the Mulroney regime and the attrition perpetuated by the Chrétien regime. It is perennially in urgent need of renewal, most recently, as I write in 2003, having fired all of its in-house directors and placed itself in the hands of freelance indies from coast to coast, desperately searching for an expanded vision and an extended mandate in the cyber-digital era. Regardless of the instability of the last decades, few would deny that the board's queer documentary cycle of the 1980s, 1990s, and, 2000s, a corpus of almost fifty documentary films (depending on how you count) has had a major impact on queer cultures and on larger political cultures in both English- and French-speaking Canada and, moreover, that it constitutes an important repository of queer voices and visions by queer artists, one recognized around the world.

This chapter is devoted to this bursting suitcase of films, sprawling, contradictory, and uneven, often inspired and brilliant, often infuriatingly outdated and beside the point, full of holes. (For example, not a single film on the AIDS crisis in relation to its domestic gay-male epidemiology emerged from the English programs—perhaps the most shocking betrayal in a sea of small betrayals.) This suitcase can be opened and unpacked through several methodological frameworks. The films constitute a pan-national documentary tradition and invite a perspective in terms of Canadian cultural themes, landscapes, and iconographies, with the usual gulf between anglophone and francophone constituents and the usual regional mosaic. But at the same time they form a genre cycle determined by its dialogue with a political constituency that overflows national boundaries, what we could call the international "sexual diversity" or queer-documentary genre cycle; the corpus contains within its margins, often within the same film, both "affirmation" and "postaffirmation" energies and stages (to use Dyer's terms for the initial waves of post-Stonewall "positive image" community-building, and the subsequent post-AIDS tide of self-reflection and diversification [*Now You See It: Studies in Lesbian and Gay Film* (New York: Routledge [1990] 2003, 215–64]. At the same time, the NFB queer corpus is work produced within a single production studio (and its regional branchplants) and thus calls for analysis from a "studio as auteur" perspective. In this light, the work reflects the personalities who came and went through the cavernous labyrinth in suburban Montreal and its regional garrisons, from persistent staff directors like Margaret Wescott and powerful producers like Don Haig to young independents like Atif Siddiqi. But the work is also stamped by one of the weirdest bureaucratic subcultures in the world, combining both the idealism and the inertia, the profligacy and the tokenism, of any civil service—but especially ours. This chapter will intermingle all three of these angles upon the elephant, commencing with an overview of the studio as auteur and building a chronology of the quarter century in which the queer corpus emerged. [...]

Two or three of the films nurtured within this microclimate have received wide international attention (i.e., from Americans), especially *The Company of Strangers* (aka *Stranger's in Good Company* in the United States, 1990) and *Forbidden Love: The Unashamed Story of Lesbian Lives* (1992). Such films are canonized by chapters in anthologies from American university presses, by entries on U.S. queer websites, and by their inclusion in a whole critical literature; the foreigners are not likely to situate the films within the historical frameworks I am trying to scan, but they sometimes see things insiders can't.

Dozens of the other films and videos make the domestic rounds of the proverbial church basements, school AV centres, and community library loan shelves, flow out through cassette and DVD merchandising online and over the counter, occasionally make it onto cablecast, and even stream down from increasingly common cyber servers. This everyday product is unrecognized by cultural arbiters but reaches huge numbers of people efficiently and quietly, providing invaluable resources for isolated individuals and grass roots groups. My study attempts to redress both the oversights and the taken-for-grantedness, as well as to go beyond the prototypical Canadian carping [...] to come up with a coherent analysis and overview of this critically important collection of our images. But it begins with a personal story.

J'ACCUSE

On 10 November 1986, in one of my more militant moments I wrote an angry letter to the government film commissioner, François Macerola, John Grierson's successor at the helm of the NFB and figurehead of one of the most prestigious documentary studios in the world. The state film studio was then getting set to celebrate, in 1989, the fiftieth anniversary of its founding, but I wasn't in a celebratory mood. What sparked my *J'accuse* was *Passiflora* (1985), an ambitious, bold, and expensive French-language NFB feature documentary about the simultaneous visits of the pope and Michael Jackson to Montreal's Olympic stadium in 1984. The visits were the backdrop against which a Breughelian foreground of dramatized sex/gender transgressors, including gay men, transgendered characters, abortion seekers, refugees from psychiatry and from domestic violence, and alienated young people with great haircuts were all teeming. All these people were excluded from the visits but integrated into the postmodern urban landscape of dissent/consent depicted in the film. Highlights included the celebration of queer street theatre (a procession of "papettes" mocking the liturgical drag at hand)[1] and queer desire (the public performance of homoerotic exchange and transgender transgression in public space). As if this were not enough to frighten the horses, the filmmakers Fernand Bélanger and Dagmar Teufel—respectively an experienced and out gay documentarist with anarchist and pro-youth sympathies and a feminist who had championed disempowered rural women in several documentaries—were perhaps the first to puncture the realist sobriety of the NFB documentary ethos with their irreverent graffiti-ization of real-life voices and bodies, overlaying image tracks and sound tracks alike with mischievous doodles (the pope's "re-mixed voice" booming out "[B]ow down and obey!" from his giant video screens). It was probably this irreverence for "reality," in combination with the film's more literal dissidence around sexual identity and reproductive rights, that was guaranteed to raise eyebrows.

Even before *Passiflora* was released, Bélanger and Teufel sensed that there was funny business afoot from the studio brass around the sensitive issues of ecclesiastical show business, queer sexualities, and reproductive rights that the film had tackled. They were furious that the board had without precedent declined to subtitle the film for its prestige invitation to the 1986 Toronto International Film Festival and that the board's strategy of damage control was being abetted by its internal festival and release bureaus (little pockets of absurdly unaccountable and refractory bureaucracy, which seemed this time to be taking orders from on high). Bélanger and Teufel blew the whistle. Recognizing an ambitious, experimental work that, moreover, was clearly the first unabashed gay lib work from the old uncle, I rushed to champion the film, programmed it in its original French version at the 1987 Grierson Documentary Seminar in Toronto, and got onto the CBC's *Journal* denouncing the suppression of the film. The board denied everything and said festivals around the world had rejected the film, and we all watched the noses grow on their faces. My partner at the time, José Arroyo, championed the film in *Cinema Canada* (128 (March 1986): 28). as a film "in concept and form much more daring than any other Québécois film I've seen recently ... [and one that will] continue to be talked about long after the awards being given to some other films have turned to dust" (1986). And the Scotsman Ian Lockerbie (not my partner and not even gay) proved him right a few years later, claiming that with *Passiflora* and an earlier Bélanger work, the documentary "has acquired a complexity of language and a richness of texture and meaning of which there are hardly other examples in all its history" and that the films "should endure, and become reference points for measuring many works to come" (*Cinémas* 2, no. 2 (Spring 1994): 119–32).

Since I had been smarting under the NFB silence for a decade, the ham-fisted suppression of this artistically innovative, bravely anarchist, and prophetically queer film by the NFB was the last straw. So I wrote my letter, indicting the institution for failing to fulfil its mandate with regard to Canadian lesbians and gays and just happened to "cc" the letter to not-yet-out MP Svend Robinson and a few others. I did not mince words and could be accused of slight exaggeration (10 November 1986):

> I have frequently criticized the National Film Board for failing to fulfil its mandate with regard to two million lesbian and gay Canadians (a conservative estimate), a criticism that is bitter and widespread in the gay media throughout both Quebec and English Canada. Throughout its history the NFB has represented every conceivable Canadian minority in its films, from the Inuits to the Hutterites to the handicapped, with the glaring exception of this large stigmatized minority still struggling for its rights.
>
> The NFB's unacceptable record of contemptuous silence has been broken on only two exceptional occasions: a passage in *Some American Feminists* (1978) that deals with *American* lesbians and an inept short *New Romance* (1975) riddled with derisive stereotypes, a film fortunately now absent from the catalogue. I suppose we should be grateful that the independent short film *Michael a Gay Son* is distributed through the NFB, that a few recent NFB co-productions in Quebec theatrical fiction have included sympathetic gay characters (*Anne Trister, Pouvoir intime, Déclin de l'empire américain*), or that regional NFB offices occasionally contribute small amounts to independent gay and lesbian productions. However, this is clearly less than we are entitled to according to the NFB's mandate, and in view of our investment as taxpayers in the world's leading producer of documentaries of social conscience.[2]

I urged the commissioner to "expedite the preparation of an English version of *Passiflora* ... and to furthermore implement immediate plans for affirmative action in fulfilling the NFB's mandate to gay and lesbian Canadians."

Svend complained to Flora MacDonald, the Tory minister of communications in charge of the NFB, who responded with the usual "arm's length" line but passed on the complaint to Macerola (27 January 1987). Two months after my letter, the commissioner replied timidly that no, the New York queer film festival had refused *Passiflora* on the grounds that it was irrelevant to the event and would not be of interest to gays and lesbians, and that no, "unquestionably, no one had deliberately obstructed the production of films for this minority group. As you know, film proposals are generated through filmmakers and producers—it may well be that good ideas on the subject have simply not emerged. However, I am told that Studio D has identified the need for such films, and is currently investigating the possibility of a one-hour documentary looking at the heterosexual institution and the history of lesbianism throughout the ages" (8 January 1987) .

Government cultural institutions specialize in this kind of feeble self-justification and damage control. Who had they expected to come up with "good ideas"? [...] [T]he blinkered male fraternity who were having trouble dealing even with mild liberal feminism in their Town of Mount Royal bungalows and Outremont duplexes, let alone gay liberation and AIDS downtown? What kind of documentary filmmaker could have looked at thousands of angry queers surging through the streets of Toronto after the bathhouse raids in 1981 or rallying there in the very month that I was writing my letter (pushing the new provincial Liberal government for protection from discrimination in the provincial human rights legislation), or more recently at the "waves of dying friends" precipitated by the HIV pandemic,[3] and not said immediately, "Wow, there are some films there!"? And the particular thrust of the self-justification—passing the buck to the women in the convenient feminist Studio D, founded in 1974—further inflamed me.

I therefore continued the tirade into a new instalment, which I happened to run as an open letter in four film and gay magazines and which I sent to a dozen well-located NFB people:

> I am glad to be informed that "no one has deliberately obstructed the production of films for this minority group." However I am not reassured by your conjecture that "good ideas on the subject have simply not emerged." This of course is the crux of the matter: the silencing of minorities through omission and institutional inertia is perhaps the most insidious kind of censorship because no one can point to "deliberate obstruction." Over the years NFB filmmakers have come to understand this problem and remedied it through affirmative action with regard to almost every Canadian minority or disenfranchised group—whether determined by gender, class, race, age, language, religion, handicap or ethnic or regional identity—every group in fact *except* homosexuals. If NFB filmmakers have avoided coming up with "good ideas on the subject," then it is the institution's responsibility to initiate affirmative action. Gay Canadian taxpayers are no longer willing to accept this silence. (1987)

I continued, spelling out three demands: consultative meetings between studio brass and producers and gay community representatives across the country, the distribution of eight independent films through NFB channels as a stopgap measure, and the publication of an audiovisual resource guide for gay and lesbian film users. For good measure I appended a list of "good ideas," including films on AIDS, the history of gay-rights struggles, a history of Toronto's *The Body Politic* (the legendary gay lib magazine had just given up the ghost after fifteen years of battles with the Ontario police and court system), a Canadian *Before Stonewall* and a Canadian *Times of Harvey Milk* (evoking the major American queer historical-documentary features of the decade, both from 1984, the latter an Oscar winner), a male *Firewords* (referring to Studio D's just completed feature by Dorothy Todd Hénaut on three Québécois lesbian writers), and finally, topical treatments of parents/teenagers/seniors/couples/ghettos, of freedom of speech/civil rights issues, and of public sex and policing. Finally, I presented Macerola with proof that either his festival office had lied to him about the New York queer festival refusal (or that my friend, festival director Peter Lowy, was lying to me), and repeated my demand for the subtitling of *Passiflora*, since I was about to show the film in Winnipeg in April. The letter ran in gay magazines but, most importantly, filled a whole page of *Cinema Canada*, and the egg hit the fan.[4]

Macerola responded on the same page, but did not add anything new to the discussion, continuing to pass the buck to women. For instead of the two male program branch directors, Georges Dufaux and Peter Katadotis, who he promised in his letter would contact me, the latter's first lieutenant, Isobel Marks, programming director for English production, soon showed up fairly nervously at my office. Marks tried to convince me that ongoing projects were just what the doctor ordered:

1. The forthcoming Puberty Package was surely exactly what I was looking for, since it included a brief reference to AIDS and a nonjudgmental treatment of homosexuality (this project apparently ended up as the *Growing Up Series*, 1989). In this connection she also mentioned West Coast producer Jennifer Torrance, a youth and woman specialist, who, in addition to the "Growing Up" series of 1985, had co-produced then-heterosexual Moira Simpson's *Lorri: The Recovery Series* (1985). This instalment in a Vancouver substance abuse series profiled a recovering alcoholic who happened to be a lesbian depicted in conversation with her therapist for fifteen minutes, and everyone was going on about it as if this brave and articulate woman absolved the NFB in perpetuity from developing programs on queers. [...]
2. Marks was also thinking about short dramas on teen issues, perhaps even homophobia, to follow up on existing pregnancy films (what turned out to be the 1994 Teen Pregnancy Package [...]).
3. The good news from Edmonton was that there was an "investigate" (the studio's quirky noun) underway on masculinity, which apparently was to end up as the homophobic *Life after Hockey* (1989 [...]).
4. She also had on her mind some programs on families in transition (which would become a major theme of late-1990s productions).
5. And finally, don't forget good old Studio D and Margaret Wescott (who, as Macerola had intimated, had just undertaken her "history of lesbianism since Sappho" project, which was not to emerge for another decade, in 1997, as *Stolen Moments*, but I'm getting ahead of myself), who were going to let the male directors off the hook and bear the entire weight of the institution's responsibility to both gender and sexual minorities and everything else.
6. And oh yes, there's already plenty of factual material available on AIDS (!!!) that shouldn't be duplicated, but she'd met with Margaret Somerville in Medical Ethics at McGill (an early champion of the rights of people with HIV), and perhaps something to help teenagers with the issues might be appropriate.[5]

Marks was acting and speaking in better faith than her boss, and in fact the momentum of educational materials aimed at children and teenagers turned out to be a creditable one as far as it went in its isolation and however isolated it was. However, I couldn't believe her utter obliviousness to the political problematics of sexual minorities and wouldn't have any of the pathetic crumbs that she was tossing my way—or rather, at straight teenagers. When I threatened to initiate a lesbian and gay boycott of board products, she looked at me as if I had just started speaking Klingon.

Though the institution clearly was not budging on *Passiflora*, it was, admittedly, like all liberal sociocultural microcosms, capable of yielding slightly to guilt. Soon after, they briefly entertained a film proposal, developed in response to the controversy, by Montreal indie gay producer

Hugh Campbell in cahoots with my friend, Toronto video bad boy John Greyson. Their film would be called *Flaunting It!* and would treat *The Body Politic* as a symbol of the trajectory of the gay and lesbian movement in Canada over the previous fifteen years. The proposal was brilliant, strategically savvy ("to both gay and straight audiences"), and sensitive to the emerging political agenda of community diversity, and it tied the pandemic into a concluding wrap-up of the work: "*Flaunting It!* will present and challenge *The Body Politic*'s very engaged version of the history of the movement. It will capture from within those turbulent decades when *TBP* was the very subjective eyes and ears of the community. Just as *TBP* did in its day, *Flaunting It!* will acknowledge a wealth of contradictory opinions and voices. Each in itself is incomplete. Together they present a richer, fuller version."[6] [...]

Three opinions about the proposal were solicited by John Taylor; of the Toronto office, one positive and two negative evaluations apparently from conservative, older gays hostile to *The Body Politic* or to Greyson's style. One of these offered a very chip-on-the-shoulder assessment, e.g., "I would like to see less emphasis on the reminiscences of those involved with *TBP*," and "While *Flaunting It!* may only be a first or working title it reflects a flamboyant male homosexual 'queen' image. If the gay community wants a serious and honest examination of its history represented then it's going to have to straighten up a little ... (On a very personal note, I was not a supporter of *TBP*'s "Men Loving Boys Loving Men" article. I didn't then and I don't now think that we are struggling for the recognition of sexual orientation so that men can fuck little boys.)"[7] Well, the consultant's last parenthetical segue seems to have frightened the horses. These lukewarm and contradictory assessments from three homosexuals selected in heterosexual Taylor's wisdom who knows how and assigned full representativity in relation to the "gay community" became the pretext for closing down discussion—and the project. Immobilized by the apparent assumption that a single film about homos could cover the whole issue, the brass gradually stopped jerking and quietly dropped the whole baton. [...] The world was never to know what an unrealized project directed by Canada's most important queer filmmaker and produced by the NFB might have looked like. Taylor moved on within the next couple of years to act as executive co-producer of two films on AIDS—but certainly not AIDS in Canada—of which one, *Karate Kids* (1990), was one of the most hateful and homophobic works ever to have shamed the institution. [...]

Nineteen-eighty-seven was otherwise a key year in NFB history, or, rather, in the history of Studio D, then in its twelfth year of sales surges, Oscars, and international acclaim and the source of such causes célèbres as *Not a Love Story* (1981) and *If You Love This Planet* (1982). The studio was in the process of passing the reins of power to an outsider, Rina Fraticelli, an imaginative cultural administrator and activist with no background in film. Fraticelli immediately embarked on a project of shaking things up through various inclusiveness programs (as well as through edging out into the male studios their established stable of white middle-class directors like the heterosexual *Firewords* director Dorothy Hénaut and Wescott, the resident lesbian director, until then relatively discreet). To celebrate the studio's fifteenth anniversary Fraticelli commissioned a feature-length package of five-minute films selected from proposals from independent female practitioners across the country, which was to appear in 1990 as *Five Feminist Minutes*. The result was electrifying on several scores, a triumph of rainbow representativity that recharged the aesthetic batteries that the now tired baby boomers at the studio had let run low. The package also, from our point of view, revealed a groundswell of lesbian cinematic energy that had previously been untapped. Of the seventeen selected projects, one, an explicit programmatic manifesto by lesbians of colour, *Exposure*, by Toronto first-time director Michelle Mohabeer, stands as *the* first NFB lesbian documentary in terms of both public authorial identity and explicit subject matter. Fully six others of the shorts in the package were of varying degrees of queer—crypto, quasi, partly, implicitly, or authorially.

The momentum continued: Fraticelli went on to commission another independent project from two freelancers, Lynne Fernie and Aerlyn Weissman, who had been around at the start of the Wescott epic and were itching to get out. The new project would be fully explicit and unabashedly hip in its identity discourse, no pussy footing around this time: a monumental epic of community and history. *Forbidden Love: The Unashamed Stories of Lesbian Lives* (1992) went on to standing ovations at the new breed of viable community queer festivals around the world and even had successful theatrical runs in such places as New York and London as one of the most internationally canonized and award-winning feminist or queer documentaries of the 1990s. And its commercial success did no harm either. *Forbidden* almost single-handedly restored the credibility of the NFB in the eyes of anglophone queer constituents and, I would conjecture, was the impetus that maintained the NFB on its queer boom over the next decade.

A corpus of almost fifty documentaries accumulated, long and short, almost a quarter from the French studios and the rest from the English-language studios. Almost none is by old-guard or staff directors, for the new boom was bolstered by the increasing reliance of the savagely defunded institution on freelance-initiated projects and increasingly rooted regional bases. The changing political tide did not hurt either. The studio might seem to have treaded cautiously during the last years of the budget-slashing Mulroney regime, but the floodgates were wide open starting in 1993 after the Tories' cataclysmic defeat at the hands of Jean Chrétien's Liberals. This party, traditionally more favourable to multiculturalism and diversity, had decriminalized sodomy in the first days of Trudeau's leadership back in 1969 and traditionally favoured public funding of the arts, so, at the very least, it did not continue the Tories' homocidal sabotage of the studio.

Thus, on a roll after the surprise commercial success of *Company of Strangers* (1990 [...]), the pastoral idyll of geriatric homosociality, and especially of *Forbidden Love*, the board had the brazenness in 1994 to put together retroactively a Lesbian and Gay Film Package, bringing together ten films of full or partial interest to the queer audience. Alongside the mega hit *Company* (1990), in which one of eight characters briefly comes out to another, were assembled and marketed together the following films (listed in chronological order of their release date): *Lorri: The Recovery Series* (1985, Vancouver); *Sandra's Garden* (1990, Winnipeg); *Forbidden Love* (1992, Montreal); *Father and Son* (1992, Vancouver); *A Kind of Family* (1992, Winnipeg); *Toward Intimacy* (1992, Montreal/Atlantic); *Long Time Comin'* (1993, Toronto); *Out: Stories of Lesbian and Gay Youth* (1993, Toronto); and *When Shirley Met Florence* (1994, Montreal). Unfortunately, Her Majesty's Loyal Opposition, already harping on *Forbidden Love*, discovered the package and behaved in its best imported Jesse Helms mode on the floor of the House of Commons. Then Reform Party cultural critic Monte Solberg (Medicine Hat), who was typically confused, having as usual not seen the materials addressed, announced to the House that the "unaccountable"

NFB had produced "a series of videos … on lesbian love. They were restricted videos, ones that contained very explicit scenes." He called for guidelines to prevent the expenditure of "taxpayers' dollars" on "anything that is pornographic in nature or is x-rated" (1 November 1994). Ottawa, unlike Washington, is used to weathering such tempests within our long history of arm's-length state-funded cultural products, knowing that the attention span of Alberta philistines is as limited as it is erratic, so aside from whatever behind-the-scenes pressures might have been brought to bear, no serious consequences ensued.

In fact, the package was not quite as dangerous as the Reform Party contended, as an analysis of its contents reveals. The fact that the package was cobbled together post facto is immediately evident: only two of the films could boast applied focus on the issue of sexual identity, *Forbidden* and *Out*, but four others involved queer authorship (director or scriptwriter), discreetly including sexual-identity politics within the scope of another or related issue, whether racial identity *(Long Time Comin')*, aging *(Company)*, female homosocial friendship/post-Holocaust Jewish diaspora *(Shirley/Florence)*, or abuse *(Sandra's Garden)*. The other four belonged only by the narrowest and most incidental of threads, neither through authorial identity (at the time, to my knowledge) nor by concentrated focus, all more or less clinging to the package through the "who happen to be" connection: *Lorri* (the eponymous lesbian is one portrait alongside four heterosexual women recovering from substance abuse); *Father and Son* (an effective first-person essay on masculinity based on the testimony of six male witnesses, of which three are constructed as gay with varying degrees of up-frontness); *Toward Intimacy* (in this serial exemplary portrait of four disabled women and their sexuality, the ratio of one to three wasn't bad); and *A Kind of Family* (this straight-authored, warm-hearted portrait of a gay adoptive father, future Winnipeg mayor Glen Murray, is the best of the four in this category, thanks to a central subject who is proud and "matter-of-fact" [which is different from "who happens to be"], and a magnetic portrait of his adopted HIV+, sometime hustler, prodigal son Michael Curtis).

Though the ten films represented a vivid spectrum of regional representation, two huge gaps were immediately apparent. First, French-language films from Quebec and elsewhere were conspicuously absent. And although the French studios lagged behind the English studios in waking up to queer politics, their absence from the package was not because there were no obvious candidates: the two arts biopics *Firewords* and *Les Trois Montréal de Michel Tremblay* (Michel Moreau, 1989), as well as the anomalous and beautiful Sudbury film *Lettre à Tom* (Paul Crépeau, 1987, about gay fatherhood), would have been obvious inclusions. Apparently, several conditions were lacking for a bicultural queer package. Extra investment would have been required for versioning, that is, money where the mouth was—though that does not explain why *Firewords*, whose original version was English, was not included. Were certain films not included because the packagers actually ended up believing their own bowdlerized descriptions for the films and did not realize how flaming many of them actually were? ("Controversial" is, hilariously, the code substitute for the L-word in the NFB catalogue descriptions in both English and French for this forthright, richly coloured tapestry of lesbian culture and writing from a queer-friendly hetero-feminist point of view.) The other condition lacking was simply the vision necessary to look over the high walls between the two distrustful linguistic solitudes that had existed at the board since the implantation of Québécois nationalism there in the 1960s (which was probably an important factor in the anglophone blinkers about *Passiflora* in the first place). The second gap was around gender representation: it's hard to believe that of the ten films, only two pertain to gay men, and one, *Out,* by the only gay male author, examines the only mixed-gender thematic in the whole package. [...] The residue of passive homophobia that tainted the male New Left (the familiar tune of "sexuality is not a class issue") was clearly still at play within the progressive male cadres outside of Studio D at the board, presumably including the branch directors that Macerola had promised would contact me; sexual identity politics had clearly not even entered the radar screen as a political issue on the testosterone side.

Nevertheless, the NFB got away unscathed with their queer collection, and their queer roll continued, churning out two extremely strong films by gay men in 1995 in the Montreal English and French studios respectively (*Anatomy of Desire,* by freelance couple team Jean-François Monette and Peter Boullata-Tyler; and *Quand l'amour est gai,* by NFB veteran Laurent Gagliardi). An eclectic array of other films reflecting the divergent interests of independents in various regions gradually lined up, including everything from a large number of low-cost trigger films about youth, family diversity, and homophobia for use in schools to Wescott's long-awaited *Stolen Moments* (1997). The latter must be the largest-budget lesbian-history film in the world if one calculates the director's full salary over the film's decade-long gestation. Unfortunately, this particular film's commercial record, despite some rave reviews, was embarrassing and must have broken the hearts of the producers, who were hoping for another *Forbidden Love* or *Strangers.* By this time budgetary stress had led to the closing of Studio D in 1996, but the queer productions continued elsewhere within the institution with no sign of abating to this day, reflecting evolving political priorities within both the NFB and the queer cultural environment.

The inevitable transgender film appeared from the Toronto office in 2000, *In the Flesh* (Gordon McLennan), an uneven and erratic serial portrait (two MTF and one FTM), buoyed mostly by the effervescent energy of star Mirha-Soleil Ross. Two later, more promising additions reflected the NFB's "diversity" agenda: both Atif Siddiqi's *Solo* (2003) and Jose Torrealba's *Open Secrets* (2003) were born from the studio's Reel Diversity competitions, whereby winning "visible minority" filmmakers had their proposals produced in-house at the standard budgets (and with the producer-director relationships so entailed), which the erstwhile indie video artists Siddiqi and Torrealba, born in Karachi and Caracas respectively, could never have dreamed of in the real world. That invisible minorities and visible minorities come together in these two films is a sign of the new maturity of the institutional politics. And that Torrealba's project, an archival/interview, historical/topical essay moved beyond the burden of ethno-cultural representation in the narrow sense (his documentary addresses the issues of gay soldiers within the Canadian Forces during World War II, and the entire handful of survivors encountered belong to the then hegemonic white caste) may be a hopeful and healthy sign of the open-endedness of queer problematics and positions *chez* the old uncle during the new decade.

Perhaps an even more hopeful sign was the sudden appearance in 2002 of another "package," the "Celebrating Diversity" collection, six films yoked together retroactively again and intended to "equip you to deal constructively with a broad spectrum of issues in the lives of today's young people." Aside from such euphemistic and bowdlerized copyspeak one more time, the package is a strong assortment of queer perspectives and voices, formats and genres, with a valid focus on youth and educational contexts that makes more sense than the encyclo-pedic "catch-up" compendium invoked the first time around. The new package nevertheless perpetuates some of the same contradictions that were evident a decade earlier: only one male author was squeezed in among the six, and he was David Adkins, whose *Out* was recycled from last time. One "adult" film was also a most welcome addition to the NFB repertory but was not specifically part of the youth/educational focus: Weissman's *Little Sister's vs Big Brother* is an outside production brought within the fold and represents, thirty-three years after Stonewall, the old uncle finally sticking his neck out on a contemporary politico-legal struggle, indicting another finger of the federal hand that feeds it, Customs Canada. As far as "adult" films go, however, another absence is much more striking: the board had mys-teriously withdrawn *Forbidden Love* from circulation, still burningly relevant a decade after its release, without even informing the filmmakers that their labour of love was now itself *really* forbidden. The other four items, all with lesbian creative input, are "trigger" shorts geared specifically for elementary or secondary classroom use (the short, open-ended format is designed to spark discussion), and with their constructive focus on bigotry, bullying, and name-calling, they shift the onus away from earlier identity essentialism that activists and intellectuals were themselves calling increasingly into question: *In Other Words* (Jan Padgett, [2001], a "consciousness-raising" forum about name-calling); *One of Them* (Elise Swerhone, scenario Nancy Trites Botkin, Winnipeg [2000], dramatization of a high school antibigotry initiative that leads to a coming out in an unexpected place); *Apples and Oranges* (Lynne Fernie [2003], a fresh classroom consciousness-raising exercise with younger participants than in the Padgett film, bountifully interpolated with didactic cartoon narratives); and *Sticks and Stones* (Jan Padgett, 2001). The last named, another trigger work for elementary school children, was a matter-of-fact excursion into the fraught territory of lesbian and gay-male parents for its discussion of familial diversity, and it thus unexpectedly became one of the only NFB films to date to have chanced upon in a fleeting way the urgent problematic issue that equally unexpectedly became a political front-burner of the first decade of this century, the queer-family/same-sex-marriage issue.

I make no assumption that my letter had had anything to do with this proliferation of the NFB queer corpus over the last fifteen years as I have described it. Rather, it can be attributed to aspects of the institution's production system and apparatus as they evolved in the new era of tight budgets, low overhead, and proliferating cable outlets and to the increasing importance of TV window financing—in combination with alterations in the Canadian political environ-ment conducive to the emergence of "new ideas" from both personalities entrenched within the institution and the new generation of independents that increasingly found a foothold there.

The new abundance of films must also be connected to the genres that were available to these filmmakers as vessels for the "ideas" that were emerging, the funding opportunities that were on hand, and the audience/market niches that were identified. [...] The corpus is extremely diverse, including many different modes and styles of documentary film production, reflecting different regional and cultural differences and coincidentally incorporating all but the scariest of the topics suggested in my original letter.

GENRES AND GENDERS

What all these modes and styles and topics have in common, however, aside from their NFB logo and their public financing (often "commissioned" by various federal ministries), is of course their pedagogical mandate or their didactic premise, what Bill Nichols might call their "kinship" to the

> nonfictional systems that together make up what we may call the discourses of sobriety. Science, economics, politics, foreign policy, education, religion, welfare—these systems assume they have instrumental power; they can and should alter the world itself, they can effect action and entail consequences. Their discourse has an air of sobriety since it is seldom receptive to "make-believe" characters, events, or entire worlds ... Discourses of sobriety are sobering because they regard their relation to the real as direct, immediate, transparent. Through them power exerts itself. Through them, things are made to happen. They are the vehicles of domination and conscience, power and knowledge, desire and will. (*Representing Reality: Issues and Concepts in Documentary* [Bloomington: Indiana University Press, 1991], 3–4)

Paradoxically, despite this instrumentalist modality and this mandate of sobriety, all these film frames, furthermore, exhibit a general tendency toward narrative, all the while remaining for the most part within the documentary format. They indulge wholeheartedly in the pleasure of the story, rather than being stuck in the expository or analytic structure that one might have expected to prevail after the board's first decades. The narrative thrust is no doubt a populist acknowledgment of the NFB's nonspecialist constituency, the studio's track record of reaching their audience through clarity and directness rather than enigma, ambiguity, and challenge, their potential to win hearts, if not minds, through entertainment and identification (as well as the obsession of certain executive producers, I am told). This narrative thrust is reflected twice in the films' subtitles alone—*Stories of Lesbian and Gay Youth* and *Unashamed Stories of Lesbian Lives*—and is otherwise evoked in the narrative desire solicited by others of the more pulpy titles, from *When Shirley Met Florence* to *Stolen Moments* and *Open Secrets*.

*****

As I write this under the commissionership of Jacques Bensimon, a francophone Moroccan-born Jew, who may be the first in a line of leaders to replace political appointees like Macerola at the helm of Grierson's great creaking ship, attention is being refocused on the board's mandate of instrumentalist sobriety, and social development schemes are being reinvented. [...] Still, history exerts a powerful force even on a studio forever in search of renewing itself. The old patterns of labyrinthine bureaucracy linger, and the two linguistic solitudes seem as entrenched and irrational as ever. [...] I write this at the end of 2003, the year of both the Siddiqi and Torrealba releases, and it seems that the corpus has continued to proliferate in spite of everything, acquiring its own post-affirmation and idiosyncratic queer sensibility, fostered by a combination of the sixty-five-year-old reflex to represent people and places in the here and now, however queer they've turned out to be, the reflex to fall back on familiar genres, narratives, conventions, and modes to move those cassettes and reach those audiences, and the twin parents of arts governmentality and rights governmentality. [...]

NOTES

1 A French pun that combines the word for pope "pape" with the word for faggot "tapette."

2 Cited correspondence and documents related to the *Passiflora* affair are from the author's personal archive.

3 I am obviously borrowing the title of the late Toronto activist and professor Michael Lynch's poetry collection *These Waves of Dying Friends: Poems* (Bowling Green, NY: Contact II Publications, 1989).

4 "Open Letter to Mr. François Macerola," *Cinema Canada* 141 (May 1987): 4. This was the issue that presented on its cover then closeted Patricia Rozema and arch-homophobe Jean-Claude Lauzon gloating over their forthcoming trip to Cannes, with the first lesbian feature *I've Heard the Mermaids Singing,* and the most antigay film yet made, *Un zoo la nuit,* under their arms, respectively.

5 Somerville showed her true colours on sexual-minority politics in the late 1990s, campaigning against adoption and reproduction rights for queer parents and against same-sex marriage. See her *The Ethical Canary: Science, Society and the Human Spirit* (Toronto: Viking, 2000).

6 John Greyson, "Flaunting It!" unpublished documentary film proposal, 10 August 1987.

7 Untitled document for "investigate" re "Flaunting It," (September 1987). The anonymous consultant is referring to Gerald Hannon's notorious article about men-boy relations (1977–78), which had sparked *The Body Politic*'s three-year ordeal in criminal court in the late 1970s.

CHAPTER 36

The Noble Savage Was a Drag Queen: Hybridity and Transformation in Kent Monkman's Performance and Visual Art Interventions

Kerry Swanson

The idea of the North American Indian man—stoic, primitive, dark, Other—can be largely credited to the epic paintings of celebrated 19th-century white European-American artists whose work remains housed in the national institutions and galleries of Europe, America, and Canada. In their romanticized landscapes of the New World, colonial artists such as George Catlin, Albert Bierdstadt, and the Hudson River school of painters mythologized the "dying" race of Red Men while propagating their own personas as heroic adventurers in a wild, undiscovered land. The iconography created in these works and those that followed, which depicted the Indian man as the doomed noble savage, are among what the late Native theorist Louis Owens called the "hyperreal."[1] These paintings gave birth to an imaginary Indian—the highly masculinized noble savage—that became the popular model for authenticity, challenging the identities of all those who did not fit into this limiting construct. They created a mythology that cast the Native people of the period, and therefore those who followed, as either brutal animalistic warriors, or sad victims of Darwinian destiny. In a current body of work that is gaining attention both in Canada and internationally, Canadian Cree visual and performance artist Kent Monkman challenges this imagery, and the mainstream Christian version of history perpetuated by 19th-century colonial artists, by appropriating their landscapes, language, and propaganda to create a space for himself, and queer identity, in the story of the early Wild West. In Monkman's version of history, his half-breed drag-queen alter-ego, Miss Chief Share Eagle Testickle, runs riot on the unspoilt vistas of the 19th century, affirming her existence and (re)negotiating her queer sexual power. Prior to colonization, queer identity (known in Native communities as Two-Spirit in honour of the existence of both the male and female spirit in one body) was widely accepted among many different North American tribes,[2] although this fact has been virtually eliminated from historical renderings of the period. Through his humorous and provoking interventions, Monkman reclaims that history and, using Foucault's concept of sexuality as a site of cultural power, insists on the existence and continued survival of queer Native identities.

In the performance art piece *Traveling Gallery and European Male Emporium,* which emerged from the series of paintings entitled *Eros and Empire,* Monkman celebrates and utilizes the concept of hybridity to offer an alternative mythology that transforms the prevailing fixed and static notions of Native sexuality, identity, and history. José Muñoz writes: "*Hybrid* catches the fragmentary subject formation of people whose identities traverse different race, sexuality, and gender identifications."[3] Identifying as mixed-race/mixed-gender in his work, Monkman effectively embodies and applies the concept of hybridity as a method for cultural navigation, demonstrating its transformative power in creating new identities and historical perspectives. Homi Bhabha argues that by occupying a hybrid space, the colonized can renegotiate the terms of colonization, effectively moving beyond the identity constructs that have been created around him/her.[4] Through his alter-ego Share, the ultimate hybrid who incorporates past and present, male and female, Native and white, Monkman renegotiates the terms of power in Western society and seizes the most powerful and transformative role available: the role of storyteller.

INTRODUCING *MISS CHIEF SHARE EAGLE TESTICKLE'S EUROPEAN MALE EMPORIUM*

Share Eagle Testickle is a glamorous character who flounces around the 19th-century past/present in an ankle-length feather headdress, Louis Vuitton quiver, and spiked heels. Partly spoofing gay pop icon Cher, particularly during the period of her 1970s hit song "Half-Breed," Monkman's persona plays with Native stereotypes, pop culture, and queer culture. Appearing first in Monkman's 2004 landscape paintings, a nondescript early incarnation of a prototype Share morphs into the artist himself as the series progresses. As Share's persona becomes more undeniably linked to that of the artist himself, Monkman gives his alter-ego a physical incarnation in his first "colonial art space intervention," *Miss Chief Share Eagle Testickle's Traveling Gallery and European Male Emporium.* Staged in August 2004 at the McMichael Canadian Art Collection, famous for housing many of the works of Canada's Group of Seven painters, Share's *tableau vivant* focused on the Group of Seven landscape paintings and the Edward Curtis film, *In the Land of the Headhunters.* The Group of Seven refers to Canada's renowned white landscape painters of the early- to mid-20th century, whose paintings mythologized the Canadian landscape as wild and untouched by human contact. The Group of Seven are part of the Canadian colonial establishment, and their work is considered to mark the beginning of "Canadian art," thus obliterating the importance and existence of Native Canadian artists and their preceding work. In his challenge on Canada's institutional "untouchable" artists, Monkman announces his subversive agenda. He challenges not only the white artists who claimed Canada's landscapes as their own private discoveries, but also the institutions that have, until very recently, chosen to exclude Native perspectives in their galleries. In a recent article profiling Monkman in *Canadian Art Magazine,* David Liss explains the significance of choosing the McMichael Gallery and the Group of Seven as the site of intervention for Share's debut performance:

> As the premier home of the art of the Group of Seven, the McMichael is significant in the accepted canon of what constitutes Canadian identity, or at least one version that is readily identifiable. As an institutional gatekeeper, the McMichael exercises a certain power over what is included and what is not. The Group's romanticized depiction of Canadian landscape as an unpopulated, undiscovered wilderness is not lost on Monkman, who regards history as a mythology forged from relationships of power and subjugation.[5]

In this performance, Share arrives on the back of a white horse, resplendent in elaborate headdress, Louis Vuitton and Hudson Bay Company accessories, and cartoonish drag-queen heels. On her way into the gallery space, she entices two young white men dressed in loincloths, who become the subjects of her "taxonomy of the European male." Bringing to mind the work of Mexican *mestizo* performance artist Guillermo Gomez-Peña, whose work is heavily infused with humour and a taste for the ironic, Monkman's Share is performed with a wink and a nudge, allowing mainstream audiences access to the larger theme of cultural subjectivity and bias, while leaving those without specific historical and cultural knowledge on the outside of some of the subtler messages and references. Just as Gomez-Peña's romantic Mexican stereotype "El Mariachi Liberace" creates an exaggerated caricature as a method of subverting mainstream stereotypes,[6] Monkman's Share reveals the ridiculousness and subjectivity of colonial artists who created mainstream Native mythologies through their work. Like Gomez-Peña, Monkman uses his hybrid, mixed-race identity to his advantage, demonstrating his authority and power as cross-cultural navigator. Lisa Wolford writes that Gomez-Peña's work is characterized by a type of artistic and political strategy that he describes as "reverse anthropology,"[7] which Monkman also effectively employs. By virtually travelling back in time in order to occupy the romantic landscapes and scenes that became the source of manly noble Native stereotypes, Monkman claims them as his own territory—a territory free of the borders of time and space, where he is the master of his own history, sexuality, and identity. Muñoz writes that masculinity is "a cultural imperative to enact a mode of power that labours to invalidate, exclude, and extinguish faggots, effeminacy, and queerly coated butchness."[8] In the creation and performance of Share, Monkman refutes the static and masculinized imagery of the Indian; his location in the present/past allows him to speak from within but beyond the boundaries and confines that have kept this image in the fixed past for over a century.

REVERSING THE COLONIAL GAZE

Share's taxonomy reverses the gaze of white colonizer and Native subject, using text taken directly from the letters and notes of famous colonial artists George Catlin and Paul Kane, who were two of the most prolific artists in documenting Native peoples and lives during the 19th century. Both have been highly celebrated in their respective countries, the United States and

Canada, for over a century. In a typical quote from one of his letters, George Catlin writes: "I find that the principal cause why we underrate and despise the savage, is generally because we do not understand him; and the reason why we are ignorant of him and his modes, is that we do not stoop to investigate."[9] In Monkman's performance, it is Share who plays the role of Catlin and his contemporaries, investigating the savage and primitive white man, in an earnest attempt to understand their strange habits, dress, and physical make-up before they become extinct. The performance immediately highlights how strange and uncivilized the white man is in comparison to the glamorous, immaculately dressed Share. Share takes her complicit models to her studio (the gallery), where she plies them with whiskey, forces them into more European-style clothes, and ultimately exploits her position of power and authority over them by making them pose for her. In the final act, Monkman's original landscape paintings become a part of the performance, when Share reveals them as the final product of her efforts at the easel. In this final scene, Share highlights the commodification of the Native that has been generated through image production and consumption. In turning the tables and becoming the creator of the image, as opposed to the subject, Share further confirms her position of power. While Share is still subjected to the gaze of her audience, it is now Monkman, the Native and artist, who controls the image. In this instance, and in other live performances I have seen by Monkman, Share is the ultimate embodiment of Guy Debord's concept of the spectacle. Debord writes that "[t]he world at once present and absent that the spectacle *holds up to view* is the world of the commodity dominating all living experience."[10] By becoming a commodity producer, Share transforms the role of Native as victim of commodification without denying her past. The Louis Vuitton and Hudson Bay accessories indicate that she has moved beyond her commodification but maintains her past knowledge of this legacy, again demonstrating the transformative power of her hybridity as a tool for agency, affirmation, and power.

Renowned Native American performance artist James Luna has said that performance art and installation offer an opportunity like never before for Native artists to express themselves without compromise.[11] Part of the freedom that is available to Native artists through perform- ance is access to a continuation of oral storytelling traditions in a modern context. Performance art as a language and a discipline allows Native artists to speak in a language that is not the colonizer's, and is closer to traditional Indigenous perspectives and worldviews as opposed to European. Performance, in Monkman's work, allows him to move beyond the colonial language of landscape painting, which he mimics. As Homi Bhabha argues, mimicry can be a dangerous form of agency that maintains the colonial power structure.[12] In occupying the performance art space, Monkman demonstrates that he is aware of the limitations of speaking solely through the language of colonialism. Through performance, Monkman is able not only to reimagine, but to *relive* colonization with the roles of colonized and colonizer reversed. He is able to utilize the physical, namely his skin colour, voice, mannerisms and physique, to corporeally demon- strate his occupation of the hybrid and his use of this fragmented identity as a site of cultural power. Muñoz writes that "identity practices such as queerness and hybridity are not a priori sites of contestation but, instead, spaces of productivity where identity's fragmentary nature is accepted."[13] Monkman not only embraces hybridity, he effectively demonstrates its many uses for renegotiating colonial power structures in the here and now. His performance shows that there is a space where time, space, gender, and race can be embodied as a whole. Here, he is free to adapt the storytelling and myth-making traditions of both European and Native cultures to create a space for himself, and Native gay and transgendered sexuality, in both the historical past and present.

HUMOUR, IRONY, AND THE TRICKSTER CHARACTER

Humour and irony are used heavily to bring audiences into the ruse of Share's performance and to challenge the mock-innocence of the original diarists and painters who expressed pity and childlike fascination for the Indigenous people with one hand, while exploiting them with the other. The hegemonic power relationship that exists in any colonial relationship is acknowledged through the complicity of the white models; like well-behaved children they dress up for Share, play the piano, and dance. As in the paintings, in the performance Share is a sexually charged entity, displaying the hyperfemininity of the drag queen with an authority that is distinctly masculine. Foucault writes that sexuality is "endowed with the greatest instrumentality: useful for the greatest number of manoeuvres and capable of serving as a point of support, as a linchpin, for the most varied strategies."[14] In bringing Share to life, Monkman uses his own sexuality as an instrument of power to support his goal of deconstructing imperial historical constructs. This is a highly effective strategy that allows him to physically reclaim and affirm the lost history, sexuality, and social status of the Two-Spirited person.

An androgynous character capable of shape-shifting and time travel, Share's role as a trickster is fundamental to her character. As trickster, her identity is firmly rooted in both past and present, comprising part of her hybrid identity. A central figure in Native storytelling, the trickster is a mischievous rebel, a jester who consistently challenges authority and is unbound by the rules of time. Owens writes, "appropriation, inversion, and abrogation of authority are always trickster's strategies."[15] In traditional trickster fashion, Share disarms her audiences with humour while mocking and dismantling their assumptions, in this case regarding the history of Native sexuality and its history. By mimicking a colonial structure in the guise of trickster, Share is making it very clear that she is undertaking a process of dismantling, of (re)telling the false stories we have been told and (re)imagining our version of the world. Thomas King, one of Canada's master trickster storytellers, writes, "[t]he truth about stories is that that's all we are."[16] While we cannot change history, we can change, subvert, and dismantle the stories we tell ourselves, and the stories that are told about us. By affirming the Two-Spirit identity in a historical context, Monkman's performances retell the story of colonization and create a worldview that pays homage—albeit cheekily—to the traditional values of accepting and honouring sexual diversity, which will be discussed in greater detail further in this chapter.

(RE)CONSTRUCTING SEXUALITY AND CULTURE

Foucault argues that sexuality is a not a "natural given," but rather a historical construct in which physical stimulation and pleasure are controlled and manipulated according to the dominant power structures and ideologies.[17] In the tradition of Foucault, Monkman approaches his examination of Native sexuality by examining the existing power relations of colonial North America. Native North Americans are still living in a colonial world in which their traditional lands, cultures, and identities remain colonized; therefore, Monkman makes no clear differentiation between past and present, as Native lives and identities continue to be shaped by the colonial power structure as it existed in the 19th century. Monkman's work addresses and bridges the ongoing relationship between the colonial past and the colonial present, and also confronts the significant lack of discourse and knowledge regarding the history of Two-Spirited people and their suppression through Christian indoctrination. Prior to colonization, many of the North American tribes, including the Cree, Ojibwe, Mohave, Navajo, Lakota, and Winnebago, honoured Two-Spirited people as accepted and even sacred members of tribal society.[18] Monkman's work returns to the source of the original propaganda that culminated in modern stereotypes about Native peoples, thereby revealing and challenging the subjectivity of the artists and their self-serving mythologizing. By returning to the site of colonization, Monkman works to decolonize Native sexuality by offering up an alternative to the accepted version of history, an alternative that also happens to be closer to the realities of the period.

Often tied to the creation stories of the tribe, the concept of Two-Spiritedness is not centred on the physical act of sex; it is the European worldview which essentializes sexuality in physiological terms. Historically, many tribes gave credence to the existence of what ethnographer Sue-Ellen Jacobs calls "the third gender," which is as much a spiritual as it is a physical state of being. The Cree word *ayekkwew,* for example, means "neither man nor woman" or "man and woman."[19] This is a fitting example for a study of Monkman, who embodies both gender and racial hybridity as a fundamental aspect to his identity and work. Monkman refers to these traditions, and his alter-ego is likewise androgynous, resisting black or white identity markers with her medium-toned skin and careful balance of male and female. As mentioned in the introduction to this chapter, the modern term, Two-Spirit, reflects the concept that a person can house both the male and female spirit in one body, that not every individual can be categorized in a heterosexual way. The term "Two-Spirit" has gained popularity within the Native gay community because it reflects an Indigenous worldview and rejects the previous white/colonial term of "berdache," which was used to describe traditional Native Two-Spirited individuals, and the Arabic roots of which imply the meaning of male sodomized slave.[20] As mentioned, Monkman's use of performance is particularly suitable to relaying the Two-Spirit concept of "undefinability," as the artist is able to utilize the masculine elements of his physique, voice, and mannerisms, along with the hyper-feminine *modus operandi* of the drag queen, in a physical incarnation not possible on canvas. Bhabha writes that freedom exists in a decolonization of the imagined spaces created by colonizers and imperialists and that those who are marginalized must create a "third space."[21] Like the third gender, the third space is a free zone that exists somewhere beyond the margins of definable cultures or identities and their inherent limitations. This is the space occupied by the hybrid Share, who, as trickster, cannot be defined or bound by time, sex, or geography.

THE SUPPRESSION OF NATIVE SEXUALITY IN HEGEMONIC NORTH AMERICA

The diversity of Native sexuality in pre-colonized North America is seldom mentioned or illustrated in mainstream art and media, although we know that it existed. In her groundbreaking anthropological work, Jacobs researched centuries of written documents for references to the third gender or Two-Spirited people in Native North American tribes. Out of 99 tribes, 88 referred to Two-Spirited culture, including both male and female homosexuality or transgender.[22] In 19th-century Europe, however, views towards non-heterosexual practices were extremely different. Foucault writes that by this time

> [n]othing that was not ordered in terms of generation or transfigured by it could expect sanction or protection. Nor did it merit a hearing. It would be driven out, denied, and reduced to silence. Not only did it not exist, it had no right to exist and would be made to disappear upon its least manifestation—whether in acts or in words.[23]

The diverse sexual practices of Native people were quickly suppressed by Christian European colonizers—with remaining repercussions. In Jacobs's research on modern tribes, "eleven tribes denied any homosexuality to the anthropologists and other writers."[24] The denials came from tribes with the longest history of contact with white Christian cultures that severely punished homosexuality.[25]

Foucault defines power as a relationship forged through a series of tactics, in which both the subject and object are complicit.[26] At a time when the Indigenous populations of the Americas were being swiftly killed off, both through war and disease, the denial of beliefs that made them further vulnerable to persecution was a tactic of survival. Under the heavy influence and rhetoric of Christianity, many tribes had also "become ashamed of the [Two-Spirit] custom because the white people thought it was amusing or evil."[27] As a result, many individual tribes suppressed their long-held beliefs and denied the expression of sexual diversity, taking on the Christian worldview that held any sexual practices other than heterosexuality as deviant. Just as shamanism became taboo, so too did homosexuality. What was once deemed sacred and spiritual became something to hide and be ashamed of. As a mode of self-protection and self-preservation, a hegemonic power relationship was forged between the Native population and the white rulers. Trinh T. Minh-ha writes that "[h]egemony is most difficult to deal with because it does not really spare any of us. Hegemony is established to the extent that the worldview of the rulers is also the worldview of the ruled."[28] This is the challenge faced by Monkman, who through his work attempts to reclaim a worldview that has been suppressed, from both sides, by centuries of colonial rule. By incorporating elements of Native, European, colonial, and modern cultures and traditions, the artist references the complexities of the present hegemonic colonial landscape, where the boundaries between "us" and "them," "then" and "now," are blurred.

SEXUALITY AS "DIVINE" INTERVENTION

In the meticulously rendered landscape paintings that preceded his performance art debut and gave birth to Share, Monkman steps back to the very point in time when colonial mythmaking and sexual suppression is beginning to take shape. Share debuts, literally with a bang, in the 2001 painting *Heaven and Earth,* in which she sodomizes a muscular frontiersman under a halo of celestial light that announces the mythological proportions of the event. Monkman aligns the mythologizing of the American frontier with the epic mythology of ancient Rome and Greece.[29] The light signifies the arrival of a new dawn, in which Native peoples reclaim their sexual identities and their authority over their own history. It also alludes to a literal coming-out, both from the shadows of historical marginality and from the shadows of Monkman's past work, which depicted ambiguous homoerotic characters barely discernible under heavy Cree text. In *Heaven and Earth*, Share is distinctly masculine; her femininity and persona as the artist's alter-ego emerge as the series progresses. It is through the act of performing sexuality that Share comes into her own existence and that the artist recognizes himself in her. The series also begins with more ambiguities than Share's gender; this first scene could be interpreted as an act of rape or as a complicit act. This is an interesting point, given Foucault's notion of complicity as being a necessary component of power. Share is using her sexuality as a site of power, and stamping her authority on land, culture, and history; yet there is the suggestion that perhaps her partner is ready. Performance plays heavily in the painting, as sex is performed as a function of transformation; Share's act insists on the existence of queer Native identity on the colonial landscape.

RE-MYTHOLOGIZING THE WEST

Monkman continues to create new myths in the subsequent paintings in the series. In *The Trilogy of St. Thomas,* a tragic love story unfolds between Miss Chief Share Eagle Testickle and her Orangeman lover, the young Thomas Scott. The trilogy uses the standard tragic love affair format to draw parallels to the complex relationship between Native peoples and their colonizers. The first painting in the trilogy, *The Impending Storm*, references Albert Bierstadt and Thomas Cole, the highly religious Hudson River School painter, using the storm as an allegory for the "end of innocence" and "impending doom of civilization" that are about to encroach on Native life.[30] Next, *The Fourth of March* references the execution of Thomas Scott by Louis Riel, a historical event that had a significant political impact on what was to come for the Cree people of Manitoba, Monkman's ancestors.

In this series, Monkman inserts himself in the role of Share, a decision that will later allow him to give life to his alter-ego off-canvas. Monkman writes that by inserting himself in the series, he "relate[s] the importance of this historical event to [his] own identity as a Native person."[31] In his decision to create Share in his own image, the artist blatantly references his own sexuality as a site of power. Share and her overt sexuality are always the focus of each work, with a blunt refusal to play second fiddle or to be upstaged by even her own lover's death. Minh-ha writes that "the return to a denied heritage allows one to start again with different re-departures, different pauses, different arrivals."[32] By making himself the subject of his intervention on 19th-century colonial art, Monkman is effectively creating a place for himself, a place that previously did not exist, in the history books. Putting himself in his works also serves the purpose of overtly mocking "the self-aggrandisement of the original artists like George Catlin, who would occasionally place themselves in their work."[33] The "Eagle Testickle" in our hero/ine's name is also a play on the egotism of the 19th-century artists who saw fit to create the mythologized Native image for world consumption. Monkman's challenge to the subjectivity of ego-driven colonial artists is most obvious in an earlier painting, *Artist and Model*. In this piece, Share paints a petroglyph-style image of her handsome white hostage, whom she has tied to a tree. Share's image looks nothing like her subject, yet she appears swooning, her back arched with pride over her work. Below her easel is a Louis Vuitton quiver or paint brush holder, a symbol of the commodification of both the original paintings and their Native subjects. In claiming a modern symbol of wealth, status, and luxury, Share reaffirms her power and further identifies herself with both the present and the past. She negates the hierarchy of class, power, and wealth that has left many Native people living as impoverished citizens in their own land. In the final painting in the trilogy, *Not the End of the Trail,* Share buries her lover, but hope springs up in the lingering gaze of the white priest presiding over the funeral. Again, Monkman denies the sacredness of Christianity while alluding to a new chapter for Two-Spirited people.

PERFORMANCE AS ORAL TRADITION, SPECTACLE, AND AUTHORITY

In the conscious decision to take his paintings to the forum of performance, Monkman gives a traditional voice to the story he is retelling, employing the oral tradition as opposed to the landscape art introduced to the continent through colonization. Minh-ha writes, "[s]/he who speaks, speaks to the tale as s/he begins telling and retelling it. S/he does not speak about it. For, without a certain work of displacement, 'speaking about' only partakes in the conservation of systems of binary opposition."[34] Share is the s/he who, rather than condemning the actions of her predecessors through didactic lectures or tales, retells the tale in a way that speaks directly to Two-Spirit identities, in a way that encompasses both their past and present, and dismantles the authority of the colonial patriarchal ideology. Monkman effectively re-imagines a new space where what Homi Bhabha calls "hybridity," the culture between cultures, can exist.[35] Catlin wrote that his work "will doubtless be interesting to future ages; who will have little else left from which to judge of the original inhabitants of this simple race of beings, who require but a few years more of the march of civilization and death, to deprive them of all their native customs and character."[36] Catlin and his colleagues were convinced that they were recording the last gasping breaths of a soon-to-be-extinct race. In the McMichael performance, Share takes on the role of Catlin/colonizer, occupying the position of authority as a means of discrediting it. As the artist in the piece, it is she who is singularly responsible for creating the stories and images that will reinforce the power relationship between herself and her subjects. Monkman's simple use of role reversal, emphasized by switching references to white man and red man, savage and civilized, is a humourous way of highlighting the arbitrary nature of racist classification. In giving his community audiences a new history that is in opposition to the accepted version that denigrates Native people and their customs and excludes Two-Spirited people, Monkman, like Catlin, offers a perspective that can be used as insight for future ages, as perhaps the era of white male supremacy nears its end. The "traveling gallery" is a reference to Catlin's traveling gallery, where his images reached mass audiences for the time. The traveling gallery served as one of the key methods by which Catlin's mythology of the Native people and tribes with which he came into contact was consumed. The Native person thus became a spectacle, an object of fascination, and an "other" offered up for public consumption. Share, similarly, will travel colonial galleries as a method of intervention on the spaces that continue to give ownership and authority of history to the colonial worldview. Share uses the concept of spectacle to her advantage; she embraces the idea of herself as "other," as a positive dichotomy to the oppressive identity constructs of hetero-Christianity.

CONCLUSION

As Homi Bhabha writes, freedom for those marginalized by colonization exists through the creation of new hybrid spaces beyond the confines, constructs, and definitions created by the colonizers. Freedom is the act of creating and existing in a place beyond definitions, beyond black and white, somewhere in the blurry space beyond the culturally safe margins of identity. Sexuality and its many taboos are nothing more than imaginary constructs that are given codes and rules as a method to enforce power. Names, rules, and acceptance levels change according to the dominant ideology of a specific time and place. In this way, something that was once a source of pride can easily become a site of shame, as in the case of non-heterosexuality under Christianity. Monkman refuses to accept the Christian constructs that were established and reinforced by colonial rule, and continue to deny and suppress the once-celebrated sexual diversity within Native tribes. Through his visual and performance art, Monkman successfully creates a third space, where a time-traveling half-breed drag queen can take ownership over her history and sexual identity. From this position, the margins are the centre, and the power of definition belongs to the once-marginalized. In creating this space, Monkman acknowledges the rightful place of the Two-Spirited person in traditional history, and encourages discourse that reflects on and amends the loss of Native sexuality through Christian imperialism.

NOTES

1 Owens, Louis. *Mixed Blood Messages: Literature, Film, Family, Place.* Norman: University of Oklahoma Press, 1998, p. 13. Of mixed Cherokee, Choctaw, and Irish heritage, Owens focuses on the theme of mixed blood identity in much of his writing, in which he disputes the notion of the "real Indian" and the imagery proliferated by this limited social construct. Owen's own life, cut short by suicide in 2002, was deeply affected by his inability to prove his Native ancestry, thereby branding him a non-Indian in the eyes of the American government.

2 Deschamps, Gilbert. *We Are Part of a Tradition: A Guide on Two-Spirited People for First Nations Communities.* Mino-B'maadiziwin Project: www.2spirits.com. Toronto: 2-Spirited People of the First Nations, 1998. This short guide offers the history of the Two-Spirit in a modern context, explaining some of the basic philosophical approaches and the current issues that continue to affect Two-Spirited people.

3 Muñoz, José Esteban. *Disidentifications: Queers of Color and the Performance of Politics.* Minneapolis: University of Minnesota Press, 1999, p. 31. Muñoz looks at queer theatre as a process or outcome of what he terms *disidentifcation.* He describes this as a point of departure, of building, where queer artists build identities and politics in the present and in the future, a concept that fittingly describes Monkman's work.

4 Bhabha, Homi. *The Location of Culture.* London and New York: Routledge: 1994, p. 7. Although I have argued that, for Indigenous people, we are not living in a postcolonial world, Bhabha's theory of postcolonialism is effective for an analysis of the methods of utilizing the concept of hybridity as a source of agency. Bhabha theorizes that agency exists in the moment of enunciation, in the spaces between language, which I would argue is the space in which Monkman's performance, which creates a new language, exists.

5 Liss, David. "Miss Chief's Return." *Canadian Art Magazine.* Volume 22, Number 3, Fall 2005, p. 82. This is one of the first major pieces written about Monkman's current work, which is quickly gaining

popularity in the Toronto and international art scene.

6 Wolford, Lisa. "Guillermo Gomez-Peña: An Introduction." *Theatre Topics.* Volume 9, Number I, March 1999, pp. 89–91. A further comparative examination of the Gomez-Peña and Monkman's work is an area of future research interest for me.

7 Ibid.

8 Muñoz, 1999: 58.

9 Catlin, George. *Letters and Notes on the Manners, Customs, and Conditions of North American Indians: Written During Eight Years' Travel (1832–1839) Amongst the Wildest Tribes of Indians in North America.* London: D. Bogue, 1844, p. 102. The most striking things I found in reading Catlin's letters were how earnestly he believed he was doing the right and just thing, and the important role he felt he played in recording what appeared to be a dying race. While he claimed to like the "red man" and considered him to be human, his letters reflect a tone of colonial and patronizing racial superiority.

10 Debord, Guy. The Society of the Spectacle. Bureau of Public Secrets website: http://www.bopsecrets. org/SI/debord/. October, 2005. Monkman's performance as spectacle could provide the basis for another paper, but I thought it was worth addressing briefly in the context of this paper.

11 Luna, James. "Allow Me to Introduce Myself." *Canadian Theatre Review.* Issue 68, Fall 1991.

12 Bhabha, 1994. Muñoz also discusses Bhabha's concept of mimicry as a complex, "double articulation," disavowing as it affirms the dominant power structure (1999: 78).

13 Muñoz, 1999: 79. Muñoz affirms my contention of hybridity as a site of power for cross-cultural/cross-gender identity politics.

14 Foucault, Michel. *The History of Sexuality, Volume One: The Will to Knowledge.* London: Routledge, 1990, p. 103.

15 Owens, 1998: 26.

16 King, Thomas. *The Truth About Stories: A Native Narrative.* Toronto: House of Anansi, 2004, p. 1. King, also of mixed heritage, is one of Canada's foremost Native authors, writing trickster narratives and texts asserting the importance of storytelling and the need to revisit history from the perspective of Native worldviews.

17 Foucault, 1990: 106.

18 Williams, Walter. *The Spirit and The Flesh: Sexual Diversity in American Indian Culture.* Boston: Beacon Press, 1986. Although Williams employs the "berdache" terminology, he offers a thorough history of Two-Spirit life and identity pre-colonialism, affirming its existence and positive status while highlighting the difficulties of researching a topic that has been so deeply shut down through systematic colonial oppression.

19 Ibid., p. 82.

20 Deschamps, 1998.

21 Bhabha, 1994: 8.

22 Jacobs, Sue-Ellen. *Two-Spirit People: Native American Gender Identity, Sexuality, and Spirituality.* University of Illinois Press, 1997.

23 Foucault, 1990.

24 Jacobs, 1997.

25 Deschamps, 1998.

26 Foucault, 1990: 95.

27 Williams 1986: 187.

28 Minh-ha, Trinh T. *When the Moon Waxes Red: Representation, Gender and Cultural Politics.* London and New York: Routledge, 1991, p. 145. Monkman is careful to acknowledge the hegemonic colonial relationship that has oppressed Native sexuality. His work speaks to both Native and non-Native audiences.

29 Monkman, Kent. Artist notes, *The Trilogy of St. Thomas,* 2004.

30 Ibid.

31 Ibid.

32 Minh-ha, 1991: 14.

33 Monkman, *Trilogy of St. Thomas:* 2004.

34 Minh-ha, 1991: 12.

35 Bhabha, 1994.

36 Catlin, 1884: 16.

ABOUT THE AUTHORS

Barry Adam is Professor of Sociology at the University of Windsor and Senior Scientist and Director of Prevention Research at the Ontario HIV Treatment Network. He is the author of *The Rise of a Gay and Lesbian Movement* (1987, 1995) and *The Survival of Domination* (1978) and co-author of *The Global Emergence of Gay and Lesbian Politics* (1999) and *Experiencing HIV* (1996).

Deborah Brock is an Associate Professor in the Department of Sociology at York University. She is the author of *Making Work, Making Trouble: The Social Regulation of Sexual Labour* (2009) and the editor of *Making Normal: Social Regulation in Canada* (2003). Most recently, she is co-author of *Power and Everyday Practices* (2011).

Chris Bruckert is an Associate Professor in the Department of Criminology at the University of Ottawa. She is the author of *Taking it Off, Putting it On: Women in the Strip Trade* (2002) and co-editor of *Stigma Revisited: Negotiations, Resistance and the Implications of the Mark* (2012, forthcoming) and *Mais oui c'est un travail!, Penser le travail du sexe au-delà de la victimization* (2010).

Martin Cannon is Assistant Professor of Sociology and Equity Studies at the Ontario Institute for Studies in Education at the University of Toronto. He is co-editor of *Racism, Colonialism, and Indigeneity in Canada: A Reader* (2011). His book *Undoing Citizenship Injustice: Indigenous Peoples, Racialized Violence, and the Law in Canada* is forthcoming.

Sheila Cavanagh is Associate Professor of Sociology and the Coordinator of the Sexuality Studies Program at York University. She is the author of *Queering Bathrooms: Gender, Sexuality, and the Hygienic Imagination* (2010) and *Sexing the Teacher: School Sex Scandals and Queer Pedagogies* (2007).

Elise Chenier is Associate Professor of History and the Director of the Archives of Lesbian Oral Testimony at Simon Fraser University. She is the author of *Strangers in Our Midst: Sexual Deviancy in Postwar Ontario* (2008).

Brenda Cossman is Professor of Law and Director of the Mark S. Bonham Centre for Sexual Diversity Studies at the University of Toronto. She is the author of *Sexual Citizens: The Legal and Cultural Regulation of Sex and Belonging* (2007) and *Censorship and the Arts in Canada: Law,*

Controversy, Debate, Facts (1995). She is co-author of *Secularism's Last Sigh?: The Hindu Right and the (Mis)rule of Law* (1999); *Bad Attitude/s on Trial: Pornography, Feminism and the Butler Decision* (1997); and *Subversive Sites: Feminist Engagement with Law in India* (1996). She is also co-editor of *Privatization, Law and the Challenge of Feminism* (2002).

Karen Dubinsky is a Professor in the departments of Global Development Studies and History at Queen's University. She is the author of *Babies Without Borders: Adoption and Migration Across the Americas* (2010); *The Second Greatest Disappointment: Honeymooning and Tourism at Niagara Falls* (1999); and *Improper Advances: Rape and Heterosexual Conflict in Ontario, 1880–1929* (1993). She is co-editor of *New World Coming: The Sixties and the Shaping of Global Consciousness* (2009).

Karen Duder is an independent researcher, editor, and writer. As Cameron Duder, he is the author of *Awfully Devoted Women: Lesbian Lives in Canada, 1900–65* (2010) and *The Ashburn Clinic: The Place and the People* (2007).

Jonathan Eaton is a Senior Policy Advisor at the Ontario Ministry of Labour and is affiliated to the Yeates School of Graduate Studies at Ryerson University. His publications include "Transitions at Work: Industrial Relations Responses to the Emerging Rights of Transgender Workers" (2004).

Rachel Epstein is the Coordinator of the LGBTQ Parenting Connection at the Sherbourne Health Centre in Toronto. She is the editor of *Who's Your Daddy?: And Other Writings on Queer Parenting* (2009).

Margot Francis is Associate Professor of Sociology and Women's Studies at Brock University. She is the author of *Creative Subversions: Whiteness, Indigeneity, and the National Imaginary* (2011).

Richard Fung is Associate Professor of Integrated Media at OCAD University. His work as a video artist, writer, and filmmaker is the subject of the anthology *Like Mangos in July: The Work of Richard Fung* (2002), and he is co-author of *13: Conversations on Art and Cultural Race Politics* (2002). His articles on sexuality, race, film, and video have been included in many anthologies.

Andil Gosine is an Associate Professor in the Department of Sociology at York University. He is the author of the forthcoming *Queers in Development*.

Gerald Hunt is a Professor in the Department of Human Resources Management at Ryerson University. He is the editor of *Laboring for Rights: Unions and Sexual Diversity Across Nations* (1999) and, with David Rayside, co-editor of *Equity, Diversity, and Canadian Labour* (2007) and the forthcoming *Equalizing Labour: Union Response to Diversity in Canada*.

Samantha King is an Associate Professor in the School of Kinesiology and Health Studies and Department of Gender Studies at Queen's University. She is the author of *Pink Ribbons, Inc.: Breast Cancer and the Politics of Philanthropy* (2006).

Gary Kinsman is Professor of Sociology at Laurentian University. He is the author of *The Regulation of Desire: Homo and Hetero Sexualities* (1996). He is co-author of *The Canadian War on Queers: National Security as Sexual Regulation* (2010) and co-editor of *Whose National Security? Canadian State Surveillance and the Creation of Enemies* (2000).

Kiss & Tell Collective. This Vancouver-based performance and art collective collaborated on two books, *Her Tongue on My Theory: Images, Essays and Fantasies* (1994) and *Drawing the Line: Lesbian Sexual Politics on the Wall* (1991). The Collective was composed of three artist activists, Susan Stewart, Persimmon Blackbridge, and Lizard Jones.

Sarah Lamble is Lecturer in the School of Law at Birkbeck, University of London. Her published papers include "Liabilities of Queer Anti-Racist Critique" (2011) and "Retelling Racialized Violence, Remaking White Innocence: The Politics of Interlocking Oppressions in Transgender Day of Remembrance" (2008).

Steven Maynard is an Adjunct Lecturer in the Department of History at Queen's University. He is currently completing two projects: *Infamous Men: Perversion and Policing in Toronto, 1880–1940* and *Sodom North: Explorations in Lesbian/Gay History in Canada*.

Tim McCaskell is a writer, educator, and activist. He is the author of *Race to Equity: Disrupting Educational Inequality* (2005) and is a founding member of AIDS Action Now!

Viviane Namaste is Associate Professor and Concordia University Research Chair in HIV/AIDS and Sexual Health at the Simone de Beauvoir Institute at Concordia University. She is the author of *C'était du spectacle!: L'histoire des artistes transsexuelles à Montréal, 1955–1985* (2005); *Sex Change, Social Change: Reflections on Identity, Institutions, and Imperialism* (2005); and *Invisible Lives: The Erasure of Transsexual and Transgendered People* (2000).

Charmaine Nelson is Associate Professor of Art History at McGill University. She is the author of *Representing the Black Female Subject in Western Art* (2010) and *The Color of Stone: Sculpting Black Female Subjects in Nineteenth-Century America* (2007). She is the editor of *Ebony Roots, Northern Soil: Perspectives on Blackness in Canada* (2010) and co-editor and contributor to the anthology *Racism Eh?: A Critical Inter-Disciplinary Anthology of Race and Racism in Canada* (2004).

Bobby Noble is Associate Professor of English and Cultural Studies in the School of Women's Studies and Department of English at York University. As Jean Bobby Noble, he published *Sons of the Movement: FtM's Risking Incoherence in a Post-Queer Cultural Landscape* (2006) and *Masculinities without Men? Female Masculinity in Twentieth-Century Fictions* (2004). He is co-editor of *The Drag King Anthology* (2002).

Brian Pronger is an Associate Professor in the Faculty of Physical Education and Health at the University of Toronto. He is the author of *Body Fascism: Salvation in the Technology of Physical Fitness* (2002)and *The Arena of Masculinity: Sports, Homosexuality, and the Meaning of Sex* (1990).

David Rayside is Professor of Political Science and the former Director of the Mark S. Bonham Centre for Sexual Diversity Studies at the University of Toronto. He is the author of *Queer Inclusions, Continental Divisions: Public Recognition of Sexual Diversity in Canada and the United States* (2008); *On the Fringe: Gays and Lesbians in Politics* (1998); and *A Small Town in Modern Times* (1991). With Gerald Hunt, he is co-author of *Equity, Diversity, and Canadian Labour* (2007) and the forthcoming *Equalizing Labour: Union Response to Diversity in Canada*. He is also co-editor of *Faith, Politics, and Sexual Diversity in Canada and the United States* (2011).

Becki Ross is an Associate Professor in the Department of Sociology and the Chair of Women's and Gender Studies Undergraduate Program at the University of British Columbia. She is the author of *Burlesque West: Showgirls, Sex, and Sin in Postwar Vancouver* (2009) and *The House That Jill Built: A Lesbian Nation in Formation* (1995).

Debra Shogan is Professor Emerita at the University of Alberta. She is the author of *Sport Ethics in Context* (2007); *The Making of High Performance Athletes: Discipline, Diversity, and Ethics* (1999); *A Reader in Feminist Ethics* (1993); and *Care and Moral Motivation* (1998).

Miriam Smith is a Professor in the Department of Social Science at York University. Her books include *Political Institutions and Lesbian and Gay Rights in the United States and Canada* (2008); *A Civil Society?: Collective Actors in Canadian Political Life* (2005); and *Lesbian and Gay Rights in Canada: Social Movements and Equality-Seeking, 1971–1995* (1999). She is editor of *Group Politics and Social Movements in Canada* (2008) and co-editor of *Critical Policy Studies* (2007) and *New Trends in Canadian Federalism* (2003).

Carolyn Strange is a Senior Fellow and Graduate Director of the School of History at the Australian National University. She is the author of *Toronto's Girl Problem: The Perils and Pleasures of the City, 1880–1930* (1995) and co-author of *Griffith Taylor: Visionary, Environmentalist, Explorer* (2008); *True Crime, True North: The Golden Age of Canadian Pulp Magazines* (2004); and *Making Good: Law and Moral Regulation in Canada, 1867–1939* (1997). She is editor of *Qualities of Mercy: Justice, Punishment, and Discretion* (1996) and co-editor of *Isolation: Places and Practices of Exclusion* (2003).

Kerry Swanson is an independent arts consultant in Toronto and Managing Director of Media Arts Network of Ontario.

Heather Sykes is an Associate Professor in the Department of Curriculum, Teaching, and Learning at the Ontario Institute for Studies in Education at the University of Toronto. She is the author of *Queer Bodies: Sexualities, Genders & Fatness in Physical Education* (2011).

David Townsend is a Professor in the Department of English and the Centre for Medieval Studies and a founding Director of the Sexual Diversity Studies Program at the University of Toronto. He is co-editor of *The Tongue of the Fathers: Gender and Ideology in Twelfth-Century Latin* (1998).

Mariana Valverde is Professor of Criminology and the Chair of the Centre for Criminology at the University of Toronto. She is the author of *The Force of Law* (2010); *Law and Order: Images, Meanings, Myths* (2006); *Law's Dream of a Common Knowledge* (2003); *Diseases of the Will: Alcohol and the Dilemmas of Freedom* (1998); *The Age of Light, Soap, and Water: Moral Reform in English Canada, 1885–1925* (1991, 2008); and *Sex, Power and Pleasure* (1985). She is co-editor of *Police and the Liberal State* (2008); *The New Police Science: The Police Power in Domestic and International Governance* (2006); *Nietzsche and Legal Theory: Half-Written Laws* (2005); *Wife Assault and the Canadian Criminal Justice System: Issues and Policies* (1995); *Studies in Moral Regulation* (1994); and *Gender Conflicts: New Essays in Women's History* (1992).

Rinaldo Walcott is Associate Professor and Chair of the Department of Sociology and Equity Studies in Education at the Ontario Institute for Studies in Education at the University of Toronto. He is the author of *Black Like Who?: Writing Black Canada* (1997, 2003). He is also the editor of *Rude: Contemporary Black Canadian Cultural Criticism* (2000) and co-editor of *Counseling Across and Beyond Cultures: Exploring the Work of Clemmont E. Vontress in Critical Practice* (2010).

Tom Warner is a gay and lesbian rights activist and a former Ontario Human Rights Commissioner. He is the author of *Losing Control: Canada's Social Conservatives in the Age of Rights* (2010) and *Never Going Back: A History of Queer Activism in Canada* (2002).

Thomas Waugh is Professor of Film Studies and Interdisciplinary Studies in Sexuality, the Concordia University Research Chair in Documentary Film and in Sexual Representation, and the Director of the Concordia HIV/AIDS Project at Concordia University. He is author of *The Romance of Transgression in Canada: Sexualities, Nations, Moving Images* (2006); *Gay Art: A Historic Collection* (2004); *Outlines: Underground Gay Graphics from Before Stonewall* (2002); *The Fruit Machine: Twenty Years of Writings on Queer Cinema* (2000); *Hard to Imagine: Gay Male Eroticism in Photography and Film from their Beginnings to Stonewall* (1996); and *Show Us Life: Towards a History and Aesthetics of the Committed Documentary* (1984).

John J. Guiney Yallop is an Assistant Professor in the School of Education at Acadia University. He is the author of *Of Place and Memory: A Poetic Journey* (2010).

COPYRIGHT ACKNOWLEDGEMENTS

Chapter 1: Margot Francis, "On the Myth of Sexual Orientation: Field Notes from the Personal, Pedagogical, and Historical Discourses of Identity" from *Inside the Academy and Out: Sexualities and Social Action.* © University of Toronto Press, 1997. Reprinted by permission of the author.

Chapter 2: Rinaldo Walcott, "Outside in Black Studies: Reading from a Queer Place in the Diaspora" from *Black Studies: A Critical Anthology.* © Duke University Press, 2005. Reprinted by permission of the publisher.

Chapter 3: Jean Bobby Noble, excerpted from "Our Bodies Are Not Ourselves: Tranny Guys and the Racialized Class Politics of Incoherence" from *Sons of the Movement.* © Women's Press, 2006. Reprinted by permission of the publisher.

Chapter 4: Martin Cannon, "The Regulation of First Nations Sexuality" from *Canadian Journal of Native Studies* 18 (1): 1–18. © *Canadian Journal of Native Studies*, 1998. Reprinted by permission of the publisher.

Chapter 5: Gary Kinsman, excerpted from "The Canadian Cold War on Queers: Sexual Regulation and Resistance" from *Love, Hate, and Fear.* © University of Toronto Press, 2004. Reprinted by permission of the publisher.

Chapter 6: Sarah Lamble, "Unknowable Bodies, Unthinkable Sexualities: Lesbian and Transgender Legal Invisibility in the Toronto Women's Bathhouse Raid" from *Social and Legal Studies Journal* 18 (1): 111–130. © Sage Publications, 2009. Reprinted by permission of the publisher.

Chapter 7: Tom Warner, excerpted from "Faith, Politics, and the Transformation of Canada" from *Losing Control: Canada's Social Conservatives in the Age of Rights.* © Between the Lines, 2009. Reprinted by permission of the publisher.

Chapter 8: Miriam Smith, "Identity and Opportunity: The Lesbian and Gay Rights Movement," from *Group Politics and Social Movements in Canada.* © University of Toronto Press, 2008. Reprinted by permission of the publisher.

Chapter 9: Becki Ross, "Like Apples and Oranges: Lesbian Feminist Responses to the Politics of *The Body Politic*" from *FUSE Magazine* 16 (4). © *FUSE Magazine*, 1993. Reprinted by permission of the author.